PENGUIN BOOKS

THE BATTLEFIELDS OF ENGLAND

A. H. Burne was born in 1886 and educated at Winchester and RMA Woolwich, and was commissioned in the army in 1906. He served in the First World War and was awarded the DSO. During the Second World War he was Commandant of the 121st OCTU, 1939–42. He was editor of the *Gunner* from 1938 to 1957 and Military Editor of *Chambers Encyclopedia*. Described by Sir Arthur Bryant as 'one of the most distinguished living authorities on the history of land warfare and one of its finest teachers', he was the author of many works of military history, including *Lee, Grant and Sherman* (1938), *The Art of War on Land* (1944), *The Noble Duke of York* (1949), *The Battlefields of England* (1949), *More Battlefields of England* (1953), *The Crecy War* (1954) and *The Agincourt War* (1956). He died in 1959.

THE BATTLEFIELDS
OF ENGLAND

Alfred H. Burne

With an Introduction by Robert Hardy

PENGUIN BOOKS

PENGUIN BOOKS

Published by the Penguin Group
Penguin Books Ltd, 80 Strand, London WC2R ORL, England
Penguin Putnam Inc., 375 Hudson Street, New York, New York 10014, USA
Penguin Books Australia Ltd, 250 Camberwell Road, Camberwell, Victoria 3124, Australia
Penguin Books Canada Ltd, 10 Alcorn Avenue, Toronto, Ontario, Canada M4V 3B2
Penguin Books India (P) Ltd, 11 Community Centre, Panchsheel Park, New Delhi – 110 017, India
Penguin Books (NZ) Ltd, Cnr Rosedale and Airborne Roads, Albany, Auckland, New Zealand
Penguin Books (South Africa) (Pty) Ltd, 24 Sturdee Avenue, Rosebank 2196, South Africa

Penguin Books Ltd, Registered Offices: 80 Strand, London WC2R ORL, England

www.penguin.com

The Battlefields of England first published by Methuen 1950
Second edition published 1951
More Battlefields of England first published by Methuen 1952
Published in one volume, with a new introduction,
as *The Battlefields of England* by Greenhill Books 1996
Published in this single, merged edition as a Classic Penguin 2002

2

To
Alan W. Lidderdale
who sowed the seed

and to
Peter Young
who by his penetrating but kindly criticism did his
best to improve this book

CONTENTS

THE BATTLEFIELDS TRUST

THE Battlefields Trust is a registered charity, which has been formed to help save battlefield sites (both in Britain and abroad) from destruction, and preserve them for posterity as educational and heritage resources. That such an organisation was necessary did not occur to its founder members until Naseby battlefield was partially destroyed by the construction of the A1/M1 link road in 1992. It seemed quite incredible that such an important, and until then, largely unchanged battlefield should be consigned to the bulldozers with such ease. If such a fate could befall Naseby in the year of the Civil War's 350th anniversary, then what chance would other, less well known sites have if faced with development plans?

A conference was arranged on the theme of 'Ancient Battlefields as National Treasures' by Mr Kelvin van Hasselt. The feelings of delegates were so strong that The Battlefields Trust was set up with the aims described above. Already it has helped to prevent gravel extraction at Blore Heath in Staffordshire (1459), has sat on the English Heritage Battlefields Register Panel and campaigned against developments which would threaten the battlefields of First and Second Newbury (1643, 1644) and Tewkesbury (1471). In addition many events furthering the interpretation of battlefields have been staged, including field days, study days and conferences, the latter attracting delegates from as far afield as Japan, South Africa and the U.S.A.

The Battlefields Trust is keen to work with owners of battlefields to help them improve the presentation and interpretation of their sites, so that through encouraging more visitors and by raising the profile of battlefields any threats from development will disappear. With the publication of English Heritage's Battlefield Register, planners will have to consider the importance of any battlefield listed before any development can take place. However, battlefields still have no legal protection, and only major English battlefields are included on the Register.

The interest and value of battlefields as a historical source can be seen clearly from Colonel Burne's writings. It is to be hoped that these sites of national importance will remain, unspoilt, for future generations.

If you would like to receive further details about The Battlefields Trust and/or become a member, contact:

Mr Michael Rayner
The Coordinator
Meadow Cottage
33 High Green
Brooke
Norwich NR15 1HR
Tel: 01508 558145

Michael Rayner
1996

SKETCH-MAPS & PANORAMAS

xii   *Sketch-maps & Panoramas*

FOREWORD TO *THE BATTLEFIELDS OF ENGLAND*

THIS book is calculated to give a great deal of pleasure to many people interested in their country's past. It provides them compendiously with the means of studying the principal English Battlefields with knowledge and intelligence to aid their imagination. It would be a splendid way of spending a holiday, to motor round the Battlefields with this book, which provides sketch maps (e.g. p. 436) enabling the visitor to find the actual sites of conflict, even where modern enclosure or planting has broken up the ground across which Rupert and Cromwell freely charged.

And for the home-staying reader there is here collected a great amount of careful information, thought and discussion on English battles. The wonder is that no such book has appeared before. We are grateful to have a really good one at last.

In the case of some of the battles there is uncertainty as to the precise location of particular incidents in the fighting within the radius of a few hundred yards or so. Where there are differences of opinion, Colonel Burne tells us, and argues the case for his own opinion. His opinion has the value of being a soldier's. And in other matters besides location his military experience is most valuable. For instance, I am delighted to find that his professional knowledge makes him sceptical (p. 137) on a point about which I have always felt instinctive doubt—the point of the Normans at Hastings carrying out the very delicate operation of a feigned flight. And the Colonel's estimate of the strategical and tactical qualities displayed by the commanders in the various campaigns and battles is most interesting. As a professional historian, I am bound to cock a sceptical eye at the location of Badon and the generalship of 'Arthur'. It may have been so; who can tell? But the Colonel does not claim it as certain. As to the other battles, the theses that he advances are most valuable arguments from well ascertained facts. I think Englishmen ought to be grateful to Colonel Burne.

G. M. TREVELYAN

PREFACE TO THE SECOND EDITION OF
THE BATTLEFIELDS OF ENGLAND

I AM indebted to various friends for pointing out a number of misprints and careless slips in the first edition, which have now, I hope, been rectified. In that edition I did not, for reasons of space, give the grounds for my belief that some of the statements of Geoffrey of Monmouth regarding the battle of Mount Badon should be accepted. As a certain amount of scepticism on this point has been voiced by reviewers and others I have added a short note on the subject of the credibility of Geoffrey of Monmouth's *Histories of the Kings of Britain*. There is also a short note on the reputed grave-pits of First Newbury. Otherwise there are practically no alterations in the text of the first edition.

I receive so many enquiries as to why this or that battlefield has been omitted that it may be well to explain that most of them have been written up but had to be omitted for reasons of space. I hope, however, that these slaughtered innocents may be re-vivified in a further volume of battlefields, with which England is studded.

A. H. B.

September 1950

PREFACE TO *THE BATTLEFIELDS OF ENGLAND*

TWO motives have inspired me in writing this book. The first was to provide the intelligent inhabitants of this land with a book by means of which they could discover our fields of battle and follow their course on the ground. The second was, by going back to the sources, to reconstruct the story of these battles from a purely military point of view; in other words, to provide an informed military commentary.

Since the first was the primary motive I have entitled the book *Battlefields* rather than *Battles*.

As my researches proceeded I became increasingly aware of the fact that this aspect of our national history has been surprisingly—even shockingly—neglected and disregarded during the present century. The ignorance that exists to-day, not only among the general educated public, but also among those whose duty it is to hand on the knowledge, is deplorable. This is partly due to the fact that the subject has evidently ceased to interest most professional historians, and consequently, with the exception of Hastings, Flodden and possibly of Naseby, none of our battles have received adequate attention in local or national histories or in the pages of historical publications. The consequence is that there is a real danger of detailed knowledge of the subject dying out as the older generation passes on. Only recently we have lost Sir Charles Oman, and no one has appeared to take his place in this field. No book with the least claim to comprehensiveness has been written during this century; the last was that of C. R. B. Barrett (written in 1895) and this book contains few and inadequate maps; moreover, his conclusions are in my opinion frequently erroneous. Prior to that date, we have to go back another forty years; in 1857 Richard Brooks published his *Visits to Fields of Battle of the Fifteenth century*, but this book is confined to the Wars of the Roses.

But the trouble goes deeper than this. Not only is the pasture barren, but amid the scant herbage there is, in my judgement, an undue proportion of weeds. Here I must speak frankly. Sir James Ramsay was a great and painstaking historian, and students of English military history are under a deep debt of gratitude to him for searching out and placing upon record the principal sources for our battlefield history.

Unfortunately Sir James was not content to let the matter rest there. As he himself admitted, he took great interest in battles, and took a good deal of trouble in producing these beautifully clear coloured maps of most of them, which now adorn his various historical works. But it is no disparagement to that great historian to point out that he was not a soldier himself and that on military grounds many of his conclusions are open to criticism; indeed, Gross, the bibliographer, declares that his survey 'must be used with caution'. This caution has not been observed by some of his followers, and this has caused the chief of them, C. R. B. Barrett, to fall into many errors. Some of these errors have been pointed out in the pages of local societies, such as the *Transactions of the Shropshire S. & N.H. Society* for the battle of Shrewsbury, but the average reader is unaware of the fact, and continues to accept Ramsay's account of this and other important battles.

It thus seems high time that the public should have access to a reasoned and up-to-date account of those battles that have helped to mould our Island story. For it is beyond question (though unfashionable to proclaim it) that battles *have* had an influence on the course of our history. To give but two examples; but for the issue of Hastings this country might never have experienced the Norman domination and culture; but for the battle of Bosworth there might never have been an Elizabethan age. (That profound historian, James Gairdner, declared 'that which gave the death-blow to feudalism in England was undoubtedly the battle of Bosworth.')

This brings me back to my first motive—that of helping Englishmen to find for themselves the actual sites of the battlefields in their own neighbourhood or on roads along which they may be travelling. At present there are almost insuperable difficulties in the way of the average person who may be interested in this subject. His normal sources of information would be histories, general and local, guide-books, and local inhabitants. General histories are too brief to indicate the exact sites, and unlikely to provide a map; local histories are difficult to procure outside the local public library; guide-books are nowadays usually out of print, except municipal guides (probably produced by the town clerk, who may not be well versed in battlefields); lastly, local inhabitants, in my experience, either display an abysmal ignorance of the subject, or if they are communicative are also dogmatic, wedded to the story as told them when young, and which may have become distorted in the telling. To give but one example, the field of Naseby is in the heart of the country; there are but two human habitations in the vicinity. I recently visited both of them. At one I learnt—nothing; at the other I was pointed out an oak-tree up which Cromwell, or it might have been Prince Rupert hid—my informant was not certain on the point.

I have not included battlefield monuments in my list, and for a good reason—more often than not either they do not exist or if they do they are misleading. Taking Naseby again, the old monument is over one mile from the centre of the field, and the new one erected by the Cromwell Association to mark the locality where Cromwell charged is, in my opinion, 700 yards out of place. Furthermore, such monuments as exist and *are* correctly sited are sometimes so neglected and over-grown that the traveller may have difficulty in finding them, or in deciphering them when found. Such is true of Towton, and in a greater degree of Sedgemoor. Though possessed of a local guide-book I on one occasion twice walked past the monument without finding it, and a friend armed with a one-inch Ordnance map spent a fruitless day looking for the field. I have had such instances in mind when writing this book, when preparing the maps, and when deciding on the sketches; and I claim that the result is 'foolproof'; that is to say, that anyone armed with the book should be able to find his way to any battlefield and, having found it, follow the course of the battle without assistance from any other source.

A word is due in explanation of what may seem to some a tiresome reiteration of the expression '*Inherent Military Probability*', sometimes contracted into I.M.P. This reiteration is of intent. The fact is, reliable records of our English battles are distressingly meagre. When one has discounted the exaggerations inevitable in a medieval chronicle, the distortions due to misconception, the errors due to absence of maps, and sometimes even deliberate fabrication—there is not much pure grain left. To complete the picture many gaps have to be filled in. Ancient history, as it is presented in the history books, is a compound of fact and inference or conjecture, and the conjecture will vary with the individual. *Quot homines tot sententiae*. This is particularly true of battles. When we consider that the actual participants were seldom literate, that the records were consequently written by absentee scribes ignorant of the conditions of warfare and unprovided with maps, it is surprising that our old records are as complete as they are. Even so, something more is required if the battle is to be depicted with any precision and detail. My method here is to start with what appear to be undisputed facts, then to place myself in the shoes of each commander in turn, and to ask myself in each case what I would have done. This I call working on Inherent Military Probability. I then compare the resulting action with the existing records in order to see whether it discloses any incompatibility with the accepted facts. If it does not, I then go on to the next debatable or obscure point in the battle and repeat the operation. It is important that the reader should understand this procedure, because I do not load the script with a mass of qualifying clauses, 'in all probability', 'as it seems to me', etc. These must generally be taken for granted; though in the most problematical or controversial cases I devote a section to explaining my reasoning at the end. Thus those who are prepared to accept my reconstruction will get their narrative in a fairly smooth, continuous flow, without distracting interruptions, whilst those of a more inquiring or critical turn of mind can satisfy their curiosity.

For much the same reason, namely that the average reader hates distractions, I have generally omitted references to sources in the narrative but have appended a select bibliography of the sources that I have found most useful, followed by a short list of modern books, one or more of which contain a bibliography of the sources. Only books which are readily obtainable in a normal library are listed. Unfortunately the most worthwhile modern accounts of battles are contained almost invariably in the pages of some learned or local society. Thus, the basic account of the battle of Flodden, to which all subsequent writers have been indebted, appeared 57 years ago in the pages of the Northumbrian publication *Archaeologica Aelina*. Hence it should not be supposed that I have not consulted every relevant source known to me. In this connection I should like to express my indebtedness to Mr. N. O. R. Serjeant for literal translations of some obscure medieval passages, and to Miss Cynthia Borough of the Bodleian Library for transcribing some Latin Manuscripts in that Library.

I wish also to express my thanks to the following gentlemen for reading and commenting on various chapters: Mr. H. C. Brentnall, F.S.A., Dr. Arthur Bryant, Mr. Winston Churchill, Mr. J. N. L. Myres, the late Sir Charles Oman, Major-General J. F. C. Fuller, Professor R. F. Treharne, Colonel Peter Young and others.

Chapters II, XVIII, XX, XXII and XXXVII, and the Appendix, appeared in their original form in the pages of *The Fighting Forces*.

PREFACE TO *MORE BATTLEFIELDS OF ENGLAND*

THIS book is in all essentials a sequel to *Battlefields of England*. The battlefields included in it are not necessarily of lesser importance than those in the previous volume—indeed some of them, such as Ethandun and Brunanburh are of extreme importance—but for various reasons they were not included in the previous volume.

The dual purpose of the book is similar to that of its predecessor, namely to provide the intelligent Englishman with a medium whereby he may discover our fields of battle and follow their course on the ground, and secondly to provide an informed military commentary on those battles.

The Bibliography gives the main sources for each battle. I have not attempted (as I did in the previous volume) to name the modern works on the battles since in the case of most of them there is practically nothing except articles in the transactions of learned societies, which would not be accessible to the general reader.

Chapter I appeared in its original form in the *Transactions of the Shropshire Archaeological Society*, Chapter XV in *Durham University Journal*, and portions of Chapter IV in the *New English Review Magazine*, and of Chapter VI in *Wiltshire Archaeological Journal*.

I wish to thank the following for helpful comments on several chapters; Major Peter Young, D.S.O., M.C., Miss Lily F. Chitty, F.S.A., Mr. H. C. Brentnall, F.S.A., Mr. John Prest, and Miss Dorothy Greene, F.S.A.

INTRODUCTION

WHY re-publish battlefield studies that might be thought obsolete when there are plenty of new ones, with aerial photographs and Ordnance Survey maps to boot?

Because Burne's battlefield studies are very far from obsolete. There is nothing in them that is not of value to the amateur or professional strategist or tactician today, to the newest student or the most experienced professor of military history. Because all the good modern published studies owe a very great deal to the work of Colonel Alfred Burne. Perhaps most importantly because of all the writers on such a subject he has brought most clearly the right mixture of military discipline and controlled historic imagination to the examination of each site and each campaign that comes under his eye.

He is not always right. No one can inhabit the misty fields of the past without some wrong assumptions, some mistaken directions. He has been accused of applying First World War military values to ancient armies and encounters. His yardstick of 'inherent military probability' has been dismissed as specious; yet without some such yardstick, made from the appreciation of ageless and unchanging absolutes of warfare, and without the informed interpretation of meticulously consulted contemporary records, no one can advance a step in the study of ancient conflicts and their hallowed fields.

The first time I visited Agincourt I had Monstralet in my hand; the second time I had Burne. Burne illuminated Monstralet, crowded the battlefield, lit the appalling struggle there and in the end so carefully explained the causes and the outcome that a kind of calm was left at last over those turbulent and terrible acres.

The strange and awe-filled heritage of battlefields catches the imagination of more and more people; the places where great heroism, great cowardice, sometimes great genius, sometimes great stupidity were shown, the places above all where men met to try their cause to the ultimate, fascinate a growing number. If you would understand that fascination and that instinct, partly of reverence, partly to find truth, then go to your chosen places of battle with Burne in your hands. Consult all the others, some good, some less so, but go first to Burne.

Robert Hardy
1996

THE BATTLEFIELDS OF ENGLAND

MORE BATTLEFIELDS OF ENGLAND

CHAPTER I

Caradoc's Last Fight: A.D. 51

IF Cassivellaunus was our first great British hero Caradoc was certainly the second. So delighted were the Romans at his capture, after seven ineffectual campaigns against him, that they carried him all the way to Rome to grace the victor's triumph. Moreover, so important was the event considered in high quarters that their historian Tacitus devoted considerable trouble to collecting evidence and space in describing the last fight which resulted in the capture of their redoubtable antagonist.

After the abortive attempt of Julius Caesar to subdue Cassivellaunus and conquer Britain the Romans had left the island severely alone for nearly a century. In A.D. 43 Aulus Plautius invaded the country and was soon followed by the emperor Vespasian, who in four years conquered the greater part of southern Britain. In A.D. 47 Plautius was succeeded by Publius Ostorius, who carried the war into what is now Wales. The British leader was Caradoc (Caractacus in the history books, Caratacas to the pedants), and for seven years he eluded all attempts to defeat and capture him.

In A.D. 51 Ostorius set out in earnest to subdue this slippery opponent. His first step was to construct a powerful base, near but just outside the debated territory. The spot he selected for this purpose was at the foot of the Wrekin, in Shropshire. He called this camp Uriconium, and here he stationed two legions, the 14th and 20th.

★   ★   ★   ★   ★

While the Roman general was constructing his base at Uriconium, what was Caradoc doing? Though history is silent on the point the following seems a reasonable supposition. The danger was clear; Uriconium was evidently intended as 'a pistol pointed at the heart of Wales' (if I may be allowed a slight anachronism). Counter-measures of a defensive nature were obviously called for. Now, ten miles to the south-west of this 'pistol' and about two miles north-east of the modern Church Stretton, lay a steep hill, admirably suited for the type of hill-fort usual in that age. Here, as a first step, Caradoc constructed such a fort. The steep end of this hill points towards Uriconium, and the vallum that girdled it was not weakened by an entrance at that end. The sole entrance was made on the other, the south-west end. Here the

slope is more gentle than elsewhere, and provides the only obvious line
of approach. The hill to this day is known as Caer Caradoc, the castle
of Caradoc.

The second step was to make a second and still stronger fort, further
away from the Roman base, but within supporting distance of Caer
Caradoc, and if possible within sight of this British forward camp.
Again nature provided the obvious: 15 miles south-west of Caer
Caradoc (Church Stretton) as we will hereinafter call it, a hill, similarly
shaped in all but its south-western end, points its nose straight towards
the forward camp, and the Roman base.[1] Here Caradoc constructed
his second and main camp, and a most impressive piece of military
engineering it is, in some ways reminding one of Maiden Castle,
Dorset. Tremendous labour was spent in the construction,[2] much more
so than in the first camp, though there is a distinct family resemblance
between the two. The main difference is that the new camp contained
a narrow entrance to the front in addition to the main entrance in rear.
This was necessary because if the Romans penetrated so far, the remnants of the garrison of Caer Caradoc (Church Stretton) falling back
before them, would require an opening, albeit a narrow one, on the
front side to enter by.

The fort is sited rather further forward than might be expected,
but the reason for this probably was to bring the camp into visual connexion with the forward camp, so that smoke signals could be exchanged between the two. By this means warning of a Roman advance
would quickly reach the commander in his headquarter camp. This fort
also has, at least since the year 1572 when Humfry Lluyd visited it, been
known as Caradoc's Castle. The inhabitants told him that 'a certain
king Caradoc' fought there. Gough in his edition of Camden's *Britannia*
(iii, 13) writes that 'if not the royal seat of Caradoc it was probably his
fortress during the war'. Most writers suppose that Caradoc's queen
resided there, in which case it would be his royal seat.

The third step was to connect the two forts by a military road. I
think this road can be traced through the greater part of its course without much difficulty (see Sketch-map 1). Starting from Caer Caradoc
(Church Stretton) a deep-banked track, betokening its great age, winds
down the hill into the valley, taking the line of the by-pass road as far
as Little Stretton, it then hugs the foot of the Long Mynd through

[1] Bigbury Camp, held by the Britons against Julius Caesar, also pointed its
nose towards the enemy.
[2] The ditches had to be hacked out of the naked rock.

Minton and Hamperley, reminiscent of parts of the so-called Pilgrim's Way. Crossing the river Onny at Horderley, it mounts the bank, past Castle Ring to Ridgeway (significant name). Sometimes the modern road follows it and occasionally it diverges. Down the hill it goes into Edgton (one of the most secluded villages in England) and presently passes through the fields, joining the Kempton road just north of that village. It then crosses the river Kemp and reaches the Clun–Craven Arms road at Purslow. When going over the ground, my companion and I could see no trace of it crossing the Clun valley, but this did not worry me because I assumed that it made for the defile between Clunbury Hill and Purslow Wood (see Sketch-map 3).

However, while after fording the river, we were clambering up the steep slopes of that wood, we came across its unmistakable tracks in the undergrowth. It takes the slope on a natural diagonal.[1] On attaining the crest the track disappears again in the open fields. We did not pursue it further but the map shows a fairly obvious and direct continuation through Cwm and Obley (where it is joined by an alternative track via Hopton Castle). Thence, again hugging the foot of the hill, it drops into the valley of the Redlake at Chapel Lawn, a few hundred yards from its destination, Caer Caradoc.

Now if a ruler be lined on the two Caer Caradocs, it will be seen that this track, twisty though it may be, never diverges as much as a mile from this straight line.

*　　*　　*　　*　　*

So much for topography. Now for the strategy of the campaign. After subduing the Brigantes in the north, Ostorius turned against the Silures in South Wales. Then comes a passage in Tacitus that has caused much speculation. Caradoc, we are told, cleverly transferred the war (*astu transfert bellum*) into the territory of the Ordovices. The puzzling thing about this statement is that the initiative is normally in the hands of the attacker, in this case the Romans. Yet the expression seems to imply that in some way the British general took the initiative and decided where the campaign should be fought. After much thought I can only see one reasonable solution. If we agree with Collingwood that the 2nd Roman Legion was based on Gloucester, Ostorius would presumably employ that legion in South Wales, possibly reinforced

---

[1] The 6-inch O.S. map shows a footpath continuing the line from the foot of the hill to the river, but I cannot trace it on the ground. Evidently it preserved the line of the old trackway—an interesting survival.

from the others. Now, if Caradoc had reason to suppose that the garrison of Uriconium had been weakened for this purpose, and that Ostorius himself was absent from this station, he might attempt a sudden concentration of the local tribes in his own domain on the borders of the Silures and Ordovices, with a view to counter-attacking the

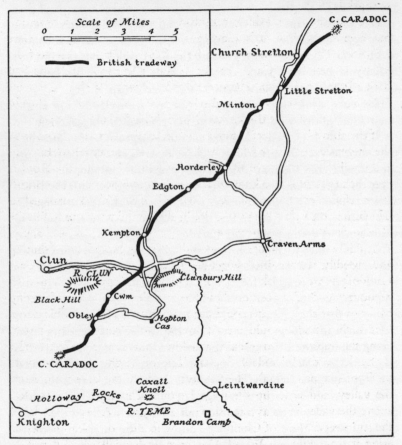

SKETCH-MAP I. THE CARADOC COUNTRY I

Roman base. Caradoc evidently did collect an army in that neighbourhood. Parry quotes from the *Triad LXXIX* 'an ancient tradition'. 'When the British hero Caractacus went to battle none would stay at home, they followed him freely and maintained themselves at their own expense. Unsolicited and unsoliciting, they crowded to his banners.' If, as Tacitus seems to suggest, Caradoc took the initiative here, it would seem that Ostorius, getting wind of his opponent's intentions, hurried back to Uriconium, no doubt taking a portion of his troops with him. Then, collecting the 14th and 20th Legions, he himself took the offensive from that base. Thus it could be said that Caradoc cleverly brought the operations into that part of the country where his greatest strength lay.

We may therefore, I think, postulate the two Roman legions setting out against the British headquarters on the line of the two Caer Caradocs. The sequel would then be as follows. The approach of the enemy is seen from Caer Caradoc (Church Stretton) and signalled back to the main camp. The general rides forward with some of his followers to relieve his advanced post, but it is too late: it has already been overrun. Met by the survivors he falls back along the trackway.

If the above is a correct reconstruction Caradoc was now faced with the alternatives of either falling back to his main camp, where his wife and family were living, or of taking up a position barring the Roman approach to it. Now we know that on at least two occasions the British leader eluded capture by the Romans; indeed they never managed to take him in the field.[1] He was no doubt elusive and wily, a man like De Wet in the Boer War, to whom the adjective 'slippery' would apply. A general with such a character would not allow himself to be shut up and speedily starved into surrender in a hill-fortress, such as Caer Caradoc; he would look for a position barring the approach to his own headquarters. Such a position should be as wide as possible, with strong flanks so that the Romans could not easily turn it and reach his camp. One such position would meet Caradoc in the course of his retreat along the trackway. On reaching Purslow from the north, the traveller is struck by the formidable-looking line of heights immediately in his front (see panorama). The trackway leads, as we have seen, across the valley, and slants up the ridge beyond. This ridge rises 450 feet above the valley at an average slope of 20 degrees. Away to the left is the still steeper slope of Clunbury Hill, with a dip or re-entrant separating it from Purslow Wood. On the right hand Black Hill rises to over 1,400 feet, with a slope equal to that of Purslow Wood. It would form an extremely strong position, at all ages of warfare, and in such a strategical situation as I have sketched, 'it cries out' to be occupied. There appear at first sight to be two weak points about it. First, it is

---

[1] The undisguised delight of the Romans at eventually getting Caradoc into their hands, probably indicates that they had made many previous attempts to capture him.

markedly concave; but there is no real objection in this so long as the flanks are firm. This they are, both of them resting on commanding localities. The other point is the wide extent of the position—over three miles. Such an extent is far beyond the normal conception of defensive positions in those days. But there are exceptional features in this case. If Caradoc was as slippery as we give him credit for, he would above all things be careful not to occupy a position that could easily be outflanked. It was therefore most desirable to hold Clunbury Hill as well as Purslow Wood.[1] Moreover it would be unnecessary to hold the whole extent of the line everywhere in strength. Nature, in the shape of steep slopes, helped Caradoc to economize in the number of men required. A hastily constructed wall-rampart added to this strength. Finally from the top of the ridge at point 966 every move of the attackers could be seen, and a mobile reserve could be dispatched in good time to that point of the line where attack threatened. The river crossing would impart a measure of delay to the attackers, and the steepness of the slope would make progress slow and add to the time available for reinforcing the threatened point or points. This brings us to the strength in numbers of the two armies. Haverfield computes that the strength of a legion together with its auxiliary troops would be about 10,000. Thus with two legions the numbers would be about 20,000. Tacitus says that the Britons were inferior in strength. This does not necessarily mean in numbers, though this is generally asserted: the superiority of the Romans might show itself in training, discipline, arms or armour. But even allowing that the Britons were inferior in number they might still amount to about 15,000 men, which would seem ample to hold the position I have indicated in the manner suggested.

The troops, having been apportioned to the ground, would start constructing defences where the slope of the ground made this desirable. The subsoil is shallow here and a very little digging would throw up stones and chips of rocks. With these a loose stone rampart would be constructed. It would run along the crest of the hill, so sited that the steepest part of the slope lay just in its front, i.e. along contour 850 feet most of the way. Caradoc would take up his position at the top of the hill at point 966, and await with calm confidence the Roman onslaught.

*　　　*　　　*　　　*　　　*

Thus far, it will be observed, I have selected a position for the battle purely on strategical and tactical grounds, endeavouring to place myself

[1] The wood is modern.

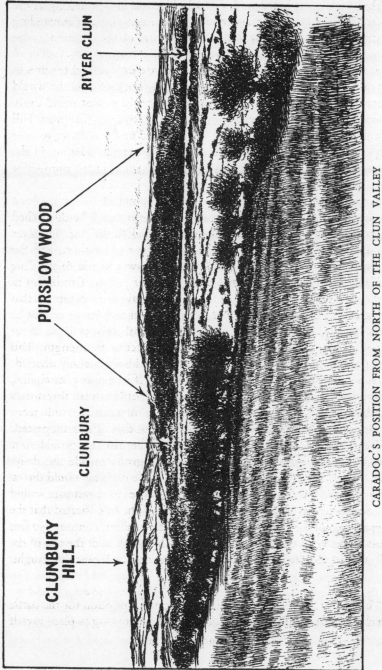

RIVER CLUN

PURSLOW WOOD

CLUNBURY

CLUNBURY HILL

CARADOC'S POSITION FROM NORTH OF THE CLUN VALLEY

in Caradoc's shoes, and thus deciding on his probable course of action, the whole reconstruction being based on the assumption of the Roman distribution of forces with which I started, and without any reference to the description of the position given by Tacitus. We will now examine in some detail the account from his pen, noting at each successive point how far it agrees with my suggested position.

TACITUS' DESCRIPTION OF THE POSITION

There is no need to quote in full the famous passage which the Latin historian devotes to the battle; crucial words and phrases only will be given in the original.

A river flowed in front of the position of uncertain or doubtful depth, *vado incerto*. This has usually been construed 'with shifting fords'. But why should Tacitus mention shifting fords? (Incidentally it would be only one ford—not much for an army of 20,000 men to use in the face of the enemy!) Fords do not shift every few hours, and are not likely to have shifted while the army was about to cross. The natural translation of *vado* in this context is depth; after a little rain the water of the Clun becomes muddy and thick, the bottom cannot be seen. If heavy rain fell just before the Romans arrived the depth of the river would at first look doubtful and uncertain. The description would thus fit the Clun at this spot. It has however been asserted that the Teme, and so all the more the Clun which is about 25 per cent smaller, is too small a river. Now, whatever its size it could not be bigger than the Severn, the biggest river in those parts. Tacitus uses the word *fluvio* to describe the Severn, and *amnis* for this river. The presumption is that by *amnis* he means to denote a smaller river than the Severn. The word can of course mean a big river, but it can also mean a mountain stream, and the Clun at this spot is little more. We do not know at what time of year the battle took place, but even in the summer, after heavy rain it can be a considerable obstacle. It seems likely that such was the case. An anonymous article in *Archaeologia Cambrensis* (but written by E. Rogers) states that 'it is recorded and proved by its channels, to have brought down formerly a much larger body of water than at present'. Ostorius was loath to attack, one reason being specified as the river; but the troops clamoured to be allowed to attack, and we are told Ostorius acceded to their wish. This is not the action of an experienced general who considers the chances of victory unfavourable —to be jockeyed into attacking by clamour. He hesitated, for how long we do not know, but Tacitus is apt to foreshorten time, and it may be he paused for a day or more. Now, if the river was in spate when he reached it, a brief pause for the level to fall would be only natural and prudent. This is what probably happened, with the result that when they did attack the troops got across without difficulty. According to Tacitus, the position was such that advance and retreat alike would be difficult for the Romans and easier for the Britons. The meaning of this is rather obscure, but the only ground that could suit it, as far as I can see, is a position where the attackers have to mount a steep slope to reach it, but the defenders can retreat from it by a gentle slope. This condition is achieved by the position of our conjectural defensive line, which runs along the crest of the hill, just below the top.

There was high ground beyond the position to which the defenders eventually fell back (*decedere barbari in juga montium*). This agrees with our position, whether we picture the retreat to the immediate top of the ridge, which is about 300 yards from the rampart, or whether we envisage the massive bulk of Black Hill immediately in rear of the position.

Parts of the position were impenetrable, and parts were negotiable. Now, since the ground was level at its foot, being in the river valley, it follows that where the slope was gentle a dip or re-entrant would be formed in the ridge. There are two such: a big one, already noticed, between Clunbury Hill and Purslow Wood, marked 'A' on the map, and a small one on the left marked 'B' on the map. It is these re-entrants in particular that the Britons defended with a stone rampart. This then is in keeping with Tacitus, and moreover the fact that Ostorius did a reconnaissance to find these weak points seems to imply an extensive position of varying nature.

There are however two objections that might be lodged against this position; there is an absence of 'rugged and frowning rocks' and a 'craggy hill', 'craggy rocks . . . a rugged and inaccessible eminence', and many similar expressions. But the words of Tacitus do not necessarily imply these things. *Arduis montibus* can mean merely 'steep mountains or hills'; *Saxa* need not mean more than 'stones': the fact that the Romans were able to pull down the rampart with their hands in the middle of the fighting seems to indicate this. Even *imminentia juga* need not mean 'overhanging' but 'adjacent mountain ridges'. If they had been overhanging the heavily armed Roman legionaries would not have been able to climb them, as we are assured they did. In short, if we bear in mind that Tacitus' informants would tend to exaggerate the physical difficulties even unconsciously (for the size of obstacles grows in the imagination with the passage of time),[1] his description of the ground adequately fits our position.

THE BATTLE

The course of the battle now becomes perfectly comprehensible, and one can stand on the ridge-top and in imagination follow it from beginning to end. The position is too extensive for Caradoc to deliver the usual speech to the assembled army; he is obliged to flit hither and thither. Ostorius on the far side of the valley hears the Britons cheer —the prevailing south-west wind would carry the sound. (Such would not be the case in the other sites suggested for the battle.) The morale of the British troops is high and when the Romans, toiling painfully up the steep slope, arrive within range of missiles, they suffer heavy casualties. Closing up to the rampart however and forming their famous testudo of shields, they pull down the stones and engage the defenders on more level terms. Eventually the Britons fall back up the hill and the Romans pursue.

As a result of his reconnaissance Ostorius no doubt directed his legionaries principally against one or both of the two re-entrants, while the light armed auxiliaries were thrown against the steeper parts of the hill. It seems in the natural course of things that the breakthrough should occur in these re-entrants. The effect of that in re-entrant 'A' would be to cut off the defenders of Clunbury Hill, whilst the successful penetration of re-entrant 'B' would force the left of the line backwards up the long slope of Black Hill. If this indeed happened, it leads to an interesting speculation. We know that Caradoc's brother surrendered after the battle; the general's wife and daughters were also captured. The natural presumption is that this took place in Caer Caradoc fort. But Caradoc himself made his escape. How came it that he got away but not his brother and his family? The speculation is as follows. The portion of the position on Clunbury Hill, being somewhat detached, would require a local commander. What more natural than that Caradoc should place his brother in this command, himself

---

[1] Anyone who takes a big fence out hunting and visits the spot years later is surprised to find how it has grown in his imagination. Moreover Tacitus 'writing up' the scene would envisage it like the rocky, mountainous, Italian scenery. A Scottish Chronicler described the terrain of the battle of Shrewsbury in similar exaggerated language.

retaining the command on Purslow Wood ridge? A break-through at
'A' would split the army in two, separating the two brothers. Frater, as
we will call him, would either be cut off on Clunbury Hill and captured, or would make his way across country to Caer Caradoc. In the
meanwhile Caradoc would be fighting a rearguard action on Black
Hill, resisting fiercely, while the break-through troops pushed on to
the camp, and surrounded it. Alternatively, Frater may have been sent
to the camp by Caradoc with a message to warn Uxor, as we will call
her, to escape and join him in the north. But Uxor delayed collecting

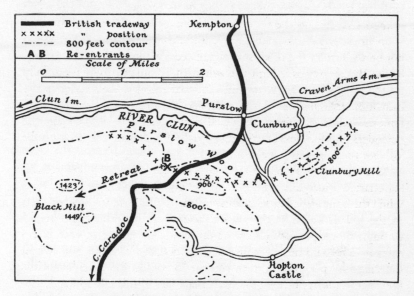

SKETCH-MAP 2.   THE CLUN: THE BATTLE II

her goods and chattels, till it was too late. No doubt the garrison fought
bravely before surrendering. There are indeed traditions of a battle.
A farmer on the spot told us that the enemy approached from the
south-west. This seemed an improbable direction until I reflected that
the Romans, wishing to capture the garrison rather than to storm a
formidable barbarian hill-top, would be likely to sweep round the camp
and approach it from the rear, which also was the easiest line of approach. So the farmer's story may not be entirely baseless. He also said
that the inhabitants from the dwellings in the valley below used to
bring up food to the garrison, but that one of them betrayed the where-
abouts of the camp to the Romans. The river Redlake at the foot of

the camp is said to owe its name to the fact that it ran red with blood—an almost invariable tradition about any watercourse near a battlefield.

RIVAL SITES

In the above thesis I have tried to show that what one might describe as the inherently probable course for events to take on military considerations, fits closely the narrative passed down to us by Tacitus. It cannot, in the nature of things, be proved, but the case for it is strengthened if it can be shown that rival sites have less claim to our credence. Let us therefore briefly examine them. Those most generally advanced are CEFN CARNEDD, six miles north-east of Llanidloes: the BREIDDEN, six miles north of Welshpool; COXWALL KNOLL, five miles east of Knighton; and HOLLOWAY ROCKS, two miles north-east of Knighton.

CEFN CARNEDD was suggested by Hartshorne in 1841, but only 'conjecturally'. I have not heard anyone else advocate it, and it is not likely that many people have visited it with that object. The reasons that Hartshorne gives are unconvincing, the locality has no connexion with Caradoc. His assertion that the attacker was bound to cross the river Severn before making the attack is not true—an attacker advancing up the river valley could approach the hill from either bank; the hill is isolated and not the sort of position that a canny general like Caradoc would allow himself to be trapped in. Even Hartshorne's observations do not seem very accurate. He writes: 'It is fortified with a single vallum on the North Western and with a double one on the North Eastern side.' Presumably he means the south-eastern, not north-eastern side. On this side, so far from there being a double vallum, there are only the slightest signs of a single one. Indeed, I climbed the hill from this side and arrived at the top without passing any apparent entrenchment at all.[1]

The BREIDDEN I should like to believe the site of this great battle on personal and family grounds, but I fear it is impossible to reconcile with strategic considerations, for the river is the wrong side of the hill, i.e. on the west. What would bring Ostorius to attack it from that direction? Advocates of the site make various attempts to explain it, the most usual being that Ostorius advanced from Welshpool, on the north bank of the Severn. But why should he advance by the north bank, if he knew the enemy was on the opposite bank? His natural course would

[1] Wynn Ffoulkes in 1851 asserted that he could find no trace of a 'double wall' on the Breidden that Hartshorne stated was there.

be to cross the river at once and advance straight towards the hill. If the Britons were holding a position facing the river he would thus turn its left flank. A curious reason was advanced at a meeting of the Shropshire Archaeological Society in 1908, namely that the Breidden was 'isolated'. I should consider that an argument against the site, not in favour of it: Caradoc was not the man to allow himself to get trapped on an isolated hill. As a result of his excavations on the hill in 1937, Mr. B. H. St. J. O'Neil pronounced against this site for the battle.

COXWALL KNOLL is more generally favoured than any other site, the main argument being that there was a Roman camp at Brandon, three miles to the south-east, with the river Teme between, which the Romans would have to cross. The river, in fact, laps the foot of the hill, which rises steeply almost from the water's edge. A crossing *haud difficulter* in these circumstances is hard to conceive: the attackers would be within easy missile range of the defenders whilst wading across the stream. The slope is at its steepest at this spot, indeed it would be almost inaccessible to the heavily armed legionaries. Moreover there would be no necessity for the Romans to cross the river at this point and attack the most difficult side of the hill. Once again the natural course for them to take would be to cross the stream just to the north of their camp, and approach the knoll over the open ground which would lead them to the east end of the hill, where the gradient is easiest. Just as in the case of the Breidden, if the Britons were holding a line facing the river they would have their left flank turned. Furthermore the premises seem to be weak. It is improbable that there was a Roman camp at Brandon in A.D. 51. The camp stands just to the west of the old Roman road connecting Caerleon with Uriconium, and is evidently sited to give flank protection to this road against an irruption from the Welsh hinterland down the valley of the Teme. It is hard to conceive of this road being built whilst Coxwall Knoll was occupied by Caradoc, for it passes within three miles of it. No doubt there was fighting at some time between Romans and Britons hereabouts—there is a good deal of evidence pointing to this—but it presumably occurred during the struggle subsequent to the defeat of Caradoc. Coxwall Knoll is an isolated hill and the 'isolation' argument applies here even more than in the case of the Breidden because the hill is smaller in area.

Lastly we come to HOLLOWAY ROCKS. So far as I can ascertain, the case for this site has been put by only one investigator, Sir Roderick Murchison. In the course of his argument he said: 'The chief resistance must have been made in the rocky precipices which lead up from the Teme to Holloway Rocks and Stow Hill. Driven from that line Caractacus would necessarily fight in retreat to the Caer Ditches (Caer Caradoc).' I think Sir Roderick took Tacitus' description concerning the precipitous rocky nature of the terrain rather too literally, for the reasons already given. After all, we know that the slope was not too steep for the Roman legionaries to negotiate. Nevertheless this site does fit in fairly well with the description of the historian, the weakest point, to my mind, being that which has vitiated the other proposed sites, namely that there would be no necessity for the Romans advancing up the valley to cross the river at that point; they could have approached along the northern bank. But, if we except the question of the river, this position is one that I should expect Caradoc to hold on the grounds of inherent military probability if he had to defend his headquarters against an attack from the south-east. I find it preferable to all the other sites noticed, and if the assumption on which I have built my thesis is wrong—namely that the Roman base for the campaign was Uriconium —then I fancy Holloway Rocks must be the site we are looking for. A slight variant, that has never been propounded, suggests itself. If for some reason Ostorius advanced from due south, i.e. from Presteign, making for Caer Caradoc, he would be obliged to cross the Teme in the face of the enemy. In this case the British position would presumably be along the high ground immediately north of Knighton, extending eastwards to Holloway Rocks. But if (as I think) the Roman campaign against the Ordovices was based on Uriconium, an advance from Presteign towards Knighton seems out of the question.

CONCLUSION

The verdict in a murder trial is frequently influenced by the consideration: 'Someone must be the murderer, if not the prisoner in the dock, then who?' If Caradoc did not fight his last battle on the banks of the Clun, then where did he fight it? I have visited the other suggested sites, and in addition have examined all the ground up the Severn from the Breidden to Cefn Carnedd, and can find no locality that fits the description of Tacitus, for in no case need Ostorius have crossed a river in order to attack his opponent. Of course Tacitus' reference to the crucial river may be a falsehood (not on the part of the historian but of some unscrupulous informer), but if we cannot build on Tacitus' account we cannot build at all. Accepting, then, his account as essentially correct, I have come to the conclusion that there is only one site on the Welsh border that adequately fits his description and that is on the Black Hill–Clunbury Hill ridge on the southern bank of the river Clun in Shropshire. A suitable name would be the Battle of the Clun.[1]

[1] Since writing this chapter I have been informed that a piece of Roman arrow has been excavated in Re-entrant A.

CHAPTER II

The Battle of Mount Badon

EVERY schoolboy knows how William the Conqueror slipped on the beach at Pevensey and defeated Harold at Hastings. Every schoolboy knows, or thinks he does, how Julius Caesar defeated that mighty British chieftain Cassivellaunus and thus subdued his country. But what schoolboy evinces interest in the defeat of the pagan Saxons by the Britons under their renowned leader Arthur at the Battle of Mons Badonicus, or Badon, about A.D. 500? Yet the result of that resounding victory was that the Saxons were driven back to the east, and Christian Britain had peace for half a century.

Mount Badon therefore is one of the most important battles ever fought in this island. Lack of interest in it is no doubt largely due to lack of information. But, thanks to our modern historians, a flood of light has recently been shed over the Dark Ages, and as a result it is now possible to reconstruct the story of the fifth century with a fair degree of probability. As a result 'King' Arthur emerges as an historical personage in the opinion of most historians of the period. His restoration to historicity is, in part, due to the partial rehabilitation of Geoffrey of Monmouth and his *Histories of the Kings of Britain*. It is now recognized that, interlarded in the hotch-potch of myth and fable that constitutes his story of 'King' Arthur, there is a solid residue of historical matter. I have made use of this matter in the following reconstruction of the Battle of Mount Badon, and discuss the credibility of Geoffrey of Monmouth in the final section of this chapter.

The Battle of Badon was fought between the Saxons under Aelle and Aesc, and the Britons under Arthur. It is impossible to define the boundary between the two peoples at that time; intermittent warfare had been waged between them for fifty years, and the situation may perhaps be likened to that which occurred in the Great Civil War where one party held the east of England and the other the west but these boundaries had little bearing on the operations, which resolved themselves into a series of marches and counter-marches by the contestants. It is, however, established that at about that time there was a Saxon settlement in the Thames Upper Valley, and a British settlement around Silchester, considerably farther east. But it does not follow that at the time of the battle these settlements were occupied by the respective armed forces. All that it is safe to assume is that the main forces of the Saxons came from Kent and Sussex, with probable contributions from East Anglia, and that the main British forces were centred in the south-west, with probable contributions from Wales. The paramount king of Britain was Ambrosius Aurelianus, 'the Last of the Romans', but he was now an old man and he had long before deputed the command of all the troops in the field to his nephew Arthur.

Badon has been identified with numerous places, such as Badbury Rings in Dorset, Bath and Strathclyde, but historians seem to despair of locating it with any approach to probability, let alone certainty. Yet I believe I know where it was fought, though I have no claim to be the discoverer. The site has been suggested by several writers, most recently by Mr. T. D. Reed, whose book *The Battle for Britain in the Fifth Century* gives a location which seems to me a convincing one. I ought, though, to say that while I accept Mr. Reed's general location I do not accept all his reasons for it. My own reasons I will give at the end, for the edification of the curious. Let it be understood, then, that, while I spare the reader an endless reiteration of 'probably' or 'it seems that', the reconstruction that follows is merely a series of reasoned surmises.

The northern edge of the Marlborough Downs passes four miles to the south of Swindon. The highest point (905 feet) on these Downs, Liddington Castle, lies six miles south-east of Swindon. I identify Liddington Castle with Mons Badonicus, and the actual battlefield as ranging between the castle and the village of Badbury, a mile to the north-west. Before describing the ground and the battle in detail let us read the account given by Geoffrey of Monmouth, as translated from the Latin by Dr. Sebastian Evans in 1903. Read every sentence carefully, as I shall have occasion to revert to the passage. Geoffrey relates how Arthur armed himself:

'Then, stationing his companies, he made hardy assault upon the Saxons that after their wont were ranked wedge-wise in battalions. Natheless, all day long did they stand their ground manfully maugre[1] the Britons that did deliver assault upon assault upon them. At last, just verging upon sundown, the Saxons occupied a hill close by that might serve them for a camp, for, secure in their numbers, the hill alone seemed all the camp they needed. But when the morrow's sun

[1] In spite of.

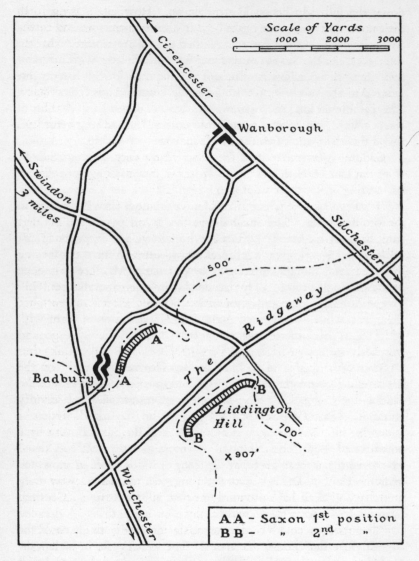

SKETCH-MAP 3.   MOUNT BADON

brought back the day, Arthur with his army clomb up to the top of
the hill, albeit that in the ascent he lost many of his men.   For the
Saxons, dashing down from their height, had the better advantage in
dealing their wounds, whilst they could also run far more swiftly

down the hill than he could struggle up. Howbeit, putting forth their utmost strength, the Britons did at last reach the top, and forthwith closed with the enemy hand to hand. The Saxons, fronting them with their broad chests, strove with all their endeavour to stand their ground. And when much of the day had been spent on this wise, Arthur waxed wroth at the stubbornness of their resistance, and the slowness of his own advance, and drawing forth Caliburn, his sword, crieth aloud the name of Holy Mary, and thrusteth him forward with a swift onset into the thickest press of the enemy's ranks.'

Geoffrey goes on to describe how 'many thousands' of Saxons were slain and how the rest took to flight, pursued by the Duke of Cornwall. But we need not quote him further.

Bearing the above passage in mind, we can now place the troops on the ground. The sketch map shows the Saxon position. The left flank lies on the southern end of the modern village of Badbury. It follows thence the crest of the hill in a north-easterly direction for one thousand yards, and the right flank, sharply refused, rests upon the edge of the steep nullah-like valley that points up towards Liddington Hill. This must be reckoned a strong position, skilfully selected to neutralize as far as possible the effect of Arthur's heavy cavalry—the arm with which he is believed to have won most of his battles. The ground falls fairly steeply in front and very steeply on the right flank, thus forming a formidable obstacle to the British cavalry. Only on the left would the horsemen have much chance of action, and here the Saxons doubtless massed their defenders and constructed anti-cavalry obstacles. No wonder the battle lasted all day, and the Britons obtained no spectacular success. None the less, the Saxons were hard pressed, and from the standpoint of morale they were weakened by the very fact that they had a strong position in rear on which to fall back if necessary. Often during that tremendous day they must have glanced back enviously at that hill-top, towering several hundred feet above them with a slope so steep that the dreaded British horsemen could hardly negotiate it. There they would be safe—if only they could get there! The evening shadows lengthened, and the customary slackening of tension enabled them to break off the fight and fall back under cover of the growing darkness to the hill-top.

Arthur did not pursue that night. His cavalry were worn out and were obliged to go back some distance to obtain water in any quantity. But the British leader took stock of the situation, noticed that the

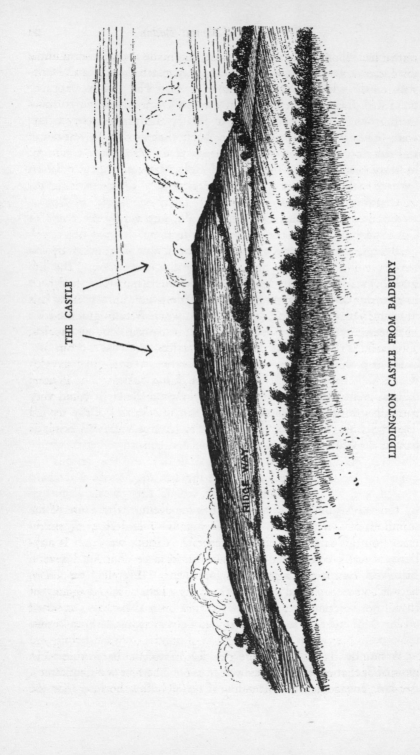

THE CASTLE

RIDGE WAY

LIDDINGTON CASTLE FROM BADBURY

retreat had stopped short at the hill-top, and made a somewhat unusual resolution for those days. He decided on an attack at dawn. Considering the ground, it looked a hopeless enterprise, for the approach was too steep for his horsemen; it rises for 300 feet at a slope of one-in-three—or 20 degrees. Even light cavalry of the present day would scarcely face it; for the heavy British horse of those times it was out of the question. Geoffrey's account rings true. 'They could run far more swiftly down the hill than he could struggle up.' It is indeed a 'struggle up', as anyone can testify for himself if he follows in the steps of the British army.

Geoffrey makes no mention of the Iron Age camp on top. This camp is too small to have been of much assistance. It forms a rough quadrangle 200 yards by 150 yards. The position occupied by the Saxons would extend almost the whole length of the crest of the hill, which is just 1,000 yards long. If the defenders remaining had been so few that the narrow confines of the camp sufficed for them it is unlikely that any would have got away when Arthur mounted his final attack. This attack would no doubt be delivered by his cavalry, approaching from the only feasible direction—the east. From any other direction the ascent would be too steep. Enveloping cavalry attacks were unusual in ancient days, though not unknown: at Poitiers such an attack had great effect. Even though difficult, it would very naturally be attempted as a last resort towards the end of the second day of battle. And it would be likely to have as decisive a result as that of the Captal de Buch at Poitiers.

ARTHUR'S GENERALSHIP

Can we, at this length of time after the event, and in spite of the scantiness of our material, descry any signs of leadership or skilful tactics on the part of the British general? I think we can. If anything is really certain about Arthur it is that he conducted several successful campaigns against his opponents. Therefore, *a priori*, he was an accomplished general. Luck may help now and again, but it will not account for a series of victories, such as Arthur is credited with. Moreover, he may be presumed to have acquired some knowledge of his opponents, of their method of fighting, of their strong and weak points. Now there were two features of the battle that were unusual at that epoch so far as we can tell. The first was that after a day-long engagement the defending army fell back a short distance and offered battle next day in a fresh position. The other unusual feature was that on the day after a long engagement the attacker made a dawn attack on the second position.

Consider the state of the British troops early that morning. They had marched some distance and fought a battle throughout the previous day, suffering heavy casualties. During the night the enemy had fallen back and occupied a still stronger position. Yet in spite of their fatigue, losses and consequent disorganization, Arthur somehow managed to get them forward to the assault on the new and formidable position at or soon after daylight.

What a strong hold over his troops he must have possessed to be able to achieve this! Only a leader who was implicitly trusted could produce such a result. Note also his good judgement. The difficulties and the dangers of such an enterprise must have appeared obvious to all, and the prospects of success, after their previous day's experiences, must have seemed remote. But Arthur judged aright. On what did he base his calculations? I suggest he shared that gift possessed by all great generals—the power of being able to picture the enemy's position and attitude and to penetrate his frame of mind. The Duke of Wellington once said he had spent most of his life 'guessing what was happening the other side of the hill'. What did Arthur discern on the other side of the ramparts of Castle Liddington? I suggest two things. In the first place, moral despondency, to which no retreating army is entirely impervious however great its discipline and homogeneity. We know nothing of the discipline of the Saxon host, but its homogeneity must have been slight, for it consisted of three allied contingents.[1] The Saxons, after holding one strong position precariously throughout the day, had abandoned it in the evening. This reverse was almost bound to effect their morale. Moreover, the disorganization in that loosely-knit army, struggling to carry out one of the most difficult operations in war—that of taking up a fresh position in the dark—must have been considerable. In the second place, physical weakness induced by hunger and thirst. The troops would start the second day's battle with an almost empty stomach, and suffering from extreme thirst, for no water would be procurable on the summit of the hill. They would also be short of missiles, whereas the British would recover their own missiles as they advanced.

The net result of all this was that the Saxons were in a weaker state than would naturally appear to their opponents. But the

[1] Sussex, Kent and East Anglia.

experienced eye of the old war leader, Arthur, discerned their weakness (just as Wellington used to discern Soult's). He appreciated the factors aright. In spite of the disappointing first day, he saw victory before him. His greatness of soul would not admit of defeat; he was a shining example of the truth of Marshal Foch's famous aphorism: 'He is the victor who refuses to admit himself defeated.' No wonder Arthur became the darling of the British race and that he became endowed with kingship and knight errantry—a national hero '*Sans peur et sans reproche*.' He deserves a prominent place in that illustrious band of heroes who saved our country in its hour of need, that band that starts with Cassivellaunus and Caradoc and ends with Churchill.

PROBLEMS OF THE BATTLEFIELD

From the general distribution of the forces the conflict would naturally take place in South England. Communications were few, forests and marshes were widespread; hence the lines of operations were limited, and dependent on the few trackways. Following Geoffrey, the numbers were considerable on each side, the Saxons concentrating from Sussex, Kent and East Anglia, while the British contingents were probably drawn from all the country comprising Wales and South-West England. The obvious concentration point for the British army would thus be Cirencester, the best Roman road centre in the country, and conveniently situated to oppose the threatened attack from the east. As for the Saxons, the Sussex men would march by the pre-Roman Harrow Way (Pilgrims' Way) as far as Basingstoke, thence up the great Roman road, Winchester to Cirencester. The Kentish contingent would traverse London and Silchester, thence taking the Silchester-Cirencester road. These two forces would thus converge at a point four miles east of Swindon, near Wanborough. The direct and natural approach for the East Anglians would be by the Icknield Way and Ridgeway, which contacts the other two roads just under Liddington Hill. What a meeting point! The roads seem almost fore-ordained for the purpose.

Assuming, then, that the opposing armies concentrated at Cirencester and near Liddington Hill respectively, where should we expect them to join battle? According to Geoffrey, the British advanced and the Saxons took up a defensive position. The site of the battle would therefore be decided by the Saxon commander Aelle. We can picture him acting as follows. He has ordered the concentration of the three contingents at Liddington, and goes there himself to meet them. His scouts now bring word that the Britons are advancing and he decides to offer battle in a position of his own selection. Naturally he would like to make it in advance of the junction point of his three bodies, but this would involve going forward into the low country to the north of the Downs. All armies in those days had a strong penchant for hill positions, and Aelle was probably no exception to the rule. Clearly the strongest position was on Liddington Hill itself. Liddington Camp could form a nucleus for the defence, and if time allowed it might be roughly extended. Entrenched on that hilltop he would be well protected from the dreaded British cavalry. The weakness of the position lay in the fact that it was behind instead of in advance of the Ridgeway—the line of communications of the East Anglians.

Aelle therefore cast his eye forward, in the hope of finding another position in advance of the Ridgeway, yet not so far forward as to involve abandoning the Downs. A position almost exactly meeting his requirements does, in fact, exist and has already been described. It possesses the double advantage of being sufficiently advanced to cover the Ridgeway while still retaining the advantage of high and commanding ground. It is a natural position, such as might well have been occupied in modern times right up to the Boer War. As to extent, we do not, of course, know the strength of the Saxon army, but Geoffrey implies that it was large, as it would naturally be. If it was about 10,000 strong a position with a frontage of 1,200 yards would be appropriate. Here, then, was a position simply crying out to be occupied. It satisfies all the known facts and inferences, and I know of no other place that does.[1] The site strikingly resembles the supposed site of the Battle of Barbury Castle fought in A.D. 556, and only six miles to the west. Finally, some authorities identify the name of Badon with the modern Badbury. The combined effect of all the above considerations convinces me that the historic Battle of Badon was fought on the ground that I have described.

Sitting on the crest of Liddington Castle with the landscape laid out below, it is easy for anyone with a spark of imagination and knowledge to picture the course of the second day's battle, to watch the British struggling painfully and slowly up the hill, the Saxons charging down on them every now and then (plying axe and spear, and even stones), and then the final cavalry charge, as the light is failing, coming

[1] I deal with the claims of BAYDON and BADBURY RINGS in an article in HISTORY of September 1947.

through on the right and driving along the flat hill-top, led by Arthur in person. What a setting for a pageant!

GEOFFREY OF MONMOUTH

I HAVE spoken above of 'the partial rehabilitation of Geoffrey of Monmouth.' The most exhaustive critical examination of the *Historia Regum Britanniae* was made by Mr. Acton Griscom in 1920. Among his conclusions are the following: 'Certain important contributions are not imaginative' (p. 101), and '(Geoffrey) had another source in the *Historia* (besides Nennius) and he had additional material' (p. 186). The most recent (1950) contribution to the controversy has been made by Mr. T. D. Kendrick in his *British Antiquity* where he writes: 'It seems likely that he did have a collection of fragmentary sources of a derived and inferior kind . . . there are signs that he did in fact compose his *Historia* under some kind of guidance and restraint.' (p. 6).

Accepting the above opinions I had to decide which statements in Geoffrey's description of the battle of Mount Badon I could accept. In selecting what I deem worthy of credence I have applied the test to every statement of Geoffrey: 'Had he any reason for distortion or fabrication in this case?' Where the answer appears to be in the negative I accept it, especially if it seems to throw light on a difficult point. To take but one example: In his account of the battle of Mount Baden he states: that the Saxons 'were formed up in wedges (*cunios*) as was their custom': Geoffrey could have no obvious reason for inventing this, and indeed it rings true. It is generally agreed, as pointed out by Mr. J. N. L. Myres, that Arthur relied largely on his cavalry arm for his successes against the Saxons. The latter would naturally after a few defeats, apply themselves to the problem of the most effective counter that their infantry could apply. This would probably take the form of a series of small clumps of men, thickly knit, shoulder to shoulder—the expedient that Wellington adopted at Waterloo against the French cavalry attacks. These clumps would be additionally effective if they were in diamond formation, the sharp point facing the enemy, for the effect of this would be that the attacking horsemen would normally have to approach either side of the wedge aslant. Now a horse approaching an obstacle obliquely (whether a fence or a line of men) tends to 'shy off'; hence the British horsemen would find it difficult to penetrate the clumps of wedges. We should therefore expect that the Saxons would evolve a formation of wedges (*cuneos*)[1], which is precisely what Geoffrey asserts that they did.

If the *Historia* is correct in this reference to the battle it may also be in others, and I have applied the same test to them all, viz: Had Geoffrey any motive for inventing or distorting the truth in this case? If the answer seems to be in the negative I have accepted it. But when, for example, he states that Arthur killed 690 of his enemies with his own hand there is the obvious motive of the glorification of his hero (apart from the essential improbability of the story), and I therefore have rejected it. ...

[1] Major Godsall, in his *Conquests of Ceawlin* coolly turns *cuneos* into *cuncum* in his endeavour to establish the battlefield on a wedge-shaped hill near Bath.

CHAPTER III

The Battle of Deorham, A.D. 577

THERE is a general agreement that the battle of Deorham was one of the most important battles ever fought in this country. After nearly a century of slow and chequered progress, the Saxons at a single blow finally split the British forces into two parts, the northern portion becoming the inhabitants of Wales, the southern of Cornwall.

In the middle span of the sixth century the Anglo-Saxons were pushing steadily north-westwards through what is now Wiltshire, Oxfordshire, and Gloucester. In the words of the *Anglo-Saxon Chronicle* (our only real authority):

'A.D. 552. This year Cynric (son of Cerdic) fought with the Britons at the place that is called Sarum and put them to flight. . . .

'A.D. 556. This year Cynric and Ceawlin (his son) fought with the Britons at Beranburh [Barbury Castle, six miles south of Swindon] . . .

'A.D. 577. Cuthwin and Ceawlin fought with the Britons and slew three kings, . . . on the place that is called Deorham and took from them three cities Gloucester, Cirencester and Bath.'

Seven years later Ceawlin is reported fighting in the north Midlands.

The implication of all this seems to be that Ceawlin made his first objective the Severn estuary, thus cutting Britain into two parts for all practical purposes, and that being accomplished he turned north to extend his sway over central England.

It is almost universally assumed that the three kings, whose capitals were Gloucester, Cirencester, and Bath, had concentrated their armies inside the triangle made by these three cities, and that the modern Dyrham represents the Anglo-Saxon Deorham. Here unanimity ceases. As to the line of Ceawlin's approach and the precise place of the battlefield there have been marked divergences of opinion through the centuries. Roughly speaking there are three schools of thought. One school makes Ceawlin, the Saxon commander, advance along the Roman road from Cunetio (Marlborough) to Bath, and thence northwards. A second gives his route as along the Roman road towards Cirencester, skirting to the south of that city and approaching Dyrham from the north-east, Bath being his objective. A third school pictures him advancing along an ancient road between Braden Forest and Box Brook, on a road running approximately east–west. A fourth school (if Major Godsall may be so described) makes the Saxons approach Bristol and Bath from a position on Wansdyke to the south, with the co-operation of a fleet on the Avon. This last theory is so fanciful that it need not be seriously considered.

Let us now see how these varied schools of thought arose. The literature of this subject is surprisingly meagre. We will start with Camden —the usual starting-point. He places the battle at Hinton Hill Camp, one mile north of Dyrham; he asserts that the Saxons occupied the camp and the Britons concentrated against it from both north and south. Next comes Samuel Ryder, writing in 1774. He follows Camden for the most part, but does not go further than saying that the Saxons 'are supposed to have occupied' the camp. Dr. Guest is the next antiquary of note to contribute to the subject. He held that Ceawlin took the northern route, just short of Cirencester, with Bath as his objective. T. G. P. Hallett adopted this theory in 1884, and worked it out in some detail. According to his theory Ceawlin marched along the Fosseway towards Bath, but found his route blocked at the combe on which is sited Castle Combe, and forced to make a detour to his right. To do this he took the old track leading through Nettleton straight on to Hinton Hill Camp, which was occupied by the enemy. Thus came about the battle at that spot.

We now jump to 1904, when the Rev. C. S. Taylor throws out an entirely fresh theory. Ceawlin advanced along the old track south of the Forest of Braden, via Christian Malford, Stanton St. Quinton, Nettleton, to Hinton Hill, making for the Bristol Channel. This we will call the Middle Road. In 1907 F. F. Fox brought the Roman camp on Sodbury Hill into the picture, stating (like Ryder) that the Saxons were 'supposed to' have occupied that camp on the day before the battle. Presumably therefore they were advancing south on Bath, as Hallett had affirmed.

The last reference is in 1929 by St. Clair Braddel. He adopts the middle road, but places Ceawlin inside the camp, where he is attacked by the Britons.

It will be noted that none of these writers sponsor the southern route via Bath (though some historians, notably Sir Charles Oman, voice that view)—still less the Godsall theory.

Let us now test these theories in the light of the *Anglo-Saxon Chronicle*, and of considerations of inherent military probability. The first thing to note is that six years elapsed between the campaign of Cuthwulf in the Chilterns (571) and the campaign of Deorham (577).

Modern historians are apt to foreshorten the events of ancient history and to picture Ceawlin advancing from Oxfordshire to the Cotswolds in six days rather than in six years. Now a great deal can happen in six years (the whole of the World War was comprised within that period). This six-year silence in the *Anglo-Saxon Chronicle* probably conceals a series of swings of the pendulum, several advances and retreats by the Saxons, from different directions, though no decisive battle was fought and the general upshot was to push the Britons further back towards the Cotswolds and the west. If Ceawlin consolidated as he advanced there could be little element of surprise in that advance. He had been under arms fairly continuously for a quarter of a century and any youthful dash that he may once have possessed had probably been replaced by caution—especially if the battle of Barbury was a moral defeat for him, as I suspect it was.

Not only would Ceawlin have grown cautious, but prudent too. I cannot see him advancing by either the northern or southern route, skirting the hostile strongholds respectively of Cirencester or Bath. If his objective were Bath I can see no object in approaching it by a circuitous route that would run him into gratuitous danger *en route*. Nor, conversely, if his objective were Gloucester, is it likely that he would pass Bath, leaving it a menace to his communications. If Ceawlin was a strategist (and there is every reason to suppose he was), he would realize the immense strategical advantage in an advance to the Bristol Channel, for such a move would cut the enemy's armed forces in two. If that were his objective he would naturally select a route that avoided passing near either Cirencester or Bath. Alternatively, if he knew that the enemy were concentrated on the Cotswolds he would prefer to strike at the hostile army in the field rather than at fortified towns. For that has always been sound strategy: if the hostile field army can be disposed of the towns will fall like ripe plums into the victor's lap. (Naseby spelt the knell of Bristol and Oxford.) By either of these suppositions Ceawlin would be expected to take the central road south of Braden Forest, as suggested by C. S. Taylor.

Now we know that when Ceawlin did reach the Cotswolds the concentrated army of the enemy was there, and it is a reasonable assumption that it was the combined army of the 'kings' of Cirencester, Gloucester, and Bath. (No doubt the *Chronicle* exalted the local leaders into kings to add prestige to the victory.) One theory (Carden's) is that they concentrated upon the Saxon army at Dyrham from north and south. This may look attractive on paper, but all history emphasizes

the practical difficulties of concentrating on exterior lines against a
centrally situated enemy. It is much more likely that the Britons were
already concentrated before the Saxons approached. It is usually the
simplest that happens in war. In this case the simplest solution would
be that Ceawlin's advance was slow and methodical, heading straight
for the Bristol Channel, that the Britons were alive to the strategical
danger threatening and that they consequently took up a position barring the enemy's approach. Where would one expect to find such a
position? Surely astride the main existing trackway. This we may presume to have been the 'middle' road. How far along it? One might
expect them to take up a position as far east on the Cotswold massif as
possible, say about Nettleton. But for reasons we do not know this did
not prove possible, so they fell back to a position covering the hill fort
of Hinton Hill, which would serve for them as a sort of depot or
arsenal of stores and food. The position thus taken up would be strikingly similar to that at Barbury—a not surprising coincidence if, as I
believe, the Barbury position had served them well. In each case the
position adopted was just on top of the massif or plateau, with the
escarpment only a few hundred yards in their rear; in each case there
was a broad valley immediately in their rear; in each case they held
a position a few hundred yards in front of, and covering a hill fort
situated on the very edge of the escarpment—in each case a 'promontory' camp. Finally (if I locate the actual line held correctly) in each case
the position was on commanding ground, sloping gently down towards
the enemy, with sharp slopes on or near the two flanks.

Full of confidence then, in the strength of their position and encouraged by the recollection of that battle at Barbury twenty-one years
before, Kings Commail, Condidan, and Farinmail arrayed their combined hosts in battle order. The seriousness of the situation must have
been clear to all in that army. Each man had only to glance over his
shoulder, over a dozen miles of flat ground to the gleaming waters of
the Bristol Channel. There would be little hope of escape if they were
worsted, nor for their country if the Saxons prevailed. It was do or die!

If the above premises be accepted, the precise site of the battlefield
should not be difficult to define. A glance at the sketch-map will show
that 300 yards in front of the camp there is a slight ridge, running
astride of and exactly perpendicular to the road by which the Saxons
were approaching. What could be better for a line of defence? But
there was one objection to it. Six hundred yards further forward there
is another and slightly higher ridge. (Though only a very gentle

ridge it is as well marked as that probably occupied by Egbert at Ellandun.)

This forward ridge also runs astride of and perpendicular to the road, and in front of it the ground slopes very gently down, affording a splendid distant view of the approach of the enemy. This strikes me as being as near ideal for the purpose as could well be conceived. Here then, on the line marked AA on the sketch-map I place the defending army of the three kings, their reserve line being on the ridge BB in the rear.

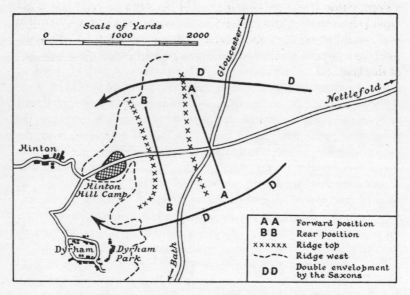

SKETCH-MAP 4. DEORHAM: THE BATTLE

As for details of the battle we only know one fact, but the full significance of that has not, I believe, been sufficiently recognized. (Godsall hints at it.) This fact is that all three commanders of the allied army lost their lives. Such an event was, so far as I know, unique in Wessex warfare. At Ashdown one Danish commander was slain, but the other leader got away. Here all were 'put in the bag'. The implication seems inescapable: they were surrounded. How did this come about? To get at the probable answer let us once more look at the map.

As the pressure of the attackers increased the Britons would be gradually pushed back to the line BB. Now the flanks of this line would rest almost if not quite on the escarpment. The least additional retreat, or the least overlapping of the line by the attackers, would enable the flank men to charge headlong and exultantly down the steep hill. Swinging inwards instinctively (as troops do) they would join hands below and in rear of the camp. All this would happen in a matter of a few minutes, and long before the defenders could organize any counter-action.

In this fashion, then, I picture the course of this historic battle. The three kings, falling back to the refuge of the camp, would find their further retreat cut off. They would be besieged, if still alive; and such a siege, unless speedy relief came, could have but one end, for water would be unobtainable in the hill fort. Commail, Condidan, and Farinmail would be captured by Ceawlin, and summarily knocked on the head. The battle of Deorham thus marked the downfall of the defenders of this land.

CHAPTER IV

Wansdyke and Ellandun, A.D. 825

WANSDYKE is the name given to that mysterious earthwork that wanders right across southern England. For over three hundred years it has excited the curiosity and baffled the researches of antiquarians and historians alike. It remains a mystery which is never likely to be entirely dissolved. But I have a theory as to its origin which seems to me to be so inherently probable that I feel justified in including it in this book. Although we have no records of any part of the dyke ever having been the scene of a battle, yet if my theory is correct its existence may help to solve another minor problem, namely the otherwise inexplicable military operations of King Egbert in that fateful year A.D. 825. I say 'fateful' advisedly, because the battle of Ellandun, fought in that year, attained for Wessex and its royal House the leadership of all the states comprising England, a leadership that it never lost. Therefore in this chapter I link Wansdyke and the battle of Ellandun.

Wansdyke is the name given to a bank, *vallum*, or dyke that runs practically without a break from the Bristol Channel to Inkpen Beacon in Berkshire. Starting at Portishead on the Bristol Channel, it runs south-east for 20 map miles to the south of Bath. After circling the southern perimeter of this town as far as Bathampton, it takes an easterly course along the old Roman road, for 13 miles, to the north of Devizes. Thence it follows the line of the Wiltshire Downs, passing to the south of Marlborough, through Savernake Forest as far as Chisbury Camp, a distance of 15 map miles. The final section bends back in an east-south-easterly direction for 8 miles to Inkpen Beacon. Only short sections of the dyke are visible in Savernake Forest, but over the remainder of its course it is fairly continuous for those who have eyes to see, while along the top of the Wiltshire Downs between Devizes and Marlborough only the blind could miss it. Here, for mile upon mile, it winds its gently sinuous way, observant of the contours, as every well-conducted military work should be. This section is most impressive and cannot have changed greatly during the many centuries that have elapsed since its construction.

I have described the dyke as a bank—not a ditch, for that is the correct meaning of the word. But a bank usually presumes a ditch also, from which the soil for the bank is dug.

Wansdyke has a ditch, and the significant point about this ditch is that it lies on the northern side of the bank throughout its course. It can hardly be a coincidence that this should be so; it is evidence of consistent design—a military design. The dyke is in other words a barrier—not a mere boundary—a barrier against a potential enemy on its northern side. I do not fancy anyone nowadays disputes this proposition. It provides us with a base of operations, as it were, in our quest. We have to identify some ruler in the course of our history who governed or controlled the portion of England that lies to the south of a line running roughly from Bristol to Newbury, and who might be expected, in the nature of things, to construct such a dyke.

There are signs of difference in the detail of construction in various sectors of the line, and it is quite possible that in places short stretches of older works were utilized in the major work—we shall note the bearing of this later on—but the work as a whole is evidently the creation of one brain.

★   ★   ★   ★   ★

We must now make a brief and rapid survey of our ancient history in our quest for this creator, noting the various theories put forward as the centuries roll by. First of all comes the pre-Roman period, that of the 'Ancient Britons'. The theory that Wansdyke was dug as a boundary between the Belgae and Ancient Britons, though once popular, has long been abandoned. It was killed by the investigations of General Pitt-Rivers, who in 1889 discovered by the spade that portions of the dyke are built upon a Roman road. From this he made the obvious deduction that the dyke must be later than the road, i.e. late Roman or post-Roman. I think the cautious general might have gone a stage further and limited it to post-Roman, for what Roman would construct a bank right on top of his own road? He would build it to the side—the enemy's side, leaving the road for lateral communication, like the lateral road along another Roman bank, Hadrian's Wall. If this is agreed it rules out the next two theories, namely that the Romans built it against incursions from the north either in A.D. 186 or 367.

This brings us to the departure of the Roman legions and to the defence of the country by the Roman-British general Arthur, against the invaders from the east. Now if Arthur, or Ambrosius Aurelianus, had built such a defensive work it would presumably have faced east instead of north. Sir Charles Oman gets over this difficulty by suggesting that it formed the boundary between two Celtic tribes in the peaceful period between Arthur's great victory of Mount Badon in about 500, and the advance of Ceawlin about fifty years later. This he deduces from certain passages in Gildas, the almost contemporary British writer. Now, I have the greatest respect for Sir Charles as a military historian, and have learnt much from him, but I feel that in this case he has extracted from Gildas' few and brief sentences more than they warrant. He has squeezed the juice out of the orange till almost 'the pips squeak'. I cannot believe that two native kings would spend so much trouble in marking out boundaries against one another at a time when the foreign invader was in possession of parts of the land. This invader may have been badly winded after the Arthurian blow, but he might yet come up for the count. With Anglo-Saxon settlements already in South Hampshire and possibly in the Upper Thames Valley, the idea that the neighbouring British sub-kings should ignore such threats to their very existence does not make sense. I am not aware that any expert has definitely accepted this theory of Sir Charles. Moreover, was there sufficient coherence among the 'conglomeration of, for the most part, insignificant kingdoms, whose small-minded rulers were solely concerned with petty schemes of aggrandizement' as Dayrell Reed describes England in those days? When the land was in such a condition it does not seem a likely period in which to construct an immense line across southern England which would require even more men than the construction of the Great Pyramid. Moreover, during this period Cerdic, based on Hampshire and South Wiltshire would be threatening its rear. There is yet another objection, relating to parish boundaries that I will touch upon later.

As opposed to Oman's theory, some modern writers hold that Wansdyke was constructed about this time, but as a defence by the Britons against the invaders. Alban Major, who made an exhaustive survey of Wansdyke, is representative of this view, though he states it with cautious reservations. The foregoing objection (i.e. that it faces north instead of east) applies here also.

The next school of thought regards the dyke as belonging to the era of the Saxon king Ceawlin (556–591), though as to whether it was built by the Britons against the Saxons or vice versa they are curiously at variance. The most popular book on this subject is *The Conquests of Ceawlin* by Major P. T. Godsal. In this book he asserts that Wansdyke was made by Ceawlin between 556 and 577, that is, in the midst of his victorious advance from the Thames to the Severn. What a peculiar time at which to devote resources and to deflect labour from the battle-line to the construction of a defensive work sited miles behind his frontier! Moreover the western area covered by the dyke was not then in his possession. These seem sufficient reasons to put the suggestion out of court without invoking the argument of the parish boundaries. Major Godsal's bull-point is that the dyke was called Woden's Dyke from the start, and as Woden was a pagan god it must have been made in pagan times. But was it thus known at the start? All we know for certain is that in 903 a portion of it was so known: that is four centuries later, by which time a mistaken origin might well become attached to it, in the absence of written records. Alternatively, there may have been one or more short lengths of dyke of pagan origin which were utilized in the construction of the work in Christian times. (Alban Major has established that Wansdyke was in its origin a composite work.)

Diametrically opposed to Major Godsal's theory is that of those who allot it to the same period but assert that it was built by the Britons against the Saxons to the north of them. In the one case the Saxons are placed to the south of the dyke, in the second to the north. This illustrates the obscurity of the history of that period. Neither theory will hold water, for Ceawlin's advance was from the Thames in a westerly direction, and it would be futile for the Britons to seek to oppose the invaders by constructing a line parallel to the line of the hostile advance: the Saxons could render the whole system valueless by advancing from the Lower Thames along the south face of the dyke instead of along the northern face, thus turning it. There were also the Southampton invaders to be watched. Once again the parish boundary argument is against this theory, and it is time to examine this argument.

In 1904, the Rev. C. S. Taylor pointed out that the existing parish boundaries ignore Wansdyke, except where they run along the Roman road. This seems fairly conclusive evidence that the parish boundaries were fixed before Wansdyke was made, for it is almost inconceivable that they would not have taken advantage of such a good landmark as the dyke, especially where it runs along the top of the Wiltshire Downs, which in themselves form a rough dividing line between the parishes. The very fact that the parish boundary follows the Roman road shows that advantage was taken of any existing landmark when the boundaries were fixed. This consideration runs counter to Alban Major's theory of early construction. And his method of explaining it away does not seem very clear or convincing.

Taylor held that the dyke was constructed by Cenwahl, King of Wessex, between 648 and 652. Objections to this are that: (1) Bede does not mention it; if such an important work were constructed within fifty years of his own time the great historian would scarcely have passed it over in silence; (2) parish boundaries were probably not then in existence; (3) Cenwahl was hardly the King, nor was Wessex at that period the country, to produce such a comprehensive and united work; there was then little internal coherence in Wessex, and the numerous sub-kings would have been unlikely to combine in such a work. Furthermore, the Western portion of the line ran through territory still held by the Britons.

The parish boundary argument was taken up quite recently by Mr. Shaw Mellor in the *Wiltshire Archaeological Magazine* for 1945. He thinks the parish boundaries were started at the end of the seventh century. He does not commit himself to a definite date, but he quotes with apparent approval Pitt-Rivers' suggestion that it is possible that Wansdyke was a boundary thrown up by the West Saxons as a defence against Offa, King of Mercia, in the eighth century. But Pitt-Rivers made so many suggestions, none of which he would sponsor himself, that this suggestion of his has not received the attention it deserves.

*   *   *   *   *

By this time the reader will perhaps be exclaiming: 'It is all very easy to pour destructive criticism on the various theories that account for Wansdyke, but there must be *some* explanation for it; the thing exists; if it was not made at any of the epochs suggested above, then how came it and when?' When studying the problem myself I felt like this. This merely made me the more anxious to solve it, for after all, Wansdyke exists; the fact cannot be gainsaid. It was a chance reference, in a book, to Offa's Dyke that set me thinking. Was there any similarity or relation between the two? Though I did not know it at the time, John Aubrey, three hundred years ago, had asked himself the same question. Now Sir Cyril Fox made an estensive survey of Offa's Dyke twenty years ago, and so I examined his writings on the subject with interest. I was at once struck by the following points of similarity between the two dykes. (1) They possess a generic similarity, being of great length, with flanks resting on natural obstacles—Offa's Dyke, the Irish Sea and the Bristol Channel—Wansdyke the Bristol Channel and Inkpen Beacon. (2) There is a similar wideness of conception and unity of purpose about them which indicate that they must each be the handiwork of a great mind and personality. (3) Their general form of construction is the same—a vallum with a ditch always on the same side.

(4) Each exhibits a variety, within these general limits, of details of construction. (5) There is evidence that each was constructed by sectors, each sector being on a tolerably straight line, and the junction between contiguous sectors not always being clear.

There is no space in which to develop these arguments; I confine myself to the mere assertion that it is so. The similarities point to the likelihood (I will not put it stronger) that the two dykes are fairly contemporaneous. My next step was to examine the inter-state situation at the time Offa's Dyke was built, to see if it would support this supposition.

For the benefit of those readers whose early English history has become rusty I will here make a small historical digression. King Offa reigned over Mercia from 758 to 796. During his reign Mercia was the dominant power in England. Offa enlarged his boundaries in all directions, and in or about 784 he constructed the dyke that bears his name running from the mouth of the Dee to the mouth of the Wye, as a barrier-boundary between his dominions and Wales. In 777 he had driven Kenulf, King of Wessex, south of the Thames in a battle fought at Bensington near Wallingford, having already subdued the sub-kingdom of Kent. Wessex was then left in peace by Offa whilst he turned his attention to his Welsh opponents. So far historical facts; now for the first time I enter the land of speculation, and I shall use the present indicative rather than the subjunctive in relating what I picture to have happened.

It is the year 784. Kenulf of Wessex is eyeing closely the doings of Offa his rival. The latter has been at war with the Welsh ever since his victory over Wessex seven years ago. Presently rumours begin to seep across the border to Kenulf that Offa, having come to terms with the Welsh, is building a stupendous military work all along his Welsh frontier. Enemies of one country may be accounted friends of one another. Wales and Wessex come under this category (just as England and Russia did in 1941). Welsh mariners bring Kenulf word that confirms the rumours, and they give a description of the great dyke that Offa is constructing, together with the warning that it may only be the prelude to another attack by Offa on his old foe Wessex. No centrally situated power courts a war on two fronts. Offa's motto evidently is 'One foe at a time'. If he can make his western frontier secure he can return with an easy mind against his southern enemy. Forewarned is forearmed; Kenulf decides to copy the action of Offa while yet there is time. (The military thought and procedure of the dominant military power is always copied by its neighbours, as was notably the case regarding Germany after the Franco-Prussian War.) Kenulf therefore sets to work feverishly to make a prototype of the 'Maginot Line' well inside but parallel to his northern frontier (again like the French). Like Offa he can anchor it on the sea on one flank, but on the other he must be content to 'refuse the flank' slightly and rest it upon the great massif of Inkpen Beacon. Thence to the south-east his frontier is no longer contiguous with that of Mercia, albeit Surrey and Kent are now vaguely subordinated to Offa. That at any rate is the best Kenulf can do, and he hastens to put his project into effect. Thus we see the two dykes being traced out and dug almost simultaneously, the northern one having a few months lead.

*   *   *   *   *

Such in brief is my reconstruction of the origin of Wansdyke. Is there any event in the subsequent history of Wessex that lends countenance to it? I think there is.

Within twenty years of the construction of the Dyke, Egbert, the founder of our Royal House, came to the throne of Wessex. Wansdyke was then almost brand new; it had been built during Egbert's lifetime; he may indeed have assisted in the work, and the new king would take care to maintain it in good order so long as there remained any potential danger on the side of Mercia. For twenty years there was peace between the two countries; and then Egbert did a thing which would seem incomprehensible were it not for the existence of Wansdyke. Though Beornwulf, King of Mercia, had an army in being, and was still the paramount military power in England, Egbert, ignoring the danger from the north, took his own army to attack the Britons in Cornwall, thus apparently leaving his own frontier open to attack by Beornwulf. How could Egbert afford to take such a risk? Wansdyke seems to be the answer. If it was still in good repair and if he left a garrison—even a skeleton one—to hold it, Beornwulf might be discouraged from attacking it in spite of the absence of the main Wessex army. Whatever the reason, Beornwulf did not attack, though he kept his own army within striking distance of the frontier while Egbert was subduing the enemy in East Cornwall. The presence of the Mercian army in a menacing position near the frontier probably shortened Egbert's campaign in the west; he hurried back, probably via Bath, Devizes, and Avebury, picking up the garrisons of Wansdyke as he passed along it. Beornwulf was now near Swindon, and Egbert came upon him near Wroughton. Here was fought the decisive battle of Ellandun, a battle that finally decided the long contest for pre-eminence between Mercia and Wessex in favour of the latter. The Kings of Wessex thus became the Kings of England, and their descendants still sit upon its throne.

Thus Wansdyke can be claimed to have played a prominent part in the shaping of affairs in the critical years that decided the future of England and gave us what is now the Royal House of Windsor.

★   ★   ★   ★   ★

Two objections may be raised against the foregoing reconstruction. How did the dyke come to be connected with the pagan Woden if its creator was the Christian Kenulf? And why did not Asser mention the fact, considering that he mentioned the contemporary creation of Offa's Dyke? Asser was a Welshman, brought up in Wales. He would be bound to be aware of the existence of Offa's Dyke which was still the boundary between the two countries. But after Ellandun the rapid enlargement of the bounds of Wessex left Wansdyke far in rear of the frontier, like seaweed left high and dry behind the receding tide. Its *raison d'être* would be gone and it would fall into disrepair. The century that followed the death of Bede in 731 was one of the bleakest in our historical annals:[1] there was no contemporary or near contemporary chronicler, and by the time that one arose in the person of Asser a century later no written record of the origin of Wansdyke existed. Small wonder then that the explanation of it was lost, and that it came to be attributed to pagan times and origin especially if portions of pagan works were incorporated in it. Errors get passed down from mouth to mouth—even among historians—and, if my reconstruction has substance, it seems high time that this particular error was unmasked and that Wansdyke, 'this mighty bulwark', should be brought back into its rightful place in our Island story.

High up on the presbytery wall of Winchester Cathedral stands a mortuary chest containing the bones of two Saxon Kings, and their names—believe it or not—are Kenulf and Egbert. The inscription on the chest runs:

'HIC REX EGBERTUS PAUSAT CUM REGE KENULPHO.'

---

[1] The period 768–814 is described by Professor Chambers as 'one of the most obscure periods of English history'.

To it I should like to add:

'WODENSDICIS CREATOR ET OCCUPATOR.'

$\star$ $\star$ $\star$ $\star$ $\star$

We can now pass on to a more detailed examination of the battle and battlefield of Ellandun. It was fought in A.D. 825, and has been described by Sir Frank Stenton as 'one of the most decisive battles of English history'. I have mentioned above that Egbert came upon the Mercian army 'near Wroughton', leaving the exact site and the course of the battle to be considered later.

THE BATTLE

As is the case in all Anglo-Saxon battles, few details have come down to us. It would seem, however, that Beornwulf with his army had taken up a position of observation a short distance to the north of the Wessex border, a few miles west of the modern town of Swindon. For the best part of twenty years (a period more devoid of records than almost any other in Anglo-Saxon history) Egbert had been steadily building up his armed forces, his ultimate intention being to challenge the position of predominance held for so long by the rival state to the north, Mercia. Beornwulf was a king with but little spirit of enterprise and he was conscious of the fact that his army was now inferior to that of Wessex; hence he did not dare to take advantage of the temporary absence in Cornwall of the main rival army, but contented himself with collecting his forces and watching the frontier. It is of course possible, though we have no records on the point, that he was waiting for reinforcements, either from his own people or from Northumbria.

Be that as it may, the summer wore on, and Beornwulf made no offensive move. Thus Egbert was able to return from his victorious campaign in Cornwall to find his northern frontier still inviolate. Passing Barbury Castle, the scene of a great battle 270 years before, the Wessex army descended from the downs into the low ground west of Swindon by the ancient trackway that leads to Cricklade. Somewhere on this road, in the vicinity of Lydiard Tregoze, the Mercian army was drawn up to accept battle. (I will deal with the precise spot later.) The two armies ranged themselves on opposite ridges astride the road and about 1,200 yards apart, with a shallow valley separating them.

The details of the engagement that followed are, with two small exceptions, confined to the *Annales de Wintonia*. The *Anglo-Saxon Chronicle* merely states that Egbert won the victory and that there was great slaughter, while *Henry of Huntingdon* states that the river ran red with blood. Now let us see what the *Annales de Wintonia* have to tell us. These have never been translated in full, but the rough sense of the passage is as follows.

It was summer time; the weather was hot. 'More soldiers were suffocated with sweat than with blood.' The two armies evidently ranged themselves in battle array with deliberation. It then became perceptible to Egbert that the Mercians heavily outnumbered his own army. He held a council of war to decide whether to accept battle. The situation reminds one of the celebrated night council of the Black Prince on the eve of Poitiers. The decision was the same; Egbert would fight. The Winchester scribe maintains that not only were the Mercians overwhelmingly superior in numbers but that they were physically in fitter condition, 'healthy and ruddy of the soil', whereas Egbert's troops were 'wan and thin'. It is hard to believe this; after a summer campaigning in Cornwall the Wessex men would look at least as ruddy as their opponents, who had been inactive. Thin perhaps, but certainly fit; whereas the Mercians were probably fat and soft in comparison. Indeed this disparity in physical condition may go some way to explain the decisive victory that ensued. For all accounts and the sequelae, confirm that the defeat was absolute and the slaughter prodigious.

The lyrical passages describing the fighting do not advance the matter, but it is clear that the Wessex army advanced to the attack, that the engagement was long and fiercely contested, and that Beornwulf himself took to flight. The scribe uses of him the curious expression: 'he sought for flight for himself and would not have wished to lose his spurs for three halfpence'.

With the king's disappearance from the field his country disappeared as a power to reckon with in this island.

THE SITE

Until fairly recently the favoured site for the battle was Amesbury. Sir Charles Oman advocated this site, but recanted in favour of Wroughton three miles south of Swindon, in the last edition of his *England Before the Norman Conquest*. The Wroughton site was first brought to notice by Plummer in his *Two Saxon Chronicles*, in which he quoted the Rev. C. S. Taylor as advocating that site. Dr. Grundy took

the matter a stage further in his *Ancient Highways and Trackways, etc.*
He showed from the Saxon charters that the Ellandun estate was but
partly in Wroughton parish and in so far as it was, in the north part of
that parish. He further showed that it must have included parts at least
of the modern parishes of Lydiard Tregoze and Lydiard Millicent, and
he placed the southern boundary approximately along the line of the
Old Canal.

Dr. Grundy also established the course of a pre-Saxon road running
from Barbury Castle through Salthrop and continuing straight on to
Lydiard Tregoze. This road continues to Cricklade and so by the
Roman road to Cirencester. He suggests that Beornwulf, King of
Mercia, had advanced by this road to the neighbourhood of Lydiard
Tregoze, and that Egbert, King of Wessex, advanced to confront him
by the same road. This would be in accordance with the general custom
of the age, which, as we have seen, was for armies to confine their
movements mainly to the old tracks and roads. I accept this view as
being inherently probable, and this has the effect of simplifying the
problem of locating the battlefield. For we have only to follow up the
line of the road and ascertain what point in it conforms most closely to
the recorded facts relating to the battle.

The story related by the *Annales de Wintonia* seems to imply that the
two armies were drawn up in sight of one another but out of range: a
matter of a few hundred yards at least (like Saxons and Danes at Ashdown forty-five years later). Where two armies meet one another in a
head-on collision each almost instinctively seeks out a ridge running
roughly parallel to his front. What we have to do, therefore, is to seek
out two ridges, each roughly perpendicular to the road which formed
the axis of their advance and parallel to one another. These two ridges
should be within sight of one another, but some hundreds of yards
apart. Finally there should be a stream or streams a short distance to the
north of the northern ridge.[1] I think we can find two ridges that
answer to all these desiderata. The southern one runs through the cross-
roads, point 352 on the Swindon–Wootton Bassett road: the northern
one crosses the old road 1,200 yards further north, and is slightly

---

[1] This is implied by Henry of Huntingdon, who states that the river ran
red with blood. Now there are two small streams (soon to merge into one)
that cross the old road in Lydiard Tregoze parish: the southern one just north
of Wick Farm and the other at Roughmoor, 1,000 yards further north. Both
are now mere brooks but may have been wider in those days and would certainly be boggier and more formidable obstacles.

oblique to it but not far from parallel to the southern ridge. These ridges are very small and the dip or undulation between the two is slight. The dip between the two armies at Waterloo was only slightly more pronounced, and the distance between the two ridges is almost exactly the same. No other locality even approaches this in probability if we are to accept the essential accuracy of the *Annales*. As for local tradition, I elicited from the incumbent of Lydiard Tregoze recently that there was a tradition of some fighting near Windmill Hill. This (misnamed) spot is in no-man's-land between the two ridges, near the centre of my suggested battlefield.

For all these reasons I place the battle that secured the hegemony of Wessex for good and all, at Lydiard Tregoze.

CHAPTER V

The Battle of Ashdown, January 8th, 871

OF no great battle in English history is there so much dispute as to its site as of Alfred the Great's first victory. It was the only clear victory of the six battles fought in 'Alfred's Year of Battles', so it holds a prominent place in our military history. It is unique in another respect, namely that it is the only battle prior to Stamford Bridge and Hastings of which we have a good second-hand account. I say 'good' advisedly, for Bishop Asser, its chronicler, was the friend, confidant and companion of King Alfred, and his description of the battle no doubt derived from Alfred himself. Further, though not present at the actual battle, Asser passed over the battlefield at a later date, probably in company with the King, and so was able to describe it with fidelity. Thus, if we can make sure of the spot it should be comparatively easy to reconstruct the battle. I believe this can be done, but in accordance with the scheme of the book this problem will be dealt with in detail at the end of the chapter.

The story starts in the year A.D. 868, when Ethelred was King of Wessex and overlord of the 'Heptarchy', or loose confederation of the states composing England. Ethelred's position as suzerain had, however, been shaken by the invasion of the Eastern Counties by the Danes, who laid siege to Nottingham. King Burgred of Mercia applied to Ethelred for help. Ethelred acceded to this request, and, accompanied by his younger brother Alfred as second-in-command, marched to meet the Danes at Nottingham where he engaged them, though without great success. Two years later these Danes, under their King Bagsac, invaded Wessex, probably sailing up the Thames. Disembarking at Reading, they threw up a defensive line between the Thames and Kennet, on December 28th, 870.

Three days later they sent out a force westwards, with the object of obtaining food and hay for their horses. This detachment was engaged at Englefield, six miles to the west, by the Elderman of Berkshire, Ethelwulf by name, and put to flight. On January 4th, Ethelred, with the main army, advancing along the Ridgeway from his base at Wantage or Swindon, joined his lieutenant, and together they attacked the Danish outposts and drove them back into Reading. Following up too rashly, the Saxons were themselves surprised by a sudden charge of Danes emerging from inside their fieldworks. The Saxons fell back, Elderman Ethelwulf being slain. The Saxon army retreated by the way it had come, through Englefield and north-westwards up the Ridgeway. It may safely be assumed that the King sent orders for reinforcements to come forward along the Ridgeway to join him, and that he also sent requests to his vassal, Burgred, to come to his aid, fixing the meeting-point at Lowbury Hill, 16 miles north-west of Reading. This is the highest point on the eastern Berkshire Downs—crowned with an ancient earthwork, and would be a well-known spot, a track junction. It would be easy to find—an important point before the advent of Ordnance maps.

The Danes did not immediately follow up their success. It was not their practice to do so, or had not been so far. Their main design was to swoop down on a tract of rich country and settle there for as long as it would support them. They therefore returned to their camp and (in the words of Walter Morrison) 'sat down to a steady drink'.

Meanwhile Ethelred and Alfred reached Lowbury Hill, probably late on January 5th and halted there to await their reinforcements and allies, making their camp round the track junction on the Ridgeway, half a mile south-west of the hill. King Bagsac, learning this, considered that the Wessex army was too near to be pleasant, and, puffed up with an easy victory (no doubt also with mead), he resolved to finish off his opponents for good and all. Moving out as soon as possible—which would probably be early on the 7th—he came in sight of the Saxon camp at dusk that day. Here he halted for the night, in the slight hollow where now Starveall Farm stands, with scouts on the ridge immediately in front. (See Sketch-map 5.)

From the top of the ridge the Saxon camp could be easily seen on the lower ridge, astride the Ridgeway, and just 1,000 yards distant.

Ethelred can hardly have expected to be followed up like this, else he would doubtless have occupied the higher ridge in front that was now in the hands of the enemy. That ridge, called by the gipsies (and hereinafter) Louse Hill, 'the Hill of Destruction', would have covered more effectually the track junction, on which Ethelred was now encamped, and along which his friends from Mercia might be expected to come—if they answered the call in time. But whether they should do so or not, the Saxon host was in good heart, for the reinforcements had now arrived, the army was concentrated, rested and refreshed.

We cannot even guess at respective numbers. But in view of the fact that the morale of the Saxons was so high, and that, as will be

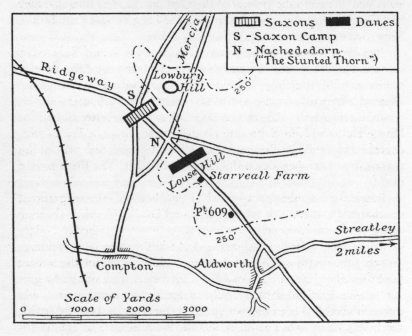

SKETCH-MAP 5. ASHDOWN

seen, they took the offensive, they evidently considered themselves superior in numbers (though no contingent had arrived from the Mercians).[1]

As soon as it got light on that eventful 8th of January, A.D. 871, the Danish army drew up in battle array, in full view of their opponents. In those times there was little finesse or manœuvring about battles; either one accepted battle or one did not. If one accepted it, the two armies drew up in obligingly parallel lines. The Saxons narrowly watched their opponents slowly and clumsily marshalling their line

---

[1] The reason why Burgred did not come to their assistance is that he was otherwise engaged. He had 'a war on two fronts' at the time—with the Welsh in the west, with the Danes in the east.

of battle in two big columns; as it became light they could descry the Royal banners of Kings Bagsac and Halfden waving over one column, that of the Danish earls over the other. The Ridgeway presumably divided the two columns. A council of war was then held in the Saxon camp, and a plan of action drawn up. By this plan the Saxon army conformed to the lay-out of their opponents; that is to say, they also formed up in two columns, that of the King opposite the Danish King, that of Alfred opposite the earls' column.

A pause seems now to have ensued, each side waiting for the other to make the first move. At this moment of tension the King decided to hear mass in his tent! The explanation no doubt is that, seeing no forward movement on the part of the enemy, Ethelred assumed they would await attack. There was no hurry. Much better obtain the Divine blessing before venturing on the attack. But the Danes were pagans, and whether they were aware that their rival was at his devotions or not, they seized this moment to make their first forward move.

Ethelred no doubt was apprised of this, but with the magnificent nonchalance that was not matched again till Drake refused to abandon his game of bowls over 700 years later, King Ethelred refused to budge; he would see the service through. Drake knew what he was doing; probably the tide was foul and nothing could be done for the nonce; but Ethelred had not such an excuse for inaction. Our sympathy goes out to the youthful Alfred (only in his twenty-third year). No entrenchments had been thrown up; the Danes had not been expected; and in any case it was not traditional for the Saxons to sit behind entrenchments and await attack by the Danes. The morale of the army was high and Alfred reckoned that in order to keep it high it was essential to assume the offensive. Could he take it upon himself to order an advance? The enemy—the hated invaders—were by now half-way down the hill, only 600 yards away; their jeering battle cries could be heard; the men around the second-in-command looked towards him inquiringly, if not apprehensively, for had it not been planned that the Saxon army was to take the offensive? There was no time to dally, or to send back a messenger to the Royal tent with a fresh message and a request for orders. Long before the reply arrived the Danes would be on them and it would be too late to do anything except just fight it out where they stood. Alfred's mind was made up. Giving the pre-arranged signal for the assault, he led his own column at a double ('like a wild boar', says Asser), down the

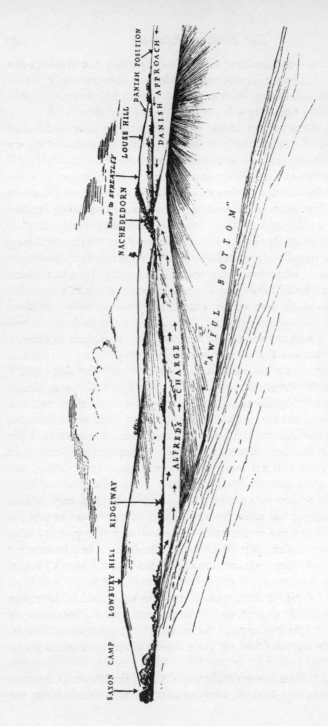

DANISH POSITION →

DANISH APPROACH →

LOUSE HILL →

NACHEDEDORN

Road to STREATLEY

"AWFUL BOTTOM"

ALFRED'S CHARGE →

RIDGEWAY

LOWBURY HILL

SAXON CAMP →

THE BATTLEFIELD, ASHDOWN

slight slope into the shallow valley that separated the rival armies. The King's column followed suit, whether spontaneously, or in response to a definite order it is impossible to say, and needless to speculate. (See panorama).

We can picture the two armies meeting head-on in an awful clash at the bottom of the valley (it is still called 'Awful Bottom' by the gipsies). The weight of the Saxon onset forced the Danes to fall back slightly up the hill down which they had just come. Nearly half-way up this hill is a road junction where five ancient tracks meet. It was the old meeting-point of the Hundred, and the spot was marked by a single stunted thorn-tree. It is conjectured that this tree had formed the scene of Druidic rites, and in Saxon times became the centre of the Hundred. Though the Wessex men were not Druids it might very well be a spot venerated by them. Whatever the reason, Asser assures us that the fighting was most severe round about this venerable tree. When riding past the spot in later years, probably with the King himself, this thorn bush had been pointed out to him. There is still a thorn bush at the spot. The name of this hundred in Domesday is Nachededorn, that is, the Naked Thorn.

Of course we do not know the details of the fight that ensued. In the nature of things that would be impossible. Like most battles, it doubtless swayed backwards and forwards for some time, and it is asserted by one chronicler that when King Ethelred arose from his knees and joined in the fight, he brought some fresh troops with him; these would be his own Household troops, the pick of the army, such as the House-carls that accompanied Harold at Hastings. They would correspond approximately with Napoleon's Old Guard.

What at any rate is certain is that long before the early winter evening the Danes had taken to flight, and a relentless pursuit was put in hand. 'Their dead bodies were strewn all over the plain of Ashdown,' declares Asser, and we need not doubt it. The continuation of the valley to the east is known to the gipsies as Dead Man's Hollow to this day.

Right up till nightfall the pursuit was continued, and in the course of it, or of the battle itself, King Bagsac was killed. Halfden managed to get away. The higher ranks in the earls' column suffered heavily too; the *Anglo-Saxon Chronicle* gives the names of the five earls who were killed.

Though Ethelred called off the pursuit at nightfall, the Danes continued their flight. With so many of their leaders out of action, few

or no fresh orders probably reached the routed invaders. It became a
'*Sauve qui peut*', and right through the night the flight went on.
Indeed, it did not stop till the Danes were safely behind their earthwork
defences at Reading. The victory was complete.

PROBLEMS OF THE BATTLEFIELD

I can find no authority who places the battle precisely where I have
sited it. The popular place is on or near White Horse Hill above
Uffington, 15 miles further west. Other suggestions have been East
Ilsley; Compton; Aston (three miles north of Lowbury Hill); and
even sites in Sussex and Buckinghamshire.

The case for the White Horse was founded largely on the belief
that Alfred constructed it as a memorial of the victory. Since it has
been established that the White Horse dates from the Iron Age, adherents of this site have had to fall back on the various place-names
that abound in the vicinity. They also assume that the Danes, after
their success at Reading, pursued the Saxons for four days, which
they argue would necessitate the site being over 20 miles from Reading.
But there is no warrant for this assumption. All that Asser says is:
'After four days [after the battle of Reading] with all their strength
and with good heart, they went forth to battle against the same army
to the place that is called Ashdown.' After all, why should Ethelred
fall back as much as 33 miles into the heart of his country, leaving
Wantage and Lambourne, royal demesnes, at the mercy of the enemy?
Moreover, how could the whole of the Danish army, stragglers and
all, arrive back at Reading the next day if they fought the battle
33 miles away? From the description of the pursuit a distance of
between ten and twenty miles would seem more nearly the figure.

But I agree that the direction of the Saxon retreat would be along
the Ridgeway *towards* the White Horse. They would naturally fall
back upon their base, and as far as possible towards their Mercian
Allies.

Now Lowbury Hill is situated about midway in this stretch of
Ridgeway, 10 to 20 miles from Reading. Furthermore, it makes a
natural rendezvous for the Mercians as we have seen; water was
available at the sources of the River Pang, a short mile to the
south-west of the camp; and Lowbury Hill itself would afford a good
look-out point. It is true that the Danes *might* have advanced up the
Thames valley, as some suppose, and fought the battle at Kingstanding

Hill, 2½ miles north of Streatley. But this would be by a summer route; in January, armies would probably be confined to the Ridgeway on the downs, which was an all-weather track.

The Compton and Ilsley sites have also the objection that they are some distance off the Ridgeway.

The next question is: What other possible positions are there in this ten-mile stretch of the Ridgeway? The answer is, only one that conforms to all our requirements, and that is the Starveall Farm dip. At first I favoured this site; the objections are that the slope is so steep that Alfred would hardly have dared to commit his troops to this valley in the presence of the enemy; and that the place-names do not fit. Louse Hill, the 'Hill of Destruction', must obviously be the one over which the Danes retreated, not the one on which they did not set foot; Awful Bottom and Dead Man's Hollow would lose their meaning and application for the same reason. The presence of thorn-trees favours both sites; their abundance is most notable; indeed they flourish in that area to the almost complete exclusion of any other tree. There is still a Thorn Hill and a Thorn Down Folly in the vicinity, which all point to the ubiquity of the thorn-trees in that area.

Finally, we come to the most striking of all the place-names: Nachededorn, the Naked Thorn. It reminds us at once of Asser's 'single stunted thorn-tree'. It may, of course, be only a coincidence; but when so many factors all point in the same direction, and when we visit the spot and, having decided on military grounds that the description fits, find a meeting-place of tracks and a mass of thorn-trees at the very spot where we should expect to find them—well, I for one am satisfied! That and no other is for me the Naked Thorn and the site of the Battle of Ashdown.

It is a fine setting for a battle. The wide sweep of the downs, the wildness and solitude—the natural arena for a conflict; all these conspire to make Louse and Lowbury Hills a worthy site for Alfred's great victory.

CHAPTER VI

The Battle of Ethandun, A.D. 878

THREE months after the battle of Ashdown (A.D. 871) Alfred succeeded to the throne, on the death of his brother Ethelred. The history of the next seven years is one of gradual expansion by the Danish army in all directions. In the south Alfred was driven further and further west, till by the beginning of 878 most of Wessex had been overrun, many of its inhabitants had fled overseas to Gaul and the remainder were incapable of offering a concerted resistance. Alfred himself, with a small band of followers, took refuge in the almost inaccessible island of Athelney at Easter, 878. His fortunes were at so low an ebb that according to popular legend, he was reduced to living disguised in the cottage of a swineherd.

Then came one of the most astonishing reversals of fortune in our history. In the short space of seven weeks the military situation had been so transformed that the King with a powerful army was able to defeat in pitched battle the hitherto victorious army of the Danish King Guthrum, who submitted to baptism and by the treaty of Wedmore promised to retreat from Wessex. How this sudden reversal of fortune came about and where the decisive battle was fought, it is the purpose of this chapter to investigate.

*　　*　　*　　*　　*

The story of 'Alfred and the cakes' is largely responsible for the false picture that is usually conjured up of a fugitive king, hunted from pillar to post, with no army and no resources. But the contemporary records do not support this. What the *Anglo-Saxon Chronicle* does state is that the King 'with his little force raised a work at Athelney from which he assailed the (Danish) army'. Moreover, a Danish landing in North Devon was defeated by a force under one of his thegns at Countisbury Hill. All this does not sound compatible with the swineherd story; yet there is generally a grain of truth embodied in folk-tales such as this. Here the explanation may be that in the course of one of his raids some local setback overtook his force, and for the time being he had to fly for his life, and to live for a day or two in disguise and concealment. At this time the Danish army of Guthrum (the Danish leader who had ravaged Wareham in 875) was based on Chippenham, 50 miles away.

Even if, as I think likely, the clashes usually occurred in the region of the Mendips it would be a long day's march back to Athelney. As for the inaccessibility of the island, all prudent generals establish a firm and if possible impregnable base before undertaking operations, especially when they are so fluid and mobile as were those of the year 878. An inaccessible base does not therefore necessarily indicate weakness.

The natural inference is that during the spring of 878 Alfred was busy reorganizing the army that had recently met with a severe reverse, hardening and training it by a series of raids, exactly as the British army was hardened and trained after its reverse in the spring of 1918.

And what was happening in the rest of Wessex during those fateful months? We do not know; but there is no record of any Danish operations in Hampshire, southern Wiltshire or Dorset. That army could not be everywhere, and we know that it had settled down at Chippenham a few months previously. The inference is that during that period Alfred was in communication with what remained of the Wessex forces in those counties, encouraging, instructing, and preparing them for the great day, whether by 'underground' methods or not. No other inference is possible when we consider the upshot.

Let us now examine Alfred's problem. Let us assume that the nuclei of his army-to-be were forming at Winchester, Old Sarum, Dorchester (accepting Oman's surmise that a Dorset contingent was included), and Athelney. Taking the hostile base at Chippenham as centre of a circle, the Wessex contingents were spread out on one-third of the circumference of this circle. In other words, they were spread over a front of 100 miles, while their opponent was only 50 miles distant from each contingent. This gave a great advantage to an enterprising enemy, operating on 'interior lines', whilst presenting a difficult problem to the English King. Under modern conditions, with modern means of communication and transport, the Wessex army would profit by its position on 'exterior lines' to attack the enemy simultaneously from two or more directions. But such an operation was clearly beyond the power of Alfred's troops; his policy was that of Napoleon—to concentrate *off*, not *on*, the field of battle.

Where, then, should that point of concentration be? Obviously it should be out of sight of the enemy, yet not so far off that the individual contingents would have a long march round the perimeter before reaching the rendezvous. The sooner they were assembled after starting on their marches the better the chance of surprising the enemy. The two most distant contingents were based on Athelney and Winchester respectively. If Alfred had a primitive map in his possession at Athelney we can imagine him drawing a straight line on it joining up these two places. Midway on this line would theoretically be the best place for the rendezvous (provided there was no fear of molestation on the part of the enemy), for this would involve the shortest possible marches by the various contingents. Unfortunately we do not know Guthrum's dispositions nor how far from Chippenham he had pushed forward his forces. The further forward they went, the thinner on the ground they would be,[1] and it does not seem to have been the military policy of the Danes to disperse their forces. On the other hand, there was a natural disposition on the part of all armies in those days to go for the high ground. All the Wessex battles that can be located were fought on high ground. There is such a line of high ground about 20 miles to the south of Chippenham, extending from the Mendips to Salisbury Plain, and we may accept as a working hypothesis that this line was occupied, though not in strength, by the Danes during the spring of 878, Chippenham being the base and the site of the army reserves.

We can now return to our imaginary line connecting Athelney with Winchester. Midway along it, on a lofty plateau overlooking East Knoyle, several ancient trackways converge at the place now known as Willoughby Hedge. I believe it also to be the site of Egbert's Stone. The spot is 8 to 10 miles from the Salisbury Plain massif, where, according to our hypothesis we have placed Guthrum's advanced line or temporary boundary. Alfred, working it out on his primitive map, or in his mind's eye, could hardly wish or expect to find a more suitable place for a rendezvous for his scattered forces. Strategically it was the best site, tactically it was sound—near, but not too near, the hostile border, convenient roads led to it from the required directions, and finally it was a place that could be easily indicated to distant contingents who had no maps, and it could be as easily found by them for it was the place where the great King Egbert had erected his Stone of victory after his campaigns in the far west.[2]

Orders were accordingly sent out indicating Egbert's Stone as the rendezvous, and fixing a day by which all contingents must be concentrated there. I compute that May Day was selected.

If Alfred himself took the direct route he travelled by Langport, Castle Cary and along the old Hardway by Kingsettle Hill (on which Alfred's Tower now stands) and thence by the primeval Long Lane to

[1] For the quadrant of the circle forming their front would vary as the radius.
[2] For the site of Egbert's Stone see the note on p. 60.

Willoughby Hedge. On the King's arrival at the rendezvous the assembled hosts, in the simple words of the *Chronicle*, 'were fain [glad] of him'.

The *Anglo-Saxon Chronicle* states that on the very day after his arrival at the rendezvous Alfred set out with his newly formed army, marching that day straight towards his enemy, and attacking the Danish main army under its king on the following day.

There are two puzzling points about this narrative: First, how did Alfred manage to march and fight a victorious battle only a few hours after the assembly of this army in contingents from all over the south of England? Second, how came it that the Danish main army was concentrated in position about 20 miles to the south of his base camp of Chippenham, before the Saxon army had concentrated? (For it must have been in position before Alfred set out, else he would not have advanced with such precision and speed in exactly the right direction.)

I suggest that there is a common explanation to these two puzzles, and it is that the Saxon army did *not* concentrate only the day before the advance commenced, but quite a number of days earlier. The *Chronicle* does not say that the *army* arrived at Egbert's Stone two days before the battle, but that Alfred in person arrived on that day. It is inconceivable that the Saxon contingents would all arrive on the same day, or that this conglomeration could be organized and welded into a fighting machine in a few hours. The practical difficulties were more than usually great on this occasion, but there is no space in which to enumerate them.

On the morning after the arrival of the King the army set out on its march, and halted for the night at Iglea, which is now held to be East-leigh Wood, two miles south-east of Warminster and seven miles due north of the rendezvous. Near here (one mile west of Sutton Veny) there is an ancient earthwork which would provide security for the army that night. This was highly desirable for they were now nearing the hostile position. Where was this position situated? It is time to enquire.

Assuming that the Saxon host began to assemble a week or more before Alfred's arrival, news of the concentration would be brought to Guthrum by his scouts. When the size of the concentration became evident the Danish king would set out from his base camp with his reserves, calling in at the same time his outlying parties and concentrating his army in a defensive position somewhere on a line between Chippenham and Egbert's Stone, on the massif to the south of Edington or Bratton. Having arrived here he would select the strongest possible position supplied by nature, reinforcing it artificially if time admitted (i.e. digging a protective ditch).

In the direct line of approach from Egbert's Stone one of three ancient tracks might be used by the Saxons, the right-hand one passing to the left of Scratchbury Camp, and the other two to the right and left of Battlesbury Camp (see Sketch-map). Guthrum would therefore look out for a position astride these three tracks, on the forward slope of some cross ridge, but only just over the crest, after the manner of the time. Such a position leaps to the eye if the contoured map, one-inch, or preferably 1/25000 O.S. be used. This ridge is 6,000 yards due south of Edington village; it runs from north-east to south-west and is in fact the ridge already referred to, three miles north-east of Warminster. The ideal position would be on the forward slope of this ridge, covering a front of about 2,500 yards, and curving with the contours in order to attain the greatest possible field of view, about 150 yards below the crest line. That would, in my opinion, be the ideal position for the purpose. The fact that Alfred marched so directly and promptly towards it would seem to imply that he was aware of its situation before he set out, and that therefore the Danes had at least two days in which to dig.[1] We might therefore expect to find faint traces of such a ditch as I have suggested and in the place that I have suggested. *And we do find it*, precisely where I have suggested. It is marked on both the one-inch and 1/25000 maps as 'Ancient Ditch'. (In the case of the 1/25000 an extension to the east is shown that I believe is in reality a separate work.)

It may of course be a mere coincidence that the ditch is just where we should expect it to be; it may be that it was dug previously and perhaps made use of by the Danes. We cannot be sure. But what we can be sure about is that it is a military work (closely resembling Wansdyke in its siting) and that it was dug for a specific purpose, a defence by a northern army of the Edington position against an expected attack from the south. There may be some other occasion in our history which would fit into this position but I fancy there is none in recorded history. So it seems the most reasonable course to associate it with a piece of recorded history into which it does fit.

Assuming that this was the position [2] taken up in the first instance by

[1] William of Malmesbury supports this contention: he speaks of Alfred 'learning exactly the situation of the pagans from scouts he had sent out for the purpose'.
[2] Marked AA on the sketch-map.

the Danes, it would be visible to the Saxon scouts from Battlesbury Camp, only 2,500 yards away, and the first clash would take place on the intervening ground. Hence perhaps the name Battlesbury, just as we have a Battlebury on the site of what I hold to be Mount Badon.

THE BATTLE

Of the momentous events of the following day we have only two accounts and they are so short that they may be quoted in full.

From the 'Anglo-Saxon Chronicle': 'He proceeded to Ethandun, and there fought with all the army and put them to flight, riding after them as far as the fortress, where he remained a fortnight. Then the army gave him hostages with many vows that they would go out of his kingdom.'

From 'Annals of the reign of Alfred the Great', by Bishop Asser: 'The next morning he removed to Ethandun, and there fought long and fiercely in close order against all the armies of the pagans, whom with the divine help he defeated with great slaughter, and pursued them flying to their fortification. Immediately he slew all the men and carried off all the booty that he could find without the fortress which he immediately laid siege to with all his army. And when he had been there fourteen days the pagans, driven by cold, famine, fear, and last of all by despair, asked for peace. . . .'

It must be confessed that Asser's account reads like a mere embellishment of the Chronicle, and it is odd that Alfred had not given him some first-hand details of the battle, as he did in the case of Ashdown. In effect all Asser adds to our knowledge is the fact that the English fought in close order (*densa testudine*), a fact that is curiously omitted in Giles's standard translation, and misquoted in Lee's *Alfred the Great*.

The whole battle is therefore a matter of pure conjecture. My own picture of the course of events is as follows:

When dawn appeared on the morning of the battle, the Saxon scouts on Battlesbury Hill who had previously reported the approach of the Danish army, spotted and reported to Alfred their precise dispositions, lining the ridge in front of them. Alfred came up to the hill, examined the position and decided on his method of attack. There was no obvious way of outflanking the position, even if such a manoeuvre ever entered the head of the impulsive king who only seven years before at Ashdown had charged 'like a wild boar' straight in the face of the enemy. One may assume that he employed the same tactics, charging in close order in an endeavour to pierce a hole in the enemy's long line. The attack, whatever the tactics employed, was successful; the Danes fled towards their own base camp, even as they had fled seven years before. Those on the western end of the line presumably took the track leading over Bratton Camp, and those on the east the track leading past Edington. The former may be supposed to have attempted a stand on the top of the ridge 500 yards south of Bratton Castle (marked BB on the sketch-map). It forms a strong position. The Edington fugitives might try to hold the defile between Edington and Tinhead Hills. This position (marked CC) resembles the position of the field of Wodnesbeorh, in the two battles of A.D. 592 and 715. The third phase of the battle would be the pursuit to Chippenham, a further 14 miles to the north. A possible argument in favour of some of the fighting at least taking place on site BB is the proximity of the Bratton White Horse, believed by many to have been cut, in its original form, in celebration of the victory. In favour of site CC is the proximity to Edington, from which the battle drew its name. But this argument is not as strong as it may appear to modern eyes, for place-names in that area must have been few and far apart. Witness, the name Hastings for the battle fought on the Sanlake brook.

The fall of Chippenham crowned the victory of Edington and paved the way for the Christianization of the Danes and the extirpation of paganism in the land of England.

A NOTE ON THE RIVAL SITES

Considering the importance of the battle of Ethandun it is not surprising that numerous attempts to identify the site have been made through the ages. Camden was the first writer to equate Ethandun with Edington in Wiltshire. His view held the field for some centuries. Heddington in Wiltshire, Edington in Berkshire, Yattendon, Yatton, and Edington in Somerset have also been suggested, but all have been dropped except the last-named which still receives some support in Somerset. The claim for this Somerset site was first advanced by Dr. Clifford in 1877. It was repeated by the Rev. C. W. Whistler in 1906, but there are weighty objections to it. In the first place it cannot be supported on philological grounds: for it derives from Edwinetune (Edwin's town), whereas the Wiltshire Edington has consistently appeared as Edendone, the Norman equivalent of Ethandun. In the second place, it does not fit in with the situation of Iglea, over thirty

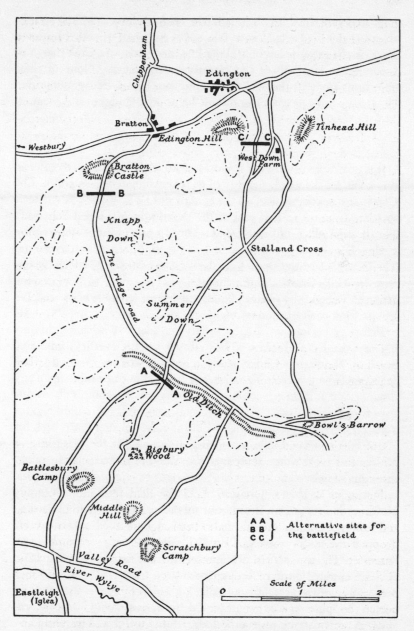

Chippenham

Edington

Bratton

Tinhead Hill

← Westbury

Edington Hill

West Down Farm

C   C

Bratton Castle

B   B

Knapp Down

The ridge road

Stalland Cross

Summer Down

A

A   Old Ditch

Bowl's Barrow

Bigbury Wood

Battlesbury Camp

Middle Hill

Scratchbury Camp

Valley Road

River Wylye

Eastleigh (Iglea)

A A
B B
C C
} Alternative sites for the battlefield

Scale of Miles

0   1   2

SKETCH—MAP 6.   ETHANDUN: THE BATTLE

miles away. In the third place, it is contrary to Inherent Military Probability that Alfred would have selected as his point of concentration a place on the extreme left of his long line, necessitating a flank march of 100 miles on the part of the Hampshire contingent. None of these objections apply to the Wiltshire Edington. It is moreover supported by the two most recent historians of the period, Hodgkin and Stenton.

A NOTE ON EGBERT'S STONE

It is obviously of primary importance to ascertain the correct site of this stone, for the whole strategy of the campaign depends upon it. The *Chronicle* states that it was 'on the eastern side of Selwood'; Asser states that it was 'in the eastern part of the wood which is called Selwood'. The modern village of Penselwood is about 7 miles west of Willoughby Hedge, but the extent of the wood in the ninth century is unknown. The O.S. Map of the Dark Ages shows it as being of considerable extent. Dr. G. B. Grundy, in the *Archaeological Journal* of 1918, placed the Stone at Willoughby Hedge and his view seems to have been accepted by the most recent historians of the period.

Before going further we must briefly consider two other neighbouring sites that have advocates. The first is Brixton Deverill, 3 miles due north of Willoughby Hedge. It lies in a valley, and seems an odd place for King Egbert to erect his Stone, for it could not be visible from any distance, nor is it on a junction of highways. The second is about one mile to the north-east of Westbury. This seems still more unlikely, for a march from this place to Iglea would involve turning sharp back for about five miles and then advancing along almost the same line—a nonsensical proceeding. Moreover the Westbury site is north, rather than east of Selwood.

Returning to the examination of Willoughby Hedge, Dr. Grundy confined his argument almost exclusively to the system of ancient trackways, a subject on which he was an unrivalled authority. He showed that tracks converged on Willoughby Hedge from all directions, making it a natural rendezvous for contingents coming from widely separated districts. To particularize, a track runs west by Kingsettle Hill (whereon is situated Alfred's Tower). This is the track by which the Somerset contingent would travel and would lead to Cornwall. A second track runs almost due north to Iglea. This would be used in Egbert's time by his North Wiltshire troops. A third goes north-east to Andover and North Hampshire. A fourth runs due east to Old Sarum and South Hampshire and a fifth goes due south to Shaftesbury and Dorset. The spot is 717 feet in height.

We have now to consider why King Egbert should elect to place a stone there. We may safely assume that it would be erected to mark or celebrate some outstanding event, such as a great victory or treaty.

Now in A.D. 815 and again in 825 Egbert conducted victorious campaigns against the men of Cornwall. It is probable that he would return from these campaigns along the ancient ridgeway, coming from the Mendip Hills. At the point where the trackways diverge near Willoughby Hedge, the South Hampshire contingent would take the right-hand fork heading for Southampton; those for North Hampshire the central track, whilst those for North Wiltshire would strike due north. At this spot therefore the victorious army would disperse. There would be leave-takings and perhaps the King would show his gratitude by giving a banquet. Is it too fanciful to picture that during the feasting some chieftain might make the suggestion that the spot would be a good place to erect a memorial-stone to record the victory? Willoughby Hedge was the highest point they had encountered since entering Wiltshire; it is a commanding site, and a stone erected here would be visible for many miles around in every direction. Here, then, I think is the most likely place we could find for the erection by Egbert of his memorial stone. Its site would become well known throughout Wessex, and Alfred in notifying the rendezvous would merely have to name the stone without any further specification. Nor, in referring to it afterwards did the chronicler or Asser think it necessary to define its position. Everyone knew where it was.

CHAPTER VII

The Battle of Brunanburh, A.D. 937

OF this battle, Sir James Ramsay wrote: 'The question as to which Power in Great Britain should rule the destinies of the Island was put and settled once and forever.' Yet the site of the battle remains unknown. Upwards of thirty-two sites have been claimed for it. It has been in dispute for over 300 years. Leland suggested Axminster and Camden Northumbria. In the nineteenth century Yorkshire and the neighbourhood of the Mersey were the favourites, but opinion has since veered in favour of a Scottish site. At the end of the century Dr. T. Hodgkin tentatively, and Dr. G. Neilson positively, picked on Burnswork Hill in Annandale, 6 miles north of the Solway Firth. Sir Charles Oman subsequently inclined strongly to this view and Dr. Neilson claimed Professor W. G. Collingwood as an adherent. On the whole it may now be considered the most favoured site, though Dr. Neilson's theory has been subjected to severe criticism by Alice Law in the *Scottish Historical Review* (1909), while the last book but one to be published on the battle (*The Battle of Brunanburh*, by Alastair Campbell) comes to the depressing conclusion: 'all hope of localizing Brunanburh is lost'. Nevertheless I will be so bold as to make the attempt to 'localize' it.

We will start in the year A.D. 934 when Athelstan, greater son of a great father, sat on the throne of England. The northern boundary of the country directly ruled by him ran roughly on an east–west line through Manchester, Sheffield, and Lincoln.[1]

Northumbria, stretching from the Forth to the Humber, was in some vaguely defined degree subject to him, though its predominantly Danish population made it an unreliable dependency. North of the Forth Constantine, King of the Scots, reigned over a small territory called Alban roughly bounded by the Moray Firth, the sea, the Firth of Forth, and the backbone of the Highlands. Strathclyde in the south-west of Caledonia, was inhabited by Britons. What we now call the Celtic Fringe, including the islands to north and west, was dominated by the Norse men. Over the rulers of these territories Athelstan claimed a general suzerainty, but in 934 the King of the Scots in some way offended him and Athelstan led a great army northwards, part by land

[1] The original course and name of the Great Central Railway.

and part by sea. He was practically unopposed and ravaged the whole land of Alban at will.

For three years nothing happened; but Constantine was preparing his revenge. It was framed on heroic lines. His own country was too small to carry out his purpose unaided so he allied himself not only with the other rulers of Caledonia but with the Norse element in Ireland. He was also joined by some contingents from Scandinavia of unknown strength. By 937 his plans had matured and the great invasion of England began. All signs point to the fact that his intention was the utter subjugation of England and the establishment of northern rule over London and Winchester. The most direct evidence of this appears in a royal grant to Worcester in which Athelstan refers to 'Anlaf [Olaf] who tried to deprive me of both life and realm'. (Olaf, recent claimant to the throne of York, was the commander-in-chief of the expeditionary force of his father-in-law, Constantine.)

The allied forces from all over modern Scotland and northern Ireland managed to effect their concentration somewhere in North Britain, and advanced southwards against their common enemy. But where was this concentration? It is at this point that opinions begin to differ; they divide into two schools—those who accept the statement of Florence of Worcester that Olaf's fleet sailed up the Humber and the school that rejects this statement. We will call them the Eastern and Western schools, and I must now decide which school to adhere to. Florence of Worcester ranks high as a Chronicler. Alastair Campbell writes of him that 'he had some source for his account of the battle unknown to us'.

Florence's statement is supported by nine other medieval chroniclers but as they, or most of them, probably copied Florence we will leave them out of account, except to remark that, living nearer the time than we do, they found nothing incredible in the statement; they had no difficulty in accepting it.

Let us put ourselves in the shoes of Constantine, when forming his plan. His ultimate objective, as we have seen, may be taken to be London. The shortest line from eastern Scotland to London is on what the railways would call the East Coast route. Constantine could come by land or by sea or both. To come by land would involve traversing the potentially hostile land of Northumbria all the way from Edinburgh to the Humber. Of the lords of Bamborough, who ruled this wide area under Athelstan, history has very little to say; but there is no reason to suppose that they would side with the invader; indeed, if we accept the Egil Saga (of which more later) these lords—Alfgeirr and Gundrek—did offer opposition. But if the Scots came by sea, landing in the shelter of the Humber, they would successfully side-track Northumbria, whether or not a land contingent followed up and joined them later. This seems such an eminently sound strategy (provided Constantine possessed a large fleet) that even without Florence's positive statement, we would be inclined to credit it. And we know that Constantine had a large fleet, for Simeon of Durham says so, and historians do not dispute his assertion that Olaf had 615 ships. Now Simeon would not be likely to have this precise information if he lived on the western side of the Pennine range, but residing at Durham as he did, he was in a good position to narrate events that took place on that side, and his authority for such statements is usually acknowledged to be good. Thus Florence and Simeon between them combine to make it probable that Olaf's fleet did sail down the east coast and up the Humber.[1]

The objections of the western school to this is that the fleet in question set out from Dublin, and would not have sailed right round the island of Great Britain, whether by the north or by the south, but would have landed on the western coast. There is obvious substance in this—if the premises are correct; but are they? They are based on the statement in the *Anglo-Saxon Chronicle* that Anlaf (Olaf) sailed back to Dublin after the battle. Now if this was the same Olaf who commanded Constantine's fleet it certainly would seem that the fleet landed on the west, not on the east coast. But there were two Olafs not one, and the *Anglo-Saxon Chronicle* seems to have merged them into one.[2] Other chroniclers are vague and misleading about them, and modern historians have shared the mystification that troubled these old chroniclers. I suspect that some modern historians have been more bothered by the involved relationship of the two Olafs than they care to admit. I certainly have been bothered by it myself. I defy anyone, for example, to make head or tail of Ramsay's exposition of the subject.

As I understand it, there were two Olafs, who were cousins or uncle and nephew, it matters not which. One of them was the son of Sibtric, late king of York, and son-in-law of Constantine, and his commander-in-chief. He was later known as Anlaf Cuaran. The other was son of Godfrey, king of Dublin, sometimes known as Godfreyson. Owing to

[1] Two recent writers, R. L. Bremner (1923) and T. D. Kendrick (1930) accept this. The Humber in time became a usual landing point for invaders.

[2] Florence of Worcester, Simeon of Durham, and some modern writers have also muddled them up.

the fact that Cuaran afterwards became king of Dublin it is not surprising that the Saxon chronicler mixed them up.[1]

The result of the above examination is that I accept Florence's statement that Olaf (with the Scottish contingent) entered and sailed up the Humber. The next question to decide is where did he land? Now since his plan involved a junction with his allies and since they would be approaching from the west or north-west, it would be to Olaf's advantage to sail as far west as possible. This 'furthest west' would be at or near Tadcaster. This old Roman town possessed one of the most important strategical sites in the north. A glance at the Ordnance Map of Roman Britain [2] shows that Tadcaster is almost exactly midway between the mouths of the Humber and the Ribble. It was the site of an important ford over the deep river Wharf, it was the junction of four Roman roads, and it was the direct road over the Pennine Range, linking York with the mouth of the Ribble and so with Dublin.

Now let us look at the military problem of concentration of forces from the point of view of Constantine's allies—the Britons of Strathclyde and the Norse-Irish (in future Irish for short). These two contingents would have to join forces with each other and with the Scots. The best direct line of approach from Strathclyde would be via Carlisle and along the Roman road to Ribchester, thence via Ilkley to Tadcaster. That of the Irish contingent would be via the estuary of the Ribble [3] to Ribchester and thence of course by the same road as the Britons. Ribchester would thus make the natural junction point for the Britons and Irish.[4]

If we accept this, the course of the ensuing campaign clarifies considerably. Which contingent would one expect to reach Tadcaster first? The Scots had nearly twice the length of sea voyage, and they were the prime instigators of the invasion and the prime movers in it.

---

[1] A few fresh Christian names in Anglo-Saxon history would have removed many stumbling blocks to the struggling student of that period. One cannot but sympathize with the author of *1066 and All That*.

[2] The map of *Britain in the Dark Ages* is valueless for the purpose owing to the incomprehensible omission of the Roman roads. Whether or not Saxon civilians used these roads, there can be no doubt that Saxon soldiers did. They were made for soldiers—and the soldiers made good use of them centuries after they had been constructed.

[3] *Annals of Clanmacnoise* states that they crossed from Dublin to England, which would seem to rule out the Solway Firth, still more the Clyde.

[4] Unless the Cumbrians had already joined the Scots, as seems possible from Egil's Saga.

Their allies would not wish to commit themselves in open opposition to the dreaded Athelstan unless and until they were assured that the Scots had actually arrived on the scene of action. This hesitation would be reinforced by the fact of the long sea voyage of the Scottish fleet. It might take days or it might take weeks.[1]

The most they would venture would be to land secretly, hoping to avoid detection, and await definite news from their allies across the Pennines.

Thus we would expect the Scots, having disembarked at or near Tadcaster, to experience an anxious period of waiting, whilst the Northumbrian earls to their north, and Athelstan to their south, were collecting their forces and advancing. The *Anglo-Saxon Chronicle* is silent on this phase, but the Egil Saga fills up the gap. It tells how the Northumbrian earls collected their forces and engaged the invaders (just as Morcar and Edwin did 130 years later, to suffer the same fate). Gudrek was slain and Alfgeirr fled. The fugitive made his way south and warned the King, then in London, of the peril in the north. Athelstan lost no time in collecting an army and advancing north against his Scottish foe. At what period he learnt of the other landing in the west we have no inkling; but it matters not; his true objective was the army of the 'hoary headed traitor' as the *Anglo-Saxon Chronicle* calls Constantine.

At this stage it seems legitimate to make two assumptions. The first is that Olaf, while awaiting his western allies, threw out forces to the south to contact the English army approaching from London; the other that the allies effected their junction before the arrival of the enemy; this is indeed implicit in the records.

By what route did Athelstan approach? There were two Roman roads to choose from; on the east that from London to Lincoln, the other along Watling Street to Venone (High Cross) [2] and thence along the Icknield Way and so to Nottingham or Derby. From the Saxon charter No. 703, it is clear that Athelstan took the western road in his 934 campaign. He would be disposed to take this road again—especially if Alfgeirr informed him of the position of Olaf in the Tadcaster area.

Derby would have obvious advantages as a temporary halting point

[1] The invasion by William the Conqueror was delayed by foul winds for six weeks.

[2] High Cross would be a likely rendezvous for the Mercian levies; it was a strategic road-junction in the Roman military lay-out.

whilst the situation up north was still obscure; for, from it roads diverged to the east and west of the long Pennine Range; there was the road running west to Chester, one running north-west to Manchester, and the Ryknild Street running due north to Rotherham and Castleford. At this point I picture him halting, levies meanwhile trickling in from the Welsh border, until it became quite clear that the main invading army was committed to the eastern route. If he then marched along Ryknild Street he was almost bound to encounter them.

So we have now reached the position, working on considerations of Inherent Military Probability, that some time in the month of August A.D. 937 the English army was advancing north towards Derby whilst the northern army was concentrating around Tadcaster. What then? It would obviously be to the advantage of the allies to advance with the minimum of delay, once they had concentrated all their forces. It is for the aggressor to take the initiative, else he loses the manifold advantages conferred on that side that takes the offensive.[1] We shall therefore be fairly safe in assuming that the allies advanced south into Mercia. Indeed it is no mere assumption; there are many indications that this was done. The most specific is that of William of Malmesbury who declared that they advanced 'far into England'. Egil's Saga also implies that the battle of Brunanburh took place far inside Athelstan's domains. Simeon of Durham records how Athelstan 'drove these kings from his kingdom', i.e. from Mercia; from which it follows that his enemy had actually penetrated into Athelstan's territory. If this be so it is clear that Olaf must have advanced southwards from Tadcaster, for that town was about 30 miles north of the Mercian border. Boundaries between states in those times are hopelessly obscure to us, and probably were only slightly more clearly known at the time. The best guide we have in defining the northern border of Mercia is the line of the castles thrown up during the campaigns of Edward the Elder twenty years before. If we accept this as the boundary, the line will run through Thelwall, Runcorn, Manchester, and Bakewell, thence over the Pennines to Castleford and thence to the sea.

Castleford would be the natural place to cross the Aire. (The Yorkists crossed it there on their way to the battle of Towton.)

Derby is about 60 miles south of the Mercian border, and if the Northern patrols pushed as far south as this whilst Athelstan was halted there it could be said that Olaf had penetrated 'far into Athelstan's

---

[1] The Earl of Lincoln in 1487 appreciated this principle when he advanced by the same road to attack Henry VII.

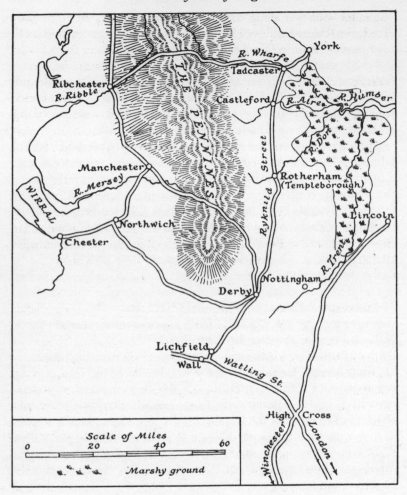

SKETCH-MAP 7.   BRUNANBURH: THE CAMPAIGN I

kingdom'. I picture them doing this, and, on the arrival of Athelstan's main army, falling back before it towards their own supports.

The next question to discuss is by what road the Northerners would advance. This looks a fairly simple problem. A glance at the maps of Roman Britain of the Dark Ages shows that the area Castleford to Rotherham (Templeborough) formed a bottle-neck. To the west was the Pennine range, to the east were the boggy valleys of the Aire, Don, and Trent. The passage between the hills and the bogs was only about

15 miles wide and along this passage there was only one pre-Saxon road, the Ryknild Street. This street—made or at least utilized by the Romans—ran due south through Rotherham and thence to Derby and Wall (Lichfield), and would be the obvious one for the invaders to take, especially if they learnt of the presence of their opponents at or near High Cross or Derby. Now armies in those times, when approaching each other for battle, and when actually engaged, almost invariably met head-on along an established road. What then more natural assuming the respective armies approaching along the Riknild Street— then that they should meet and engage at some point on that road?

If the reader has accepted my argument so far there is little more to be said. The battle will take place somewhere along Ryknild Street between Derby and Rotherham. And that is about as far as one can define it without having recourse to Egil's Saga. At this point, therefore, I will break off the argument and examine the grounds on which the Scottish school locate the battle north of Solway Firth.[1]

*   *   *   *   *

We come, then, to an examination of Dr. Neilson's claim, that the battle of Brunanburh was fought at Burnswork in Annandale. He expounded this thesis originally in 1899 and elaborated it in 1909 in the pages of the *Scottish Historical Review*. As his case is based mainly on Egil's Saga we must first examine the credentials of this famous poem. Controversy was once hot on the subject but it is now almost unanimously agreed that Egil's Vinheith corresponds to Simeon's Vendune, which is Brunanburh. Most authorities accept the Saga as a valuable source, and Alastair Campbell is almost alone in dismissing it. This he does in the following words: 'The Saga . . . in view of its frequent gross errors and confusions cannot be used as a source for the war. . . .' There follows the sombre sentence: 'If we abandon it, and abandon it we must, all hope of localizing Brunanburh is lost.' And even more strongly, on p. 60 he writes: 'I do not consider that Egil's Saga throws any light on the battle.'

[1] It has been objected to any site east of the Pennines that, according to the *Anglo-Saxon Chronicle*, the Northerners after the battle fled to their ships and sailed for Ireland, the implications being that the ships were close to the battle-field and based on the Irish Sea. But I cannot read into the text that the ships were close (though the fleet at Tadcaster would be only 35 miles away). If the Irish were defeated near Rotherham they would naturally attempt to retrace their steps to their ships, whether on the Ribble or the Humber—and that is all the *Anglo-Saxon Chronicle* says or implies.

On p. 70, however, Campbell writes in seeming contradiction: 'The main outline of the tradition of the battle of Vinheith is correct and may be safely assumed to refer to the battle of Brunanburh.'

This as a matter of fact provides us with all that we require, namely that, mingled with the myths and fantasies of the Saga are some historical facts. The problem then is to sift the good grain from the chaff.

Now the Saga was composed for the glorification of Egil and his companion Thorolf. Throughout the narration all the credit for the victory is given to these two Norse heroes. Since they had but recently enlisted under the banner of the English King, with a tiny following only 300 strong, it seems strange that the King of England should hand over the ordering of the battle to this foreigner. Yet Athelstan himself hardly comes into the picture. It reminds one of Geoffrey of Monmouth's account of the battle of Mount Badon, in which his hero, King Arthur, performs prodigious feats of valour, but which also contains traces of historical facts. I therefore propose to deal with the Saga's account of Brunanburh in the same manner as I have dealt with Geoffrey's account of Mount Badon: that is to say, where the Saga makes statements of a topographical nature for which there can be no motives for falsification I accept their essential accuracy, though allowing that slight exaggeration and errors of detail may well be present.

Since Dr. Neilson bases his identification of the battlefield site on this Saga we must first establish, on the criterion of Inherent Military Probability, which of the Saga's statements can be accepted, and then examine the use Dr. Neilson puts them to. At the same time we must remember that the Saga was committed to writing nearly 300 years after the event, and allow for slight errors of geographical detail creeping in. The essential story according to the Saga is as follows. Egil and Thorolf, two Icelandic Norsemen, took service under King Athelstan, with 300 of their retainers, and formed part of the army that he led against the Northerners. Olaf (Anlaf) with a Scottish army invaded England, over-running Northumbria and defeating its two earls, Alfgeirr and Gudrek. The latter was killed and Alfgeirr fled south and warned Athelstan. The English King then hastily assembled an army and marched north against the invaders. Whilst the two armies were still several hours distant by horse (at least 20 miles), each occupying a 'borg', i.e. an inhabited place of some sort, peace pourparlers passed between the two armies. They however led to nothing and the fully concentrated rival armies met in battle at Vinheith. The battlefield was bounded on the west by a watercourse, and on the east, which was on higher ground, by a wood. The ground between was heath and fairly flat. To the north it sloped (apparently downwards).

On the basis of these facts Dr. Neilson sites the battlefield on Burns-work Hill, 6 miles north of the Solway Firth. This hill rises to a height of 920 feet above sea level and 500 feet above the surrounding country. Its slopes are steep on all sides, and it has a flat top, 350 yards long and 200 yards wide from north to south—about the size of a polo ground.

On this tiny oval Dr. Neilson places two armies that may have been as strong as 20,000 each. The imagination boggles at the idea of 40,000 soldiers milling on a polo ground on the top of a mountain. It would resemble a monstrous Rugger 'scrum'. He sites the Northern 'borg' in an existing earthwork distant only 180 yards from the hill-top, and the English 'borg' 180 yards on the other side, i.e. the two camps were for two days only 400 yards apart, the length of Rugby railway platform. This is to reduce the battle to an affair of boy scouts or schoolchildren on Tom Tiddler's ground. Incidentally the watercourse—a mere trickle at that—is on the east, not the west.

Apart from its minute dimensions, the shape of the hill is inconsistent with Egil's description which implies that the slopes were gentle and that there was a slight and fairly uniform slope upwards from the watercourse on the left to the wood on the right, the whole of the intervening ground being occupied in the battle by the English army. Nor does the situation of the northern 'borg' tally with Egil's account. Instead of being in wide open country where ample supplies could be obtained, it was amid narrow valleys with barren hills in rear.

Egil says he buried his dead brother Thorolf on the battlefield. Now there is a tumulus on the hill-top, a very natural spot for a prehistoric burial-mound. But Dr. Neilson identifies it with Thorolf's grave. This tumulus is 70 feet in length and 10 feet in height. It must mean that at least 18,000 cubic feet of earth have been raised upon it. Can anyone believe that a Norse warrior of the tenth-century would, while the army was engaged in a relentless pursuit, stop back to perform this almost herculean task. I.M.P. says that he would not. A further objection to this site, if we are to accept Egil's account of the preliminaries, on which Dr. Neilson relies, is that Athelstan challenged the Northerners to battle, and himself named the spot. Would he be likely to name as a site for the battle a steep hill in Annandale, a spot of which he could have had no previous knowledge, and distant over 100 miles from his own territory? And if he had, would the Northerners have consented to fall back this distance, undefeated? The idea is nonsensical.

Most of these objections to the Burnswork site have been noted by W. S. Angus in *Antiquity* (1937) but the author proceeds to favour a site 2 miles south-east of Burnswork, called Middlebie Hill. Apart from the fact that this site loses whatever weight is to be attached to the place-name Burnswark (Burnanswerc) the site is not one that appeals to me as a battleground for two great armies facing one another on an east-west line; for it is astride a ridge only 1,200 yards wide and bounded by watercourses on *both* sides. Moreover Angus bases much of his argument on belief in a childish ruse in connexion with the English tents which I frankly do not credit and will not waste space to discuss. I therefore find Middlebie Hill only slightly less improbable than Burns-work Hill.

Apart from any real or supposed resemblance between these hills and Egil's description, on what grounds do these writers place the battle in Caledonia? Such a site does not seem consistent with the general course of the campaign. The Northerners, we are told, advanced far into England. The next we hear of them is engaged in the battle of Brunan-burh. There is no indication that the Northerners retreated upwards of 100 miles before the battle. And even if they did they would scarcely fix on such a curious place on which to make their stand, for it is 6 miles north of the north shore of the Solway Firth, on which shore Dr. Neil-son locates their fleet. Thus if they were defeated (as they were) they would be cut off from their ships and be reduced to retreating over the wild and almost trackless country of the Dumfriesshire hills to the Firth of Clyde. They would obviously have selected a line somewhere to the south of Solway Firth. Even Solway Firth seems to me improb-ably far north for their fleet; if it was in the Ribble these objections become still stronger. The same applies even more so to the ships in the Humber. How could Constantine and Olaf on the Solway Firth escape to Scotland by ships that were at that moment 150 miles further from their home than they themselves were?

There is in fact every indication that the battle was fought in England. Simeon states that Athelstan 'drove these Kings from their King-dom'. The English king also, according to Egil, told the Scots immedi-ately before the battle to 'go back into Scotland', an unlikely ex-pression if they were already north of the Solway Firth.

Both Dr. Neilson and Mr. Angus base this general location on a passage in *Alia Miracula S. Johannis Episcopi*, by William Ketell, which purports to place the battle 'in finibus' near the 'flumen quod dicitur Scotorum Vadum'. Dr. Neilson maintained that this referred to the

Solway Firth, and Mr. Angus gives a qualified agreement. But the passage in reality refers to the Firth of Forth. It describes Athelstan's invasion of Alban in 934, when he crossed not the Solway but the Forth. The passage fits his expedition exactly. 'Vadum Scotorum' would be a natural name for the Firth of Forth in 934 for it divided Scotland from England. (Compare the 'English Channel' which divides England from France.) It is unreasonable to suppose that the Solway Firth would be known as 'Scots Water' in 937, when it was distant over 80 miles from the nearest point of Scotland.

If further proof were required that William Ketell was not referring to a battle that he believed to have been fought on the Solway Firth it would be found in his subsequent statement that Athelstan returned to England after the battle via Dunbar, i.e. via the east coast. This is quite incompatible with a battle fought on the Solway Firth.

If it is agreed that *Vadum Scotorum* could not be the Solway Firth, the last vestige of grounds for locating the battle of Brunanburh just north of that Firth vanishes.

Before proceeding further it should be stated that some people still favour Bromborough in the Wirral peninsula of Cheshire as the site. Apart from the similarity of name, Bromborough has nothing in common either with Egil's Saga or I.M.P.

*   *   *   *   *

If the reader accepts my arguments up to this point, we should look for the site of the battle of Brunanburh somewhere in the neighbourhood of Rotherham, and astride some road running in a north–south direction.

The position should have a river on one flank and a wood on the other. Now there is a village 2,500 yards south–west of Rotherham bearing the suggestive name of Brinsworth, and J. H. Cockburn in his book applies the still more suggestive name Brunesburh to the Roman fort of Templeborough in the south–west angle of the rivers Don and Rother, one mile south–west of Rotherham, which he identifies with the fort Brunesburh (rather than Bremesburh) constructed by the Lady Ethelfleda in A.D. 910. I find his arguments rather flimsy and fanciful. Templeborough is a Roman fort without a vestige of Saxon work in it; how then could it be maintained that such a fort was 'built' by Ethelfleda? But though I cannot accept these arguments I think it quite possible that the Saxon fort was in the neighbourhood of the modern Brinsworth.

I therefore set out one day to examine the ground on the east bank of the Rother just south of Rotherham since Cockburn marks Ryknild Street as running on that side of the river. But I soon found that it held no position likely to be held by Athelstan, nor was it in agreement with Egil's Saga.[1]

I then crossed to the west bank of the Rother and found a very different situation. We should expect Athelstan to take up a position on commanding ground and also on a ridge running roughly at right angles to the direction in which he was facing. The position should also be astride of the road by which he was advancing. These two features seem common to all Anglo-Saxon battles of which the sites can be identified. As regards the second point, I believe armies in those days were more wedded to existing roads than we are apt to imagine, but have not space here to substantiate my argument. As regards the predilection for commanding ground, I believe there were three reasons: (1) that a charge downhill would have more impetus than one on the level; (2) that movements of the enemy prior to the battle could be the better observed; (3) a position on the higher ground tended to induce heightened morale in the occupiers of it. So I attach considerable importance to these two features—a position astride the road and on commanding ground.

Can we find a position that satisfies these two requirements on the west side of the Rother? Undoubtedly we can. The Roman road that runs south from the ford over the Don at Templeborough ascends the ridge just to the south of Brinsworth.[2] Moreover this road is evidently part of the old Ryknild Street, connecting Castleford with Derby. The ridge in question is roughly at right angles to the line of the road and commands the approaches from the Don valley admirably. Thus our two factors are satisfied. From the top of the ridge where the road crosses it a splendid view could be obtained of all the ground down to the river Don, though the slope is gentle and infantry could easily operate on it.

So far so good. Now let us see how far it satisfies the accounts in Egil's Saga. There should be a river on one flank—the left flank according to the poem. The river Rother is on the right flank. In this case I think we need not attach infallibility to the word 'left' in the Saga. Written nearly 300 years after the story of an event has been in oral circulation, it is likely to contain errors. As for a wood, there is now

[1] The fact that the ground was heathy (cp. Vin*heath*) is a mere coincidence.
[2] Miss Dorothy Greene, F.S.A., in 1951 established the course of this road where it crosses the ridge.

none; in such a locality one would not expect one. There is, however, good evidence that the area was once densely wooded. But there is another point in Egil's description: he states that Athelstan occupied the space between river and wood 'where it was at its narrowest. This implies that either river or wood or both bulged inward at this point. Now the river does make an inward bulge at this point as a glance at the map will show. I do not attach much weight to this, but mention it for what it is worth, since the final verdict is the resultant of *all* the considerations and factors.

The final factor in the case I have not hinted at yet; indeed it came to me at the last moment and almost by chance. It is that there is a strong local tradition that a very big battle once took place in the area between Catcliffe and Rotherham. What could this big battle have been? It has been suggested that it may have been between the Roman general Petifius Cerealus and the Brigantes in A.D. 69. Apart from the fact that I should expect such a battle to be fought further north, would such a tradition survive? There had been two partial or total changes in population between A.D. 69 and 937: Saxons had replaced Britons and Danes had to a certain extent replaced Saxons in this area. No other specific traditions of Roman battles have survived in this part of England, and for the foregoing reason this fact is not surprising. On the other hand, if the uniquely big and important battle of Brunanburh was fought hereabouts in the comparatively late Saxon era, surely some trace or tradition of it would survive? Put it in another way: if the battle was fought elsewhere why is there no tradition of such a battle elsewhere? Thus I attach importance to this tradition, especially as the ground so strongly fits the facts and deductions. For if a position was to be held, facing north in the area of Rotherham–Catcliffe, there is one obvious place for it and only one, namely on the Brinsworth ridge.

To sum up, if we piece together all the known facts and reasonable deductions therefrom, the probability points strongly to Brinsworth being the site of the mighty battle of Brunanburh.

If the preceding arguments carry general conviction it should now be easy to establish the actual line held by the English with some precision. I mark my conception of it on the sketch-map. It will be noted that its centre lies on Ryknild Street; that it runs along the forward slope a very short way in front of the crest—the Saxon practice; that the right flank rests on either of the two short forks into which the ridge splits; and that the extent is about 1,800 yards, a convenient frontage for an army of 20,000 in those days.

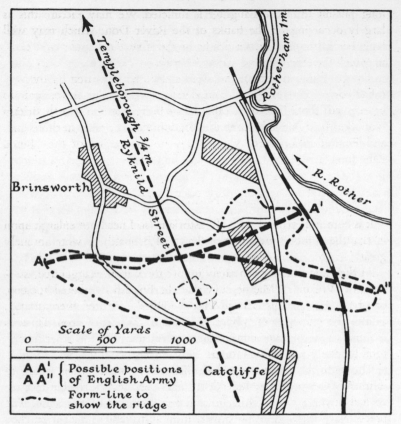

SKETCH-MAP 8.　BRUNANBURH: THE BATTLE II

THE BATTLE

Of the battle itself there is little that can safely be said. King Athelstan, it seems, hesitated on the eve of the battle, as he well might when he saw the huge host arrayed before his own hastily assembled army. He temporized and tried to come to terms; but these the allies rejected, so a battle became inevitable. The King therefore selected the strongest position available, hoping to make up for lack of numbers by strength of position—like the Black Prince at Poitiers 400 years later. Indeed the two battles may well have taken a similar course. The English take up a defensive position, against which the enemy breaks himself in vain. Then, seizing the psychological moment, the English commander puts in a counter-attack, the enemy is hurled back, and in the course of a long pursuit immense slaughter is inflicted. We may picture this as largely occurring on the banks of the River Don; which may well have been the scene of the deaths of the 'five kings and seven earls' of which the *Anglo-Saxon Chronicle* speaks.

The component parts of the allied army each retreated by the way it had come. The short-lived confederation was broken, never again to be revived. If the Southern capital had been captured North Britain would probably have become the 'predominant partner' in this island, and Edinburgh or Perth would now be the capital of the United Kingdom.

A NOTE ON THE NUMBERS

It is common ground with all historians (so I need not enlarge upon it) that the numbers present at the battle of Brunanburh were uniquely great.

At the same time we can safely ignore the wildly exaggerated assertions of William of Malmesbury that the English numbered 100,000, or of the *Clanmacnoise Annals* that the allies' casualties were 30,000; as also the estimates of modern historians, such as Sharon Turner's estimate of 40,000 to 60,000 for the Scottish army, or J. H. Cockburn's total for the two sides of 120,000.

The truth is we have singularly little to go upon when trying to estimate these numbers. Indeed the only seemingly credible fact recorded in our sources is that Olaf's fleet consisted of 615 ships. The precision of this figure has caused most historians to accept it; they point out that Simeon of Durham (the author of this statement) is a fairly reliable source for events in his own part of the country. Let us therefore accept this figure provisionally and see what conclusions we can draw from it.

The first point to ascertain is of course the number of soldiers (as opposed to the total complement) carried in each ship. Equating them with Duke William's ships 130 years later, we should put them at about 20 foot-soldiers per ship (there is no mention of mounted men). This would make about 12,000 in all. Of these, owing to casualties in the Yorkshire fighting and sickness and ship-guards after landing, one could not count upon more than say 9,000 available for the battle of Brunanburh. Making a pure guess that the Irish and Strathclyde contingents between them equalled the Scottish army, there might be 18,000 present at the battle.

But modern writers generally reckon the Viking ships as carrying a larger number of fighting men than 20. Averaging the total capacity of the ships at 50–60, of whom threequarters might be fighting men, we get a total of about 22,000 fighting men. Deducting as before for casualties, &c. we get say 18,000 foot-soldiers, or say a grand total for the whole force of 36,000.

It seems unlikely that the small area and population of Scotland (Alban) at that time, even with the help of soldiers of fortune such as Egil on the English side, could muster so many troops. So I prefer to stand by my own figure of 18,000.

Of the English numbers we know nothing. But the fact that they were numerous enough to defeat the enemy implies that their numbers were at least comparable to that of their opponents. And that is as far as we can go.

CHAPTER VIII

The Battle of Maldon, 11 August 991

ON the 11th of August A.D. 991,[1] was fought the battle of Maldon. Of this battle it has been said that we have more authentic details than of any other battle in our history previous to the battle of Hastings, for it is described in almost the only great battle poem in our language. In the battle the English commander was Britnoth (I scorn the spelling of modern historians, Byrhtnoth or Beorhtnoth, just as I spurn the spellings Aelfred (Alfred), Boudicca (Boadicea), and Knut (Canute). Britnoth, in spite of being defeated in the battle, became a national English hero and remained so even in Norman times. Unfortunately his name has subsequently almost sunk into oblivion. If for no other reason than that it was he who commanded the English in the battle, the fight deserves to be remembered; for Britnoth was a very remarkable man. He stood 6 foot 9 inches (as was ascertained when his headless skeleton was discovered in Ely Cathedral in 1769); at the time of the battle he was about sixty-five years of age, older even than Simon de Montfort at the battle of Evesham; he was conspicuous by his silver white hair; he was the personification of chivalry, even in that dark age; he was the most eminent subject of King Ethelred the Unready.

But the battle deserves to be remembered for other reasons. For a century the Danes had not won a stand-up fight against the English during those palmy days of the great House of Alfred; they had to content themselves with 'tip and run' raids on the coast of this island. Maldon was their first real victory, and it strengthened their morale, encouraging them to attempt a permanent invasion of the country. It was the direct occasion of the first imposition of the fatal Danegelt and it led to the complete occupation of England which occurred (as we are apt to forget) a quarter of a century later. It was thus an event of supreme importance in our history, but the site of the battle has been disputed by modern historians.

The formidable historian Freeman thought he had done so, and such was the prestige of his name that for a generation after his death no one dared query his conclusions. We must therefore start by examining the grounds on which he based his identification of the battlefield.

[1] Three sources out of four give A.D. 991, the fourth gives 993. The date 11 August is given by a Clerk in the Abbey of Hyde at Winchester.

THE BATTLE

Our main authority for the battle is a poem (of which the beginning and end are lost) written in the Anglo-Saxon tongue within a few years of the battle. In the year 991 a Danish (and possibly Norwegian) raiding force[1] harried the coast of Kent and then sacked the town of Ipswich. It then sailed up the Blackwater and fought the battle near Maldon against Britnoth the aldorman of Essex. At the beginning of the battle the river Blackwater separated the two armies at a spot where there was a bridge or causeway. This crossing-place was immersed at high water, the river being tidal. When the English army approached the river crossing it was high water and the two armies faced one another, powerless to engage. During this pause a Danish herald stepped forward to the river bank and shouted across the demands of the invading army. These were that the English should pay tribute in gold and that on its payment the invaders would depart and leave the islanders in peace. Britnoth then stepped forward and in turn shouted his reply. It was short and simple: the English scorned to pay tribute and challenged the enemy to attack. This was of course impossible till the tide fell, and a tedious period of waiting ensued. (Some of the English leaders filled in the time hawking in a nearby wood.) As soon as the tide had fallen sufficiently the Danes rushed forward along the causeway. But it was guarded by three English heroes, Wulfstan, Aldere, and Caccus, who, standing on the causeway, kept them at bay. Now comes the surprising and seemingly incredible part of the story. The Danes shouted across, asking that the English should fall back from the river-bank as otherwise it would be impossible to have a battle. To this cool request the chivalrous Britnoth 'over confident', acceded, if we are to believe the poet. This I think we must do; for a contemporary poet would hardly name the three heroes on the bridge if his readers were aware that they had failed in their stand; the lie would be too transparent.

So the English host fell back a few hundred yards, sufficiently far to allow the Viking army to draw up in good order on the flat meadow-land. This we know because the invaders then advanced to attack in wedge formation which they could hardly have done if they had

---

[1] It may have been commanded by the famous Olaf Tryggvason, King of Norway 995–1000, M. Ashdown's *English and Danish Documents* cites the reasons in favour of this, but E. D. Laborde in *Burhtnoth and Maldon* gives perhaps stronger reasons against. The question must remain an open one.

fought their way piecemeal across the bridge. The battle opened with an archery duel: the Anglo-Saxon words relating it could almost be used to-day: 'Boan Waeren Bysige' Bows were busy.

Then the infantry got to grips, wielding sword, spear, and javelin or dart. The carnage was great. Quite early in the battle Britnoth led forward a body, presumably from his second or reserve line. In so doing the English leader was wounded by a spear thrust. He threw a javelin at his opponent, but he himself was then wounded a second time by a javelin. An officer named Wulfmaer who was at his side, pulled out the javelin and Britnoth then drew his sword and mortally smote his opponent. Simultaneously he was himself struck in his right arm by a sword and dropped his own sword powerless. The Danes then gathered round him and hacked him to death. They then cut off his head and left his body on the ground where he fell.

As was normal in ancient battles, when the leader fell his army began to disintegrate. One of the leading men on the English side, Goderic, mounted Britnoth's own charger and galloped off the field, followed by many others. All seemed over 'bar the shouting', when suddenly the battle took a turn that rendered it famous. A faithful band of Britnoth's followers, swearing not to yield a yard, seem to have formed a circle round the dead body of their revered chief and there they fought it out to the death. Thus the battle lasted for several hours and when eventually all resistance came to an end the Danes were so exhausted and depleted that they did not attempt any pursuit, indeed according to one account they had scarcely enough men left to man their ships. This may be an exaggeration, for they certainly demanded and received from Ethelred, as I have said, the first consignment of Danegelt, to the tune of £10,000. The body of Britnoth was recovered and taken to Ely where it was buried in the cathedral, a lump of wax replacing the head.

THE 'FREEMAN' SITE FOR THE BATTLEFIELD

Such was the battle of Maldon as given in the English poem, and we have now to examine the alternative sites proposed for it. First comes Professor E. A. Freeman, in his *Norman Conquest*. He places the battle at Heybridge, one mile north of Maldon in Essex. The reasons adduced by the great historian are few and simple. The battle was fought near Maldon, a tidal river dividing the two armies at a spot where there was a bridge. A study of the map is at this point indispensable. It will be noted that the tidal rivers, Blackwater and Chelmer, unite just to the north of the town. Maldon itself lies on a hill, and was a fortified burgh in those days, presumably holding a garrison. Freeman placed the Danish army between the two rivers and he made Britnoth approach from the north, as he (the historian) knew of no ancient bridge other than that at Heybridge. But there are considerations that make this site most improbable. In the first place he completely ignored the existence of the fortified town of Maldon lying under a mile in rear of the Danish army. In that position it would find itself between two fires, Britnoth to the north and the town garrison to the south. In the second place there is no mention of the town in any of the records of the actual battle, although in order to reach the suggested position the Danish army would have had to pass under its walls. Herded between the two rivers, its position would have been constricted and hazardous, with no line of retreat open to it. Thirdly there is no evidence that there was a bridge at Heybridge in Saxon times, and in any case a bridge that was submerged at high tide would be a queer one. Fourthly, if the Danes found themselves blocked at the bridge there was nothing to prevent them moving quite a short way to their left up stream where they would be able to cross by a ford. Fifthly and finally, according to the poem the Danes crossed the river in a westerly direction, but Freeman's siting would make them cross to the north.

Clearly we must look elsewhere for the battlefield. An alternative site was suggested by Dr. E. D. Laborde in the *English Historical Review* for April 1925. He places it at the causeway joining the island of Northey (nearly two miles downstream from Maldon) to the southern bank of the estuary. Let us now examine the Laborde site in detail.

THE 'LABORDE' SITE

The island of Northey, approximately 2 miles long from north to south and 1 mile wide, is situated in a desolate neighbourhood. There is no habitation within a mile of it, and only an unmetalled road and a causeway, submerged at high tide, joins it to the mainland to the south. But it can be easily and directly approached on foot from Maldon along the sea dyke. Now the first thing to note, on which Dr. Laborde largely based his localization, is the fact that the Anglo-Saxon word *bricge* can mean either a bridge, or a causeway. Since this particular 'bricge' was under water at high tide it is much more likely to

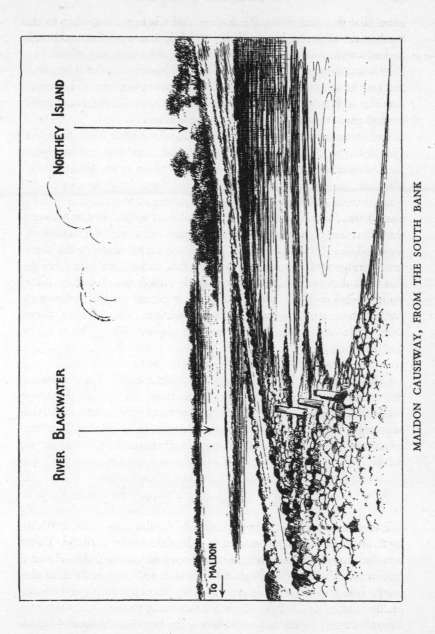

MALDON CAUSEWAY, FROM THE SOUTH BANK

be a causeway than a bridge. If this is the correct site it also throws light on an otherwise obscure phrase in the poem: 'the water-streams locked together', for at the causeway the tides approach from both sides simultaneously, and there they meet. I have verified this by standing on the causeway as the tide was rising and saw the two streams actually 'lock together' between my feet; the expression is exact, and it cannot apply to any other point on the estuary.

Assuming that the Danes had made the island their base, the causeway was their only approach to the mainland, and this would explain their urgent plea to Britnoth to be allowed to cross the causeway. The next question is, was the island of Northey a likely place for a base? From a study of both the map and the ground, and in view of Danish precedents, I say emphatically, yes, it was. The Vikings had always shown a propensity for a base surrounded by water. This might be an island, e.g. Sheppey, Thanet, Isle of Wight, Northey, or the water might be an artificial ditch such as their camp at Reading before the battle of Ashdown, or by the moat they dug round themselves at Fulham (still visible, though few Londoners are aware of the fact). On the score of Inherent Military Probability then, Northey Island would be a likely base for a force intending to raid up the valley of the Blackwater.

There remain, however, a few questions to be settled. Why could not the Danes cross over the practically dry land at low water instead of asking for a free passage? Was the estuary-bed too boggy to pass on foot except by the causeway? The simplest and most satisfying way of answering this question was to make the attempt myself, and I did so. I had not gone more than a few yards before I sank half-way up my calves and did not dare go any further. I had got my answer. It was oozy black mud: hence no doubt the name Blackwater.

Next problem: was the channel narrow enough for the herald to be heard by the English? Laborde states that this would be easy as the causeway is only some 80 yards long, and E. V. Gordon in his edition of the Poem repeats this figure. It is in fact about 170 yards long. This merely shows how easily it is for a mis-statement to become encrusted tradition. (Another mis-statement is as to the width of the causeway which is given as 8 feet. I measured it as about 12 feet). Could the voice of the herald carry intelligibly in a foreign accent across this distance? Probably it could, for the sound of the human voice does travel well over water.

A third question is, why should the Danes allow themselves to be

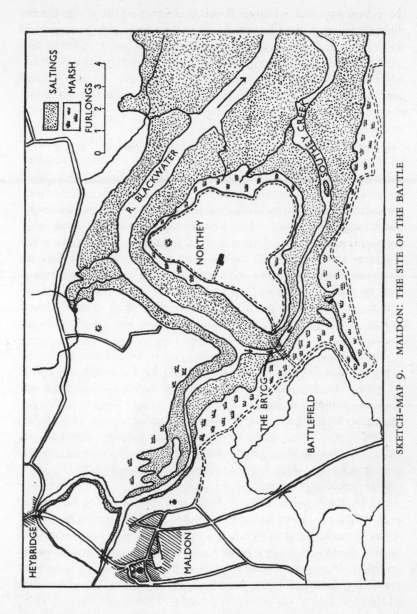

SKETCH-MAP 9. MALDON: THE SITE OF THE BATTLE

cooped up on the island, dependent on a single ford? But it should be remembered that they had their ships with them; they were not surrounded, but still retained freedom to sail away. The reason for their plea for a free crossing was merely in order that the battle, which both sides desired, might take place. It was not unusual in those days, or even later, for a battlefield to be selected by mutual agreement,[1] and this was all that the Danes were suggesting—or so it seems to me.

We do not know for certain where Britnoth assembled his army nor his route to the battlefield; but it seems reasonable to suppose that the last stage of his advance would be through the burgh of Maldon where he might pick up some reinforcements. It is thus easy to picture the preliminary stages leading to the battle. Sitting on the shore of the island, looking westwards, I could see the town of Maldon, 2,600 yards away, and in my mind's eye I saw the English scouts riding down the slope out of the burgh towards the island. Before them the Danish foragers hastily fall back, fearful lest they may be cut off by the rising tide. The causeway can be used on foot till within about 1½ hours of high water, so we may picture those scouts recrossing to safety about that time. As the main body of the English army approached, the causeway became completely submerged and a sheet of water 170 yards wide then separated the two armies.

The rest is easy. Both armies are marshalled in battle formation, the English all dismounting first, and receiving their instructions for the battle from their trusted leader, while the Danes look on from the other side. A painful pause of an hour or more then ensues. During this time the parley between the Danish herald and the English leader is carried on. The waters slowly 'unlock' themselves, the foremost Danes dash eagerly into them ere the causeway is completely uncovered, splashing their way across, and the battle begins.

The place fits the story like a glove. Here, and nowhere else, stood brave Wulfstan, like Horatius on the bridge. With tolerable assurance one can stand and picture the exciting scene. One can even get excited oneself, for of what other battle fought nearly one thousand years ago can one stand on the very spot, practically unchanged from that day to this, though seven hundred thousand tides have since ebbed and flowed?

---

[1] The English challenged the Scots to fight on a specified battlefield just before Flodden. The French did the same at Agincourt.

But of outward signs of the battle there are none. Though our fore-fathers there fought to the death in defence of their fatherland, their ghosts can now say:

> Never a story and never a stone
> Tells of the martyrs who died like me
> Just for the pride of the old countree.

CHAPTER IX

The Battle of Assingdon,[1] *18 October 1016*

THE battle fought on St. Luke's Day, 1016, enabled a Danish dynasty to reign over this country for a generation.

In order to put the reader 'into the picture' we must hark back a few years. Ever since the battle of Maldon the Danes had been almost consistently victorious in their campaigns, and for a short period Sweyn had been acknowledged King by the greater part of the country, Ethelred the Unready having fled to the Continent. Then there arose a national hero in the person of Edmund Ironside. By astonishing efforts, of which we have not the details, he raised a formidable army, and defeated the redoubtable Canute, son of Sweyn, in at least five battles in the space of six months. The campaign of 1016 was in truth one of the most remarkable and sparkling in our annals.

Briefly, on the death of Sweyn, his son Canute claimed the crown; but he was opposed by an Anglo-Saxon army, under Edmund Ironside and Edric Streona, the King's favourite. We shall hear more of this Edric and may here quote Freeman's description of this astonishing man. He was 'a man of low birth, shrewd intellect, of an eloquent tongue,—which he used only to persuade men to mischief—proud, cruel, envious and faithless'.

On the approach of Canute, this Edric deserted to him, taking with him his own portion of the army. Consequently Edmund had to fall back to the north to recruit fresh troops, before meeting the Dane in the field.

On St. George's Day, 1016, Ethelred 'did England the only good service that was in his power by dying', as Sir Charles Oman scathingly puts it. But the capital still held out and Edmund, now King, used it as the pivot of his six months' campaign. London should indeed be proud of its record during those hectic but heroic six months. Even when all seemed lost, with the Danes apparently triumphant in most parts of the country, the capital was proof against all the attacks which continued intermittently throughout the summer. With their details we are not here concerned. While Canute was attacking London, Edmund, who had raised a fresh army in Mercia, attacked and defeated

[1] Most historians, for some obscure reason, adopt the spelling of Florence of Worcester, *Assandun*, in place of the *Anglo-Saxon Chronicle* version.

a Danish army near Penselwood (where his ancestor, Alfred, had concentrated his forces before his great victory of Ethandun). He then
turned on a second Danish army led by the traitor Edric, engaged it
at Sherston and drove it back towards London. Edmund followed
them up, and, in another battle, raised the siege of London, which
Canute was conducting in person. Edmund then entered the city,
defeated the Dane in a battle at Brentford and drove him back to his
camp at Greenwich. Thence Canute sailed away and landed in the
mouth of the Orwell. From here he raided Northern Mercia, as com-
compensation for his defeat at London.

At this stage the English King appeared to have the upper hand;
the country as a whole rallied to him, and when he advanced towards
the Orwell his rival hurriedly re-embarked and sailed away—only
to land again in the Medway. Edmund followed him up by land,
engaged him at Otford in Kent, and won his fifth great victory. The
Danes fell back into the Isle of Sheppey, where they established a
practically unassailable base—for Edmund had no fleet.

Such was the situation, the month being September, when Edric
the traitor, seeing how things were shaping, turned his coat once more
and, astonishing to relate, was forgiven and reinstated by the English
King. On this affair the austere *Anglo-Saxon Chronicle* allows itself a
rare comment 'than which nothing could be more ill advised'. The
reason for this comment we shall shortly see.

A few days later the restless Canute sailed with a portion of his host
and disembarked in the river Crouch, near the modern Burnham.
From here, true to form, he carried out yet another raid, this time over
Southern Mercia (i.e. Buckinghamshire and perhaps Oxfordshire).
Edmund fell back temporarily into the West Country, where he
recruited fresh forces for what he foresaw must be the supreme contest
between the two young antagonists.[1]

Edmund Ironside now had an army superior in numbers to that of
his opponents, though necessarily less homogeneous and less well
trained or experienced. Canute fell back hastily before it (just as he
had done in the Orwell raid), intent on getting his booty safely on
board ship, and thence to his Sheppey base. The Dane was a cautious
general and like William the Bastard before Hastings and Montgomery in the Normandy landing, prepared a defensive bridgehead.
This was on the high ground at Canewdon, two miles south-west of

---

[1] Edmund was only 22 years of age.

his disembarkation point on the Crouch (near the famous Burnham roadstead).

The Anglo-Saxon army pursued the retreating Danes with all speed, and by the evening of 17 October it camped at Ashingdon hill, in full view of its opponents on Canewdon Hill, just 3,000 yards away. The enemy had his back to the wall; he could not retreat any further if he was to retain his fleet; he must stand and fight. Canute recognized this necessity and took appropriate measures.

THE TERRAIN

The terrain of the battlefield is easily described. The whole promontory of Essex between the Crouch and the Thames to the east of Ashingdon is completely flat except for a low ridge that joins the villages of Ashingdon and Canewdon, culminating in two slight hills at the two extremities. On these hills the rival churches of Ashingdon and Canewdon are now perched. The low ridge joining them is not straight but sags, or bulges towards the south. Hence if one takes a straight line between the two churches one has a drop of nearly 100 feet into the bottom of the Crouch valley. There is also a slight but nameless swell of ground on the ridge 1,000 yards west of Canewdon. At the time of the battle the ground was quite open, though there are now some scattered farms on the low land which must have been marshy at the time of the battle. In October, however, it would probably be passable for troops, though the normal trackway would run along the line of the ridge or watershed.[1] The two armies would be in full view of one another, and as the sun rose on St. Luke's Day Canute would have a good view of the approach of his antagonist. This is important.

THE BATTLE

(It must be understood that the following description of the battle is necessarily conjectural. We have only five sources from which it is safe to take any details, and even in these sources the story is so encrusted with mythical details beloved of the medieval scribe, that

[1] The most likely route for the Danish retreat would be via the old Roman bridge over the Crouch at Hullbridge, five miles west of Ashingdon (existing till about 1850), thence along the watershed to Ashingdon, and still, following the watershed, thence to Canewdon.

there is very little that can be accepted as absolute fact. In order, however, to avoid constant use of qualifying words and phrases, such as 'in all probability', 'as I believe', 'it seems that', &c., I give my rendering of the story in an uninterrupted narrative for the most part, and in the final section, 'Problems of the Battlefield', I give my reasons for the controversial conclusions I have come to.)

The Danes had been caught up before the embarkation of their booty was complete. Canute was therefore obliged to stand and fight. His position was uncomfortably close to his fleet, and he would like, if he could do so advantageously, to join battle a little further forward, thus giving himself more 'depth'. But the Danish general was, as I have said, a cautious commander though a youthful one. He had no intention of throwing away the advantage of holding a hill position up which his opponents would have to climb if they wished to engage. It would however be possible to advance about 1,000 yards along the ridge and halt on the swell of ground to which I have referred. As soon, then, as Canute saw that his enemy was indeed advancing down the hill from Ashingdon with the evident intention of attacking, he adopted the course that he had predetermined, and advanced to this forward position on the swell, where he halted his army and prepared to receive the onslaught of the Anglo-Saxons.

Meanwhile Edmund had drawn up his army in line on the hill-top where Ashingdon church now stands, shortly before dawn. He formed it in 'three lines'. Freeman interprets this as three ranks, but this is highly unlikely. The phrase probably means little more than that it was in considerable depth. Edric Streona had been given the command of the West Mercian section of the army, including some Welshmen. It can be assumed that, having been restored to favour, Edric again shared the command with the king, Edmund taking one wing and Edric the other, just as Ethelred and Alfred had divided the command at the battle of Ashdown. To placate the returned traitor the more the King may be assumed to have given him the position of honour on the right. Having drawn up his army the King passed along the line haranguing each division in turn.

It was now close on nine o'clock and the sun was getting high in the sky. The enemy could be clearly seen, also drawn up for battle. Canute was at last at bay. Edmund, full of confidence after his recent succession of victories, and rendered all the more so in that Edric and his followers were once more on his side, decided to advance without more ado and give battle.

Emulating his ancestor Alfred, in a strikingly similar situation, he dashed impetuously down the hill, at the head of his division, expecting Edric's division to follow suit. The latter—assuming he was on the right had not such a steep slope to descend and would naturally be outpaced by the left division. Thus they lagged behind. Edric was at their head, regulating the pace, and the further the advance continued, the greater became the distance between the two wings. By the time Edmund's wing had reached the modern Hyde Wood the Danes had occupied their forward position on the swell. One thousand yards now separated the antagonists. The impulsive Edmund did not draw rein. To do so would mean losing for the moment the momentum, the élan, of the attack, which might be fatal, for they

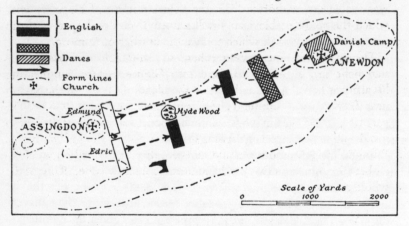

SKETCH-MAP IO.   ASSINGDON: THE BATTLE

were now about to mount the slight rise between them and their opponents. On then they went without a pause, breasting the gentle slope without appreciable slackening of the pace. Another minute and the two lines were engaged in close combat.

But Edric, instead of speeding his wing forward to join in the battle, abruptly halted it and remained a cold spectator of the fight. The effect of this was inevitable. The left wing of the Danes, having no enemy in their immediate front, wheeled round to their right and thus enveloped the exposed flank of the King's contingent which was already fully engaged (see Sketch-map). Thus Edmund was both outnumbered and outflanked. Even so the attack was persevered in and the battle lasted, if we are to believe a contemporary source (*Encomium Emmae*) from 9 a.m. till vespers.

By this time the traitorous Edric had cleared right off the field and the fate of the King's army was sealed. The fact that they had fought valiantly is shown both by the length of time they had held out though outnumbered, and by the number of dead they left on the field. The records only mention those of high rank, but these included and indeed comprised 'the flower of the English race'. A large portion of the army was surrounded, due to the above-mentioned enveloping movement, and these men died to a man. Assingdon was indeed the prototype of the battle of Flodden, where the chivalry of Scotland perished almost to a man, but, as at Flodden, the victors were too exhausted to pursue. Darkness fell and this formed a convenient excuse for the absence of any pursuit—as also at Flodden. Thus King Edmund was enabled to withdraw from the field a nucleus of his army with which this undauntable man—well named Ironside—hoped to form yet another army with which to face the invader once more.

The sequel does not concern us here, so I must confine myself to the statement that Edmund retreated into Gloucestershire, augmenting his army as he fell back, and that on the island of Olney on the Severn near Tewkesbury [1] Edmund and Canute met, and as a result, agreed to partition the kingdom between them. Something at least had been saved out of the wreck of Assingdon. But not for long. The heroic Edmund Ironside, worn out and diseased, died at Oxford on 30 November (St. Andrew's Day) and Canute was acknowledged King of the whole country.

THE SITE

The first problem is to discover the general site of the battle. Here we have sure foundations at least, for the *Anglo-Saxon Chronicle* states clearly that it was in Essex. After the sojourn at Sheppey the Danes 'returned into Essex' (*A.S. Chron.*), 'crossed the river into Essex' (Florence of Worcester). Somewhere in Essex then Canute left his fleet and conducted a raid into Mercia. Where did he leave his fleet? Clearly not on the north bank of the Thames, for it shelves so gently that the tide recedes nearly a mile in places. There remain three possible regions, the estuaries of the Crouch, Blackwater, and Orwell. The previous raid had been based on the Orwell, and the fact that the *Anglo-Saxon Chronicle* does not again mention it by name seems to imply that it was not used the second time. Moreover it is on the northern confines

[1] Probably at Deerhurst.

of the county, a good 40 miles from Sheppey, whereas Florence's account seems to suggest that Canute did not sail far. The same objection applied, though with less force, to the Blackwater (used by the Danes in the Maldon campaign twenty-five years before.) There remains the Crouch, which is a mere 15 miles from Sheppey. The estuary of this river forms the famous roads of Burnham where landing would be easy and expeditious, and—even more important—a re-embarkation. This river would fit what we know of the strategical elements of the campaign. From the Orwell Northern Mercia had already been raided. This time it was the turn of Southern Mercia. Marching due west from the Crouch the Danes would skirt London—a danger spot for it was still held by Edmund—and they could then traverse Buckinghamshire and Oxfordshire into the heart of Southern Mercia.

If this be accepted, the next point to decide is, on which bank of the Crouch did the Danes land? Either bank would suit equally as far as strategy is concerned, so we must have recourse to other factors—place-names and battle relics. The name of the battle is given variously as Assingdon, in Essex (*A.S. Chron.*), Assendun (William of Malmesbury), Assendune (Roger of Hovedon), Assandun (Florence of Worcester). Now there is an Ashdon on the northern border of the county, which has been claimed as the site; but this village is over 20 miles from the sea, whereas it is implicit in the story (as we shall see) that the battle was fought close to the fleet. We will return to this point later.

There remains Ashingdon, 5 miles north of Southend. The spelling is practically the same as that in the *Anglo-Saxon Chronicle.* Let us accept this site as a working hypothesis and see where it leads to.

We must, in this case, picture the Danish fleet as lying up in the Burnham roadstead, while the army advances into Mercia along the high ground on the south of the Crouch, returning by the same route some time later, heavy with booty. Edmund with his army in hot pursuit, and travelling lighter (not being burdened with booty) travels faster, and catches up the Danes before they can get on board ship. It is obviously Canute's policy to avoid battle with a numerically superior army as long as possible; his sole aim is to reach his fleet with the minimum of delay, in order to get his booty on board while he holds off the enemy as best he can from some nearby position. So we must look for such a position within a mile or two of the roadstead. It is easily found. Under two miles from the river, and to the south-west of Burnham is a hill which exactly meets our requirements. Moreover it has the suggestive name of Canewdon.[1] May this not be Canute's hill or down? Dr. Reaney, the Essex etymologist, says no, and J. W. Burrows, who has written one of the best papers on the problem, rather meekly accepts the dictum. I do not. It seems to me that etymology can be a 'snare and a delusion' when dealing with place-names which have come down to us from the Norman scribes who spelt phonetically.

It is hard to prove a negative, and a bold thing to say categorically that such and such a spelling of 800 years ago cannot be related to a very similar word to-day, such as Canewdon and Canute's Down. Be this as it may, the place now called Canewdon is precisely the spot where I should expect the Danes to make a stand, having already made an entrenched camp there as a bridgehead for their army and fleet. Moreover, there is so strong a tradition that the Danes did have a camp on this hill, that it is so marked on the 1/25,000 O.S. map. One would hardly expect to see signs of this entrenched camp now, but, walking round what I imagined to be its perimeter, I detected at one spot signs that might indicate ditch and vallum. If so the vallum was used as a target butt in later Ages, for the place is still called Butts Hill.

Let us carry our working hypothesis a stage further. Let us assume that Burnham was the landing place, Canewdon the Danish camp, and Ashingdon the position of the English army. How far does this hypothesis fit in with the course of the battle? Again admirably. The two armies evidently formed up on ground visible to one another, which implies that both were on higher ground than the intervening terrain.

The *Encomium Emmae* describes the Assingdon position as a hill 'in Aesceneduno loco, quod nos latina montem fraxinorum possumus interpretare', 'hill of the ash trees'.

The same chronicle also seems to suggest that the Danes were on an eminence, for they ran (*occurrunt*) against their enemy. This is stated more explicitly by Florence: 'Canute by a slow march led his troops *down* to a level ground.' Thus we require two hills with lower ground

[1] Canewdon is pronounced Can-u-don by the inhabitants, reminiscent of Canute. Pronunciations of place-names sometimes outlive their spelling. Near my native home in Staffordshire is a wood spelt Deansbridge, but pronounced Danesbridge. It happens to lie on the old boundary of the Danelaw, as far as can be ascertained, and possibly marks the site of a bridge from the Danish territory to the Saxon.

between them. A primeval track almost certainly ran along the low ridge connecting the two hills, for the bottom of the valley would be waterlogged most of the year. In October, however, the ground would be at its firmest, thus allowing of Edmund's advance to the very bottom of the hill, as I have made him do.

On another line of reasoning, one might expect the point of engagement to be nearer Canewdon than Ashingdon. We are told by Florence (and can well believe it) that Canute advanced slowly and cautiously, whilst Edmund advanced rapidly. Thus, if one army started as soon as it saw the other on the move, the engagement would open on or near the swell of ground where I fancy Canute took up his final position.

The final piece of evidence is the presence of battle relics. There have been found in the churchyard at Ashingdon parts of a shield, a spear, and also a silver penny of Canute.

Putting all the above factors together, and having no contrary factors to set off against them, I have no hesitation in maintaining that the battle of Assingdon took place in the area bounded by the villages of Ashingdon and Canewdon.

THE CLAIMS OF ASHDON

In the foregoing paragraph I have, for the sake of clarity and brevity rejected the Ashdon site in a single sentence. For the benefit of those who may retain doubts on the subject I will here give my reasons in greater detail. It will be convenient to examine, point by point, the case for Ashdon put forward in an article in the *Journal of the British Archaeological Association* for 1926 by Miller Christy, since this article claims to be definitive—in his words to 'finally dispose of this centuries-old controversy'. Some may find the article somewhat cocksure, if not arrogant. The author is severe on adherents of other schools who give their views in a positive form, yet his own account teems with such expressions as 'There can be no doubt that . . .' in places where I, for one, do experience considerable doubt. However, let that pass. His three main arguments for the Ashdon site appear to be as follows. First, Ashdon is far removed from the sea and from the fleet and is 'just where one would expect to find it according to the guidance afforded by the *Saxon Chronicle*'. I will return to this argument presently. His second argument is that at Hadstock, two miles north-west of Ashdon, is a stone Saxon church which he identifies with the stone 'mynster' that Canute had built 'for the souls of the men who were there slain'. Third, that the word Ashdon is more closely related to Assingdon than is Ashingdon. As regards the second argument, his 'bull point' is that Hadstock church is made of stone and is large for a village church, about 100 feet in length, which he supposes the mynster would also be. These are pointers in the right direction, but, standing by themselves, as they do, they do not carry the argument far. On the opposite side of the account there are some difficulties. The mynster was at Assingdon; but Hadstock is not Assingdon, nor even Ashdon. If, as the author asserts, Canute had his camp on top of the hill at Ashdon, he would have strong reason for building the mynster there in preference to anywhere else. Though it is agreed that it is a Saxon church, he would be a bold man who would aver: 'It is the right style for 1020, *but no earlier*', which is what the author implies. Moreover there are other stone Saxon churches in Essex. (Hadstock, by the bye, lies practically on the borders of Essex, Cambridgeshire, and Suffolk.) Finally, there are no battlefield relics at Ashdon as there appear to be at Ashingdon. Standing by itself, therefore, the 'mynster' argument amounts to little.[1]

Miller Christy's third argument is that the word Ashdon is more nearly Assingdon than is Ashingdon. In this he runs counter to the main authorities. I will quote but one. Dr. Reaney states: 'From a philological point of view, whilst Ashdon cannot be the site of the battle, Ashingdon may be.'

I now return to the first argument—that the battle must have been fought far away from the sea and the fleet. This is fundamental to his argument, so I will examine it in more detail. He starts by quoting the relevant passages in the *Anglo-Saxon Chronicle* and in Florence of Worcester. The latter is quite clear and explicit: The Danes having raided Mercia and carried off much booty, 'regained their ships; Edmund Ironside went in pursuit of them . . . and came up with them as they were retreating at a hill called Assandun. . . .' Miller Christy admits that this can only mean that the battle took place near the coast, and he gets out of it by the cool assertion that Florence was guilty of

---

[1] For centuries a piece of skin hung on the door of Hadstock church, and Mr. Christy suggested that it might be that of Edric who had been buried just outside London Wall. His idea was that years after his death, Canute had the body exhumed, conveyed to Hadstock in order to blacken the name of the man to whom, more than to anyone, he owed his crown. Those who have a weak case will clutch at any argument however preposterous.

'an obvious misconception'. Previously he had stated that Florence was 'the most trustworthy' of the chroniclers, and he accepts most of his account. It is easy to accept an account. when it agrees with one's pre-conceived standpoint, and to reject it when it does not. His excuse is that Florence is not consistent with the *Saxon Chronicle*. The relevant passage in the *Chronicle* is as follows: 'When the King understood that the [Danish] army was up, then collected he the fifth time all the English nation and followed them and over-took them in Essex on the down called Assingdon. . . .'

Where is the inconsistency in these two accounts? To follow and overtake a hostile army implies a pursuit, and this pursuit, coming from the direction of the West Country, must have been towards the coast of Essex, even if Florence had not specifically mentioned the ships. Yet Miller Christy asserts that this passage 'cannot possibly mean that they were retreating to or had reached the coast, or were even near it. Clearly they were some distance, *and were going still further inland*' (my italics). I had to read this astonishing passage twice, in order to take it in! Was the author standing on his head when he wrote it?

In doubtful points of military operations it is a sound thing to apply the test of Inherent Military Probability. What would one expect the action of Canute to be when in the midst of his raid he heard that his opponent was raising 'all England' against him? To be surer of our ground we should study the character of the commander in question. Fortunately we get a clear picture of the military character of the young Danish leader from the *Encomium Emmae*, a work that is almost com-pletely ignored by Christy (and by other writers). I hold it in high esteem as a source. The author was a contemporary and had him-self met Canute. It appears that Canute was a prudent, cautious commander, taking no avoidable risks in war. The Encomiast describes an episode, probably relating to this campaign (though his chronology is weak) wherein Edmund challenged the Dane to stand and fight, but Canute made reply that he would only fight when he was on ground favourable to himself, and continued his retreat. The ground most favourable to himself would, as we have seen, be the Canewdon position, with the fleet close in rear. Handy in case he should be obliged to re-embark, it was the position that would afford him the best chance of getting safely away with his booty. Until this precious booty—intended probably for the half-beleaguered garrison on the Island of Sheppey—was safe on board, he had no desire to risk his field army, any more than the Black Prince had when trying to get his booty back to Bordeaux past Poitiers. The *Encomium* also depicts Edmund as a young impulsive leader, the prototype of King Harold (who half a century later probably consciously based his strategy on that of England's Darling of his boyhood).

Thus the picture is complete: on the one side a young and headstrong leader, driving forward impetuously and full of confidence, with an army grown greater than ever and filled with confidence after its recent succession of victories: on the other hand, the cautious Dane, fearful of his formidable opponent and mindful only of one thing, to get his booty on board and out to sea before this whirlwind scattered or captured it but eventually forced to fight in order to cover the embarkation of the booty. Florence's description is in full accord with I.M.P. and I accept it unhesitatingly and without qualification.

It follows that I reject Ashdon.

THE CONDUCT OF EDRIC STREONA

This is a real puzzle. I have done the best I can to make sense of the extraordinary story of Edric's treachery. At the first blush one is disposed to reject the whole story; the defeated side clutches at any excuse and welcomes a scapegoat. However, in this case not only the defeated but the victors assert his treachery. The *Encomium* is most explicit on the subject, and after describing how Edric withdrew his troops at the outset of the battle, adds: 'And as some say, this he did, not because of fear, but of craftiness, as afterwards was made evident; which he secretly had promised the Danes.'

The English account of Edric's treachery comes from two sources, the *Anglo-Saxon Chronicle* and Henry of Huntingdon. The latter puts it in the middle of the battle, when the Danes were beginning to waver. 'Flet Engles!' he cries; 'Ded is Edmund.' The shorter *Chronicle* version is not inconsistent with this. But it is improbable, to say the least. How could one man, in the noise and bustle of the battle, make his voice heard by a great number, and how could he manage to extricate them from the battle, once engaged by prearrangement with the Danes? If the cry 'Ded is Edmund' had spread, the English King would have taken the natural step to show its falsity, by uncovering his head, as did William, Duke of Normandy, half a century later almost to the day. Florence of Worcester has the still more preposterous story that Edric beheaded a soldier who resembled the King and held the head up as proof of Edmund's death. Incidentally he attributes the story to the battle of Sherston when Edric was fighting on the other side, which makes it still more incredible.[1] The Danish account is the much more probable version, and I accept it. According to this, the traitor hung back from the beginning, and never entered the conflict at all. Somewhat like the Stanleys at Bosworth Field, he watched the battle from afar, standing aloof. He must have produced some plausible excuse afterwards, some quibble or other, for in spite of his villainy, he managed to worm his way back into the royal favour. The *Encomium* explains it by saying that 'he was a man of good counsel'. There was something rather baffling about this man.

THE CONDUCT OF EDMUND IRONSIDE

I have ignored the lyrical account of Henry of Huntingdon (which Freeman swallowed so easily). Every medieval scribe felt that a battle description was not quite complete without the two commanders coming into personal combat. Henry makes the English King dash into the midst of his foes, hewing a path before him right up to Canute's bodyguard, &c. But one must accept that the young prince was as hot and impulsive as his ancestor, young Prince Alfred, 150 years before. He had already, it would seem, become the darling of his country, and perhaps it is a pity that he did not die on the field of battle instead of painfully in his bed at Oxford only a few weeks later. He would thus have become as well known a figure in our national history as Harold Godwinson.

[1] Though accepted by Freeman!

CHAPTER X

The Battle of Stamford Bridge, 25 September 1066

PROFESSOR FREEMAN described 1066 as 'that terrible year', and terrible for England it was. Thrice was the country invaded, if we include Tostig's landing in the Humber as an invasion. Even had there been no battle of Hastings the year would have been big with fate for this land. The trouble started on 5 January when Edward the Confessor died and Harold, son of Godwin, was elected King in his stead. When William, Duke of Normandy, heard of this, he swore a great oath that he would come and take by force the crown that was rightfully his. Harold consequently had to keep watch and ward along the south coast with fleet and army throughout the summer. Moreover, in the month of May, his baleful brother Tostig, the exiled Earl of Northumberland, with a fleet of 60 ships, made a series of attempts on the southern and eastern coasts. Repelled everywhere, he was obliged to take refuge within the territory of the Scottish king, Malcolm. Thus started the tradition, that survived for some centuries, of Scotland siding with the enemies of England to her hurt. Tostig was enabled to refit his fleet and even to recruit Scottish volunteers.

We have reached the second week in September when almost simultaneously Harold disbanded his levies, retaining only his House-carls, or household troops, and withdrew his fleet to London, to refit. At the same time Duke William made his first approach to England, taking advantage of a partially favourable wind to move eastwards up the coast to St. Valery, whence the crossing would be comparatively short.

And now a new threat appeared from the north. Harald Hardrada, King of Norway, the foremost captain in western Europe, was also on the war path. In league with Tostig, he collected a powerful army and fleet of 300 vessels in Bergen and the nearby fjords, and in early September set sail for the conquest of England. The fact that he left his eldest son as ruler of Norway and took his youngest son Olaf with him, suggests that his intention was to stay in England, not merely to raid it. Touching at the Shetlands, he picked up the Earl of Orkney, and no doubt, a contingent of troops there.

By a good piece of staff-work, of which we do not know the details, the expeditionary forces of Harald and Tostig met at a rendezvous in the mouth of the Tyne, and together continued south to the Humber, raiding Scarborough and other places *en route*. Sailing and rowing up the estuary, the scene of Tostig's recent defeat, they pushed on up the river Ouse, the few English ships in those waters retreating before them up the river Wharfe as far as Tadcaster. But the combined fleets did not follow them up that river; instead they disembarked on the east bank of the Ouse at Riccall, 10 miles south of York. Here young Olaf was left with a guard over the ships while the army set out for York.

It was 19 September; the whole of the north had been alarmed. Morcar, who had succeeded Tostig as Earl of Northumberland, and Edwin his brother, Earl of Mercia, speedily collected their forces and marched south from York to meet the invaders. At Fulford, two miles south of the city, battle was joined. The fight was long and bloody on both sides, but at last the invader prevailed; many of the English were swept into the river by a flanking movement and drowned. The rest dispersed, leaving York practically open to Harald Hardrada. Some histories state that the Norwegian King captured the city, but it does not appear that he actually entered it. On the contrary he took the surprising course of falling back to his base-camp at Riccall, whilst conducting negotiations with the garrison of the city. The result of these parleys was also surprising. Not only did the city consent to capitulate but also agreed to accept Harald as King and to co-operate with him in the subjection of southern England. The explanation of this humiliating decision was probably threefold. In the first place Harold Godwinson had only reluctantly been accepted as King in Northumbria. In the second place the spirit of nationality was not fully developed: possession was nine-tenths of the law: the Norwegian monarch seemed to be all-powerful and the commonalty was prepared to accept him as King. In the third place Harold was under a papal ban and the superstitious Northumbrians may have seen 'the hand of God' in the Norwegian victory. Hostages were exchanged on both sides and arrangements made for further hostages to be handed over at a spot 8 miles east of York, where four Roman roads met at the crossing of the river Derwent. No satisfactory reason has been advanced for this curious selection of place, a good dozen miles from the base-camp of the invaders. Freeman suggests that the proximity of a royal residence at Aldby would account for it, but this is a flimsy reason.

The battle of Fulford had taken place on 20 September, and by the evening of the 24th the Norwegian army (less a division left to guard the ships) had reached the rendezvous on the banks of the Derwent where there stood a wooden bridge, that went by the name of Stamford Brigge.

Whilst Harald Hardrada was thus having an easy triumph in the north, what was the other Harold doing? Details are scarce. We neither know the date at which news of the invasion reached the English king, nor his situation at the time. Harold had now to make the second most important decision of his life: whether to remain on guard against the threatened invasion from the south, trusting to Morcar and Edwin to deal with the northern invasion, or whether to march north himself, gambling his crown on being able to beat the Northmen and return in time to beat the Normans. A man of action, accustomed to taking rapid and bold decisions, Harold decided on the second course. Few men can have had such a difficult decision to make, and it was rendered still more difficult by the fact that he had only that month disbanded the bulk of his army, which he now had to reassemble before setting out. How long this took we do not know, but, judging by what followed it was a matter of a very few days. During those days he evidently sent orders to the shire-levies in the districts through which he would pass, to meet him *en route*. This they did, and some volunteers also came flocking to his banners.

Marching rapidly up the Great North Road, his army steadily increasing in size as he progressed, Harold reached Tadcaster on 24 September, four days after the battle of Fulford. Here that evening he inspected the ships that were assembled and probably gave them instructions for co-operation with the army against the hostile fleet at Riccall after he had disposed of the hostile army. No doubt he was joined by stragglers from the defeated army of Morcar and Edwin. But on all these points there is a tantalizing silence in the records.

The English king, although physically ailing, appears to have been full of fire. The story is well known how when told that Harald Hardrada aimed at seizing the whole land he remarked grimly: 'I will give him just six feet of English soil; or since I hear that he is a tall man I will give him seven feet.'

At Tadcaster, if not before, Harold would receive particulars of the battle of Fulford and the subsequent movements of his opponents and of their rendezvous at Stamford Bridge. This unexpected move on the part of the Northerners left the road to York open, for not even the troops left at Riccall were in a position to intervene. Tired though Harold and his army must have been with the exertions of their forced march, he resolved to take immediate advantage of this favourable situation. Marching at or before dawn next day, 25 September 1066, the English army, after a 10-mile march, entered York unopposed amid the rejoicings of its fickle inhabitants. In the city, according to one account, were Morcar and Edwin with the remnants of their army, and here it might be supposed the English army would halt to rest and to absorb the army of the two earls. This presumably was Harold's intention; but the news that greeted him in the city, namely that the Northern host was camping, unsuspecting danger, only seven miles beyond the city, spurred Harold to instant action. The enemy must be taken by surprise; the army in spite of its fatigue must resume its march. This unhesitating and immediate assumption of the offensive was typical of the English king. He had shown it in his hurricane march to the north, and he was to show it again by his still more rapid return march to London and on to Hastings. All things considered, it was one of the most remarkable decisions in military operations that I know of. It must have required a supreme exercise of will-power on the part of that ailing and weary man, and also remarkably good discipline in his rather motley army that they were got on the move again so expeditiously just as they were hoping for well-earned rest and refreshment in the northern capital. But it was done. Indeed one account asserts that he reached Stamford Bridge at dawn, which is manifestly impossible. Still, he arrived sufficiently early that day to fight a long and bitter battle and conduct a pursuit of several miles—a feat of endurance that it is hard to match, far less to beat.

*   *   *   *   *

The river Derwent approaches Stamford Bridge from the north-east and there makes a slight bend to the south. The river is about 40 feet wide, sluggish and deep. It flows through a shallow valley, the eastern slopes being the more pronounced of the two, rising as they do to a height of about 50 feet above the valley bottom. At the time of the battle there was a wooden bridge 400 yards above the modern bridge, and four ancient roads converged at this point. This may have been the reason that induced Harald Hardrada to select it as the spot for the receipt of hostages and supplies.

But the allied army—as we must describe one that included Norwegians, English, Flemings, and Scots—was quite oblivious to the proximity of the hostile army: so much so that many of the leaders had discarded their mail corselets, for the time being, leaving them in the base-camp at Riccall. Nor had they troubled to send out scouts towards York.

The fact that the invader's army was lying on the wrong side of Riccall to defend the base-camp if attacked from the south is striking corroboration of the statement by the chronicler that Harold's approach to Stamford Bridge was unexpected. The fact that Harald Hardrada had hurriedly to send to his base-camp for the troops left there is a further indication of unpreparedness. The Norwegian king evidently calculated that the English king would not dare leave southern England whilst the threat of invasion from Normandy hung over him.

THE BATTLE

The army was encamped on both sides of the river, awaiting the arrival of hostages and supplies. Suddenly a cloud of dust was seen on the road to the west, about 1½ miles away on the slight swell of ground now occupied by Great Helmsley. It was Harold, driving furiously. A council of war was hastily held to decide on the action to be taken. Tostig recommended a retreat to the fleet, but this was not to the liking of the soldier King of Norway, who decided to stand his ground. The plateau to the east of the river valley is practically flat, a convenient place for a hurried forming-up position. Here Harald resolved to make a stand with his main body. To provide time for this operation he ordered the troops on the west of the river to fight a delaying action.

Meanwhile the English army was getting close. Before actually gaining contact, Harold seems to have sent emissaries to his brother, offering him favourable terms if he would abandon the contest. This Tostig refused; surrounded by Norwegians he could scarcely do otherwise, whatever his private inclinations may have been. So the battle began.

The bend in the river to which I have referred had the effect of making the English line of approach oblique to the line of the river, as the sketch-map shows. Thus, as the leading units approached they found themselves engaging the extreme left flank of the Northerners on the near bank of the river. At the same time their own right flank was exposed to missile weapons from the opposite bank. But these two factors did not cancel out, since the allies on the opposite side were in process of massing on the plateau, not lining the bank. Thus the progress of the attackers was rapid, resistance being ill-organized. In a short space of time the whole of the western bank of the river was in English hands and the surviving defenders were pushed back across the river;

many being drowned in the process for the river was unfordable, being deep, with a muddy bottom.

The first phase of the battle was over. Now came an incident with which the battle of Stamford Bridge will always be associated. A Norwegian saga, which gives a vivid account of the battle, is curiously silent about this famous exploit on the part of one of its own countrymen; it was left to the English chronicler to relate it. It tells of an unnamed Norwegian of immense stature and strength who alone and unaided held the bridge, standing surprisingly on the English end of it. He is reported as holding the bridge against all comers for an incredibly long space of time.[1]

The end of the brave bridge-defender came from an unexpected quarter. An Englishman procured a swill-tub (according to local tradition) and managed to propel it unobserved, probably under cover of overhanging willow branches, to the end of the bridge. Once under the bridge he was comparatively safe and he was able to manoeuvre his awkward-shaped boat to a spot exactly underneath the feet of the Norwegian hero. The bridge was roughly and crudely made of logs with numerous chinks between them. One such was, fortunately for his purpose, exactly under the feet of his quarry. Seizing his spear he thrust it up through this gap in the bridge and pierced the Norwegian in an unprotected spot between the legs. The defender fell, the English rushed forward, and the bridge was won.[2]

The capture of the bridge ended phase two of the battle. Phase three can be quickly narrated. The fact is, all details are lacking. All we know is that the final struggle, and the principal one, took place on the plateau—still called Battle Flats—that both Harald Hardrada and Earl Tostig were killed,[3] that there was great slaughter and that it ended in the complete defeat of the invaders.

The statement in the saga that reinforcements, fully armoured, arrived from Riccall during this phase is quite likely to be true if the battle was very prolonged. The Norwegian king is believed to have

[1] It is difficult to conceive one man standing unscathed against a concentration of missiles at short range; but the fact that the story is told against themselves by the attackers obliges us to accept it.

[2] The story of the boat is hard to swallow, but I do swallow it. Similar instances occurred at Boroughbridge and at the taking of the Tourelles in the siege of Orleans. In the excitement of action extraordinary things can be done, even in modern battles.

[3] The story that our Harold struck down the Norwegian Harald was only to be expected, but cannot be accepted by the historian.

been killed towards the end of the day, and, like his antagonist a fortnight later, his death, when it became generally known, would put an end to the fight. For what object can there be in risking one's life for a dead king? We see much the same sudden collapse at Wakefield, and Bosworth.

The remnants of the allied army were pursued all the way back to Riccall, a distance of 12 miles, in spite of the extreme weariness of the English troops who had fought a hard battle on top of an 18-mile march. Such a feat of endurance would scarcely be possible nowadays.

In the moment of his triumph King Harold showed remarkable leniency and restraint. He allowed Prince Olaf to depart with his survivors (24 ships were sufficient to convey them) after he had promised that Norway would never again invade England—a promise that was kept.

* * * * *

We cannot leave this tremendously important battle without attempting to assess the causes of the victory. They are unusually difficult to assess, the records being so tantalizingly scanty, and an unusually large measure of conjecture must be resorted to.

Victory in battle is the resultant of various forces or 'strands of war'. These strands can be classified under four headings:

A. The quality and capacity of the commander.
B. The quality and capacity of the troops.
C. Morale.
D. Resources: (numbers, weapons, &c.).

Let us consider each of these strands in turn.

Strand A, of course, includes planning, strategy, and tactics. Our knowledge of the actual battle is too meagre to draw conclusions as to tactics, but in the realm of strategy we can at least note that there is a marked contrast between the two commanders.

No coherent plan can be descried in the case of the Norwegian. Why did he waste time in raids along the Yorkshire coast? Why did he not, after his victory at Fulford, march boldly into the city of York, or dispose of the English fleet cooped up at Tadcaster? Why did he remove his army 12 miles on the far side of his base-camp from the direction of the English approach, and why did he allow himself to be surprised at Stamford Bridge? To all appearance he 'dithered'.

The action of the English king was very different. The closer we examine such evidence as we have the deeper becomes our respect and indeed enthusiasm for his conduct of this brief campaign. The grounds for this enthusiasm have, it is hoped, been made manifest in the preceding pages. Professor Freeman may have been led too far in his hero-worship when he wrote of 'the great northern march which must rank among the greatest deeds of its kind that history records', for we have no details of that march. But taking the campaign as a whole Harold's conduct of it was such as to rejoice the heart of the professional soldier. Clear vision, quick and correct appreciation of the situation, a bold decision made and resolutely maintained, a sound objective kept ever before his eyes, and a sure execution made possible only by a steely will-power and the enthusiastic loyalty and support of his army—all these qualities entitle Harold Godwinson to be considered one of our greatest captains of war.

As for Strand B, the English House-carls had a reputation second to none. It was said that one of them was the equal of any two other soldiers, and their fame had spread to the Continent. On the other hand the hastily raised shire-levies cannot have been fully trained troops. Still their endurance in this campaign, and in the following fortnight, was proof that at least they were in splendid physical condition. More than that we cannot say. And we cannot say even that of their opponents. We simply do not know; but the probability is that after being cooped up in ships, and in the absence of any considerable land marches, they were in comparatively soft condition.

As for Strand C, Morale is always difficult to assess. More than ever it must be guesswork here. Invaders, led by a trusted leader, flushed with a recent victory, may be expected to enjoy high morale. But the supreme confidence shown by the English king seems to indicate that his men also were imbued with high morale. Many of them had fought with their leader in his victorious past campaigns, and they must have trusted him implicitly, while their discipline as shown by their unhesitating advance from York must have been high. Moreover they were mainly of one race, speaking the same language, and inspired with the motive of defending their own hearths and homes. The allies, on the other hand, were a polyglot collection of warriors, many being mere soldiers of fortune, whose allegiance and reliability could not compare with that of the defenders of this island.

As regards resources (Strand D), we are completely in the dark. Judging by the reputed size of the Norwegian fleet, they may have had as many as 5,000 in the battle; but it is quite impossible to assess the English. Nor can we discriminate between the weapons carried by the two armies. It is safest to omit the strand of resources and to conclude that the English won because Harold was a better leader and possessed better troops than his Norwegian opponent.

PROBLEMS OF THE BATTLEFIELD

There is really only one problem that requires close investigation—to fix accurately the site of the bridge. All we have got to go on is the local tradition that it was about 500 yards above the present bridge, and

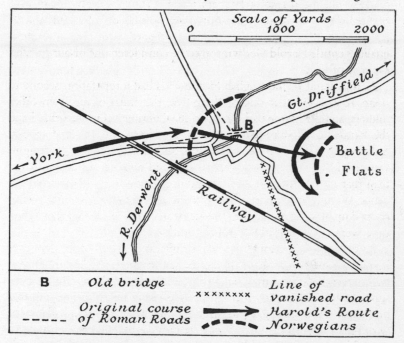

SKETCH–MAP 11. STAMFORD BRIDGE: THE BATTLE

the evidence of the map and of our own eyes. Of course the river may have changed its bed since the battle, thus making the problem still more difficult, but I doubt this.

A cursory glance at the map shows that at least four roads—evidently old ones—converge in the vicinity of the river. Let us take first that approaching from the north. It looks like a Roman road, but 300 yards south of Primrose Hill it bends abruptly to its right, as if to cross the modern bridge—which no doubt is the reason. But if we prolong the line of the straight road it cuts the river only 400 yards above the present bridge. Are there any visible signs of such a track still existing? I looked for them, starting just south of Primrose Hill. At first there was nothing to be seen, but presently I noticed a slight depression, perceptible only to one who was looking for it. This depression deepened as it approached the river, till it became an unmistakable track. On reaching the valley bottom it disappeared. This was to be expected, for before the valley was drained it would be boggy, and crossable only on a stone causeway. When it was drained the stones would gradually disappear.

This track, if prolonged, would cut the river about 400 yards above the present bridge. So far so good. If this was the old Roman track it would imply that the course of the Roman road had been slightly diverted to the west, probably when the wood along which it now runs was planted.

Now take the road approaching from the west, from York and Great Helmsley. This also is obviously a Roman road, but it also has a slight kink in it at 500 yards from the present bridge. I prolonged the straight stretch of road with my ruler, and found it cut the northern track practically at the river. This also was satisfactory, but did the original road take this course? I went to see. This time there could be no doubt about it from the outset. I was able to trace its course every yard from where the modern road left it to where it entered the valley bottom. It is significant that this old track, not the present road, is the county boundary.

Next take the road approaching from the east, again indubitably a Roman road. If we prolong the line of the west road we find it cuts our road only a few yards east of the river and practically runs along it. Excellent! But there is yet a fourth track to consider. If we prolong the line of the northern road south-east of the river, we find that 200 yards beyond the river it meets a faint track marked on the O.S. Map 'Roman Road'. Moreover for 400 yards, rising from the river, a slightly winding road almost exactly follows the course of the dotted line (shown thus on my sketch-map). Best of all! We now have four Roman roads converging exactly (if we allow of a bend on to the causeway) at the river. The point where they meet is 400 yards above the present bridge, and about 20 yards below the junction with the modern cut (not shown on my map). At this precise spot then, I unhesitatingly place the famous Stamford Brigge.[1]

[1] It is to be noted that the exact convergence of these roads on the river shows that the river-bed has *not* been changed.

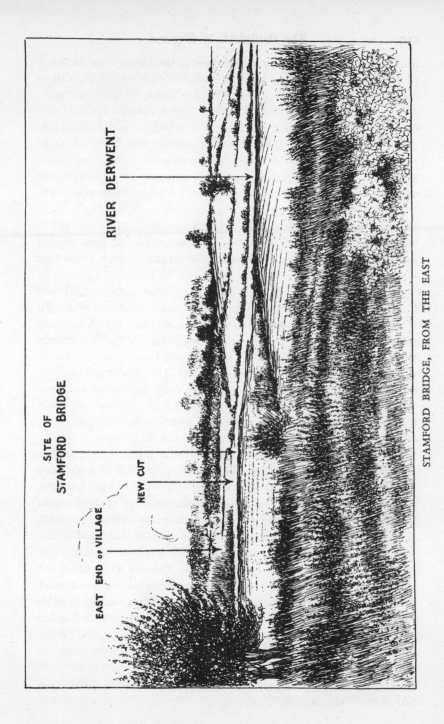

RIVER DERWENT

SITE OF
STAMFORD BRIDGE

NEW CUT

EAST END of VILLAGE

STAMFORD BRIDGE, FROM THE EAST

The site of the bridge being ascertained, the location of the main battle becomes obvious. For it must be on the ridge beyond the bridge, the centre being approximately opposite the bridge. At a spot 600 yards south-east of the bridge, just where we should expect is a field still called Battle Flat, and the area round is vaguely called Battle Flats. Here we may put the centre of the Norwegian army in its last stand, and here have been ploughed up from time to time swords and other battle debris. There is no monument to commemorate the battle, but either here on Battle Flats or down by the old bridge a memorial should be erected.

There is another minor problem that troubled me. I wanted to accept the story of the Norwegian hero on the bridge, but found it difficult to believe that the whole army could be held up for any length of time by a single man, or even a party, on the bridge of a river only 12 to 15 yards wide. Why did not the English cross higher up or lower down and thus turn the bridge? So I hired a boat from the boat-yard in the new cut, rowed upstream and took soundings both above and below the bridge site. I found the bottom was heavy with mud, the banks steep, and the depth 6 to 8 feet. The river has since been canalized, but there would be no need to dredge it to this extent, and the conclusion I came to was that it was not only unfordable but quite uncrossable by anyone in mail armour. Individuals, lightly clad, could and no doubt did, swim across, but their efforts would most likely be spasmodic, devoid of concerted action, and the effect would be small. Moreover, if the stand of the Norwegian at the bridge had been only a fleeting affair the Anglo-Saxon chronicler would hardly have gone out of his way, in his brief account, to relate the incident—the only one he deemed worthy of narration. So I accept the legend of this Norwegian hero and only wish we had his name and knew more about him.

A subsidiary problem is to discover the reasons that induced the Norwegians to fall back from the river-bank without a serious fight and to offer battle some hundreds of yards to the rear where the water line could be of no benefit to them. One is reminded of the voluntary withdrawal of Britnoth from the causeway at Maldon, and it is possible that there is some common reason. There is, however, no indication that Harald Hardrada was impelled by motives of chivalry, and I fancy the dominating motive was a more prosaic one. The Northmen's conception of a battle in those days was based on the operation of the shield-wall; which implied a stand-up static fight at close quarters. In this the Norwegians probably considered themselves pre-eminent, and their one thought was to form this shield-wall on a fair battleground, the preliminary skirmishing down by the river being merely to gain sufficient time to form the battle-array. In this the Norwegian king was evidently successful and we can only presume that he had left such a large covering force on the river line that he eventually found himself hopelessly outnumbered and consequently outflanked. His army, it must be remembered, was not wholly concentrated and the reinforcements from his base-camp arrived too late. Our Harold was too quick for his opponents.

A NOTE ON PROFESSOR FREEMAN'S ACCOUNT OF THE BATTLE

The only apparently detailed account of the battle that we possess is that of Professor E. A. Freeman in his *Norman Conquest* (Vol. III). It extends to thirteen pages; but the historian of the Norman Conquest veils the paucity of reliable details about the battle by eking out his account with the story told in the Norwegian Saga. He devotes four pages to this story, though prefacing it with the statement that it is 'hardly more worthy of belief than a battle-piece in the Iliad'.

Towards the end he gives vent to his own fancy, and I cannot find much to choose between his fancy and that of the author of the Saga. This for example: 'We may see how, step by step, inch by inch, dealing blow for blow even in falling back, Northman and Scot and Fleming gave way before the irresistible charge of the renowned Thingmen'. Yet there is no indication in what accounts we have that such a thing happened, nor in my opinion is there any likelihood of it. The main battle took place on Battle Flats, and the simplest explanation surely is that given in my account, namely that while the advanced Norwegian troops were disputing the river crossing the main body was being marshalled in battle order on the flats above. Thus, once the bridge was captured the English progress would be fairly rapid until Battle Flats were reached. Battles where both sides move forward or back in line 'step by step, inch by inch' are infrequent, to say the least of it, nor are they compatible with Freeman's picture of an 'irresistible charge'. How can a 'charge' progress 'inch by inch'?

My own tentative conception of the final stages of the battle is that they followed a similar course to that at Hastings a few weeks later, *mutatis mutandis*; that is to say, the invaders formed the shield-wall which was gradually surrounded and battered to pieces by the defenders of the soil. It was essentially a static battle.

CHAPTER XI

The Battle of Hastings, October 14th, 1066

ON September 28th, 1066, William the Bastard, Duke of Normandy, set sail from St. Valery to enforce his claim to the throne of England. His army was something short of 10,000 strong. This may seem a small force with which to essay the conquest of a foreign country, but:

1. William may have counted upon a rising in his favour of a portion of the population, for he claimed to be the rightful king.

2. He may have counted on help from King Harald of Norway, who had landed in Yorkshire a few weeks previously.

3. His army consisted for the most part of picked men, well armed, and it included bowmen and cavalry, in both of which arms Harold was deficient.

Nevertheless, in spite of the fact that he found the coast undefended, and was able to land at Pevensey unopposed, William exhibited signs of considerable nervousness and caution. This is admitted by the Norman chronicler, William of Jumièges, whom I consider the most reliable of all the chroniclers. This writer asserts that the first thing William did on landing was to throw up 'strong entrenchments,'[1] in which he left 'brave knights' when he moved out; that he 'came hastily to Hastings'; that he kept his troops under arms all night long, in fear of attack; and that for a fortnight he hung about, within reach of his fleet, presumably because he feared he might be obliged to evacuate. Very different was the conduct of Julius Caesar when he invaded the country in 54 B.C.; he pushed inland in search of his enemy on the very day of his landing.

Harold received the disturbing news of the landing of his rival at York, where he was in the midst of celebrating his victory over the other Harald at Stamford Bridge. Now our Harold was a very remarkable man. William of Jumièges (an enemy, be it noted) says of him that 'he prepared himself vigorously for fresh combats; for

---

[1] According to one account, materials carefully measured to fit together, were brought with them, with which they constructed a defensive perimeter —a species of land 'Mulberry'.

he was extremely brave and bold, very handsome in all his person, agreeable in his manner of expressing himself, and affable with everybody'. A fine soldier, his previous operations against the Welsh had been characterized by celerity and decision.

At this supreme crisis in his and our history he surpassed himself. Instantly his mind was made up. Announcing his intention to march straight against the bold invader, and despatching orders to the shire levies of the southern half of the country to muster at London, he set out for the capital with his army on October 1st. The distance is 190 miles, and he covered it in about six days, which is at the phenomenal speed of 32 miles per day. This is all the more remarkable inasmuch as his army consisted solely of foot-soldiers (apart from a few mounted thegns). How did he manage it? It seems generally assumed that his army arrived in London with Harold, but a simpler explanation is that he rode on ahead, and that the troops trickled in behind him during the ensuing days. Even so, they must have marched rapidly, for only five days later he was again on the move, this time for Hastings, and this time his troops most certainly did accompany him.

It is not certain whether he departed from London on October 11th or 12th, which is unfortunate, for a good deal hinges on it. The distance from the capital to the battlefield is about 58 miles. If Harold started on the 11th he could easily arrive before nightfall on the 13th. In this case he would have time to reconnoitre the position before dark, and it would be evidence that he intended all the time to await attack there. But if, as I think, he set out on the 12th, he could scarcely arrive with his whole army till well after dark on the 13th, and may have intended to continue the march next day. In other words, the date of his departure from London is a pointer to his future intentions. On this the evidence is conflicting. On the one hand, it is asserted by several chroniclers that he intended to attack the invaders as soon as he could come up with them; on the other, we know that he did in fact stand on the defensive. Can these two be reconciled? I think they can, if we allow that the departure from London was on the 12th. In that case, the English army would be trickling into camp far into the night; it had to traverse the Weald Forest by a single un-metalled track, and would get badly strung out; the march discipline of the hastily-assembled levies could not be good, and some of them probably marched direct to 'the hoar apple-tree' as a rendezvous; indeed, I go so far as to suggest that they were still coming in after daylight on the very day of the battle. There is one item of direct, and several of indirect evidence that this was the case: the Anglo-Saxon Chronicle states explicitly (it is almost the only thing about the battle that it does state!) that the English were attacked before they were ready or all assembled; and some Norman chroniclers imply, and one definitely asserts that the English army had not all arrived when William attacked, and William of Jumièges goes so far as to say that Harold, 'wishing to surprise and attack the Duke, having ridden a whole night, arrived next morning on the field of battle'.

Weaving all these statements together, we get the picture of the ardent Harold driving his army forward by the force of his indomitable will-power, and with desperate speed, till it was hopelessly strung out; so that when morning dawned on that fateful October 14th, his leading troops (no doubt his House-carls or Household troops) were bivouacked near the hoar apple-tree and the Sandlake stream (the battlefield to be), and the remainder were straggling through the forest[1] —how far back no one around Harold exactly knew. It would clearly be imprudent to approach the Norman camp till his army was more consolidated, especially as a great portion of it consisted of freshly-raised levies whom the King had never seen before.[2] Harold therefore felt obliged to make a late start that morning. This seems an inherently natural course to take—always assuming that Harold left London on the 12th, and I cannot understand why most historians assume that he always intended to adopt the defensive,[3] unless they have been influenced by the formidable Professor Freeman, who sees in Harold's selection of a purely defensive position 'consummate generalship'. But though Freeman states that Harold did not leave London till the 12th, he asks us to believe that 48 hours later the English army was drawn up in a position 58 miles away in 'what is distinctly spoken of as a castle[4] surrounded by a threefold palisade'. I should be inclined to characterize this as 'consummate foolishness'.

The question must now be considered, what was the cause of Harold's extreme haste and eagerness to take the offensive? It is not

[1] There was a two-thirds moon which would help them.

[2] The fact that he would have to meet the Norman cavalry in the open field may also have influenced his decision to assume the defensive.

[3] General Fuller in his *Decisive Battles* is a notable exception.

[4] The actual words used by Henry of Huntingdon are '*Quasi castellum*', so it looks as if the great historian of the Norman Conquest could not even translate correctly!

an easy question to answer. Time was so obviously on his side, that efforts to hasten the issue seem pointless. The longer he delayed the greater and better organized would his army become, whereas the Norman army, so far from increasing, would be more likely to diminish from sickness, casualties, detachments, etc., as time went on. Hence, unless William advanced on London and thus forced the issue himself, Harold's game should have been a waiting one.

That is the theory of it, but the personal equation comes in. Harold was hot-headed, and possibly not over-endowed with brains. He could see a few essentials clearly, and little else. He lacked a cool staff officer to draw up for him a balanced appreciation of the situation, from which to compile a sound plan. He could see one thing and one thing only—his rival had invaded his country and was laying it waste. The English King was the personification of the offensive spirit: 'Show me the enemy!' was all he asked, and like an enraged bull, with lowered head, reminiscent of Prince Alfred at Ashdown, he charged full tilt at the enemy.

The Duke of Normandy, in glaring contrast, was prudence personified. We have already had an example of this, on his landing at Pevensey. He realized the general soundness of establishing a firm base from which to operate. Moreover he knew his opponent of old, for they both had fought on the same side in Brittany, and he had a healthy respect for Harold. Hence he restored the castle at Hastings that Harold had dismantled earlier that year, and under cover of it he remained till he had received information that the English army was approaching.

He now had to decide whether to accept battle within his own defensive position at Hastings, or to sally forth and seek out his opponent in the open. As we have seen, time was on the side of his enemy, which was a good reason why William should force the pace; in the second place, his cavalry, in which arm he possessed a monopoly, would be comparatively useless cooped up in a defensive position; finally, it was essential to maintain the morale of his troops, employed on what must have been a hazardous venture, by cultivating the offensive spirit. All three were sound reasons, for which we may give Duke William full credit.

Sometime during the night of October 13th, news of the approach of the English army through the Forest of the Weald must have reached the Norman camp, and William ordered his host to stand to, in preparation for an advance at dawn. We may dismiss the Norman reports that they spent the night at their orisons while the English spent it eating and drinking. Such stories were commonly spread by the winning side after a battle. Unfortunately for the English troops there were no public-houses in the middle of the Weald Forest, nor would they be inclined to sit up all night after a 30-mile forced march. As General Fuller dryly remarks: 'Harold's men were dog-tired and slept like logs.'

THE ENGLISH POSITIONS AND DISPOSITIONS

After the battle William celebrated his victory by erecting an abbey on the field, so sited that the altar marked the spot where Harold fell. The ruins of this abbey thus pin-point the English command-post. This provides unprecedented precision in siting a medieval battlefield, and it might be supposed that the exact line held was beyond controversy. But such is not the case. I show on Sketch-map 13 six different solutions by six leading historians. On Map 12, I show my own solution, which it will be noted does not agree with any of the others. It almost seems a case of '*Quot homines tot sententiae*'. In *Battlefield Problems* at the end of the chapter, I discuss the matter and give my reasons for my own solution. Here it will suffice to say that it covered a frontage of 800 yards, stretching 375 yards east and 425 yards west of Harold's command-post, and that it ran in an almost straight line, along the crest of the famous ridge.

If Harold was to stand on the defensive he could scarcely have found a better position for his purpose. He was probably aware of the place previously, for he had spent the summer on the south coast, preparing to repel the expected invasion. Moreover, his native heath was not far away. The Duke of Wellington had noted the possibilities of the Waterloo position some time previously, and Harold had probably done the same at Sandlake[1] (Old French—Senlac). It was indeed rather an obvious position for any army facing south. Immediately behind it, stretching for miles, lay the broad acres of the Weald Forest, in which fighting was out of the question. A few miles in front lay the sea. The position was admirably devised for defence against cavalry, and it crossed and barred the direct road from the coast to the capital.

To describe it in greater detail, in Sketch-map 12, I have marked the two contours which best bring out the essential shape and features of

[1] See note p. 140.

the position. It will be seen that the ridge faces south, connected by a *col* to the high ground and forest to the north. On each side of the *col* there are ravines, steep enough to deter hostile cavalry, and almost all round there are boggy valleys, also bad for cavalry. The ground was open (though the Bayeux Tapestry shows a few trees), but too rough for cultivation. A glimpse of this roughness can still be seen at the hillock, marked "H" on the map. This hillock is about 15 feet high, and incidentally forms a good spot from which to view the western half of the field. Straight in front, one mile away, stands Telham Hill, and the ridge over which winds the road to Hastings.

Harold's command-post was situated in the obvious position, on the highest point, in the centre of the line, and on the roadside.[1]

The dispositions of the English army were simple in the extreme. A single line of House-carls, or Household troops, covered the whole front. Standing shoulder to shoulder and protected by their long shields, they formed an imposing line, known traditionally as the 'shield-wall'. We are told, and historians all seem to accept it unquestioningly, that these shields were 'interlocked'. In what manner could they be interlocked? The nearest approach to interlocking would be overlapping, and it is true that the Bayeux Tapestry in one scene does convey this impression; but it is so crudely depicted that it would be dangerous to draw fixed conclusions from this. Judging from church effigies of a slightly later period the shields could hardly have been more than 15 inches wide. Even if the House-carls stood shoulders touching, say 20 inches apart, this would not allow of the shields touching, still less overlapping or 'interlocking'. Moreover, if the soldiers were wedged so close together, how could they wield their weapons? Least of all could they wield their special weapon, the two-handed axe. To use the axe it was necessary (as shown in the Tapestry) either to place the shield on the back, or on the ground behind them. If we assume that axemen and spearmen alternated, the latter would protect the former while they were in action. But this would remove all semblance of an interlocked shield-wall. Moreover, this expression is a dangerous one; it conjures up a kind of

[1] On no maps is this road shown: all show the line of the modern road. But it will be noted that there are two straight sections of road on each side and in direct prolongation, and that the modern road makes a detour from them round the Abbey grounds. Surely the natural conclusion to draw is that the road originally ran straight, but had to be diverted to allow of the erection of the Abbey.

field defence, against which the opposing horsemen could not force a way. In point of fact, the only method by which the shield could in the least serve such a function would be if the point were thrust into the ground, as to which there is not a particle of evidence. Otherwise they could be no more of an obstacle to a horse than if the soldiers had no shields at all, for it is as easy to push a man backwards or knock him down when he is holding up some object as if he is empty-handed. Finally, if this shield-wall were devised as an obstacle to the hostile

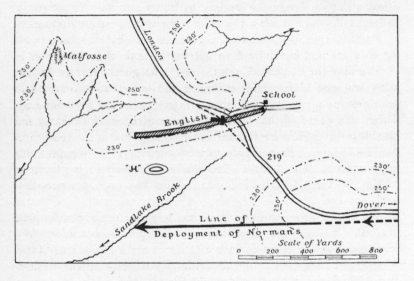

SKETCH-MAP 12. HASTINGS

horsemen, it would dissolve at the very moment when it was required, namely at the moment of contact, for at that moment the soldier would require to use his axe, dispensing with his shield, as we have seen. No; the 'interlocked shield-wall' may be dismissed as a poetic fantasy. The shields were designed and used (as the Tapestry shows) primarily as a protection against hostile missiles, arrows, darts, etc. in the early stages of the battle.

The surplus of House-carls not required for the front line were grouped around the Royal Standard of Wessex, in the centre. The shire levies closed up in rear, in serried ranks, ten to twelve deep. Though a threefold palisade (as asserted by Freeman) is ruled out, some modern historians suppose that a rough wall of stakes or hurdles was hastily erected. This is harder to refute; it suffices that if there were such defences at any part of the line, they had no influence on the course of the battle.

The House-carls wore chain-mail to the knees,[1] and helmets; their principal armament was the English double-handed axe, but some had swords or spears. The shire-levies had a wide assortment of arms, ranging from swords and spears to stone-headed clubs, javelins and even country pitch-forks. They wore no armour. There were also a few archers. The whole army constituted a solid, compact mass, the sight of which made a profound impression on their opponents.

As to the numbers engaged, every historian has had his guess—for they are nothing more than guesses. I deal with the matter in 'Problems of the Battlefield', p. 132. My own guess is that the English army was just under 9,000 strong at the outset, and increased in numbers during the day as fresh contingents and stragglers came up. The Norman army (which had had to leave garrisons at Pevensey and Hastings) was slightly less in numbers, but better in quality, apart from the House-carls, who probably had not their peers in Europe. But the Normans enjoyed three important advantages: a large force of cavalry; archers and cross-bowmen; and mail armour for probably every man on the field.

We cannot neglect morale, but this, as is usually the case, is hard to assess. It is at least safe to say that it was high on both sides. We might put it as highest in the House-carls, who had just returned from winning the battle of Stamford Bridge, and lowest in the freshly-formed and inadequately-armed shire-levies, the Norman morale coming somewhere between these two extremes.

THE NORMAN ADVANCE

At break of day on that memorable Saturday, October 14th, 1066, the Norman host set forth along the road to the capital. The Duke of Normandy had thrown off all his seeming hesitation and doubt; approaching action showed him for the grand leader that he undoubtedly was. His prelude had been distinctly *piano*. When he stumbled on the beach at Pevensey he got, literally, a bloody nose, and it was not he that passed it off with a ready quip but one of his

---

[1] This interpretation of the Tapestry is nearly universal, but Mr. T. C. Lethbridge, in *Merlin's Island* (p. 11), suggests that it might be 'some kind of quilted material'.

courtiers. But now he was quite himself. We can picture his invading army winding its way along the leafy lanes of Sussex on that October morning in a snakey column a good three miles in length. After marching silently for an hour or more, and as the advanced guard is approaching Telham Hill, a mile short of Sandlake, a scout comes spurring down the hill. He seeks out the Duke who is a mile in rear, near Blackhorse Hill, and reports in some excitement that masses of Saxons are visible on the ridge beyond.

The hour has struck! Duke William orders the head of the column to halt and the remainder to close up, and then gallops up the hill himself to verify the report; then he returns, announces to his circle of subordinate officers his intention to fight, issues his orders, and dons his armour—an action in which the whole army joins.[1]

At this point the chroniclers regale us with long-winded harangues by the good William to his army, which we are to picture as gathered in a circle around him (much as General Montgomery harangued his units before the invasion of Europe in 1944). Unfortunately for the historicity of these reports, the rear of the army at this moment must have been some miles away—distinctly out of earshot. This does not worry Professor Freeman, who devotes twenty lines to retailing the monk-composed 'speech'.

The march of the Norman column is resumed. On topping the crest, the army deployed in a line parallel to that of the English: French and Flemings on the right, Normans in the centre, and Bretons on the left.[2] Each division then marches down the hill in three sections, archers leading, followed by heavily-armed infantry, the cavalry bringing up the rear. The whole manœuvre must have been carried out in full view of the defending army about 600 yards distant. In those days there was little thought of outflanking moves or oblique attacks, and the Normans no doubt obligingly conformed to the frontage adopted by their opponents, taking up their dressing, as it were, from the hostile line. We can picture the House-carls gazing on the scene in grim silence, while the shire-levies hastily closed up the rear, with a good deal of chattering and argument.

The Norman formation presaged the Norman plan, which was simple but sound. It envisaged three phases.

[1] Of the many anecdotes relating to the battle, the story that in his nervous excitement he put on his hauberk the wrong way round, is the most worthy of credence.

[2] See p. 138 *for the method of deployment.*

PHASE ONE

The archers engage, and shake the morale of the enemy. ('Artillery preparation' or 'softening-up'.)

PHASE TWO

Under cover of this, the heavily-armed infantry advance and fracture the shield-wall of the English.

PHASE THREE

The cavalry then charge through the shattered and disorganized ranks and deliver the *coup de grace*.

This plan was very nice in theory, but in practice it did not work out quite like that.

THE BATTLE

PHASE ONE

The battle opened probably at about 9.30 a.m.[1] The Norman archers advanced steadily and resolutely until they were only 100 yards distant from their opponents, while the cross-bowmen on the left no doubt lined the edge of the rough ground at "H" hillock, at a range of 150 yards. The English received the hissing cloud of arrows unflinchingly, but found it trying, because they had no means of replying for the moment; they had merely to 'stand and suffer'. But there was a weak feature in such an attack—the ammunition supply was strictly limited. The Bayeux Tapestry shows an enormous quiver placed in position in front of each archer; but even so, by firing several arrows per minute the supply could not last long; and it could not be eked out by using the spent arrows of the English, for they had scarcely any archers. In fact, this shortage of archers in the English army redounded to their ultimate advantage, in so far as the artillery preparation could only be of short duration. The *Draco Normannicus* states explicitly that the 'ammunition supply' gave out.

PHASE TWO

The shield-wall of the English was thus still intact when the infantry advanced up the hill to the attack. But now everything was in favour of the defence—the slope of the ground, the shield-wall, the serried ranks of the defenders, the stout hearts of the islanders defending hearth and home. Moreover, William's army was not entirely Norman. The Bretons on the left were probably of inferior

[1] I cannot accept the well-known Taillefer story, on which chroniclers and historians love to dwell. See *Chronology of the Battle*, p. 139.

quality (though one historian, Horace Round, denies it). At all events these Bretons met with such a murderous reception that after a short encounter they broke and fled. Now we are told that Harold's orders were that his troops were on no account to break ranks in such an eventuality.[1] But in the heat of battle only the sternest discipline can ensure such an order being obeyed, and this pitch of discipline apparently was not attained by the raw shire-levies. They broke ranks and exultingly pursued the enemy down the hill. This retrograde movement began to spread along the Norman line, as often happens in such a case: each man in turn falls back in order to conform to his neighbour, and maintain the dressing. Worse was to follow, for in the confusion that arose the rumour circulated that the Duke had been killed. It should be remembered that in those days helmetted knights were practically unrecognizable (heraldry was in its infancy), so that such a mistake could easily be made. But William proved equal to the occasion. Dashing into the midst of the fugitives, he removed his helmet so that all around could see that he still lived. By such means, aided by his voice, he managed to stay the flight. But he did more. (We must give him personal credit for it, though definite proof is lacking.) After a considerable amount of confused fighting he launched a portion of the hitherto unused cavalry of his centre against the pursuing English. Wheeling to their left, the horsemen struck the pursuers in their left flank somewhere in the valley below *H* hillock. The English were overrun, and very few of them succeeded in regaining their old position. But the gap thus made in the line had been filled by the troops in rear, albeit it is likely that the shield-wall in this part of the line now had some gaps in it.

If the Norman leader accompanied this counter-attack he would find himself riding close to "H" hillock, and it is tempting to picture him ascending it at the conclusion of the operation to obtain a better impression of the state of affairs than he could get from the ground at its foot.[2]

In the course of this charge some of the cavalry ran into a spot of difficulty in the Sandlake stream which runs below "H" hillock,

---

[1] I accept this here, but there are grounds for doubting it and I give them on p. 130.

[2] Freeman places here the scene depicted in the Bayeux Tapestry of English on a hillock being assailed by cavalry from both sides. I reject this; I think it refers to the closing stage of the battle when the English position was contracted and attacked from each side.

The tapestry clearly indicates horses getting bogged, but the episode seems to have been exaggerated by the chroniclers.

The second phase of the battle was over; honours easy. A pause probably now ensued. No such pause is specifically recorded though it is hinted at in one account, but pauses in battle seldom are recorded, even in modern ones. Such a pause was almost inevitable. Consider the facts. A large portion of one army had been marching through the night; the other had been marching since dawn; immediately on top of that had come the battle, a battle that was not over till dusk, ten hours later. For knights weighed down by heavy chain-armour, such an ordeal, if continuous, would require superhuman strength and endurance. Men would faint for want of food.[1] There must indeed have been several perceptible pauses, and the conclusion of Phase Two must have been one of them. Indeed the pause was probably a prolonged one. Both armies were in a state of disorganization. It would seem that William rallied his men by the skin of his teeth. Half his army was in a state of confusion, and his plan had gone wrong. A fresh plan must be made; subordinate commanders must be summoned to discuss it and to receive fresh orders. The problem was, whether to commit the main body of his cavalry to the attack before the hostile line showed any signs of disintegration.

On the opposite side of the line Harold also had to do some 'tidying-up'. A gap had been made in the line on the right flank owing to the pursuit of the Bretons. No doubt Harold rode over in person and expostulated with his young brother Gurth (if it were he) for his impetuosity or lack of control; Gurth seems to have been impetuous by nature. The King may also have utilized this pause to bring up some water-skins in order to relieve the thirst of his weary warriors, and possible (but not likely), some food.

Reserves of missile weapons would also be brought up by both armies, and those thrown by the enemy collected and distributed (as happened in a similar pause at Poitiers). In short, this pause may have been upwards of an hour in duration.[2]

PHASE THREE

William now launched his 'Old Guard', his precious cavalry, in

[1] At the battle of Agincourt the Duke of York actually died of exhaustion, unwounded.

[2] In the middle of the battle of Waterloo, the British Horse Artillery commander found time to attend a funeral, as did a Cavalry general in the middle of the battle of the Marne.

a general assault. One chronicler asserts that he had hoped to retain them for pursuit, but it was not to be. The day was getting on and the English line appeared to be as intact as ever. So the cavalry had to be put in. And it is hard to believe that they enjoyed it—still less their horses! Medieval knights wore the most villainous-looking spurs, but even so, it must have required consummate horsemanship and strong legs to force the reluctant and terrified steeds up that hill in the teeth of spears, arrows, javelins and stone-headed clubs, all hurtling through the air, to be confronted at the top by a grim-looking line of motionless House-carls with axes poised above their heads, quietly waiting till horse and rider should come within reach of them.

The battle at this juncture must have presented a remarkable spectacle, the knights kicking and cursing their reluctant steeds, the House-carls grunting as they wielded their great double-handed axes, contenting themselves with the brief, breath-saving but pregnant words: 'Out! Out!' The Norman casualties are known to have been heavy, and most of them were probably incurred at this juncture. It was a one-sided contest and the vaunted Norman cavalry came off worst. Groups of them here and there fell back in despair, and the morning's episode against the Bretons was repeated on the other wing. Groups of Englishmen broke ranks and followed up the retreating cavalry only to meet the same fate as their comrades of the right wing. Scattered, breathless and disordered at the bottom of the hill, they were charged by fresh bodies of cavalry and overwhelmed; for now the horsemen had the advantage of the slope; they could come thundering down the hill on top of the unprotected foot-soldiers with devastating results. I think we must see the hand of the commander in this prompt counter-attack. William had profited by the experience of the morning.[1]

PHASE FOUR

The final phase of the battle shows a significant development in Duke William's tactics. Hitherto each arm had acted in turn and on its own: artillery (for archers are artillery), infantry and cavalry. Each arm in turn had failed to produce the decision. William now applied the principle of co-operation. In the first phase the archers had used low-angle fire directed against the front rank, which was the most highly-protected portion of the army. The House-carls had

[1] My reasons for rejecting the story of a 'feigned' retreat are given on p. 137.

intercepted the arrows on their shields. It had been 'direct fire.' The archers were now ordered to use high-angle 'indirect fire' against the invisible enemy in the rear ranks. This nature of fire had the disadvantage that the striking velocity, and hence the penetrative effect, was less than that obtained from direct fire. On the other hand, the bulk of the troops in the rear ranks were less well protected than those in the front ranks, so that an equal penetrative effect was not needed to produce the same result. Hence the effect was considerable. The English troops were now for the first time really 'softened up'. But that was not all. As long as the archers employed direct low-angle fire it was impossible for the other arms to advance under cover of it; but by using high-angle fire the Normans could advance under its cover, and this they did. The attackers in this case were probably a confused mass of infantry and mainly dismounted cavalry, for it is difficult to believe that many of the horses that had been engaged in the mêlée of the first cavalry attack, unarmoured and offering a huge target, can have emerged from it unscathed; and William must have retained the remainder of his precious cavalry, like the prudent general that he was, for the final pursuit of the defeated foe.

Approaching through the loosely-extended lines of archers, they once more assailed the English position. By this time there was not much left of the shield-wall, especially in those places where the defenders had broken ranks, that is, mainly on the two wings. As the footmen burst through the now dissolving ranks, the archers increased their range. To employ modern parlance, they put down a 'creeping barrage'.[1]

The rot in the English ranks no doubt set in more markedly on this, the western flank, where the Bretons had first attacked, than elsewhere. The slope up to the position is more gentle here than anywhere, and thus more favourable to cavalry. But another big penetration seems to have been made on the eastern flank. Thus a *double envelopment* was effected, pointing towards Harold's command-post in the centre, as pictured in the Bayeux Tapestry. There were, in addition, minor infiltrations here and there all along the line, as

[1] In this I accept and develop the theory of H. B. George, who envisages the archers opposite the centre co-operating with the cavalry on the left, switching their fire always more to the right as the horsemen progressed. If this is so, the fire came probably from the top of 'H' hillock, from where the progress of the cavalry could be traced. It sounds almost too good to be true, and I feel that most of the co-operation must have been done by purely overhead fire.

disintegration set in and gaps in the shield-wall became wider and more numerous.

In the midst of the confusion an arrow struck King Harold in the right eye. He pulled it out with an effort and cast it to the ground. He still apparently remained on his legs; but the shock had grievously weakened him, and the report spread that he had been struck down. The result was much the same as in the earlier case of his opponent. Something like panic began to spread among the shire-levies, but the reserve of House-carls continued to stand their ground, grouped round their sovereign. Their opponents could not refrain from praising them for this. *Draco Normannicus* declares that 'the valour of the English and all their glory raged', and William of Poitiers writes: 'They were ever ready with their steel, those sons of the old Saxon race, the most dauntless of men'.

The dusk was descending—the twilight of the Anglo-Saxon race. Harold's two brothers, Gurth and Leofwine, had by now fallen. The Normans were closing in. The circle round the English King grew ever smaller. The devoted House-carls continued to fight on. But all was now lost save honour. A party of Norman knights hacked their way right up to the King, standing bowed over his shield, under the Royal Standard of Wessex. The leader struck him a savage blow on the thigh. The dying Harold sank to the ground and the party finished him off with their swords.

There was no one left to take the command. It was 'each for himself'. But even at this dread hour of Anglo-Saxon history the hearts of many of the House-carls did not fail. In little knots and islands of desperate resistance they fought on, till merciful darkness intervened, and enabled a few of them to find refuge in the forest.

In spite of the fatigue of the day, William ordered an implacable pursuit. This was carried out far into the night, though some of the pursuers met their end by falling into a ravine afterwards known as the Malfosse.[1]

The epoch-making battle of Hastings was over. The English troops were all dead or dispersed, and Duke William was left on that ridge-top, lord of all he surveyed.

COMMENTS

It is interesting to compare the generalship of Harold and William. Taking strategy first, though time was against him, William proved

[1] See note on the *Malfosse* on p. 138.

justified in holding back at the outset, and luring his opponent on to destruction, though it must have cost him much anxious thought. For it was always possible that Harold would not take the bait, but that he would remain at London till he had amassed an overwhelming army, including the strong contingents that he had instructed Edwin and Morcar to bring down from the north. William gambled on it, as every commander has to do in war; but he gambled on the sure foundation of his knowledge of his rival. He had seen him dash hot-headedly into the sands of the river Cousenon in Brittany and rescue some of the Duke's own men; he now no doubt expected that Harold would act in the same impulsive way; and he judged correctly. The English King certainly made a dire strategic mistake when he took the offensive so prematurely. Not only was he impulsive, but over-confident. He had always gained successes in the past by quick, vigorous, offensive action, and he could not see that actions in war as much as anywhere else, must be attuned to the actual situation. He paid for his mistake with his head and his kingdom.

Coming to tactics, William's battle plan seems sound—if rather obvious. There were not many alternatives open to armies of that era. Enveloping or flanking moves were seldom attempted; it would be intriguing but irrelevant in this place to discuss the reason. William's claim to good generalship in his tactics must lie in his flexibility, quick eye, decision and resource. His quick eye spotted disaster overtaking the Bretons, his instant decision to quit his command-post (probably up on Telham Hill) and intervene personally in the fracas saved what might otherwise have been a very ugly situation; his resourcefulness was shown at least twice; first, by turning to account the premature break-out by the English, and later in the battle on the other flank; his flexibility, by changing his tactics when he saw what little impression his cavalry was making on the shield-wall. As far as one can judge, and always remembering that we only have reports from his own side, his tactical conduct of the battle appears almost flawless.

When we turn to Harold we are met with this difficulty that none of the reports were written from his own side. No reporter was on the spot to interrogate him and afterwards write an article entitled: 'Why I lost.' We can only deduce his intentions and thoughts from the bare recorded facts. And they do not tell us much, for the reason given above. In truth there was probably little to tell. Having apparently elected to fight a purely defensive and static battle, all he could do, once his host was marshalled, was to stand and suffer, and to put in a counter-attack at the end of the day. I write 'apparently', for the chroniclers and historians are unanimous that Harold gave strict instructions to his men that they were on no account to break ranks. This *may* be so (and I have tentatively accepted it in my narrative), but how did the Norman chroniclers ascertain it? It is just possible that they merely guessed it. Not only was Harold not alive after the battle to tell them; most of his senior officers were dead, the rest dispersed, and the single English chronicler passed over the battle with understandable brevity.

Now it is generally assumed that the break-out in pursuit of the Bretons was made by the raw, ill-disciplined shire-levies; but if this is so, they must have leap-frogged over the House-carls who at that early stage in the battle held the front line intact (as most historians agree). What if the House-carls themselves joined in the charge? The possibility cannot be summarily dismissed. William of Poitiers asserts that 'the greater portion' of the English army sallied out. But if the House-carls took part in this counter-attack, it would presumably be by the order or with the approval of their king or of their local commander—probably Gurth. A purely passive defence leads nowhere—a fact that Harold must have realized, and he must have indicated that a counter-attack would eventually be delivered. Again, he may have feared that the ordeal of standing motionless under fire throughout the day would prove too much for many of his troops. Wellington's men proved equal to it at Waterloo, but they were better trained and disciplined. Moreover, prompt local counter-attacks, if not carried too far, have much to recommend them. If then Harold's plan was to make use of local and strictly limited counter-attacks, and to end the battle with a concerted general counter-attack, one cannot but approve of it. Possibly the death of his two brothers before the moment to assume the offensive had come, prevented such a concerted attack. It cannot be proved either way. All I ask the reader is to suspend judgement on Harold, realizing his immense difficulties, and not to accept everything that the Norman chroniclers tell us at its face value.

At any rate, we can all agree that Harold possessed an 'eye for country' in his selection of position, and it is difficult to suggest how his dispositions could have been improved upon.

Finally, we must record the rather palpable fact that, apart from generalship, training and morale, the superior armament of the

Normans—cavalry and archery—won the day, and as at Badon, cavalry in the end bested infantry.

PROBLEMS OF THE BATTLEFIELD

I.—ENGLISH POSITION AND NUMBERS

I have already alluded to the disparity in views of our modern historians on this question. Sketch-map 13 shows the approximate siting of the English position by Professors Freeman, Oman, Ramsay and Messrs. George, Baring and Saltzmann. How are we to judge between such eminent authorities? When the doctors disagree, who shall decide?

One method clearly is unsound, namely to argue in a vicious

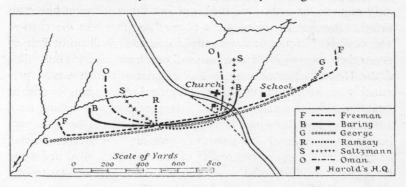

SKETCH-MAP 13

The English position as given by various writers

circle, as there seems a tendency to do. It goes thus: Harold probably had about X men, therefore his frontage at Y men to the yard must have been Z yards. But if the frontage was Z yards, the number of troops to hold it must have been X men. By this deft method of reasoning we solve two knotty problems at one blow!

It is obviously sound to start with a consideration of the number of men—not of the ground. Here we get no help from the chroniclers, since their figures are quite impossible. An attempt has been made to establish the Norman strength from the number of their ships; but here also we get exaggeration; the figure 3,000 is out of the question and there is something suspicious about Wace's figure 696, though it may not be far out.

General James, in what I consider the most satisfying account of the battle,[1] accepts the figure 696, and from it calculates an original strength of 3,600 cavalry and 7,400 infantry. I can see no reason against accepting his calculation, which is based on the assumption that the size of ships did not increase greatly between the time of the Conquest and that of Edward III's invasion of France, when his ships carried about 20 men each. Accepting his figures, and remembering that garrisons were left at Pevensey and Hastings, and allowing for sickness, etc., one may place the strength of the Norman army at the battle of Hastings at about 9,000 men.

As for the strength of Harold's army, the Norman chroniclers are emphatic that the English vastly outnumbered their opponents. They had an obvious motive for this assertion, and we can ignore it. Considering the haste with which Harold had assembled his army, and the statement of Florence of Worcester (who was probably following a since lost version of the *Anglo-Saxon Chronicle*) that Harold had only one-third of his army with him,[2] it is unlikely that the English army much exceeded the Norman. I have compiled the following table giving the (sometimes qualified) approximate computations as to numbers by some of the leading modern historians. It will be noted that Freeman—the doyen of them all—does not commit himself to any figures. Neither does George, while the others do it with manifest reluctance.

Author.	English.	Normans.
Foord . . .	15,000	?
Oman . . .	12–13,000	The same
Baring . .	10,000 or less	8–10,000
Round . .	?	5–10,000
Stenton . .	Not more than 7,000	Probably similar
Ramsay . .	5–10,000	Under 10,000
Corbett . .	5,000	4,400
James . . .	10,000	8,600

My own computation is that the Normans were nearly 9,000 and the English about the same at the start, with considerable reinforcements flowing in during the course of the battle.

[1] *R.E. Journal*, January, 1907.

[2] Sir Frank Stenton is the first to comment on this important passage in his *Anglo-Saxon England*.

Accepting this computation of the English army at about 9,000, we can now compute the approximate extent of the position. A depth of ten to twelve ranks seems reasonable. This gives a frontage of about 800 yards.

Knowing the approximate centre and extent of the position, and the direction of the enemy, there would not appear to be much more to do. But, as we have seen, the authorities are far from agreement. The next logical step is therefore to examine the terrain closely, trying to establish what appearance and shape it possessed 900 years ago.

We know that it was in a clearing of the forest, which must have extended at least as far south as Telham Hill, as the position could be viewed from there. We also know that it was on ground then too rough to be cultivated, that there were some boggy ditches, and that (from the Bayeux Tapestry) there were a few trees on the position. What changes in the actual shape of the ground have supervened? The centre was evidently levelled slightly when the abbey was built. The ridge running westwards seems to retain its natural contours, but that running east has clearly been cut into in the vicinity of the school. Before this excavation was made, there must have been a well-marked hummock at this spot, just 375 yards east of Harold's command-post.[1] There do not seem to be any other appreciable alterations in the contour of the ground.

Bearing these facts in mind, let us glance at Sketch-map 13, showing the several solutions of some of the leading historians. On the line of the right flank all except Ramsay trace their position along the ridge, but they differ as to its termination. All, with the exception of Oman, place the flank in the valley, and all refuse it fairly sharply except George. On the left flank there is more diversity. Freeman and George take it right along the ridge for about 800 yards. Baring makes it stop short near the church, whilst Oman and Saltzmann made it bend back sharply towards the north. Ramsay plays a 'lone hand' throughout, making the position practically a semi-circle with a diameter of under 400 yards. His position does not even cross the London road. It is hard to believe that Harold would have adopted such a narrow front if he wished to ensure barring William's approach to the capital. The objection to Oman's and Saltzmann's lines, as

---

[1] It is curious that Baring, who seems to have made as close an examination of the terrain as anyone, ignored this excavation, and indeed explicitly stated that there was no sharp slope of the ridge at this point. Consequently he places the left flank 200 yards further west.

I see it, is that they pass over what the French call *terrain accidenté*, so that the line must either go up and down, or if it is to keep at all level, it must bend sharply in and out, an unusual formation for those days.

It is time to arrive at our own solution to this vexed problem. When in doubt about an ancient battlefield, it is a sound practice to place oneself in the shoes of the commander, stand where he stood, and issue the orders that seem most natural under the circumstances, remembering that in war the simplest course is the most likely the one to be adopted. This procedure is made the easier for us in the present case inasmuch as we know to within a few yards where Harold stood; it is on the one obvious spot. Riding straight up the road to the ridge-top, he would halt and look around him. Let us repair to the Abbey grounds and do the same. Standing by the high altar it is now unfortunately impossible to see much; but by a preliminary reconnaissance it is easy to picture the lie of the land. Let us reconstruct the scene that was there enacted nearly 900 years ago. To do so can prove quite thrilling.

It is just fully light, about 7.30 a.m., as King Harold, having been warned by his scouts of the enemy's approach, rides up accompanied by his two brothers, Gurth and Leofwine. Halting on the top and glancing right and left, he sees the ridge stretching away, slightly oblique to his front, but not enough to matter. The King points out the ridge to right and left. 'Since Duke William offers me battle, I shall accept it here. Brother Gurth', he says, 'you will command the right wing. Line this ridge; you can certainly extend as far as what looks like the end of it at that point about 400 yards away. Later on, if sufficient reinforcements come up you can extend it further, but do not, on any account extend into the valley. Put a single line of House-carls in front, and send the surplus to report to me here in the centre, where I shall make my headquarters, and mark it with my standard. Password: "God and King Harold" . . . Brother Leofwine, you will command the left wing. You will line this ridge in the same manner, reaching as far as that hummock 400 yards away that seems to mark the end of the ridge. You may both carry out strictly limited counter-attacks, but I shall reserve my general counter-attack until I am satisfied that the enemy have shot their bolt. Any questions? Then go!'

The position thus indicated by Harold is marked on Sketch-map 12. It is practically a straight line. I see no point in refusing the flanks, which would necessitate descending into the valley where the cavalry might meet them on level terms. In this I agree with George, as against the other historians cited. At the same time I take note of the argument that the 'wedge-shape' of the English army might point to refused flanks. But, in the first place, how came the Norman chroniclers to know that it had this wedge-shape? The refused flanks would be out of sight from the Norman side, so how could the Normans know that they existed? In the second place, does 'cuneus' (the word used of the English position) mean more than a clump or close formation? That they were wedged together? The word is certainly used in this sense in the course of the fight by the chronicler of the *Relatio Brevis*, who speaks of a *Cuneus Normanorum* with this connotation.

To sum up, I place the left flank with some confidence on the spot now occupied by the school; and I place the right flank on the slight swell of ground 425 yards west of the high altar, with the proviso that if the English army exceeded 10,000 men, it probably extended another 200 yards to the far end of the ridge.

II.—THE PALISADE

It may have been noticed by those familiar with the battle that, in my narrative, I made but scant allusion to the famous palisade and ditch which Freeman claimed that the English built along the front of their position. The reason is that the contention has long been abandoned by English historians. The controversy raged fiercely, however, in the last decade of the nineteenth century, and still retains its interesting and even entertaining side to a generation which knew not the participants. J. H. Round, the chief of them, himself described it with evident relish, as 'the fiercest controversy of the generation'.[1]

Freeman, in his *Norman Conquest*, based his case for the palisade on an obscure passage in Wace's *Chronicle*. Now, apart from the fact that Wace wrote 90 years after the event, and in badly rhymed verse which necessitated the inexact use of words, none of the other chroniclers, nor the Bayeux Tapestry mentions it. A 'threefold' palisade of timber would have played a prominent part in the battle, and it is inconceivable that there should be such a 'conspiracy of silence' about it. Moreover, since the English only took up their position at dawn they had no time to construct such a formidable defence. The verdict of history is that there was no palisade.

[1] *Sussex Archæological Collections*, 1899, p. 59.

III.—THE NORMAN DEPLOYMENT (*See Sketch-map 12.*)

The precise point at which the Norman army deployed has been slurred over, if not entirely disregarded, by most commentators; possibly because it presents considerable difficulty. William was confronted (if he was aware of the fact) by a kind of Hobson's choice. If he continued in column of route along the London road from his halting-point on Blackhorse Hill (which is two miles from the battle-field) till he reached the valley immediately in front of the Anglo-Saxon position, he would find himself opposite its left flank. If he deployed at this point, as General James asserts,[1] the greater part of his army would have to file to its left, across the front of the enemy, and only 150 to 200 yards from them. This seems dangerously close, for it would be just within bow-shot, and William could not be aware that Harold had scarcely any bowmen.

Moreover, the peculiar danger of deploying to a flank was that during the operation there would be, immediately on the Norman left hand, a boggy bottom (the source of the Sandlake stream). Should the Anglo-Saxons charge down on them whilst in the act of deploying they would be driven into this boggy ground, where the cavalry would be at a disadvantage. Further, if the army deployed in this manner, the whole of it being on the north side of the stream, it would have no depth; but this seems inconsistent with the pursuit episodes in which struggles took place in this boggy bottom which were ultimately terminated by cavalry charges. From whence did these horsemen charge? Surely from the slope *behind*—that is, to the south of—the stream, not from in *front* of it. If one tries to picture the scene on the ground no other solution seems plausible. William's own headquarters would (in the early stages) be sited on the high ground on the south side of the stream (as General James seems to agree), when he could survey the whole field.

But if we conclude that the deployment must have taken place before the valley was reached, we are confronted with the objection that the army would have rough, hilly country over which to advance after deployment. From Telham Hill there are two ridges to cross. Over such terrain it would be difficult for a long line to keep its dressing. But this is the lesser objection of the two, and it is overcome if the deployment was started from the top of the Telham

[1] *R.E. Journal*, Jan. 1907. Ramsay's map shows that he shares this view.

Court Ridge, at the bend in the road, 900 yards from Harold's head-quarters. From this point the army would deploy to its left down the crest of the Ridge, moving almost due west, till the head reached Sandlake stream. The whole army, then turning to its right, would be in line roughly parallel to the hostile position. This would con-stitute an unusual manœuvre for those days, but the terrain seems to demand it. The fact that it was carried out without any notable hitch or delay speaks well for the state of training of the Norman army. (See Sketch-map 12 where I have marked the suggested line of deployment.)

IV.—THE FEIGNED RETREAT

There are many difficulties in connection with the various Norman retreats that are recorded during the battle. The chronicles are obscure and contradictory as to facts and chronology. The con-sensus of modern opinion is that the first retreat, on the part of the Bretons, was a genuine one, and that the second and the third (if there was a third) were feigned. I simply cannot bring myself to believe that a feigned retreat could have been mounted, as an after-thought, in the midst of the battle. Consider the difficulties. By what means was William to get his orders right up to the individual horsemen who were at grips with the foe only a few feet from them; how explain to them, without their opponents noticing it, that they were to fall back in such a way as to make the enemy believe they were driven back, so that the English should break out and pursue them; that they were only to go back such and such a distance, and then suddenly to wheel round and attack again. One has only to stand upon that open slope at the present day and picture the scene to realize the utter improbability of it. If done on a large scale, nice co-ordination would be necessary. Had William a trained staff, sufficiently expert and numerous, and available at hand at that advanced hour of the battle to organize and execute such a complicated manœuvre?

But if the 'feigned retreat' did not happen, how are we to account for the positive assertions of two of the best chroniclers, Guy of Amiens, and William of Poitiers, that it did occur? I suggest the following explanation. To start with I accept the first genuine retreat. This was made by the Bretons, and the Norman chroniclers would have no qualms about admitting that the retreat of their allies was genuine; but not so in the case of their fellow Normans, and it was the

Normans who appear to have been involved in the 'feigned retreat';
it could not have been the Bretons, for the English in that part of the
line had been caught once, and would not be likely to try it again.
So some excuse had to be found for the retreat of their Norman com-
peers. A feigned retreat was the obvious excuse to make.

I will allow that these retreats did end in more setbacks for the
English, but hold that the explanation that I have given in the narrative
(though so far as I know it has never been advanced by any previous
writer) is the natural, and therefore the most likely solution to a
difficult problem.

V.—THE MALFOSSE

There has been much speculation as to the site of what is described
by expressions ranging from 'fearful precipice' to a 'ditch covered
with grass'. Freeman sites it immediately behind the left wing.
My objection to this is that the ridge here is so narrow that the cavalry
which would be blown and reduced to a walk on reaching the top
of this ridge, would not have space to get into a gallop before en-
countering the ravine. I think this is fatal to the site, for unless they
had been at a gallop they would not have plunged headlong into the
ravine. The same objection applies to the similarly placed but not so
steep ravine behind the other flank.

Baring's location is much more likely, and I adopt it on my map.
Here the pursuers would have time to get up speed, though they were
going slightly up-hill, and rather oblique to what one would suppose
to be the general line of retreat, but no doubt the defeated army
scattered in all directions. Also, to derive the word from 'Mansers'
seems rather far-fetched, and is rejected by the last writer on the subject
that I can discover, namely E. H. Stevenson, who thinks 'Mansers'
represents an owner's name. It is no great matter, for the extent of
the disaster was probably grossly exaggerated, and in any case it
occurred too late to affect the issue of the battle. Just such an exaggeration followed a mishap to a few French cavalrymen in the famous
chemin creusé at Waterloo.

VI.—THE CHRONOLOGY OF THE BATTLE

There are certain difficulties about establishing this that are conveniently slurred over by nearly all the historians. The chief difficulty is that so much seems to have happened in the $2\frac{1}{2}$ hours between
sunrise and the opening of the battle. I think the best way to obviate

this is to extend the time at both ends—i.e. to assume that the march of the Norman army started not later than 6 a.m. After all, none of the chroniclers of the battle were standing watch in hand to record the exact moment when the first arrow was discharged, and the utmost we can accord to the figure 9 a.m. is that the battle opened after 8 a.m. and before 10 a.m. On these two assumptions I have compiled the following comparative chronology.

TIME	NORMAN	ENGLISH
6.0	March begins	
6.30		
6.45	Scouts spot English army	
7.0	Scouts inform William (at Blackhorse Hill)	Harold dons his armour
7.15	William reaches Telham Hill	Scouts spot approach of Normans
7.30	William back at Blackhorse Hill	Scouts inform Harold Harold reconnoitres
7.45	William gives out his orders Army closes up to Blackhorse Hill	Harold gives out his orders
8.0	William dons his armour	
8.15		Army begins to file into position
8.30	Army resumes the march	
8.45	Army begins to deploy	
9.0		Position completely occupied
9.30	Battle opens	

VII.—TELHAM HILL

It seems always to be assumed that the point from which William viewed the Anglo-Saxon army was on the main Hastings-London road, as it exists to-day. I think there can be little doubt that the present road did then exist, at any rate in the vicinity of the battlefield. Harold would be likely to draw up his army astride the road leading to London; moreover, the road approached Battle from the south along the line that would naturally be expected, that is by the watershed dividing the Sandlake valley from the valley running north-east. But the highest point on the ridge along which the main road runs is on Blackhorse Hill, and from nowhere on this hill can the Battle position be seen. I have made a section from the six-inch map, from which it appears that, even were there no trees or scrub, the position would not come into view till the 300 feet contour is reached, only 800 yards from the field. It is the more surprising that even Mr. Baring, who has made the most detailed examination of the ground, is guilty of the *suggestio falsi* contained in the sentence: 'The view between Telham and Battle is now much interrupted by modern plantations' (op. cit. p. 226*n*). Though this is strictly true it implies that, but for the plantations, the battlefield could be seen from 'Telham'. By Telham he refers evidently to point 425 on the main road, from which point the battlefield could *not* be seen, with or without plantations.

Whence then did William gain his distant view of the Anglo-Saxon army? A glance at the contours would suggest that the spot would be Telham Hill as marked on the one-inch O.S. map. This hill is $\frac{3}{4}$ mile to the left, or west of the main road. From this hill a good view of the field can be obtained, for it looks over the shoulder of the two intervening spurs (Loose Farm and Telham Court on the one-inch map) which blot out the view from point 425. Even if the intervening ground was heavily timbered the view would still be unimpeded, for the ground slopes down very steeply from the crest of the hill. From this spot, then, it seems to me, William must have first cast eyes on his opponent's army, and from here he must have made his plan and probably given out his orders. No visit to the battlefield can be considered complete without including this historic spot.

N.B. It will have been noted that I give the name Sandlake to the stream that runs at the foot of the English position. This name is well attested. The Norman writers obviously spelt it as it sounded to them—Senlac. I hold Freeman warranted in naming the battle Senlac, though I should prefer the English Sandlake.

CHAPTER XII

The Battle of the Standard, or Northallerton, 22 August 1138

SO little is known of this battle and its interest is so predominantly ecclesiastical rather than military that it is worth no more than a brief and cursory description. I am, however, induced to include it by the fact that the only popular account of the battle contrives to reverse the positions of the contestants, showing the English as facing south and the Scots north. As a matter of fact there is probably no battle fought in England, of equal importance, that has so little controversy attached to it. Furthermore the site is easy to find, as the Great North Road bisects it, and a prominent monument by the roadside correctly marks the site. This spot is three miles north of Northallerton on the Great North Road.

★　　★　　★　　★　　★

In the summer of 1138 during the troubled reign of King Stephen, David, King of Scotland, decided to add to those troubles by invading the country at a moment when Stephen had his hands full in the south. There was, however, in the north a man of action, Thurstan, Archbishop of York. Stephen had made him Lieutenant of the North, much as in later days the Bishop of Durham was made the King's deputy on the northern border. Thurstan was too old and decrepit to take a personal part in the forthcoming campaign, but he lent it full ecclesiastical aid; that is to say, he preached a Holy War, and had a sacred banner prepared to go forward at the head of the army, accompanied by his deputy, the Bishop of Orkney. Fired by the Archbishop's lead and spiritual aid, the able-bodied men of the northern shires came forward eagerly. Soon a large army was collected at York. It contained a curious admixture of races: Normans, Anglo-Normans, English, and some Scots. (For the line of demarcation between the two countries was not then clear-cut. As an example two of the leading men in the English army were named Bruce and Balliol; the latter name came from Bailleul, a town in Picardy well known to soldiers in the 1914–18 War.)

The army thus formed, though still smaller than the Scottish army, moved forward from York to Thirsk, and thence to Northallerton. Here news was received that the enemy was approaching down the road from Darlington and the advance was resumed. Rising very gently from the town of Northallerton, the road, at the third milestone, crosses an almost imperceptible dip between two hillocks, 600 yards apart, immediately on its right hand. Both of these hillocks (I am informed by the inhabitants) are impartially known as Standard Hill. In order to distinguish between them I shall call the northern hillock Pseudo-Standard Hill. The ground was completely open, and sloped down very gently to right and left of the hillocks.

Early in the morning of 22 August 1138 the English army reached the southern hillock and the (anonymous) commander raised on its summit the sacred standard, amid the prayers of the priests. This standard must have been a remarkable sight. On a four-wheeled wagon a tall mast was erected. To its head a pix was affixed, containing a consecrated wafer. Immediately below it cross-pieces were nailed on to the mast, and from them hung four sacred banners.

At the foot of this inspiring banner the army was drawn up in line of battle, for the enemy had by this time appeared upon the opposite hill and it was obvious that a battle was impending.

All we know for certain about the formation of the English order of battle is that all the troops were dismounted, that three lines were formed, that the first line consisted of archers, the second of spear-men, and the third of men-at-arms. The banner clearly represented the centre of the line, but as we do not know the strength it is impossible to compute where the flanks rested.

Almost equally little is known about the composition of the Scottish army. The King presumably commanded in the centre, and his son Prince Henry, had the right wing. David originally ordered his armoured troops and archers to occupy the front line. But the semi-barbarous men of Galloway set up a clamour, demanding the privilege of forming the front line. Reluctantly the King acquiesced.

We may picture the two lines as being drawn up in equal and parallel lines in the dip between the two farms, with a space of about 300 yards dividing them before the action commenced. The first to take the offensive were the Picts from Galloway. With an impetuous charge they rushed down against the line of English archers. Being completely unarmoured, they offered an easy target to the English bowmen at a close range. The slaughter was immense; the attackers came to a halt just short of the English line, and then recoiled from the deadly hail of arrows. In falling back they seem to have involved many of the troops behind them in their rearward motion.

Prince Henry rose to the occasion. Rallying his own men, who were also beginning to waver, he led them forward in a charge which slightly outflanked the English left. Now at the bottom of the slope behind Standard Hill, and about 400 yards in rear, the led horses of the men-at-arms were being held or were tethered.[1] The spot is still known as Scotspit Lane, and there are a number of grave-pits there. The horse guard put up a strenuous resistance, which lasted sufficiently long for the third line to turn about and attack these intrepid Scots. The fight was fierce, and bloody. Few of Henry's men managed to regain their own lines, and the Prince himself only effected his escape with difficulty. By the time he had returned the decision had been reached. The King and his whole army was in full flight—all except a little band of English and French knights who attempted to form a rearguard and protect the flight of their sovereign.

Though the numbers of prisoners taken was not numerous the Scottish army had completely disintegrated. Retreating via Carlisle, what was left of the army was across the border a few days later, and the land had rest.

THE BATTLEFIELD

As I have said, there are few controversial points to be examined. By putting oneself in the shoes of the English commander as he reached the top of Standard Hill, and saw the advanced patrols of the Scottish army appearing on Pseudo-Standard Hill, one perceives an almost inevitable course of action. The slight dip between the two armies (reminding one of the dip between the two armies at Waterloo) formed an admirable theatre for a medieval battle. Both flanks, it is true, were in the open, but that affected each army equally; and medieval armies did not concern themselves greatly about their flanks. Each army doubtless drew up its line on the forward slope in front of its own hill, leaving the centre of the dip between them. In this dip most of the fighting must have taken place, quite near and to the east of the present monument. Battle relics are still occasionally ploughed up, though the plough-boy that I questioned seemed delightfully vague about the whole affair. The owner of the farm on Standard Hill, however, assured me that her father had dug up some relics, which she supposed might now be in the museum at York.

The only place-name connecting with the battle is Scotspit Lane,

[1] The spot is still known as Scotspit Lane, and there are a number of grave-pits there.

400 yards south of Standard Hill. And this brings me to the extraordinary battle line shown by Barrett in his *Battles and Battlefields*, to which I have referred. His map shows the English on Pseudo-Standard Hill and the Scots on Standard Hill, but his text does not attempt to explain how the two armies got reversed in this fashion. There is of course no evidence whatever that this occurred, and the only reason that I can think of why Barrett thus shows the two armies is the existence of Scotspit Lane in rear of the English position. Barrett must have mistaken Pseudo-Standard for Standard Hill; and have argued thus: The Scots pit marks the scene of the chief slaughter; this must have been behind the Scottish, rather than behind the English position. The northern hill is known as Standard Hill. Therefore the English must have been on the northern hill and consequently the Scots on the southern.

Now I must admit that I usually attach great significance to the position of the battle grave-pits, as probably indicating the approximate centre of the battle, but this must not be taken as an absolute rule, especially when it conflicts with other evidence. Several explanations might be given for the presence of grave-pits in Scotspit Lane; the most obvious will suffice. It marks the spot where Prince Henry received his chief casualties, that is, in his desperate fight behind the English line. The corpses in this fight would be buried near the lane. As for the other grave-pits, they have been levelled in the course of centuries as has happened on most battlefields. Probably not a tenth of the original grave-pits still exist on any of our battlefields. Indeed, Hastings, where the number slain was very much greater, and which was fought only seventy years before, has no pits whatever to show.

To what is this signal victory to be attributed? At this distance of time and in view of the paucity of the evidence it would not do to dogmatize. But one thing at least seems clear: the English morale was raised to fever pitch by the holy crusade that had been preached, and is probably largely responsible for the result.

The battle is also an example of the effect of missile weapons when in steady hands, especially when wielded against an unarmoured foe. Finally the discipline of the English was probably superior. The conduct of the Galloway men points to lack of cohesion, and the action of Prince Henry seems to have been the result of his own promptings, not the orders of his King.

CHAPTER XIII

The Battle of Lewes, 14 May 1264

'WARS (and battles) settle nothing', is a trite and untruthful remark. The Barons' War, and the battle of Lewes settled a parliament on England. Is that nothing? Had Henry III won, parliamentary government would have been indefinitely postponed. So the battle that made parliament possible seems worthy of study. Like most medieval battles there are a number of points to be unravelled, and the unravelling process will be deferred to the Battlefield Problems at the end of this chapter.

Apart from constitutional and political considerations, the battle possesses a certain dramatic quality—it was a duel between the monarch and his leading subject, Simon de Montfort. Of the King it is hard to find anything good to say. Certainly he was pious, in a narrow, superstitious way; but he was, in my opinion, the most despicable monarch that has ever sat on the English throne. His father, King John, had at least the redeeming feature that he was a good general and a first-class strategist; but poor Henry, in spite of having to do a good deal of fighting, was no general. And what are we to think of a sovereign who, while still trembling with fright from a thunderstorm, meets his leading baron with the remark: 'I tremble still more at your presence'?

The days are past when the name of Simon de Montfort would raise such heated arguments as the name of Oliver Cromwell still occasionally conjures up, but there was much resemblance between the two. Both were pre-eminent in war, and that is all that we are concerned with here. They both built up a formidable army by careful training and the inculcation of morale—enthusiasm for their cause.

We must not, however, look upon either his or the Royalist army as well trained or homogeneous in the modern sense. Military science had not advanced greatly since the battle of Hastings just two hundred years before, in spite of the experience of the Crusades. Fortification and armour admittedly had advanced, but not tactics and manoeuvre.

As for numbers, the usual exaggeration and obscurity of those days is so much in evidence that few modern commentators dare give any estimate, contenting themselves with the statement that the Royalist army was much the most numerous. We are, however, approaching the time when a chronicler would on occasion approximate to the truth, and there are two passages in the chronicles which seem to be near the mark. The first is a statement in the Chronicle of St. Pancras Priory at Lewes to the effect that the royalist dead numbered 2,700, 'more or less'. The Abbot of the near-by Priory would be likely to know. The other is in a fragment of a manuscript in the British Museum which was brought to light some years ago by Mr. J. P. Gilson. It appears to be a contemporary document, and though unfortunately the end is mutilated, it has a certain value. There is no printed translation, but I hope there are no gross errors in my own rendering. 'It is said that the King had with him more than 3,000 cavalry; the Earl of Leicester [Simon de Montfort] had with him 500 cavalry, and a few other irregular cavalry and more infantry.' Now, in the Appendix to the second edition of Blaauw's *The Barons' War*, Mr. C. H. Pearson states that in 1810 about 1,500 skeletons were discovered in three large pits near the modern gaol, and large numbers on the Downs near Offham chalkpits. Putting all these facts together we may roughly compute the King's army at a little under 10,000, and the Baron's army at not much more than 5,000.

PRELIMINARY MOVES

At the outbreak of the Barons' War, the King's strength was in the midlands and the Barons' in the capital (rather like the situation in the Great Civil War). Operations opened with the King reducing the towns of Northampton, Leicester, and Nottingham, after which he made a dash for Rochester which de Montfort was besieging. Prince Edward (later Edward I), the King's eldest son, covered the distance with his cavalry—160 miles—at the rate of 32 miles per day, wearing out his horses in so doing. But it was a foretaste of the driving power and forcefulness of the youth who was later to be known as 'The Hammer of the Scots'.

Rochester was relieved, the King came up with his infantry and captured Tonbridge. He then marched to Lewes where he arrived on 6 May 1264. Meanwhile Simon had returned to London where he recruited a large contingent of raw troops, a welcome addition to his tiny army. Marching out from London on the same day that Henry marched into Lewes, the Baronial army proceeded at great speed to Fletching (8 miles north of Lewes in a straight line). What was the need for such haste? We cannot say, any more than we can say in the very similar case of Harold's hurried march from the capital to Hastings. Simon, one would suppose, might have borne in mind the sad results of Harold's undue haste and been influenced thereby. But, as we shall see, the similarity did not end there.

An exchange of letters of a curious nature now took place. Neither army was particularly anxious to engage in a pitched fight, but the overtures came from the Barons. Their letter was outwardly conciliatory and reverent. He tried to maintain that they were in arms, not against the King, but against 'certain persons among those who surround you', and they proposed only to resist 'those persons who are not only our enemies but yours'. When two hundred years later the Barons again took up arms against their King, they used almost precisely the same language. I fancy the Duke of York at St. Albans must have deliberately copied Simon de Montfort. The unnamed 'certain persons' included no other than Henry's own brother Richard, the King of the Romans (who preferred England to the Holy Roman Empire!), and his own son, Prince Edward. This letter therefore, not unnaturally, produced a savage reply from Henry. He ended, too angry to preserve grammar: 'We therefore value not your faith or love, and defy you as their enemies. Witness myself at Lewes, on May 13th, in the 48th year of our reign.'

Not content with this, his brother and his son threw a lance of their own, in which this amiable sentiment occurs: 'We therefore let you know that you are all defied as public enemies by each and all of us your enemies, and that henceforth whenever occasion offers we will with all our might labour to damage your persons and property. . . .'

The sword was unsheathed; the arbitrament of battle must decide.

On 12 May, while these letters were passing, a curious little affair took place in the neighbourhood of Offham. It is only recorded in the above-mentioned fragment, and was only an affair of outposts; but it is of importance as disproving the contention of some writers that Simon managed to surprise the King in offering him battle on the morning of the 14th. The skirmish on the 12th, which seems to have taken place in the hollow immediately to the south-west of Offham (see Sketch-map), gave the King full warning of the proximity of the Baronial advanced troops, and the upshot of his letter must have been obvious to all. Henry therefore placed a picquet on the high ground overlooking Offham and awaited developments in a sanguine state of mind.

It did not take the Barons long to decide on their course of action,

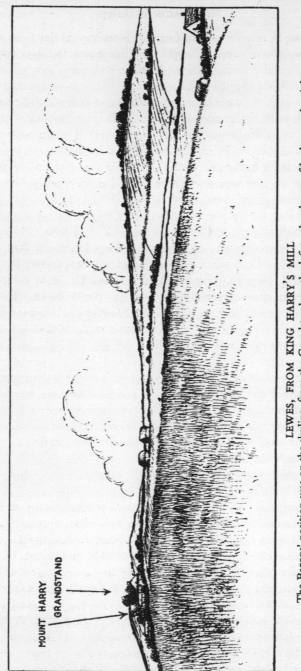

LEWES, FROM KING HARRY'S MILL

The Barons' position was on the skyline, from the Grandstand on the left to the clump of bushes on the right

MOUNT HARRY

GRANDSTAND

though we have no record of their deliberations. At dawn on 14 May the Baronial army broke camp at Fletching and marched down the winding road towards Lewes. But Simon did not intend a direct approach. The skirmish on the 12th must have acquainted him with the lie of the ground (probably that was the reason for it), and must have shown him that if he attempted to keep the direct road south of Offham, his army would be cooped up between a steep hill on his right and the river and marsh on his left. It was almost a Pass of Thermopylae, and Simon, good soldier that he was, had no intention of getting his army caught in it. Reconnaissance had, however, disclosed a convenient track (it must have been centuries old even in those days) leading diagonally up the hill from Offham, on to the plateau now named Harry's Hill, just 400 feet above the valley. Up this steep chalky track the army wound in file, to debouch at the top on to a flat plateau, almost exactly 1,000 yards wide. Here on the smooth and flat-topped Harry's Hill, de Montfort drew up his array. The right column was under his two sons, Henry and Guy, the centre under the Earl of Gloucester, and the left consisted of the Londoners. He kept his own column in reserve—an uncommon practice in those days.

Though the Londoners were completely untrained the morale of the whole army was high. Simon had inspired them with a burning enthusiasm for their cause; he imbued them with the crusading spirit, and partly in order to enhance this spirit, and partly for the more prosaic reason of distinguishing friend from foe, he had large white crosses sewn on their tunics, front and back. Prayers and the customary pre-battle harangue put the finishing touches to his arrangements. It was now about 10 a.m.

THE BATTLE

We have seen how the King had posted picquet on top of Harry's Hill, after which he slept soundly in his bed. Next morning he held a council at which he countersigned a document of secondary import-ance, a thing he would hardly have done had he known that the sentry on the hill-top was fast asleep, 'his head reclining on the ground', while the Baronial army was fast approaching. A foraging party out on the Downs was the first to give the alarm. Immediately a great din arose. The battle-trumpets blew the assembly. The chronicler Wykes surpasses himself in recording it: 'Tubis terribiliter clangentibus' should convey the sense of stir without the necessity for the reader to know a word of Latin!

The dispositions of the royal army were peculiar. The columns of the King and of his brother were billeted in or near St. Pancras Priory, just outside the town to the south; whereas Prince Edward's column was billeted in the castle, inside the town, 300 yards away.

It was no doubt the Prince's foragers who had given the alarm, and they would naturally give it to their own people first. Thus the Prince's

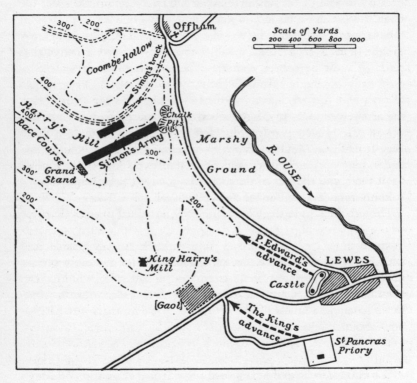

SKETCH–MAP 14.   LEWES: THE BATTLE

column got a flying start, and, urged on by the impetuosity of the youthful Prince, it sallied out well ahead of the rest of the army. From the castle to the top of the hill where the rival army was in the act of drawing up, was threequarters of a mile, a steady uphill slope all the way. Now the Prince's troops consisted mainly of cavalry, and a steady trot would cover the distance in approximately ten minutes. Moreover Edward seems to have recognized the Londoners from afar, and he had a grudge to work off against those Londoners who had recently

insulted his mother the Queen. Throwing caution to the winds, therefore, he let drive his mounted troops straight up the hill and into the
ranks of the enemy. The encounter was brief and decisive; the
Londoners who must have lacked coherence and discipline broke and
fled to the rear down the steep hillside with Edward's clumsy horsemen
careering down on top of them, completely out of control. It is only
necessary to visit that almost precipitous hillside to picture the scene of
uncontrollable disorder on *both* sides.

'Rider and horse—friend, foe—in one red burial blent.' The charge
like most charges got out of hand. Some of the cavalry pursued the
fugitives in a north-easterly direction across the river and marshes;
others pushed straight north up the valley past Offham. The further
the pursuit went, the more disorderly and out of hand it became.
And as the pursuers fanned out, the more scattered they necessarily
became. Chroniclers give the distance of the pursuit as from 2 to 4
miles. It matters not. Once they got really going, nothing would stop
the Londoners till they got within sight of Paul's great spire. They were
out of the battle and out of the war. And so was Prince Edward too,
for many months to come—if he had but realized it. To explain this,
we must go back over the hill and see how the rest of the royal army
was acquitting itself.

By the time the King's two columns were drawn up outside the
Priory, the right column had already launched its attack, and there was
nothing for it but to join in as speedily as possible. Up the hill the
columns therefore set out, the King taking the right and his brother
the left wing. Of details of the fight that ensued we have practically
none, but it is safe to assume that Simon met the onset in his stationary
position at or near the hill-top, much as Harold did at Hastings. But
we know how Harold's passive defence led to disaster. De Montfort
had learnt this lesson, and kept a reserve, with every intention of using
it. The column of the King of the Romans, rather breathless from the
long climb, soon recoiled from the strong fresh line that it encountered
and started trickling down the hill. This gave Simon his opportunity;
he flung his reserve into the battle against the King's own column
which had held its ground and was thus becoming isolated. The overwhelming concentration of two columns against one, the slope of the
ground in addition being in favour of the Barons, decided the issue.
The King, fighting stubbornly, fell back, until the vicinity of the
modern gaol was reached. Here his troops turned at bay, in a desperate
attempt to hold up the enemy while their sovereign was hurried back

into the safety of the Priory. To give him his due, King Henry had fought well, and showed courage—the courage of despair perhaps. 'The King was much beaten with swords and maces, and two horses killed under him, so that he escaped with difficulty.'

It was noon, the battle was over, the royal army was back in the Priory and the rebels were storming into the streets of Lewes; and still the right column was absent from the field. It was not till two hours later that Prince Edward appeared from over the hill, with the remnant of his cavalry, returning from the pursuit. It had taken him the best part of four hours collecting his troopers after that mad onrush. On the way back a party of his men came across the 'chariot' of Simon, a specially constructed litter on wheels for him to ride in on the line of march (he had recently broken his leg). The inmates were four Londoners, hostages, but in the excitement of the moment they were run through by mistake. Historians are apt to explain the long absence from the field of the right column by this incident. The sober fact is that it can only have delayed about ten or twenty men, for a matter of fifteen minutes. It was a colourful but unimportant incident.

Similarly unimportant was the fate of Richard, King of the Romans, who took refuge in a windmill half-way down the hill (King Harry's Mill on the Sketch-map). Presently a mob of Baronial infantry surrounded it, but the entrance was firmly closed and all the baffled soldiers could do was to hurl insults at the most unpopular man in England.[1] 'Come out, you bad miller,' they shouted, 'you forsooth to become a wretched mill-master—you who defied us all so proudly,' &c. There is something a little ludicrous in the spectacle of the King of the Romans, perched high up in an English windmill, with the ribald English troops like a pack of hounds baying at him from below. Doubtless his mind went back to a certain letter that he had penned so light-heartedly only a couple of days before. 'We will with all our might labour to damage your persons and property.' Had that letter been delivered? No wonder the King of the Romans was reluctant to 'come out'. However, towards the end of the day he did descend—to receive unexpected leniency. He was imprisoned at Kenilworth, and thus missed the battle of Evesham next year.

Meanwhile Prince Edward had returned to the battlefield, to find, as did another Prince of the royal blood nearly 400 years later, that the battle had gone badly in his absence. Confused fighting was still

[1] Richard had proved himself a capable general in Gascony—far finer than his brother, the King.

going on in the town and its outskirts, and the lion-hearted Prince promptly planned a fresh attack. But alas! His troops had had enough, and one by one, they trickled away and took refuge in flight. There were scenes of carnage at the various river-crossings, which need not concern us here. Edward himself tried, some say successfully, to regain the castle. Later that evening, he managed to join his father in the Priory. The meeting of the bruised and battered sovereign with his headstrong and impetuous son must have been stormy. In the course of the night Simon made advances for a truce, which culminated in the 'Mise of Lewes', whereby Simon ruled the country for the next fifteen months, with the King 'in his pocket' and Prince Edward in confinement. One of de Montfort's first acts was to summon the first Parliament in our annals.

COMMENTS

Sir James Ramsay sums up the battle in a crisp sentence. 'A most signal exhibition of foresight and skill on the one side, and of presumption and rashness on the other.' In this he was not far out. But we must first glance at the opening strategy of the two sides. It is not easy to surmise what was the intention of the King in marching from Tonbridge to Lewes. But it is fruitless to look for a coherent strategical plan in any of Henry's campaigns. That in which he lost Poitou was perhaps the most inept and futile in all our history; the King merely sat down and waited for something to happen. In this he seems to have been like the Bourbons, who 'learnt nothing, and forgot nothing'. The wonder is that such a father produced such a son. Simon's strategy, on the other hand, had something clear-cut and purposeful about it that commands respect. As we have already noted, it had much in common with Harold's strategy in the Hastings campaign—without Harold's mistakes. A point that has escaped remark is that he must have been well served by his intelligence agents. For, on the day de Montfort left London (6 May), the King was at or near Battle Abbey, and Simon doubtless took the road trodden by Harold's army at the outset. But Henry was marching across his front towards the west, yet de Montfort reached Fletching on the same day that the King reached Lewes, only 9 miles distant. This shows good intelligence and good march discipline on the part of the Barons. Probably they marched along the Hastings road as far as Tonbridge, and from there bore off to their right towards Lewes, rightly guessing that the royalists were making for that town. This is one of the first qualities of a general—to guess correctly the enemy's plans and moves. De Montfort had the King's army marked down, and like a ferret on the track of a rabbit, he did not abandon the trail till he had the enemy in his grasp.

We pass on to tactics. Unfortunately the tactical details of the battle are obscure. One thing at least is clear—Simon's 'eye for country' Instead of blundering straight ahead along the Lewes road till he got into hopeless difficulties 'twixt river and mountain, he looked ahead, and thought ahead. With unerring instinct he led his army along a route that a first-class officers 'syndicate' could not improve upon at the present day. Then, having arrived on the summit of the Downs he formed up his army with a careful precision and with an attention to detail that was unusual in those happy-go-lucky days. His prolonged pause on the hill-top was construed by two of the chroniclers as a sort of chivalrous gesture, to allow the King ample time to come out and fight. This it may in part have been. But in the other part it was due to a more prosaic motive—namely to allow time for the army to close up and draw up in proper battle order, and to break their fast, for they had had an early start. Clambering up that steep slippery chalk lane the column must have strung out considerably, and I calculate that it would take ninety minutes to pass a given point, so that two hours at least would be required in which to form up. Thus when the royal army came panting up the hill in driblets, the Baronial army was drawn up in perfect order, cool and collected, on an extremely strong position with flanks—especially the left flank—protected, and with the advantage of the slope. Hastings again! And the opening phases of Hastings (as regards the main body) were probably re-enacted. But the early stages of the battle were to give Simon an opportunity to display another quality of generalship—what Lord Wavell has called 'the quality of robustness—the ability to stand the shocks of war'. The overwhelming of his left wing was indeed such a shock; but Simon seems to have been quite unperturbed and to have continued to stand his ground just as if nothing had happened. Possibly he guessed that the young Edward would have difficulty in recovering control over his cavalry. Right through the ages this has been the great problem of cavalry; it has never been completely solved. Finally there was that comparatively rare feature, a reserve. Simon seems to have handled this in a masterly way. I say 'seems', for there is a regrettable absence of specific detail about this. At any rate it is clear that he refused to disperse it in a wild goose-chase after Edward's galloping cavalry, and in that he showed good judgement.

As for the King's tactics, there is little worth saying. His billeting arrangements and precautions were slipshod; he evidently had little control over his impetuous son, who, it is to be supposed, had a poor view of his father's military abilities. Under such circumstances good co-ordination and homogeneity, which were such a marked feature of the Baronial army, were noticeably absent. Add to all this, Edward's inexperience as a cavalry leader, and the unfavourable nature of the ground, and the result was almost a foregone conclusion. There is no need to advance the plea that Henry was surprised (though most of the chroniclers and historians unite in doing so) for Simon was in no hurry to attack. It suited his game to start on the defensive. It was early in the war, and, just like the Duke of York after him, at St. Albans, he probably had qualms about striking the first blow against an anointed king. To defend himself when attacked was quite another matter. Henry thus played into his hands, or perhaps it would be fairer to say Prince Edward did the playing, and the poor King felt he must back up his son by following him into battle. The greater part of the actual battle was a confused mêlée, out of which it would be foolish to try and extract any tactical lessons.

THE SITE OF THE BATTLEFIELD

There are two schools of thought, one which favours the lower slopes of the Downs, of which we may cite Oman as a leading exponent, and the other that favours the upper slopes, of which Ramsay is the leading light.

One could add the intermediate view of Pearson in the Appendix to the second edition of Blaauw's *Barons' War*, that Prince Edward's battle was engaged on top of the Downs and the main battle on the lower slopes. Ramsey characterizes this as 'a most funny arrangement', but it is not nearly so funny as Ramsay's own siting of the battle-front at Barnet, where he places the Lancastrians in line parallel to their line of march. Indeed the battle line at Barnet did screw round in much the same way that Lewes did before it, and Edgehill after, to take two notable examples. Such a screwing movement was not unnatural in the days when the 'right of the line' was considered the post of honour of both armies; with the resulting tendency for both right wings to make ground and both left wings to give it.

But it is not necessary to assume that the main battle *started* at the bottom of the hill. My solution, it will be remembered, was that they engaged at the top in the opening clash and ended in strife at the bottom. But let us subject the problem to my usual test. The Baronial army was first upon the scene. Let us follow in de Montfort's footsteps on that mid-May morning. Leave your car or bicycle at Offham Church crossroads and take the old chalky track that winds up the hill in a south-westerly direction (it is marked on the one-inch ordnance map and on my Sktch-map). When about a hundred yards from the top you will instinctively veer off the track half left, and reach the top of the hill by the railings of the reservoir. Simon is now by your side, the only difference being that he cannot share your binoculars. But he can see what you cannot—the tower of St. Pancras Priory, peering over the lower shoulder of the ridge. Straight below, between you and the town are some grooms grazing their horses, and others mowing grass (the royal army was short of forage). The captured sentry is here also, still stupid with sleep, and not much can be got out of him. Looking along the top of the ridge to the right, Simon sees something to rejoice the heart of a sergeant-major—a parade-ground! For that is exactly what it is to this day, a beautiful parade-ground, level and straight, just the right size for the army, and facing square to the front.[1] The advanced guard is therefore halted, and Simon parcels out the ground to his column commanders who have accompanied him up the hill. Meanwhile, the army is strung out over a distance of about 3 miles. Moreover the narrow hollow trackway constitutes a bottle-neck which will cause more delay. Here then, and nowhere else, does Simon de Montfort elect to make his stand and cross swords with his King—if the latter is so foolish as to throw down the gauntlet.

So far it is plain sailing; but how are we to account for those 1,500 graves down by the prison? One might well retort: 'How account for the graves by the chalk-pits? The bodies are hardly likely to have been carried uphill to burial there.' But bodies might have been carried *downhill* to the other burial place. However, I do not base my case wholly on this argument, for I allow of prolonged fighting, as my narrative shows, down by and in the town. All who fell inside the town would probably have shared the grave by the gaol.

Finally the argument from silence—the absence of any graves discovered on the centre and western side of the hill-top position—is unimpressive: a good many thousand corpses buried at Hastings nine

[1] I have drawn on my Sketch-map the contours best suited to show this.

hundred years ago, have completely vanished. May not other graves seven hundred years old also have disappeared?

THE ROUTE OF DE MONTFORT'S APPROACH

Though all modern historians are agreed that Simon diverged from the Lewes road at Offham, all seems rather vague as to the precise track followed by the Barons from Offham, except Ramsay, who marks it following a circuitous track further to the north and nearly half a mile longer than the one favoured by me. I can see no reason why Simon should take this unnecessarily devious route, and there is nothing in the record to suggest it. Ramsay's route is not marked as a track on the one-inch ordnance map, and it may not have existed at the time of the battle, whereas mine indubitably did. It is a small point, but of interest to those who wish to visit the field and re-enact the battle on the spot—a wish which it is the chief object of this book to satisfy.

DID SIMON INTEND TO SURPRISE THE KING, AND DID HE SUCCEED?

The chroniclers are fairly unanimous that the King *was* surprised, and most historians, most notably Prothero, maintain that Simon did intend a surprise attack. His divergence from the direct road at Offham is cited in support of this view. But this thesis fails to account for the assertions of the *Waverley Annals* that Simon scorned to take such an advantage of his opponent. Surprise attack when two rival armies faced one another in the field was hardly thought of in those days. Either you agreed to fight a battle or you did not. If it was to be a battle, one side would draw up in a straight line and the other would obligingly conform. It is true that small flanking parties were sometimes sent out with a definite mission (indeed it is asserted that some Londoners were thus sent out to fire the town of Lewes, but the story is vague). But it was recognized that 'it takes two to make a fight', and the element of surprise seems hardly to have been considered in a set-to battle. A battle resembles a duel; witness the previous exchange of letters. De Montfort's climb to the top of the Downs was not in order to get closer to his opponent undiscovered; that he would have better achieved by keeping to the direct road, whereby he might have got almost up to the town unseen. No, Simon climbed the hill for a simple reason: he wished to fight on the top.

THE LENGTH OF EDWARD'S ABSENCE FROM THE BATTLEFIELD

This problem does not seem to have exercised other commentators as it has me. According to some accounts the battle started soon after dawn; according to some it ended at nightfall, sixteen hours later. Now Edward's onset opened the battle, and the Londoners must have started to flee shortly afterwards. The pursuit progressed for from 2 to 4 miles. At a speed of 6 miles per hour this would take up to forty minutes, say one hour from the beginning of the action. Yet historians seem quite happy to record that Edward's cavalry returned when the day was far advanced, or at 8 p.m. (One chronicler who mentions eight hours, evidently means 2 p.m.) Even so, what was Edward doing between say 6 a.m. and 2 p.m.—eight hours? Some explain the delay by the attack on Simon's chariot, but as I have pointed out in the narrative, this could have made no appreciable difference. I have therefore been driven to conclude that the battle opened much later than has been hitherto suggested. I work out the time-table thus :

Head of Baronial army departs Fletching	4.30 a.m.
Head of Baronial army arrives Harry's Hill	7.30 a.m.
Rear of Baronial army arrives	9 a.m.
Army drawn up and Edward's attack	10 a.m.
Edward's pursuit ends	11 a.m.
King's attack	11 a.m.
King retreats to lower position	12 noon
Edward returns to Lewes	2 p.m.

This allows Edward two to three hours to collect and reorganize his scattered troopers—not an excessive period under the circumstances. How long did it take to collect the 9th Lancers after their charge at the battle of Mons? A matter of hours, I fancy. Part of the interval was no doubt spent in watering and feeding, before Edward attempted to return to camp.

THE POSITION OF DE MONTFORT'S CHARIOT

Most historians place it right on top of the hill. I think this is not only improbable but impossible—for the simple reason that it could not have got up the hill. It was a heavy, cumbrous contraption, and anyone who will walk up that track will find it hard to picture it getting safely to the top. There are three other reasons against this siting. First, the chariot was with the baggage, and there could be no object in the baggage slavishly following the army up the track— even if it were possible. Simon's ultimate destination was Lewes; either he would succeed in getting there or he would not. In either case the baggage was better situated on the low ground near Offham, either for a forward or rearward move. Secondly, if the clash took place at the top of the hill, there would scarcely be elbow room for the baggage behind the combatants. Thirdly, if it was on the top of the hill, hard by the Baronial line of battle, Prince Edward, on seeing it, would have realized that the Barons had advanced beyond the hill-top and that the King had been defeated, whereas we are told he was surprised to find on his return that this had happened. The most natural place for the chariot would be near the road in the vicinity of Offham.

CHAPTER XIV

The Battle of Evesham, August 4th, 1265

THE unique interest of the battle of Evesham rests upon the strategical rather than the tactical plane. This is most unusual for a medieval battle, where the strategy is generally almost non-existent but the tactics full of interest. Robert of Gloucester, one of the most reliable chroniclers (for he spent the day of the battle within 30 miles of the spot), describes it as 'the murder of Evesham, for battle it was not'. It will thus repay us to devote special attention to the strategical movements immediately prior to the battle. Quite apart from their intrinsic interest, they, as is usually the case, throw considerable illumination on the staging of the battle itself. For this battle is no exception to the rule that the course of a medieval battle is shrouded in mystery and controversy. In this particular case the two leading participants are two famous medieval historians—Sir James Ramsay and Sir Charles Oman.

It will not be necessary to go back further than the escape from captivity of Prince Edward on May 20th, 1265, and his rapid assembly of an army in the West. The subsequent campaign in Wales, though replete with interest, has no direct bearing on the brief Evesham campaign. We can therefore take up the story on July 31st, 1265, when Prince Edward, aged 26, was at Worcester, Simon de Montfort Earl of Leicester at Hereford, and his son Simon junior at Kenilworth Castle. It is generally accepted that Simon Junior reached Kenilworth on the 31st, but this seems incredible. Kenilworth is 34 miles from Worcester, and we are asked to believe that Simon with his army marched into that town from the south on the 31st and that the news of his arrival and of his dispositions, or absence of them, reached Prince Edward at Worcester the same day, and that the latter had time to make his preparations and set out on a 34-miles march with an army composed in part of foot-soldiers on the same evening, and arrive at Kenilworth at early dawn next day. Such a swift succession of events would have done credit even to the age of radio and mechanization; if it happened in 1265 it was an utterly unique and most astonishing occurrence. However, it matters little for the purpose of our reconstruction; its only value is as a corrective, putting us on our guard against dubious statements of the chroniclers, even though they be unquestioningly accepted by a succession of historians, as this statement has been.

Consider the strategical situation that confronted Prince Edward when he heard of the arrival of Simon junior at Kenilworth. He found himself in a position of what is called interior lines. If we exclude the situation of Harold in the Stamford Bridge-Hastings campaign, this is the first example in our history of such a strategical situation being exploited by the possessor of interior lines. In olden days, before the perfection of communications, such a position conferred a big advantage on its possessor. By speedy movements he might defeat first one and then the other of his opponents without the possibility of their joining forces and thereby defeating him. Now de Montfort at Hereford was 27 miles from Worcester, and Simon junior at Kenilworth was 34. Not much in it, and it is not as clear to me as to some historians why Edward elected to attack the son before the father. The river Severn can have had nothing to do with it, for it flowed through Worcester, midway between the two hostile armies. The Kenilworth army was believed to be stronger than the Hereford army, but this strength was probably more than redressed by the presence of the great war leader and victor of Lewes with the Hereford army. I am therefore inclined to think, *pace* Sir Charles Oman, that Edward elected to settle first with the army that he feared the least. This would undoubtedly be sound strategy. Nothing is certain in war, but one is more likely to defeat the weaker of two armies than the stronger (strategy is as simple as that) and therefore Edward was right to attack Simon Junior before his father-He evidently gave this matter much anxious thonght before decid. ing on his plan of action, for Wykes states that he spent a sleepless night on July 30th—an unusual and interesting personal note.

If Edward's army reached Kenilworth by, say, 7 a.m. on August 1st, and if it averaged 2½ miles per hour through the night—good going—it must have left Worcester 14 hours previously, i.e. at 5 o'clock on the afternoon of July 31st—at the moment when Simon is supposed to have been entering Kenilworth. This alone shows that he must have arrived much earlier. Moreover, a convoy of supplies was arriving at Kenilworth for Simon Junion simultaneously with the arrival of the hostile army. If Simon Junior had only reached his destination a few hours previously it is hard to believe that he could have arranged for a convoy of supplies to arrive almost simultaneously. (Incidentally this supply convoy is one of the rare references we have to the problem of the supply of armies in the field in the Middle Ages.)

A large portion of Simon Junior's army, himself included, were billeted or encamped in the town outside the castle walls, and they were taken utterly by surprise, many of them being killed in their beds. Simon escaped by swimming or rowing across the river, but much booty was captured, including many horses and 13 banners. Prince Edward made use of both: the horses to provide mounts for his footsore infantry, and the banners—we shall see presently. Having no engines of war, Edward could not attempt to storm the castle. The remainder of the day (August 1st) he therefore rested his weary troops, who no doubt refreshed themselves by bathing in the river. In the course of the night his army started on its return journey, and reached Worcester probably late on August 2nd.

Here exciting news greeted him. In his brief absence de Montfort, taking King Henry III with him, had moved out of Hereford with the intention of joining forces with his son at Kenilworth; in fact he must have set out very soon after Edward set out from Worcester. If he was aware before he left Hereford that his son had reached Kenilworth, which is reasonable to assume, that fact also shows the unlikelihood of Simon junior arriving at Kenilworth as late as July 31st.

Prince Edward had called in such picquets as were lining the bank of the Severn before his dash on Kenilworth. Consequently de Montfort found the river unguarded and was able to cross at his leisure at Kempsey, four miles south of Worcester. This he did by boats on August 2nd, and the operation must have taken most of the day. When Edward's army returned to Worcester it was much too tired after two 34-mile marches in three days to attack de Montfort the same day. And next morning, August 3rd, his enemy had disappeared. De Montfort slipped away before daylight on the road to Evesham. The direct road to Kenilworth would have taken him through Alcester, but this would have entailed marching within three miles of his opponent's army at Worcester. De Montfort's plan was to unite his two armies before joining battle—a sound strategy which, if successful, would eliminate Edward's advantageous position on interior lines. At the same time de Montfort, unaware of the mishap at Kenilworth, sent a message to his son, beseeching him to join him, but not apparently prescribing the road by which he should come.

Simon junior responded to the message, and elected to approach by the Alcester road.[1]

THE OPENING MOVES

Let us now consider the difficult problem that confronted Prince Edward on the morning of August 3rd. The first step in his plan had been carried out with swift and remarkable success. He had struck his eastern opponent what he considered a reeling blow. The next obvious step after his return to Worcester was to turn west and strike his other opponent more or less at his leisure. But this opponent was showing most annoying signs of mobility; not only had he accomplished the great achievement of forcing the Severn barrier, which had withstood him throughout the campaign, but he had since disappeared, moving in an easterly direction. The enemy might have any one of three objectives: London, Evesham or Kenilworth. The probability is that during the course of the day news reached Edward that his opponent was crossing the river Avon at Pershore, midway between Kemsey and Evesham (see Sketch-map 15). This would point to Evesham as being his destination for the night. And after that? If London, he had a big start, and Edward could not count on catching him. On the other hand, if he was attempting to join forces with his son, his march next day would take him through either Alcester or Stratford. Prince Edward, either from the information of spies[2] or from his own military intuition and correct reading of his opponent's mind (and I like to think that this was so), judged that de Montfort would make for Kenilworth. In that case there was still time to circumvent him; for the Earl's army would be delayed by the river crossing at Pershore and he could hardly get much beyond Evesham that night. If, then, Edward started off late that afternoon, he could reach Alcester, 17 miles, during the night and be across the the Avon in the vicinity of Cleeve Prior[3] well before dawn, thus

---

[1] No chronicler makes these specific statements, but deeds are sometimes more eloquent than words, and the fact is that Simon did indeed advance upon this road, which he would scarcely have done so soon after his beating at Kenilworth, had he not come to some agreement to join his father.

[2] Wykes states that this was so. He had a female spy of the name of Margot, dressed in male attire.

[3] The crossing at Cleeve Prior is disputed by some historians. Rishanger uses the word CLINEMAN, which is transcribed CLIVE VIAM in the Rolls Series of 1865, and accepted by Herbert New in 1876 and G. W. Prothero in 1877.

blocking whichever of the two roads to Kenilworth de Montfort attempted to take.

Orders were issued accordingly, and the much-tried army set out late that day on yet another night march, the third in four days. Oman seems to throw doubt on the story that in order to delude his enemy, Edward set off for three miles due north from Worcester, and I agree with him. Edward was a great general, and I cannot believe he would do so nonsensical a thing as this. His men could not have fully recovered from the exertions of their 70-mile march—they had had a bare 24 hours rest—and the extra three miles would entail an additional hour or more on the journey, apart from the additional weariness engendered, with the prospect of a battle at the end of it. To march out by the northern road, and after traversing three miles to reverse his steps, as some aver, seems quite unthinkable. Such a sudden and drastic change of direction in a long column in the darkness of night would be beyond the tactical ability of a scratch army of those days, such as Edward's was. Moreover, if spies could witness his motions in a northerly direction and report them to Evesham, other spies could witness and report his subsequent reversal of march an hour later, and also report it. Even if it were reported to old Simon that the enemy had retreated north, he would probably 'smell a rat', for such a movement was intrinsically improbable on the part of the enterprising Prince Edward.

Historians seem to assume that Edward expected and intended to do what he eventually did do, namely, surprise his enemy in their Evesham camp; but his march to a point well to the north of Evesham shows that such was not his expectation or intention; his object was to intercept de Montfort's march towards Kenilworth and prevent the junction of the two hostile armies; the project of surprising Simon senior in Evesham, as he had surprised Simon junior in Kenilworth, cannot have been his intention, else he would have marched with all speed direct for Evesham.

Prince Edward's army was divided into three columns: those of Richard de Clare, Earl of Gloucester, Roger Mortimer and himself.

The exact route taken by Edward to the Avon at Cleeve Prior is conjectural. Oman pictures Edward's column as hitting the Evesham-Alcester road at Dunnington, three miles south of Alcester, and we can accept this. But from this point onwards the whole course of the campaign and battle, both strategically and tactically, is hopelessly controversial. It is here that those two giants, Ramsay and

Oman, part company, and I must follow one of them. Though I respect Oman's scholarship, admire his military acument and insight, and revere his memory, I find myself bound here to reject his conclusions. The matter is so important yet so involved that I will deal with it in detail in a separate section at the end, in order not to make a big break in the narrative. The conclusions I have come to here agree broadly with Ramsay's, until the actual battlefield is reached. The narrative therefore continues as follows, but readers must remember that it is all highly conjectural.

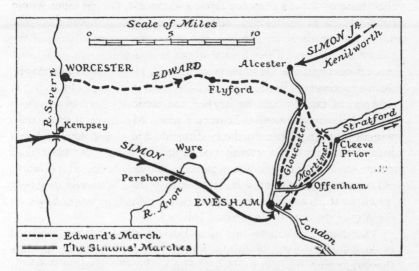

SKETCH-MAP 15. EVESHAM: THE APPROACH MARCHES

Finding no sign of movement of the enemy along the Alcester road, the Prince detached Gloucester to advance down the direct road to Evesham, while with the remainder of the army he continued on his march. He crossed the Avon by the ford at Cleeve, in the very early hours of the morning of September 4th, and reached Kenilworth via Stratford road at that place. Thus both roads between Evesham and Kenilworth were successfully cut. Still there was no sign of the enemy; so Edward did the obvious thing—he turned south and approached Evesham by the eastern bank of the river. This old road crossed the river just south of Offenham, two miles north of Evesham, (by an old bridge, the foundations of which are still visible.) Here he detached Mortimer to push still further south and block the Bengeworth bridge and London road, while he himself crossed the Offenham bridge and regained touch with Gloucester's column.

It was now fully light and hostile scouts spotted the column. Possibly as a decoy, Edward had the captured Kenilworth banners carried in the van. De Montfort's scouts, at first misled by these banners, approached to close quarters; then discovering their mistake they spurred back to town with the news of the enemy's approach.

Meanwhile, de Montfort's army was resting quietly in Evesham, all unaware of the net that was closing in on it. For the great loop of the Avon that almost surrounds the town left only a gap to the north 1,500 yards wide, and this gap was now practically blocked by Edward's army. There was a single bridge across the river, on the south-east side, leading to Bengeworth and London, and Mortimer was fast approaching this bridge.

Meanwhile an enterprising barber had climbed the abbey tower (loftier than the present Bell Tower), whence he had discerned the approach from the north of a thick column. The arrival of the scouts confirmed what had previously been in doubt, that it was indeed the enemy who was bearing down upon them in overwhelming strength.[1]

This news naturally startled de Montfort, who was expecting the appearance of his son from this very quarter. At about the same time

[1] The above is my interpretation of many conflicting stories. They have no essential bearing upon the course or upshot of the battle, but are significant as an illustration of the mass of contradictory accounts that the historian has to plough through and try to make sense of. These accounts state variously that the barber climbed the tower, once, twice, that Simon also climbed it, that he ascended a nearby hill, that the news was brought by scouts—at least five variations of the story. I think we can boil down these stories and state the matter thus. The approach of the hostile army was spotted both by scouts and by a watcher on the tower, but the former were at first misled by the banners at close quarters and the watchers on the tower merely could see the approach of a column, and when its great size became apparent, concluded that it must be the enemy. The story, as related in several of the accounts that the banners could be recognized from the tower, is ridiculous. The distance would be at least two miles. They were approaching from the north or north-east. The prevailing wind in August is towards the north or north-east. Thus they would float in the direction of the line of approach, while the speed of the march would enhance the tendency for them to float to the rear. Thus, whatever their size, they would fly parallel to the line of vision of the watchers on the tower, and could not be recognizable till they got within a few hundred yards of it, which they never did till the battle was over.

a fresh blow fell; another enemy column (Mortimer's) was seen approaching the only bridge over the Avon, on the south-east side of the town. Retreat was thus cut off in that direction, the river hemmed him in on the two flanks, and the main body of the enemy was bearing down upon him from the fourth side. The military perception of the old warrior interpreted the dreadful situation. 'May God have mercy on our souls, for our bodies are theirs!' he exclaimed.

He was indeed caught like a rat in a hole, and there was only one thing to do—what a rat does in such a case—to make a dash for it. His army was already arrayed, for he was about to start off on the road to Kenilworth, taking the unfortunate King Henry III with him. It was probably to the King that the delay in starting was due; for he had desired time for the celebration of mass. There may have been collusion with his son in this, or it may have been a genuine display of piety. The chroniclers give no clue whatever to this problem. But even an earlier start would not have affected the issue of the battle, though it might have affected its duration.

THE BATTLE

The ground slopes up gently from Evesham for $1\frac{1}{2}$ miles to a ridge called Green Hill (see Sketch-map 16). The spot where the Alcester road crosses the ridge is marked by cross-roads, and the modern Twyford House. The road to the left is the old Worcester road, along the top of the ridge, the lane to the right, now called Blayney's Lane drops down to the river, where a bridge used to carry it across.

It was on the ridge formed by Green Hill that Edward decided to draw up his army. We may picture him, on the arrival of his column at Offenham bridge, spurring eagerly up the hill to the cross-roads, whilst his army was crossing the bridge. Hereabouts he would find Gloucester in the act of forming up his column, covering the road.[1] Edward instructs him to extend his line to the right, from the road inclusive, thus making room for Edward's own column on the left. (It may here be noted that whilst Edward's column was visible from the abbey tower, while it was still on the far side of the river,[2] Gloucester's

[1] Colour is lent to this supposition by a statement in Tindall's *History of Evesham Abbey* (1794) that Edward held a war council under a thorn-bush on the road between the bridge and cross-roads.

[2] All this ground is visible from the present Bell Tower.

column was hidden from view until it reached the cross-roads. This explains the statement of Wykes that at first only Edward's column was visible, Gloucester's being hidden from view by a hill —Green Hill, obviously.

Prince Edward's object was to prevent the escape of the Earl and then to bring him to battle. It was therefore necessary to ensure that de Montfort could not slip past either flank. This could only be done by forming a somewhat extended line at the outset, for the width of the gap between the two branches of the river through Green Hill approached 2,000 yards. Unfortunately we have no reliable statement as to the actual strengths of the two sides. Judging by the reports of the casualties in de Montfort's army it must have been at least 5,000 strong. In that case Edward's and Gloucester's columns may have been near 10,000. If so, a distance of 800 yards would have been a convenient frontage. Th s would leave a gap of 500–600 yards on each flank. The line may have been extended initially to cover this whole front, (as Oman suggests) or these gaps may have been merely picquetted, and the army ordered to be prepared to sideslip to either flank if necessary.

It was not necessary. De Montfort's experienced eye told him at a glance that escape without a fight was impossible. Orders had already been issued to march out up the Alcester road, and he let them stand. He had decided on novel battle tactics. In that age it was the almost universal practice, when two armies engaged in battle, to draw up the respective arrays in opposite and parallel lines. The Earl himself had done so at Lewes in the previous year. But now he introduced a novelty. Probably guessing that Edward had unduly extended his frontage in order to cover the whole of the 2,000 yards gap, he resolved to concentrate his whole army on a narrow front and attempt to drive a wedge through the centre of the hostile line. To achieve this he drew up his army in compact formation on a narrow front, cavalry leading, then English infantry, with the Welsh infantry in the rear. Oman computes that the frontage was 50 to 60 horsemen. I will not quarrel with this figure, though it may err on the small side. If we give the frontage as 150 to 200 yards we shall not be far out.[1] The route was up the road, or slightly to the left of it. The Royalist army was drawn up just in front of the cross-road, on the crest of the ridge

---

[1] T. Wykes says that Simon *formed* his army in a circle (*in forma circulari suum inglouveravit exercitum*) but it is more likely that he was eventually *forced into* this formation by the action of his enemies.

(Sketch-map 16). When the Baronial army reached the top of the rise (700 yards beyond the modern railway), the hostile army broke into full view at a distance of 600 yards. Along the whole ridge appeared a serried mass of defenders. The spectacle must have been an unnerving one. The time was about 9 o'clock; the heavens were black with clouds and presently a tremendous thunderstorm broke though there was little rain. The poor King was placed by

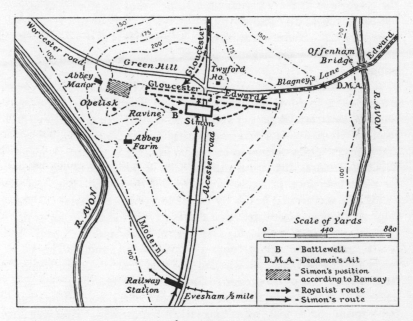

SKETCH-MAP 16.　EVESHAM: THE BATTLE

de Montfort in the midst of the army, in armour and helmeted, so that he was practically unrecognizable.

All the accounts of the battle that ensued are brief. Most are taken up with relating the words of the Earl of Leicester, who seems to have been somewhat loquacious. But it is legitimate to inquire who was the nearby scribe who took them down. The Earl himself did not survive the battle. His companions were all but exterminated. Possibly his son, Guy, may have overheard a sentence or two and afterwards related it to some monkish chronicler. But as he afterwards fled the country his opportunities cannot have been great. On the other hand, most of the chroniclers were anxious to apotheosize the earl, and would be tempted to put into his mouth ennobling sentiments, such as his behest to his companions to save themselves. We can safely ignore all of them except the one I have already quoted, as showing the military insight possessed by this veteran warrior.[1]

De Montfort's troops were in a trap, and they knew it. Such knowledge is not conducive to high morale, and the morale of the Baronial army sank so low that a large part of the Welsh foot fled at the very outset of the engagement. Some swam the river, and were pursued as far as Tewkesbury by Mortimer's army, which was well posted for that service. It was the only one that it performed in the battle, apart from the negative one of preventing escape across the bridge.

The course of the battle, though it is said to have lasted two hours, is soon told. De Montfort's battle-arm tactics seemed at first to be successful. He struck Gloucester's column so fiercely that it momentarily recoiled. It may be (as I have hinted) that it was unduly extended, and that Gloucester was obliged to reduce its frontage at the last moment. What is certain is that it was pushed back at the point of the blow, for a short distance, probably to the line of the road.[2] But then it rallied. It was assisted in this by the action of the two wings. The ridge was bare and cultivated, thus the exact size and formation of the baronial army was visible in all its narrowness and weakness. It was a case of 'line versus column', and the line won. The two wings pushed forward and wheeled inwards, that of Edward along level ground, that of Gloucester rushing downhill into the ravine that descends to the Avon on the west. The head of this ravine is marked by a spring or a well, now known as Battle-well. This well is 130 yards to the west of the main road, and 200 yards short of the cross-roads.

De Montfort's doomed army was thus first outflanked, then encircled, and finally completely surrounded by its opponents. There was nothing for it but to die fighting, for quarter was not granted by the infuriated Royalists, who had grudges to repay, and there was by this time no hope of escape. No wonder Robert of Gloucester, in one of the earliest poems in the English tongue, calls it a 'mordre' (murder). Old Simon died fighting, as did one of his sons; Guy fell severely wounded; all of his knights save three seem to have been killed.

---

[1] His age is unknown, but is computed at about sixty-four years.

[2] Dr. Richard Pococke stated, in 1757: 'They say the battle was in the road and in UPTON (Offenham) Lane.'

Fugitives towards Offenham were cut down in numbers just short of the bridge, and the spot is still known as Dead Men's Ait.[1]

Henry the King narrowly escaped death, but he managed to gasp out: 'I am Henry of Winchester, your King!'[2] The battle was over; and so was the Barons' War.

COMMENTS

What are we to say about this amazing battle, fought in a raging thunderstorm? Robert of Gloucester, who lived the nearest of any scribe to the battlefield, and himself trembled during the storm, seems to come nearest the truth when he writes (as recorded above): 'Such was the murder of Evesham, for battle it was not.' But if there was no battle worthy of the name, there was a campaign in every respect worthy of that name. I entirely endorse Oman's high praise of Edward's strategy during those brief five days. It probably excelled that five days' campaign of another Edward in an adjoining county just 200 years later. How he managed to accomplish three long night marches in four days and fight a battle at the end of them it is difficult to say. It is a great pity that the old chroniclers pass over in almost complete silence the logistics of military campaigns. We would give a good deal to know just how many wagons, how many pack-horses, what forage, what ammunition were taken, what was the number and state of the roads, the bridges, the fords, etc. Without this information it is hard to assess the extent to which personal driving power on the part of the commander was responsible for the success. It seems, however, reasonable to suppose that in this case the personality of the young commander was a big factor in accomplishing the result. Endowed with a remarkable stature and physique, Edward was 'every inch a prince', and his troops probably followed him devotedly. After his escape from captivity he was probably invested with a romantic glamour, such as attached itself to Bonnie Prince Charlie. Moreover, the early phase of his campaign west of the Severn had gone in his favour, and the morale of his troops would be correspondingly raised thereby. The conclusion seems pretty clear that it was the leadership and strategy of the commander more than anything else that brought victory to the Royalist arms.

[1] Tindall, in 1794, reports bones being dug up there.

[2] This episode is depicted on the battle obelisk.

What are we to say of Simon, Earl of Leicester? This French-man had come to England 35 years before, already possessed of a high military reputation. This he had enhanced, notably at the battle of Lewes. Yet it is difficult to descry any military genius in his conduct of this campaign. Possibly he was grown too old; possibly he had bad councillors; possibly he was handicapped, in some way we know not, by the King. But the fact is that his movements were character-ized by slowness and almost inertia. On August 2nd he was crossing the Severn whilst Edward was returning with a dog-tired army in the opposite direction. The coast was clear; he could make a dash either for London or for Kenilworth; yet we see him 48 hours later, only 14 miles further on his road. Nor was his son, Simon junior, much more rapid in his movements, though here the data is too flimsy to be positive. It looks, however, as if the Simons, father and son, were lacking in true military genius.

PROBLEMS OF THE BATTLE

I.—OMAN'S RECONSTRUCTION

According to Sir Charles Oman, Edward's army departed from Worcester in three columns: his own via Flyford and Dunnington, thence due south to Evesham; Gloucester via Wyre and Chadbury, approaching the town from the north-west; Mortimer via Pershore, round the south bend of the Avon to Bengeworth Bridge. If these dispositions are correct they present a most interesting strategical operation—based on exterior lines, such as had never previously been seen so clearly in English history. I wish I could believe it happened. But an examination of Sir Charles's reasons for it do not carry con-viction. Before proceeding to this examination we must consider Oman's assertion that Edward did not cross the river at Cleeve, but marched due south from Dunnington. In the first place his thesis has to reject the testimony of Rishanger (supported by Trivet) that he crossed a river at 'Clineman' or 'Clive viam', usually identified with Cleeve. This is the more surprising in that Oman admits that it was his primary object to cut the Cleeve road. The reasons for his rejection of Rishanger's statement are two-fold: first, that there is no mention of the re-crossing which must have been necessary if Edward attacked from the north of the town; second, that his re-crossing at Offenham would have been spotted by some of Simon's troops.

As for the first, an 'argument from silence' is not impressive, for none of the chroniclers seem to have been present, and all seem to have been vague as to geographical conditions. Rishanger is the only one who even mentions a river.

As for the second reason, again silence does not imply that the approach was *not* spotted. The column first seen from the abbey tower was thought to be that of Simon junior. As we have seen, the reason for this cannot have been that they recognized the banners at a distance of about three miles, but that the column was approaching by the most direct road from Stratford. Actually Simon junior was approaching via Alcester, but he halted at that town to feed, and does not seem to have proceeded further; but if de Montfort was expecting his son's approach by the direct Stratford-Offenham road he would be likely at first to mistake Edward's army for that of Simon. As for Oman's objection that Mortimer's approach to Bengeworth would be seen, no doubt it was: but the distance from Offenham bridge was only 1½ miles, and Montfort would not have time to issue orders and cross the bridge before Mortimer blocked it.

Let us now examine Oman's conception of the approach by the three widely-separated roads. This is based on a passage in Hemmingburgh's Chronicle which, translated, reads:

'. . . He advanced towards Evesham, and having formed his army into three columns, he came (there), himself with his own column from one direction, Count Gloucester from another, and Roger de Mortimer from the west and from behind.'

This passage implies that, setting out in one body, Edward and Gloucester approached by separate columns from the north, and Mortimer from the rear, i.e. from the south. It is generally agreed that the latter attacked the Bengeworth bridge, thus blocking de Montfort's escape to the south. So far I agree with Oman. But he maintains that the words *ab occidente* must indicate that Mortimer took the Pershore road. Now if Hemmingburgh showed any knowledge of the lie of the land there would be some force in this. But he shows no indication of such knowledge. He does not even seem aware of the big effect of the narrow bend in the river, or even of the existence of the river, and he speaks vaguely of Edward approaching from one direction and Gloucester from another. Exact directions and distances meant nothing to this monk, writing in his abbey in Yorkshire, without the help of even the roughest map. He merely set down what he had heard by word of mouth from some first- or second-hand

witness.   He grasped and recorded the essentials, namely the attack by
two columns from the front and one from the rear, but by a slip he
wrote *occidente* for *oriente*.   That at least seems more likely to me than
that Edward should have adopted the remarkable manœuvre favoured
by Oman.   For, consider its implications, and judge then by the criterion of Inherent Military Probability.

According to this thesis, Edward's army split up from the outset,
and marches by three widely-diverging routes, one via Dunnington
21 miles, one via Wyre 14 miles, and one via Pershore 16 miles;
the first two being separated by as much as six miles, and the last two
by as much as three miles and a river.   It is difficult to understand how
Oman can claim that 'they are sufficiently close to leave no danger
of the two columns getting out of touch with each other', especially
when we remember that much of the march must have been done in
the night.

It is just this early separation that makes such a disposition unlikely.
A prudent general does not separate his forces beyond the pitch that
they can be concentrated in time for the fight.   But could Edward
be sure of this?   Yes, if we assume that Simon was at Evesham and
intended to *remain there for the time being*.   But how could Edward
assume this?   It is not even clear that he was aware of his opponent's
exact location at the moment when he started on his march; and he
would have looked foolish, and have been dubbed a mediocre commander, had he set a snare round the town of Evesham in this manner
only to find that 'the bird had flown', and that the two Simons were
joining forces in the Stratford area.   As a matter of fact, the earl was
on the point of setting off when his rival approached; a few hours'
delay on Edward's part would have resulted in a battle somewhere
near Cleeve.   Edward would then, according to Oman's thesis, have
had to fight certainly without the help of Mortimer's column, and
possibly without Gloucester's either.   Oman maintains that he could
well have done this, as he was three and a half times superior in
numbers.   But this statement of the *Melrose Chronicle* is not supported
by any other, though most of them emphasize the big disparity in
numbers between the two sides.   As most of the chroniclers favoured
de Montfort, this assertion must be discounted.   In any case Edward is
unlikely to have been in possession of accurate information as to the
number of troops that de Montfort had brought with him from Hereford, and therefore would not needlessly disperse his forces before he
had ascertained the approximate strength and position of his opponents.

There is a further objection to this extended application of exterior lines by the Prince. Such an operation, to be successful, demands good communications between the various separated columns. Such communication and co-operation between three columns that had not seen each other since setting out from Worcester, and which (marching in the dark) were separated by several miles of country would be abnormal, if not impossible in those days. Either column might easily find itself confronted by the Earl's whole army, and that experienced war leader, with the prestige of Lewes still fresh upon him, would have been quick to take advantage of it. Thus we come to the conclusion, on the grounds of Inherent Military Probability, that Oman's reconstruction is unlikely to be the right one.

If it be objected that my reconstruction makes Edward separate his own and Gloucester's columns by about two miles after passing Dunnington, the risk here was less than in the other case, for the distance was less, the period of separation was less, and for most of the way the two columns must have been in view, once day had dawned. Moreover it is difficult to see what else Edward could have done. Oman himself admits that the Cleeve road was the one 'which the Earl was the more likely to adopt',[1] and that it was important for Edward to block both roads. At the moment that the Prince reached Dunnington he could not know by which road, if any, de Montfort would march; therefore he approached the town by both.

As for separating Mortimer's column from his own near Offenham, that was only at the last moment when he must have become aware that the Earl was still in Evesham and when it was at length possible, for the first time, to evolve a detailed plan to circumvent him. Even so, the separation of the columns did not exceed two miles.

II.—RAMSAY'S SITING OF THE FIELD

Sir James Ramsay sites the battle in the grounds of Abbey Manor, as shown in Sketch-map 16. He explains it thus: 'Simon had only managed to reach a jutting spur or promontory, abutting on the cross-road where Edward was arrayed, but not the road itself. This jutting spur, the battlefield pointed out by local tradition, and identified by an obelisk, presents a little plateau, some 300 yards long and 200 yards wide, protected on flanks and rear by steep slopes, a fairly defensive position to withstand attack, but not one to offer much hope

---

[1] *Transactions of the Bristol and Gloucester Archæological Society*, 1909, p. 72.

of escape in case of defeat. Here the Earl drew up his forlorn band. . . .'[1]

Ramsay does not give any authority for this site, apart from 'local tradition' and the presence of the obelisk. There is in fact no suggestion in any chronicle that Simon took up such a position on a promontory, or indeed that he took up a defensive position at all. It is implicit in nearly all the accounts that he took the initiative and made a desperate attack, as described in my account. Nor does Ramsay indicate the source of the 'local tradition'. I cannot trace any such tradition anterior to the erection of the obelisk by Mr. E. J. Rudge in 1845.

On the contrary, a local tradition that Simon fell at Battlewell can be traced much further back—indeed almost to contemporary sources. George May, in the second edition (1845) of his *History of Evesham Abbey*, refers it to MS. *Cotton. Cleopatra* A1, folio 109 (which I have not checked) where it is stated that on the spot where Simon fell a fountain was erected, and that it is sometimes called 'The Earl's Well'. This is now known as Battlewell. It now consists of an open pit about 12 feet long by 6 feet wide. At one time there was a ring of trees round it, the well was bricked in and surmounted by a roof. Many miraculous cures are recorded as having taken place to persons bathing in the water.[2] Relics have been dug up near the well and there can be little doubt that it was the scene of some of the heaviest fighting.

There is admittedly now a local belief that the obelisk marks the spot where de Montfort fell, and Ramsay accords it his imprimatur, but the inscription on it does not claim this. It merely states that the battle was fought 'here'. What does it mean by 'here'? The obelisk is only 450 yards from Battlewell, where I locate the centre of the battle. The obelisk might therefore easily be within the confines of the battle without marking its precise centre. As a matter of fact, it is so symmetrically placed on the centre of the promontory, so nicely calculated to command a wide view (though latterly obscured

---

[1] *Dawn of the Constitution*, p. 245.

[2] It is easy for the visitor to miss the well, as there is nothing to indicate it. On my first visit to the field I failed to discover it at all. It is as shown on Sketch-map 16, 130 yards to the left of the Alcester road and 200 yards short of the cross-roads. A small portion of the wall of the well can still be detected, but the whole place was in a shameful state of delapidation when I last visited it, and there was nothing to mark this famous and once hallowed spot.

by trees) that I make no doubt Mr. Rudge selected that precise spot with such a purpose in view.

Let us now check Ramsay's site by the test of Inherent Military Probability. It will be noted that, according to Sir James, Simon started out on the left of the road with the intention of establishing himself on the cross-roads. But finding that he was forestalled he must have inclined to his left, and marched diagonally across the front of his opponent who was in position only a few hundred yards away. He then dipped into the ravine and climbed the steep slope out of it on to the summit of the promontory, still in view of the enemy, who were in position (as Ramsay elsewhere tells us) at the lodge gates of the Abbey Manor, i.e. only 100 yards away. Now it is hard to conceive that Edward would be so supine as to allow his adversary unopposed to establish himself on such a position; nor is it easy to see why de Montfort should attempt to do so. He could hardly expect to succeed against such an enterprising opponent as he knew from experience Prince Edward to be. His whole object—a sound one—was to try and cut his way out, not to sit down and allow a superior force to chew him up at its leisure. In short, Ramsay's thesis does not stand the test of I.M.P.

CHAPTER XV

The Battle of Neville's Cross, 17 October 1346

THE battle of Neville's Cross was fought on 17 October 1346. A battle with such an alluring name as this may be expected to possess some romantic details. It does. Fought within one mile of the city of Durham, and sometimes indeed known as the battle of Durham, it has close associations with that ancient city. Indeed the battle has almost as close a connexion with ecclesiastical history as the Battle of the Standard, fought just two centuries before and under very similar circumstances. In each case something resembling a sacred crusade to oust the barbarous invader was proclaimed; in each case a sacred banner was carried and set up on the field of battle by the church dignitaries; in each case clerics took an active part in the battle; in each case a Scottish king, taking advantage of the absence abroad or the preoccupation of the English king, crossed the Border with the intention of making trouble, and finally in each case the attempt ended in disaster complete and irretrievable.

It is exasperating that we have such scanty details of this important battle, the most considerable ever fought in County Durham; and that the evidence, such as it is, is so conflicting. This, however, is but normal in medieval battles, and it is possible to reconstruct a fairly plausible and rational account. The task is not rendered the easier by the fact that no serious attempt has ever been made to construct a map, or to give the respective positions of the two armies, with any degree of precision.

PRELIMINARY MOVEMENTS

On 26 August 1346 the King of France was defeated by the English army at Crèçy. In his distress he turned to his ally David II of Scotland, begging him to create a diversion across the Border into England. To this the twenty-three-year-old King of Scotland was not averse. Collecting what by all accounts must have been a very large army, he crossed the Cumberland border early in October. Laying waste various strongholds, and the famous abbey of Lanercost, he worked his way towards Durham, reaching the vicinity of that city on 16 October. In the pleasant park of Beaurepaire (now Bearpark) he halted, and pitched his tents and pavilions. He then sent out plundering parties in all directions, little suspecting that a hostile army was already in the neighbourhood. He then settled down to enjoy his easily won success. His troops, according to Andrew of Wyntoun, 'made them great mirth'.

Meanwhile the city of Durham, momentarily expecting to be attacked, was verging on panic. It seems strange that the Scottish King did not attempt to win so great a prize. Possibly he was aware of its great natural strength and that it had never been captured by assault through its recorded history; possibly he believed that time was on his side, and that he was awaiting siege engines before summoning the city to surrender. The last thing that he can have supposed was that a considerable army could have been raised in such a short time to oppose him; was not the English King besieging Calais, calling almost daily for more reinforcements? England must be quite denuded of troops. The ball was at his feet. There was no need for haste.

Let us now cross to the 'other side of the hill'. In the absence of the King, the task of defending the Scottish Border fell normally upon the Prince Bishop of Durham. Unfortunately Bishop Hatfield of Durham was at that time in France with the King. It is unfortunate in one sense only, for had he been present in his see we should not now possess the report on the battle written to him by his prior Fossor (or Forcer)— the best account of the battle that exists. In the absence of the Bishop, the Archbishop of York took his place. Assisted by the northern barons, notably Ralph Neville and Henry Percy (and probably Edward Balliol, the ex-king of Scotland), he summoned an army from all the shires north of the Trent to assemble at Bishop Auckland. The response was astonishingly prompt, with the result that at the moment when King David was serenely settling down to enjoy life at Bearpark, an English army of comparable size to his own was assembling only 8 miles to the south.

I have described this army as 'of comparable size', deliberately employing a vague term; for it is as impossible here as in any battle of the time to assess the strength of either army with any exactitude. The sources themselves vary widely in their figures, but they are in agreement that the Scottish army was superior in numbers. The most precise and reliable figure we possess for the English host is the number of the archers, of whom Lancashire provided 1,200. If other northern shires acted on the same scale, the total strength of the army could easily have reached 15,000. I will tentatively accept this figure, putting the Scots at somewhere in the region of 20,000. Froissart asserts that both armies were well ordered, and we may certainly accept this statement in the case of the Scottish army, which had had ample time to assemble and shake together.

On 17 October the English army resumed its advance. Evidently getting news of an intended Scottish raid on Darlington, they took a route somewhat to the right of the direct line to Durham. The result was that at Merrington, 3 miles north-east of Bishop Auckland, the van ran into a raiding party commanded by Sir William Douglas. It put the Scots to flight, and a running fight ensued as far as Sunderland Bridge, only 3 miles south of Durham. Douglas managed to escape and to warn David of the proximity of the foe. On the purblind and conceited monarch this information made little impression, and a suggestion that the army should beat a retreat was received by him with contumely.

Meanwhile the English army, heartened by this opening encounter, pushed forward with speed. The army contained a large force of 'hobilars' or mounted infantry. By means of these it was possible to keep in touch with the retreating enemy and to discover the position of the Scottish camp. On passing Sunderland Bridge therefore, an important decision had to be made—whether to march on straight to the relief of the threatened garrison of Durham, or whether to seek out the Scottish army and engage it in battle. No doubt a council of war was held and the latter course was decided on. Thus it happened that at some hour before noon the English army ascended the hill leading due north from Sunderland Bridge, and after covering 2 miles found themselves on the ridge-top, and in sight of Bearpark. The spot they had reached was marked by one of the several ancient crosses which girdled the city; this one was known as Neville's Cross. It was a pure coincidence that it bore the name of the leading soldier on the English side; but if Ralph Neville was aware of its name at the time it might have seemed to him a good omen, and been an inducement to take up a position there. Be that as it may, from this vantage point the Scottish army could be descried advancing from the direction of Bearpark. With or without a council of war, Lord Neville (for we must consider him the commander in the field) decided to occupy a defensive position. In order to discover the reasons for his dispositions we must now examine the ground.

THE TERRAIN

Those who are unfamiliar with the ground but who have read some account of the battle will probably be surprised, as I was, to find that it is a very hilly and intricate locality; the French word *accidenté* expresses it well. From the city of Durham the ground rises sharply for nearly 200 feet, on to an irregular-shaped ridge with numerous promontories. This ridge runs roughly north–south, with an average breadth of 500 yards. It is known as the Red Hill, and on this ridge the battle was fought. The first thing that strikes one, when one remembers the great numbers of troops engaged, is the narrowness of this ridge. The next surprising point is that there is no mention in any of the accounts either of the ridge or of the ravine-like valley of the little river Browney to the west of it. Yet this river must have had its effect on the battle.

Standing by the side of Neville's Cross, Lord Neville could note both these features.[1] The steep bluff on the eastern edge of the ridge would clearly mark the eastern flank of the battlefield and the river valley the left. By siting his line 300 yards in front of the cross and resting his two flanks as above indicated, Neville could form up on a frontage of almost exactly 1,000 yards (just the same frontage as adopted by the English at Poitiers ten years later).

The ground slopes down gently to the front, not so steeply as to induce the enemy to shun battle, but steep enough to make their advance slow. Thus Neville's archers, armed with the now formidable long bow, would have full scope for their business, and the front rank at the outset was probably composed almost entirely of archers. There did not appear to be much scope for mounted cavalry owing to the cramped nature of the flanks, and some people have supposed that the English retained no mounted men. The only reason for rejecting the positive statement of the chroniclers is the negative one that it was against the custom of the English to use them. This is not a strong enough argument, especially as we have very little reliable evidence as to how battles were fought in those days; it is, I think, likely that in all our battles we retained at least a small force of mounted men-at-arms. If cavalry could not be usefully employed at the beginning of the battle their opportunity might come later. Neville therefore placed them behind the centre of the line in reserve—probably just behind Neville's Cross. The line taken up by the English is very easily found for it crosses the railway embankment where it is crossed by the by-pass road. The right flank rested on the end of the spur and the left flank on the edge of the river bluff just to the north of Quarry House (see sketch-map). It formed as strong a position as could be wished for. The frontage

---

[1] Unfortunately the ground near the cross is now built over and it is necessary to move northwards 300 yards to the railway cutting to obtain a good view.

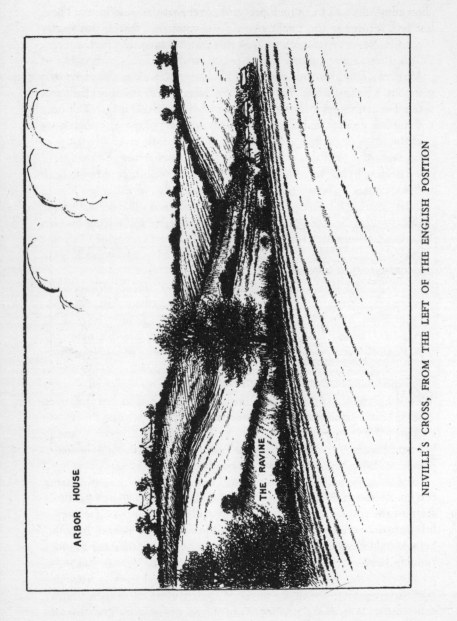

ARBOR HOUSE

THE RAVINE

NEVILLE'S CROSS, FROM THE LEFT OF THE ENGLISH POSITION

allowed of some 12 to 15 men per yard, a very satisfactory figure. The line was formed in the customary three divisions or wards, Percy on the right, Neville in the centre, with the Archbishop and Sir Thomas Rokeby on the left.

Meanwhile the Scottish army was slowly lumbering forward, with complete self-confidence, for David could not bring himself to believe that a big army could have been raised against him. On approaching the English position it became necessary to deploy for battle. But on

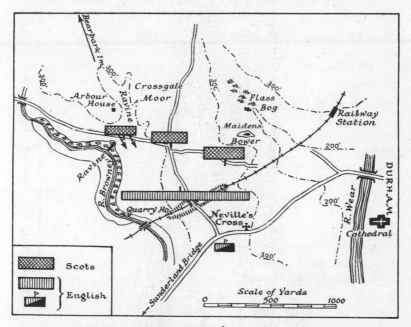

SKETCH-MAP 17.   NEVILLE'S CROSS: THE BATTLE

reaching Crossgate Moor, the ground became difficult, as an examination of the contours on the sketch-map will show. Whereas the English were drawn up on a ridge 1,000 yards in width, the ground that the Scots would have to occupy was cut in two by a deep valley or ravine running between Crossgate Moor and Arbour House. It was thus impossible to form a continuous line facing the enemy, and it became necessary to place the right division, led by Sir William Douglas, to the right of the ravine and the other two divisions to the left of it. Even so the three divisions must have found themselves in echelon, with appreciable gaps between them. But the trouble did not end there. Though

Douglas's division formed up on a forward slope, the right portion of his line had in its front a small but steep ravine running down to the river. The effect of this ravine we shall shortly see. King David commanded the centre division and Robert Steward the left.

*   *   *   *   *

Before describing the battle we must briefly refer to the activities of the monks. The patron saint of the city was St. Cuthbert, whose relics were jealously preserved and honoured. As we have already seen, this campaign against the ravaging Northerners was regarded almost as a sacred crusade. Had not the invaders plundered the revered monastery of Lanercost, apart from their other ravages and killings? The .Archbishop was himself in the field; the lesser brethren must also do their part. What this would be is clear. They would invoke the support of their Saint. As the two armies drew near each other, the extraordinary spectacle could be seen of a procession of priests from the cathedral to a hillock in the no-man's-land between the two armies known as Maiden's Bower, carrying with them the sacred corporas cloth of St. Cuthbert held aloft on the point of a spear. Planted on the little hillock that forms the Maiden's Bower, this cloth acted as a holy standard. Round it therefore they clustered, kneeling in prayer, while the two armies drew near. Eventually they found themselves well in the Scottish area. Yet such was their exalted demeanour that they were left unmolested. Another party of clerics ascended the cathedral tower. Tradition avers that the party at the Bower were also engaged in the more mundane task of signalling to the party on the tower the latest news of the progress of the fight.[1] Unfortunately for tradition in this case, the party on the tower were better placed to see how the battle was going than the party in the hollow occupied by the tower.

THE BATTLE

Amid the usual welter of contradictory stories there is little to be gathered for certain regarding the course of the battle. The lie of the ground, applied to these various stories, does however seem to indicate pretty well what happened. It seems then that the opening move was made by the Scottish right wing. Being the vanguard they would be

[1] The tower was lower than it is now, but even so the bower would be in full view.

formed up before the other two divisions, and no doubt they exhibited impatience to begin the fight. Unfortunately, as they reached the foot of the slope their right wing encountered the before-mentioned small ravine, which they would find it difficult to cross.[1] The natural result was that they swerved to their left, thus crowding on top of their neighbours on the left of the line. The English bowmen were quick to take advantage of the resulting congestion and confusion. Pouring in their shafts with the speed and precision which had recently made the English archers famous, they exacted a heavy toll, and as the Scots struggled slowly and painfully up the slope in front of the English position, the casualty list rapidly rose. When eventually the two lines of spearmen got to grips, the slope of the ground favoured the English and the Scottish attack was held up.

The Scottish centre, under the eyes of the King himself, engaged upon more favourable ground, and obtained an initial advantage. A portion of the English line had been thrown into temporary disorder by an impetuous mounted charge by a Scottish lord on his own initiative, and the left division of Robert the High Steward had a style more pronounced success. How far the English in this part of the field were driven back cannot be precisely ascertained. But it matters not; all the ground on the top of the ridge was flat, suitable for a cavalry charge. This was the opportunity for which the cavalry had been so wisely held in reserve. Sweeping forward into the now disordered ranks of the attacking Scots, they pressed back the foremost elements. All battles have their critical moment, and that of Neville's Cross was come. If King David could counter promptly by swinging a portion of his own division to their left; if the High Steward could support his advanced troops from his own reserve, the hostile cavalry would be snuffed out. But neither of these things happened. David was doubtless absorbed in his own portion of the battle, and Robert did nothing. He was afterwards suspected of treachery; but the simplest explanation is that, as the King's nephew, he was next in succession to the throne (he afterwards became Robert II), and seeing what looked to him like a Scottish disaster, he reflected that if David were defeated and slain or captured, it would be well for the country that he himself should get safe back to Scotland. At all events he did nothing to stop the rot, and presumably abandoned the field. The rot did not stop; it spread. Neville put in the remainder of his mounted troops all along the line; Rokeby's

[1] This is my interpretation of the chronicler's statement that the ground on this flank was difficult and enclosed (see Sketch-map).

division on the left sprang to the attack and Douglas's division after a brief struggle broke and fled.

But the Scottish centre, fired by the example of its young King, stood firm. Thus it happened that the two English wings, finding opposition vanishing on their own particular fronts, very rightly swung inwards and attacked the Scottish centre. If my conception of the battle is correct, the King's last stand took place on the present by-pass road, a few hundred yards north of the railway cutting. It was the last phase of the battle. How long it continued it is impossible to say, but if, as seems likely, the battle lasted nearly three hours, we can allot fully half that time to the dogged stand made by the King of Scotland and his division. But there could be no doubt as to the upshot. Fresh troops under Lord Lucy were hastening to the battlefield on the English side, while none came to the relief of King David. At last, seeing that there was no hope left, the Scottish King managed to slip away, wounded and unarmed, only to be captured shortly after quitting the field. There are varying stories regarding his capture, as is normal in such cases. Perhaps the most likely is the tradition that he was captured under the bridge which still stands over the Browney to the west of Arbour House. Taken in triumph to London, he languished in the Tower for some years.

Next year Percy invaded Scotland with a small avenging army. Little resistance was put up and large tracts of the country were ceded to England. As Professor Tout remarks: 'In thus playing the game of the French King, David began a policy which, from Neville's Cross to Flodden, brought embarrassment to England and desolation to Scotland. It was the inevitable penalty of two independent and hostile states existing on one little island.'

We can ascribe this remarkable victory to three main causes: better leadership and choice of ground on the part of the English commanders; the power of the long bow; and the high morale of the English army, stimulated by the recent victories in France, and brought to red heat by the fervour and ardour of the monks.

PROBLEMS OF THE BATTLEFIELD

Considering that the battle took place so close to the city walls of Durham, one might expect that the ground would now be almost completely built over. It is a pleasant surprise to find that this is not so,[1] and

[1] Maiden's Bower, only 1,200 yards from the cathedral, is still in what appears to be the heart of the country.

that though the face of the country has changed greatly, the contours of the ground remain the same, and the general lie of the land can be picked out, if not from one spot, then from another. This is important, for Neville's Cross, like almost all medieval battles, suffers from an absence of exact statements as to the topography of the field.

There is of course ample evidence that the battle took place on the ridge to the west of the city. But almost any point on this ridge from near Bearpark to the cross ridge just south of Neville's Cross could be reconciled with the statements of the chroniclers. It is here that the process of reasoning on the grounds of Inherent Military Probability, combined with an approach to the position in the steps of the commander, can be of help. Lord Neville must have marched up the road to Neville's Cross from the south. From there he must have seen the ground much as we now see it from the railway cutting only 300 yards further forward. He must have known of, and indeed seen the approach of the enemy. The rest seems simple. The ground offered him an obvious position: a forward sloping front, firm flanks, a convenient width, a position abreast of the town that he had come to help. The more one studies it, the more does the position almost clamour to be occupied.

But reasoning in accordance with I.M.P. is not by itself enough. We must examine all the references to the battle and decide if any of them which appear to be reliable run counter to our solution. The only passage that I have queried is the statement that the ground on the west was difficult owing to being enclosed with fences and ditches; I have considered that the presence of the small ravine is sufficient to account for this (without denying that there may in addition have been some fences, &c.). I claim to find further corroboration for my siting in a statement regarding the Maiden's Bower. It is usually represented as being situated between the two armies (a most inconvenient place in which to hold a prayer meeting). But I place it definitely behind the Scottish line.[1] If it can be shown that this is correct, it obviously rules out the possibility that the line of battle ran further north than I place it. Now the following passage quoted by Surtees from Davies in his *History of Durham* (I, p. 50, note) seems to indicate that the Bower *was* behind the Scots line: 'A great number and multitude of Scots running and passing by them with intent to have spoiled them yet they had no power . . .'

It is difficult to be positive about the exact formation of either army.

[1] That is, once the two armies had engaged.

Contemporary writers do not trouble to describe what is common knowledge to those living at the time. Both sides possessed a number of 'hobilars' who are described in England as a form of mounted infantry, but in Scotland as ill-trained country bumpkins. In any case what happened to their horses in battle? It has been asserted that they merely let them loose, but this seems hard to credit. I have shown the English line, for simplicity, as continuous. But doubtless there were intervals between the divisions, but of what extent it is quite impossible to say. Assuming as I have done that the archers formed the front line at the outset, there must have been intervals left for them to pass through to the rear immediately before the spearmen became engaged. Each Scottish division consisted of three 'schiltrons' and it is reasonable to suppose that, owing to the narrow frontage imposed upon the Scottish army, these schiltrons formed up in column, one behind the other. This helps to explain Robert's action—or lack of it. The initial success was won by his leading schiltron. When that was eventually forced back, or broken through, Robert led his two rear schiltrons off the field. On the other flank, Douglas's rear schiltrons would be huddled in the narrow valley between Arbour House and Crossgate Moor. It is possible that these, or some of them, also left the field when the English cavalry attacks began.

As for these cavalry attacks, most historians slur over them, if they do not deny them altogether. I claim support for the line I take in a source that I believe has never been printed, so I transcribe here the relevant passage. It is found in *MSS. Bodley* 302 ff. 142–3 and *Ashmole* 789 f. 160.[1] It takes the form of a circular letter apparently contemporary, describing the battle, written by one Thomas Samson to his friends. The passage runs thus: 'Et sassemblerent e combatierent bien e trop longement de lhoure de noen tantq al hour de vespres avant que les enemis finirent pleynement desconfits en la bataille. Deux fois se retrairent les archers e comunes de nostre partie, mais nos gents darmes se combatierent e se continuerent durment bien tantq les archers e comunes reassemblerent Et dieu, par sa grace e virtue nos dona la victoire . . .' The implication seems to be that a reinforcement of mounted troops came up and restored the situation. It is from the same source that we learn of the tardy arrival of the English reinforcements under Lord Lucy with 'grant nombre de gens darmes'. The whole letter deserves printing.

[1] As they differ slightly they have been transcribed and combined for me by Miss Borough of the Bodleian Library.

Finally, a word about Neville's Cross. It is now agreed that a cross of that name existed before the battle, which was fought 'apud Neviles Croys'. Now Lord Neville must have made his command post well within bow-shot of this old cross, and the fact that it bore his name must have been an additional inducement to him to select that spot to erect his own memorial to his victory. The cross he erected was destroyed in 1589 by 'some lewde and contemptuous wicked persons'. All that remains now is the socket with an old milestone where the cross had been. A few years ago this was moved a few yards to allow of road widening, but it is still visible by the roadside—a venerable object indeed.

CHAPTER XVI

The Battle of Otterburn, 19 August 1388

'KNIGHTES and squyers were of good courage on both parties to fyghte valiauntly, cowards there had no place, but hardyness rayned with feates of armes. There the Scottes showed great hardynesse, and foughte meryly with great desyre of honour; the Englysshe men were three to one. Howbeit I say not but Englishemen dyd nobly acquiyte themselfe, for ever the Englysshemen had rather ben slayne or taken in the place than flye.'

This passage from Froissart, in Berner's matchless translation, explains in part the widespread fame that this battle has acquired. But in part only; for never was battle fought on English soil that had less effect on the fortunes of old England. In truth, the battle was fought for the possession of a small piece of embroidered silk—a mere boy scouts affair. There was no military occasion for the fight; it was a case of just one more Border raid, this time by the Scots under James, Earl of Douglas. His army was on its way back to the northern kingdom—it had but a day's march before it—when Henry Percy ('Hotspur') pursued it, not in order to defeat the invaders or to hasten their retreat, but to regain the pennon that Douglas had snatched from his lance in a mêlée outside the gates of Newcastle.

We must therefore look elsewhere to discover the peculiar hold on the imagination of both countries that this battle has always evoked. It is no explanation to say that it became famous owing to two ancient ballads descriptive of it, for there must have been a solid reason for these ballads. The truth is, it caught the imagination partly from the peculiar and romantic conditions in which it was fought—a night-long battle fought under the light of the moon—and partly because it was, in A. G. Bradley's words:

'A chivalrous and fiercely contested duel between the great rival houses of Percy and Douglas at the moment when they were at their zenith and led by the most warlike of their respective names.'[1]

Walsingham describes them as 'duoes tam praeclaros juvenes', 'two such illustrious young leaders'.

Froissart who was then in the prime of life and who met and talked to several of the participants on each side in the battle, was evidently

[1] *Romance of Northumberland*, p. 300.

deeply impressed by the gallantry displayed on all sides, and he went out of his way to emphasize the fact.

'Of all the battles that have been described in this history, great and small, of which I am now speaking was the best fought and the most severe, for there was not a man, knight or squire, who did not acquit himself gallantly, hand to hand with his enemy.'[1]

＊　　＊　　＊　　＊　　＊

The preliminaries of the battle need not detain us long, for, as I have hinted, there was no strategic interest in the battle.

In 1388 England had fallen on evil days, under the feeble rule of the young Richard II. The glory and the power of the southern kingdom, that had been so much in evidence during the long reign of his grandfather Edward III, had vanished for the moment, and internal discord was only a short way below the surface. At the same time France was threatening an invasion.

Taking advantage of the troubles of the southern kingdom, as was their wont, the Scottish nobility collected two armies and crossed the Border. The larger army made for Carlisle and need concern us no more. The smaller one, under James, Earl of Douglas, crossed the Border to the west of the Cheviots and advanced down Redesdale, crossed the Tyne, and ravaged County Durham. Then, gorged with the spoil, and elated with an easy success, they advanced on Newcastle, hoping to capture that city. In this they were disappointed, but in a scuffle outside the north gate Douglas captured the pennon of Percy's lance, as already related, and made off with it to Scotland. Percy vowed he would recover it, and twenty-four hours after the Scots had decamped he set out in pursuit.

The Scottish army naturally took the shortest route back to their own country, via Redesdale, through which they had come. (The main road to the Border now follows this route.) It was in the early morning of 18 August that Douglas set out. Passing Ponteland Castle, he took it without difficulty or delay, and resuming his march camped that night at Otterburn, 32 miles from Newcastle. This was good going, but the Scots must have been in hard condition after a succession of long and rapid marches.

Douglas pitched his camp astride the road, his right flank resting on the river Rede, a stream about 20 yards wide, and his left stretching up a slope to the moors. The camp was about one mile beyond the

[1] Froissart, Johnes' translation.

castle of Otterburn, which he left unmolested for the time being. The day was far spent and his army was dog-tired. Here, then, the Scots settled down in their bivouacs and tents[1] and slept soundly no doubt, for the enemy was far away.

Next morning, 19 August, Douglas attacked the castle. Details of this operation we have not; all we know is that it was unsuccessful. This is not surprising; the Scots would have no breaching engines with them on such a raid, and in face of a determined defence a long siege would be required.

In the afternoon, seeing that the attempt was fruitless, Douglas held a war council to decide on future plans. There was a strong party, probably a majority, in favour of resuming the march and getting their booty safely over the Border while the going was good. But the youthful and chivalrous Douglas, who was aware of Percy's vow to recover his pennon ere the Scots left England, persuaded the council to await the advent of Percy, in order to give him an opportunity to fulfil his vow.

By this time the afternoon was far spent and there was no news of the approach of the English. The camp was however strengthened, while Douglas made a personal reconnaissance and then a plan to deal with Percy, should he pursue. (We will consider this plan later.) This being done, and the enemy still not appearing, the army began to settle down for another quiet night's repose.

We must now return to the English army. Scouts had during the morning of the 19th informed Percy of the position of the Scottish camp, their approximate numbers and the fact that they were halted and besieging Otterburn castle. It cannot have been far short of 1 p.m. when Percy received this exciting news. His troops had just finished their dinner and he ordered an immediate advance.

The army that he had collected consisted of about 2,000 men-at-arms and 5,000 infantry. As all had horses[2] a pace of about 5½ miles per hour might be maintained. Thus, if they set out at 1 p.m. they should be in sight of the Scottish camp at 7 p.m. just as dusk was spreading.

The country was heavily wooded and no sharp look-out was kept up.

[1] It is hard to credit Froissart's story that they made huts out of trees and branches. It was a hot day at the height of summer. Tired troops would hardly trouble to do more than cook their food and drop to sleep.

[2] I think we must accept this, though Froissart evidently believed they had some dismounted troops.

Consequently the Scottish army was surprised. Though inferior in numbers to the English army, it was not markedly so, in spite of Froissart's assertion. The most careful computation was made by Robert White in his *Battle of Otterburn*, where he puts the total at 6,600 including grooms and varlets. Since these were armed there is no reason why they should not be included in the total. Indeed, as we shall see, the grooms played an appreciable part in the battle. The English army was possibly 8,000 strong.

The broad outline of the battle that ensued is not controversial and can be related briefly as follows. Percy, having located the hostile camp, divided his army into two divisions. While he himself led the main division directly upon the enemy the second division attacked and took the Scottish camp in rear and captured it. Meanwhile the Earl of Douglas (in accordance with his prearranged plan) made a flank attack, with a portion of his army, on Percy's division. In the course of this attack he was killed. However, in a battle which lasted for a great part of the night, the Scots gained the upper hand. Both Percy and his brother Ralph were captured.

The rest is controversy, contradiction, and conjecture. But it is these very points of detail—where precisely the battle was fought, how it was fought and by what routes the various forces moved—that it is the object of this chapter to resolve.

THE SOURCES

It will be as well to open this examination with a review of the evidence, or sources. The primary source is Froissart's *Chronicles*. This may be described as a neutral source, Froissart being a Fleming who had visited both England and Scotland and may be regarded as impartial. Moreover, he wrote his account of the battle after talking with various participants on both sides only one year after it took place. Furthermore it is the most detailed and most readable account, and forms the basis of all reconstructions of the battle. But (there is always a 'but' where Jean Froissart is concerned) the chronicler suffered from an incorrigible habit of embroidering, and even of fabricating the story in order to heighten the effect. Consequently we cannot rely on it absolutely unless it is either corroborated by other sources or unless it passes the test of Inherent Military Probability (which I call I.M.P. for short).

Passing to the Scottish side we have three accounts. One is a Latin poem written less than thirty years after the battle by a Glasgow canon named Thomas de Barry. Unfortunately the poet seems more intent on his rhymes and puns than on presenting a straightforward historical account. Here is a typical couplet:

> Clamor inardescit docti, sapiens sapientem
> Lancia mordescit, jaculis jaciunt jacientem.

The poem is contained in the *Scotichronicon* or Scottish Chronicle of John de Fordun, who wrote shortly after, also in Latin.[1] Fordun's account of the campaign and battle is under sixty lines, but it is factual and valuable and substantially in agreement with Froissart.

The third earliest Scottish source is the *Oryginale Cronykil* of Andrew de Wyntoun, written about thirty years after the battle in English (or rather Scotch, requiring a glossary, as it has never been translated). Being in the form of a rhymed poem it cannot be relied upon for exact details, any more than Barry's poem, but it tallies in all important respects with Froissart.

The above three accounts are of course frankly partisan and must to a certain extent be discounted, but they are probably nearer the mark than their English fellow scribes to whom we must now refer.

There are three main English sources: Walsingham's *Historia Anglicana*, and Higden's *Polychronica*, both in latin prose, and John Hardyng's *Chronicle* in English verse. The two first are of about equal length to Fordun's, and are valuable as giving the English plan and movements more explicitly than the Scottish sources, as is only natural. But they slur over the defeat and indeed speak of pursuit to the Border. John Hardyng's account has the advantage that he was a soldier, and fought at Agincourt. He wrote his poem in 1465, seventy-seven years after the battle, and it is not rated highly as history, but he had taken service with Percy only two years after the battle and no doubt received and passed on Percy's own version.

The reader may wonder why I have not included the three famous ballads of the battle, *Chevy Chase* and the two versions (English and Scottish) of the *Otterburn* poem. Alas! Modern research attaches no historical importance to any of them. They give the broad outline of the story correctly enough, but in no other respect can they be credited; they are fanciful to a degree, and some of their incidents probably refer to other raids and have been transplanted to this more famous raid in

---

[1] Neither has ever been translated, as far as I can discover, and my rendering may not be perfect.

error. But even without them we have a good deal of material to work upon, and a fairly coherent story can be built up.

Astonishing as it may sound, only one real attempt to construct a detailed and independent account of this famous battle has been made. That was nearly a century ago. In 1857 Robert White published his *Battle of Otterburn*, a work of erudition and a storehouse of information. In later years he intended to publish a revised edition but unfortunately died before it was done. Consequently it is now a very rare book.[1] But Robert White was a civilian, without practical knowledge of war and, like Sir James Ramsay, he sometimes enunciates military absurdities. But his is the standard work and nearly all subsequent accounts are based on his (generally without acknowledgement). Consequently there is no need to refer to them minutely.

The only really independent account is that of Sir James Ramsay in his *Genesis of Lancaster*, to which I shall refer later. Nothing of substance has been published on the battle in the present century.

* * * * *

Two main problems have confronted the above historians in their attempts to reconstruct the battle. The first is the position of the Scottish camp, and the second the routes of the flank movements by the Scottish and English forces respectively. It will be noted that I do not mention the site of the battlefield, for I consider there can be no reasonable doubt about that, though Sir James Ramsay ploughs a lonely furrow here, as in many other battles. I must therefore deal with the question.

THE SITE OF THE BATTLE

The approximate site, at least is beyond doubt. The chroniclers agree that it was near Otterburn, in Redesdale, on the road from Newcastle to Scotland. Now, until 1777 there stood in an open field near Otterburn and near the road and river Rede a stone obelisk in a stone socket that was known as Battle Stone. Local tradition asserted that it marked the spot where Douglas fell. Now there are circumstantial accounts of Douglas's last moments, how many times he was wounded, and where, and the exact words he uttered, &c. Most of these stories have been unquestioningly repeated by the historians. But how could anyone in the midst of a mêlée in the middle of the night be in a position

[1] There is a copy in the British Museum but it is difficult to find in the catalogue.

to observe and hear all this? Satisfied that it was mostly moon-shine, I was interested to note in the earliest Scottish account, that of Wyntoun, the explicit statement that 'no man knew in what manner Douglas died'. The English marched over his prostrate corpse in the dark according to Froissart, not knowing what a prize lay beneath their feet. Nevertheless, the Scots remained on the battlefield next morning and recovered the body of their dead leader, so they must have known the spot where he fell and it is inherently probable that they would mark the spot before their departure. Thus the tradition that Battle Stone marked the spot where Douglas fell may be accepted;[1] and if we accept it we know within fairly narrow limits the battle-area. For we still know where Battle Stone stood to within about five yards. Robert White was shown the spot by an inhabitant who lived there in 1777[2] and he paced the distance from it to the new Percy Cross and found it 180 paces, say 165 yards, north-east. This spot is now marked on the six-inch O.S. map, and I show it as B.S. (Battle Stone) on my sketch-map.

Modern writers with one voice declare that this second monument is erroneously named Percy Cross and that it ought to be called Douglas Cross. This is not so. The history of its erection is as follows. In the year 1777 the Duke of Northumberland, wishing to mark adequately a battlefield so closely connected with his ancestor Percy, approached the local landowner for permission to erect a monument. The landowner, fearing that the Duke might later lay claim to the ground on which the monument was erected, refused permission but said he would erect a monument himself. He then proceeded to remove the old Battle Stone, and to use the base socket for his own monument. This he erected nearer the road in order that it might be easily visible from the road, and he planted the belt of trees from the road to the monument, which still exists. The cross therefore has no connexion with Douglas, and owing to the Duke of Northumberland's initiative it may fairly be connected with Percy Hotspur. Further corroboration as to the site is furnished by the fact that battlefield relics have been dug up all around Percy Cross and that the ground is still called Battle Croft or Battle Riggs.

[1] The exact spot where Lord Audley fell in the battle of Blore Heath is also marked by a stone, and no one queries the accuracy of its siting. Both stones are on the side of a slope, near, but not on, the crest—an unnatural spot to select unless it happened to be the right one.

[2] White was a native of Otterburn.

THE TERRAIN

Having thus established the approximate area of the battlefield we are in a position to describe the terrain. This need not take long if it is examined in conjunction with the sketch-map. The river Rede (here about 20 yards wide, and swift) winds through a valley with an average width of 1,000 yards. Along its north-eastern bank runs the turnpike road, constructed in the eighteenth century but almost certainly following the route of the old road or track to Scotland. Otterburn Castle (now represented by Tower Hotel) lay 150 yards to the north of the road; 3,000 yards further on the valley narrows to 500 yards and is here flanked on each side by two rectangular or square earthworks of Roman type if not workmanship. Obviously they were so placed to command the 'pass' traversed by the road and river. To the north the ground slopes up fairly gently to a ridge about 700 feet high. Apart from a few modern plantations on the ridge it is open but generally cultivated land, but at the time of the battle most of it was forest. The season of the year being summer, the valley was probably dry and passable everywhere.

THE PROBLEMS

We are now in a position to tackle the problems of the battlefield, of which I have said there are two main ones: the situation of the Scottish camp and the routes followed by the two flank marches.

Froissart is responsible for the confusion concerning the position of the camp. He wrote: 'They (the Scots) placed their baggage and servants at the entrance of the marsh on the road to Newcastle.' Then came the attack. 'They forced their way into the camp . . .' The English made their first attack on the servants' quarters, which checked them a little. Then, while the knights were donning their armour the Scots 'ordered a body of their infantry to join their servants and keep up the contest'.

The picture the passage conjures up is that of the servants' quarters being in front, and the marsh and the combatant portion of the army being in the rear. What an astounding formation that would be, for Douglas was deliberately awaiting the arrival of the English army in his camp at Otterburn! How are we to get round it? And how to reconcile it with the other chroniclers who state or imply that the camp was in rear? The evidence on this point is strong. They state that Percy

divided his army into two divisions and that while he led one division
to the direct attack the other division (variously described as being
under Sir Thomas Umfraville and Lord Grey or Sir Matthew Red-
mayne and Ogil) stationed itself in the enemy's rear where it did
execution among the tents.[1] The conclusion is inescapable that Froissart
misunderstood his English informants or had by oversight omitted
from his account the fact that the servants' camp was attacked by
an enveloping force. If he understood 'the entrance to the marsh' to

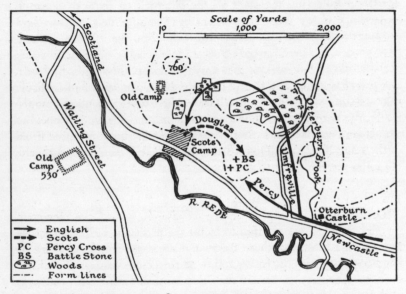

SKETCH-MAP 18. OTTERBURN: THE BATTLE

be the 'pass' that I have described, his story can be reconciled with that
of the others. But I confess that the passage has caused me much trouble.

Let us then assume, as a working hypothesis, that the Scottish camp
was astride the road (as Froissart says) and just to the east of the pass
between the two earthworks, as marked on the sketch-map. From this
camp Douglas, looking towards the English approach, would see a
slight ridge running down from the main ridge to the river, and
distant 500 yards. This would be a natural line to hold in case of attack.
A few outposts would be stationed on this ridge while the army made

[1] Walsingham in particular is most explicit on this point; and Higden, whom
Grose describes as 'one of the best authorities for the period' states that Red-
mayne (Umfraville) was to fall on the enemy from the rear.

itself ready for the night. This ridge stretching from the river up to the top of the first slope is 500 yards long and the modern Percy Cross is in the exact centre of it. We will call it Percy Cross Ridge.

So far so good. Now Froissart tells us that Douglas had reconnoitred the country and made a plan to circumvent the English, should they attack. This plan was, to leave a division to engage them in front, while another division would move round their flank. So important did Douglas regard the task of this division that he decided to lead it in person. Can we trace its course? I think we can. Froissart says 'they skirted the side of a mountain which was hard by'. The word 'mountain' can of course mean merely a hill, and there is such a hill at the back and left flank of the camp. Now if at the outset the battle was waged on the Percy's Cross Ridge and Douglas wished to outflank this position by moving along a hillside, there is only one line possible for him to take, and that line I have marked on the map. I walked it myself, and found that, if Battle Stone marked the approximate flank of the English position, Douglas could approach it from the north and be under cover owing to a slight crest for the last 200 yards. More distant cover would not be required for it was thickly wooded country, and in any case dusk had fallen.

The rest is easy. Douglas, leading his division, comes over the crest on Percy's right flank, charges down the slight hill into the unsuspecting English line at about Battle Stone and there gets swallowed up in hand-to-hand fighting. At some time in the course of it—it is fruitless even to speculate at what hour—the Scottish leader fell, and was trampled under foot in the darkness and confusion of the mêlée.

If the above reconstruction be accepted as at least not at variance either with the Chronicles or with I.M.P., let us pass on to my second perplexity, namely how Umfraville's division avoided contact with Douglas's during the two enveloping movements. C. R. B. Barrett, in his account,[1] explains it airily by saying that they missed one another 'by good luck', but his map seems to give another explanation, for it shows Douglas performing the extraordinary evolution of wheeling through three-quarters of a circle whose diameter is less than 300 yards with a force of some thousands of men, and in semi-darkness. Robert White and James Robson do not seem to regard it as a problem at all, while Ramsay gets out of it by the drastic device of denying Umfraville any enveloping movement at all. He puts the camp down by the river

[1] *Battles and Battlefields in England.*

on the Scottish right flank (apparently following Froissart literally) instead of in rear, and incidentally he sites the battle 1½ miles to the east of the generally accepted site.

I must admit that I at first toyed with the idea that Umfraville could have moved by the south instead of the north, but I had to reject it decisively; the river makes it quite out of the question. Eventually I came to the perhaps obvious conclusion that Umfraville made a fairly wide detour, as marked on my map, in order to ensure getting well to the rear of the Scots, which kept him clear of the track of Douglas.[1] The gathering darkness and the trees would also help to conceal his march.

Perhaps I ought to explain why I do not follow Robert White and his school who all site the Scottish camp in the old earthwork on hill 760. This earthwork was described and carefully mapped by a friend of White for his book, and it is in apparently just the same condition to-day as it was one hundred years ago. Therefore four hundred years earlier, when it was already at least one thousand years old, it cannot have been in very much better condition than it is in now, that is a mere scratch in the ground. Romans did not dig deep ditches round their camps. Hence this earthwork would have been of little protection to the Scots, and would offer no inducement to them to climb the hill, away from water and away from their homeward road. Moreover, have our historians stopped to consider whether this camp could hold the Scottish army? I paced it and found the inside measurement to be 97 yards square. How could one get some 6,000 men, with their tents and cookhouse fires, &c., to say nothing of their horses, into this tiny space? It would be tighter packed than a prisoner-of-war camp. Historians writing on battles often jump to the conclusion that any old earthwork in the battle area must have some connexion with the battle. I do not follow their reasoning.

THE COURSE OF THE BATTLE

We are now in a position to reconstruct the course of the battle, omitting all personal details and stories, which may or may not be true, but which have no bearing on its course and result.

[1] The Latin poem in Fordun seems to point to this, if my translation of 'Angli descensum montis consulte lucrantur' is correct: 'The English manoeuvred to gain the advantage of the hill'; for only by making this wide flanking march along the ridge-top could Umfraville take advantage of the hill.

It would seem, then, that on the afternoon of Thursday, 19 August,[1] 1388, the Scottish army rested from its labours of attacking Otterburn Castle and began going into bivouac for the night. They had a plan ready in case Percy should appear but there seemed little chance of him approaching till the morrow. If Percy then came, Douglas would fight him on the ground he had himself selected and by the plan he had himself formed. Suddenly a mounted scout gallops into the camp shouting excitedly 'Arm speedily!' (Wyntoun states this and it seems inherently probable—just the thing that might happen.)

All is confusion and bustle. In his excitement the Earl of Dunbar forgets to put on his bascinet (another natural incident reminiscent of William of Normandy putting on his hauberk the wrong way round at Hastings). But the English attack does not come at once. Percy, though young and impulsive, makes his plan. This involved the flanking march by Umfraville's division to the rear of the enemy, partly to beat up his camp and cause confusion and partly to prevent the Scottish army escaping.[2] For the English were in superior numbers and were confident of victory.

By the time Umfraville had got right round to the rear of the camp the bulk of the combatants had left it and were forming up on the Percy Cross Ridge or were accompanying Douglas in his flank march.[3] Consequently Umfraville's men made short work of the grooms and camp guards who now had the camp almost to themselves. It was by this time dark and Umfraville could hear increasing sounds of battle on Percy Cross Ridge but could see nothing. After waiting some time his patience gave out; leaving a smallish party to hold the camp he returned by the same route by which he had come, to rejoin the main fight.

Meanwhile Percy's division had engaged all along the line. Superior in numbers, they were pushing their opponents back when the sudden irruption of Douglas restored the position. The surprise was complete, the Scots being shielded by the ridge and the trees.[4] Douglas's men had the advantage of the hill and the English were gradually pushed down it and squeezed together in the centre. At such close quarters and in

[1] Sources are almost equally divided as to between 5 and 19 August. On the 5th there was no moon, on the 19th there was. This seems conclusive.

[2] In John Hardyng's words: 'To hold them that they ran not away.'

[3] Fordan implies that Douglas did not emerge from the camp till later, but this is impossible to reconcile with the other accounts.

[4] Wyntoun states explicitly that Douglas came out of the wood.

the dark the English archers could not use their long bows. With this trump card not available, they were at a disadvantage. The Scots were probably in harder fighting trim, having been marching for many days. Moreover, the English were tired out by their long march that day, followed by an immediate attack. They were fighting on empty stomachs whereas the Scots had had several hours rest and also food.[1] As the hours of darkness passed the purely physical factor loomed more and more important, till it eventually became dominant. The English could no longer wield their weapons with sufficient force to strike death-dealing blows. In the hopeless obscurity of the night, lit up from time to time by the fitful rays of the moon, the confusion became utter. The English leader Percy and his brother Ralph were captured and the English army, little by little, filtered off the field.

The dawn found the Scots in undisputed possession of the arena. Pursuit was attempted. But even in defeat the English were formidable, and over 200 prisoners were captured from the too rash pursuers. The battle of Otterburn was over; the voice of the ballad-maker was about to be heard.

[1] Only a small proportion of the army could have been actively engaged in the attack (probably little more than a demonstration) on Otterburn Castle.

CHAPTER XVII

The Battle of Shrewsbury, July 21st, 1403

ON 21st July, 1403, was fought 'the sory bataille of Schrovesbury between Englysshemen and Englysshemen'; an engagement described by a French chronicler of the time as 'a battle unparalleled in history'. It was certainly one of the decisive battle of the Middle Ages, deciding, as it did, which should be the reigning family in England for the next 60 years.

Though this book is primarily concerned with the fields of battle, rather than manœuvres and events leading up to them, there were elements of unusual interest in the strategy of the campaign that may well be included.

In 1399 Henry of Lancaster had been helped on to the throne by the powerful north-country family of the Percys, Earls of Northumberland. Four years later the King marched north with a strong army to assist the Earl of Northumberland to repel the Scots. When he reached Burton he was thunderstruck to hear that the Earl had turned against him, in alliance with Owen Glendower, the Welsh chieftain, and Edmund Mortimer; further, that Harry Hotspur, the Earl's son, had marched south with a following and had reached Chester on the 11th of July where he was rapidly collecting an army.

This necessitated an abrupt change of plan. Instead of continuing his journey north, the King turned sharp to his left, reaching Lichfield on July the 16th. From here he sent out summons for military levies in the surrounding counties, and waited for a few days while they came rolling in. No doubt he was also collecting information as to the movements and intentions of his enemies, and it seems clear that he learned of the plan whereby Glendower would bring an army out of South Wales to join Hotspur at or near Shrewsbury.

Shrewsbury, the chief crossing-place over the upper Severn, thus became the focal point of the campaign. But for some unexplained reason Henry did not march for the Salopian capital by the direct route along Watling Street; instead on the 18th he marched north to Stafford, where he spent the night of July 19th. Evidently he had not up to this day received clear intelligence of the southward move of Hotspur. But this news he must have received during his short sojourn at Stafford; Hotspur was heading for Shrewsbury. The King's eldest son, Prince Hal of Shakespeare (afterwards Henry V), was dangerously isolated at Shrewsbury with a force which had been carrying out a raid in North Wales. Henry's course was clear; he must march with all speed to the help of his son. This he did with a vengeance: marching all next day, the 20th, via Newport and Haughmond, he reached Shrewsbury, 32 miles away, the same day, just in time to prevent the enemy breaking into the town. Hotspur had marched south from Chester, presumably by Whitchurch and Wem, and it must have been an exciting race. Having been foiled in his purpose there was only one thing for Hotspur to do: that was to work his way upstream till he could either find a crossing, or at least get into touch with Glendower, who should be approaching from the other side. He therefore fell back from in front of the town, three miles in a north-westerly direction and halted for the night in the village of Berwick, near the river bank. From here scouts must have been sent across the Severn in search of the Welsh allies, or for news of them. Percy Hotspur must have spent an anxious night. It is true that the Earl of Worcester had most unexpectedly come over to his side, joining him at Chester, but his strategical situation was bad. The armies of the Confederates, as we will call them, were in three widely-separated portions: in the north there were still considerable forces under the Earl of Northumberland; somewhere to the south-west was the army of Glendower; and in the centre, confronted by the concentrated army of the King, was Hotspur's hastily-raised army, chiefly consisting of Cheshire volunteers. With a Napoleonic stroke of decision, the King had pounced upon the centre army while it was still isolated.

Morning came, the morning of July 21st, but with it no news whatever of Glendower reached Hotspur. (He was, as a matter of fact, still in Carmarthenshire, delayed—so he afterwards averred— by floods.)[1] But with the morning came news of a disturbing nature from the opposite direction; the royal army was on his tracks. A glance at Map 19 will show that if Percy dallied at Berwick he ran the risk of being hemmed in by the enemy with his back to the river, with his line of retreat to Chester cut. Instant and hurried action

---

[1] There is, alas, no truth in the story that he watched the battlefield from the top of the oak at Shelton, $1\frac{1}{2}$ miles west of Shrewsbury. The shell of this oak still stands.

was indicated, and taken—so hurried that Hotspur left his favourite sword behind in the house of the family of Betton at Berwick. Regaining the Whitchurch road at Harlescott, the natural course might appear to be to march straight up it. But there had been some skirmishing with the Royal army, which was now in fairly close contact with it—it is likely that while a detachment under the Prince had taken the Berwick road the King with the main body was marching up the Whitchurch road due north: this would easily account for Percy's extreme haste. When two armies are in close contact it is difficult to disengage during daylight, and Hotspur probably did not choose to attempt it. We must remember that his army, apart from a tiny nucleus, was only a few days old—an unknown quantity; to retreat with the enemy on their tails might end in this new and unblooded army disintegrating altogether. That is probably the clue to the problem: that shrewd judge of character, William Shakespeare, paints Hotspur as a hot-headed youth (though he was in fact 39); when Sir Richard Vernon points out that their horses are in need of a rest after the long march of the day before, he replies curtly and truthfully: 'So are the horses of the enemy.' This is an age-old military problem—if we wait to increase our strength will the enemy increase his in a quicker or slower ratio? At any rate, Hotspur decided to put a bold face on it: to stand and face the enemy. A position favourable for this purpose had therefore to be found. If the reader will place himself at Harlescott, in the shoes of Hotspur, I have no doubt he will make the same decision as he made that morning. For an obvious position strikes the eye at once. In a district where the terrain is for the most part flat and featureless, one ridge does stand up, distant a little over a mile to the north-east. It is possible that Hotspur had made a mental note of it when passing in an opposite direction just 24 hours before. The ridge in question runs approximately east and west, and just in front of the centre of it there now appears a handsome church tower. Thither, then, Hotspur directed his army and drew it up on the ridge, 300 yards north of the present church, with a frontage of about 800 yards.

The Royal army pursued the same route, and the two armies drew up in full view of one another, outside bow-shot, say 300 to 500 yards apart, on the ground now known as Battlefield. The King's army was considerably the more numerous and the more homogeneous, for the bulk of it had marched as an army from London. We may compute it at 12,000 to 14,000 strong, and the Rebels at about 10,000.

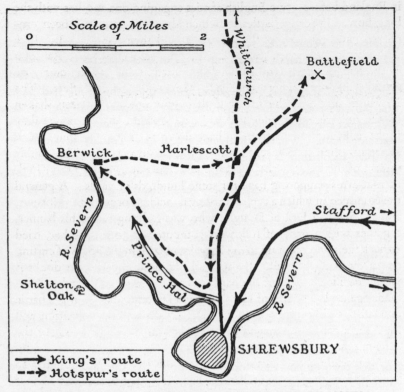

SKETCH-MAP 19. SHREWSBURY: THE PRELIMINARY MOVES

THE BATTLE

After the two hosts had been drawn up opposite one another in the prescribed deliberate method of medieval times, an incident occurred not unusual in those days of civil war. Neither side stirred and an emissary, the Abbot of Shrewsbury, passed between the two armies in the hopes of averting a conflict. This involved a pause of an hour or two, and is well portrayed by Shakespeare. But the details do not concern us here. On the failure of the negotiations the Royal army advanced to engage. The main body under the King—that is, the army that had advanced from London—took the premier position on the right. The railway embankment crosses Kings Croft, which no doubt marks the position of the King's own division. Prince Hal, with his own division, took the left. And now ensued a fight, as noted by Sir Charles Oman, the like of which had never been seen in England before—two English armies engaging one another with the long-bow. Previous battles in which the long-bow had been employed had been against the cross-bow and men-at-arms. But here both armies had their front lined with long-bowmen. As soon as the King's archers (probably dismounted) came within range the skilful Cheshire archers engaged them with deadly effect. The Royalists answered the fire, but their aim must have been shaken by the rude reception they had had, and after a fierce exchange they broke ranks and came streaming back down the hill. Hotspur, quick to see his opportunity, sent his men-at-arms in pursuit. The double impact of the flying archers and the rebel men-at-arms sent the King's men-at-arms staggering back for some hundreds of yards. A general mêlée ensued in which a typical medieval incident occurred. Hotspur, and the Scottish Earl of Douglas who was fighting under his banner, together with a band of followers computed at 30 in number, tried to hack their way right up to the Royal standard, in the hopes of cutting down the King himself. If this could be accomplished no doubt it would decide the fate of the battle. Just the same attempt had been made against the person of Harold, it will be remembered, at the battle of Hastings. The King's chief of staff, realizing their intention and the King's danger, managed to persuade him to fall back out of the danger zone.

Meanwhile the Prince's division on the left had not suffered so heavily from the hostile archers; it had stood its ground, and now it actually advanced, driving back Hotspur's right wing. Wheeling round to the right in pursuit it gradually got in rear of the rebel main body, while they were engaged with the King's division. Moreover, the rebels were inferior in numbers; thus they gradually found themselves being surrounded, and the mêlée and confusion became greater than ever. At some period in the course of it, probably quite early, the Prince received an arrow in the face. There is the usual story of his refusing to quit the field, which may or may not be true; but he certainly cannot have had the breath or ability to utter the long and rounded phrases that a chronicler puts into his mouth. In the course of this indescribable mêlée, when the bulk of the casualties must have occurred, Percy Hotspur fell, transfixed with an arrow sped by an unknown hand. When the dire news spread through the rebel ranks the natural and inevitable result followed: the whole line gave way and quitted the field. A merciless pursuit was launched by Henry, and continued for three miles or more. The victory was complete.

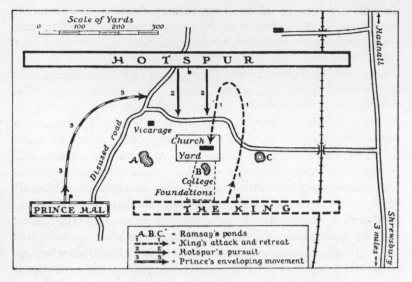

SKETCH-MAP 20.   SHREWSBURY: THE BATTLE

PROBLEMS OF THE BATTLEFIELD

I.—RAMSAY'S RECONSTRUCTION

The above narrative is my own reconstruction from somewhat slender and perplexing sources, though it is based in the main upon the reconstruction of Hastings Wylie, the historian of the reign of Henry IV.   It has little in common with the most widely-known and standard account of Sir James Ramsay in his *Lancaster and York*. Ramsay was, of course, a great historian, as far as amassing and compiling facts is concerned, but the military conclusions that he comes to as a result of those facts cannot be accepted in their entirety. For example, he makes Henry's troops march 45 miles in a single day, and the very next morning march another few miles and fight a battle for several hours; he makes Hotspur, when within a few miles of the crucial river crossing at Shrewsbury make a two-mile detour to his right, to Berwick, and only approach the town the next morning, to find that the King had got there first—the act of an imbecile, not that of the victor of Homildon Hill.   Thirdly, he makes the rebels draw up in a line only 170 yards long, leaving the road (to Hadnall) along which he was retreating uncovered.   Fourthly, he makes the King alter the organization of his army, turning three divisions into two on account of the existence of three tiny ponds, 26, 9 and 16 yards wide respectively—moreover, ponds which it is almost certain did not exist at the time of the battle.

For the above reasons I find Ramsay's reconstruction untenable.

II.—THE SITE OF THE BATTLE

Since Battlefield church was built on the battlefield it might be supposed that there is no problem to solve: that the church obviously marks the site of the battle, just as Battle Abbey marks the site of the battlefield of Hastings. But even in the case of Hastings (where we are positively assured that the altar marks the exact spot where Harold's headquarters were stationed), a number of subsidiary points remained to be settled. In the case of Shrewsbury we are not told what part of the field is marked by the church, nor even whether it is on the field at all (though one may safely assume that it is). Let us therefore approach the problem with an open mind, applying to it the touchstone that we have applied in previous battlefield problems—that of Inherent Military Probability. Given certain premises generally accepted by the historians, what would one on purely military grounds expect the lay-out to be, and what the course of events resulting from it?

The most interesting way of approaching the battlefield is undoubtedly by the road followed by the King from Shrewsbury to Harlescott (assuming my interpretation is correct: Ramsay makes both armies take the Market Drayton road, and turn abruptly off it to the left to fight the battle—an unnatural proceeding). From Harlescott the visitor will then follow in the steps of both armies to the actual field of battle—always the best way of approaching a battlefield. Unfortunately the old road between Harlescott and Battlefield no longer exists. You are therefore reduced to crossing the fields on foot. This of course will not matter if you have a car driver who can meet you with the car at the other end. It is only a walk of a mile. But the usual way to reach the field is to take the Market Drayton road, and after going three miles turn sharp left under the railway. You emerge on the other side within 400 yards of the church; in fact, you are already on the field before you have realized it. This approach has great drawbacks and is not to be recommended. But if it must be so, I recommend an immediate halt and a climb to the top of the railway embankment, whence a better general idea of the lie of the

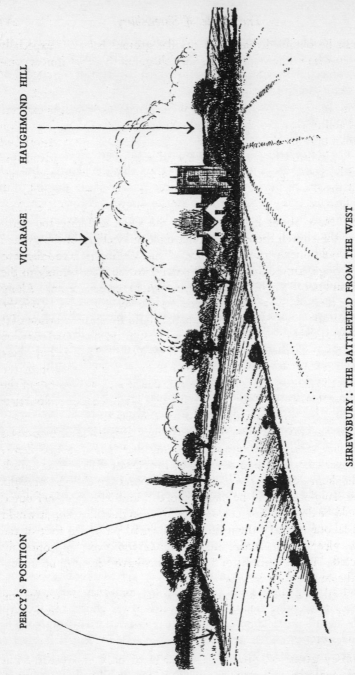

PERCY'S POSITION

VICARAGE

HAUGHMOND HILL

SHREWSBURY: THE BATTLEFIELD FROM THE WEST

land can be obtained than from the flat ground below. Expecially is this the case in the summer, for the foliage on the trees almost completely obscures the ridge that stood up so plainly from Harlescott. So restrain the obvious temptation to rush straight to the church.

From the railway embankment we realize at a glance the extreme improbability that the church marks the centre of Hotspur's position (as shown on Ramsay's map). Why should Hotspur, having reached the only obvious ridge in the neighbourhood, give up the advantages offered by it and place his troops at the foot of it? It seems an unnatural proceeding, and is ruled out by me on these grounds. A position somewhere on the forward slope would appear the obvious choice. Now about half-way down the slope and just 300 yards short of the church there is a distinct crest or swelling in the ground which would suit the case admirably. This swelling (it is too slight to call it a ridge) runs approximately parallel to the road leading to the church and passes just below the farm shown in the panorama. Along this line, then, with some confidence, I place Percy's army. (Brooke also places the position here.) Immediately in front of a portion of it there was a field of peas, fully grown. The soldiers attempted to twine the peas together to make some sort of obstacle. But it is not likely to have been very effective; we do not hear anything of it in the course of the battle; just as the famous hedge at Poitiers dies out of the story long before the end of the battle. Both obstacles doubtless were soon flattened under the feet of the contestants.

There remains one question to be faced. If the line of battle was a good 300 yards above the church, why was it not erected there? The answer seems to me to be given by the narrative: the rebel onrush brought them down to the level ground around the church; here the greatest slaughter would be likely to occur, and here the chief burial pit would be dug. Many corpses would be on the ridge, but it would be less labour to carry them down to a burial pit at the foot of the hill than vice versa. On this site the church would very appropriately be erected. Indeed, masses of human bones have been dug up underneath the church foundations.

Thus all the evidence seems to show that Percy's position was on the ridge behind the church. We must now consider its extent.

III.—THE EXTENT OF THE POSITION

Ramsay gives the position a frontage of only 170 yards. But Ramsay was the accepted exponent of the small-numbers school.

In the case of expeditionary forces, such as Crécy, Poitiers, etc., no doubt his thesis is fully justified.   But in this case he gives no reasons for the extremely small numbers he evidently allots to the two sides. According to his account the whole Royal army which the two most recent historians (Wylie and Dimock Fletcher agree in making over 20,000) attacked the enemy, through two gaps between tiny ponds, on frontages of 110 and 130 yards respectively (*A—B* and *B—C* on Sketch-map 20).   Yet these ponds are so small that they would have been invisible to the King as he approached them along the flat ground. If the reader doubts it let him experiment for himself.   But in any case, from my observation of these 'ponds' and from what I can gather as to their past history, I think the western one (*A* on Ramsay's map) may be the clay hole from which the bricks were made for the construction of the vicarage in 1861; the centre one *B* in the words of Richard Brooke, writing in 1857, is one of 'several shallow holes or pits in the meadow which have been dug into in the hopes of discovering something of interest; but nothing remarkable was discovered'.   Alternative suggestions are that they are the remains of fishponds belonging to the college that was built in addition to the church after the battle; or that they may represent the foundations of the college.[1]   In any case they are only a few inches deep.   The third pond *C* has the typical appearance of a Shropshire marl-pit, the marl from which was used in the eighteenth century and possibly earlier as a fertilizer for the fields.   In short, the whole elaborate theory built up by Sir James Ramsay seems to have an unsubstantial foundation. The probable explanation of Ramsay's theory of the ponds is a passage in the *Scottichronicon* that the King's army had to pass through a *strictum passum*, and Sir James found two *stricta passa* between the three ponds. Wyntoun, writing far away in Scotland, may have pictured the Shropshire terrain as similar to his own mountainous country; but it is more likely that the word was used in the usual medieval sense of a temporary narrowing in the approach, such as a ford, bridge or sunken road.   The King would encounter such a sunken road 2,000 yards north of Shrewsbury, leading up from the old bed of the river; it is the only one in the neighbourhood, and is probably the one referred to.   Indeed, it tends to establish the route by which the King advanced.

[1] There are objections to all these, and I incline to the view that it is an ornamental garden made by some vicar after the dismantlement of the college in 1548.   There are some rare water plants in the 'ponds'.

Apart from Ramsay's estimate, and that of C. R. B. Barrett in *Battles and Battlefields in England* (1896), which follows Ramsay closely, I can only find one explicit estimate as to the extent of the position, and that is Richard Brooke (quoted above) in *Visits to Fields of Battle in England*. He gives both armies a frontage of just 1,000 yards, 500 yards each side of the church. This takes the line on the east side a few yards over the Hadnall road. Allowing 12 men per yard of front this gives each side 12,000 men, which is not far from my own guess. But I am inclined to give a front of 800 to 900 yards, and place the eastern flank about midway between the railway and road.

CHAPTER XVIII

The First Battle of St. Albans, May 22nd, 1455

SINCE this is the first battle of The Wars of the Roses it will be as well to preface an account of it by a brief picture of the setting or background. Mark the plural—'The Wars'—for they constituted a series of disjointed and almost spasmodic operations extending over more than 32 years from St. Albans to the bloody fields of Bosworth and Stoke. Yet there was one idea latent through them all—who should govern England.

The year 1453 saw the last of our conquests in France (except Calais) wrested from us. The country was in an exhausted condition and feeling was bitter against the government for the sad ending to the once glorious French war. Moreover, the government was inert and poor King Henry VI was weak and spiritless, in striking and melancholy contrast to his father Henry V. He had just recovered from a mental malady, during whose course the country had been governed, and well governed, by his third cousin once removed—the Duke of York. The Duke had, in the opinion of many, a better right to the throne, which made the situation rather piquant. The King 'threw the fat in the fire' directly he recovered by dismissing York and reinstating the hated Duke of Somerset, his third half-cousin once removed, who was third in succession to the throne, being a Beaufort. Thus York and Somerset were in two senses rivals, and that was the original cause of the trouble.

The Duke of York hurried off to his estates in the North, where he collected his retainers, and was joined by his brother-in-law the Earl of Salisbury and his son the Earl of Warwick ('the Kingmaker'). The combined army did not amount to more than 3,000 men, but a large proportion of it had fought in France, so it was fairly well trained and experienced for the outbreak of a civil war—very different from the undisciplined bands that constituted the early armies of the Cavaliers and Roundheads. It consisted almost entirely of archers and foot soldiers armed with pikes, axes, etc., conveniently described as 'bowmen and billmen'; the knights constituted the officers. At this period armour had almost reached its heaviest and most cumbrous form, and as the men-at-arms almost invariably dismounted at the beginning of a battle there was a complete absence of mobility and manœuvre once battle was joined.

The Lancastrians were similarly placed. Neither side possessed field artillery or 'hand-guns' at the beginning of the war.

PRELIMINARY MOVES
(Sketch-map 21)

As soon as the King heard that the Duke of York was marching south he hastily collected what troops he could. They only amounted to 2,000, but were well officered, for it is calculated that no less than one-quarter of the nobility of the land marched with their king to battle. The King acted with speed and apparent resolution; speed was essential because he did not wish to fight near London, where opinion was Yorkist in sentiment, but rather in the north of England. The Yorkists consequently were anxious to reach London before the King had time to set out. Events therefore moved rapidly.

On May 20th the Yorkist army, coming down the Great North Road, reached Royston, 40 miles north of London. The King was evidently unaware that they were so close and next day, the 21st, he set out for Watford, *en route* for Leicester. Simultaneously York continued south for 20 miles to Ware. Thus, when night fell the Yorkists were 20 miles to the north-east of the Lancastrians and the road to London was open to them. The odds on the two armies making contact next day appeared small. But each side was well served by its spies, and became aware in the course of the night of the position of the other. Both came to the same decision—to advance direct upon the adversary with all speed. We thus get the most unusual spectacle of two armies approaching each other by night, or early morning, marches. The chief town between the two was St. Albans, and it looks much like a race for this town. The King had only eight miles, while York had to cover twice that distance. He seems, however, to have started out earlier, with the result that the race nearly ended in a dead-heat, one account describing the King as entering the town at one end while the Duke entered it at the other. But this is a slight exaggeration. The King's army arrived at 7 a.m. and the Duke's halted at about the same time in Key field, just outside the city to the east.

A curious episode then occurred. Both sides seemed averse to bloodshed. The Hundred Years' War had wiped out memories and traditions of civil strife, and York had, at this time, no designs on the throne: he merely wished for the downfall of his rival, the Duke of

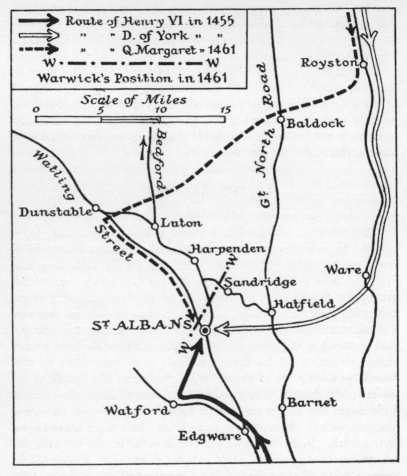

SKETCH–MAP 21. ST. ALBANS: THE PRELIMINARY MOVES IN BOTH BATTLES

Somerset. He therefore did not stir from his camp but essayed to negotiate. He had previously sent a letter to the King setting out his intentions, but it was intercepted by his rival, who wisely suppressed it. After three hours of curious inactivity on both sides—like the calm before the storm—the King sent the old Duke of Buckingham, York's father-in-law, to parley with the Yorkists. Back he came with

a cautiously worded answer, which mentioned no names but respect-
fully requested that the King would deliver to them 'such as we will
accuse' and that they would not desist 'till we have him which have
deserved death'. In other words, they demanded the head of the
King's friend and counsellor, the Duke of Somerset. In this they may
have consciously followed the example of Simon de Montfort on the
eve of the Battle of Lewes.

And now for once the King exhibited a touch of the imperious
spirit of his great parent. 'By the faith that I owe to St. Edward and
to the crown of England,' he exclaimed, 'I shall destroy them (the
traitors) every mother's son, and they shall be hanged and drawn and
quartered. . . .' So that was that! The gage was thrown down—
and the Duke of York picked it up.

THE BATTLE

(Sketch-map 22)

The battle that ensued has a special place in our history, for it
ushered in the long-drawn-out Wars of the Roses, and was in its
nature quite unlike any other battle of that or any other medieval
war. Two considerations may deter the historian or the tourist from
attempting to examine this battlefield. Like all other battles of the
time, only scanty accounts of it have come down to us, and the shape
and appearance of the town in which it was fought have so changed
that one may easily suppose it impossible to reconstruct and picture
it. In refutation of this view here are two points. First, an eye-
witness of the battle did in fact write an account of it; namely, the
Abbot of St. Albans Abbey, John Whethamstede by name. I make
little doubt that he stationed himself on the top of the great Abbey
gateway (which still survives) from where he could follow almost
every detail. In the second place, the line of the streets (with one
exception) have not changed, and some events of the battle can be
pinpointed to within a few yards. Of what battle fought out in the
open country can that be affirmed? Thus, provided with a fair knowledge of the appearance and methods of medieval warfare, and of the
lay-out of ancient towns, and gifted with a vivid imagination, one
should be able to take one's stand upon the clock tower or town hall
roof in the middle of the town and witness, in imagination, the scene
enacted before one's very eyes, as did the horrified Abbot of St.
Albans nearly 500 years ago.

The town of St. Albans is situate upon a hill; or to be more exact, upon the south-western extremity of a ridge some hundred feet or more above the surrounding plain. The ground slopes down fairly steeply to the River Ver, whence the Brito-Roman city of Veru-

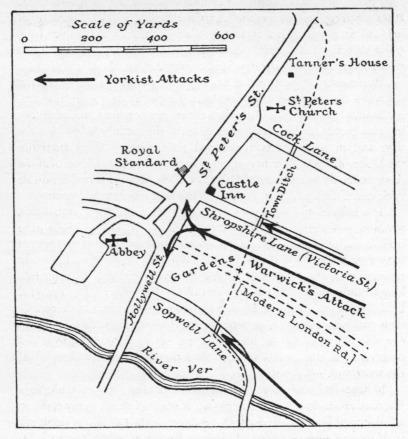

SKETCH-MAP 22. ST. ALBANS I: THE BATTLE

lamium on the far bank took its name. The buildings clustered round the great abbey; the eastern boundary was provided by St. Peter's Street, and its southern extension Holywell Street. It was not a walled city, but during the Barons' War it had been half-heartedly fortified; that is to say, a ditch had been dug round it surmounted by a palisade, but it had long since sunk into decay, and the only remaining practical obstructions were the 'bars' or wooden barriers that could be swung across the streets at need. (These 'bars' must have resembled the tree-trunk obstacles again seen in those parts 500 years later, whose object was to prevent ingress by hostile armoured cars.)

The course taken by the aforesaid ditch was a peculiar one, but the only part that concerns us is the eastern face, which ran parallel to St. Peter's Street, and about 200 yards to the east of it. Three roads led into St. Peter's Street from this side: Cock Lane, Shropshire Lane (now Victoria Street) and Sopwell Lane. (The modern London Road runs between the two latter. See Sketch-map 22.)

When early in the morning of May 22nd the King's Army entered the town the eastern face of the ditch was hastily and somewhat un-methodically occupied. But when the troops saw the Duke of Buck-ingham go out for his parley they assumed the battle was 'off' for the day, and in many parts abandoned their posts. When therefore the Duke of York, after haranguing his men after the fashion of those days, suddenly advanced to the attack there was a hurried scramble back to the ditch and bars, with the result that will shortly appear.

The bells of the Abbey of St. Peter's were rung as a signal that invasion was imminent. The type of fight that ensued must have been quite unprecedented in those days of chivalry when contests took two forms: sieges, in which the one side sat down deliberately to encompass the other, and battles, in which one side drew up in a long straight line, and the other side obligingly conformed in a parallel line. The First Battle of St. Albans refuses to conform to either of these patterns. Rather, it resembles a boy-scout battle, in which one side has to hold a locality and the other to penetrate into it un-observed. In this case Warwick 'the Kingmaker' played the part of the successful boy-scout.

It happened this way. The Yorkists confined their attack to a direct advance along the southern two roads. Naturally they came to a full-stop at the two barricades.[1] As a result the battle was resolving itself into an impasse when suddenly a fresh turn was given to it by Warwick's column which managed to cross the ditch unobserved between the two lines. Oman, in his *Warwick the Kingmaker*, credits the Earl with a 'quick military eye' in this manœuvre, but there does not seem much to go upon. If blocked in one spot it is only natural to 'feel' for another. Or it may be, even more simply, that one of his men came in with the intelligence that he had discovered a spot

[1] One in Victoria Street near Pageant House factory, one in Sopwell Lane near the 'Hare and Hounds.'

where the ditch appeared to be undefended (Hall, the chronicler, indeed asserts this). We can at least claim for Warwick that he was quick to take advantage of it. That a spot in the centre of the line should be unguarded seems surprising, but it corroborates the statement that the King's men were taken off their guard. Moreover, there had been but little time to make clearances and a decent field of fire round the old ditch; and at the point penetrated there were gardens and enclosures which would make surprise the more easy. Further, the length of ditch to be held was a good 1,000 yards, and the garrison was only 2,000 strong.

Certain it is that Warwick not only crossed the ditch at a spot a few yards to the north of the present London Road, but got right up to the back sides of the houses lining Holywell Street unmolested. He then proceeded methodically to hack holes through the walls of what is now know as Battlefield House, and thus gain access to the main street. He emerged just by The Chequers (now Queen's Hotel) 'blowing up his trumpets and shouting with a great voice "A Warwick A Warwick!"' Thus did the 25 year old Earl of Warwick make his debut, and his mark, in battle.

The Lancastrian line was thus broken in two, and Warwick's men, flushed with success, wheeled outwards right and left, thus turning the flanks of the parties manning the two road-barriers. These in turn fell back and the whole Yorkist army burst into the town.

Now came the last phase of the battle, graphically described by old John Whethamstede, from his vantage point on the Abbey gateway. 'Here you saw one fall with his brains dashed out, there another with a broken arm, a third with a cut throat, and a fourth with a pierced chest, and the whole street was full of dead corpses.' Clearly the street to which the Abbot refers was at St. Peter's Street. This fine broad street now acts as the market place at its southern end, where the bulk of the fighting took place. Henry VI set up his Royal Standard here, and here he remained himself throughout the fray, quietly seated under a tree. But his troops were not only outnumbered they were taken off their balance. They had trusted to defences and they had trusted in vain. The battle is in fact a good example of the eternal inherent weakness of the defensive, namely, that 'the strength of a chain is its weakest link'. It is no use being strong *nearly* everywhere; you must be strong *quite* everywhere.

The struggle was short and sharp. A fierce flight of arrows at deadly range wounded both the King and the Duke of Buckingham, the King in the neck and the Duke in the face. No doubt they had their vizors open. When the enemy surged round the King he gently reproved them: 'Forsooth! Forsooth! Ye do foully to smite a king annointed so.' At this moment panic seems to have set in: his own Standard-bearer, who had fought valiantly at the outset, threw down the Royal Standard and basely fled. The rot set in, and presently the King was left almost alone.

And there, at the corner of Shropshire Lane, only a few yards away, huddled up on the steps of the Castle Inn (now occupied by the National Provincial Bank) lay the dead body of the man who had been the cause of all this trouble—the Duke of Somerset.

The battle was over. The King of England, bleeding at the neck, was led quietly away to the house of a tanner situated just to the north of St. Peter's Church. Here he was sought out by the victorious Yorkist leaders; but not to claim him as their prisoner, as might have been expected. Instead, they approached on bended knee, and 'besought of him grace and forgiveness'! This the King was graciously pleased to grant (he could, under the circumstances, scarcely do otherwise!). Both sides appear to have been tactful enough not to refer to the little matter of 'hanging, drawing and quartering', though the Duke was hardly gifted with tact when he bade the King rejoice that Somerset was dead. With all reverence, the King was conducted through that fine old gateway into the Abbot's house, where he remained for the night. Next day he was taken back to London and lodged in the palace of the Bishop.

Thus was fought that strange and muddled affair, the First Battle of St. Albans. The casualties among the rank and file were small, but nearly all the Lancastrian leaders were struck down or captured. This is a feature common to the time. Armour was so heavy and the knights elected to fight on foot. Thus when the day went against them they had not the power to run away, unless they could find some kind friend to release them from their armour. The bowmen and billmen, however, were not so impeded in their flight. Thus was waged, in the streets of St. Albans, the only 'Boy Scout' battle of the war.

Unlike all the battles with which we have dealt, First St. Albans presents no problems for investigation. All that is required, in order to follow it, is a knowledge of the lay-out of the ancient streets. This can most conveniently be obtained from the map in Ramsay's *Lancaster and York*.

CHAPTER XIX

The Battle of Blore Heath, 23 September 1459

THE bloody battlefield of Blore Heath is one of the easiest to approach and to locate, as it is almost exactly bisected by a main road—that between Market Drayton and Newcastle-under-Lyme. Yet it is the most neglected of all the major battles of the Wars of the Roses. The reason for this neglect is not far to seek: the sources for it, strategical and tactical, are very obscure and scarce. This scarcity has led to considerable divergence in the reconstruction of it by modern historians. This very fact adds to the interest of the battle; it is like building up the story of a murder on flimsy and conflicting evidence.

The opening moves of the campaign were simple and straightforward, in my opinion, but an early historian of the battle—W. Beaumont—has needlessly complicated them in a paper read by him to the Chester Archaeological Society in 1850. This account would probably not have achieved much notice had it not received the *imprimatur* of that great historian of medieval battles, Sir James Ramsay. It will therefore be necessary to devote some space to this subject, for Ramsay is usually followed unquestioningly by subsequent historians.

*   *   *   *   *

After the first battle of St. Albans a settlement was patched up between Queen Margaret and the Duke of York. But after an uneasy four years the war broke out again in September 1459. The strategical situation then was that the Yorkists were dispersed: the Duke of York with his retainers was at Ludlow, the Earl of Warwick (later 'the Kingmaker') was marching from London towards Warwickshire, while the Earl of Salisbury was marching from Yorkshire to join the Duke at Ludlow.

On the Lancastrian side the King was collecting an army in the Midlands, while Queen Margaret was at Eccleshall, 10 miles south-east of Market Drayton, possibly accompanied by a few troops. A royal army had just been raised in Cheshire and Shropshire by Lord Audley, and it was concentrated about Market Drayton. As soon as the Queen heard that the Earl of Salisbury was marching to join the Duke of York at Ludlow, she ordered Lord Audley to intercept and 'arrest' him. Thus far the facts are not in dispute.

The next definite indication that we get is that on 23 September a battle was fought between the two at Blore Heath, 2½ miles east of Market Drayton. What we may call the Beaumont-Ramsay version is that the Lancastrians were encamped 1 mile west of Drayton (Audley himself being at Audley Brow, 4 miles further west), with Salisbury one mile to the south of them, on the day before the battle; that Salisbury fell back to Blore Heath in order to draw Audley into a trap that he had set at Blore Heath. This fantastic conception is neatly disposed of by F. R. Twemlow, in the only modern study of the battle, *The Battle of Blore Heath* (1912), in the following passage:

'The obvious comment is that it is most unlikely that an experienced general like Salisbury would have had his small force divided at night time, detaching part of it on something like a wild goose chase; that he should have followed at dawn with the remainder, taking a bee line across two boggy valleys and a wood, disregarding all roads and fords, when pursued by a force of more than twice his strength, which commanded the ordinary road between his point of departure and his destination; and still more unlikely is it that, having done all this, he should have been rewarded by a crushing victory.'

The explanation of this curious theory is the incorrect interpretation of place-names. Audley Brow, where Beaumont supposed Audley to be encamped, was so named long before the battle, and had no connexion with the Lancastrian general's position. Salisbury Hill was no doubt so called because the Yorkist general camped there, but that was on the day following, not the day before the battle. All that remains, therefore, in support of the theory is the fact that Salisbury is reported by one authority[1] as starting to retire before the battle, and then reversing his steps and engaging in battle. This was evidently a tactical move on the actual battlefield, and had nothing to do with a complicated ruse such as is suggested.

What really happened, then, is simply that the two armies advanced towards one another along the Market Drayton–Newcastle road, each having good information of the movements of the other by their 'espials', and that they met head on at Blore Heath.

THE BATTLEFIELD

And now to locate the precise field of battle. We know that it was fought near Mucklestone, one mile north of Blore Heath, and that it

[1] Hall, copied by Grafton, Holinshead, and Stowe.

took place on 'Blore Heath'. Further than this we get absolute precision by the fact that a monument was put up on the field to commemorate the death of Lord Audley, and according to Plot (writing in 1685) he was 'slain just in that spot'.[1] There is no reason to doubt this. The actual spot is not one that would be selected for a monument unless it was the precise spot, for it is neither on a road, or on the top of the ridge, but half-way down the slope in an inconspicuous place.

With the aid of this cross it might be supposed that there is nothing more to decide: the battle would presumably be fought astride the road at this spot—that is, facing roughly east–west. But Twemlow, whose book I have already quoted from with approval, and to whose topographical researches I am much indebted, places the battle line entirely to the south of the road, and facing north–south (see sketch-map). By what line of reasoning does he arrive at this peculiar result? Before giving the answer to this question I will describe the preliminary moves on the battlefield.

The most detailed account comes, curiously enough, from the pen of a foreigner, Jehan de Waurin,[2] the Burgundian chronicler. He had however visited England and although he is frequently wrong in his names, he probably obtained some of his battle details from eye-witnesses; they certainly ring true. Let us then follow his account in detail. According to him, the Yorkists approached at dawn, and having traversed the forest they spotted the Lancastrian army behind a great 'forest hedge', above which they could only see the tops of the pennons. So they dismounted behind the forest and formed their line. They rested one wing on the wood and at the other they made a laager of wagons and horses tied together; behind them they dug a good trench for security, and they fixed stakes in their front. When they were ranged in order the Lancastrians advanced, the whole army being mounted. The Yorkists were then all shriven and lay down and kissed the ground. The Lancastrians presently came on, and when they were within bowshot they opened a very heavy fire, to which the Yorkists replied. Many horses were killed and 20–22 Yorkists and 500–600 Lancastrians. (Waurin is writing from the Yorkist viewpoint and probably exaggerates the Lancastrian losses.) Audley was obliged to fall back just outside bowshot. A second attack, however, was soon mounted and this time only 10 Yorkists fell and about 100 Lancastrians.

[1] According to Beaumont, battle relics, sword-hilt, stirrup, and iron banner-head, have been found near the site of the cross.

[2] Or Wavrin—the letters U and V were the same in medieval times.

The Lancastrians now changed their tactics; they dismounted and sent up the hill 4,000 men on foot. These engaged in a hand-to-hand contest lasting over half an hour. They counted on the support of their mounted cavalry but these, seeing that the affair was not going well, rode right off the field, leaving the dismounted men to their own devices; 500 of them even deserted to the Yorkists. Thus the battle was lost, the Lancastrian dead numbering 2,000 and the Yorkists 56.

Thus Waurin. We need not take his figures too seriously, but his account provides some valuable indications as to locality. And we can add to it from Hall's account, which states that a small stream divided the two armies at first, that Salisbury started to retire, in order to induce Audley to attack; that Audley crossed the stream and did attack; and that Salisbury then returned to his old position. Twemlow arrives at his conclusion from a combination of the above statements, together with deep research (for which we should be very grateful) into the nature of the terrain at the time of the battle. He finds that the forest behind the Yorkists was as shown in my sketch-map; that the stream flowed in the same channel as at the present day, but that the road from Newcastle made a sharp bend as shown on the sketch-map, instead of continuing straight across the heath, as does the modern road. Thus for 750 yards it hugged the stream, now known as the Wemberton brook, a narrow, muddy road with steep banks. Twemlow proceeds: 'So that for a distance of about 750 yards the road passed through a narrow defile. . . . Here then was the "Pass" mentioned by the Chronicler Rapin. . . .' And it was the existence of this defile and the determination to contest the passage of it which caused Audley to take up the position that he did. Twemlow marks this position on his map as shown on mine by the letters AA, facing the 'pass'.

I suggest that the author has here fallen into two errors. Rapin was not an original source for the battle, but a French eighteenth-century historian, and the word 'pass' does not appear in any original source; it is merely a translation of Rapin's own word. Therefore no special significance need be attached to it.

Secondly, the word 'pass' in medieval battle accounts need not mean more than a narrow spot, not necessarily a defile or pass as the word now indicates. This narrow point may be no more than a gap in a hedge (it is so used at the battle of Shrewsbury), or a ford over a stream (it is so used as late as the battle of Langport). The natural inference is that Rapin merely meant that the army crossing the brook might be bunched up at the crossing place. He probably, being a foreigner, had never seen the brook and envisaged it as a much more serious obstacle than it actually was, Waurin, it may be observed, did not trouble to mention it at all. But apart from the above considerations the Twemlow theory does not satisfy the test of Inherent Military Probability. Consider for a moment what it implies. Apart from the complexity of the manoeuvre—inclining off the road to the right, and then wheeling to the left in line, a difficult operation for a raw army such as this—it would take some period of time to complete, and when concluded, the bulk of the army would be in full view from the Yorkist army on the march, for there would be rising ground behind them. Could Salisbury, who was an experienced soldier, sixty years of age, have been guilty of the egregious blunder of solemnly marching his army along a narrow hollow road, whence he could not quickly debouch, along the front of a hostile army drawn up at a distance of 150 yards—bowshot range? To state the thing is to dismiss it out of hand. Any general still in possession of his senses would do one of four other things: (1) Continue across the heath towards the ford (there would almost certainly be a track leading to it, and in September the going should be at its best); (2) diverge further to his right in order to slip past out of sight of the Lancastrians;[1] (3) advance and attack the enemy; (4) halt and form a defensive line of battle.

There are other objections to the Twemlow thesis: (1) It is not consistent with Waurin's account that only the tops of the pennons could be seen; this presupposes ground either flat or sloping down to the rear of the Lancastrians. (2) It places the spot where Audley fell on the very flank of the field, hardly a likely place for the commander. (3) If such an unusual manoeuvre had been carried out, some reference to it would surely have been made by the chroniclers. (4) Audley too, was an old, experienced soldier, who had fought in France and had been selected by the Queen for the task. Could he have been capable of such an inane proceeding? (5) Burial pits—always a sure sign of where the heaviest fighting took place—are suspected at Audley Cross Farm, 250 yards in front of Twemlow's battle line.

But if we cannot accept the Twemlow thesis what other solution is there left except the natural, simple, straightforward one that Audley marched straight up the road for a mile or two from Drayton, that on hearing that the Yorkists were approaching, he spurred forward to find a convenient position to take up, blocking the Newcastle road; that he reached the brook when the Yorkist patrols were debouching from

[1] His object was to join forces with the Duke of York at Ludlow.

the forest (or perhaps a little earlier), that he noticed a clearly defined though shallow ridge sloping down to a stream which crossed the road in his front, and that he said to his officers: 'This is the very position for us! Deploy your companies to the right and left of the road here.'

That, at any rate, was the conclusion that I came to as I approached the brook, in the steps of the commander (as I always do in such cases).

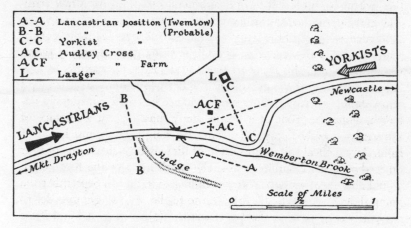

SKETCH-MAP 23.   BLORE HEATH: THE BATTLE

This position runs parallel to the brook and 400 yards short of it, the right half being behind the lane just to the east of Blore Heath New Farm, a lane that Twemlow shows as being in existence at that time. The hedge of this lane would thus hide all except the tops of the pennons from the Yorkists on the opposing crest. There is now no corresponding hedge to hide the left half of the line, but as it is on lower ground that fact in itself would hide them. In short, this position seems to fit exactly the situation given by the chroniclers.

THE YORKIST POSITION

Let us now consider the Yorkist position. Here, if we accept my siting of the Lancastrians, no difficulties present themselves. Everything seems to flow along inevitable channels. The Yorkist 'espials', as they reach Audley Cross Farm descry the Lancastrians ranging themselves in line on the opposite side of the brook. Salisbury is informed of the fact; he makes a reconnaissance, verifies the information, spots the pennons behind the hedge (a sure indication), and decides to take up an opposing position in the hopes that Audley will do the attacking. He has only about 5,000 men, and a position about 600–800 yards in front-age is indicated. If he extends 300 yards on each side of the track leading across the heath, his left flank will rest on the boggy bottom through which the stream runs, a strong flank; the right flank will, on the contrary, be 'in the air'; so he copies the Black Prince at Poitiers, who held a strikingly similar position, his left flank on a boggy bottom and his right flank on higher ground on no natural feature; the Black Prince therefore strengthened this flank by forming a laager of his wagons. Poitiers was fought only a century before Blore Heath, and its details were probably known to most soldiers of the time, so that conscious imitation by Salisbury is quite likely. Thus I site his position running north and south through Audley Cross Farm, and 120 yards east of the spot where Audley fell.

THE FEIGNED RETREAT

There remains one final problem to be solved—the so-called 'feigned retreat' of the Yorkists. This feigned retreat was stretched by Beaumont, as we have seen, to a distance of 3 miles. Twemlow, who throws justified scorn on this, accepts the story of a retreat, but only half-heartedly, stating that 'it was probably confined to his centre, and did not extend to his entrenched flanks'. Considering that his flanks cannot have been much more than 350 yards from his centre, it certainly could not have proceeded very far. But what an odd manoeuvre it would have been. What would Audley have made of it? The flank most easily visible to his opponent was obviously the flank on the ridge which was terminated by his laager of wagons. Audley would note that though the men in the centre had apparently disappeared the wagons were still in laager. He could hardly have supposed that this indicated a retirement. The usual procedure is to send off the wagons first. No, I cannot believe that Salisbury was as fatuous here as Twemlow makes Audley at the beginning. Salisbury was twenty-nine years of age when his father-in-law, the famous Earl, who was the leading general of his day, died. It is hard to imagine that the great Salisbury could have such an inept son-in-law. Yet I do not think that we are justified in rejecting the story of the feigned retreat in its entirety. A feigned retreat *in the course* of a battle is a most difficult, indeed impractical operation, but before the battle starts it is a different matter, and Salisbury would have every inducement to attempt some such subterfuge. For the defence possessed great advantage over the attack in those days, and was in the English

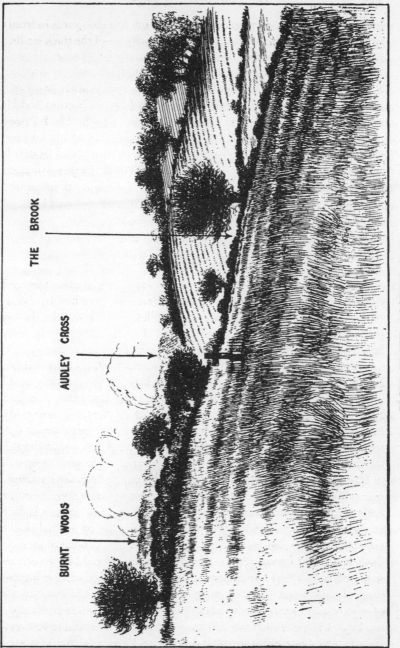

THE BROOK

AUDLEY CROSS

BURNT WOODS

BLORE HEATH, LOOKING EAST

tradition. Crécy, Poitiers, Agincourt, all pointed that way. Moreover a brook divided the two hosts and this would add to the difficulties of the attacker. No doubt there was a distinct pause when both armies were drawn up: each hoped that the other would begin. When neither side showed any sign of moving it probably occurred to Salisbury to make as if to retreat in order to induce his opponents to cross the stream. But the obvious way to do this would be to start loading up the wagons ostentatiously and harnessing up the draught-horses. I feel little doubt that this is what Salisbury did. Audley's troops would spot it. 'They're harnessing up,' the excited cry would ring throughout the ranks. Audley would react immediately. 'The Queen has ordered me to arrest Salisbury. I must not let him slip away, especially when I have a much larger army,' he would reason. His mind was made up. 'Avaunt, banners!' he cried, and the whole Lancastrian army advanced in line, the horses leaping the little brook or splashing through the water. On reaching the other side they were within the range of the arrows, and the accustomed artillery duel then took place. The sequel was as described by Waurin.

*   *   *   *   *

The actual details of the fighting are sparse, and it is not even certain at what period in the battle Audley fell, though it is conjectured that it occurred in the second mounted charge and that the change of tactics —a dismounted in place of a mounted attack—indicates a change in the command.

What is significant is the traitorous conduct of the 500 Lancastrians in going over to the enemy, for it reminds us that in civil wars divided allegiances are a factor that has always to be taken into account. It is this, and the better training of the Yorkist army (which had been in being the longer), that decided the issue.

The slaughter of the losing side was great—again a common feature of medieval warfare, when knights encased in armour and dismounted, could not remount without the assistance of their pages, most of whom had probably run off the field.

All we know (if we pass over Gregory's confusing story) is that the pursuit lasted for two hours, and that a field on the banks of the river Tern, 2 miles in rear (a natural place for a slaughter), is still known as Deadman's Den.

Local tradition avers that Queen Margaret watched the battle from the tower of Mucklestone church. As she would have had to pass round the rear of the Yorkist Army in order to get to Mucklestone we can dismiss this story. On the other hand, nothing is more likely than that she rode out in the direction of the battle to see what she could see. If she ascended any church tower it was probably Cheswardine, 3 miles south of the field. It is clear from her action that very few, if any, of her troops had reached Eccleshall by the day of the battle—in spite of Ramsay's reference to 'The Royalist forces at Eccleshall'. Two other local traditions that I heard as a boy (my home being near) are that the Queen escaped by reversing the horseshoes on her palfrey, and that the brook ran red with blood for three days. It is hard to say which is the least unlikely of these traditions.

CHAPTER XX

The Second Battle of St. Albans, February 17th, 1461

IN more ways than one this is the most remarkable battle of the Wars of the Roses—and the most tantalizing. Remarkable inasmuch as it included three tactical features almost unheard of in medieval warfare —a night approach march followed by a dawn attack; a flank, instead of a frontal, attack; and an army occupying a position several miles in length. Tantalizing because the records of the battle are more than usually scanty, even for that period. As a result, scarcely a single historian has ventured to compile a map of the battle, and most of them slur over the inherent difficulties and problems as if they did not exist, and pass on as quickly as can decently be done to subsequent events. If therefore I try to disperse some of the fog that obscures the battlefield it must be understood that a great deal of my reconstruction is pure conjecture. In accordance with my usual practice, I retain most of my reasons for this reconstruction to an end section, to be studied by the curious and skipped by the rest.

PRELIMINARY MOVES
(Sketch-map 24)

On New Year's Eve, 1461, the Lancastrians won the great victory of Wakefield, and captured and beheaded the Duke of York; after which Queen Margaret advanced on London with the object of rescuing the King, who, though nominally still ruling, was in the power of the Earl of Warwick. Hearing of her advance, the said Earl hastily collected an army of Londoners and Kentishmen, and advanced north on February 12th to St. Albans, where he halted.

Meanwhile, Margaret was pushing slowly south with an enormous but ill-disciplined and heterogeneous army of Northerners, Scots, Welsh and French, pillaging as they went. Indeed we track her course by the towns she pillaged—Grantham, Stamford, Peterborough, Huntingdon, Royston. In other words, she was advancing approximately down the Great North Road. Why, then, did Warwick take the St. Albans road? A glance at Sketch-map 21, Chap. 18, will show that by this road he should fail to meet the Lancastrians. This is one of the many problems of the campaign. The presumption is that Margaret turned west from Royston, for some obscure reason, and that news of it reached Warwick before he left the capital. Undoubtedly Margaret did turn west, and we next hear of her army entering Dunstable on the 16th, after the Yorkists had been stationary at St. Albans for four days.

Warwick occupied these four days of waiting by preparing a widely extended position, covering a front from St. Albans on the left to No Man's Land (1½ miles north-east of Sandridge) on the right, a distance of about four miles. Obviously this position was not held in one unbroken line, but probably in four detachments, covering the lines of approach from the north and north-west (see Sketch-map 21, Chap. 18). The Lancastrian army was clearly moving across his front from east to west, and it seems probable that when Warwick took up these dispositions the Northerners were on the axis Bedford—Luton—Harpenden. Now, from Harpenden two roads led towards the capital, one via St. Albans, the other via Hatfield. Warwick therefore selected positions astride these two roads at Barnard's Heath and Sandridge respectively, and placed flank detachments in St. Albans on the left and No Man's Land on the right. This is a very modern form of disposition—quite unprecedented in the Middle Ages. Nowadays it would be sound and natural, owing to improvement in communications and in speed of concentration. But the Yorkist flank communications were very bad and slow, as we shall see.

The striking fact may be noted in passing that Warwick occupied the very line that the Belgae (according to Dr. Mortimer Wheeler) constructed against the older Britons shortly before the coming of the Romans. It ran from St. Albans to Wheathamstead one mile northeast of No Man's Land, and parts of the great ditch are still visible as Beech Bottom (see Sketch-map 24). Warwick was encouraged to occupy this extensive position by the knowledge that he had with him some defensive devices that were novelties, calculated to give the oncoming Lancastrians some nasty shocks. The quaint description that Gregory, the chronicler, gives of them seems worth quoting fairly fully:

'The (gunners) had such instruments that would shoot both pellets of lead and arrows of an ell of length with six feathers, three in the middle and three at the other end, with a great mighty head of iron at the other end, and wildfire withal. Also they had great nets made of cord, of four fathoms (24 feet) of length, and four feet broad, and at every second knot there was a nail standing upright, that there could no man pass over it by likelihood but he should be hurt. Also they had pavises (shields) and loops with shutting windows to shoot out of, they standing behind the pavis, and the pavis as full of 3d. nails as they might stand. And when their shot was spent and done they cast the pavis before them; then there might no man come over the pavis at them for the nails that stood upright, but if he would mischief himself. Also they had a thing made like unto a lattice full of nails as the net was, but it would be moved as a man would; and that served to lie at gaps (in hedges) where horsemen would enter in, and many a caltrap.'[1] Warwick had not only cannon but also Burgundians with 'hand-guns', till then practically unknown in this country.

While the Earl was methodically constructing his position, his opponent, Queen Margaret, was on the move. It is thought by some that the real commander of her army was one Andrew Trollope, described as her 'great captain'. But the manoeuvre carried out by the Lancastrians was so unlike the normal of those days and so unpredictable that a feminine hand may be detected in it. Indeed it reminds one of the feminine hand of Joan the Maid. Margaret of Anjou was herself French, the Maid was a popular French heroine, and it is quite possible that Margaret was striving to emulate her. This Margaret of Anjou was certainly a remarkable woman. Wedded to the unfortunate Henry VI at the early age of 16, she had for many years played a big part in the government of the country of her adoption. Possibly she deserves Fortesque's stinging description of her: 'That pestilent, indomitable woman'; but we cannot withhold a tinge of admiration for dexterity, and even brilliance; for the manoeuvre about to be narrated seems to deserve that description.

This manoeuvre was made possible, or at any rate easy, owing to treachery within the Yorkist ranks—a feature all too common in those unhappy civil wars. A Kentish squire named Lovelace, who commanded a contingent in the Yorkist army, conveyed to Margaret information of the Yorkist position, evidently adding that when the moment arrived he would come over to her side. We can place the Lancastrian army somewhere between Bedford and Luton when this

---

[1] A device consisting of four spikes so arranged that whatever its position on the ground one spike sticks upwards. They had the same effect against cavalry as the modern minefield has against tanks.

intelligence arrived. Margaret promptly decided to take advantage of this knowledge in a novel way. Instead of advancing straight down the road through Luton and Harpenden and attacking the hostile army in its front, in accordance with all the precedents of chivalry, she decided to attempt a surprise flank attack, and to roll up the position from left to right, thus taking full advantage of the faulty dispositions adopted by the enemy. Moreover, to ensure surprise, speed was necessary. Warwick had scouts ('prickers') out in front who would keep him informed of her change of direction if she maintained her previous crawling pace. Margaret therefore resolved first to make a dash to Dunstable, then by an abrupt change of direction to follow it up by a night march to St. Albans, arriving on the left flank of the unsuspecting enemy at dawn on February 17th.

THE BATTLE

This bold and original plan was put into operation. A Yorkist detachment of 200 men was holding Dunstable, but the sudden attack took them by surprise and they were quickly overwhelmed, all being accounted for as killed or prisoners. Consequently none got back with the important news to Warwick. The first stage had been successfully carried out. Next came the night march, on top of the previous rapid march and action. This was hard going, and it speaks well for the Queen's hold over her loosely disciplined host that she got her army on the move again in the dead of night. The distance from Dunstable to St. Albans is a good 12 miles, but it is straight down the Watling Street, so it was easy for the army to find its way in the dark. All went well, and according to one account they reached St. Albans at three o'clock in the morning. This seems hard to believe, for it would be over three hours before dawn. Unless there was a full moon, the action that ensued would be impossible, for it consisted of a fire action by archers, which would be impossible in the pitch-dark. Probably it was just getting light when the advanced guard of the Lancastrians passed through the old city of Verulamium, crossed the River Ver and ascended what is now George Street into the heart of the town (see Sketch-map 24). So complete was the surprise that the barrier where the town ditch crossed the road was not in position, nor apparently any defenders. But the alarm had been given, and on reaching the top of the hill, just opposite the Abbey Church, the leading men were heavily engaged by the detachment of archers that had been detailed as garrison of the town.[1] In the confines of the narrow street it was impossible to escape the arrows which the Yorkists shot with deadly effect, just as they had done at First St. Albans, six years previously. The advanced guard of the Northerners fell back discomfited across the river and halted by St. Michael's Church. Here a council of war was held, after which scouts were thrown forward to endeavour to find some other unguarded entry into the town. Just as in the first battle, after an unpropitious opening, a way in had been discovered, so in this case the scouts presently returned with the cheering intelligence that the

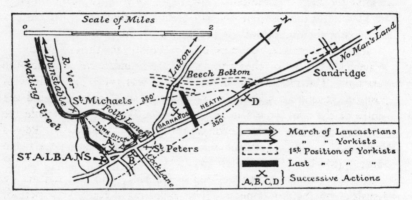

SKETCH–MAP 24.   ST. ALBANS II: THE BATTLE

entrance through the ditch by Folly Lane and Catharine Lane was unguarded. Prompt advantage was taken of this; the army moving off along the indicated route and entering the town by Catharine Lane. From this lane they debouched into St. Peter's Street, just opposite Cock Lane.

An interesting situation now developed. The rear of the Lancastrian army had not yet passed St. Michael's Church, so the garrison of the town had still to watch that quarter in case of a resumption of the attack; and meanwhile they now found themselves cut off from the main Yorkist army. They were encompassed on both sides. But so were the Lancastrian vanguard, for they had the garrison on their right and the main Yorkist army on their left; *they* also were encompassed! This is a situation that frequently occurs in war—indeed every time one army makes or threatens a double penetration.

[1] Marked A... on Sketch-map 24.

Each side is geometrically encompassed to the same degree. But in practice things are seldom equal: the side that has the better morale ignores the threat to its flanks and attacks boldly; the other side conforms and defends. In the present case one might suppose that the Lancastrians, having the initiative, would have the better morale, and that, ignoring the garrison, they would swing to their left and attempt to roll up the Yorkist army. Such was no doubt Margaret's intention. Unfortunately for her, the superior morale was now possessed by her immediate opponents. These had only a short time before decisively defeated the first attack; they were archers with a deservedly high reputation. Moreover, they were comparatively fresh, whereas their opponents were tired after their night march, and the Northerners could not afford to ignore them.

Instead, therefore, of pushing on boldly to their objective—Warwick's left flank—they turned aside to liquidate the troublesome garrison. The First Battle of St. Albans was re-enacted, but with positions reversed. This time the Yorkists were ranged round the centre of the town, the southern end of St. Peter's Street, while the Lancastrians were to the north of them, and the broad St. Peter's Street became for the second time in six years the scene of a fierce battle. (Marked B on Sketch-map 24.)

The Yorkist bowmen resisted stubbornly, and exacted heavy casualties on their opponents. The battle raged for a long period, and by the time the town was completely in the possession of the Red Rose the sun was high in the heavens. Why, the reader may well ask, did not Warwick attack Margaret's rear during this contest? It is one of the many problems of the battle. The reader must push up the slope, past St. Peter's Church, and out of the town on to Barnard's Heath in order to discover the answer.

I have said above that the position selected by Warwick followed approximately the line of the old Belgic boundary. These Belgae were the comparatively civilized and latest invaders of south-east England, and they dug and manned Beech Bottom (see Sketch-map 24) in order to repel the more barbarous denizens of the North. History was curiously repeating itself, for the White Rose Kentishmen were more civilized than their Northern opponents, and they found themselves defending the same line. The question we have now to consider is: did they occupy the line of Beech Bottom or the top of the ridge to the south-east of it? Along this ridge, about 100 feet above the valley followed by Beech Bottom, runs the modern road to Sandridge and Wheathampstead. Warwick was in two minds whether to hold the one or the other. In favour of Beech Bottom was the fact that it provided a splendid and formidable obstacle. Even to-day this impressive ditch is over 30 feet deep in places, and at the time of the battle must have been even deeper. And it strides the direct road to Luton. Its drawbacks were that it is not continuous—it only extends for a mile—its left flank 'is in the air', and it runs along the bottom of the valley. In favour of the ridge position is the fact that it has the advantage of the slope in its favour—like Crécy or Poitiers—and that its left flank joins up naturally with the town of St. Albans. I have come to the conclusion that Warwick originally occupied and fortified the Beech Bottom, and that on hearing of the approach of the Northerners from the Dunstable direction he hastily withdrew his left wing up to the top of the ridge and started fortifying it. My reasons will be given in the final section.

Thus while the battle was raging in the town below, a complicated and difficult manœuvre was being carried out on Barnard's Heath. Warwick had decided to 'write off' the devoted defenders of the town, and to concentrate his efforts on preparing and occupying his new position. Having set this operation in motion, the Earl departed to visit his widely extended and distant centre and right columns with the intention of bringing them over to the aid of his left. We will for the moment leave him so employed and see how things were faring in the town.

As soon as all resistance came to an end the leading troops of the Lancastrian army had to be reorganized, and as far as possible refreshed. Remember, they had made a rapid march on the previous day, followed it up by a night march a few hours later, and had fought two sharp actions, the last of considerable length. Next, the new line held by the Yorkist left wing had to be reconnoitred and a line of battle drawn up in the opposite direction to the one in which they had just been fighting. This was clearly a difficult job, and it must have been midday before the new battle was joined. We can picture the new Yorkist line astride the Sandridge road and ridge, about half a mile beyond St. Peter's Church, in fact across Barnard's Heath, with the right flank resting on Beech Bottom, where it is crossed by the Harpenden road.[1] This makes the line about 900 yards long, quite a reasonable position, and one which the respite had allowed the defenders to fortify hurriedly with the queer contraptions that we have

[1] The position is Shown in Sketch-map 24, marked C.

described. Thus when the Lancastrians advanced once more to the attack, for the third time that day, the Yorkists, though heavily outnumbered for the moment, were able to put up a good fight and offer strenuous resistance.

At first things went badly with Queen Margaret's troops. They could make no impression on their opponents, and were somewhat taken aback by the new 'secret weapons' employed. Trollope himself was caught in a caltrap, but he managed to fight on. The handgun men no doubt had moral if not material effect, though we are told that the artillery acquitted itself badly. When the occasion arose 'they could not shoot one of these, but the fire turned back upon them that would shoot these things', *i.e.* the aforementioned pellets of lead, etc. They were, in fact, 'hoist with their own petard'.

In spite of these minor setbacks things were going well for the Yorkists, and it seemed that when the remainder of the army came up victory would be assured. But when would that be? There was still no sign of reinforcement from the centre column, and men began to look back over their shoulder, scanning the horizon, like Sister Anne, for any signs of approach. But signs there were none. Meanwhile, snowflakes were beginning to fall; their numbers were becoming steadily depleted by casualties while those of the Northerners were steadily increasing as Margaret's huge army gradually deployed and entered into the battle. As long as the Yorkist morale remained high there was ground for hope. But 'hope deferred maketh the heart sick'. Hope *was* deferred: the Yorkist heart *did* become sick. In other words, the Yorkist left column turned and fled from the field, falling back on the centre.

We have reached the haziest period of the battle, and once more we must turn our gaze in the direction of the Earl of Warwick. What was he doing? Why did not the centre column appear? We left the Earl on his way to this centre column. It is fair to suppose that he was somewhat flummoxed. His intelligence had served him badly. Whilst leisurely fortifying his position, he had little idea that the Northern army was so close as it really was. He had sent out patrols the previous night, but they had served him ill. Only one returned with a report, and this report was misleading. The scout asserted that the Lancastrian army was nine miles away at dawn on the day of battle, when in reality it was hard on the town of St. Albans. The first report of contact therefore caught Warwick unawares; it was a bad start for the day. He resembled the Duke of Newcastle who got up half an hour late and spent the rest of the day trying to catch it up; but Warwick had got up several hours late.

To add to his difficulties he had to deal with insubordination. It must be remembered that the Lancastrians, wild and unruly though they might be, were battle-hardened, having utterly defeated their chief opponent at Wakefield only a few weeks before. They had been welded into a force and their behaviour on the field of battle proved better than when 'behind the line'—as has since often been the case with irregular troops. But the bulk of the Yorkists had been hastily raised, and hurried to the battlefield, and they had not yet experienced the welding effect of a battle. Warwick himself was probably in two minds as to what was the best thing to do now that his elaborately prepared position had been turned, in an unheard of and despicable manner. He had never welcomed a fight at this juncture: the young Earl of March, son of the Duke of York (shortly to be Edward IV), was marching from Wales to join him. Would it not be prudent to cut his losses and fall back on London in an effort to join up with his friends? Evidently some of his lieutenants were of this opinion, and when he tried to induce them to march to the help of the left wing he encountered opposition. All this consumed time, and meanwhile the left wing was getting into sore straits, as we have seen. By the time Warwick had prevailed upon his obstructive subordinates and had got his centre column on the move from Sandridge towards Barnard's Heath the left wing had broken. Midway between village and heath, Beech Bottom merges into the Sandridge road (the road, in fact, for some way runs along the remnants of the old ditch) and from that point the road climbs the gentle slope of the Barnard's Heath ridge. The tree-lined road now winds up the hill, and there are on each side plentiful fields and crofts now, as there were on the day of the battle. As Warwick's men drew near, a terrible sight met their gaze. Pouring down the slope, over hedges and ditches, in a vast torrent, came the remnants of the defeated left wing. Their wild flight infected the oncoming column (in just the same way that, 100 years earlier, the flight of the Dauphin's column at Poitiers infected the oncoming column of the Duke of Orleans). The one merged into the other, and the flight became doubled in volume after a brief engagement (at the point marked *D*.)

The disorganized masses flowed on to and through Sandridge. But Warwick was not with them. In later days he was quite unjustifiably suspected of cowardice owing to his absence from the front line. The truth is that in a normal medieval battle, once the two lines have been ranged opposite one another and the rival commanders have delivered their rival addresses, informing all ranks that the Deity was on their side, there was little that the commander could do to influence the fight; he therefore naturally plunged into the thick of it. But this was far from being a normal medieval battle. Warwick might still influence the fight if he could induce his distant right wing to close on the centre. To that wing he had therefore hurried. But here a fresh contretemps awaited him. Treason, as so often in civil war, had shown its ugly visage: Lovelace with his Kentish detachment had taken the opportunity quietly to slip away and join the Lancastrians. The result had a shattering effect upon the remainder of the column, and the *coup de grâce* was delivered by the sight of the rest of the army hastening towards them in full panicky flight. It must have been a terrible moment for the still youthful Warwick (only 30 years of age), but by some means he managed to 'form front to his flank', to swing the right column, or what was left of it, round to the left and make some sort of a line on which to hold up the oncoming Lancastrians. This line no doubt ran along the ridge 500 yards to the south of No Man's Land; and here till dusk he managed to hold up the enemy, and indeed to leave the field with an intact force still estimated at 4,000 men. With this force he managed to skirt round his opponents and join the Earl of March at Chipping Norton in Oxfordshire, though how he did it and the route he took remains a complete mystery.

The last scene of all brings the unfortunate King Henry VI into the picture. Warwick had made him accompany the army from London, ostensibly as monarch but in reality as prisoner. Poor Henry must by this time have become accustomed to being a helpless spectator on the battlefield. The last scene finds him seated under an oak near No Man's Land, 'smiling to see the discomfiture' of what was nominally his own army. He met his Queen and her young son Edward on the field of battle, and then proceeded to St. Albans Abbey, where he spent the night.

COMMENTS

Queen Margaret's strategy had been unusual, brilliant, and phenomenally successful. It must have made the leading soldiers of the time do a little quiet thinking. Hitherto it had been assumed—indeed chivalry demanded—that armies should engage front to front; but here was an army engaging front to *flank*. What did they make of it? One can imagine old generals giving it up in despair, with a shrug of the shoulder and the observation, 'Well, she's a woman: what more can you expect?' At any rate, her example was not followed in any other great battles fought in this country.

By contrast Warwick's strategy was plebeian. He approached his problem in a defensive spirit. His object was to defend London. Before setting out he had sent to request the Earl of March in Wales to collect an army and march to the defence of the capital. Meanwhile he seems to have thought that if he could construct a sufficiently formidable-looking position Margaret would obligingly form up opposite it, and equally obligingly come to terms.

But the battle shows up the inherent weakness of a passive defence. It requires two to play the game: if the enemy refuses to play, all your efforts and your gadgets are in vain. Warwick was badly served by his information service, and Margaret was correspondingly favoured thereby. This in itself tipped the balance against the Earl and in favour of the Queen. But even had he the best information service in the world it was rash of him to spread out his army on such a wide front without the means of speedy communication and concentration. If he had possessed anything approaching modern means and methods there would be much to say in favour of his dispositions. They were certainly original—but he was up against a still more original opponent. What a story they could have told if each had written what we should now call a commander-in-chief's despatch describing the campaign and battle—or, better still, their memoirs years later!

But the last word lay with Warwick. While Margaret remained irresolutely at St. Albans he not only joined forces with March at Chipping Norton, but induced him to march straight on London, where they arrived only 12 days after the battle—a 12 days in which Warwick's remnant had covered 120 miles. Margaret's tactics were in the end nullified by Warwick's strategy.

PROBLEMS OF THE BATTLE

The reconstruction of the Second Battle of St. Albans is hedged about with problems, but no one reading cursorily any modern history would suspect it. The historians have a disarming way of skating quietly over a difficulty as if it was not there. The silences of the original chroniclers and of the modern historians are devastating. Let me give some examples.

First, the route and rate of Margaret's southward march. We know she was at York on January 20th and at Dunstable on February 16th. The intervening space and period have to be interpolated as best we can, assisted by the list of some of the towns that her army pillaged on the way. We do not even know if this list is complete: probably not, for one chronicler asserts that she left a trail of devastation 30 miles wide. It seems, however, tolerably certain from this list that the Northerners marched down the old Ermine Street to the latitude of Royston and then turned west to Dunstable. Assuming that they left York the day after Margaret's arrival, namely January 21st, I reckon that they must have averaged nine to ten miles per day.

This does not allow of a halt on the line Bedford—Luton, as suggested in my narrative; but if it was not so why did not Warwick advance along the York road instead of Watling Street? The Lancastrian army could, by marching 12 miles per day, have reached the neighbourhood of Luton by February 9th, which fact could have reached Warwick before he set out. The only other possible theory is that Warwick deliberately veered off to his left in order to approach more nearly to the Earl of March, hoping and assuming that Margaret would conform, as did York and Warwick, under very similar circumstances in the campaign of First St. Albans.

Next problem: who commanded the Northern army, Trollope or the Queen? The statement that Trollope was 'grand captain' seems to have satisfied most of those who have given the matter any thought; but, though Trollope was afterwards well thought of, I think he would have received greater notice had he been the architect of such a resounding victory. He was knighted shortly after the battle, when he apologized for having slain only fifteen men! This aeems hardly the *metier* of a commander-in-chief. But probably he scted as adviser to the Queen, who, however, had views of her own as to how the campaign should be conducted.

But the greatest silence of all concerns the dispositions of Warwick's army. The chroniclers are hopelessly vague. The narrative of the best of them (William of Worcester) is unfortunately deficient of the pages dealing with the battle. They have been mysteriously torn out. My theory is that this account of a Yorkist defeat was *too* truthful for the Yorkist régime under which it was written. Gregory's *Chronicle*, from which I have quoted, is the best extant account of the actual battle, but he is silent as to movements and localities. We, however, get the names Barnard's Heath, Sandridge and No Man's Land, and are pretty well left to do the best we can with them. It is, however, tolerably clear that the battle resulted in a running fight; a passage in the Latin account of the *Registrum* of St. Albans states explicitly that the casualties occurred over a wide area ('in diversis croftis').

If there is silence regarding the *general* line taken up by Warwick it is greater still regarding the *exact* line. It is surprising that no account of the battle mentions Beech Bottom, yet that very remarkable feature must have had its bearing on the battle. In considering the problem I eagerly scanned every shred of information that has come down to us, but I drew an almost complete blank. What influenced me in deciding that Warwick originally held Beech Bottom was the fact that we know he did change his position at the last moment. If to the line on Barnard's Heath, then from where? From Beech Bottom seems to be the only answer. And, such a position, though it has its drawbacks, is an obvious defensive locality. I hesitated for a long time, revolving the matter over in my mind, and then the thought suddenly occurred to me that perhaps Warwick experienced a similar tormenting doubt when making his decision! It gave me an unexpected fellow-feeling for the 'last of the Barons'!

There still remains a narrow strip of common land alongside the Sandridge road just where it reaches the top of the ridge—all that is left of the old 'Barnet' or Barnard's Heath. If the reader will stand there and then descend the hill to Beech Bottom he will comprehend the cause of Warwick's hesitation.

A final difficulty is to fill in the long period of time during which the battle lasted. There is good evidence that it opened at or before dawn, and did not finish till dusk. In all this period of about twelve hours there is no indication in the accounts that have reached us of how it was divided up between the different phases of the battle. Exact chronology in the course of a battle—even of a modern one—is notoriously difficult to reconstruct. I can only say I have done the best I could; I can at least claim that my account is not in conflict with any of the known facts, nor with I.M.P.

CHAPTER XXI

The Battle of Towton, March 29th, 1461

ON Palm Sunday, March 29th, 1461, was fought 'the most sanguinary and important battle that ever took place in the civil wars of England'. So at least declared Richard Brooke in 1857. There may be perhaps some slight exaggeration regarding the latter assertion, but that it was the most sanguinary battle, and fought by the biggest armies that ever assembled in this country, there can be no doubt. All the more astonishing is it that it has been so scantily chronicled. Apart from Hall's *Chronicle*, written some 70 years later, we have only fragmentary details from a handful of sources. Yet in spite of this paucity of records the battle remains one of the least controversial of the battles of the Wars of the Roses. This account will consequently be shorter than the importance of the contest might appear to warrant. All historians are agreed as to the approximate site of the field, and as to the main course of the battle. It remains to fill in the details as far as possible.

PRELIMINARY MOVES

The preliminary moves throw little light on the course of the battle, so they can be sketched in very briefly. In spite of the victory of the Lancastrians at St. Albans, Queen Margaret dallied so long that Edward, Earl of March, after winning a victory at Mortimer's Cross on the Welsh border, made a dash for the capital and entered it first. Here he had himself proclaimed king on March 4th, and promptly set about concentrating an army to oppose Queen Margaret in the north, whither she had retired. For Edward had no illusions as to the necessity to fight for his crown.

His steps seem to have been methodical and thorough. On March 7th he sent the Earl of Warwick with 'a great puissance of people' to raise the Midlands and West.

On the 11th, Lord Fauconbridge led out another division, consisting chiefly of Kentishmen and Welshmen. On the 13th, Edward himself set out with the remainder of the army. Marching slowly via Cambridge, he reached Pontefract, where his whole army concentrated from all parts of southern England.

Meanwhile, Queen Margaret, who was with King Henry VI at York, on hearing of the approach of the enemy, concentrated her army around Towton, 10 miles south-west of that city, where it awaited the enemy. Advanced troops of both armies met on the line of the River Aire, at Ferrybridge, two miles north of Pontefract. At dawn on Saturday, March 28th, there was a clash of outposts at Ferrybridge, the Yorkists being surprised. Warwick behaved in a theatrical, almost hysterical manner, but the cooler-headed Edward proved equal to the occasion. Sending a force out to the left, he was able, by crossing the river four miles higher up-stream, at Castleford, to threaten the enemy's flank. The threat had immediate effect: the Lancastrians fled. They were rapidly pursued and cut up at Dintindale, under two miles south of Towton. The main body of the Yorkist army followed via the ford at Castleford, while the rearguard remained constructing a new bridge at Ferrybridge. This was no doubt required for the artillery and train of wagons, which might find the ford at Castleford in the swollen state of the river impracticable.

The vanguard discovered the Lancastrian army drawn up on the high ground between Towton and Saxton. Though there was still sufficient daylight to fight a battle, Edward prudently refrained from attacking till his huge and unwieldy army, stretching many miles to the rear, could all come up. Thus night fell upon the rival hosts, partially drawn up facing one another, with a certain amount of bickering going on. There is no mention of tents, and both armies must have spent a chill and cheerless night, bivouacking on the exposed upland, while threatening snow-clouds gathered.

THE TWO ARMIES

The new King Edward led his army in person. It is time to say a word about this remarkable youth. For youth he was—19 years and one month precisely on the day of the battle. Handsome, over six feet three inches in height, he possessed a genial manner and had already made himself very popular. He fortunately was absent from the field of Wakefield where his father, the Duke of York, had suffered defeat and death. He collected an army in the west with which to avenge his father, and with it he won the battle of Mortimers Cross in Herefordshire. Though little is known about the details of this battle, the promptness of his attack and the vigour of his pursuit betokened budding signs of generalship. Indeed, he seems to have had a sagacity beyond his years, though it is true that men developed at an earlier age then than now. In default of definite records we may safely assign to him the credit for the successful operations on the Aire at Ferrybridge, though it might be natural to suppose that he was in Warwick's tutelage. The fact is, Warwick was not a great general, and young Edward was already assuming the lead in his own right. His chief lieutenants were Warwick (whom we may imagine as chief of staff), the Earl of Norfolk who was temporarily indisposed and lying at Pontefract, and Lord Fauconbridge, much the most experienced of the leaders, who commanded the vanguard.

All the chroniclers are unanimous that the army was of enormous size. Various figures are given, but it became fashionable 50 years ago to scale down their figures very drastically. According to Hall, the Yorkist army numbered 48,640, and this figure was accepted by the old historians. But Oman writes: 'Perhaps so many as 15,000 or 20,000 may have been present'; while Ramsay does not even trouble to suggest a figure, merely remarking: 'All England had been under arms for two years; but the reader must bear in mind that in those days 5,000 men represented a considerable army.' This can mean anything—or nothing.

I give in the end section my reasons for accepting Hall's total, but must note here that I regard it as including the pages and camp-followers, perhaps 25 per cent of the whole. This would make the combatant force about 36,000. The Lancastrian army was still more numerous.

As for the Lancastrian army and leaders, there is little to go upon. It is not even certain whether the King and Queen were in the vicinity (though Shakespeare makes them present).[1] Certainly the King had no influence over the course of the battle. All we know is that he was reluctant to fight on Palm Sunday. Edward did not share his qualms; and it takes two to make a truce as well as to make a fight. The commander of the army in the field was the young Duke of Somerset, 24 years of age, the son of that Somerset who was killed at First St. Albans. The other chief leaders were the Earl of Northumberland, and Lord Dacres.

[1] The most recent biography of Queen Margaret passes over this point in silence.

THE BATTLE

(*Sketch-map 25*)

A low massif or ridge rises out of the flat York plain between the villages of Saxton and Towton, to a height of just under 100 feet. The rise is very gentle on all sides except the west, where the slope is very steep—up to 40 degrees—forming a line of bluffs down to the valley of the little river Cock. A slight east-west depression crosses the top of the ridge, thus forming two cross-ridges. This dip is less than 20 feet on the east, but steepens into a gulley on the west where it drops into the Cock valley. On these two cross-ridges the opposing armies were ranged in battle order. The ground was unenclosed, chiefly heath-land, with hanging woods along the line of the bluff.

Nothing is known of the order of battle of either army, but all historians seem to assume that in each case the three wards were drawn up in line—van-ward on the right, rear-ward on the left; the commanders of each ward have even been named. For reasons that will appear later, I cannot accept this formation; I think both armies formed up in column of wards or divisions, van in the first line, rear in the third. It may be presumed that Fauconbridge commanded the Yorkist van, as he had done on the previous day; certainly he gave the opening orders in the battle. King Edward's command-post cannot have been far from the modern Air Ministry tower, on the top of the ridge and in the centre of the line. From here he could easily see and control the whole field. Similarly Somerset's position must have been near the spot marked *G.P.* on the Sketch-map. The Lancastrians had also done something unusual; they had laid an ambush in the Castle Hill Wood on the bluff, a very good spot for one.

The sun rose, or should have risen, shortly before 6 a.m. on that fateful Palm Sunday; but the sky was overcast, presaging snow, and there was a sharp south wind blowing. For over four hours nothing much happened; the Yorkists no doubt were adjusting their position as laggards gradually came up. Still there was no sign of Norfolk's division. But the battle could not wait indefinitely; indeed, the Yorkists eventually took the initiative at about 11 o'clock. It had begun to snow, and the south wind blew it into the faces of the Lancastrians. Fauconbridge took instant advantage of this; he ordered his archers, who occupied the front line, to fire a single arrow each, and then to fall back out of range. This had the expected effect; the Lancastrian bowmen replied, not with one arrow but several, and went on shooting until their precious stock of ammunition was almost exhausted. It was blind shooting, into the teeth of the wind and the snow. The bowmen naturally calculated that if they were in the range of their opponents so must the Yorkists be. But the combination of the wind and the withdrawal of the hostile bowmen had the effect that the arrows fell on an average 60 yards short.

The wily Fauconbridge must have chuckled as he saw the success of his ruse. When the shooting came to an end his men quietly stepped forward (still covered by the veil of snow) and seized the bulk of the enemy's arrows (just as our men did at Poitiers). The bulk, but not all; Fauconbridge had ordered them to leave a portion in the ground so that their sloping shafts might incommode the enemy when they advanced. Probably this inconvenience was not great, but the incident is of importance as showing that the infantry attack was made by the Lancastrians, the Yorkists standing on the defensive, and that the Yorkists were a disciplined host acting to orders.

Thus the first phase of the battle was an artillery bombardment (for bow and arrow is strictly a form of artillery). Any cannon that were present must have joined in this bombardment; the Lancastrians are pretty certain to have had some, but those of the Yorkists may have been in Norfolk's division, crossing the Aire by the bridge at Ferrybridge. Whatever guns were present, their effect cannot have been appreciable.

And now came the second phase—the Lancastrian attack. Sinking the slight hill into the dip the line of billmen and spearmen began to ascend the opposing slope. They were received with a heavy fire from the Yorkist bowmen, now well furnished with ammunition, and losses must already have been heavy. But with casualties made good from the serried ranks in rear, the long line slowly drew near. The Yorkist bowmen stepped back through the intervals of the billmen and the close-quarter contest commenced. The scene must have beggared description, and its very horror probably deterred the survivors from passing on stories of the fight, which would account for the paucity of details in the chronicles. One lurid, but probably true, detail has however come down to us; it is that so great was the slaughter that the corpses formed a positive impediment to the living, a wall of dead and dying gradually getting built up between the contestants.

As the men in the front line fell or became exhausted their places were taken from the lines in rear, and the battle was continued. After about two hours of this, Norfolk's division began to make its welcome

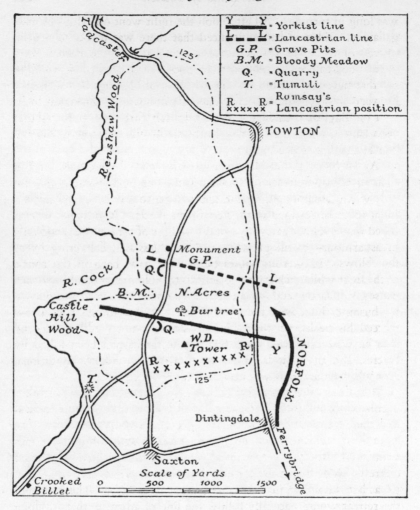

SKETCH-MAP 25.   TOWTON

appearance. The Lancastrians by weight of numbers seem to have
been getting the better of it, and their ambush in Castle Hill Wood
may have upset the order of the rear lines, for at one time there was
a panic on the part of the Yorkist horseholders.

As Norfolk's men[1] gradually came up on the right flank the
fortune of the battle veered in favour of the Yorkists; but the tide

[1] It is not certain that Norfolk himself was present.

was long in turning. All afternoon the fight went on with obstinate gallantry. Edward had announced that there was to be no quarter offered or taken, and though this was not strictly observed it must have added to the desperation and ferocity of the fight. It is safe to say that never in our history since the day of Hastings had such fury between the contestants been witnessed; nor was it ever again to be seen on English battlefield. Both sides felt that they were fighting with halters round their necks—in the sight of two kings of England —if Henry was indeed present.

As for his rival, Edward seems to have played the correct part in such an action—that of feeding the front line from his reserves, not only when casualties required it, but in order to give relief and refreshment to those engaged in the heat of the battle. It must be remembered that a soldier carrying a heavy weight of armour—even if only breast armour—would grow hot and breathless after delivering a very few blows. Numerous pauses there must have been in the course of the fight while each army replaced its front line troops. In one such pause Lord Dacres sat down and removed his helmet in order to quench his burning thirst with a cup of water. At that moment an arrow pierced his neck and killed him. (We need not credit the legend that he was recognized by a boy whose father had been killed by Dacres, and that this lad fired the fatal arrow, but the traditional spot whence the arrow was fired can still be identified.)

And now we come to the third phase. As evening fell Norfolk's numbers became sufficiently great to enable the front to be extended and thus to outflank the hostile left. This extension would give the impression of superior numbers, and the waning morale of the Lancastrians, having no inspiring leadership to sustain it, collapsed entirely. Men began to trickle to the rear, first singly, then in groups, till at last the whole mass became dissipated in flight. The course of the retreat would naturally follow the line of advance, that is, along the old Tadcaster road (the present road running north from Towton is modern). This road turned north-west at Towton and crossed the river Cock by a ford or possibly a bridge.[1] Hereabouts the river is on an average ten feet wide, with a firm bottom—not muddy as has been asserted. It is swift-flowing with a maximum depth at

[1] The present bridge is of wood (no doubt well known to the Bramham Moor Hunt). The stones of a previous one are visible in the river bed, but it is not likely that it was as old as the date of the battle. It is a beautiful secluded spot—well worth a visit.

normal times of two feet. But the banks are perpendicular, three feet high, so that when the river is in spate (as it probably was during the battle) it can be as deep as five feet except at recognized fords. The fugitives therefore concentrated on the ford from all parts of the field, hotly pursued by the triumphant Yorkists. The congestion became terrible and the slaughter correspondingly great. It may seem a picturesque touch that the dead blocked up the river and made a solid bridge of corpses over which the pursuers are said to have passed; but it is quite possibly true. At a sharp bend at a shallow point, the dead bodies might quite well stick, and other bodies floating downstream pile up on them. At any rate, the slaughter at this point was great, as also at Tadcaster, where some of the fugitives attempted to stand. The total killed on the actual field is recorded at a figure varying between 28,000 and 38,000 on the field. The latter figure may be an oral error, in mistake for 28,000. Accepting the smaller total, and assuming that up to the moment of retreat the losses were roughly equal, say 12,000 on each side, and adding a few thousand for the Lancastrian losses after quitting the field, we can put the Lancastrian total at about 20,000 killed, which agrees with another account. If to this we add those wounded and captured, we may say that the Lancastrian army lost well over half its strength. For the time being it ceased to be an army, most of its leaders were dead and the King and Queen were in flight to the north. It was the most decisive victory that the Wars of the Roses had till then produced.

PROBLEMS OF THE BATTLEFIELD

I.—NUMBERS

I must here attempt to justify my rejection of modern estimates as to numbers. The deeper one examines this brief campaign the clearer does it appear that the numbers on each side were altogether exceptional. Though the chroniclers disagree in details they are at one on this general principle. Hall gives the pay-roll as his authority; none could be better. The vast numbers given as killed is indirect corroboration of the vast numbers engaged. The references to the grave-pits are exceptionally detailed and emphatic. King Edward afterwards felt it incumbent on him to reward the grave diggers for their herculean task. There were at least three big burial grounds: at G.P. on the Sketch-map, in Bloody Meadow (where four grave-pits are shown on the six-inch O.S. map, and were in existence as recently as 1896 when Mr. Barratt saw them), and five great pits north of Saxton church. The *Croyland Continuation* states that 'those who helped to inter the bodies, piled up in pits and trenches prepared for the purpose, bear witness that 38,000 warriors fell in that day, besides those who were drowned in the river'. *Harleian MSS.* 795 is quoted by Leadman as stating that the graves shown as *G.P.* on my map were deep trenches 19 yards in breadth and 32 yards in depth. Each of these might well have taken 500 corpses.

The various figures of killed given can be tabulated as follows:

Whethampstede's poem .	Lancastrians over 20,000
Paston Letters . .	'computed by the heralds at 28,000'
Croyland Continuation .	38,000
Hearne's Fragment .	30,000
Polydore . . .	30,000
Hall	36,766
Gregory . . .	35,000 commoners
Edward IV (in a letter to his mother shortly after the battle) estimated .	28,000

If over 26,000 combatants were killed, 75,000 is not an impossible total for those present.

Another indirect corroboration is the duration of the battle. Anything over two hours for a battle was in those days exceptional, for the simple reason that the physical exertion required of heavily-armed men was so great that prolonged conflict was impossible. The Duke of York at the battle of Agincourt died from sheer exhaustion. Thus the only way in which it is possible to account for a battle lasting several hours is by the assumption that the troops were present in great depth, one ward behind another, as I have suggested in the text, and that there was a continual flow of fresh troops to the front.

The only ground on which modern historians base their disbelief in the numbers given by the chroniclers is that the population could not have produced the numbers given. But we do not know for certain what the population was. Contemporary chroniclers must have had a pretty fair idea as to what was and what was not possible, and they would not have given figures which anyone living at the time would know to be impossible. At any rate, careful chroniclers such as Hall, would not. Hall's grandfather, Sir David Hall, was the Duke of York's most trusted councillor, and Hall was evidently in

touch with authoritative sources.   The mistake that modern historians
perhaps make is in including only the adult manpower, ignoring the
fact that probably over 50 per cent of the soldiers were boys under
20.   Harry Hotspur commanded a successful assault on Berwick at
the age of twelve.   Thus considerably more soldiers could be raised
for a given population than to-day.

No one knows what the population was in 1461.   *The Historical
Geography of England before* 1800 computes it as 4,688,000 about a
century later.   If we accept a conservative estimate of $3\frac{1}{2}$ millions in
1461, with a fighting age of 15 to 40, we get something in the neighbourhood of 500,000 potential soldiers.   If we allow that 75,000
took part in the battle, that comes to 15 per cent of the potential
soldiers.   This would admittedly represent a vast effort, but we
are assured that a vast effort was in fact made by both sides.   Moreover, it is likely that the ranks of the northerners included many Scotsmen.   Taking everything into consideration, especially Hall's statement, I consider 36,000 Yorkist combatants and 40,000 Lancastrians
a reasonable figure.

II.—THE SITE AND EXTENT OF THE POSITION

As already pointed out there is a general agreement on this subject,
the only dissident being Ramsay, who places the Lancastrian line on
the forward slope of the southern ridge on a front of under 800 yards
enclosed between the two roads and not embracing either of
them (marked R—R on Sketch-map).   Apart from the ridiculous
narrowness of this front, there is this to be said for the southern
ridge, that it would be a natural one for the Lancastrian vanguard
to occupy in the first instance.   Its right would rest on the bluff near
Castle Hill Wood and it would command a good view to the south.
Further consideration, however, would show that there was danger
attached to such a position, for if the right flank were repulsed it
would be driven down the bluff into the river.   By falling back 700
yards to the northern cross-ridge the double advantage was obtained
of removing the above-mentioned danger, whilst shortening the line.
The right flank would still rest upon the bluff, but at a point where the
ridge is at its narrowest.   The defenders would still have the advantage
of a forward slope, the only disadvantage compared with the forward
position being that the view to the front was limited.   In practice
this would be no very great disadvantage, for patrols would be left
on the forward ridge till the last moment, when they would fall back,

leaving the ambush in position on the right flank. Incidentally, it would be interesting to know how this ambush fared, and what effect upon the battle it had.

Thus by the test of Inherent Military Probability the Lancastrians would select their position upon the forward slope of the northern ridge, with their right flank resting upon the bluff. But where did their left flank rest? History is completely silent upon the point, but it is reasonable to suppose that the position extended well beyond the Ferrybridge road—the direct line of approach to Tadcaster. On the other hand it would hardly extend to the flat ground, which would be boggy at that time of the year. Indeed, there were boggy patches on this slope; conditions would be still worse in the bottom. This bottom reaches to within 500 yards of the road. If the Lancastrian position covered the top half of this slope, say 200 yards, that would give a total frontage of 1,300 yards. Allowing the vanguard 12,000 to 15,000 men, this would give then 10 men per yard—not a bad proportion. The middle and rear wards would be formed up on the slope between the ridge top and the village of Towton.

If the Lancastrian position was as here suggested, the site of the Yorkist line becomes obvious. There could scarcely be any alternative to the one I have indicated in the text, and the point need not be laboured.

Let us now see how far tradition and battlefield relics sustain the position arrived at from a study of the topography. Tradition concerns two sites, that of the Bloody Meadow and that of the 'bur tree' (elder bush), from which a Yorkist shot Lord Dacres. This is marked on the six-inch O.S. map in the hedge running east from the Bloody Meadow, and 300 yards from the road (see Sketch-map 25.) It is the southern border of a field called North Acres. On my visit to the ground I was delighted to find just about the spot indicated two or three elder bushes. If the tradition has any truth in it one of these bushes may be the lineal descendant of Lord Dacre's 'bur tree'. From here to the top of the ridge in front is 300 yards—within crossbow range. (It was a crossbow bolt that killed him.) The bush is opposite the spot which I have suggested as the Lancastrian command-post. What more likely than that during a pause in the fighting Dacres should stroll over from his command post to head-quarters to report on how things were going in his part of the front and to discuss matters with his chief, the Earl of Somerset? Relaxing and removing their helmets, the two would start refreshing themselves, when the fatal shaft cut short all further discussion.[1] The situation of the Bloody Meadow accords absolutely with our conception of the battlefield. Here is reported the greatest slaughter, and it is here that the Lancastrians had the steepest slope in front of them; the slow climb out of the head of the gully would give the Yorkist bowmen a better opportunity to exact casualties here than anywhere.

Thus far, then, we find that tradition supports our view. Lastly we come to battlefield relics. These consist mainly of bones in gravepits. The two main ones, those in the Bloody Meadow and at G.P. also accord with our view and are precisely where we should expect to find them. These mounds were visible in 1896, but have since disappeared. The burials near Saxton church may be the result of the Yorkist panic when the horseholders fled; one of the forward movements in what we know was a swaying battle may have penetrated almost as far as the church; but on the whole it is more probable that these corpses were removed from the field for burial near sacred ground. The tumuli in the river valley may, or may not, be grave pits. There is no information existing on the point, though the largest of them has evidently been excavated at some period. It measures 12 yards in diameter and is about three feet high. If it had any connection with the battlefield it probably indicates a fight on the part of the ambush in the wood just above the spot.

N.B.—Bloody Meadow is also known as the Field of the White and Red Rose, a dwarf rose—with white petals and a red spot, that used to grow there. It had become scarce by 1896 and has since entirely disappeared. The inscription on the monument is also in course of disappearing. Motorists dash past it without being aware of its existence.

[1] Chroniclers do not explain how the lad could have seen (let alone have recognized) Dacres when he was seated behind the line, and historians do not pause to consider the absurdity of the story.

CHAPTER XXII

The Battle of Barnet, April 14th, 1471

CONSIDERING that the battle of Barnet was one of the most important battles of medieval times, and that it took place almost on the front doorstep of London, it is remarkable how much it has been neglected. Yet the battle of Barnet has many claims to be remembered and studied. There were unusual attendant circumstances. In the words of an old chronicler: 'Both sides fought for their kings [Henry VI and Edward IV], both kings having been crowned, and by several Parliaments acknowledged. And indeed the question was so subtil that even among Divines it had been long held, and at that day remained not absolutely settled.'

But the battle settled things with a vengeance. It settled the doom of Henry VI; it settled the doom of the greatest man of his age, Warwick the Kingmaker; and it planted Edward IV and the Yorkist dynasty firmly on the throne of England. In short, it was a really important battle.

No doubt one reason for the neglect of the battle is the impression that its details are too obscure to repay study. This is probably due to an egregious reconstruction of the battle by Sir James Ramsay over 50 years ago, which set the experts at loggerheads. But, after examining all possible material and studying the problem on the ground, I have come to the conclusion that the course of the battle is clearer than that of many other battles of that epoch.

In one of those strange topsy-turvy episodes that characterize the Wars of the Roses, a sovereign in exile, Edward IV, returning and landing in the Humber, marched boldly on London, cutting through the cordon of three Lancastrian armies that opposed him. The Earl of Warwick, who by deserting the Yorkist cause had caused the flight of Edward and the restoration of Henry VI on the throne, had concentrated his armies (mixed Lancastrians and Yorkists) and pursued. On Good Friday, April 12th, 1471, he reached St. Albans. On Saturday he continued his advance to Hadley Green, three-quarters of a mile north of Barnet, where he arrived about midday and halted.

Meanwhile, Edward, taking with him King Henry (who had been

handed over to him on his arrival in London), advanced straight up the road to Barnet. Poor Henry must have known what this journey meant, for he had had previous experience of this sort of thing.

On reaching Barnet, Edward's advanced guard swiftly ejected the advanced patrols of the Lancastrians, who fell back upon their main body, just as it was getting dark. Both Edward and Warwick (who had fought together for several years) must have been familiar with the ground. It was on the main road out of London to the North, and was the highest point between London and York. Edward therefore, sharing the gift of the Duke of Wellington, guessed correctly what was happening 'the other side of the hill', and formed up his troops as they arrived in line of battle astride the road, half a mile north of the town (see Sketch-map 26). But it was done in the dark—a difficult and unusual manœuvre till quite recent days. It is not surprising, therefore, that his line did not exactly coincide with that of the Lancastrians. Not only was it rather closer to them than he intended or suspected but his right flank overlapped that of the enemy while his left flank was in turn overlapped by theirs.

Numbers are always a problem in ancient battles, but there seems less difficulty than usual as regards the Yorkists. Writing quite soon after the battle, their official chronicler puts them at 9,000. It is unlikely that he would *over*estimate their numbers, and we shall be safe in putting them at a good 10,000. The Lancastrians were more numerous, 15,000 at a guess.

Warwick selected a position along the flat crest of the cross-ridge that intersects the main Barnet—Wrotham Park ridge just to the south of High Stone, on the junction of the Hatfield and old St. Albans roads. The position extended 800 to 1,000 yards on each side of the road, and consequently faced fairly square to Barnet, though the flanks were slightly refused. On the west of the road it ran along a hedge (still partly visible), on the east of the road it traversed Hadley Green, passing about 150 yards to the north of Hadley Church.

All through the night the two armies were so close to each other that their voices could be plainly heard, though the slight swell in the ground probably hid their camp fires from one another. One of the unusual features of this remarkable battle was that 'harassing fire' was employed by the Lancastrian artillery. The Yorkist chronicler records it in these quaint terms: 'Both parties had guns and ordnance, but the Earl of Warwick had many more than the King. And therefore in the night, hoping greatly to have annoyed the King and his host, with

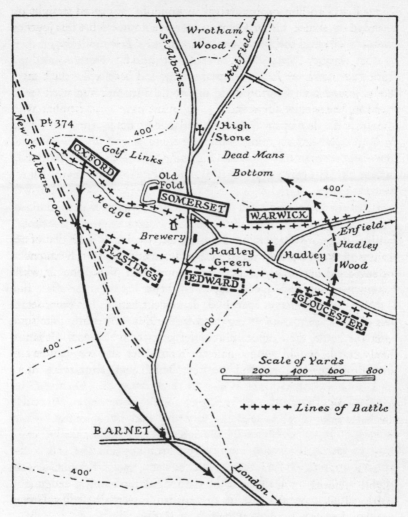

SKETCH-MAP 26. BARNET

shot of guns, the Earl's field shot guns almost all the night. But, thanked be God, it so fortuned that they always overshot the king's host, and hurted them nothing. And the cause was (that) the king's host lay much nearer to them than they deemed. . . . The King suffered no guns to be shot on his side, all that night, or else right few, which was to him great advantage, for thereby they might have esteemed the ground that he lay in and have levelled their guns near.'

Such artillery tactics are not unknown at the present day.

Edward, true to his impetuous nature, had resolved on taking the offensive whatever the conditions, and to make a dawn attack—another unusual feature. Very early on that memorable Easter morning, April 14th, 1471, ere it was properly light, and despite the thick mist that obscured both sides, Edward ordered the trumpets to sound as a signal for the general advance.

The battle then opened, with a brief artillery duel—guns and bows. As both sides were shooting blind (the equivalent of what we should now call 'programme' or 'map shooting'), little damage was done, and the Yorkist army advanced all along the line to engage in the hand-to-hand fight.

It is time to describe their dispositions (see Sketch-map 26). Each army was organized in three divisions, as was the custom of those times. Edward placed his youngest brother, the Duke of Gloucester, in command of his right wing, in spite of his tender years—he was only eighteen, but carried himself like a veteran. The King himself commanded the centre with the division of his other brother, the Duke of Clarence—'false, perjured, fleeting Clarence'. Clarence had only a few days previously deserted from Warwick, so the King no doubt preferred to keep him under his own eye. Lord Hastings commanded the left wing. (Eleven years later the commander of the right wing sent the commander of the left wing to the block!)

The Lancastrian army was also in three divisions. On the right was the Earl of Oxford. The place of honour in the centre Warwick allotted to his new Lancastrian ally the Earl of Somerset, while Warwick himself commanded the left. We are told that he, contrary to his usual custom, dismounted from his charger and commanded on foot. If he remained on the flank, which I doubt, he can have had but little influence on the battle. He was now at the height of his natural powers, 44 years of age, 16 of which he had spent in warlike operations. Although at the second battle of St. Albans he had been out-generalled, his experience of war was unsurpassed in England.

THE BATTLE

As the two lines loomed out of the mist into the ken of one another it was seen that Oxford's wing outflanked that of Hastings. The Earl took immediate advantage of this. Charging forward, and partially outflanking his opponents, he drove them back, along the line of the present main St. Albans road into Barnet, and out again to the south. Some of the fugitives from this impetuous advance did not turn about till they had reached London, where they loudly proclaimed that all was lost. (Compare the action of the fugitives from Waterloo to Brussels.)

But Oxford experienced great difficulty in halting and rallying his excited troops. When we remember the fog, which was still thick, we shall not be surprised. Moreover, to add to his difficulties, many of his men 'fell to ryfling'. (Compare the action of Prince Rupert's troopers after his charges in the Great Civil War.) Eventually he managed to collect about 800 of his scattered men and led them back to the battlefield. It is usually maintained that in doing so he intended to attack the enemy in their rear, but that he lost direction and swung right round the rear of his own army and attacked Somerset's division in their left rear by mistake. I simply cannot believe this story. Armies in those days did not have the benefit of ordnance survey maps; but when you have advanced through a town, down a main road towards London, crossed a causeway over the bog (1 mile south of Barnet), it should not be a difficult matter for the formed body to retrace their steps up the road, at least as far as Barnet, though on doubt individuals would be straggling all over the place, completely lost. I assume then that Oxford succeeded in leading back up the road the nucleus of his force into the town of Barnet. Emerging from it in the gradually thinning mist, not knowing what had happened in his absence, he was fired on by those of Somerset's men who had extended to their right in his absence in a natural and instinctive movement. Such a mistake on the part of Somerset's division was not only natural but almost inevitable. The light was still bad; the unknown troops were approaching from the enemy's side of the line, and moreover their banners looked similar to those of Edward's. But the reaction of Oxford's men could not have been foreseen. Instantly they suspected treason—of which there had been a good deal of late. Some of them stood and answered the fire, others, crying 'Treason!' simply decamped from the battlefield.

The effect of this unfortunate mistake need not have been fatal. The rest of Warwick's army probably still outnumbered that of its opponents, and the line was still intact. But the cry of 'Treason!' spread from Oxford's men to those of Somerset, with fatal results. For, fearing that Oxford had gone over to the enemy, some of Somerset's divisions turned against the remainder of Oxford's troops, while others began a trickle to the rear. The whole Lancastrian army was now in a state of confusion and disarray.

Now was the chance for the young Edward. Earlier in the battle his brother, Gloucester, fighting valiantly on the right flank, had made appreciable progress, whilst in the centre the battle raged between the road and Hadley church.[1]

But Edward, like all good generals, had retained a reserve in his own hand till the critical moment of the battle. That moment he, with his discerning eye, realized now had come. At this moment we get a glimpse (all too rare in accounts of medieval battles) of Edward's demeanour. 'He is mounted on his white steed, with his teeth firmly set, the spurs pressing his charger's side.' With his eagle eye he had detected the confusion that was developing in the hostile ranks, though he may not have realized the cause of it. There were evident signs of disintegration: this was the moment to strike. 'Up, Guards, and at 'em!'

On the other side of the line, Warwick realized to the full the seriousness of the situation. Attempting to steady his already rattled troops, he cried: 'This is our last resource. If we withstand this charge the day is ours!'

Down into the dip now known as Dead Man's Bottom—a significant name—Edward launched his reserve. Gloucester was still pushing forward on the right and was mounting the slope towards Wrotham Park. A brief, fierce fight took place, but the result was soon seen; Warwick's army slowly gave ground, then turned and dissolved in flight.

The Earl of Warwick, whose command-post was probably near High Stone, seeing that the issue was decided, struggled, though sorely hampered by his cumbrous armour, to regain his charger, which he had rashly left well in rear of the line. He got as far as Wrotham Park, 'flying somewhat', as the Yorkist chronicler quaintly puts it, but here he was entangled in the undergrowth and set about by foes. Overtaken in the thicket, he was wounded, forced to the ground, his visor prised open, and a sword-thrust finished him off. Thus perished Richard Neville, Earl of Warwick and Salisbury; a man who 'stands out in character and genius above all others of his generation. He was the best beloved man in the kingdom. When he was away from England,' says Hall, 'the common people thought the sun had gone out of the heavens.'

[1] Not the present church.

But Warwick had been defeated by the greatest general of his age. Edward IV, elated with victory, seized the banner of the dead Earl of Warwick, and rode hot-foot to London. Arriving at St. Paul's as the afternoon service was in progress, he marched proudly up the aisle and laid the banner on the high altar, thus proclaiming to the assembled congregation that his enemies were vanquished and that he had retained his crown.

THE PROBLEM OF THE BATTLEFIELD

I have written above that the hedge behind which part of the Lancastrian army lay is still in existence and can be identified. I must attempt to justify this claim, particularly as at least one historian of the battle roundly declared that the hedge is no longer there.

Confusion has been occasioned in fixing the exact site and alignment of the battle by a passage in Sir James Ramsay's *York and Lancaster* (incidentally, the most detailed modern account of the battle) which states that the hedge bounded the Barnet—Hatfield road. This would make Warwick's line face east, instead of the more natural south as it would do if it lay astride the road along which he was advancing. This identification by Ramsay can only be characterized as preposterous and I will not waste time in discussing and refuting it, but will proceed straight to my own appreciation.

In fixing the exact site of a disputed battlefield it is a sound and fruitful method of procedure first to set out the agreed facts immediately preceding the battle (which are likely to be more accurately given than the details of the subsequent battle), and secondly to place oneself in the shoes of the respective commanders on the actual ground, go where they went and see what they would be likely to do. This procedure, which I have followed throughout, is particularly applicable to Barnet.

First, then, the agreed setting. The fact is not disputed that on Saturday, April 13th, the Earl of Warwick advanced by the old St. Albans road, leaving Wrotham Park on his left, to Hadley Green. Nor is there any doubt that that same afternoon King Edward advanced from London to Barnet and formed line of battle roughly parallel to his opponent's line. Let us now put ourselves in Warwick's shoes. Knowing or suspecting that Edward, true to his nature, would boldly advance from London to offer battle, it was desirable to find a suitable position on which to oppose him. Even were

Warwick not familiar with the ground round Barnet, he would, when about 300 yards short of High Post, notice on his right front a low ridge at right angles to his line of advance, and apparently extending across the road to the left. If the visitor will go to this spot he will find a convenient opening on to the Barnet golf links. At the point where he is standing the main ridge along which the Lancastrian army was advancing is only 200 yards wide—far too narrow for the purpose of a battle. But the golf links ridge looks just made for his purpose—always provided that this cross-ridge extends to the left of our road too.

We will see. Push on to High Stone and turn sharp left down the Hatfield road for about 300 yards. A lane runs down from the road to the right at this point. Follow it a short distance until it opens out into a field. From here we get our answer: the ridge *does* extend across the road. There it is, plain to see—Hadley Common Ridge—crowned by Hadley church tower. What more could a medieval general want? It exactly fits the description of the old chronicler Polydore Vergil: 'An hill, in the top thereof is a place fyt for araigning of a battayle.' Holinshed's account is also worth giving: 'There is a fair plain for two armies to meet upon named Gladsmuir Heath (Hadley Common) on the further side of which plain towards St. Albans the Earle pight his campe.' The Yorkists met his patrols in Barnet and 'chased them somewhat further than half a mile from the town where, by an hedgesyde they found ready assembled a great number of the Earl of Warwick's people'.

What other locality in the neighbourhood of Barnet could these facts possibly fit than the cross-ridge marked by a 400-foot contour? Moreover, the extent of the ridge, approximately 2,000 yards, would be a convenient length for an army of 15,000.

I suggest, then, that, on reaching the aforementioned gap in the hedge, Oxford was ordered to incline half-right and occupy the golf links ridge, while Warwick's own division occupied the Hadley Green ridge, and Somerset took the centre with his troops astride the road.

Can we define the position even more closely? I think we can. If we now follow in Oxford's footsteps on to the golf links ridge we naturally push on till we reach the top of the ridge. Now what about the 'hedgeside'? Note that Holinshed does not say that the *whole* army was behind it but only 'a great number of' the army. On which side of the road would this hedgeside be likely to run? Obviously not on the Hadley Green side, which was open heath. Therefore it should be on the golf links, on or near the top of the ridge, which is five to six furlongs from Barnet, as required by Holinshed's account. And precisely where we should expect to find the hedge there *is* such a hedge! Though there are gaps in it and the golf links run through it, the bank and ditch are almost continuous, running from the moat that surrounds Old Ford Manor, thence along the top of the ridge, and dropping down gradually to the modern St. Albans road at point 374. I make no doubt that this is the hedge behind which Oxford's division lay on that misty Easter morn nearly 600 years ago.

(The visitor can best reach this hedge by leaving the main road opposite the brewery on Hadley Green and following the footpath over a stile and across the golf links. About 300 yards beyond the stile the path reaches the hedge, from which point its course can be traced in each direction.)

I am not aware that this hedge has ever been identified as that mentioned by Holinshed, but there is nothing unusual in a hedge existing for 600 years. Hedges near villages, especially crooked ones such as this, are apt to be of great age, especially when accompanied by a bank and ditch. Such is the famous hedge at Poitiers which I firmly believe still exists and can be identified, though over 700 years old.

The position on the eastern side of the road need not detain us long. It is quite obvious, running as it does in an easterly direction and gently sloping down till the flank rested, as I estimate, on what is now the edge of Hadley Wood.

Thus, if my location is correct, Warwick's line ran some 300 yards in advance of High Stone, and his own command-post would most naturally be near that spot. Now the battle memorial stands at High Stone, and an old tradition avers that that was the spot where Warwick fell—all of which fits in naturally with my siting of Warwick's battle-line.

A last point. If this siting is correct the line ran within 200 yards of the church, yet it is mentioned in no accounts of the battle. But neither is the old windmill, which also must have been in the middle of the battle. Apart from the fact that the old church may have had a very squat tower, or none at all, our worthy ancestors were not partial to climbing church towers in the course of a battle. Their cumbrous armour would make the operation almost impossible, whether it be the narrow spiral staircase of the church or the rickety ladder of the windmill. Such things were seldom done—though it is true that the King of the Romans ascended a windmill on the battle-field of Lewes—but that was in order to avoid capture.

CHAPTER XXIII

The Battle of Tewkesbury, May 14th, 1471

EDWARD IV won the battle of Barnet in the very nick of time. On that same fateful Easter Day Queen Margaret and Prince Edward, the legitimate heir-apparent, accompanied by a small band of French and Englishmen, landed at Weymouth. Next day (news travelled fast in those days), the news of Barnet reached her. Now there is for us a danger of belittling the gravity of the Queen's attempt, for we know the outcome. But, in spite of the Barnet disaster, it might have become a formidable threat to the Yorkists. Margaret herself did indeed nearly give way to despair when she heard the news, and contemplated returning to France. But her followers persuaded her that her chances were still good. The Earl of Pembroke undertook to raise an army in Wales; other adherents prepared to do the same in Lancashire and Cheshire. The precise details we do not know, but it is significant that one of the Lancastrian Pastons, who had been wounded at the Battle of Barnet, wrote a cheerful letter to his mother, with mysterious hints that good tidings might soon be expected. It must also be remembered that if King Edward was proving himself a general of the first water, Queen Margaret had defeated the formidable Warwick the Kingmaker in battle.

So it is worth while studying the brief campaign that ensued with some care. Nearly all the important facts come down to us from a single source, but that a reliable one. *The History of the Arrival of King Edward IV*, which I shall discuss later, and shall call by the name of its owner, the *Fleetwood Chronicle*.

King Edward heard of the landing two days later. He was 'caught on the rebound', for he had already given orders to disband his army. But he did not hesitate. A new army must be raised rapidly, and fresh stores collected. The King acted vigorously, and only three days later (April 19th) he set up his headquarters at Windsor, to which place all contingents were summoned.

Meanwhile the Queen was processing through the West Country towards Exeter, collecting an army, with the intention of advancing with it to Wales and the North in order to join up with her friends (precisely the same procedure as was adopted just 200 years later by the ill-fated Duke of Monmouth). She also sent patrols in the direction of London in order to create the false impression that she intended marching on the capital.

Edward was well served by his spies, and as soon as he had ascertained the probable plan of his opponents and had assembled his army, he set out to confront the Queen's host. Marching via Abingdon, he was at Cirencester on April 30th, on which day the Lancastrian army was at Bath. (Sketch-map 27).

The marches of the first four days of May must now be established in detail. From Bath the Queen turned westward to Bristol. The King suspected this to be a change of plan, the result of his approach, but it seems more reasonable to believe that the real motive was the acquisition in Bristol of artillery and stores, of which her army was in sore need. This she succeeded in doing in the second city of England, which received her with apparent warmth. Even so, her army was inferior in ordnance to the Yorkist army, which was distinctly strong in artillery. Edward naturally followed, and reached Malmesbury that night, both armies having made a 12-mile march.

But Margaret had acquired her guns at the price of a big risk. A glance at Sketch-map 27 will show that when she was at Bath and Edward at Cirencester, she was already in a fair way to be cut off from her objective—Wales. For the Severn had to be crossed and the nearest crossing place was at Gloucester. Now Edward at Cirencester was 15 miles nearer Gloucester than the Queen at Bath. Furthermore, her detour next day to Bristol accentuated the risk of being cut off. I am assuming that Gloucester was her first objective; all the facts point to that, as do also her movements next day. It must be remembered that Margaret was ten years older than when she had so signally defeated Warwick at St. Albans; the fire was departing out of that fiery frame, and she had her precious son and heir to think of. If anything should befall him—with his father in captivity, if still alive —the future of the Lancastrian dynasty would be at stake. Everything therefore conspired to play for safety at that juncture, in other words, to get across the River Severn as quickly as possible, and it is not surprising that her stay at Bristol was of the shortest. At this point we are particularly handicapped by not having the Queen's own account of the next three days. It may be that she received false intelligence at Bath which prompted the visit to Bristol next day.

We come to the exciting events of Thursday, May 2nd.[1] Whatever false news the Queen may have received at Bath, she became aware of the true and hazardous position in which she was at Bristol. Her course of action was obvious—a dash for Gloucester. The direct road ran along the plain, through Berkeley, leaving the Cotswold Hills on the right hand. But if she took this road the King's excellent spy service would spot it, and Edward would probably march straight towards the River Severn and she would be cut off somewhere near Berkeley. For Berkeley is five miles nearer Malmesbury than Bristol. By hook or by crook the Yorkist army had to be delayed or deluded. Now exactly midway between Malmesbury and Bristol lies Sodbury Hill, on the southern spur of the Cotswolds.[2] Edward would be likely to make for that spot if he thought the Queen was prepared to fight a battle. Therefore, in order to encourage this belief, Margaret early in the morning sent her vanguard to occupy a position at Sodbury, while she followed with the main army, as if to support the vanguard. She had correctly gauged her opponent's move; his army also was making for Sodbury, where he planned spending the next night, badly misapprehending his opponent's plan; if he had sensed it he would of course have made for Berkeley.

The immediate upshot was unexpected, and rather humorous. The King's quartermasters, each spurred on by the natural ambition to get the best billets in Sodbury for their own masters, pushed on recklessly ahead of the army, thinking only of their billeting problems. Entering the town without any military precautions, they discovered too late that the enemy was in occupation, and several of them were ignominiously captured. The news of this would naturally induce the King to believe that the enemy intended to stand, and no doubt his further advance was made more cautiously, and slower. Meanwhile the Lancastrian main body was passing Sodbury, leaving it on its right hand, and making for Berkeley. This detour cost it two or three miles, say one hour's march. But the delay caused the enemy was much more as it turned out; for by the time Edward had reached Sodbury Hill, at noon, the Lancastrian vanguard (now become rearguard) had passed on and disappeared from view. King Edward was bewildered. He had been badly served by his scouts and patrols,

[1] The *Fleetwood Chronicle* mistakenly calls it Thursday the 1st, and Holinshed blindly perpetuates this error.

[2] Close to Ogham, where in 577 A.D. the Saxons defeated the Britons in a great battle.

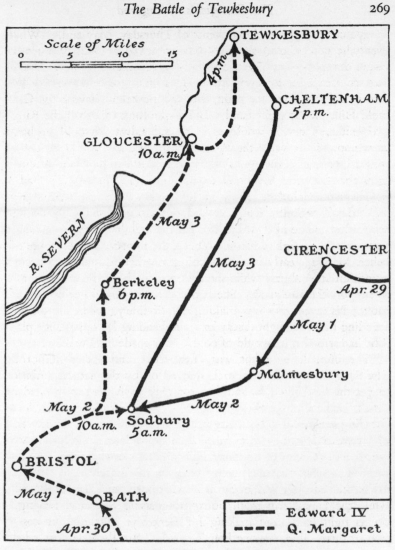

Scale of Miles
0   5   10   15

TEWKESBURY

4 p.m.

CHELTENHAM
5 p.m.

GLOUCESTER
10 a.m.

R. SEVERN

May 3

May 3

CIRENCESTER

Apr. 29

Berkeley
6 p.m.

May 1

Malmesbury

May 2   May 2
10 a.m.

Sodbury
5 a.m.

BRISTOL

May 1

BATH

Apr. 30

———— Edward IV
- - - - Q. Margaret

SKETCH–MAP 27.   TEWKESBURY: THE PRELIMINARY MOVES

though how the Lancastrians contrived to give them the slip it is impossible even to guess.   But the fact remains that from noon onwards the Yorkist army remained stationary on Sodbury Hill, wasting valuable hours whilst its patrols were endeavouring to regain touch with their elusive opponents.   The *Fleetwood Chronicle* expresses faithfully and ingenuously the utter bewilderment of the King.   'The

King, not having any certainty of his enemies, sent his scourers all about the country, trusting by them to have wist where they had been. About that place was a great and fair large plain, called a Wold, and doubtful it was for to pass further, so till he might hear somewhat of them, supposing that they were right near, as so they might well have been, if they had kept forth the way they took out of Bristol.'

But the enemy, so far from being right near, were all the time increasing the distance between the two armies, and hourly increasing their prospects of getting out of the toils with which they had entwined themselves by going to Bristol.

That evening, as the Queen's army, weary with a 23 miles march, trickled into Berkeley, King Edward, despairing of obtaining definite news of the enemy, decided to halt for the night where he was, at the top of Sodbury Hill, with outposts in the town below. If she was aware of the position of the Yorkist army Queen Margaret must have gone to bed that night in a thankful frame of mind. For she had given the slip to her adversary, and had a clear lead of 12 miles in the race for the Severn crossing. King Edward had, however, a reputation for speed when really put to it, and, tired though her army might be, another early start must be decreed. It was 14 miles to Gloucester; Margaret had friends in the city; if the gates were opened to her the way to Wales and her friends was secured. It looked as if the Queen had outwitted King Edward as thoroughly as she had outwitted the King's 'maker' ten years before.

The Lancastrian army resumed its weary march at, as I reckon it, 1 a.m. on Friday, May 3rd. Two hours later an 'espial' came spurring to the top of Sodbury Hill, and awoke the King with the astonishing news that the enemy were on the march from Berkeley towards Gloucester. The camp was aroused and the King summoned a council of war. A surprising action, under the circumstances for there could be only one immediate course of action—to pursue. But, according to his chronicler, the King was in doubt whether the enemy were making for Gloucester, or Tewkesbury. Did it matter? Whichever the Lancastrian objective, the immediate route for the Yorkists was the same, for Gloucester lay on the route to Tewkesbury. The only possible question for consideration was, should he follow the line of the Cotswolds or the lower route via Berkeley, in the tracks of the enemy? Here also, there could be but little doubt as to the answer: the lower road would be longer, and worse going—owing to woods and the bad state that the road would be in after it had been poached up by the enemy. The fact is, King Edward showed an unwonted air of self-distrust and indecision during those vital 24 hours. I attempt no explanation; I merely record the fact. It is the only flaw I can detect in his high military record.

The council did one thing, however: it decided to send messengers to warn the governor of Gloucester of his danger, and to assure him that, if he were attacked, the King would come to his immediate relief. It may here be noted that the lowest crossing over the Severn was by a bridge at Gloucester, which was commanded by the town defences; the next crossing being by ferry one mile south of Tewkesbury, ten miles further north, and the next bridge at Upton on Severn another six miles up-stream.

Early in the morning of May 3rd—(5 a.m. would fit in with the facts)—the Yorkist army set off. Now for the first time it was marshalled and marched in order of battle: vanguard, middleguard and rearguard. Patrols were also sent out in plenty. No doubt they were burning to redeem their humiliating failure of the previous day. Well did they succeed; the King was kept in constant information of the progress of rhe rival army. We are told that the two armies were only five or six miles apart. Seeing that their roads were that distance apart and that the Lancastrians had about four hours start, this is impossible. What it probably means is that the head of the Yorkist army was abreast of the rear of the stragglers of the Lancastrian army: it was a hot day, and there would be many stragglers, strung out over several miles of road.

This day fortune favoured the Yorkists. The King's messengers reached Gloucester before the advent of the Queen, and duly delivered their message to Sir Richard Beauchamp, the governor. The gates were closed and admission to the Queen firmly refused. The Lancastrians were taken by surprise at this attitude. 'Of this demeaning they took right great displeasure, and made great menaces, and pretended as though they would have assaulted the town.' But they were restrained by the knowledge that Edward was hard on their tracks; the delay necessary to launch an assault on the town would be fatal. Margaret therefore, after an hour or two's delay, gave the reluctant order to resume the march on Tewkesbury. Her army reached this town at 4 p.m. utterly worn out. They had marched 24 miles in the last 15 hours and, whatever the horse and foot might have been capable of, the newly-acquired ordnance, with their new and unpractised teams of horses and oxen, could scarcely be counted on to do

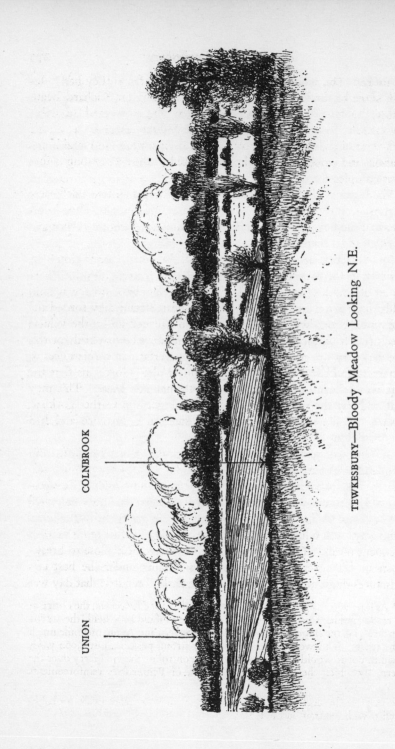

COLNBROOK

UNION

TEWKESBURY—Bloody Meadow Looking N.E.

any more. The wonder is that they had got as far as they had. Indeed, some of the laggard guns were captured by Sir Richard Beauchamp, pursuing out of Gloucester. Nor was it deemed advisable to attempt a crossing the river by the ferry at the lower Lode, a mile south-west of the town. It would entail an operation of several hours duration, and would probably be interrupted by the enemy long before it was completed.

There was nothing for it but to halt and prepare a hasty defensive position on the low flat ridge just to the south of the town and almost abreast of the ferry.[1] Here we will leave them, settling into their new position as best they could.

Meanwhile Edward was pursuing with his usual vigour along the Portway. Not only was the day hot, as the sun rose high, but there was an alarming absence of water for man and beast on the upland wolds that they were traversing. At or near Stroud they forded the little river Frome, where the water was so churned up by the vehicle wheels that it was scarcely drinkable.[2] One may be thankful for this little detail, for most accounts of medieval warfare omit references to matters of food and drink. The chronicler also informs us that the route was denuded of provender for both man and beast. This may be an indication that the populace was antagonistic to the Yorkists. Edward, at all events, had anticipated such an occurrence and had brought rations for the army with him.

At Prinknash the army left the Portway, and marching via Birdlip reached Cheltenham about 5 p.m., where his scouts brought the welcome intelligence that the hostile army having just reached Tewkesbury was preparing a position. His own army had now marched 31 miles in just about 24 hours, having had no food and little drink all the way. Men had stout frames in those days and were innured to infrequent meals. Even so, they must now have been close to breaking strain. Tewkesbury was five miles distant; under the best circumstances they could not reach it before dark. A battle that day was

---

[1] As long ago as 1793, in *A Tour to the Royal Spa at Cheltenham*, the criticism was made (and has since been repeated) that they should have held 'the MYTHE eminence', i.e. the ridge in the angle between Severn and Avon, one mile north of the town. This would have been a very strong position, just 1,000 yards in width, but it would have entailed losing control of the vital ferry over the Severn, by which the enemy might retreat, or Pembroke's reinforcements arrive.

[2] This would not apply to the vanguard, but the chronicler probably travelled with the train in the rear.

thus out of the question, but an early attack next morning was essential in order to prevent the enemy slipping away as they had done yesterday.   The King therefore ordered a short halt and served out the food he had brought with him.   The march was then resumed and as darkness was falling the weary host came to a final halt near Tredington, three miles short of Tewkesbury.[1]

If we now review the manœuvres of the last three days we shall make the surprising discovery that the two armies had covered as near as I can measure it precisely the same distance, namely 59 miles.   This figure may seem unduly precise, because evidence as to roads is scanty; but it happens to be the aggregate of my reckonings so I show it as such in the appended Table.

Date	Yorkists	Distance	Lancastrians	Distance
May Dep.	Cirencester		Dep. Bath	
1st. Arr.	Malmesbury	12 m.	Arr. Bristol	12 m.
May Dep.	Malmesbury		5 a.m. Dep. Bristol	
2nd Arr.	Sodbury Hill	12 m.	10 a.m. Pass Sodbury	11 m.
noon			6 p.m. Arr. Berkeley	12 m.
May Dep.	Sodbury		1 a.m. Dep. Berkeley	
3rd Arr.	Cheltenham	31 m.	10 a.m. Arr. Gloucester	14 m.
Dep.	Cheltenham		12 noon Dep. Gloucester	
Arr.	Tredington	4 m.	4 p.m. Arr. Tewkesbury	10 m.
	Total	35 m.	Total	24 m.
	Grand Total	59 m.	Grand Total	59 m.

The *Fleetwood Chronicle*, it is true, gives only 'thirty-six long miles' for the Lancastrians and 'thirty miles and more' for the Yorkists, apparently reckoning for the last two days; but medieval reckonings in miles are usually too small.   For example, the distance between Cheltenham and Tewkesbury is given as 'but five miles' whereas it is eight.

THE BATTLEFIELD

While the two armies are taking a few hours' rather feverish rest, both sides well knowing what was in store for them and for the kingdom in the morning, let us take a look at the ground that was likely to become the scene of the fight.

[1] Vestiges of the house where the King spent the night still exist.

All historians are agreed that the terrain has altered exceedingly, and they quote uncritically the well-known passage, given originally in the *Fleetwood Chronicle* in these words: 'Before them and on every hand foul lanes and deep dykes and many hedges with hills and valleys: a right evil place to approach, as could well have been devised.' But though I have a high opinion of the veracity of this chronicler, agreeing heartily with H. B. George, I feel that here alone

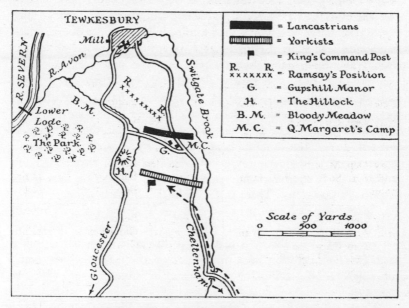

SKETCH-MAP 28. TEWKESBURY: THE APPROACH

he may be guilty of exaggeration. After all, in describing a position captured by his master, a medieval chronicler would take care to err, if at all, on the side of emphasizing the strength of the hostile position and the difficulties overcome by the conqueror. Of course, it is impossible to prove my supposition (nor yet to disprove it), but let us consider one only of his assertions, namely that there were 'Upon every hand foul lanes. . . .' Now, there were two roads to Tewkesbury from the south, on the left from Gloucester (by which the Lancastrians approached), on the right from Cheltenham (by which the Yorkists approached). Both are shown on Sketch-map 28. In this narrow space there could hardly have been any other roads except a possible cross-road. Such a road did exist along the present

hedge and ditch from Gupshill towards Bloody Meadow, at the foot
of the low ridge on which the Lancastrian army was arrayed. If
the valley to the south of it was full of dykes that at least shows
that it had been drained and was not too boggy. As for hedges, they
still abound; the same applies to trees—to a distracting extent if one
visits the battlefield in summer and hopes to get a good general view
of it. As for 'hills and valleys', unless there has since been a prodigious earthquake, these must be as they then were. The fact is,
our ancestors had a limited vocabulary, and could not express nice
distinctions between gentle slopes, knolls, hillocks, mounds and swells
of ground. In short, I estimate that except for a few farms such as
Stonehouse Farm and Lincoln Green and the new turnpike road,
the terrain is not very greatly altered since the fifteenth century.
Indeed, Gupshill Manor was then in existence, having been built in
1438, and a local tradition asserts that Margaret slept there the night
before the battle. This is hardly likely, for it was in the front line, if
not outside it. Just as in the next Civil War the name of Cromwell
is connected with almost any event where he might have fought, so
in the Wars of the Roses the name of Queen Margaret is kept green
in popular tradition. There is, for example, a five-sided earthwork,
100 feet along each side, situated 200 yards to the east of Gupshill
Manor, called Queen Margaret's Camp. Its antiquity is unknown,
but the most likely theory is that it was dug after the battle, possibly
as a grave-pit, possibly as a memorial of the battle. It is much
too small to be a camp for the Queen, or anyone else. (Sketch-
map 29.)

There is a low flat ridge one mile to the south of the town, over
the middle of which the modern high road to Gloucester passes. There
was a large field in the middle of it (in recent years built over) called
the Gastons. Somewhere in or about the Gastons the Lancastrian
position was sited. To the south of the Gastons the ground is low and
flat, with a small stream running through Bloody Meadow into the
Avon. To the south of the low ground is another slight ridge, on the
top of which is Stonehouse Farm. One thousand two hundred yards
to the west of Stonehouse Farm[1] is a wooded hill known as the
Park.

Sketch-map 29 shows the position the Lancastrians held. It runs
almost due east-west, through Gupshill Farm, its left resting on the
Swillgate Brook, its right on what Canon Bazeley calls Coln Brook,

[1] Not shown on the map.

about two hundred yards west of the present road, the right wing lining the aforementioned cross-road, the total length being just seven hundred yards. If the size of the army was about 5,000, that would be a fairly reasonable frontage. The exact strength of the army is conjectural to an unusual degree. All we know is that it was generally held to be slightly superior in numbers (though not in armament) to the King's army, which consisted of more than 3,000 foot and a smaller number of horse.

Holinshed's story that the position was strongly fortified is inherently improbable. The defending army was much too tired to do much digging on the evening of its arrival, and there was not much time next morning. Nor were field entrenchments a usual feature of the Wars of the Roses. We hear nothing of entrenchments or fortifications at the battle of Barnet fought a few weeks previously, when both armies spent a whole night in their respective positions. Even the Fleetwood Chronicler, in spite of his anxiety to stress the strength of the position, imputes this strength to the natural ground.

THE TWO ARMIES

The Queen deputed the actual command to the Duke of Somerset, and herself quitted the field either just before or during the battle, for she was not the Margaret of St. Albans. The Duke, in addition to having the somewhat nebulous supreme command, also commanded the vanguard, which occupied its normal position on the right of the line. The centre was under the nominal command of the Prince of Wales, then 17 years of age. By precedent this was not too young to exercise a command in the field; his ancestors, the Black Prince and Henry V, had done so when considerably younger, while the Duke of Gloucester, hero of Barnet, was only nineteen. But Prince Edward, about whom we know all too little, seems to have been but the pale shadow of his grandfather, and the real command rested in the hands of Lord Wenlock. Now Wenlock was a turncoat; he had fought for the Red Rose at St. Albans, for the White at Towton, and now at Tewkesbury once more for the Red Rose. This fact should be kept in mind. The left wing was under the Earl of Devonshire. The cannons made what show they could in the intervals between the foot-men. I picture the command-post on the Gastons, with a forward look-out post at Margaret's Camp prior to the battle. The Queen, accompanied by the Hope of England, her only son, processed

along the line at daybreak, uttering suitable exhortations, doubtless
in very broken English.

Early that morning the Yorkist army, arranged in the usual three
wards, van, middle and rear, 'advanced directly upon his enemies,
approaching to their field'. Edward, therefore, must have crossed
the Swillgate brook by the Tredington bridge, and taken the direct
or right-hand road thence (still marked by a thick hedge and a faint

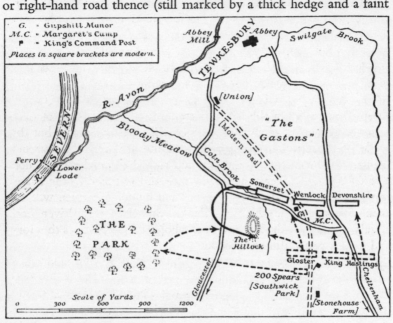

SKETCH-MAP 29. TEWKESBURY: THE BATTLE

track) towards Tewkesbury. (Sketch-map 28.) By this route he
had the brook on his right hand and a slight ridge on his left, which
would screen from view the western half of the hostile position.
I make no doubt that he then ascended this hill in order to obtain a
wider view, and found himself by the modern road, 200 yards north
of Stonehouse Farm. From here he would get a fair view of all
the hostile position, ranged directly in his front. Here then he would
make his command-post for the ensuing battle.

The van of his army was commanded by his brother Richard,
who had won his spurs so admirably at Barnet; the middle ward
he kept in his own hand, accompanied (also as at Barnet) by his unreliable brother Clarence, while Lord Hastings had the rear.

The obvious manœuvre for forming line from column of route would, under the circumstances, be for the head of the column to incline to its left towards the present Stonehouse Farm, followed by the remainder of the column. When the head reached the farm, all turned to their right and the line then made a slight wheel to the left, and found itself in line, straight opposite the hostile position. I presume this procedure was adopted, and that, at the conclusion of it Gloucester's column was on the left and Hastings's on the right. The right flank thus rested on the brook and the left flank on the modern road, or just beyond it. If, therefore, the King sited his command-post near the modern road he would be with Gloucester's division, and presumably left the centre under Clarence.

At this stage it will be as well to rehearse briefly the generally accepted narrative of the battle. It goes thus. The Duke of Gloucester, on the right of the line, opened with a fierce attack, but then made a feint retreat in order to entice Somerset out of his entrenchments. Somerset rose to the bait and rushed out of his stronghold. But Gloucester suddenly halted his men and returned to the charge. In this he was seconded by the King, and by 200 spearmen who had been posted outside the right flank. Somerset was driven back, closely pursued by the King and his whole army. So goes the story; and I must reject almost all of it.

The story of the feint retreat is the most easily disposed of. It is common to read of such feint retreats in military history, from Hastings onwards, but such an operation demands a higher state of training than any army of our civil wars was likely to possess. Nor does our one really reliable witness, the Fleetwood Chronicler, mention it. If Gloucester had devised and carried out successfully such a clever feat of arms, it is unbelievable that the official historian (for such the chronicler seems to have been) would have omitted all mention of it, the authority for it is *Hall's Chronicle*.

But Sir James Ramsay and his school (a formidable one, I admit) also places Gloucester on the right; moreover, he places the Queen's line facing south-west (as shown on Sketch-map 28). He places the 200 spearmen in Queen Margaret's Camp and therefore the whole Yorkist army to the left of the modern road.

Such dispositions make the whole course of the battle meaningless, and since Ramsay is regarded as our prime modern authority for medieval battles, I feel obliged to examine his thesis in detail. But, in order not to interrupt the flow of the narrative, I will relegate this examination to a note at the end. It will, however, be as well to set down here the salient passages in the *Fleetwood Chronicle*, for almost every word in them is of significance. (The spelling is modernized.)

'And in front of their field were so evil lanes and deep dykes, so many hedges, trees and bushes, that it was right hard to approach them near, and to come to hands; but Edward, called Duke of Somerset, having that day the van ... knightly and manly advanced himself with his fellowship, somewhat asidehand the King's van; and, by certain paths and ways therefor before purveyed (prepared), and to the King's party unknown, he departed out of the field, or close, even before the King, where he was embattled; and from the hill that was in one of the closes, he set right fiercely upon the end of the King's battle. The King full manly set forth upon them, entered and won the dyke and hedge, upon them, into the close, and with great violence put them up towards the hill, and so also the King's vanguard in the rule of the Duke of Gloucester.

'Here it is to be remembered, how that, when the King was coming before their field, ere he set upon them, he considered that upon the right hand of their field, there was a park, and therein much wood, and he, thinking to purvey (prepare) a remedy in case his said enemies had laid any bushment (ambush) in that wood, of horsemen, he chose out of his fellowship two hundred spears and set them in a plump (mass) together, near a quarter of a mile from the field, giving them charge to have good eye upon that corner of the wood, if case that any need were, to put themselves in service; and if they saw none such then as they thought most behoveful for time and space, to employ themselves in the best wise they could—which provision came as well to point, at this time of the battle, as could well have been devised; for the said spears of the King's party seeing no likelihood of any bushment in the said wood-corner (seeing also good opportunity to employ themselves well), came and broke on, all at once, upon the Duke of Somerset and his vanguard, aside-hand, unadvised, whereof they seeing the King gave them enough to do before them, were greatly dismayed and abashed; and so took to flight into the park, and into the meadow that was near, and into lanes and dykes, where they best hoped to escape the danger; of whom nevertheless many were distressed, taken and slain. And, even at this point of their flight, the King courageously set upon that other field where was the chief, Edward, called Prince of Wales, and in a short while put him to discomfiture and flight, and so fell in the chase of them, that many of them were slain, and namely by a mill in the meadow, fast by the town, were many drowned.'

THE BATTLE

And now I come at last to my own reconstruction of the battle. The opposing lines at the beginning of the battle were about 400 yards apart, just within artillery range, and the battle opened with a mild artillery duel. In this the Yorkists had the advantage, as might be expected, for the Lancastrians had only managed to collect a scratch force of guns a few days previously, some of which they had already lost, whereas the King's had no doubt been with him at Barnet. The Duke of Somerset then struck his blow. Perceiving that Gloucester's left flank rested 'in the air' on the Stonehouse Farm ridge, and perceiving that the hillock 500 yards further west remained unoccupied, and further, that owing to the great number of trees it should be possible to approach the enemy's left flank unseen and gain a footing on the hillock, he himself made a reconnaissance of the ground that would have to be passed over ('certain paths and ways therefor before purveyed') and decided that the thing was feasible. Having his own division on that wing he elected to command it himself. But this was not the whole plan. It was to be a combined operation. As soon as his flank attack got under way the centre column under Wenlock was to make a frontal attack in support. (Here the authority is *Hall's Chronicle*, the only other real source for the actual battle.)

This plan was both imaginative and practicable. From the King's command-post the approach of Somerset's men would be screened from view by the hillock combined with the trees in the valley. It was of course necessary to leave a skeleton force in the front line, to screen the movement. If this line ran as I have indicated, along the hedge and ditch that still bounds the edge of the Gaston's ridge, the screening business would be simple. At any rate we have the statement of the chronicler that the way was unknown to the King, and it is implicit in the whole story that it was a surprise attack, crossing a lane (it would have to cross the Gloucester road near Lincoln Green), round the hostile flank ('somewhat asidehand the King's van') and reached a hill whence he could attack the hostile flank ('the end of the King's battle'). Having occupied the hill, Somerset took up a position at its foot where there was a hedge and ditch ('embattled . . . the dyke and hedge . . . into the close'). The enemy attacked him here and drove him back up the hillock ('put them up towards the hill').[1]

Now came the dramatic intervention of the 200 spearmen. From his command-post the experienced eye of the King had perceived a possible danger-spot away on his left flank, formed by what is still known as The Park, really a largish wood on a hill. Realizing that the enemy might easily hide a force of mounted men therein, in order to threaten his flank during the battle, he despatched the 200 spearmen, as clearly narrated by the chronicler. The arrow on Sketch-map 28 indicates the probable line that these 200 spears would take.

Posted on the side of the wood they would, as it happened, be ideally placed to strike the outer flank of Somerset's attack. No doubt they would wait till the main body of it had passed on to the attack, for fear of drawing upon themselves the whole force of the attack. But when they did intervene it was probably the turning point of the action.

Somerset was thus beset on two sides. The enemy had recovered from their initial surprise and were now themselves attacking. Now was the time for Wenlock to join in with his promised attack. But there was no sign of any such attack. In default of it Somerset's own attack was gradually driven back till it eventually broke altogether and his men sped as fugitives back the way they had come. This took them into Bloody Meadow, whose expressive name doubtless enshrines an authentic tradition of slaughter just at the place where one would expect it. Some fugitives, we are told, tried to get shelter in the Park—again a natural step—and some made for the river. The counter-attack was completely broken; Somerset himself managed to get back into his own lines. No doubt he was mounted and would have more chance to escape than the foot-men. Burning with rage against the perfidious Wenlock, for such he deemed him, he rode up to him. Wenlock was sitting inactive. Hall's words are: 'But whether the Lord Wenlock dissimuled the matter for the King Edward's sake or whether his heart served him not, still he stood looking on.' Somerset reviled him, roundly accusing him of being a traitor. Treason and treachery were ever-present dangers during the Wars of the Roses, and indeed during all civil wars, and in view of Wenlock's past history Somerset's suspicions were natural. At all

---

[1] This 'hill' could also be taken to mean the Gastons ridge. It does not greatly matter which meaning is given it.

events he would scarcely have taken the next step that is recorded of him unless he had felt no doubt in the matter. He drew his battle-axe and dashed out the brains of Lord Wenlock.

Such an act, even in those hard times, was bound to create consternation, coming as it did at the moment when the right wing was recoiling in confusion. The centre division was now left without a leader, and there could be only one result. Whether or not the attack on the centre was immediately driven home, the issue was decided. Disintegration set in the whole Lancastrian army, rapidly, as it always does in such civil war contests. It became a *sauve qui peut*. Many were killed while trying to cross the river by the Abbey mill, and worst of all, Prince Edward, the last of Henry of Lancaster's line, was slain.

PROBLEMS OF THE BATTLEFIELD

All students of medieval battles owe Sir James Ramsay a big debt of gratitude for his painstaking compilation and citation of all the relevant sources so unerringly. So it may appear churlish if one devotes space to examining and refuting his inferences and consequent reconstruction of the battles. He is the recognized authority in this matter. But that is the very reason why it seems essential to point out any errors in his accounts of battles. For though, in this case, a subsequent writer, Canon Bazeley, has shown up some of his errors, at least 20 persons will have read Ramsay's account for one that has read Bazeley's in the *Transactions of the Bristol and Gloucester Archæological Society for* 1903.

Let us then glance at Ramsay's version of the battle. According to him, Somerset drew up his lines as marked R—R on Sketch Map 28. Edward approached by the right-hand road, inclining off it to the left just short of Queen Margaret's Camp. From this camp the King obtained his first sight of the hostile army, or rather its left flank, distant 500 yards, sited on the middle of the Gastons plateau. The line was thus almost parallel to his line of approach. Leaving 200 spearmen in Queen Margaret's Camp, he marched on, and deployed his troops for battle opposite the hostile line. Gloucester's column, which was in the lead, opened attack. 'The struggle might have been lengthy, but that Somerset [whom Ramsay places on the left] taking his men round behind the ridge . . . wheeling round, came down from the height [*sic*] upon the King's flank. Edward put them backwards up the hill, Gloucester coming to his support. Then the 200 spears

charged Somerset on his left, and between them he was routed, and
driven down the reverse slope towards the Swillgate. Edward then
pushed into the Lancastrian position by the way left open to him by
Somerset, and all was over. . . .'

Thus Ramsay—an account so different from the one I have given
that they can scarcely be recognized as referring to the same battle.
And yet both are derived from the same two sources.   For, surprising
as it may seem, for such an important battle there are only two real
original narratives of the actual battle—the *Fleetwood Chronicle* and
material used by Hall in his *Chronicle*.   This disparity in result merely
goes to show what a long way inference has to go in reconstructing
ancient battles.

Let us now examine Ramsay's narrative in the light of Inherent
Military Probability.   We shall find that he involves himself in at least
ten difficulties.

1.   He makes the Lancastrians form their line almost at right
angles to the line of approach of their adversaries, i.e. facing approximately south-west instead of south-east.[1]

If Edward had found the enemy thus drawn up, would he not
by advancing straight to his front have attacked the enemy in flank?
It is wrong to suppose that flank attacks were never made in those
times.   We have seen how Queen Margaret had done so at St.
Albans, and how Somerset did so in this very battle.

2.   Ramsay's position does not properly cover the road to Tewkesbury by which the Yorkists were approaching.   Its flank merely
rests upon the road.   (Again compare Ramsay at Barnet, and also
at Hastings.)

3.   The Lancastrian position, the chronicler tells us, was protected by ditches and dykes.   This betokens, surely, the low meadow
ground that lies in front of the position.   Yet Somerset apparently
threw away this advantage by forming his line on the middle of the
plateau, a good 400 yards behind this low watery ground, thus allowing Edward to deploy and attack along the comparatively high and
dry ground of the Gastons.   Ramsay is obliged to admit that 'the
dykes seem to have disappeared'.

4.   He makes Gloucester move across from the left flank to the
right during the battle to help the King.   But what was Hastings
doing?   His division was the nearest to 'Queen Margaret's Camp',
and so would be the natural one to help the King.

[1] He did the same thing, it will be remembered, in his account of Barnet.

5. He makes the King drive the enemy up the hill; but, according to his map Edward was already on the Gastons which are practically flat, and on the top of the hill.

6. He places the Park where there is no evidence that there was ever a park—on the east of the road—whereas 'The Park', which is on the other flank, was known as such in medieval times.

7. This 'park' he afterwards describes as merely 'the wooded lane' meaning the right-hand road. But this lane cannot have looked like 'a park, and therein much wood' (*Fleetwood Chronicle*) capable of hiding 'an ambush of horsemen'. Moreover, it ran within 100 yards of the 'camp', where the 200 were to hide. It all sounds more like a boy scouts' game than war.

8. In order to get Somerset on to the eastern flank, Ramsay has to explain away the assertion of the chronicler that the park and therefore, from what follows, Somerset's division, was on the Lancastrian right flank. Ramsay assumes that when the chronicler wrote 'right' he meant the chronicler's own right. Now it is true that ancient chroniclers were not always careful in such matters, but this chronicler was writing what amounted to the official account, and it is unusually precise and accurate, as far as we can judge. Moreover, Somerset commanded the vanguard, which would normally form up on the right. Ramsay gets round this by the quite unsupported statement that the Lancastrian line was 'fronted to its rear'.

9. If the spearmen's 'hide' was in Margaret's Camp, fighting can hardly have occurred there. But the only existing signs of what may be grave-pits are in and around this camp.

10. If the Lancastrian position was as shown by Ramsay, how came it that the retreat and slaughter of Somerset's men occurred, if tradition be correct, in the Bloody Meadow, on the opposite flank? In order to reach the Bloody Meadow—which, according to Ramsay, was 300 yards behind the Yorkist line, the fugitives would have to pass right through the hostile army!

The conclusion that is forced upon us is that Sir James Ramsay's reconstruction of the battle must be rejected *in toto*.

CHAPTER XXIV

The Battle of Bosworth, August 22nd, 1485

ON August 22nd, 1485, in a marsh on the borders of Leicester and Warwick, the House of York perished for ever, making way for the ever-memorable Tudor dynasty on the throne of England. Bosworth Field was thus one of the most important battles ever fought on English soil. Unfortunately it is worse documented than any that even approaches it in importance. Thus our reconstruction of the fight must be more than usually conjectural. Only one reasonably detailed account has come down to us, and that was written by a foreigner, Polydore Vergil, who only arrived in the country 18 years or more after the battle. The only strictly contemporary account is contained in the *Continuation of the Chronicle of Croyland*, but that is very meagre for the actual battle, and it is clear that the author was ignorant of the ground fought over. To add to our difficulties that great stand-by—the grave-pit—fails us, none having been discovered. It is not surprising therefore, that those historians who have not slavishly followed one another, are hopelessly at variance in their attempts to reconstruct the scene and course of events. But the task must be tackled.

The battle, with its intensely important results stares in the face those who try to maintain that 'wars decide nothing'. For England received the Tudor line, not as the result of a national demand, but of a few well-aimed sword thrusts in a bog.

On August 8th, 1485, Henry Tudor (loosely but wrongly called Earl of Richmond) landed at Milford Haven with a force of 2,000 French mercenaries, intent on wresting the crown from Richard III. Needless to say, Henry did not expect to be able to accomplish this mighty task with such a small following of troops: he counted on receiving sufficient adherents, from disaffected subjects of the Yorkist king, to achieve success. Notably he counted on the support of that powerful baron, Lord Stanley. But Stanley was in a delicate position. On the one hand, he was step-father to Henry Tudor: on the other, his loyalty was suspect, and the King held his son, Lord Strange, as a surety for his continued allegiance. Stanley, therefore, though willing to join his step-son, dared not show his hand till the last minute. His brother, Sir William Stanley, could afford to take a less equivocal line, for he had already been declared a traitor.

There were obvious reasons for the selection of Milford Haven as a landing place. It was less likely to be guarded by the royal fleet than the south coast, and Henry, being a Welshman, counted on receiving numerous adherents in the Principality. In this latter respect he was only partially successful in his march north-eastwards. He reached Shrewsbury on August 15th, and the news was speedily conveyed to the King, who was then centrally situated at Nottingham. Richard promptly ordered out the shire levies, and designated Leicester as the rendezvous.

Meanwhile, Henry continued his march, reaching Newport on the 16th and 'pitching his tents upon the next hill.'[1] Here he was joined by Sir Gilbert Talbot with over 500 men. On the 17th he was at Stafford where he was visited by Sir William Stanley, who had left his contingent of Cheshire troops at Stone. After conferring with Henry, he returned to Stone and resumed his march on a parallel route to that of the Tudor army. At the same time he sent word to his brother, Lord Stanley, who was falling back towards Leicester. The rebels, as we must call them, resumed their march to Lichfield next day, where they were warmly received, and 'gonnes in Lychefyld craked'.[2]

Probably taking some of these 'gonnes' with him, Henry proceeded by short stages to Tamworth and Atherstone, where on August 20th he was met by the Stanley brothers. At a war council both assured him of their support when the moment for it arrived. Obliged to put up with this rather dubious promise, Henry marched on next day, and camped that night at the White Moors, three miles south-west of Bosworth. (Sketch Map 30.)

On receiving the alarming news that his rival was approaching with an armed force, King Richard had sent out his 'scurryers' to gain information, and to shadow the enemy's movements. Receiving

[1] Probably Wilbrighton Hill, two miles east, and the scene of the Albrighton Hunt point-to-point races.

[2] *Richard the Third, his deathe*, by the Lord Stanley (Harl. MSS. 342, f. 31). This curious document has not received the attention it deserves. Incidentally, J. Nicholls, who transcribed it in Hutton's *Battle of Bosworth Field* in 1813, wrongly cited it as folio 34, and this mistake has been perpetuated by Ramsay and others.

a report from them that the enemy had now reached Lichfield, the King decided not to wait for any more reinforcements, but to march resolutely forward to meet his oppenent, whom he affected to despise. The odds certainly appeared to be on the King's side. He was comparatively experienced, while his opponent had never been in action and was not of a warlike disposition. The royal army was more numerous and more homogenous than any that his opponent was likely to be able to oppose to it. But there was a 'but'. The King was not sure how much reliance he could put on his great barons. To a direct order to march to join him at Leicester, Stanley had sent the lame and untruthful reply that he was suffering from the 'sweating sickness'. But Richard dared not tarry. On August 21st, while his adversary was marching east from Atherstone, Richard advanced west from Leicester. Presumably taking the old road via Peckleton and Kirkby Mallory, he camped that night near Sutton Cheney. The two armies were within three miles of one another, and their camping grounds must have been spotted by the respective scurryers (See Sketch-map 30). Richard had marched with all the panoply of war, wearing his golden crown upon his helmet,[1] mounted on a white palfrey and with trumpets blowing. All this was a deliberate morale-raising measure: his army had need of it. Biondi recorded that 'no jollity was observed in his march'. As for respective numbers, it is a particularly difficult matter to assess them because they were changing from hour to hour, as deserters slipped away from the Yorkist side, and adherents came in on the Tudor side. Most historians, without stating their reasons or calculations, give figures for all four armies, but there is little direct evidence to go on. The most detailed estimate for the royal army is given by Baker in his *Chronicles*, as cited by Brooke in his *Visits to Fields of Battle* (1857). I have not verified the quotation but the numbers given agree so closely with what I should expect that I will give them. Vanguard: Duke of Norfolk, 1,200 bowmen flanked with 200 cuirassiers; main guard, the King, 1,000 billmen and 2,000 pikes; rearward, Earl of Northumberland, 2,000 billmen and pikes, and on the wings 1,500 horsemen. This makes a total of 7,900, which I accept.

[1] Some writers have denied that this was a real crown, but there seems no reason against it; crowns in those days were mere circlets which could be easily fitted upon a helmet. The contemporary account (*Croyland Chronicle*) states that it was a crown 'of exceeding value.' Henry V is reputed to have worn his at Agincourt, and doubtless Richard was aware of this and may have consciously imitated it.

Tudor chroniclers afterwards averred, as was natural, that Henry was badly outnumbered: even granting that to be so, if we add the two Stanley armies the numerical superiority almost certainly became his.

But civil war is a cruel, nerve-racking affair. The leading protagonists on each side are well aware that they fight with a halter round their necks, and the two leaders are always left in doubt right up to the moment of contact how far the loyalty of their troops will remain firm. It is thus not surprising to hear that Richard spent a disturbed night, though we need not accord credence to the fanciful tales of his nightmare afterwards put about by the Tudor writers.

Nor was his rival easy in his mind on that momentous morning of August 22nd; he was but a child in arms (though 27 years of age), utterly in the hands of his own officers. The chief of these was the Earl of Oxford, who had fought at Castillon and had a good military reputation. Like Richard, his rival glanced anxiously from flank to flank, for signs of the approach of the two Stanley armies. Of these armies, that of Lord Stanley was probably situated to the south, near Dadlington, about midway between the rival armies, while that of Sir William was similarly situated on the northern flank, perhaps at Nether Cotton.[1] Thus the four armies formed a square. If football was indulged in in those days it must have seemed like two rival teams lining up, while on the two touch-lines stood the two spectators, ready at any moment to intervene on one side or the other. The terrain was open and of such a nature that at the moment of contact all four armies would be within sight of one another. Such an extraordinary situation can never have occurred on English battlefields before or since.

THE TERRAIN
(Sketch-map 30)

Sutton Cheney is situated on a low ridge, rising about 100 feet above the surrounding ground, and running from north-east to south-west. Its highest point, 417 feet, is just to the north of the village, near a tumulus at the road angle which was afterwards called (according to some) Dickon's (Richard's) Nook. At the south-western end is a hillock, 393 feet high, called Ambien Hill. From here the ground slopes down at about one in ten to the north, and at about one in twenty to the south. This southern slope was marshy in places, owing

[1] Two miles north of Ambien Hill.

to the outflow from a spring, now called Richard's Well, though it
is not a well. The ground was unenclosed, uncultivated, and nearly
devoid of trees. The name Ambien is supposed to derive from the
Saxon *Ann Beame*, meaning One Tree. The hillock would afford a
good defensive position for the Royalists, if they could reach it in

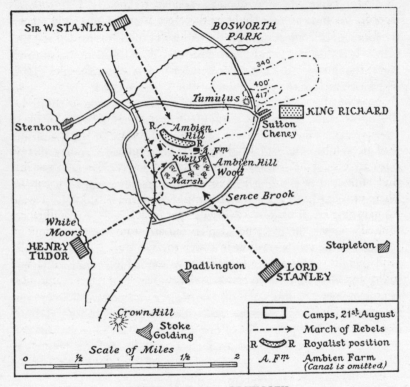

SKETCH–MAP 30. BOSWORTH

time. It was, according to my reckoning, about equidistant from the
two hostile camps.

The ground has since completely changed in appearance, being
entirely enclosed, traversed by a railway and canal, two farms erected
on the battlefield, and a wood of 90 acres covering the marsh. Practically the only thing that remains substantially unchanged is Richard's
Well. A stone pyramid was erected over the 'well' by Dr. S. Parr,
in about the year 1813. I show a sketch of it. I have not been able
to discover a photograph of this historic spot.

THE BATTLE

The battle manœuvre resolved itself into a race for Ambien Hill. The King's scurryers were probably more practised and enterprising than those of the Rebels, and were in occupation of the hill by dawn. Richard, being apprised of this, decided to make for it with all speed. As soon as it was light he therefore assembled his chief officers on Dickon's Nook, whence not only the hill, but the camps of the two Stanleys were also visible. The old chroniclers, true to form, put into the King's mouth a long speech addressed to his whole army. Needless to say such an address to the army was quite out of the question; he may have delivered it to his chief officers, but as he was pressed for time, he in all probability confined himself to the matter in hand, namely the orders for battle. General exhortations to the troops had no doubt been circulated by him overnight. We may picture him addressing his officers to the following effect: 'Do you see that hill with a single tree on it, about a mile away? My scurryers are there now and can see the rebels' camp in the hollow beyond. I want to gain that hill before the enemy can get to it. But haste will be required. I shall therefore not deploy the army now, but continue in yesterday's march formation in order to save time. You, Norfolk, will therefore continue to lead; keep to the top of the ridge; I will follow you with the main ward, and you, my Lord of Northumberland, will follow me with the rear ward. You, Norfolk, must line the whole length of the position with your bowmen, and I will thicken up your line when my ward comes up. What happens after that will depend upon what action Henry Tudor takes. If he attacks us so much the better; we shall know how to defend ourselves: but if he stands fast, we will attack him. Sound, banner, advance!'

Having given these orders the King sent a peremptory order to Lord Stanley to join him at once, but Stanley sent a procrastinating answer, and stood fast, whilst Norfolk's division moved forward at full speed.

Meanwhile in the rival camp events were not moving so fast. Henry, the amateur soldier, lacked his opponent's grasp of the situation and his driving power. He failed to get his army on the move as expeditiously, with the result that as he neared Ambien Hill he found it occupied by the enemy. His progress was still further delayed by the fact that his scurryers had not done their work well and had not warned him that almost in a direct line between his camp and the hill was a

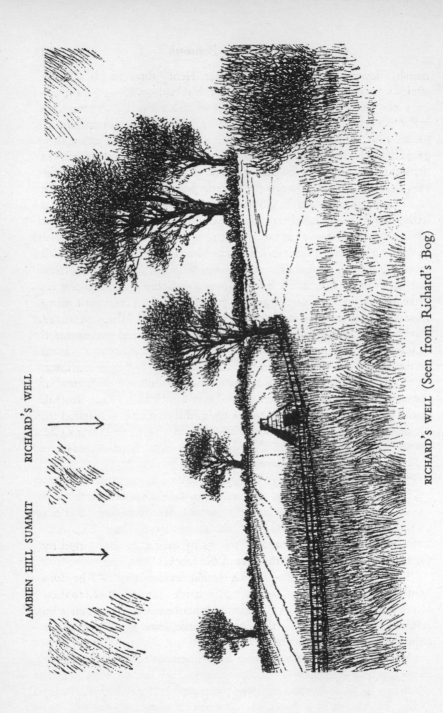

AMBIEN HILL SUMMIT   RICHARD'S WELL

RICHARD'S WELL (Seen from Richard's Bog)

marsh. Ignorant of this important fact, Henry directed his advance straight forward, with the result that his leading troops soon encountered the marsh. (See Sketch-map.) In order to circumvent it a sharp wheel was made to the left. The sun was now up, but low on the horizon and it was shining in the eyes of the vanguard as they groped their way forward. The sharp turn to the north removed the dazzle and made their path clearer. Years afterwards one of the vanguard, recounting the story of the battle to Polydore Vergil, would remark on the relief this sudden turn afforded them and the Italian took it down and recorded it in his book, little realizing what trouble he was thereby causing future historians.[1]

The sudden change of direction would be in full view of Norfolk's troops, and we may safely picture him standing by the side of the King, now arrived at the front, and narrowly watching the manœuvre. Presently the van ward emerged to the north of the marsh, following almost exactly the line of the modern railway. When the head reached what is now Shenton railway station, Oxford endeavoured to form front to the flank, facing up the hill. This operation was no doubt carried out clumsily, slowly, and with a good deal of confusion on the part of Henry's scratch army. Moreover it was in full view of the enemy, distant only a few hundred yards. The King and Norfolk must have eagerly debated whether to hold their fire and position till the remainder of the army should have closed up, or whether to take advantage of the increasing confusion visible in the hostile ranks and charge down the hill.

What would have happened if the forward policy had been adopted will, of course, never be known, but it is tempting to envisage a resounding victory for the King. But counsels of prudence prevailed; a compromise was resolved on. The troops stood fast, and a fire-action developed—a discharge of arrows by each side—supported by the fire of a few cannon on the part of the rebels.[2]

The sound of gunfire—if not ocular evidence—told the two Stanleys what they wanted to know; the battle was on. True to their secret undertaking to Henry made at Atherstone, they set their two armies in motion towards the field of battle, directing them at the exposed flanks of the royal army.

Meanwhile the King's division had closed up to the hill and lay

[1] See end of chapter.

[2] See end of chapter for a discussion as to the presence of artillery at the battle.

in support of Norfolk's division. The natural position along the end of the ridge is about 600 yards in extent. If Norfolk had 3,000 men he could hold it fairly comfortably till the rear divisions came up.

And what was Northumberland's division doing? Precisely nothing. It remained rooted to the ground on the ridge-top, near Dickon's Nook. From here Northumberland could watch the motions of the two 'neutral' armies. Till they showed their hand he also did not intend to risk action. For if they both, as he suspected, intervened on the side of the rebels, the King could scarcely avoid defeat, whether Northumberland took part in the battle or not. So the cautious Earl of Northumberland must have reasoned.

Michael Drayton, who lived near the spot in the next century, has depicted his infamy in verse.

> He doth but vainly look
> For succour from the great Northumberland
> That from the battle scarce three quarters of a mile
> Stood with his power of horse, nor once was seen to stir.

After a brief missile engagement the supply of ammunition began to run short, the fire died down, and a pause ensued, each side closely scanning the other and waiting for it to make the first move. Then, as if by mutual consent, both armies advanced against one another, and the two lines clashed into one another on mid slope. The present Glebe Farm, 250 yards west of the hill top, represents approximately the centre of the strife.

For some time, perhaps over an hour, the issue remained undecided. Little by little the King's division became engaged, as also that of Henry Tudor on the opposite side. Henry, we are told, kept well to the rear. Sensible man! If he were killed while striving for the crown, a victory for his army would not gain it him. Possibly he called to mind the example of another Henry on Shrewsbury field. Richard, on the other hand, we may picture standing well forward on the crest of the ridge, whence he could see the progress of the fight, and—what was even more important—the progress in his direction of the Stanley armies. These were steadily drawing closer, and it became increasingly clear that their intentions were unfriendly. Finally the awful moment arrived when they engaged in open action against his two wings, Sir William on the north and Lord Stanley on the south. Richard must have given a last despairing glance to the rear to see if Northumberland was coming to his help. On realizing the dread truth that the powerful Northumberland also had failed him, the King recognized that the end was at hand. Encompassed by enemies there was nothing left to him—save honour. He spurned the advice of a courtier that he should take to flight—for he was no Monmouth.

In a battle full of conjecture one fact stands out clear, testified to by friend and foe alike: King Richard died like a king. Nothing in his life, it may truly be said, became him like the leaving of it. Mounting his horse and collecting his bodyguard around him, the King of England prepared to strike his last blow. Which opponent should he strike? The chroniclers all assume that his antagonist was his rival and would-be supplanter, Henry Tudor. But if Henry was keeping well out of danger's way, how could Richard reach him? How indeed could he know where to find him? On a hot, sunny August day after over an hour's hand-to-hand fighting, such a steam of sweat and cloud of dust would arise as would effectually screen all but the front line of the hostile array. Then against whom would the King feel most bitter—against his open enemy or against his treacherous friend? Can there be any doubt that his fiercest desire at this supreme moment of his life was to cross swords with the traitor Lord Stanley? The thought of Stanley's treason was uppermost in his mind if we may believe the report that the last words he uttered were: 'Treason, treason!' Now, as I see it, Lord Stanley's army approached from the south. This would bring at least a portion of it into the marshy ground below the well. We may then envisage the King galloping madly down the slope from the hill-top, past the well and into the boggy ground immediately below it. Plunging heedlessly into the marsh his charger became bogged. Shakespeare's famous line: 'A horse, a horse, my kingdom for a horse!' may well be fitted into this episode, and may be historical. His own horse hopelessly bogged, the King called for another. But another was not forthcoming. Immobilized and surrounded by enemies, the King died fighting. Lord Stanley's own account (if we are to credit the *Harleian MS.*) puts these words into the dying King's mouth:

> Bring me my battleaxe in my hand
>> And set the crown of gold on my head so high
> For by him that shope[1] both sea and sand
>> King of England this day will I die.
> One foot away I will not flee
>> While breath will bide my breast within.

[1] Shaped.

The relation goes on:

> As he said, so did he; he lost his life.
> On his standard then fast did they light.
> They hewed the crowne of gold from his head
> With dreadful dents; his death was dyght.

So died the last Yorkist King of England, as the *Croyland Chronicle* puts it, 'like a brave and most valiant prince'.

In every part of the field, when the death of the King became known, resistance ceased. This was only to be expected; what object could there be for anyone to continue risking his life for a dead monarch? Richard was a childless widower. His heir was a nephew, a boy unknown to the army or the country. Resistance ceased and the army melted away just as completely as the English army had done on the death of the only other king to perish on an English battlefield—Harold at Hastings.

There are no indications of an organized pursuit. Why should there be? Henry's battle was against the King and his immediate supporting nobles, most of whom had been slain. The common soldiers could go their way; Henry had no need or wish to fight against his own subjects once the issue was decided. Moreover the royalists must have dispersed in all directions, discarding weapons and any distinctive marks of uniform that they wore. Thus they could merge in the countryfolk in the surrounding villages. There are, however, indications that one batch made off towards the north-east, for a large number of weapons were found in the eighteenth century to the north of Sutton. Probably the bulk of the defeated army broke away to the south, for numerous relics have been found in that direction, and after the battle Henry seems to have established some sort of rendezvous on what is now called Crown Hill, 3,000 yards south of the field. Richard's crown had been seized and secreted in a thorn-bush by one of the troops, who no doubt intended to return for it after dark. But it was found and handed to Lord Stanley. In full sight of the victorious and cheering soldiers on Crown Hill, Lord Stanley performed an act that has since struck the imagination of every schoolboy—he placed the battered crown of Richard upon the head of his victorious rival and hailed him as King Henry the Seventh. Henry Tudor had triumphed—but Lord Stanley, the traitor, had won the battle.

The country settled down with astonishing suddenness and

unanimity to accept Henry as its King. Professor C. H. Williams in the *Cambridge Medieval History* accounts for this phenomenon by the fact that the people accepted the arbitrament of battle as an Act of God. 'It was war under the eye of the Supreme Judge, and that is "trial by battle".'

PROBLEMS OF THE BATTLEFIELD

I.—THE SITE OF THE BATTLE

From what has been said above about the paucity of sources for the battle it is not surprising to find the historians at variance. Though the consensus of modern opinion is in general agreement with my siting of the field, there are some notable divergences. Hutton, who made an unusually thorough investigation of the battlefield in the eighteenth century, and to whom all subsequent historians are deeply indebted (whether they acknowledge it or not), places the fighting on the top of the ridge. Sir James Ramsay contrives somehow to screw the two armies round so far that they engage with Richard facing north instead of south-west! Professor Gairdner remarks on this mildly: 'I do not know how Sir James Ramsay could vindicate the view that he has taken.'[1] If it be hidden from Gairdner, who is the leading historian of the battle, it would be profitless to enter upon conjectures in the matter. The conclusion seems to be that Ramsay has here 'out-Ramsayed' himself.

Though I agree in general with Gairdner's siting of the field, I cannot agree in particulars. The bone of contention is the situation of the marsh. I have placed it on the slope to the south of Richard's Well, and owing its existence to that well. Hutton, and his editor in the 1813 edition, J. Nichols, take the same view. But Gairdner disagrees on the ground that Holinshed states that the marsh has since 'growne to be firme ground'. Therefore, he argues, it could not have been marshy in Hutton's time, 200 years later. Indeed it could! I know of places that were 'firme ground' when I was a boy, but which have since become marshy. Indeed, though the spring has at some period been piped, there are at the present day marshy passages due to this spring. Drainage, if not seen to frequently, deteriorates. Such has evidently been the case on Ambien Hill.

There is therefore no need to look further afield for the marsh.

[1] *Archæologia*, 1896, p. 163.

Gairdner places it just to the west of the railway and the canal, 800 yards from Richard's Well, in a flat meadow. But bogs do not necessarily require dead flat ground. Any land below a spring, if undrained, will be boggy. Ramsay, driving his lone furrow, places the marsh a good half mile to the *north* of Ambien Hill. Where two such authorities disagree I approached the problem with a completely open mind. I supposed that if Hutton was right there should at least be signs of what had been marshy ground in the wood through which the spring water had flowed. I therefore started my search in the lower part of the wood. Here, close up to the railway and canal, the slope, always very slight, has practically disappeared. Hereabouts I found large patches of coarse reedy herbage, very similar to some that I know of on my native heath, where what is now fairly firm ground was once under water. I make little doubt that such has been the case here. This area is immediately below the Well, and would, before drainage, almost certainly be boggy ground. The very fact that it was liable to bog may have been the reason why it was planted as woodland when the surrounding and drier land was enclosed in 1646. Even in the field just outside the wood and below the well there are patches of boggy ground where a horse to-day might well get bogged. Indeed, if I am right in locating Richard's death charge down into the marsh, one of these boggy patches may well be the identical spot where the last Yorkist king perished. At any rate, it aids the imagination when reconstructing the battle on the spot so to regard it. Though I did not find any boggy spots inside the wood, Mr. Bradley, the farmer at Ambien Farm assured me that it is frequently boggy there. Thus I feel on firm ground in my siting of the marsh! My sketch indicates the boggy nature of the ground immediately below the well. This I identify as the spot where King Richard fell.

II.—THE LEFT-WHEEL OF THE REBEL ARMY

The position of the marsh is bound up with another problem: how did the change of direction of the rebel army in avoiding the marsh bring the sun on to their backs? This problem seems to have baffled, or at least perplexed, all who have studied it. For long I shared this mystification. Eventually I was drawn to the solution that I have propounded in my narrative. The difficulty arises from Hall's account which reads as follows (I have modernized the spelling): 'Between both armies there was a great marsh, which the Earl of Richmond left on his right hand, and in so doing he had the sun at his back and in the faces of his enemies.'

The difficulty resides in the fact that the battle took place, as all assume, in the morning, when the sun would be in the east—the direction whence the royalist army was advancing. How then could the sun possibly be in their faces when they engaged in the battle? Both armies would have to wheel through nearly 180 degrees in order to bring this about. But there is nowhere the slightest indication that this happened. The difficulty is reduced, as pointed out by Gairdner, by assuming that the words 'and in the faces of his enemies' was added by Hall to Polydore's account merely as a presumption and a wrong one. If the rebel army followed the course I have indicated, the sun would be, if not on their back, at least no longer in their eyes after they had wheeled to the north. But, it may be argued, when they turned back towards the east to engage the enemy it would once more be in their face. Agreed—but would they then notice it so to the extent of remarking on it afterwards? When a man is engaged in some absorbing or exciting task, such as fighting, he takes little note of the weather. Moreover, the sun would be higher in the heavens by the time the battle started, and therefore would not be so much in evidence to either army. Probably very few of those engaged could have said afterwards whether the sun was out or not. The above at least seems the simplest explanation, and avoids several difficulties. Failing that, one would be disposed to suspect that Polydore Vergil had got the story wrong rather than force the battle into the pattern required by the passage. It should not be forgotten that a foreigner who starts to collect information—probably by word of mouth, and often at second or third hand—a generation after the battle is liable to error in details. However, in this case I feel that the general sense of the passage can be accepted.

III.—THE YORKIST POSITION

So far as the written records go, there is nothing inconsistent with Hutton's theory that the battle took place on the top of the hill. But medieval records are seldom an exact guide as to topography. Maps did not exist, and the chronicler was seldom an eye-witness of the battle. His informers, even if they themselves were participants, probably had never revisited the ground and were themselves vague as to the precise locality. Dwellers in the neighbourhood probably took to their heels during the battle. (We never hear reference to such folk during a battle.)   We are thus reduced to the evidence that the soil produces—relics of the field in the shape of bones, arms and ammunition, which have worked their way to the surface or have been unearthed by the plough.   This is indeed the most satisfactory form of evidence.   A chronicler can lie; the soil cannot.

In this case the soil gives us excellent evidence.   Just to the west of the hill-top, on the western slope of the hill, about on the site of Glebe Farm, four cannon-balls were dug up in the eighteenth century.   In the field between here and the hill-top the owner of Glebe Farm four years ago found a stone cannon-ball of about four inches diameter. About 15 years ago Mr. Bradley, of Ambien Hill Farm, dug up a stone cannon-ball 150 yards due east of the well.   These three finds form an adequate pattern, pointing to a royalist position along the crest of the hill.

It may, however, be asked: Could not these balls have been fired by—not at—the Yorkists, in which case their position would have been on the plateau several hundred yards further east?   The answer is that if the balls were fired by the rebels, 'the angle of incidence' would have been sufficiently big to drive them into the ground where they would remain until disturbed, whereas, if fired by the Yorkists, 'the angle of incidence' would have been small and they would probably have ricocheted to the bottom of the hill, where they would have lain on the surface and eventually have been made use of by the farmers.   The position of the well nearby adds strength to the supposition that the crest was occupied by Richard.   One need not suppose that he drank from the well just before undertaking his charge. It would have been in the thick of the fight, and a man who is about to ride to what he supposes will be his death would hardly stop, remove his helmet, and dismount from his horse (a lengthy operation when in full armour, especially in the remounting).   It was natural that a legend should connect his name with the well; compare Simon's Well at Evesham.   No, the well is merely evidence pointing to the fact that fighting took place close to it.   The evidence provided by the soil is sustained by Inherent Military Probability.   Any soldier viewing the ground from Dickon's Nook would wish to get forward to the western extremity of the ridge, partly to obtain the advantage of the slope, partly to deny the position to the enemy, and partly to get a view of the enemies' movements.   The less skilled Henry may well have been slow to apprehend the military factors or to take prompt advantage of them if he did comprehend them.   In this we shall probably be right in detecting the military genius of King Richard. Though he had not seen a deal of fighting himself, he had been brought up by his elder brother who was the first soldier of his age.

Corroboration of the fact that Richard's position was on the western crest of the hill is furnished by Polydore's statement that the sight of it 'to the beholders afar off gave a terror for the multitude'. In other words, Henry's troops could see the hostile position on the crest, whereas if it had been further back it would not have been visible 'afar off'.

IV.—RICHARD'S ENCAMPMENT ON THE EVE OF THE BATTLE

The records are particularly vague about this matter. We do not even know the route followed by Richard from Leicester. It would be natural to suppose that he camped near Sutton on the eve of the battle. Hutton, however, locates his camp south of Stapleton, i.e. two miles south of Sutton. He gives no specific reason for this except the fact that he had found traces of a camp there. This is flimsy evidence; it does not seem to have been usual to entrench a camp at the end of a day's march in those times; Richard's elder brother did not do so before Towton or Barnet, and in any case the provision of entrenching tools in that sparsely-inhabited locality would have been difficult, nor would there be much time in which his troops— wearied with the march—could do it. But Hutton managed to find entrenched camps for all four armies. Why should Stanley wish to take the precaution of entrenching when both sides, so far from having any idea of attacking him, were hoping for his support? It is almost as easy to find entrenchments where one expects them as it is to see canals in Mars, if one believes in them.

There is, however, one specific statement as to the locality of Richard's camp. Holinshed asserts that it was on 'Anne Beame' Hill. Ramsay, who follows Hutton, suggests that this may derive from Abraham's Stream, which he places south of Stapleton. But surely the obvious derivation of Anne Beame is Ambien? Now there used to be an old road from Leicester via Kirkby Mallory towards Sutton. Everything thus points to the probability that Sutton, on the Ambien Hill ridge, was approximately the scene of Richard's camp on the night before the battle. If this is accepted, the course of events depicted in my account seems to follow the line of Inherent Military Probability. It removes the difficulty experienced by modern writers who, having placed the rival camps at White Moors and

Stapleton, have to explain why the battle did not take place between the two, i.e. near Dadlington.

V.—THE BATTLE FORMATIONS

It will have been observed that instead of depicting the divisions of the two armies drawn up in line—van ward on the right, main ward in the centre, rear ward on the left, as was customary in those days, I show the Yorkists in three column of divisions, reminiscent of the French at Crécy, Poitiers, or Agincourt and probably of both sides at Towton, while for the rebels I give no precise formation. The explanation is that I hold the battle to have been a genuine encounter battle, one in which the leading division forms the frontage, and the rear formations reinforce the front division bit by bit. Thus the battle started with a head-on clash between Norfolk's and Oxford's divisions. This conception seems to be confirmed by the only contemporary account, that of the *Croyland Chronicle*, which names only those two divisions. We must picture the rear divisions closing up and reinforcing the front line in a rather confused and irregular way. We have seen the reason for Northumberland's division hanging back in rear; if Henry's rear ward extended the line of Oxford's division to the left it would have to pass behind the latter division in order to do so, and it is more likely that whatever the original intentions may have been, it got drawn into the fight in support of the van ward. There would be the less reason for extending to the left that Sir William Stanley was approaching towards that quarter; moreover, owing to Northumberland's holding back there would be no enemy in sight on that flank.

This conception of an encounter battle in which the three divisions of the royalist army were in column, not in line, is corroborated by Michael Drayton, who lived near the battlefield and who seems to have picked up some facts that are not recorded by the earlier chroniclers. He makes Norfolk's division take the lead, his line being of 'wondrous length' and wedge-shaped.[1] Richard's division follows in 'a perfect square', and in the course of the action 'the main two battles (divisions) mixed': i.e. Richard's division came up and reinforced Norfolk's division. (I may add that I formed this opinion *before* reading Drayton's poem.)

[1] If Norfolk's front line conformed to the line of the contour of the hill it might look wedge-shaped from the front.

VI.—RICHARD'S PERSONAL MOTIONS

The commonly accepted story is that the King spotted his rival from afar early in the battle, and that, taking with him a small party, he made a detour to the flank and engaged Henry in personal combat, after killing certain of his bodyguard. The old chroniclers revelled in such stories as this. No battle was quite complete without a personal encounter between the two leaders. But I fear I must reject this story *in toto*. The date was August 22nd, and we know that the sun was shining; therefore it may be presumed to have been a hot day. On such an occasion at the battle of Shrewsbury we have seen how a cloud of steam and dust obscured the combatants. We also are told that Henry hung back well to the rear. In such circumstances the chances of Richard being able to see, let alone recognize, his opponent would be but slight. Even if he suspected his position, he would have to make a wide detour if he was to get past the hostile battle line, and strike the enemy's rear, accompanied only by a handful of men. To leave his battle line to itself in such a case would be a most unprecedented act for the commander of the army. And who were the fortunate eye-witnesses who could describe with such a wealth of detail almost each stroke struck by the King in the hurly-burly of the battle? I regard it as a fairy story. It can be dismissed.

VII.—THE POSITION OF THE STANLEY ARMIES

Here conjecture is rife, no place being named in the early accounts. Hutton places Sir William near Nether Cotton, two miles to the north, without giving any reason except the existence of entrenchments; probably he bases his statement on local tradition. Ramsay and Gairdner both accept this location. As for Lord Stanley, his army cannot have been united with that of his brother—a proclaimed traitor. It is therefore natural to suppose that it was on the opposite or southern flank. Now Hall says it was 'indifferently between both armies', i.e. midway. This would put it somewhere between Dadlington and Stapleton, which is near enough for our purpose. Thus both Stanley armies would be visible from Richard's command-post at Dickon's Nook. I do not know why Ramsay places both the Stanley armies on the northern side.

VIII.—HAD HENRY ANY ARTILLERY?

It has been asserted that the rebel army had no guns. Certainly neither the *Croyland Chronicle*, Polydore nor Hall mention it, but there seems no reason to discredit the *Song of the Lady Bessy*, Drayton's *Polyolbion*, or the Stanley account, all of which mention guns.   There is nothing surprising in this.   The King of France presented Henry with some small guns, and he may have picked up more *en route* to the field.   Gairdner argues that the slowness of his march on the last three days may be due to being hampered by the acquisition of big guns, probably (he supposes) taken from Tamworth Castle.   This may be so, but it is equally likely that they were picked up at Lichfield, for it was at this point that the rate of march suddenly slowed down, and Lord Stanley's account states that on his arrival 'gonnes at Lyche-fyld craked'.   In any case, the discovery of cannon-balls is pretty conclusive evidence.   It is stated in *Parliamentary Rolls*, vol. VI, 276, that Richard's army was 'myghtily armed with all manner of armes, as gunnnes . . .'

IX.—RICHARD'S WELL

This so-called well is really a surface spring, the water from which was piped in Elizabethan times but has since broken surface in several places.   In about the year 1813 a stone pyramid about 10 feet high was erected over it by Dr. S. Parr, and a Latin inscription carved on the lintel stone of the entrance.   This inscription is now almost illegible. The wording of it is given in Brooke's *Visits to Battlefields*, p. 174.

CHAPTER XXV

The Battle of Stoke Field, 16 June 1487

THE battle of Bosworth is generally regarded as the end of the Wars of the Roses, but strictly speaking the battle of Stoke Field must claim that honour. For only two years after the crown had been placed on the head of Henry Tudor a formidable insurrection in the North threatened to remove it abruptly. The trouble originated in Ireland, where the Earl of Lincoln and Lord Lovel landed in 1487 and raised the standard of revolt.

The rebels assembled in Dublin, where the Earl of Lincoln collected 2,000 German mercenaries. Here they proclaimed the ten-year-old Lambert Simnel king, giving him out to be Edward, nephew of Edward IV. That boy was in fact then languishing in the Tower of London. The force then set sail and landed on the Lancashire coast on 4 June, 1487. Here they were joined by some English adherents. Including some wild Irishmen whom they had enlisted in Ireland, the total force may have been as much as 9,000 strong.

Marching across the Pennine Range the rebels made for York. Short of that city, however, they changed their plans and turned due south, probably via Tadcaster. Thence they passed over the battlefield of Towton, which must have evoked gruesome thoughts in the mind of Lincoln, for on that field had perished his grandfather, Richard Duke of York claimant to the throne. Pushing on south through Castleford and along the old Ryknild Street they would fork half-left at Rotherham making along the high ground to Southwell.[1]

Southwell is 5 miles west of Newark, which is generally assumed to have been their objective. But Newark was held for the King, and a direct assault on it would involve the passage of the broad Trent with Newark Castle glowering down on them from the far side. So we will leave them at Southwell wondering what to do, whilst their scouts scour the country far and wide attempting to gain information of the King's movements and intentions.

[1] Up to Rotherham their course was almost startlingly similar to that of the great allied army that was defeated by King Athelstan at the famous battle of Brunanburh in A.D. 937. One portion had sailed from Dublin, landing on the Lancashire coast where it was joined by a Scottish contingent; thence it crossed the Pennines towards York, but veered southwards via Tadcaster and Castleford, to meet its doom hard by Rotherham. For details see Chapter 7.

When news of the invasion reached the King he was at Kenilworth. Hastily collecting the near-by levies, he set out only five days after the landing of the rebels. Marching by a direct route he made Coventry his first stage (9 miles) where he picked up some more levies. On the 10th to Leicester (25 miles). On the 11th to Loughborough (16 miles). Up to this point he may have been in doubt as to which side of the Pennines the enemy was approaching, but here he was strategically well placed to meet them on either route. But at Loughborough, if not earlier, Henry must have received definite information that the enemy was taking the East Coast route, as we may call it, for it followed fairly closely the main line of the old L.N.E.R. The King therefore continued north towards Nottingham next day, but did not get very far and his army spent the night in 'the felde under a wood called Bonley Rice'. Next day, Wednesday, he did worse still, for the army seems to have lost its way, the quartermasters could not find accommodation and 'the Kinge and his hooste (army) wandred her and ther a greate espace of tyme',[1] eventually quartering in a village 3 miles short of Nottingham, probably Ruddington. Next day, Thursday, they reached Nottingham, and picked up a welcome reinforcement in the shape of the Earl of Derby's contingent, 6,000 strong, under his son, Lord Strange. Some spies were captured here and hanged on an ash tree at the south end of the old Trent bridge.

Thus on the evening of Thursday, 14 June, the rival armies, at Southwell and Nottingham, were just a dozen miles apart.

There are two sharply divergent schools of thought regarding the events of the next day and the setting of the battlefield. *School A* maintains that Henry VII fought with his back to Newark, facing southwest. *School B* maintains that he faced Newark and that the rebels had their backs to it. Historical thought has veered backwards and forwards between these two schools during the last 120 years. The leading protagonist for School A was Richard Brooke, who was one of the very few persons to make a careful study of the battle on the ground. He went over it with Sir Robert Bromley, the owner of Stoke Hall in 1825, and wrote his account in the following year.[2]

An answer came from School B in 1828 from R. P. Shilton in *The Battle of Stoke-field*. In 1865 Dr. Trollope reiterated the case of School A, and in 1904 Cornelius Brown supported this view.[3] Finally,

---

[1] *The Herald's Account* (see bibl. note).
[2] Repeating it in 1857 in his *Visits to Fields of Battle in England*.
[3] The Victoria County History appears to throw no light on the matter.

after a lapse of half a century (during which time scarcely anything of note was written about any of our battlefields), Mr. A. C. Wood in 1947 in the *History of Nottingham* sided with School B, though without stating his reasons. Which school is in the right?

Before examining the arguments of these two schools we must have a look at the theatre of operations.

The river Trent flowing between Newark and Nottingham is about 150 yards wide and in the summer was fordable at Fiskerton, 4 miles south of the former town. It flows through a wide flat valley, occasionally bordered by low escarpments. One such escarpment begins west of Stoke and runs south-west, about 150 feet above the valley. A cross spur juts out from it to the east, half a mile south of Stoke, and descending gently merges into the valley 1½ miles away. The slope down to Stoke is about one in ten, and to the south still gentler. The ground was open and unenclosed, but it is now enclosed and there is a new copse or hanger along part of the escarpment. The valley was marshy, and the straight road to the Fiskerton ferry did not exist. On the other hand there were two windmills which, though marked on the six-inch map, have now disappeared. One was known as the Rampire, on the ridge-top just west of the Fosseway (the straight road running south-west through Stoke.) This mill used to be pointed to as the camp of the Earl of Lincoln.

JUNE 15TH

We come now to the events of Friday, 15 June. School A maintains that the King, hearing of the approach of the rebels towards Newark, marched rapidly to that town in order to forestall them, which he succeeded in doing. Lincoln therefore was reduced to fording the Trent at Fiskerton, and encamping on the escarpment just south of Stoke. Next morning, Saturday the 16th, the royal army, turning in its tracks, marched straight against Lincoln's position. On reaching Stoke they found the rebels drawn up in position on the ridge awaiting attack. (This position is marked AA on the sketch-map.) Finding that he had only to do with the 'Fore ward' (or leading division) of the royal army, Lincoln gave the signal to attack, his whole line charged down the hill and the battle consequently took place on the low ground just south of the village.

According to School B, the King did not march to Newark on the Friday but only to Radcliffe, 6 miles east of Nottingham, on the south bank of the river. Meanwhile the rebels had crossed the river by the ford and encamped in much the same ground as that indicated by the rival school. On Saturday morning the King resumed his march on Newark, and by 9 a.m. Oxford's fore ward encountered the rebel army drawn up on the ridge facing him, i.e. with their backs, not faces, towards Newark and Stoke. The rebels then advanced to the attack, so the main battle—or at least the opening phase—took place just to the south of the ridge instead of to the north of it. The rebels were eventually driven back over the ridge and fled towards the river, whence they had come.

If we examine the sources closely we shall understand the reason for this startling variance in interpretation. School A is supported by all the Tudor chroniclers and historians: Polydore Vergil, Grafton, Hall, Hollinshed, Stow; School B can only claim one source, that of the anonymous Herald who accompanied the royal army. At first sight the weight of evidence seems overwhelmingly in favour of School A. Yet examining the accounts of the above five chroniclers we are at once struck by the similarity of language, which seems to imply a common source. There is neither space nor need to substantiate or exemplify this assertion: it is common knowledge to historians. It comes to this, that Polydore Vergil wrote the original account; this was copied by Grafton; Hall in his turn copied Grafton or Vergil (it matters not which), and Hollinshed and Stow copied Hall with sundry embellishments. Thus we have in effect one source on each side, Vergil as opposed to the Herald. Of these there can be no doubt as to which is the most reliable. The Herald wrote circumstantially, as an eye-witness; his account rings true throughout and we can, and must, accept it absolutely. Not so Vergil, who was a foreigner, who came to the English court nearly half a century after the battle and was quite ignorant of the geography of the country over which the operations took place. Bearing this in mind, let us look at his crucial passage, on which the whole case for School A is based. It has never been translated into English, for some singular reason, but the substance of it is as follows:

Lincoln marched towards Newark, intending to draw on supplies there prior to seeking out the royal army and attacking it. But the King, being well informed of the enemy's motions, forestalled him, and reached Newark on Friday night, whence after a little delay he pushed forward (*progressus est*) 3 miles and there encamped for the night. Meanwhile Lincoln continued his march and reached the near vicinity of the hostile camp 'which is called Stoke' and there he camped for the night. Thus Vergil.

Now it is perfectly clear that if we read this passage without a map in front of us the picture it conjures up, and which Vergil meant to conjure up, is that the King marched through and beyond Newark for a further 3 miles to a village called Stoke that must therefore have been north of Newark; that Lincoln advanced straight on the same village from the opposite direction and that a head-on collision occurred there next day.

Now let us look at the map and we see what absurdity has been enunciated. For, to reach Newark the King must have passed through Stoke, along the Fosseway. Therefore he must have turned straight back in his tracks in order to arrive at Stoke once more. But Vergil clearly did not realize that this would be the effect of his words, nor I imagine did Grafton, Hall, and the rest. Only Stow who did know a little of the geography of his own land, declined to copy Vergil in this statement about advancing through and beyond Newark.[1]

Now let us set against Vergil the sober and circumstantial account of the Herald. I have already given his credentials. The early account of the motions of the royal army I took direct from that account, including the quotations. We left the Herald's story on the Thursday night when the King was in Nottingham. That night he held a council of war at which it was resolved to direct his march on Newark next day. But there seems to have been no sense of urgency. Before setting out the King heard mass in a Nottingham church, and I suspect there was a certain amount of indiscipline and over-sleeping on the part of the troops who had spent the previous two nights in the open. Any way, only about 7 miles was covered that day, and quarters were obtained at Radcliffe, to the east of the town and on the south bank of the river Trent. From here next morning, Saturday, the march was resumed, in battle formation, that is to say in the three divisions of the day—fore ward, main ward, and rear ward—with considerable intervals between them. They seem to have made better progress than on the previous day and before 9 a.m. they came in sight of the ridge and saw the rebel army drawn up on top of it awaiting them.

---

[1] It is easy to surmise how Vergil may have made his mistake. Someone said to him: 'The King marched towards Newark in order to prevent the rebels getting possession of that town, and at Stoke, three miles from Newark, he camped for the night.' Vergil thought his informer said 'beyond Newark' not 'from Newark' and therefore naturally concluded that Stoke must lie beyond the town. This apparently trifling error, having once been committed to paper, flourished and was repeated *ad nauseam* by succeeding historians; for thus was history written in those days—and sometimes still is.

Which account are we to believe? Which witness, the eye-witness or the foreign courtier writing in London, picking up odds and ends about the battle wherever he could find them, unpossessed of a map and completely ignorant of the terrain?[1] Surely there can be only one answer—the Herald's story is the correct one.

There are other difficulties, or rather improbabilities attached to the School A version. Assuming that Lincoln on reaching Stoke heard that the enemy was in Newark what would be the obvious position to occupy? Surely not the ridge to the south of the village, whence, if defeated, retreat across the ford would be almost impossible? An alert enemy would only have to send a detachment across Stoke Hall park to the ford before the battle began and all retreat that way would be cut off. No, the obvious position to hold would be immediately to the north of the village, his left flank anchored on the river and his right stretching away towards the river Devon, 2 miles to the east. Thus his position would be a strong one and his line of retreat would be secured.

A further objection is that according to tradition the rebels in the course of their flight rushed down to the valley through a deep gully in the escarpment, where great slaughter took place and where skeletons have since been found. This gully is still known as Red Gutter. Now a glance at the sketch-map shows that by the School A version the Red Gutter was in prolongation of the rebel left flank. How then could they retreat through the gully to the river ford at Fiskerton? Fugitives from a battlefield retreat to their rear, not square to a flank. But by the School B version the gully would be in rear of the rebel position and in a direct line to the river ford.

Still more difficult would it be to account for the flight along Burham Furlong, which is south of Red Gutter (a 200 yards flat stretch on the ridge-top), but it *would* be in the line of retreat under School A solution.

There is one point that at first sight tells in favour of School A. Relics have been dug up, including skeletons just south of the church and of the village, and near the vicarage. This certainly points to fighting or slaughter taking place on the outskirts of the village, but it does not follow that the main fighting was there. Slaughter usually is greater in the pursuit than in the battle unless the battle is prolonged—which Stoke was not. The presence of skeletons in Red Gutter is an illustration of this; and the village slaughter may have been of the same

[1] Vergil's omission of any reference to the great river Trent is an indication of his ignorance of the geography.

nature. One would expect to find some battle relics south of the ridge if the battle started there. On the other hand excavations near a village are more likely to yield results than in the open fields, where there are no habitations. Besides, which relics *were* dug up in times past and no records made of them.[1] So far as I know there is only one authority for the village relics, Sir Richard Bromly, the owner of Stoke Hall, who so informed Richard Brooke in 1825.

A further difficulty about accepting School A version is that if the royal army had passed along the Fosseway through Stoke a few hours before the arrival of the rebel army, stragglers and baggage, sutlers and camp-followers (of whom there were many), would have been cut off and captured.[2] But of this there is not even a hint in any of the records.

The conclusion that the above considerations lead me to is that the battle took place in the open country to the south of Stoke, the rebels fighting with their backs to that village.

THE BATTLE

As regards the actual battle there are fewer authentic details than about any other battle of like importance fought since Hastings. The Herald, who had spread himself in the early part of the march, describing how the stocks were filled with 'harlatts and vagabounds', and like details, contents himself with a single sentence in describing the battle: 'And so in good order and array, before nine of the clok, beside a village called Stoak, a large myle out of Newarke, his forwarde rencountrede his enemyes and rebells, wher, by the help of Almightty God, he hadde the victorye.' He then proceeds to specify some of the casualties.

Certain broad facts seem, however, to emerge. It is clear that Lincoln was bent on a fight. He had been disappointed at the way the country folk held aloof (as they did 260 years later in the case of Bonnie Prince Charlie); time was not on his side, he must strike soon and boldly, and for this he had the comforting examples of Barnet and Bosworth where resolute initiative had won a kingdom. With this in mind, he formed up his army for battle on that Saturday morning, intending to fight it out, whatever the odds.

[1] They are vaguely described as being found in the fields south of the village, but how far south we are not told. The only evidence is a tradition that Lincoln was buried near a spring called Willow Rundle, which is between Elston and the Fosseway and *south* of the ridge.

[2] Including probably the Herald himself.

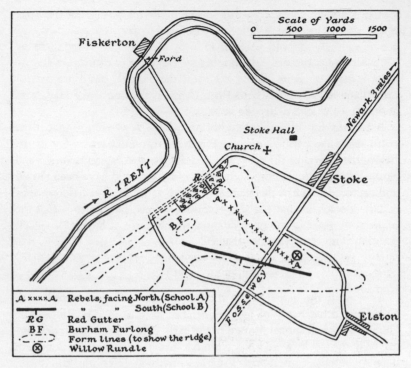

SKETCH-MAP 31.　　STOKE FIELD: THE BATTLE

If the reader agrees with my premises (or deductions) so far, and will take the trouble to ascend the ridge from the direction of the ferry in the footsteps of the Earl of Lincoln, he will feel no doubts about the line the rebel leader decided to occupy. He must have assumed, if he did not know, that the King would approach along the old Fosseway. Now the first thing he would note would be that, instead of involving a head-on encounter, i.e. at an angle of 180 degrees, the line of the royalist advance and of his own made an angle of only 110 degrees. Thus his line could not be drawn perpendicular to the hostile advance and at the same time perpendicular to his own line of retreat. A prudent general would endeavour to 'halve the difference' if the ground rendered such a course feasible.

This the ground did: it might have been made for the purpose. By resting his right flank on the highest part of the ridge, the Burham Furlong, with the river at the foot of a steep slope, it would scarcely be possible for that flank to be turned. Thence the line would follow the crest, keeping just on the forward slope[1] in an easterly direction, bending inwards very slightly in the centre in order to do so, and the left flank would rest on or about the Stoke–Elston road, near the site of the old Elston windmill. Such a line would be nearly 1,800 yards long, but this rather wide front would be necessary if the right flank—his strategic or vulnerable flank—was to be unturnable and if the line were to embrace the Fosseway. On that line I place the rebel army.

Now the effect of this line being askew to the line of advance of the royalists along the Fosseway would be that the latter's left wing would come into contact before their right. They would halt as soon as they came within sight of the ridge and endeavour to adjust their line by swinging their right shoulders forward; not an easy manoeuvre for a large force, especially when in close contact with the enemy. No doubt a certain amount of confusion occurred and was duly noted by Lincoln. He would be tempted to take advantage of this momentary confusion and would change his plan and immediately assume the offensive. I believe he had a further inducement to take this course, namely that the royalist fore ward, led by the Earl of Oxford, was dangerously isolated. To justify this belief we must return to the royalist army.

It will have been noted that the Herald's account states that Oxford, with the fore ward 'had the victory'. Why only the fore ward? If the fore ward won single-handed a battle that lasted three hours, it must have been very far in advance of the main ward. The next evidence comes from a poem celebrating the battle which was nearly, if not quite contemporary. This poem states that at first the rebels thought they were winning—a likely enough belief if they only had the fore ward to deal with. The next evidence is shared by all the chroniclers, namely that the royalist army advanced in three divisions. Finally Stow states that the fore ward was eventually strongly reinforced from the remainder of the army. The natural inference from all this is that the three divisions advanced with considerable intervals between them, and Oxford was able to attack and almost to overwhelm the fore ward before the main body came up. (One is reminded of the King of France's three widely separated divisions at the battle of Poitiers.)

We can take it then that Lincoln deftly turned to account the confusion and isolation of Oxford's division, and launched his army to the attack. Things went hard with Oxford's division, which was so badly shaken that many fled from the battlefield spreading reports that all was

[1] A contemporary poem states that the rebels drew up on the brow of a hill.

lost. However, reinforcements from the King's ward arrived in the nick of time, and the situation was saved.

Gradually, as more and more royalist troops joined in the fighting, the rebels were first arrested, then driven back over the ridge. The 'beggarly, naked and almost unarmed Irishmen' as Hollinshed contemptuously calls them, were the first to break. They had fought bravely enough, but they lacked the 'harness' of their German comrades-in-arms. It is easy to picture them careering down the steep slope through Red Gutter towards the river and safety. Probably a gun, if they had any, or a wagon got stuck in the Gutter, and enabled the pursuers to catch up and execute the traditional slaughter at that spot. The remainder made for the river as best they could, but many were cut off and perished in the water. Lord Lovell, one of the leaders, swam across and reached his home on the Windrush, only to perish by the horrible death of starvation in one of his own cellars at Minster Lovell.

The Earl of Lincoln was killed, Schwartz and his Germans died fighting, and Lambert Simnel was captured, to become famous as a scullion in the Royal household. It was reported that 4,000 were slain of the rebels and 3,000 of the royalists. If we accept these figures, and I see no reason to doubt them, it should give some rough indication as to the numbers engaged. The 3,000 royalists slain must have come almost exclusively from Oxford's division; thus we can hardly put his whole strength at much less than 6,000. Clearly it was badly outnumbered, so it is reasonable to compute the rebels at between 8,000 and 10,000. As to the proportions of English, German, and Irish in their ranks it is quite impossible to make even a guess.

Henry VII advanced to Lincoln where he hanged many of the rebels, and then returned in triumph to London. His throne was now secure.

The battle of Stoke Field gave us the Tudor dynasty.

*   *   *   *   *

It only remains to consider the question, why was Oxford's division so dangerously isolated? Why was there so big an interval between it and the second division? Partly the reason may have been that each division approached the field deployed for battle. I think we may deduce this from the Herald's words 'in good order and array'. Earlier on the line of march the troops were probably badly strung out and stragglers were many, for the Herald complains of the bad discipline. But on the Saturday morning they were formed in the order in which they would have to fight, each man in his right place, from which straggling would be difficult. To marshal such a bad and untrained army into such array would take time, and as Oxford is reported as having the pick of the men he probably got his division into battle order much quicker than the remainder of the army, and thus out-stripped them.

This might account in part for the dispersion, but I fancy there was another reason. Henry Tudor was not a good soldier and he had no pretensions to be one. Previous to Bosworth he had no experience of battle, and at Bosworth he kept himself prudently in the background, unlike his opponent Richard III. What was the result? The gallant soldier who fought in the front line lost his head and the cautious civilian gained his crown. Henry would be tempted to repeat the operation. Let Oxford and Simnel expose themselves in battle, but what use was there for him to imperil his person to a chance arrow? At that time he had no son and heir to carry on his line. The rebels since the arrival of Derby's reinforcements were heavily outnumbered, and by giving Oxford a strong force of picked men, the King might well hope that the work would be done before the arrival on the field of the main body. Therefore he held back his own division contenting himself with sending up strong reinforcements to Oxford's division. This would account for the silence of the Herald, who would be near his master, as to the details of the actual fighting. Be this as it may, the King of England seems to have played only a minor part in winning the victory of Stoke Field.

CHAPTER XXVI

The Battle of Flodden, September 9th, 1513

THE 'Fatal Field of Flodden' is famed in story—and in fable. The two earliest ballads in its honour are written in the alliterative style of the Middle Ages and I find myself unconsciously conforming to that style. For Flodden was essentially a medieval battle. It—not Bosworth—marks the end of medieval warfare in England. When it came to hand-to-hand fighting between foot soldiers it differed little from the corresponding stage of the battle of Hastings, fought nearly half a millennium before. There was the same mêlée of sword *v.* spear, of soldiers in harness jabbing at one another, of knights in armour, of standards and banners, of battle cries and trumpet calls, of prelates and pages, and of personal duels between the leaders on each side. Such had been the features of Bosworth, and although there had since been a slight development in arms and tactical formations, the two battles were decided by similar factors. The bark of the big bombards was worse than their bite; the new formation of separate columns cancelled out for it was adopted by both sides. Even the upshot was curiously similar; in each battle we see an impetuous king rushing down a hill to his death in the front line, and the dispersal of his army consequent on that event.

All this, of course, is well known; probably no battle fought in our land has had so much written about it—with the single exception of Hastings. A fresh account might therefore appear superfluous; and so it perhaps would have been had not two books written in recent years advanced a completely new theory as to the conditions of the battle. They will be dealt with in due course: here I will only observe the curious fact that whereas, as is natural, the majority of accounts of Bannockburn have been written by Scotsmen, the same also applies to Flodden. Englishmen through the ages seem to have paid little regard for, and have taken little trouble in writing up their battles, whether victories or defeats. Nor is it clear why these two battles are invariably associated, for Flodden from a purely military aspect was not such a great English victory as several others, for example, the Battle of the Standard, Neville's Cross, Homildon Hill,

Hallidon Hill or Pinkie. No organized pursuit was attempted after the battle, and on the morning after the fight a portion of the Scottish army was still on the verge of the battlefield. But because a Scottish king and his nobles elected to fight and die in the front rank, and because a famous Scottish poet has celebrated it in verse, it has become the second most famous battle fought in England.

When, in 1513, the young King Henry VIII took a great army to France it was only natural that Louis XII of France should call on his ally, James IV of Scotland to create a diversion in England. This colourful and chivalrous monarch responded to the appeal, ignoring the fate of previous attempts to stir up trouble in the Southern Kingdom in the absence of its sovereign. Doubtless he did not expect much opposition as he is supposed to have declared that, in the absence of the English army in France, 'only millers and mass priests' were left. On August 22nd he crossed the frontier at Coldstream with a vast army, collected from all over Scotland and even from the Western Isles. It included a powerful ordnance, which his Master Gunner, Robert Borthwick, had collected mainly from Flanders. The French king had also sent over the Swiss pike, 15 feet long, to replace the old spear and bill, and 40 French captains to instruct the raw Scottish levies in the continental method of war. The army was reputed 100,000 strong—a suspiciously round number. Half that figure would be nearer the mark. Even so, it was an immense army for that day. In the opinion of Dr. Mackenzie: 'No Scottish army had ever taken the field so well equipped with every appurtenance of war.'[1] It was, however, alarmingly heterogeneous, consisting of what had once been four different races—Borderers, Lowlanders, Highlanders and Islanders. It also included 5,000 French troops, commanded by Count d'Aussi. Its power of cohesion remained to be proved.

In the course of the next fortnight the army had some rapid and easy success. The famous Norham Castle fell to artillery bombardment by, it is said, the great Mons Meg from Edinburgh Castle, followed by a night attack in a great storm. Etal, Chillingham and Ford Castles also surrendered. Taking up his quarters in the last named, and camping his army on the banks of the river Till nearby, James sat down and quietly awaited the inevitable English reaction.

He had not long to wait. Before leaving the country Henry VIII,

[1] *The Secret of Flodden.*

foreseeing the possibility of his brother-in-law stirring up trouble in his absence, had appointed the Earl of Surrey (who had fought with his father the Duke of Norfolk on Bosworth Field) in charge of the defence of the north. On August 11th, James had formally declared war, but Surrey was already on his way from London with the nucleus of his army, making for the North. From Pontefract he sent out orders for what amounted to a *levée en masse* of the whole country. He then continued northwards, collecting the local levies *en route*.

On September 1st, the Earl was at Newcastle, which he had selected as the general rendezvous for the various contingents. These contingents came naturally from the north of England. Meanwhile, Queen Katherine with great vigour was marshalling what might be called a reserve army 40,000 strong in the South, and Lord Lovell had another army of 15,000 at Nottingham.

Continuing his march with ever-growing numbers, Surrey reached Alnwick on September 3rd. Here he was joined by his eldest son, Admiral Thomas Howard, who on hearing of the invasion had left the fleet and landed at Newcastle, bringing him 1,200 marines from the fleet. The 70-year-old Earl of Surrey was only too glad to appoint his son second-in-command, and virtually Chief of Staff, in modern parlance. Sailors and soldiers were almost indistinguishable in those days. At Alnwick he was now within 25 miles of the invading army, and his own army was practically complete. It was about 26,000 strong, well found in archers, but weaker than its opponents in artillery. Nor was it so well furnished with supplies and food. Apparently it had to live mainly on the country, and owing to a 'scorched earth' policy having been employed food was hard to come by. Almost worse, the beer (which Wolsey had been so careful to supply in abundance for the expeditionary force in France) ran out, and considerable discontent was thereby caused, which the rainy weather that now set in did nothing to alleviate.

However, morale was high, the old spirit of The Standard and of Neville's Cross was in evidence; indeed, the banner of St. Cuthbert was carried forward with the army from Durham cathedral. The Prince-bishop was not himself present at the battle, but he subsequently provided one of the best accounts of it.

At Alnwick, Surrey organized his many contingents into a single army, and issued precise instructions so that 'every man knew what to do'.

It was thus in good order and with a good heart that the English troops, nearly all of whom were mounted, marched forward to drive the presumptuous foe from their native land. From Bolton on the 5th, Surrey sent Rouge Croix, his herald, with a challenge, quite in the medieval style and spirit, offering to fight his opponent not later than the next Friday, September 9th. In the course of the next few days a series of messages passed backwards and forwards between the two armies. The messages are entertaining in their own way, but have no direct bearing on the ensuing battle, except in one respect which must therefore be alluded to. The upshot of it was that the English Earl pledged himself in very definite terms to fight a battle by the specified date. Now it takes two to make a battle, and it is clear—to me at any rate—that the King felt himself equally pledged to fight if his opponent presented himself. The relevance of this point will become evident in due course.

In the course of negotiations the English army pushed forward to Wooler, only six miles from the enemy. The latter shifted their camp slightly to the west, occupying an almost impregnable position on Flodden Edge (see Sketch-map 32). This position, I estimate, ran from point 50 on the east, through Flodden Edge to point 591 on the west.[1] Its extent was thus slightly over 2,000 yards. On its right flank the valley of the little brook was marshy; on its left flank the ground sloped down steeply for 300 feet, but in the centre there was a slight dip over which the road ascended obliquely. This seemed the only vulnerable point in the whole front, and James took the rather remarkable step of occupying the foot of it with guns, carefully entrenched. These must have been confined to light ordnance, the heavy culverins being retained on the top of the hill. The position was obviously skilfully selected, and probably we can detect here the influence of the French captains.

The top of Flodden Edge is almost, but not quite, visible from Wooler, and Surrey's scouts were able to corroborate Rouge Croix's reports as to its strength.[2] The Earl of Surrey was in a quandary; he had rashly pledged himself to fight by a fixed date, presumably on the assumption that his quixotic challenge would be accepted in the spirit of chivalry, and that the King would come to meet him on an 'indifferent' ground, i.e. fair to both parties. Such a ground existed—

[1] The 'three greate mountains' in *A Trewe Encountre* account.

[2] Advancing close to the position they had caused the defenders to unmask their guns.

'a fair cornefield' midway between the two camps. Surrey suggested this, adding the extraordinary proviso that the battle should take place 'between 12 o'clock and 3 o'clock', as if he was fixing a football match.[1] He received a chilling reply; the King of Scotland would fight where and when he thought fit. This was a most unmedieval attitude to adopt, and Oman is probably right in ascribing it to the influence of the French captains. Or it may have been due to La Motte, the ambassador, who was present in the camp.

Surrey called a council of war to consider the awkward situation that had suddenly arisen. (It is to be noted that neither commander came to any important decision without consulting his council.) As a result a remarkable step was taken. The whole army marched at dawn on September 8th, not towards the enemy but almost due north for eight miles in pouring rain and 'in cloggy mire and foule filthy waies', halting under the shelter of Barmoor Wood. This wood is five miles east of Flodden Edge, and the first part of the march must have been in view of the Scottish position. We are not told explicitly what at this stage was Surrey's intention, but the fact that the Admiral then carried out a reconnaissance of the Scottish position from the high ground east of the Till (probably from point 25 just north of Ford Castle), makes it highly likely that Surrey intended to attack the camp from that direction if it were feasible. As a result of his reconnaissance the Admiral evidently reported against such an attack; instead he suggested that the flanking movement should be turned into an enveloping one, and that the hostile position should be attacked from the rear, that is from the north. There is something almost breath-taking about this proposition. Consider it closely. An invading army of vast dimensions is drawn up on your flank, facing south. You have already moved out of the path of its direct advance into England. If it does advance your own retreat will be cut off. Yet you propose to increase this danger by moving your whole army right round to the enemy's rear and attack him from that direction. You will then have, a short distance in your own rear, a wide river in spate, leading into a hostile country. What abject disaster will overtake your army if your attack is driven back! One almost shudders to think of the risk that old Surrey was deliberately taking when he and his council came to this decision.

Still the die was cast, and at 5 a.m. next day, September 9th, 1513,

---

[1] There are two Manuscript copies of this remarkable epistle in the British Museum. Doubtless James destroyed the original in anger.

the vanguard moved off, in a north-westerly direction towards Twizel
Bridge. It should here be explained that Surrey had adopted a novel
formation. He divided the army into two divisions, the van commanded by the Admiral, and the rear under his own command. Each
division had two wings, about half the size of the main bodies. Thus

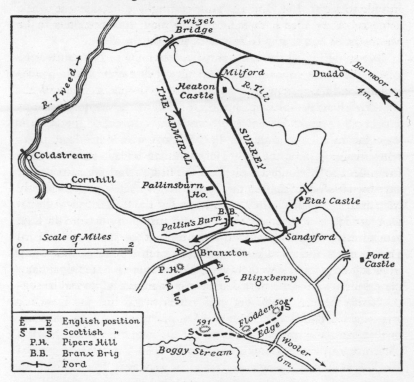

SKETCH-MAP 32. FLODDEN: THE PRELIMINARY MOVES

there were in all six separate bodies or brigades as I shall call them, the
right brigade of each division leading its division.

There is direct conflict of evidence as to whether the army marched
on foot or mounted.[1] They certainly had not their horses with them
at the end of the battle, so if they set off mounted they must have left
their horses either at the crossing of the river or later, when they came
to the bog; probably the latter.

[1] Hall says on horseback, Brian Tuke and Bishop Ruthal say on foot.
Ruthal calls it 8 miles. I make it at least 15. Probably he means 'little miles',
or leagues, which would make it 16 miles.

The route was presumably via Duddo, and the vanguard reached Twizel Bridge about 11 a.m., where they crossed. The rearguard crossed at Milford, a ford about a mile up-stream, near Heaton Castle. At the river there must have been a halt to water horses and men and to allow of stragglers catching up. There was, alas, no food for the troops, who fasted all day. Having reached the far side, the whole army was marshalled in its fighting formation, and then the advance was resumed in a southerly direction, straight for the foe.

What, during all this time, was the foe doing? No trustworthy report has come down to us. The answer is therefore purely conjectural, and full reasons for it are deferred to the end section. When the English army was seen on the morning of the 8th to be marching north it might have two objects—either to attack the Scots in their left flank or to make for Berwick and invade Scotland. This left James with three courses. He could take advantage of the flank movement to continue his own advance into England, hoping that thereby he would frighten the English into abandoning their bold intention, or he could wheel round to his left and face east, or finally he could fall back into Scotland. It was apparently decided to stand fast until the English intention made itself more apparent. No big changes were therefore made in the dispositions, but patrols would naturally be placed along the river Till, and there is a tradition, likely enough, that some guns were also moved down the hill to the left.

Next morning, September 9th, visibility was bad and there was much rain. The probability is that the morning was spent in trying to discover the direction of march and the intentions of the English. When at length it was established that the enemy was indeed crossing the Till at Twizel Bridge[1] a council of war was held. There are indications that this council was protracted, and that opinion was sharply divided. There was a party in favour of retreating into Scotland, but the King would not hear of it; he considered himself in honour bound to accept battle if the enemy offered it that day; and there was now every indication that the enemy did intend to offer it.

But his chivalry did not extend to descending into the plain and fighting an old-fashioned battle on 'indifferent ground'. He must already have been aware that Branxton Hill offered well-nigh as strong a position facing north as Flodden Edge did facing south. The distance between the two positions was only one mile. By a very simple manœuvre it could be speedily occupied. The two ridges are within

[1] It is invisible from Flodden Edge and the news would come from patrols.

sight of one another, with a slight dip between the two. All that was necessary was for the camp marshals to point out the northern ridge and to instruct each brigade to turn about and march straight to that portion that was opposite its own place in the line. Thus the order of battle would be reversed, the right flank becoming the new left and vice versa. James decided to occupy the new position and invite attack. Orders were issued accordingly. The tents were struck

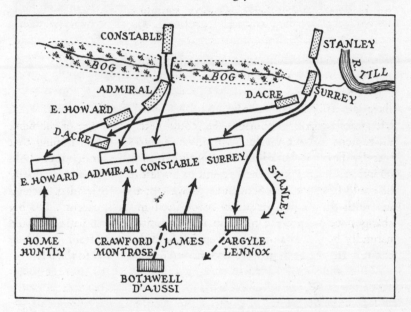

SKETCH-MAP 33. FLODDEN: THE APPROACHES

and moved behind the new position while fatigue parties set fire to the damp and foul straw that had been used as bedding in the old camp. A south wind was blowing, and thick volumes of damp straw smoke accompanied the army as it advanced, thus making still worse the already poor visibility.

It must have been about one o'clock in the afternoon when the leading troops of the various brigades ascended out of the slight dip on to the Branxton Hill ridge. They were marching in five columns, four abreast and a fifth in reserve. As the heads of the four columns reached the ridge-top they must have seen dimly in the low ground to their front several columns of hostile troops winding their way slowly in their direction. The English were evidently at last going to attack;

Surrey intended, after all, to keep his word! James no doubt felt delighted at this sign of his own good military judgement. All was going according to plan.

THE TERRAIN

(See Sketch-maps 32 and 33)

The massif which composes Flodden Edge and Branxton Hill rises 300 feet above the surrounding ground. The slope on its northern face is, at its steepest, about one in five, or 12 degrees. At its immediate foot a tiny water-course trickles from Branxton Stead Farm towards the Till. This forms a miniature valley, the ridge to the north rising some 20 feet.[1] The highest point on this ridge is Pipers Hill, the hillock on which the battle monument now stands. Continuing to the north, the ground slopes another 60 feet down into the boggy valley of the Pallin's Burn. This valley was a vast bog, about a mile in length, with only two crossing places for horses or vehicles—one at what was known as Branx Brig and the other near the mouth of the burn at Sandyford.[2] The ground was unenclosed and only partially cultivated.

THE DISPOSITIONS

On resuming their march from Twizel Bridge, the English army may at first have advanced in deployed formation, i.e. one division behind the other, each division with its wings spread out to right and left. But on the whole it is more probable that they advanced in column, as before, though not necessarily in a single line. But it matters not; for after proceeding three miles, led by a local guide,[3] they came upon the above-mentioned bog. This cannot have surprised them for the Admiral must have seen it on his previous day's reconnaissance, and that very fact may account for the presence of the guide; he would undertake to lead them across the treacherous Pallin's Burn. The Admiral's division was therefore directed upon Branx Brig, while Surrey's division, following in rear, made for

[1] This subsidiary ridge has been curiously ignored by chroniclers and historians alike.

[2] Historians state that this bog has disappeared. This may once have been true, but it is so no longer. For several hundred yards I would not care to attempt it on horseback in the winter months.

[3] Mentioned only in the *Ballad of Flodden Field* (ll. 1560–70).

Sandyford near the junction of the Pallin's Burn with the Till. The Admiral was plainly aware that the enemy had not so far moved off the Flodden massif, but thick clouds of smoke betokened a movement of some sort. He therefore hurried his division forward as speedily as possible. Visibility was bad as he dropped down into the Pallin's Burn valley, and the ridge in front then disappeared momentarily from view. The little Branx Brig was not wide or strong enough for the guns, so they were perforce ordered to go round by Sandyford with the rear division. The infantry crossed the bog, some by the Brig, and some by wading through the water, which after several days of rain was up to flood level. Emerging on the far side and climbing up the slope to the top of the ridge, the leading troops descried on the top of Branxton Hill four great columns of enemy troops who seemed to be (as they were) in the very act of occupying the position. Each column was in massed formation, nearly square in shape, with about 200 yards separating the various columns. The total frontage was about 1,500 yards. Heavy guns were also being brought into action along the hill-top, and even as the troops were crossing the bog a few random rounds, fired at extreme elevation, fell harmlessly in the bog.[1]

The Admiral hastened forward to the ridge-top, whence he calculated that he had the whole Scots army in his front. At any moment they might charge down the hill and strike his disordered column. The situation was alarming. The rearguard was out of sight, temporarily separated from his division by the bog. It also would be strung out in column as it passed through the defile presented by the brook crossing at Sandyford. I reckon that the Admiral must at that moment have been quite close to Branxton church, which was in existence at that time (though not as we know it now). It is quite possible that he ascended the church tower to get a better view. If the head of Surrey's division had at that moment reached Sandyford it would be more than $1\frac{1}{2}$ miles away whereas the enemy were less than half that distance. No wonder the Admiral in this his first battle on dry land, exhibited some signs of excitement, if not agitation. Plucking from off his breast his ornament of the Agnus Dei, he handed it to a messenger and sent him off post-haste to implore his father, the Earl, to hasten to his support. Meanwhile he wisely halted his own division before it had ascended out of the valley.

[1] One of these on the western end of the bog was dug up in the nineteenth century. Its range must have been quite 1,400 yards.

Surrey responded with alacrity, as may well be imagined, to the disturbing appeal from his son. The latter, in his message, had made the very sensible suggestion that the rear ward should join up in line with the van ward, extending the line to the left. By this means it would 'cover off' the Scottish position. The Earl agreed to this suggestion and led his division forward at top speed, though it must have become dangerously strung out in the Sandyford defile.

By this time it had become apparent to Surrey that the Scottish formation was in four columns, whereas the English army, if the two divisions formed up in line, would be in six columns. This might be awkward, even dangerous, if the Scots suddenly took the offensive and charged down the hill. Surrey and his son, doubtless in hurried consultation near Branxton village, therefore decided to conform to the fourfold formation of the Scots. This was done by a very simple procedure. The order of the march was as shown in Map 34. Edmund Howard, the young brother of the Admiral, led with the right wing, while old Sir Marmaduke Constable followed the Admiral with his left wing. Lord Dacre led the right wing of Surrey's division and Sir Edward Stanley brought up the rear. All that was necessary was to merge Constable's brigade in the Admiral's main body[1] while Dacre's brigade was placed behind the line as a mobile reserve (for Dacre still had a large proportion of his men mounted). Thus was the line formed, and the guns, coming up later, were placed in the intervals between the columns.

All this marshalling took time—possibly as much as two hours, say from 2 p.m. to 4 p.m. And all this time the Scottish army stood motionless at the top of the hill. What a temptation, what an opportunity that was for a quick attack on the scattered and un-organized English army! But it was not to be. The minutes passed, and it was within two hours of sunset before the English army was formed up in proper order along the ridge below Branxton Hill, the line running through Piper's Hill and Branxton Vicarage. Six hundred yards separated the two armies.

The four Scottish columns were as shown on Sketch-map 20, with a fifth in reserve consisting of Bothwell's column combined with d'Aussi's French contingent of some 5,000 men. The total strength of the Scottish army may have been as high as 35,000.

[1] Opinions differ on this point. It is all guesswork, but this seems the most natural solution.

THE BATTLE

The rain was still falling intermittently, dashed into the faces of the English troops by the strong southerly wind, as the opening shots of the battle proper were fired. These took the form of an artillery duel. Though the Scots had the greater weight of metal the English guns had the better of the encounter. The reason for this is not clear,

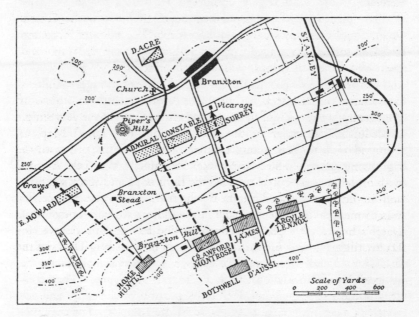

SKETCH-MAP 34.   FLODDEN: THE BATTLE

but no heed should be paid to the absurd explanation that it was due to the Scottish guns being at a greater height and that consequently their rounds fell over. The actual casualties caused were doubtlessly small; but the artillery fire seems to have had one important—possibly decisive—effect when the guns were turned upon the infantry; the Scots were galled by this fire, we are told, and stung into offensive action. This first offensive movement originated with the Borderers on the left flank. It was the first experience for most of them of combined operations with a big army; hitherto they had been accustomed to action on their own, in the form of petty border raids, and the restriction and discipline now imposed proved too much for them.

After a short time they could abide the fire no longer. With an impulsive movement they charged down the hill. Greatly outnumbering the wing of Edmund Howard opposed to them, they must have presented an awe-inspiring spectacle. The miniature valley to which I have referred does not extend so far west as the line taken by their charge, so their momentum was maintained right up to the moment of impact. It was too much for some of the young Cheshire troops who largely composed Howard's brigade. Many of them turned their backs and fled before contact was obtained. Others fought bravely enough until Sir Brian Tunstall was killed and Howard himself wounded. Then resistance crumpled up, and practically the whole brigade was swept from the field.

The situation looked ugly for the English; and worse was to follow. King James, we have seen, had intended to accept battle in a position of his own choice. It was to be a defensive battle; but the Borderers, by their indiscipline and independent action, had upset his plan. Should he follow their example and take the offensive? For some time he hesitated. Then two things happened: the English cannonade became ever more irritating to his troops and the King saw, or thought he saw, some of the Borderers[1] swinging to their right as if to attack the Admiral's brigade, though they were in fact some of the Cheshire men.[2] The temptation proved too much for the King and his companions. He ordered forward his own brigade and that of Crawford and Montrose. These two columns swept down the hill in admirable formation and in an impressive silence. They constituted the best trained and disciplined portion of the army and the French captains must have been proud of their pupils. For they had grafted a new formation and a new tactic on to these Scottish troops. This had been evolved by the Swiss as a defence against cavalry attack, though it had been used long ages before by Alexander the Great. It was, in fact, a revival of the Greek phalanx. Advancing in a serried square column, armed with lances 15 feet long (now for the first time called pikes), they formed a veritable 'hedgehog' that no horse would face; furthermore they constituted a formidable offensive weapon against hostile infantry *so long as they kept in motion*.

[1] For simplicity I call them Borderers throughout, but the column included Lord Huntley's Highlanders.

[2] This is on the sole authority of Bishop Leslie, who wrote before 1570, but whose story has been curiously ignored. Mistakes of identity of this sort frequently occur in battle—modern as well as ancient.

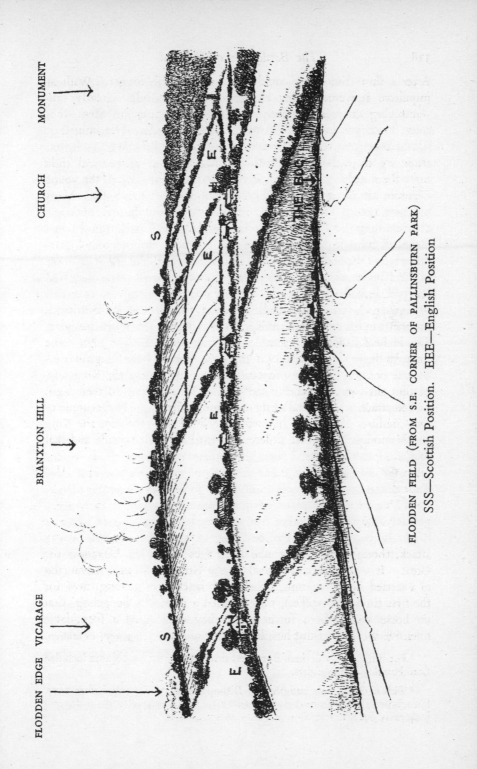

FLODDEN EDGE VICARAGE →   BRANXTON HILL →   CHURCH →   MONUMENT →

FLODDEN FIELD (FROM S.E. CORNER OF PALLINSBURN PARK)
SSS—Scottish Position. EEE—English Position

If and when they ceased to move forwards, their offensive power vanished. It is important to keep these facts in mind.[1]

As the two centre brigades advanced down the hill, they were raked by cannon balls and arrows; the former had appreciable effect, but the Scots were too well armoured for the arrows to do much harm; armour had reached its zenith. At the bottom of the hill they crossed the little stream mentioned above, and breasted the 200-yard ascent to the English line. This climb must have reduced the speed and momentum of the attack. It was no doubt during this short advance that the English guns had most effect; each cannon-ball would ricochet right through the column from front to rear. Fortunately for the Scots the distance to go was short; the compact order of the King's column was maintained, and when the clash occurred Surrey's brigade was slowly pressed back. I compute that this retrograde movement extended for nearly 300 yards until the Scottish phalanx was brought to rest about the line of the present village street. The archers had stepped back behind the billmen just before the moment of the clash, but the English guns must all have been overrun. The Crawford-Montrose column had in its front the rather uneven ground between Pipers Hill and the hillock 300 yards further east. Consequently it lost some of its cohesion and was quickly brought to a standstill.

Meanwhile what were Home's Borderers doing? Why did they not, having routed their immediate opponents, swing round upon the Admiral's column, as the King supposed they were doing? Two things conspired to prevent this. It will be remembered that Lord Dacre had been placed with his mounted troops in rear of the position as a mobile reserve ready to render quick support where it might be required. He had not long to wait; the spectacle of the Cheshire men streaming over the crest told him that help was required. With exemplary alacrity and initiative he galloped forward with 1,500 of his men, and caught the Borderers on their right flank. It must have been a double surprise. If he took the natural route (marked on the sketch-map) his advance would be under cover till it passed Pipers Hill. From this point there was a downward slope with only a few hundred yards to cover. The cavalry[2] must have been upon

---

[1] The point is well dealt with by Dr. Mackenzie in *The Secret of Flodden*.

[2] Dr. Mackenzie suggests that they were only 'mounted infantry' fighting dismounted; but Holinshed is explicit: 'Dacre gave a charge on them with his horsemen.'

the Borderers almost before they were aware of it. For, Borderer-like, they were busy plundering the dead and prisoners (of whom they had taken 60). The situation was restored; young Howard managed to reach the Admiral's column, and the fighting in this part of the field then came to a standstill. Each side seems to have stood eyeing the other closely, but neither side chose to move.

It is true that Lord Home still had ample forces at his disposal to renew the attack and to co-operate with the centre columns, and much speculation has been occasioned by his failure to do so. Three years later he was executed as a traitor, largely on this count. I suspect there was something of the scapegoat motive in this, for I can see no difficulty in accounting for his inactivity. In the first place, the spirited counter-attack of Dacre showed him that the English could still sting; next, the Pipers Hill ridge hid from view the battle that was raging to the east, and the sounds that reached him indicated that the centre columns had made good progress, and indeed were pretty well as far forward as were his own troops;[1] finally, his Borderers were an independent set of men, whose conception of warfare was summed up in one short word—loot. Now it takes some time to divest a fallen knight of his armour, especially when only improvised tools are available for the purpose. Home's men were in no mood to interrupt this important and absorbing operation when only half completed; darkness was approaching; they had had their fight, and they were not disposed for another at that late hour. It all seems perfectly natural; indeed, under the circumstances, any active inter-vention of the Borderers in the main battle would have been a matter for surprise.[2]

While the left and centre of the Scottish army was thus occupied, the fourth column, that of Argyle and Lennox—Highlanders and Islanders—was standing in position on the brow of the hill unen-gaged. The reason for this was simple—there was no enemy opposite to them. They might conceivably have joined in the attack on Surrey's column, and their gaze must have been eagerly directed

[1] To obtain a view he would have to have gone to Pipers Hill which however I make no doubt Dacre was occupying as his command-post.

[2] Dr. Mackenzie dryly remarks: 'The Borderers were no great asset on either side. Howard's first despatch contained the sentence (subsequently erased): 'The Borderers not only stale away as they lost 4 or 5,000 horses, but also took the oxen. . . .' In the French version the word 'French' was inserted before horses, thus completely altering the meaning.

upon the exciting mêlée taking place almost at their feet below. Indeed, they did ultimately prepare to help the King's column, but why was there no enemy on their front? Again the reason is a simple one. The rear brigade of the whole army was that of Sir Edward Stanley. It was bound to experience delay at the 'bottleneck' caused by the passage over the stream at Sandyford. Consequently, by the time his whole brigade was passed over and formed up in close order once more, there was a considerable interval between it and the Earl's own brigade. As Stanley advanced up the slope through Windy Law *en route* for Branxton, he must have seen the Highlanders standing on the brow of the hill, motionless and showing no signs of descending the hill towards him. But for him to advance up that formidable hill to attack them seemed foolhardy. What was to be done?

From the spot whence Stanley viewed the Highlanders he could also notice that the eastern end of the ridge on which they were posted—500 yards south of Mardon—was unoccupied. His quick keen eye also detected a covered approach to a re-entrant at the end of this ridge (see Sketch-map 33). He thereupon hatched a plan with a curiously modern flavour. He would make a holding attack on the enemy's front, with a portion of his force, whilst the remainder crept round by the covered approach, and attacked them in flank while their attention was held by fire from the front. (This is what is now called 'Fire and Movement'). And so it was. We have sufficiently good authority for the details of what ensued. The flanking force consisted of 'three bands', and Stanley led it in person. All went well; the foot of the hill was reached, apparently unobserved, and the steep climb commenced. The ground was so slippery after the rain that some of the troops removed their foot-gear in order the better to progress. Some even crawled on hands and knees. One must remember that they were weighted down by arms and armour. The rainstorm had evidently ceased and the sun emerged, for it was hot, and when they reached the summit they were perspiring and out of breath.

Meanwhile the holding attack was performing its task admirably; the Highlanders still had their eyes glued to the front—in fact, they were about to advance to the support of the King's brigade.[1] Stanley thus was enabled to halt his force for a brief space while they regained

[1] According to the *Trewe Encountre*: 'Stanley seeing the 4th battel ready to relieve the said King of Scotland's battel. . . .'

their breath. Quite clearly he was a cool as well as a quick-witted soldier. When all was ready Stanley gave the word; the archers opened a deadly fire—deadly because the Highlanders were very lightly armoured—and the whole force then charged forward. Success was immediate and absolute. The Highlanders, taken by surprise, fell back to their left, and, passing behind the line of the Scottish position, cleared off the battlefield to the west—and to Scotland.

The success of Stanley's stratagem had been complete, but there was still work to be done. In the centre the Admiral's brigade had by this time almost wiped out its opponents, and it was turning against the left flank of the King's column. James sent repeated messages to the rear for support, and Bothwell and D'Aussi dashed down the hill to his help. The combat was now concentrated on the King's column. Unlike the Borderers, Stanley's men were more intent on winning the battle than on plunder. Far below to his right, Sir Edward could see the mêlée still proceeding on the outskirts of the village. Which was having the better of it would be difficult to say. But Stanley's nimble eye spotted another opportunity for effective action. The Scots were fighting with their backs to him; by charging straight down the hill he would achieve an even greater surprise than he had just brought off. We must picture his position at this moment as on the road at the end of the screen of trees, 900 yards south of Branxton village. (Sketch-map 33.) Exhilarated with their recent success the Englishmen charged down the hill, and picking their way through the recumbent bodies, crashed into the rear of the King's own column near the present vicarage, with devastating effect.

But Sir Edward Stanley was not the only leader of initiative and enterprise on the English side. We have already had occasion to admire the prompt and opportune intervention in the battle of Lord Dacre.[1] He was at it again. The column of Crawford and Montrose had by this time been practically wiped out, and the King was hard put to it. The fact is, the prime weapon of the Scots—the pike —had become more an encumbrance than a help once the two columns had been brought to a standstill. Recourse was had to the broadsword, but the English bill (or halberd) proved more effective at close-quarter fighting than the cutting sword. But still the King fought on. Dacre therefore, realizing by this time that there was

[1] He afterwards got into undeserved ill-odour for his temporary inactivity after charging the Borderers.

nothing to fear from Home's Borderers, decided to intervene in the main battle. From his command-post on Pipers Hill he would be well posted to notice D'Aussi's advance. First he charged the Frenchman's left flank, probably without much success, then he swung round to attack the King's column in its left flank at about the same time that Stanley attacked it in the rear. The King's column was now beset on all sides, 'constrained to fight in a round compass'. The double impact proved decisive. All that was left of the King's column disintegrated, and the few survivors staggered as best they could off the field.

But not the King. Everyone, friends and foe alike, unite in paying tribute to this gallant and likeable monarch. James fought as one possessed, rejecting every thought of flight, inspiring his men with his own fiery spirit and falling, no one knows when, but in the thick of the fight with his face to the front. The precise spot cannot have been far from the vicarage.

The Scottish lords, fired by the example of their sovereign, fought also to the end, and one only, the unfortunate Home, succeeded in getting alive off the battlefield.[1] In the night the ghoulish business of stripping the dead, common to the age, proceeded, and when morning dawned the body of the King of Scotland lay naked and hidden among a pile of other naked corpses. Lord Dacre had some difficulty in identifying it, and in his first despatch on the battle Surrey could not announce his fate. Thereafter a legend arose that the King had not really died, but had escaped and gone on a crusade to Jerusalem. This legend was still given credence in some quarters more than a generation later. The body was, as a matter of fact, removed to Branxton church, embalmed, sent to London and buried at Sheen, near Richmond.

* * * * *

The military effects of the battle were not commensurate with its fame. This degree of fame was due to the fact that the King and most of his nobles had perished on the field of battle. In sober fact, Flodden, as it was called in Scotland, Branxton in England, might well have been a drawn battle but for the military genius of the two young English leaders, Lord Dacre and Sir Edward Stanley. The present monument on Pipers Hill (erected in 1910) bears the inscription: 'To the brave of both Nations.' That is as it should be. Of no battle in

[1] Three bishops also were slain, including Andrew Stewart, bastard son of the King, who at the age of twenty-one, was appointed Primate of Scotland.

which the islanders to the north and to the south of the Tweed have fought can both sides show more pride than that fought on the Fatal Field of Flodden. A Scot (Andrew Lang) has written of the Southerners: 'The English never won a better deserved victory', and an Englishman (A. G. Bradley) has crisply described the Northerners as 'beaten but not disgraced'.

THE LEADERSHIP

I.—KING JAMES

The King has been more sharply criticised by Northern than by Southern writers. There are four main counts in the charge. In the first place, he is charged with dawdling for a fortnight near the Border instead of pushing on into the heart of England. But we must not lose sight of his objective, which was not to conquer territory but to create a military diversion in support of his allies, the French. He must have realized that an English army would sooner or later be formed to drive him north of the Tweed, and the further this army was obliged to advance north the more effective would be the diversion. There was also an element of risk in proceeding south leaving the fortress of Berwick unsubdued behind him. I hold that he was justified in halting at Flodden Edge. In any case this decision can have had no effect upon the upshot of the battle. Had he won it, his strategy in 'luring Surrey to his doom' would have been acclaimed as masterly.

The second count is that he dallied on Flodden Edge while the enemy was marching round his flank. But all through the 8th of September he must have been under the impression that Surrey would engage him in battle next day. All that was therefore necessary was to change his position on the massif, turning it to face east instead of south. There are indications that he took some preparatory steps in this direction, but they were probably unduly delayed by lengthy disputes in his council. It is unfortunate that we have no authentic account of its proceedings, but it is clear that divided views and counsels held sway. All this would lead to delay. But it may be argued, why did not the King decide for himself in a case where speed of decision was obviously called for? The answer is that he dared not take any step without securing the acquiescence of the leaders of the main contingents. His was a loosely-knit army, almost as much so as was that of Marlborough, and James was not perhaps possessed of those qualities that enabled Marlborough to secure cheerful obedience to orders by all his contingents. This was not his fault. He had to take his army as he found it; even Marlborough, unlike Wellington, had to summon frequent councils of war.

The third count is that, in Oman's words: 'he is liable to grave criticism' for not marching at once to attack the English when they were only half across the Till.[1] This criticism comes surprisingly from such a sage student of military history as Sir Charles, for a simple study of time and space shows that it was an impracticable course. It took Surrey at least three hours to cover the intervening space from Twizel Bridge to Branxton. It would have taken the Scots even longer, for time would be required to get out the orders after the arrival of the messenger, to get the troops fallen in and the army marshalled. Long before the Scottish army reached the river the English army would be across it and united in one body.

The fourth count is not widely made, though it possesses more substance than the others. It is that James should have remained on the defensive instead of descending the hill and attacking. Consider the tactical situation. On Flodden Edge the King had invited attack in a very strong position, but Surrey had shirked it, at the same time undertaking to give battle within three days. The third day had now come, and James had won the race for the Branxton Hill position. (For this there is no special credit, as he had less distance to go). He was now in another strong position, with his opponent practically pledged to attack it. What could be better? He had averted what had looked like becoming an awkward situation and the favourable conditions of three days before had been restored. All he had to do was—to do nothing. Therefore it is natural to blame him for taking the offensive; this action in all probability lost him the battle. If the English columns had been forced to struggle up the slippery slope with the wind and rain in their faces, and if the 'phalanxes' had been launched to the attack when the enemy was about 50 yards short of the summit the prospects of a Scottish victory would have been great.[2]

Why then did James change his mind? For it seems clear that his

---

[1] Thomas Hodgkin, another careful and moderate historian, is even more severe: 'The English,' he writes, 'were saved from ruin by the apathy or over-strained chivalry of James' *Archæologia Aeliana*, iii, 24.

[2] Strange to relate, this criticism is best expressed in a letter written by the Regent in the name of the boy-king, James V, a few months after the battle: 'Impatient at the sight of them our dearest Father keeping no order among his men, from a position in which he could be attacked only with difficulty and danger, boldly rushed down upon the enemy.'

original intention was to await attack on top of the ridge. The contemporary Italian poem *La Rotta* (which seems to have made use of some Scottish source) says that 'Their desire was to be attacked on the hill. For awhile the English awaited them on the plain'. Each side, in fact, wanted the other to commence. But can the King rightly be blamed for what then happened? I have suggested (it is no more than a suggestion) that his course was decided for him by the independent-minded Borderers who could not stand being galled by the English cannonade. If this be a correct interpretation it looks as if the action of the English artillery, so far from playing no part in the victory, did in fact play a decisive part. Assuming that the King witnessed the success of the Borderers on his left, he was faced with the difficult alternative whether to adhere to his plan or to take advantage of an unexpected development. It is hard to blame him for doing the latter—whether or not his hands were forced by the impatience of the leaders and troops around him.

To summarize, I can see no blatant military faults committed by the King of Scotland in the campaign of Flodden.

II.—THE EARL OF SURREY

The English commander had this advantage over his opponent that he commanded a more homogeneous army. But even he felt himself tied and bound by his council. This may at first seem surprising, but councils of war were a normal feature of warfare in England. Even Richard III, with his great military reputation and the prestige attached to kingship, held one before Bosworth Field, and it was natural to follow the example of his military mentor. Moreover, Surrey was, for those days, a very old man. Owing to rheumatism he travelled in a coach, which produced the scornful Scottish description of him as 'an old crooked earil in a chariot."

Our criticism of his leadership whether favourable or the reverse, is conditioned by the doubt as to how far the decisions taken were his own or were imposed upon him by others. The evidence tends in the latter direction. The letter of challenge to James IV was signed by no less than 18 senior officers besides himself. The weather was bad, which would exacerbate his rheumatism and lack of mobility. After reaching Barmoor the natural step to take would be a personal reconnaissance of the hostile position from the new direction. The old Earl, however, contented himself with sending his son. After the battle was over he was so fatigued (we have it on the authority of Henry VIII) that he did not write his own despatch, contenting himself with dictating a short account to his son, who wrote it down. The Admiral was indeed already experienced in despatch writing.

III.—THE ADMIRAL

This brings us to this remarkable eldest son of the Earl of Surrey.[1] He is described as a little short, dark man. As admiral at sea, on hearing of the invasion he had left his fleet at sea and hurried to join up as a general. Here he soon established a position of predominance. Bishop Ruthal called him 'the very leader, conductor and setter-on of our army'. He was a fiery-spirited soldier, who declared that he would give no quarter, no, not even to King James himself. I seem to descry his influence in every decision and every action taken. It is for this reason that I have described him as Surrey's Chief of Staff.

But it is quite impossible to apportion the precise amount of credit that is due to father and to son respectively. Looking upon them as one, for all practical purposes, and denoting the couple by the word 'Howard', we must ascribe warm praise for the truly remarkable, bold and almost unique operation (in those days) of deliberately marching his whole army round the rear of a bigger army which was in the act of invading the country. 'Howard' rightly read the intentions of the enemy—one of the first signs of generalship—and decided that he could afford to take the risk.[2] But the brilliance of this manœuvre was marred and its benefits destroyed in advance by the absurd but quixotic pledge of the Earl to offer battle by the 9th of September. How are we to judge such action? It is impossible to do so by any modern standard—and profitless, to boot. If those modern historians are correct who assert that the English army approached the hostile position by widely dispersed routes[3] then 'Howard' must be strongly criticised, but I do not consider that they establish their case. If I were to attempt here to examine all their arguments in detail, this chapter would have to be doubled in length. I must sum up by saying that I can find no fault committed by

---

[1] Remarkable is the right adjective to apply to this family. Out of six successive heads of generations, one died on the battlefield, one died in the Tower, one spent some years in the Tower, two were beheaded, and the sixth narrowly escaped that fate.

[2] It reminds one of Wellington's apparently foolhardy manœuvre at Toulouse, where he accurately assessed the reaction of Soult and profited thereby.

[3] *New Light on Flodden* is the most extreme example of this school.

'Howard' during this campaign, and must award high praise for his restraint in awaiting the attack at the foot of Branxton Hill instead of taking the tactical offensive himself. At the same time, it would be absurd to attempt to assess his place as a general on the strength of a single campaign, however brilliant, of only a week's duration.[1]

PROBLEMS OF THE BATTLEFIELD

I.—THE NUMBERS

The usual vagueness and contradictions regarding the numbers do not apply to the English army in this battle. The unanimity with which the figure of 26,000 is given for the army is at first sight impressive. But further examination shows that this figure is probably derived from a single source—the broadsheet issued soon after the battle and usually known as *A Trewe Encounter*. This account allots Surrey's main body 5,000, the Admiral's 9,000 and the four wings 3,000 each. Thus the total of 26,000 is arrived at. This symmetry in the numbers of the wings tends to arouse suspicion. However it has been almost universally accepted by historians till quite recently. But in 1937 Dr. W. M. Mackenzie published a book entitled *The Secret of Flodden*, in which he suggests a figure of 13,000 to 15,000 for the English army. Anything that comes from his pen demands the closest consideration and respect, so I will give his reasoning in some detail. Dr. Mackenzie starts from the figure 26,000, derived as we have seen, from the items in *Trewe Encountre* which allots all four wings 3,000 men each. But the Doctor tries to show that in three of these cases the real figure was only about half that given; therefore, he argues, the other items will be wrong in the same proportion, and we must accept only half the total arrived at, i.e. 13,000.

Let us examine these three examples:

1. *Constable.* Hall only gives his total as 1,000, in addition to his sons and kinsmen. But Hall also says that the grand total was 26,000. Is it sound to accept his figure when it is lower than that given elsewhere and reject it when it agrees with the other?

2. *Sir E. Howard.* The *Articles of Battle* allot him 1,000 men from Cheshire, 500 from Lancs., and many gentlemen from Yorks. But in *Archæologia Aeliana*, iii, 214, Robert White credits him in

---

[1] He, Surrey, has been likened to Hannibal and Napoleon in *New Light on Flodden*, by G. F. T. Leather.

addition with 'the men of Hull, the King's tenants of Hatfield, and 200 from the south of England'. Thus the grand total is impossible to assess, but may approach 3,000.

3. *Lord Dacre* came to the relief of Sir E. Howard with 1,500 men. 'There is no reason to doubt that this represents the whole of Dacre's command' writes Dr. Mackenzie.

But this is nowhere stated. It *is* however stated that the 1,500 were horsemen, so unless his command was exclusively composed of cavalry, his total must have exceeded 1,500. Now the *Trewe Encountre* states that his command included 1,500 men of the Bishop of Ely. To this, according to Robert White, must be added 'the bowmen of Kendal, and the men of Keswick, Stanmore, Alston Moor and Gilsland. . . . In company with Dacre was the Bastard Heron commanding another troop of horse'. Thus again the total must exceed 1,500.

Colonel the Hon F. Elliot points out, in *The Battle of Flodden*, that two months after the battle Dacre had 4,000 men under him, and he finds it 'really barely credible that at such a juncture Dacre should have brought so small a force [as 1,500] into the field'. Were the Bishop of Ely's men cavalry? If not, there must have been 1,500 men in addition to the Bishop's 1,500. One would expect the cavalry to be Dacre's own men from the North. Further, Dacre states that contingents from Bamborough and Tyneside were added to him because his ranks were weak. It looks as if Surrey's aim was to have four wings of similar size, 3,000 in each, and that in order to bring Dacre's wing up to this number these contingents were added.

Be that as it may, I feel disposed to accept the contemporary figures given in the *Trewe Encountre* as approximately correct, though as they are only round numbers the exact total may well be slightly less.

For the Scots we are completely in the land of conjecture and I do not propose to spend space on a study of it. 'One man's guess is as good as another's', and possibly that of Sir Charles Oman is better than most. He puts the maximum figure at 40,000, reduced by the time of the battle to about 30,000.

II.—THE RIVER CROSSING BY SURREY'S DIVISION

Almost every possible ford between Twizel Bridge and Ford has been suggested. I have favoured the ford about a mile to the south of the bridge, near Heaton Castle. It has been objected to this that the *Articles of War* (Surrey's first despatch to the Queen) states that the

Admiral's division (with the guns) crossed the Till at Twizel Bridge and that Surrey followed him 'and passed after (*après*)', which must mean that he also crossed by Twizel. But '*après*' may only mean 'after in time'. If, then, Surrey followed the Admiral up to the river and crossed by a ford a mile short of him, the statement would be broadly correct. Indeed, the leading units of Surrey's division may have used the bridge, after which some enterprising individual may have discovered that it was possible to use the ford, thus cutting off a mile.

Another school of thought favours the bridge or ford at Etal. I liked this suggestion at one time. The climb up the bank on the far side is very steep, which would make it impossible for guns. This would explain the attachment of the ordnance to the Twizel division. But the statement of Leland that there was a decayed bridge at Etal in 1538 disposes of this argument. Nor do I think that a prudent commander like Surrey[1] would separate his two divisions by over four miles when in the presence of the enemy.

This argument applies with still greater force to the fords at Willow Ford and Sandyford, still further up-stream. Incidentally the latter ford has an average depth of about three feet, so in the swollen state of the river at that time it would have been quite impassable on foot.

Elliot thinks the Scottish army held the line of the Till between Etal and Ford on the morning of the battle; he also thinks that Surrey's division crossed at Sandyford. The two suggestions appear irreconcilable to me; for Surrey's van would have encountered the Scottish rear at the river. But of this there is no evidence; rather the reverse.

One recent writer of the Sandyford school gets over the statement in the *Articles of Battle* by suggesting that Surrey deliberately deceived his son into believing that he would follow him. If he had done this he would deserve to be beaten. In any case, the Admiral would have discovered the deception by the time he wrote the despatch—almost certainly at his father's dictation.

III.—DID THE SCOTTISH ARMY TRY TO RETREAT?

The theory that the Scottish army was in the act of retreating towards Scotland when it was surprised by the appearance of the English army at Branxton has been advanced in two modern books,

[1] He is described in the letter to Cardinal Bainbridge as 'rei militari expertissimus'.

that by Elliott already mentioned and *New Light on Flodden* by G. F. T.
Leather (1937). Since both books adopt the same general line of
reasoning I will confine my remarks to the former. Briefly put, the
contention is that James did not sit motionless throughout September
8th whilst Surrey was marching round his flank, but took up a position
covering the Till crossings in the vicinity of Ford; that next morning
he decided to fall back on Scotland, via Blinkbenny, Branxton Hill
and Coldstream; but that when the vanguard had reached the top
of Branxton Hill the English army appeared and it was obliged to
form front to its right flank.

I have not the space to deal with this contention in detail. There
is no contemporary evidence in support of it, else we should have heard
the theory put forward long ago. The only passage suggesting it
that the Colonel cites is the statement by Bishop John Leslie, writing
about 1570, that on the morning of the battle James advanced his army
towards Barmoor. But Leslie is not a good witness for the theory,
for he implicitly supports the normal contention that James stayed on
Flodden Edge on the previous day. Furthermore, Leslie quotes the
King as assuring Surrey on that day: 'I shall defend (our quarrel) at
your fixed time, which we shall abide.' There is no indication here
of a retreat into Scotland. But Elliot supposes that the King changed
his mind, and finds the views of the Scottish historians 'curiously
confusing and conflicting'. There should be nothing to be surprised at
here when it is realized that we cannot in the nature of things know
what was passing through the King's mind, or in his council. He
did not live to tell the tale of his defeat; nor did any of his council
except possibly Home, who had reason not to be talkative afterwards
on the subject of the battle. It is just possible that Sir William Scott,
his secretary, was present at the councils, but he was captured by the
English and can have had no opportunity to inform the Scottish
chronicler what occurred in the various councils. All is conjecture;
hence the confusion of the chroniclers. The only safe procedure
is to try and gauge the King's intentions by his subsequent actions.
It is not sound to *assume* certain intentions, and from them to declare
what his actions were; yet by no other means can the thesis be
established. Nor, if we for the sake of argument agree that the
King intended a retreat, can we consider the course ascribed to the
army a natural one, conforming to Inherent Military Probability.
Consider the position, map in hand. We are asked to believe that on
the morning of September 9th, the Scottish army, being at the foot

of Flodden Hill watching the crossings of the Till between Ford and Sandyford, started to retreat to Coldstream via the top of Branxton Hill. The most direct and quickest, because the levellest, route would be via Branxton village, in a straight line. But the writer makes them plod up the hill again, dragging their guns with them, only to drop down into the valley again a bare half mile further on. Why make a detour in order to include a hill in the march? Speed would be of importance? Would the oxen drawing the heavy 'Seven Sisters' of Borthwick travel quicker on the hill or on the level? There can be but one answer to this question.

Nor can I follow the author's difficulty in finding a motive for the occupation of the Branxton Hill position from Flodden Edge. There was a double motive: to occupy a good position facing north, and to deny that position to the enemy. It was a natural move to make. I see no reason therefore to reject the statement of the chroniclers that the bulk of the army moved direct from Flodden Edge to Branxton Hill.

IV.—THE APPROACH OF THE ENGLISH ARMY

I have shown the two divisions of the English army as following almost the same route after crossing the Till until the bog was nearly reached. There is no direct evidence bearing on the point, and consequently a variety of routes has been suggested. Several accounts make the divisions and even smaller units diverge widely, some units taking the road via Cornhill and others by Sandyford, the two wings being separated by several miles. There is no warrant for this curious operation and I cannot credit old Surrey with such foolhardy conduct. One of the most recent accounts makes the English army approach the position in no less than five widely separated columns, and engage in the battle on a front of $3\frac{1}{2}$ miles. Such a procedure would be exceptional in those days, and it goes flat against the best contemporary evidence, which states that the Scottish columns were only an arrow-shot apart, say 200 yards. Such solutions as this are brought about by building surmise upon surmise till, as the structure rises, one begins to assume that the original surmise was a fact. But if that surmise is proved faulty the whole edifice falls to the ground like a pack of cards. The only safe method, I suggest, is to advance by the stepping-stones of indisputable facts, filling in the gaps between the stones on the lines of Inherent Military Probability. Here the stones are few but solid. First stone: On September 8th the Scottish army was in position on Flodden Edge. Second: The English marched to Barmoor. Third: Next day the English marched via Twizel towards Branxton. Fourth: Soon after that the Scottish army moved north over Branxton Hill and attacked the English. If the gaps are filled in in the way suggested there will not be much room in the story for a Scottish retreat towards the Border.

V.—THE ARTILLERY ARM

Chroniclers and historians alike attribute more effect to this arm than is warranted. The Scottish chronicler, Lindsay of Pitscottie, relates how the Master Gunner besought the King that he might fire at the English army while it was crossing the Twizel Bridge, and that James spurned to take such an advantage of his enemy. Now the range to Twizel Bridge would be about $4\frac{1}{2}$ miles, a distance that was out of the question. Modern writers have interpreted this as either Branx Brig or Etal Bridge. The range to the latter would be at least two miles, and to the former 1,700 yards. The heaviest of the Scottish guns, of which there were only a few, might have reached this range at extreme elevation, firing 'at random' as it was expressively called. But apart from the hopeless inaccuracy of this long range, the steep angle of descent would have driven the cannon-ball straight into the ground, instead of causing it to ricochet; consequently its effect would have been practically nil. Robert Borthwick must have been well aware of this, and we can dismiss this story as a figment from the ingenious and fertile brain of Lindsay. This episode tends to shake our faith in the trustworthiness of Lindsay as an historian. Other statements by the same writer will not tend to restore our faith.

Then it has been asserted that a battery established at the encampment at the eastern foot of Flodden Edge was to cover the bridge at Ford. In this case the range would be 2,500 yards, again an impossible distance. Finally there is the story by John Leslie, another Scottish chronicler, that 'the English ordnance . . . shot fast and did great skaithe and slew his principal gunners; but the king's ordnance did small skaithe by reason of the height where they stood they shot over the English army'. I daresay the worthy Lindsay believed the story that Branxton Hill was half a mile high, and that therefore the Scottish guns could not be depressed sufficiently to hit the enemy. But anyone with an elementary knowledge of ballistics will agree that they could have shot down to their target without depressing the bore below the horizontal, for the angle of sight was less than three degrees depression.   No, I am afraid this is only a case of 'blaming it on to the ground'.   The defeated side is generally fertile in excuses.

VI.—THE SMOKE-SCREEN

Few writers now believe that the smoke-screen caused by the burning of the camp refuse was an intentional stratagem.   But they mostly accept the assertion that it impeded not only the Scottish but the English army.   But this will not do.   The campfire must have been nearly a mile behind Branxton Hill, and the English army, when crossing the bog, would be two miles away.   Smoke rises; it does not creep along the ground for two miles—downhill at that. Moreover, intentional smoke-screens are tricky affairs to put down and maintain.   It is hardly credible that the fortuitous and spasmodic smoke occasioned by the burning of some refuse would screen the approach of a whole army.   Yet it is reported that the approach of the Scottish army was invisible and a surprise to the English.   The explanation is simple, though it would be unknown to a chronicler who was not acquainted with the ground and did not possess a modern contoured map.   The screen was caused, not by the adventitious and evanescent smoke coils from the rubbish heap but by the more solid medium of mother earth: in other words, the Branxton Hill ridge hid the approach of the Scottish army till it reached the crest of the hill.

CHAPTER XXVII

The Battle of Edgehill, October 23rd, 1642

THIS is one of the best known of our English battles, though it does not deserve to be. The reason is clear: no battle had taken place on English soil, and no English king had taken the field at the head of his army for more than one hundred and fifty years. It was the opening battle of the great Civil War, and opening battles—though normally less important—have a way of being more familiar than the closing ones.

The strategy leading up to the battle was curious. King Charles I, having raised his standard at Nottingham, perambulated the Midlands, seeking to raise an army with which he might advance and capture the capital. Meanwhile the Parliamentarians (Roundheads for short) dispatched Essex with the striking-force via Nottingham to bring the Royalist army to battle. As the King moved westwards into Shropshire, Essex marched parallel with him to Worcester, where the opening shots of the war were fired, Prince Rupert with the King's horse easily dispersing some Roundhead horse.

On October 12th the King set out from Shrewsbury to march upon London. Essex allowed himself to be out-manœuvred, and instead of keeping his army between the King and the capital, hung on to Worcester too long, thus letting Charles slip past him. Thus on the evening of October 22nd, while Essex was at Kineton, Charles was at Edgecott, seven miles to the east.

The problem before the King was: should he continue on his way or turn and shake off his opponent first? Inspired by his youthful nephew, Prince Rupert, Charles decided on the latter course, and orders were sent out to occupy the high ridge of Edgehill on the following morning.

Now, had Essex advanced at dawn on 23rd October, he could have engaged or turned the Royalist position before the King had time to complete its occupation, for his billets were scattered. But Essex lost this opportunity, probably because some of his foot and the greater part of his artillery had not yet come up. Thus by the time he had advanced to and drawn up his army on the low ground to the north of Edgehill, the Royalist army was drawn up along the brow of the hill. The positions had become reversed; instead of Essex being between the King and the capital, it was the King who was between Essex and his base.

THE TERRAIN

It is now time to describe the terrain. There are here fewer points in obscurity than on almost any other English field of the Civil War.[1]

Edgehill is a conspicuous ridge, rising 300 feet out of the plain, three miles long, facing north-west—that is, square to the road to London. The slope is steep, reaching a gradient of 1 in 4. Though now fringed with a belt of trees, it was at the time of the battle open ground except for one small clump. The plain between the hill and Kineton was fairly open in the centre, though there was some scrub and furze, and a single hedge ran between what are now Thistle and Battle Farms. This hedge still exists, a road running alongside it. On the Royalist right wing there were five or six hedges in the three miles to Kineton, but the other wing was very enclosed on the Kineton side with a number of small fields and orchards. What makes the battlefield difficult to locate with precision nowadays is that some copses that were present at the time of the battle have been cut down, and others have been planted since that time. The chief of these are shown on my map—Battle Holt, the Oaks and the two small copses in the exact centre of the field, the triangular one being Graveyard Coppice, and the other unnamed.

THE RIVAL ARMIES

Since this is the first battle of the Civil War, it may be as well (though the subject is not strictly relevant to this book) very briefly to review the rival armies. The first thing to note is that both armies consisted essentially of amateurs. Since Elizabethan days there had been but little fighting, and any professional knowledge acquired was possessed by a few officers, mainly but not entirely Royalist, who had

[1] There is, however, a danger that local evidence as to the site may disappear with time, for it is now War Department land, and enclosed. The inhabitants have been ejected, so that local tradition, place-names, sites of grave-pits, etc., may in the course of time be forgotten and lost.

fought on the Continent. Thus both armies were makeshift affairs, and the muddle, confusion and obscurity that there is in the accounts of the battle reflect accurately the muddle, confusion and sheer bad leadership that was evident on both sides. That is what I meant when I said that Edgehill did not deserve the reputation as a battle that it holds. It was badly fought, and there are few lessons to be learnt from it except the negative one of 'how NOT to do it'.

The Royalist cavalry must to some extent be excluded from this indictment. Trained by Rupert to charge home in the Gustavus Adolphus manner, better mounted than their opponents, possessing better morale (which had been stimulated by the affair of Powick Bridge), they completely outmatched the Roundhead cavalry; indeed, they were the nearest approach to a trained arm, as understood on the Continent at the time, that existed in the kingdom. There was not much to choose between the infantry or artillery in the two armies. The drill of the musketeers and pikemen had not altered much since Sir Francis Vere had used them so effectively in the Low Countries; and the guns were so few in numbers, and so slow in movement that they had but little effect on the fortunes of this or any other battle in the Civil War.

Since Professor S. R. Gardiner computed the Royalists at 14,000 and the Roundheads at 10,000, a fresh assessment has been made by Godfrey Davies, who puts both armies at about 13,000, though the Roundheads had superior equipment. The Earl of Essex may not have been a heaven-born general, but at least his sway was undisputed, whereas in the opposing camp there were divided councils and almost divided command. That is to say, while Lord Lindsey was the titular commander, Prince Rupert was independent of him. It is not surprising that old Lindsey refused to put up with such a nonsensical arrangement and resigned the command on the eve of the battle. He was replaced by another elderly man, the Earl of Forth. The King seems to have held a sort of vague 'watching-brief' over the whole.

THE BATTLE

The two armies probably spotted one another simultaneously. 'A worthy divine' on the Parliamentarian side claims to have first discovered the Royalists on the top of Edgehill through his 'perspective glass', and to have reported it to Essex. Meanwhile the King himself was also engaged with a perspective glass from Knowle Hill, the right-hand edge of the ridge. Essex was then slowly marching out of Kineton and clumsily marshalling his host in line of battle about two miles outside the town. It was past noon before this operation was completed, and meanwhile the Royalists, having completed their own dispositions, stood still. A pause—typical of civil war engagements, where neither side is anxious to strike the first blow—ensued. It looked for the moment as if no engagement would take place. Essex clearly was unwilling to assault such a strong position, and the King eventually realized that if there was to be a battle that day he must take the initiative in the matter. An incident that may have decided him then occurred. A gunner in the Roundhead army spotted the King, still stationed on Knowle Hill, and laid a cannon at him. The ball was fired, but fell short, landing in a field below him (and still called Bullet Hill).[1] Charles was roused to action. He ordered the whole army to advance in line down the hill and engage. The steepness of the slope occasioned difficulties to the cannons, and the horses had to be taken out and, according to one account, harnessed to the traces or drag-ropes in the rear.

Meanwhile the Roundheads were standing motionless. It was one o'clock. Both armies were now drawn up a few hundred yards apart, somewhere between Kineton and the little village of Radway. We must now establish the exact location of the respective lines.

Here we have place-names, grave-pits, tradition and contemporary accounts to help us. As for the place-names, apart from Bullet Hill there are Battle Holt and Battle Farm and Graveground Coppice (see Sketch-map 36). As for tradition, there is a mound on the side of the Radway—Kineton road, 800 yards west of Radway, that tradition asserts to have been the spot where the King's standard was set up during the early part of the battle. Three grave-pits (confirmed by tradition) are as shown on my map, a sure indication of the scene of the heaviest fighting.[2]

Accounts assert there was a single hedge in the centre of the Roundhead position, and there still is an old hedge between Battle and Thistle Farms which exactly answers to this. Finally we are told that Essex formed his army on the top of a slight rise, up which the Royalists had to advance.

[1] A copse in the shape of a crown was later planted to mark the spot where the King stood.

[2] The one in rear of Thistle Farm was probably only a small one.

To clinch the matter let us march forward in the steps of the Earl of Essex, out from Kineton via Little Kineton. As we near the obvious vicinity of the battlefield we are mounting a very slight, gradual rise. We cross the above-mentioned hedge and road, and see the crest 300 yards in front of us. We proceed to the top; there what appears an obvious position unfolds itself. The ground slopes down very gently to the little nameless brook between where we stand and Radway village. If we advance any further we shall get involved in the probably boggy ground along the brook, and also be getting uncomfortably close to and under the frowning heights of Edgehill. In short, this ridge where we now stand seems made for the purpose. The grave-pits—a sure sign of fighting in the vicinity—are all on this ridge. Here, then, there can be no doubt, Essex decided to form up his army.

The extent of the Parliamentary position is nowhere recorded. All we know for certain is that it was in two lines. Thirteen thousand men in such formation would hardly have occupied more than two miles at the outside. Thus, if the centre rested on the Kineton—Radway road—a reasonable assumption—it could hardly have extended further to its left than the Kineton—Knowle End road, while its right would rest near the present Oaks plantation. When the Royalist army advanced, doubtless it conformed, in the accommodating way customary in those days, to its opponent's position and frontage. Thus we get the two armies ranged in battle order as shown in my Sketch-map 35. In both armies the usual formation of the day was adhered to; that is, the cavalry were on the two wings, the infantry in the centre, and the guns mainly placed in the intervals between the infantry regiments. But the heaviest guns were some way further in the rear. In the case of the Royalists this would be near the road for convenience, and about Battleton Holt.

THE BATTLE

The battle opened with a rather feeble artillery duel—of technical interest to gunners only. We therefore pass on to the next phase— the world-famous charge of Prince Rupert's horse. It is worth taking some trouble to identify the exact ground over which this charge passed. The data is not extensive, but it is possible to locate it within fairly narrow limits. We know that Rupert led his horse down

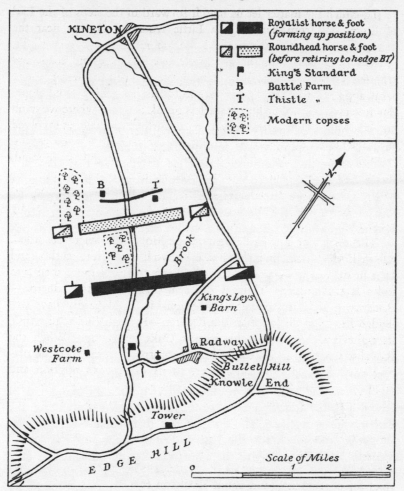

SKETCH-MAP 35.   EDGEHILL: THE BATTLEFIELD

Knowle Hill on the right flank.   This road leads straight to Kineton, and it would therefore be natural to suppose that he formed them up with the road as axis.   On the other hand, for reasons already given, it is probable that the Roundhead line did not extend appreciably to the north of the Kineton—Knowle End road; they would thus be all on the left of the road as seen by Rupert.   Now the Prince had given orders that his troops should charge right through the hostile ranks without waiting to discharge their pistols.   The implication is that the charge was made straight to the front, directly at the opposing line. If these were drawn up to the left of the road (as Rupert saw it) he would form his line to the left accordingly. But it is recorded that the opposing cavalry were stationed upon 'a hill'. This has led some people to suppose that a small hillock on the northern side of the road is indicated. But writers of that and of an earlier day had a narrower vocabulary than we possess, and the words 'ridge', 'slope', hillock', 'swell of ground' never occur in their accounts. Instead they employ words less qualified, such as 'plain', 'pass', 'hill', 'mountain', and it is reasonable to suppose that the 'hill' mentioned in this connection is no more than the northern extremity of the gentle ridge already referred to, on which Essex formed his line of battle. If this be so, and knowing that the charge took Rupert's men into Kineton, it follows that the charge was immediately to the left of the Kineton road and parallel to it. This is for us a fortunate thing, for though the ground to the left of the road is now War Department property one can follow the charge by simply going down the road.

What happened is probably as follows: Rupert, having descended the hill in column, extended his line at the bottom to his left, abreast of King's Leys Barn. His troops in two lines then trotted forward about one mile down the gentle descent to the brook which, being very narrow, they took in their stride. On the slight ridge opposite them they could see Fairfax's horse drawn up. Breaking into a canter, possibly followed by a gallop, they headed straight for the Parliamentary cavalry. The sight of this formidable onslaught was altogether too much for the half-trained horsemen of the Parliamentary army (especially as their left was slightly outflanked): they turned and fled. Rupert's men quickened their pace in pursuit, and between the ridge and the town of Kineton they jumped five or six hedges. It is still quite easy, motoring or cycling along the road, to picture the scene and identify these hedges; the ground was now almost level, and the broad pastures must have presented much the same appearance as they do to-day.

Not only the Roundhead cavalry but the contiguous infantry were affected by this onslaught, and Lord Wharton declared, in a moment of candour only a few days later, that four regiments of foot, including his own, took to flight.

Rupert's cavaliers swept on into Kineton. Here some of them stopped to plunder; the remainder continued their wild charge up the

Warwick road for close on two miles, till they encountered reinforcements for the Roundhead army at a spot since known as Rupert's headland, and their pursuit was checked. Fugitives were collected and gradually some sort of a line of Roundhead troops, including one commanded by a Captain O. Cromwell, brought the Royalist cavalry to a standstill.

The upshot is well known.

While Rupert's charge was still proceeding (the precise moment is not recorded) the Royalist infantry, forming five brigades in two lines,[1] advanced to the attack. Crossing the little brook and marching slowly up the gentle slope, they encountered the Roundheads on the ridge-top. What then happened is described in detail by only one eye-witness, and his account has been curiously ignored. That eye-witness was none other than the future King James II. He was then a boy, aged nine, and together with his elder brother Charles he witnessed the early stages of the fight at close quarters. (Later the two lads were hurried away to safety on the top of Edgehill.)

James relates that the Cavaliers fired their muskets while they were advancing—a surprising and unusual action, but we must accept it. On the top of the ridge they came to 'push of pike', and though James does not mention it, the Roundheads gave some ground, falling back at least in places to the hedge, which they lined with musketeers. To continue James's account: 'Each, as if by mutual consent, retired some few paces and then stuck down their colours, continuing to fire at one another even until night.' The fighting in the centre of the field thus became static and rather dull.

Not so on the flanks. Rupert's action on the right flank was shortly followed by similar action by the smaller body of cavalry under Lord Wilmot on the left. For some way the ground over which they charged was as open as on the other flank, and the charge was almost as successful. Fielden's regiment was swept away and Wilmot's men penetrated right behind the hostile foot. But two things altered the complexion of affairs in this quarter: the enclosed nature of the ground previously referred to impeded and disorganized the Cavaliers, and in the course of their charge they had ridden too wide to take in two enemy cavalry regiments—those of Balfour and Stapleton, which may have been drawn up partially behind the foot

[1] Most accounts say three brigades, but a plan of the Royalist army by De Gomme, recently discovered at Windsor, clearly shows five brigades, three in the front line, two in support.

of the front line.[1] These two regiments now played a big, but confusing part in the battle.

Accounts of cavalry actions are generally confusing. Events happen so fast, and when the terrain is at all enclosed it is difficult for any one eye-witness to take in all that is happening, and also to remember events in their right order afterwards. So it is not surprising that the records at this stage become fragmentary and somewhat contradictory. Out of it all we can, however, distinguish two separate charges by the Roundhead cavalry under Balfour. Opinions differ as to the course pursued by these two charges. Till recently I envisaged both as swinging round from the outer flank (Balfour's right) and thus avoiding the Royalist foot. On the other hand Balfour seems to have been formed up in rear of the Roundhead foot, so his charge would naturally strike the opposing infantry. I have now veered to the opinion that his first charge did go through the Royalist foot, as the result of examining two unpublished documents in the Royal Archives at Windsor, which I have permission to make use of. The first is a map of the Royalist line of battle made by De Gomme shortly after the battle and probably reliable. This shows in the centre of the left brigade a regiment of Welshmen. This regiment would be approximately opposite Balfour's regiment. The other document is an Almanack for the year 1642, apparently owned by one John Booker. Opposite the 23rd of October there is written a short account of the battle (evidently by a Roundhead). It ends by saying that 'all the Kings field killed or ran away from him. Two Welsh regiments ran away quite'.

If there be truth in the latter statement (which is quite likely, for the Welsh were ill armed and disciplined), then a gap would appear in the Royalist foot just opposite Balfour's horse. If he then charged through the gap thus formed it would explain the easy success that he appears to have obtained. Then, wheeling slightly to his left, he would be in a good position to attack the heavy Royalist ordnance, which I reckon were near the roadside, in or near the present Battleton Holt (see Sketch-map 36). As he approached from their left flank their escort ran away and, as the Roundheads, flushed with victory, surged round the guns, an exciting scene ensued. The gunners, cowering under the guns, were sabred, and Balfour shouted excitedly: 'Nails! Nails!' These were required for the purpose of 'nailing

[1] Some persons believed that Wilmot purposely rode wide of them. The exact truth will never be known.

up' or 'spiking' the guns. But nails were, as might be supposed, not immediately forthcoming. Balfour was therefore reduced to cutting the traces so that the guns could not be driven away. He then returned to his own lines. In so doing he was mistaken for the enemy and fired on by his own guns. Thus the upshot was disappointing. But it seems to have taught him the necessity of coordinating such attacks with his own foot. Profiting by this lesson

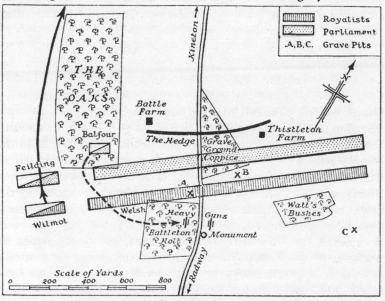

SKETCH-MAP 36.   EDGEHILL: THE BATTLE
(Cavalry on the Eastern flank not shown)

he now mounted a second attack, in which he obtained the promise of the foot regiments on the right flank to co-operate. This was the first sign on any part of the front, in either army, of the least attempt to co-ordinate the two arms in attack. The result was a deserved success. While the cavalry swept round once more, probably in a wider sweep than before, the infantry, leaving the protection of the hedge, advanced with the Kineton—Radway road as axis. While the foot attacked the opposing infantry in front, the horse struck into their left flank. The result was decisive for the moment; the Royalist infantry reeled and recoiled, first on their left flank but gradually extending in lesser degree all along the line. Thus the retrograde movement partook of a partial wheel, till the line reached and crossed the brook. This retrograde movement exposed the King's standard to danger. A homeric struggle for the standard ensued; the standard-bearer, Sir Edmund Verney, was killed and the standard captured. (It was recovered that evening.) The guns were by some unrecorded means withdrawn behind the brook, and some sort of new line was taken up roughly along the line of the brook.

It was a critical juncture for the Royalist cause. The least additional pressure and the whole line might crumble and fly. But two things combined to prevent this catastrophe: the exhaustion and shortage of ammunition of their enemies, and the reappearance of their own victorious cavalry on the field.

Prince Rupert has been unrestrainedly condemned by practically every writer for his impetuosity. Gardner even asserts that: 'Little recked Rupert how the battle fared behind him.' Such criticism betrays a lack of appreciation of the difficulties controlling a cavalry charge. Unless the commander rides ahead of the whole line (like the Marquis of Granby at Warburg) he cannot control or direct the charge once it has been launched. The leading ranks can neither see nor hear him; and if he spurs his horse forward in order to get to their head, the ranks he is trying to pass will merely quicken their pace; no horse likes being overtaken by another horse.

There is the further difficulty that, when the charge has spent itself and come to a natural standstill, the troopers are so scattered and disordered, and their horses are so blown and weary that any concerted further movement of an offensive nature is for the time being out of the question. It would have required a large, well-mounted and well-trained staff, which Rupert did not possess, to restore order and cohesion to a body of horse that was in a few brief moments scattered over several square miles of country. It looks so obvious and easy for the 'arm-chair critic' to see what ought to be done by Rupert, but it is so difficult to do it. No one has recorded Rupert's own motions and acts during the period when his horse were absent from the battlefield, but there is no reason to suppose that he did not strive as vigorously (and as unsuccessfully) as Prince Edward under similar circumstances at the battle of Lewes.[1]

Be that as it may, dusk was falling when at length he reappeared on the battlefield with a substantial proportion of his cavalry.[2] Lord

[1] Clarendon draws this striking comparison between the two Princes.

[2] It is significant of the confusion and dispersion, that some of them on return from the left flank, had ridden right round the hostile army.

Falkland at once urged him to engage the enemy once more, but Rupert, though he would have liked to accede, did not do so. His men were either still in no condition, or in no mood for a further fight; they were dead-beat—the reaction of inertia that overtakes most of the actors on the battlefield at the close of a hard-fought day was too much for them. The martial flame was now only flickering in their breasts and their bodies called out for repose.

Nor was this flame burning with a brighter light in the ranks of the Parliamentarians. The truth is that both sides were utterly exhausted. Silence descended with the dusk upon the scene. Both sides, new to warfare alike, had had their fill; they were licking their wounds. It is even probable that soldiers from each army stole down to the brook and tacitly shared its thirst-quenching water—just as did our men and the French at the brook of Talavera. The stout-hearted King was urged to abandon the position in the night, but declined to do so. Indeed, he himself spent the night at the foot of the hill.[1]

The battle was, in fact, over, and history has rejected the claims of both sides to victory, declaring it a drawn battle. I make bold to challenge this judgment of history, late in the day though it be. When two armies engage in battle each has an object in view. When one of them achieves its object while the other fails in it, there can be no doubt which side can claim the victory. What was the King's object? To shake off the pursuit of the Roundhead army. What was Essex's object? To prevent the Royalist army getting to London.

Now the upshot of this battle was that Essex, so far from holding his opponents from London, himself retired to Warwick, in the opposite direction, where he remained several days. On the other hand, the King, having held his ground next day in case his opponents should desire to renew the battle (they had received 4,000 reinforcements and guns) quietly resumed his march on London unmolested, and a week later entered Oxford in triumph. The battle of Edgehill was a victory for the King.

But it was the worst fought fight in our history.

PROBLEMS OF THE BATTLEFIELD

Though from the indications given in the above narrative the locality of the fighting seems fairly precise, it is a curious fact that none of the standard modern accounts present the line of battle with real

[1] At what is now called King's Leys Barn.

precision, and there seems a general tendency to place it too far to the north. This lack of precision may be partly due to the fact that the face of the field has changed in at least two ways. Some spinneys and furzy ground have disappeared and new spinneys have been planted. The chief of these are Battleton Holt, the Oaks and Graveground Coppice, and the little spinney 200 yards to the east of it, probably Watts Bushes. Graveground Coppice, as its name implies, marks the approximate site of one of the two main grave-pits. (The precise spot is 30 yards east of the coppice and 120 yards from the road. It is still faintly visible.) The Coppice site is vouched for by the Reverend George Miller, writing in 1890 in the *Illustrated Naval and Military Magazine*; and it was confirmed to me by an inhabitant when I visited the field a few years ago. The second grave-pit is just outside the little spinney. Writing of the hedge between the two farms, Miller says: 'The carnage must here have been great, as we see by the amount of relics that have lately been turned up in front of the hedgerow in a plantation, once called the Little Graveyard, just behind the spot that is still called the "Grave".' (p. 225). Referring to the King's right centre, he writes: 'One of the graves, that of the officers, was dug near by.' Finally, on page 228: 'The dead were buried on the field of battle in two graves, one near the hedgerow, and the other one field from the brook on the Kineton side, and one field from the old turnpike gate—this was the officers' grave. . . .' These three extracts are somewhat puzzling and conflicting, but present-day tradition points to two grave-pits approximately where shown on my Sketch-map 36 as B and C. Grave B can still be only faintly discerned. Grave C more easily.

The hedgerow still exists and borders the track between the two farms.

Writing in 1893, C. J. Ribton-Turner in *Shakespeare's Land*, gives more specific details. Unfortunately he gives no authorities for his statements. He writes as follows:

'In the fields round the Battle and Thistle Farms, and especially in one on Battle Farm, called the Lower Bladon, sloping towards Kineton, large numbers of bullets have been discovered. A few yards onwards on the left we arrive at a large coppice termed the Little Graveground, in which 500 of the slain were interred. In the centre of the field which succeeds this coppice on the left of the road, is a wych-elm which marks the site of the Great Graveground, where some 800 of the dead were buried. . . . The grass here is of a deeper emerald green than in the surrounding part. . . . About 400 yards to the east of the wych-elm in the upper corner of a field on Radway Grounds Farm adjoining Watts Bushes are the stumps of an oak and a fir-tree, which mark the grave of Captain Kingsmill. . . . In the field on the right of the road about 80 yards from the hedge is a small mound which marks another spot where a few of the dead are interred.' (*A* on Sketch-map 36).

Mr. Ribton-Turner also states that two cannon-balls of 28 lbs. each used to be preserved at Thistle Farm, which 'seem to have been fired from some foreign ordnance, as they do not fit any known form of English cannon.' These no doubt were fired from the King's heavy ordnance. It would be interesting to know what has become of these cannon-balls.

At least four traditional sites were marked by Mr. Sanderson Miller, owner of Radway Grange in the mid-eighteenth century. They are: the site of the King's standard during the battle, marked by a raised mound and a circle of trees just to the east of the Radway— Kineton road, to the west of the village (see Sketch-map 35). At this point the King took up his stand. This does not mean that he or the standard remained there throughout the battle. Far from it. At a critical moment Sir Edmund Verney bore the standard forward, and at the moment of its capture I estimate it must have been not far from Battle Holt. Indeed the one visible monument on the battlefield stands here, and misleads most visitors (it misled me), for the inscription on it shows that it was erected in memory of an officer who was killed there in the nineties, while riding in a point-to-point. Miller's second memorial is the tower on the centre of the ridge, erected to mark the spot where the King's standard was raised *before* the battle. His third memorial consisted of the clump of trees in the form of a crown already referred to, on the ridge-top at Knowle End. It was a few yards to the east of the road, but it is obscured by the plantation that now covers the whole ridge. His fourth and last memorial was a small spinney at King's Leys Barn, to mark the spot where the King spent the night after the battle. It was cut down in the 1860's.

The only other identification that need be mentioned is Lower Westcote Farm, around which numerous cannon-balls and bullets have been dug up, showing that the Royalist left wing was pressed back at least as far as this farm.

It is unfortunate that the Rev. George Miller (a descendant of Sanderson Miller) was content to record the relics so vaguely. But there are no grounds for doubting his statements, for they are consistent with surviving local tradition, and with what we know of the general course of the battle. Indeed, putting all the available evidence together, I feel as certain of the accuracy of my sketch-maps as of almost any battlefield described in this book. But it is to be hoped that some of the key points will one day be clearly marked before local tradition dies—as it seems for obvious reasons fated to do.[1]

[1] Gravel pit B has since been marked with a stone.

CHAPTER XXVIII

The Battle of Lansdown, 5 July 1643

NO two battles are alike. Certainly no battle that I have ever heard of contains the most striking feature of the battle of Lansdown, fought between the Royalists under Sir Ralph Hopton and the Marquis of Hertford, against the Roundheads under Sir William Waller. Of what other old-time battle can it be said that the cavalry attacked in the centre and the infantry on the wings?

In the summer of 1643 things were going well for the Royalist cause in the West. For this they had largely to thank the fighting qualities of the Cornish infantry and the inspiring leadership of Hopton. Following on a brilliant victory at Stratton, he had cleared Cornwall of the rebels and shortly afterwards all rural Devonshire was in his hands. Pushing east he reached Chard early in June, where he was joined by a strong force of cavalry with a few infantry under the command of the Marquis of Hertford and Prince Maurice, brother of Prince Rupert. This raised his army to over 7,000 and enabled the combined army to advance resolutely towards Bath where Sir William Waller was gathering a fresh army for the defence of the West Country.

Prospects looked promising. The only fly in the ointment was that Many of the latter were freshly raised for the most part and their discipline was lax; they were arrant plunderers, Hertford had little control over them and young Prince Maurice was believed secretly to encourage their pillaging proclivities. This was very different from the habits of the Cornishmen, on whom Hopton had imposed a strict discipline, and among whom plundering was almost though not completely unknown.

However, open dissension did not break out and the combined army advanced with little opposition, via Wells, Frome, and Bradford-on-Avon to join issue with the defenders of Bath. This town is bounded on its southern side by the River Avon, a deep and sluggish stream. It was decided to outflank it from the east. From Bradford therefore the Cavaliers advanced north to Monkton Farleigh. But though his communications with London were thus threatened, if not cut, Waller did not budge. After an ineffectual skirmish on 3 July the Cavaliers decided to continue their turning movement. Next day therefore they pushed on to a point 6 miles north-east of Bath. Waller now sensed that their intention was to attack Bath from the north, which would give them the commanding ground of Lansdown Hill and would avoid the necessity of crossing the Avon. In order to forestall this threat Waller was obliged to move out of Bath and occupy Lansdown Hill himself. Thus we have the two armies marching roughly parallel in a northerly direction on 4 July. By evening, whilst a certain amount of bickering went on between the horse on each side, Hopton, who had been placed in command for this operation, halted for the night at Marshfield, while Waller halted on the northern edge of Lansdown Hill, nearly 5 miles north of the city.

THE COMMANDERS

So far so good for the Royalists. Next morning, 5 July, their army turned to its left and marched straight towards Lansdown Hill, with every intention of engaging the Parliamentary army if it would stand. But before following its progress we must inquire as to the system of command in the Royalist host. Who was in actual command? Hopton, to whom we owe what may be called the official Royalist account, is silent on the point. Historians slur over the question, apparently assuming that Hopton was in command, but without stating their reasons. But the matter merits discussion. The fact seems to be that Hertford's army joined that of Hopton without any written or expressed directive on this essential point from the King who seems to have been content that it should be commanded by Committee. Right through the Civil War there was a marked tendency on both sides to ignore the importance of a single commander. This was especially marked in the case of the Roundheads at Second Newbury and of the Cavaliers in this campaign. The system of the high command seems to have been extremely vague and sketchy, but a careful reading of Clarendon gives at least some pointers as to the true position. The first matter to decide is who was the senior, Prince Maurice or Hertford? According to Clarendon the King originally placed Hertford in command of the reinforcements for the West, but later he says that the Prince was to be 'disposed into a command of that army', but he makes it appear that Maurice's post was really second in command under the Marquis.

Who was to be the supreme commander, when the two armies joined? Here the evidence is conflicting—Clarendon says that the

Marquis was 'thought only fit to have the supreme power over those western counties where his fortune lay'. Moreover, the capture of Taunton and Bridgwater is ascribed to Hertford. This sounds clear and unequivocal, but when we come to the events of the battle, Hertford's name disappears from the picture, and though Clarendon makes no more direct allusion to the supreme command, Colonel Slingsby, in his account, writes of the march on 4 July, 'The chief commanders resolved of a retreat towards Marshfield and committed the order of it to Sir Ralph Hopton.' That is clear enough, but who commanded in the actual battle on the following day? Here there is complete silence. Hopton himself merely says 'The chief commanders of the King's army' carried out such and such manoevures. This looks as if the battle was fought by a committee, and so it may have been, in theory. But on the morning after the battle Hopton is reported by Slingsby as riding about seeing to the wounded, and generally straightening up affairs. By this time the Marquis's name has completely faded out of the accounts and the probability is that he had gradually receded into the background, recognizing the superior military abilities and experience of Hopton and appreciating the hold he had over the Cornish foot who formed the majority of the whole army. My conclusion is thus that Sir Ralph Hopton was the *de facto* commander in the battle of Lansdown.

It is time therefore to say a word about this remarkable soldier. Sir Ralph Hopton was a Somersetshire man aged forty-five at the time of the battle. He had received his baptism of fire under the Elector Palatine in the Thirty Years War, as had a few others of the leading Cavaliers. Early in the Civil war he raised the army of Cornishmen that afterwards became so famous, and showed here both his power of organization and of leadership. His men were devoted to him; indeed Clarendon says crisply that he was 'indeed the soldiers' darling', and he elsewhere describes him as a man of the highest integrity. It is one of the unavoidable tragedies of civil war that friends find themselves on opposite sides. It happened that Sir Ralph Hopton and Sir William Waller were old friends, and during the campaign affecting letters of friendship passed between the two commanders. Indeed I have a feeling that Waller delayed making a direct assault on Devizes a few days after the battle from the knowledge that his old friend was lying within the town desperately wounded. Waller himself was one of the best Parliamentary generals. He is generously described by Colonel Slingsby as 'the best shifter and chooser of ground when he was not master of the field that ever I saw'. The two generals were worthy antagonists.

JULY 5TH

The early stages of the day's proceedings involved some rather complicated evolutions, interesting in their own way but having no bearing on the battle itself. We can therefore skim over them lightly.

When day broke the mass of the Parliamentary army was drawn up on the brow of Lansdown Hill, while the Cavaliers were billeted at Marshfield, 5 miles away. Rather more than halfway from Marsh-field lies Tog Hill, the road running along a ridge to it all the way. At Tog Hill both ridge and road turn to the left for a mile, ending in the eminence known as Freezing Hill. Here the road dips into the valley, thence to ascend Lansdown Hill.

Early in the morning the Cavaliers set out on their advance towards Bath, and contacted the enemy horse on Tog Hill. Here there was some bickering, while the full strength of the hostile position on the opposite hill could be seen. Hopton was averse to attacking this hill and as the bickering was causing the expenditure of more ammunition than he liked (for it was already scarce), he favoured abandoning the enterprise, and resuming the march to Oxford, which had always been one of his objectives.

This move could not be concealed from the enemy, and Waller was prompt to react. He sent out a body of horse to harry the flank and rear of the retreating Cavaliers. This resulted in a scrap near Cold Ashton, in which the Roundheads were at first successful; but the steadiness of the Cornish infantry finally prevailed. It was now the turn of the Roundheads to fall back and in doing so they were hotly pursued. The Cornish men, seeing the line of cannons drawn up on the opposite height, clamoured to be allowed to 'fetch off those cannon'. Such was their ardour and confidence that Hopton gave way (whether reluctantly or not he does not say), and ordered a general attack on the hostile position. This position must now be described.

THE TERRAIN

Unlike most of our battles there is not a scintilla of doubt as to the spot on which the battle was fought: such is the clarity of the various witnesses that almost every incident recorded can be pin-pointed to within a hundred yards or so. Moreover, the ground is so clearly marked on the one-inch O.S. map that a special sketch-map to illustrate this battle can be dispensed with.

The long flat-topped Lansdown Hill runs for nearly 4 miles north by west from Bath, ending suddenly in a steep escarpment with a drop of 150 to 200 feet. Just on the right of the road at the top of this escarpment is a tall obelisk erected to the memory of Sir Bevill Grenvile, the commander of the Cornish foot. This monument marks the centre of the position, and the approximate centre of the breastwork that had been erected the previous evening, along which the seven Parliamentary cannons were posted. The road descends the hill diagonally to the right, after which it ascends Freezing Hill and so on to Tog Hill. The escarpment is covered with a belt of trees on both sides of the road, but at the time of the battle it is probable that they were only thinly scattered in the immediate vicinity of the road, but further to each flank were copses (as there still are to-day). The surrounding country was for the most part unenclosed, but there was a long stone wall 'half a culverin shot' in rear of the breastwork. There is to-day such a stone wall about 400 yards in rear which is almost certainly the wall in question. And that is all the reader requires to know in order to follow intelligently the course of the battle.

THE BATTLE

The Royalist leaders, after some show of hesitation, resolved to accept the challenge so obviously thrown out to them, but it was well on in the afternoon when the Cavaliers advanced to assault the formidable looking position directly in their front. As seen from Freezing Hill (which must have been the Royalist command post), a breastwork astride the road at the summit of the hill appeared to mark the centre of the position, but its flanks could not be exactly determined owing to the above-mentioned woods to right and left. No account states where precisely the flanks did rest, but as Waller sent musketeers forward into both woods to move down the hill under cover of the undergrowth we can take it that both woods were for all practical purposes occupied for their full extent.

Hopton's intention was, in his own words, to send out 'strong parties of musketeers on each hand, to second one another to endeavour under cover of the enclosed grounds to gain the flank of the enemy on the top of the hill'. In short, to turn the enemy's flank, a task generally entrusted to the cavalry, and we may wonder, in passing, why a wider turning movement by the horse was not made. Up the central space marked by the road Hopton sent the Cornish pikemen under their beloved and redoubtable commander, Sir Bevill Grenvile. How then should the cavalry be used? or should they not be used at all but kept in reserve for the pursuit? A tame compromise was resorted to, symptomatic of Hopton's low regard for the fighting qualities of Prince Maurice's horse. They were sent up the hill after the pikemen and slightly to their right, in the fairly open space between the two woods. Thus we see a strange reversal of the normal battle order— for that or for almost any other period. Here we have the musketeers on the flanks and the cavalry in the centre. (Sir Thomas Fairfax adopted much the same dispositions at Nantwich).

The musketeers on the flanks secured entry into the woods without much difficulty, but in the centre pikes and horse received the plunging fire of the guns as they crossed the dip and began to ascend the steep hill. The picture is graphically described by an officer of horse in the Royalist army, in his delightful and informative *The Vindication of Richard Atkyns*. This little book, published in 1667 and never republished, deserves quotation. Signs that the enemy was flying induced Colonel Sir Robert Welsh to 'importunately request the Prince to have a party to follow the chace, which he gave him the command of and me the reserve. . . . As I went up the hill, which was very steep and hollow, I met several dead and wounded officers brought off, besides many running away, that I had much ado to get by them. When I came to the top of the hill, I saw Sir Bevill Grenville's stand of pikes which certainly preserved our army from a total rout, with the loss of his most precious life. They stood as upon the eaves of a house for steepness but as unmovable as a rock. On which side of their stand of pikes our horse were I could not discover for the air was so darkened by the smoak of the powder that for a quarter of an hour together (I dare say) there was no light seen, but what the fire of the volleys of shot gave.'

Atkyn's horse was severely wounded but 'did me the service' of carrying him to the rear where he obtained another mount.[1]

Meanwhile the Royalist musketeers were making steady progress through the woods, and eventually the crest of the hill was attained

---

[1] His tribute to the Cornish pikemen is worded almost precisely the same as the French tribute to the famous British square at Fontenoy which 'was a rock that could not be mined'.

all along the line. But at terrible cost. The cavalry in particular practically melted away. Hopton himself admits that at the end of the day 'of 2,000 horse there did not stand above 600'. This does not mean that the remainder were killed or wounded as some accounts would seem to imply. Then what did happen to them? Clarendon in his *Great Rebellion* is quite candid about it. They ran away. Some did not draw rein till they reached Oxford where they, as Clarendon truly and shrewdly puts it, 'according to the custom of those who run away, reported all to be lost, with many particular accidents which they fancied very like to happen when they left the field'. So much for Maurice's cavalry.

The sheer fighting qualities of the Cornishmen had accomplished the seemingly impossible. The position was captured and the Roundheads fell back to the shelter of a lateral stone wall about 400 yards in rear. This they loopholed and manned with their guns, all of which they managed, somewhat surprisingly, to withdraw. There was every sign that the next stage of the battle would begin. But nothing happened. The Royalist cavalry who might have been used to advantage to outflank the wall had been frittered away in that preposterous assault in the centre. The infantry were exhausted by their arduous climb; the guns were short of ammunition (though they did get to the top of the hill). Thus both sides sat and glared at each other as darkness fell.

Both armies were in an unenviable position, especially the Cavaliers. Except on the right, where they had crept forward into some pits that still exist, they were perched on the very edge of the hill, 'like a stone hanging on the edge of a precipice' as one eyewitness put it; the momentum of the attack had died out, the casualties had been almost crippling, ammunition was scarce, extreme fatigue pervaded the ranks after a long day of marching, counter-marching and fighting, and deep gloom had descended over the Cornishmen at the death of their commander. A single push, it would seem, should be sufficient to send the whole army rolling helplessly to the bottom of the hill.

But the aspect of things is so different when viewed from 'the other side of the hill'. Waller too had his difficulties, which seemed great to him, but which in reality were much less than those of his opponents. So far from counter-attacking, he was contemplating a retreat to within the walls of Bath. Both sides, in short, were played out. That deadening condition of mind and body, what I call *lassitudo certaminis*, which always supervenes on the evening of a hard-fought battle, had done its work—on both sides. Each was thinking only of being left in peace. It is in situations such as this that the mark of a great general becomes apparent. Which man, Sir Ralph Hopton or his friend, Sir William Waller, would show that supreme quality (so strikingly displayed by General R. E. Lee on the evening of Sharpsburg) of 'sticking it out'? In the upshot it turned out to be the general who had the greater excuse to retreat who held his ground, and the other who abandoned it. The Cavaliers held their ground, the Roundheads retreated.

During the night they crept silently away and took refuge within the welcome walls of Bath.

*   *   *   *   *

EPILOGUE

The Royalist general, by preserving a stiff upper lip, had wrested victory from what had threatened to be disaster. But the course of war is unpredictable. Early next morning Fortune struck the Cavaliers a double blow which completely reversed the strategical situation. Let Richard Atkyns tell the story in his own inimitable way:

'Major Cheldon and myself went towards the Lord Hopton who was then viewing the prisoners taken, some of whom were carried upon a cart whereon was our ammunition, and (as I heard) had matches to light their tobacco. The major desired me to go back to the rear, while he received orders from his lordship. I had no sooner turned my horse and was gone three horse lengths from him but the ammunition was blown up and the three prisoners with it together with the Lord Hopton, Major Cheldon, and Cornet Washnage who were near the cart on horseback, and several others. It made a great noise and darkened the air for a time and the burnt men made lamentable screeches. As soon as the air had cleared I went to see what the matter was. There I found his lordship, miserably burnt, his horse singed like a parched leather, and Thomas Cheldon (that was a horse length further from the blast) complaining that the fire was got within his breeches, which I tore off as soon as I could, and from as long a head of flaxen hair as ever I saw his head was like a Black-Moor . . .'

Sir Ralph Hopton was put into a litter, blind and incapable of motion. Thus suddenly deprived of both its trusted leaders and bereft of almost all its ammunition, the Royalist army with drooping spirits turned its back on Bath and its opponents and resumed its march towards Oxford.

Thus did the fickle goddess of war sport with the victors of Lansdown field.

COMMENTS

In neither the preliminary movements nor in the battle tactics did either commander distinguish himself. It should be remembered that although both men had warlike experience on the Continent in the Thirty Years War, their actual command of troops in the field had been limited; nor does it appear that they had (as Prince Rupert for example had) systematically studied the art of war before they had leadership thrust upon them.

But the most important moment in a battle is the last. Waterloo was won by a last-minute decision of the commander of one side. That moment is the supreme test of generalship, and judged by that test Sir Ralph Hopton is entitled to be considered a great general.

The Cavaliers had shown vacillation in their preliminary motions and faulty judgement in their use of cavalry, and Waller, who had a reputation for an eye for country, had been deceived by the seeming strength of the position which he selected to hold. He did not fully realize the weakness of this position with the dead ground immediately in its front and the weakness of its flanks, which could be approached under cover of the woods.

THE PROBLEM OF THE GUNS

It has been widely surmised that the explanation of the undoubted fact that the Royalist troops, both horse and foot, did climb to the top of the ridge in the teeth of the hostile fire, both musketry and cannons, could be largely explained by the fact that the Parliamentary guns could not reach the enemy ascending the hill because they could not depress their guns sufficiently. I have therefore been at some pains to resolve this problem, and give here the tentative conclusions I have come to. I advisedly say 'tentative' because the data on which to form an opinion is meagre, many of the relevant factors are unknown and indeed unknowable. In any case the problem is a technical one, but since only a few readers will have had an artillery education, I will go into the matter in some detail.

The first thing to do is to ascertain the slope of the hill. Like nearly all hills, it is not uniform, being steepest in the middle and less steep the further up and down you go. Thus we must be content with an average slope, and I calculate that this average slope is about 12 to 15 degrees. Here I must remark that the guns, posted probably along the line of the crest (the very brow of the hill), would find the greater part of the slope in dead ground. Now since indirect fire was practically unknown at that epoch it may be argued that this fact alone is sufficient to explain the matter, without going into ballistical calculations. But this will not quite do. The heads of the horsemen would be visible where the actual ground-line was out of sight (just as Mercer's Troop at Waterloo could see the heads of Ney's cavalry while their bodies were in dead ground). So we must persevere with our calculations.

I have said that the evidence is meagre; this for two reasons. In the first place, the range of two consecutive cannon balls might vary greatly, dependent on their respective 'windage'—the degree in which they fitted the bore of the gun—if the fit was a bad one and the cannon ball rattled loosely down the bore it lost a great deal of range. We do not know of course what degree of windage the Parliamentary ammunition had. In the second place exact ballistical figures for guns of that period do not exist; only a rough computation can be made. I have, however, obtained from the best authority on the subject that I know, the following figures. (It should be understood that the problem is to ascertain at what point in a slope of 12 degrees a cannon *pointed level* would reach, since if it were depressed below the horizontal the ball would roll out of the muzzle before it could be fired.)

The figure arrived at is based on the following assumptions: The gun was a 'drake', weight of shot 6 lbs.; diameter of shot 3·5 inches; muzzle velocity 400 feet per second; ballistic coefficient 0·29. Under such conditions the shot might be expected to strike the slope 180 yards from the gun. Now the slope is about 300 yards long, so the shot might be expected to strike the ground just over half-way down the hill. But the heads and bodies of the infantry and still more the cavalry would be exposed well before that, so we shall be within the mark if we say that they would be exposed to artillery fire for more than half the ascent.

Moreover, when they reached the crest they would be in full view from the guns, firing point-blank for 50 to 60 yards on the crest itself, directly in front of the guns. Here great execution could be done, and indeed one account asserts that it *was* done.

There is a further complication, or at least point to be considered. I have mentioned the road running diagonally up the hill, with a stone wall on its upper side, and said I would refer to it again. Now Gardiner makes much of this wall and of the protection that it afforded. It is incontestable that this wall would afford considerable protection to troops advancing up the road in file or single file, for they could and did hug the wall. But it is not to be supposed, as Gardiner seems to suppose, that the horse advanced up the hill on a frontage of only two men. Their normal formation would be in line three deep, and though they would lose all regular formation scrambling up so steep a hill, their frontage must have been over 100 yards wide so that the wall could only protect a very small proportion of them. Much the same applies to the pikemen. I think it probable that the pikemen had the benefit of the road and that the horse were on the slightly less steep slope immediately to the right of it.

Thus I come to the conclusion that neither the slope in general nor the wall played as great a part in the battle as might be supposed. Lansdown remains a standing example of the fact that to resolute troops no position, however, formidable looking it may be, is impregnable.

CHAPTER XXIX

The Battle of Roundway Down, 13 July 1643

THIS battle took place only eight days after that of Lansdown, described in the last chapter. It will be remembered that on the morning after the battle Sir Ralph Hopton was blinded and crippled by an explosion of powder, and that the army then resumed its march on Oxford. Its route took it through Devizes) (then called The Devizes) and its march was at times harried by Waller's horse, who cut off a few stragglers. The Royalists reached Devizes on 9 July and Waller, who had been reinforced, took up a position on Roundway Down, 3 miles to the north-east of the town and astride the road to Oxford.

Hopton was put to bed in Devizes and so far recovered that he continued to command the army from his sick-bed, though this indomitable soldier could still neither see nor move.

There was no possibility of further retreat from Devizes for the foot; a siege seemed inevitable. In such a situation his cavalry would be wasted, especially as ammunition was so short. Hopton therefore ordered his horse, under Prince Maurice, aged twenty-three, and the Marquis of Hertford to cut their way out, and make for Oxford; on arrival there, they were to ask for reinforcements to be sent to Devizes. By skirting round to the south-east on 10 July, they eluded Waller's troops, and riding all the night they reached Oxford on the morning of the 11th, having covered 44 miles during the night.

Meanwhile disaster had overtaken a convoy of ammunition that was on its way to Devizes from Oxford. Waller had got to hear of it and he sent out a mounted force which succeeded in capturing every wagon. Thus the garrison were almost 'on their beam ends', for ammunition was all but spent; the supply of match was also nearly exhausted and early capitulation seemed inevitable. But the dauntless spirit of Sir Ralph rose superior to the emergency; he had a search made through the town for bed-cords, which when collected were boiled in resin. By this means he managed to secure 15 cwt. of match; the crisis was averted. In addition King Charles had taken prompt action. Lord Wilmot was despatched from Oxford with a fresh force of cavalry, 1,500 strong. Prince Maurice and a few of his party accompanied it as volunteers. The force was despatched on the very day that Maurice had arrived, the 11th. About forty-eight hours later it was nearing the besieged town, marching along the old Bath road. On the evening of that day Waller had decided to assault the town. As a preliminary he subjected it to a heavy bombardment from the hill 600 yards to the east. Part of this bombardment was deliberately aimed at St. John's church, and pretty good practice was made.[1]

Devizes Castle was manned with cannon, but the town had no other defences, and only hasty barricades were thrown up. But Hopton hoped to be able to hold out long enough to allow of reinforcements arriving. This he calculated would not be for a few days, so he was pleasantly surprised on the afternoon of the 13th to receive the welcome news that Wilmot and Maurice were on their way. They were accompanied by 'two small field-pieces'. For these to have kept up with the horse, as they did, shows to what a degree of mobility the light artillery of the Royalist army had attained. Wilmot had arranged that when he drew near he would fire off both cannon, as a signal to notify the garrison of his approach.

An interesting situation was developing. Let us examine it. In the town were perhaps 2,000 Royalist foot. Approaching from the north-east were 1,800 Royalist horse. In between the two was the Roundhead army, consisting of nearly 3,000 foot and 2,000 horse, with 8 field guns. Thus the Roundheads heavily outnumbered each of their opponents, and the only chance for the latter would seem to rest in a combined attack. Wilmot evidently realized this, and hoped for assistance. Unfortunately the messenger with this plan seems to have been captured, and though the signal guns were heard (a surprising fact at 4 miles range, unless the wind was north-east) it was suspected in the town that the withdrawal of the besieging army was a ruse to entice them out of the town. This, at least, is the explanation given by both Hopton and Clarendon, though it does not seem very convincing. Waller had indeed drawn off his army to confront the new opponent, and if Hopton was aware of the approach of Wilmot, his right course was to join in the battle, ruse or no ruse.

Hopton, with his soldierly instinct, saw this, and tried to convince his council of officers whom he had summoned to his sick chamber. But there was a majority of opinion averse to this course. Now it is difficult to lead an army from a sick-bed and in his physical state the wounded commander may not have exerted the same forcefulness in the council as he would have done had he still been in vigorous health.

[1] The pattern of 'grazes' on the church tower made by the cannon balls can still be seen. No less than 14 of them are enclosed in a space of 2 feet square.

At any rate, he did not feel equal to ordering his subordinates against their will to ride out to battle while he stayed behind; he acceded to the opinion of the majority, and the army remained inactive.

Thus Wilmot was left with his 1,800 horse to face an army roughly thrice his own strength. For Waller had left only a few guards for the heavy guns and wagons, and with the remainder of his army he had ascended the hill on to the top of Roundway Down.

There are, as usual, conflicting views as to the precise site of the

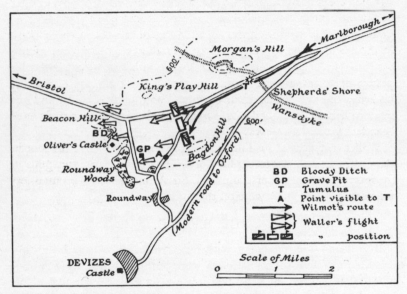

SKETCH-MAP 37.   ROUNDWAY DOWN: THE BATTLE

battlefield, and I deal with them in the end section. The course of events, as I reconstruct them, was as follows:

The road from Oxford and Swindon to Devizes did not take its present course via Shepherds Shore, 4 miles from Devizes, but left it 2 miles further on (see sketch-map). It crossed Wansdyke 500 yards to the north-west of Shepherds Shore. This spot is a point of great archaeological interest. It is marked by a tumulus, and was evidently the junction of two sections of Wansdyke. From this point the track runs west-south-west for 2,000 yards and then bends to its left, and makes straight for Devizes. When Waller, having ridden up to the top of the hill, reached A on the sketch-map, he saw the Royalist horse approaching direct from the tumulus, which is visible from this spot, and is marked by a clump of trees. In front of him was a wide plain in the shape of a shallow valley, with gentle slopes to north and south—a beautiful arena for a battle. Its breadth is about 1,500 yards. The hill to the south is marked Roundway Hill on the O.S. map, but at that time it was called Bagdon Hill. The hill to the north is called Kings Play Hill. In this shallow valley, then, Sir William Waller decided to offer battle to the oncoming foe.

From the tumulus, just 2 miles from Point A, Wilmot would catch sight of the leading men of Waller's army appearing over the brow of the hill; and it was probably at this point that he brought his two guns into action and fired the approach signal. He then proceeded to form up and deploy his tiny army. Observing that Waller was doing the same, he had no need of speed. Delay, rather than speed, was his policy for the moment; for time was required for Hopton to marshal his army and march out of the town and up the hill. At least an hour must have been consumed in this fashion, and the afternoon must have been far spent when all was ready.

Waller had formed his line in the conventional fashion, his foot in the centre, astride the track, his horse on the two wings, his guns in the intervals between horse and foot. Sir Arthur Hazelrig's cuirassiers (nicknamed 'Lobsters') were on the right.

THE BATTLE

Clarendon[1] gives a fairly vivid picture of the opening of the engagement, but all cavalry actions involve confusion, and Clarendon was not an eye-witness. What probably happened was that Wilmot's men came sweeping impetuously up the very slight slope, in two bodies. Seeing the hostile foot in the centre and the horse on the wings, they no doubt instinctively headed for their mounted opponents, as being those best fitted for their steel. Thus the battle was joined on the two wings while the main body of Roundhead infantry in the centre had the remarkable experience of having no one to engage and nothing to do but to gape at the cavalry charges on each side of them. Hazelrig's 'Lobsters' were literally, not only metaphorically, a 'tough nut to crack', for their armour was something of a novelty, and it was for the most part sword-proof. Clarendon fittingly describes Hazelrig's regiment as 'that impenetrable regiment', and Wilmot's men, in spite of their speed and *élan*, took the best part of half an hour to dispose of them.

[1] There is also, in the B.M., a manuscript account, detailed and rather involved, by Sir John Byron, who commanded Wilmot's second line of horse.

There were constant charges and countercharges. In the course of the fray four of the Roundhead guns were captured, and turned against their own side. This was all the fire the infantry had to encounter, but they must have been prevented from firing into the mêlée on each side of them for fear of hitting their own people.

At the end of about thirty minutes the issue was decided, the Roundhead cavalry turned and fled from the field, hotly pursued by the triumphant and exultant Cavaliers. Instead of retreating on the line on which they had approached the field, the bulk of the fleeing troopers took a westerly direction. The natural inference is that some of Wilmot's troops had swept over Bagdon Hill and prevented flight in that direction.

However that may be, the ground on the actual line of their flight sloped upwards very gently and with perfect uniformity. It is beautiful cavalry country, and being unhedged, offered ideal ground for shock action.

After retreating in this direction for 2,500 yards, with their pursuers thundering behind them, they, to their horror, saw suddenly appearing in their front a huge semi-precipitous slope with a drop of about 300 feet. (The drawing will show that the adjective is deserved.) There was no pulling up, the enemy being on their heels. They were indeed 'twixt devil and deep sea'. Down the hill they stumbled and tumbled and rolled willy-nilly—a hill 'where never horse went down or up before'.

The bottom of the hill became a shambles. A ditch marks its foot, and it is now known as 'Bloody Ditch'.

Waller's cavalry was utterly liquidated, and Waller himself escaped with difficulty. But in their impetuosity some of the pursuers could not pull up their horses in time and shared the fate that overtook their adversaries. Never can quite such a dramatic and harrowing scene have been witnessed on an English battlefield. The Roundheads no doubt fanned out in the course of their flight: some would strike the 'precipice' by Beacon Hill, some by Oliver's castle, and some in Roundway Woods (see sketch-map).

Meanwhile the Parliamentary foot, after witnessing the downfall and destruction of their own horse, had been left on the position intact and unmolested. And there they stood motionless, alone on what a few minutes ago had been a bloody battlefield. What were they to do? For some time they did nothing; they just stood where they were, no doubt somewhat dazed by this remarkable experience.

BLOODY DITCH

ROUNDWAY DOWN: BEACON HILL FROM OLIVER'S CASTLE

We must now return to the other portion of the Royalist forces—Hopton's army. Hearing the sounds of battle, and probably by this time receiving definite messages from Wilmot, Hopton had no further difficulty in securing agreement for an advance. The army was assembled rapidly and marched out up the hill, meeting with no opposition on the way. On reaching the top, they could see the Roundhead infantry drawn up in a body about 1,000 yards away, while isolated bodies of Wilmot's horse were beginning to come back from the pursuit and to engage the hostile foot. Wilmot had managed to collect the majority of his troops on the brow of the hill, with a view to launching an attack on what remained of Waller's army. But he showed admirable coolness. He reckoned that Hopton's Cornish infantry must be on their way; a concerted attack on the still formidable foe was indicated. There was therefore no immediate call for haste. Quietly he collected and marshalled his disordered ranks and not till he saw the Cornishmen on the hill-top and about to engage, did he launch a concerted attack. Then the unfortunate Roundhead infantry faced the fate that had overtaken their own horse. Attacked by the fresh Cornishmen from the south, charged by Wilmot's elated horsemen from the north, their guns captured, their commander missing, the Londoners were quickly overwhelmed. Over 600 were killed; the remainder were captured; scarce a man got away. Waller's army had been wiped out by an inferior force as completely as any army in the whole course of our civil wars. It was the most sweeping victory the Royalists ever won.

COMMENTS

I hope the reader will now agree with my assessment that the battle of Roundway Down was 'easily the most dramatic of the whole of the Civil War'. One might add that it was one of the most interesting strategically; for it involved a situation on 'exterior lines'. It is an illustration of the inherent difficulty of ensuring and co-ordinating the two attacks by the side holding the exterior position. Unless this co-ordination be effected the advantage lies with the enemy who is on interior lines. The Royalists were in the exterior position, and they did not succeed in launching a simultaneous attack at the outset. Moreover, they were numerically inferior, even when combined. How then, the student of military history may well ask, do I account for the victory of the Royalists? This question brings out another cardinal feature of war—the power of morale. Hopton's army had won a series of victories against Waller (for Lansdown must be included as a victory) and their morale was consequently in the ascendant. The cavalry, apart from being comparatively fresh, still were imbued by that almost contemptuous feeling of superiority over their opponents that they had shown at Edgehill. The war was still only in its first year, and the Roundhead cavalry, outside the Eastern counties, had little to be proud of. Then we must remember that it was only the Parliamentary horse that was defeated by the Royalist horse; the downfall of the foot was achieved by joint action on tactically exterior lines—Wilmot's horse from the north combining with the Cornish foot from the south. If, as it appears, Wilmot deliberately delayed his attack on the foot till the Cornishmen arrived, he was ensuring that coordination and simultaneity of attack which, as we have seen, is essential, besides being so difficult to achieve, in such a situation. Wilmot also showed sound instinct (if indeed it was his deliberate action) in avoiding contact with the infantry in his first attack. In so doing he brought about a situation which has scarcely a parallel in battle, that of the two wings engaging, and the main body of the defenders being left with no opponents in their front. No wonder they were slightly puzzled by this novel and unlooked-for situation, and stood irresolute and inactive, even after the cavalry had swept past them.

This brings our attention to Sir William Waller. What was the Parliamentary commander doing while his horse were being dispersed and his foot were standing disengaged? History does not tell. Sir William afterwards wrote about the battle, but apart from blaming the Earl of Essex for not coming to his assistance, he does not indicate the reason for the disaster nor his own movements in any detail. There can scarce have been a battle in which we know so little about the doings of the commander of the defeated side. He probably fled with his cavalry, he certainly must have made off in that direction, and he did not stop till he reached Bristol, 30 miles distant, where he was the first to bring the tidings of his own defeat. Bad news travels fast; Waller travelled even faster. He afterwards proved himself quite a good general; Roundway Down was his worst day. For his opposite number, Lord Wilmot, we can have nothing but praise. His conduct at Edgehill had not been convincing, to say the least, and it is possible that in this later battle he was inspired and urged on by Prince Maurice, of whom we know all too little.

It is interesting to speculate as to what course the battle would have taken had Sir Ralph Hopton been in the saddle. It is natural to suppose that he would have had his own way at the council, and that his infantry would have joined in the battle simultaneously with, or very shortly after Wilmot's attack. The result could hardly have been more decisive than it actually was, but it might have been over quicker. That is all that can be said. One can picture and feel for the pent-up excitement of the general, lying powerless and sightless in bed, within earshot of the battle.

PROBLEMS OF THE BATTLEFIELD

The chief problem is to locate the precise battlefield. Let us start by tabulating the relevant factors. First we will take place-names. The earliest name for the battle, given it shortly afterwards, was the 'fight on Bagdon Hill'. Now this hill was identified by J. Waylen in his *History of Devizes* (1859)[1] as Beacon Hill (see sketch-map), and his view has since been accepted by others. But Speed's map (1610) shows it as the hill now called Roundway Hill on the one-inch and six-inch O.S. maps. Another map of 1773 (two inches to one mile) also shows Bagdon Hill in the same place. The first Roundhead report (Thomason Tract E 61 (6) states ' . . . which made us draw up to Bagnall Hill' (evidently Bagdon Hill: the writer had just reached Bristol from the battlefield and would not be likely to have a map with him). To 'draw up' to Beacon Hill from their headquarters at Roundway village would have taken them not towards the oncoming Royalists but at right angles to them, but the present Roundway Hill would just meet the case. The only other place-name that helps is Bloody Ditch to which I have already referred. Kings Play Hill can have no significance.

As for relics, a grave-pit in the form of a trench 30 feet long at G.P. on the sketch-map, was many years ago partially excavated by Captain B. H. Cunnington, Hon. Curator of Devizes Museum. He informed me that he disclosed, one foot below the surface, about twelve skeletons laid lengthways but irregularly. They had evidently been stripped before burial, a sure sign that they were battle casualties. Some other skeletons have been found in a chalk-pit on the slopes of Bagdon Hill. Bullets have been dug up on the southern slopes of Kings Play Hill.

If we put all the above facts together there can be no doubt but

[1] Published anonymously and incorrectly attributed to H. Bull in the B.M. copy.

that the battle was fought on the top of Roundway Down, and that the direction of the flight was over Beacon Hill and Oliver's Castle.

To pinpoint the actual position taken up by Waller we must once again apply the touchstone of Inherent Military Probability. If we accept the course that operations took up to the point where Waller discerned Wilmot's approach, the former being at A and the latter at the tumulus 'T', with a road or track joining the two points, the natural course for the Parliamentary commander to take would be to form line astride this track, facing the oncoming enemy. If he formed this line on the spot on which he was then standing, the right wing would find itself on a sharp slope (Bagdon Hill), but by pushing forward about 700 yards he would find room to deploy his army on each side of the track on fairly level ground. Here then, in all probability, Waller drew up his army. I calculate that the foot stretched about 400 yards on each side of the track and that the horse extended this line about 300 yards on each flank. Thus the total frontage was about 1,500 yards, which would just about fill the level plain, having Bagdon Hill on the right flank and Kings Play Hill on the left. My sketch-map so shows it. The crossed sabres sign on the one-inch O.S. map is about 300 yards to the west of this line.[1]

A minor problem is how to account for the apparently great disparity between the speed of Prince Maurice's march to Oxford and that of Wilmot in the opposite direction? Exact timings are not available, but Maurice's march cannot have taken much more than twelve hours, for he started out in the dark, which in July cannot have been earlier than 9 p.m., and reached Oxford next morning. Wilmot left Oxford the same day, presumably in the afternoon, and reached the battlefield (4 miles shorter than Maurice's march) at 4 p.m. two days later, say forty-eight hours. Partly this disparity can be accounted for by the fact that Maurice's arrival in the morning does not mean more than himself and the leading troops of his column. We are told that the column was greatly strung out; Maurice probably rode furiously on a well-bred horse, or horses, leaving 'the devil to take the hindmost'. In the second place those members of Wilmot's column who

[1] In an article in the *Wiltshire Archaeological Magazine*, Vol. 53, Mr. John Prest places the Roundheads on the very top of Bagdon Hill, and on a front of only 650 yards. Apart from the fact that it does not seem in accordance with I.M.P. to occupy a position on a narrow hill-top that does not cover the road by which the enemy were approaching, horsemen retreating from such a position would have been swept down the hill towards Devizes, instead of towards Bloody Ditch.

had just come from Devizes would be tired, man and horse, and he would have to suit his pace to theirs, for it would not do to arrive piecemeal in front of the beleaguered town. But there may be a third explanation hidden away in an obscure passage in a Thomason Tract (E 60 (12)). This tract is listed as relating to the battle of Lansdown. So it does, but it carries on the story up to the eve of the battle of Roundway Down, and ends as follows, the date being either 11 or 12 July. 'The like, a gentleman of my Lord Wilmot reported, who was come within five miles of the Devizes to the aid of the Marquis [Hertford] by five of the clock that morning, and hearing the taking of the ammunition [the capture of the convoy] and of the Marquis of Hertford retiring . . . towards Oxford, was retired with his four regiments and come within a mile of Hungerford by eight of the clock.' Now this is a remarkable statement, if true, for according to all accounts Wilmot was in Oxford on the 11th. Moreover, Hungerford would not be on his direct route towards Oxford from Devizes. The story cannot be exactly correct, but if on the morning of the 12th Wilmot with his leading troops got within 5 miles of Devizes it points to the fact that his own movements were as rapid as those of Maurice and Hertford in the opposite direction, but that he had deliberately drawn off to await the arrival of his slower-moving main body. The astonishing fact is that the tract seems to have been printed in London on the 14th. London is 90 miles from Devizes. But prodigious distances were covered in twenty-four hours in those days.

CHAPTER XXX

The First Battle of Newbury, October 20th, 1643

THE short campaign that ended in the battle of Newbury is replete with strategical interest. It all started with the siege of Gloucester by Charles I, which opened on August 10th, 1643. Hitherto that year had been a year of victories for the Royalists. If Gloucester weretofall final victory would, in the opinion of Professor Gardner, crown the royal cause. But Parliament hastened an army under the Earl of Essex to the rescue. On August 26th he set out with 8,000 hastily raised men, soon increased to 15,000, to its relief. On September 5th the King rather weakly broke up the siege and marched off towards Worcester, and on the 8th Essex marched into the town. So far the honours were incontestably with the Roundheads. But the King now led the Earl a 'song and a dance'. Essex followed the Royal army up the Severn as far as Tewkesbury, where he remained irresolutely from September 10th to 15th. He then turned south and east with the intention of regaining his base at London. He reached Cirencester that night, and next day Charles conformed, marching on a roughly parallel route. Essex spent the night of the 17th at Swindon, and Charles at Alvescot, 16 miles to the north-east. The Roundheads were now 20 miles from Newbury, which was their next objective, while the Royalists were a good eight miles further away. It looked as if Essex would win the race for Newbury, but Prince Rupert delayed their march in a skirmish on the Berkshire Downs at Aldbourne next day, so that they only reached Hungerford, nine miles short of Newbury. However, the royal army also did a slow march, being still in some uncertainly as to the objective of their opponents. Thus they spent the night at Wantage, 16 miles from the vital town. It looked as if the race was already as good as won by the Parliamentarians. But military operations are not decided by a pair of dividers on a map; the human equation is the deciding factor. In this case there has been curiously little speculation or comment on the slowness of the Roundhead advance next day; but I suspect the main cause was a sort of 'delay action', resulting from Prince Rupert's aggressive attitude on the previous day.　Or it may be that Essex had knowledge of the King's position at Wantage, and that he reckoned there was no longer any need for haste.　But if so, he reckoned without the agile and resourceful nephew of the King.　Whatever the reason, when the Roundhead quartermasters, pushing on ahead, were leisurely chalking up billets in the town of Newbury late in the afternoon, they were rudely disturbed by Prince Rupert, who thundered into the town, dispersed the escort and took prisoner many of the said quartermasters.　A few hours later the main body of the royal army arrived. Charles had won the race after all.

Though the Royalists had won the race, this was not the time for celebrating.　At any moment their opponents would be upon them. The King, who was aware of the line of approach, namely south of the river Kennet, led his army out of the town and bivouacked on its southern outskirts, thus blocking the road from Kintbury, by which Essex would presumably approach.　Charles guessed right.　Essex. was approaching along the Kintbury road and halted for the night near Enborne, two miles west of the town.　The royal army now lay directly in his path to London.　Charles had won that round decisively, and his army retired to rest, tired after a four day's march, but exultant.

There was every prospect of a battle next day on the ground between Newbury and Enborne.　It is time therefore to describe the terrain over which the battle was destined to be fought.

I only know of one detailed large-scale map of the battle; that is found in Money's *The Battles of Newbury*.　This is a well known and standard work, and contains much local information that is of value; but the map of the battle gives a misleading idea of the ground.　The essential ground features can as a matter of fact be adequately portrayed by a single contour, that of the height, 400 feet, which I have adopted in my Sketch-map 38.　It will be noted, from a study of it, that the essential feature is the plateau extending over the southern half of the field.　To the north the ground shelves gently down to the river Kennet.　All this northern part of the field was flat and well enclosed —much as it is to-day.　But, curiously enough, whereas over most parts of England enclosures have increased since the seventeenth century, the ground on the northern slopes of the plateau—that is, over the centre of the battlefield—were more enclosed then than they are now.　A huge field of at least 30 acres now takes the place of the many 'closes' of which the battle chroniclers speak.　Among the hedges that have disappeared is that at which the Earl of Falkland

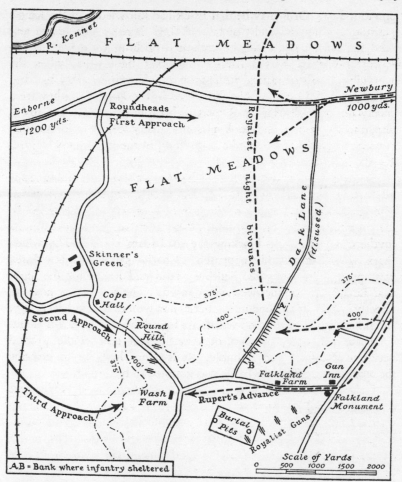

SKETCH-MAP 38.   NEWBURY I

met his death.   The 400 feet contour shows two fingers or ridges
jutting out to the north.   The eastern one is marked on the one-inch
ordnance map by the crossed swords denoting the site of the battle;
the western one, when viewed from the low ground to the north, has
the appearance of a round hill, rather than the end of a ridge.   This
fact is of great importance, for it explains much that is otherwise
obscure—that is, the position of the 'round hill' to which the
chroniclers such as Byron so frequently refer.   Byron, from his position

to the north-east would naturally describe it as a round hill, and for convenience I have named it Round Hill. At the present day it is crowned with some trees and a house. (This house should not be confused with Wash Farm, which is situated 400 yards further south on the top of the plateau.) This plateau is almost dead flat and featureless—except for the burial pits (more probably tumuli) to the south-east of Wash Farm. The plateau was then known as Enborne Heath, and even to-day there are some signs of heath between the two burial pits, now known as the Recreation Ground.[1]

No one knows for certain the respective sizes of the two armies. That of the King is estimated at about 10,000 or a little more. The Parliamentary army had shrunk considerably since its arrival at Gloucester. That is all we positively know. It will probably be near the mark if we consider both armies of equal numbers. But the Royalists were greatly superior in cavalry, both as regards numbers and quality. Seldom can an English army have ridden forth to battle that contained a greater proportion of men of noble blood. Utter contempt had they for their opponents, a contempt that the upshot was to prove unmerited.

In infantry the two sides were fairly evenly matched, though we are rather in the dark as regards artillery. Firth, in his *Cromwell's Army*, points out regretfully 'I do not know of one single account of any English battle of the period that was written by an artillery officer'. It seems, however, that the Royalists had at least one really heavy gun, probably a culverin, for there is a well authenticated story of a cannon-ball reaching the village of Enborne during the course of the battle, at a range that I estimate must have been 2,500 yards. This would mean that the piece was elevated to the utmost that the carriage would allow and fired at 'random range'.

I defy anyone who has not seen or by some means obtained a good impression of the ground to make head or tail of the detailed and graphic but incoherent accounts of the battle written by the participants. This is for two reasons. In the first place the chroniclers are vague and sketchy in their description of the exact locality of the incidents they are describing. In the second place, their accounts are coloured in favour of their own side. Thus it is difficult to reconcile much that appears contradictory, nor to be sure that in a given case both sides are describing the same event. In framing my story I have therefore given considerable weight to Inherent Military

[1] Since demolished (1950).

Probabilities, in default of specific statements. In accordance with my usual custom in this book, I reserve discussion of my reasoning to the final section.

HOW TO EXPLORE THE BATTLEFIELD

The reader who visits the battlefield with this book in his hand is recommended to take the Andover road out of Newbury. Immediately after crossing the railway a road branches off to the right. This leads to Enborne and Kintbury, the natural line of approach for the Roundheads. It is safe to picture the leading troops of the Royalist army turned down this road and forming a line of outposts on the edge of the town, facing west. The bulk of the army would follow them, extending to their right and left and eventually reaching from the river Kennet on their right to the foot of the rising ground 500 yards distant on their left. The front covered would thus be 1,500 yards, all on the flat enclosed meadows or 'closes' as the chroniclers put it. We will not follow the army down this road but continue along the Andover road. After 600 yards the road begins to rise. At the steepest point, another 900 yards farther on, an unmetalled track turns off to the right. Follow this track; after 200 yards it opens out into fields. Straight in front, reaching uphill to the left, is a low ridge, distant 500 yards. It was on the lower slopes of this ridge that the left of the royal outposts lay on that night before the battle. On reaching this ridge a path will be found leading up it to the left. Follow this path for 300 yards and then strike off to the right for about 100 yards to the crest of the ridge. You are now on the centre of the battlefield, and precisely on the spot marked by crossed sabres on the one-inch Ordnance map. From this spot there is a splendid view. In the centre you will see the 'Round Hill', with the Enborne woods behind. On the extreme left is the top of Wash Farm. Further to the left, and of course out of sight, is the flat plateau, known at the time as Enborne Heath. Away on the right, across the flat meadows, and concealed from view by the railway, is the river Kennet. From this spot practically the whole course of the battle can be followed.

THE BATTLE

The King went to bed in the town of Newbury in a cheerful and confident frame of mind. He had won the race. He had obtained ample supplies of food (collected in the town for his opponents), though his powder was ominously short. The rebels had been out-manœuvred and cut off from London. If they continued in their design of reaching the capital it would be necessary to fight their way through. The King was happy to let them attempt this; indeed, it had been his aim throughout this campaign to lead his enemy on to battle in a disadvantageous position. It was principally for that reason that he had abandoned the siege of Gloucester—mistakenly, as some thought.

Many of his troops were comfortably disposed in billets for the night, whereas the enemy were forced to bivouac out in the open on a damp chilly autumn night. They were undoubtedly in low spirits, wearied, footsore, homesick (the majority of them were hastily raised London-trained bands and desertion had been rife), more-over they were short of provender. Everything conspired to the belief that the battle next day, if there was one, would be a fairly easy and decisive Royalist victory.

Now let us move across to the Parliamentary camp. The picture we see there is not dissimilar to that envisaged by the King. The army was, in truth, in a bad way. But one point, and an important one, was overlooked by the Royalists: that desperation breeds courage; a cornered animal fights the more fiercely. The Roundheads resolved to fight fiercely that day, if necessary (even as did our army hemmed in at Dunkirk in a later age). The Earl of Essex enheartened his men, much as Winston Churchill enheartened his countrymen on a similar desperate occasion, not by promising them easy victory and a happy return home, but by stressing the hardness of the road. 'The enemy have all the advantages,' he exclaimed to his troops: 'the hill, the town, hedges and river.' Thus steeled for the fight, the Roundheads drew up in battle array at the approach of dawn on October 20th, 1643.

Essex had, as we have seen, approached Newbury via Kintbury and Enborne. He parked his baggage and artillery trains at Hamp-stead Park, just west of the village of Enborne, which no doubt constituted his headquarters. His army lay in bivouac 1,000 yards further forward, stretching from the river Kennet on his left to Skinner's Green on his right. Thus the two armies faced each other head-on during the night.

I must now hark back to an event, seemingly unimportant, of the previous evening. It obviously would not do for the King to leave the plateau on his left entirely unoccupied, and a troop of cavalry was accordingly despatched to make it good. We can picture them trotting up the Andover road as far as the cross-roads where now stand the Falkland memorial column and Gun Inn. Here they turn to their right along the lane as far as Wash Farm. From here, on the edge of the plateau they get a good view to their front and to their left. It is a good vantage-point for the protection of the left flank, and on it they settle down for the night, sending out patrols to the front during the hours of darkness. But they have been guilty of one omission. They have *not* made good the northern end of the spur (Round Hill), pointing towards Skinner's Green. Fatal omission! A study of my map will show that the line of approach for the Roundheads to this hill from Skinners Green would be invisible from Wash Farm; the enemy could thus gain the hill unobserved. Failure to secure the hill may be attributable to the lateness of the hour at which the troop was posted, or to a casual assumption on the part of the troop commander that some other unit was to hold it, or merely to sheer carelessness and weariness. Whatever the reason, the Roundheads took advantage of this lapse, and either during the night or at dawn they crept up the hill and, as daylight advanced, brought up on to it two light guns. These guns immediately opened fire on the Cavaliers in the plain below them, thus proclaiming in unmistakable terms that the Round Hill was occupied by the enemy.

The first task for the King in the battle clearly was to eject the enemy from Round Hill, and to strengthen his hold on the rest of the plateau. The latter task was given to Prince Rupert with the bulk of the cavalry, and Rupert carried it out in his well-known dashing style. The position on the Wash was secured and guns were brought up to the plateau. A battery was formed from near the Falkland Memorial corner in a south-westerly direction facing Round Hill, and as more guns were gradually brought up on each side, a protracted artillery duel developed at a range of about 1,000 yards, the Royalist guns being just behind what is now the recreation ground, and the Roundheads on Round Hill.

The other task—the ejection of the enemy from Round Hill— was deputed to Sir John Byron, who commanded his own and Sir T. Aston's Horse. The scene that followed is graphically described by his nephew, Sir John (afterwards Lord) Byron, who commanded a brigade of foot. The foot, suffering heavily, had come to a stand-still. 'Upon this,' writes Sir John, 'a confusion was heard among the foot, calling "Horse. Horse". Whereupon I advanced with those two regiments I had and commanded them to halt while I went to view the ground.'

In view of Falkland's death—an event with which the battle is most generally associated—it is desirable at this point to decide on the spot from which Sir John "viewed the ground". Actions in war and battle usually take a simple, natural course. The Roundhead guns on Round Hill were engaged with the Royalist guns on top of the plateau and the Royalist cavalry would naturally prefer to attack them from a flank, i.e. from north or north-east. Even though they started out across the plateau they would instinctively swerve away from the cannon-balls which would be sweeping the plateau, but there is no mention of cannon-balls in the account. In the second place, if the attack was to come from the plateau it would naturally have been deputed to Rupert who was in that part of the field. Thirdly, if the advance was over the northern spur of the plateau, it would approach it across the line A—B (see Sketch-map). Now a very steep bank runs between these two points, so steep that it afforded protection to the infantry from the hostile cannon-balls; they were so snug there that for some time they could not be prevailed upon to abandon their cover. The cavalry could hardly have climbed this bank. Fourthly, there is no mention of hilly ground, but rather of 'closes', which we know were mainly on the flat ground to the north of the hill. Everything therefore combines to place Byron's reconnaissance at the foot of the plateau, and within musket shot of the defenders of Round Hill. The resultant spot I have indicated on my map. Byron probably formed up his two regiments a few hundred yards to the east of that spot, on what is now completely open ground. We can now from our vantage point picture the whole scene as Byron, somewhat breathlessly, describes it. 'I went to see the ground, and to see what way there was to that place where the enemy's foot were drawn up, which I found to be enclosed with a high quick hedge with no passage into it, but by a narrow gap through which but one horse at a time could go and that not without difficulty. My Lord of Falkland did me the honour to ride with my troop this day, and I would needs go along with him. The enemy had beat our foot out of the close, and was drawne up near the hedge; I went to view, and as I was giving orders for making the gapp wide enough, my horse was shott in the throat with a musket bullet and his bit broken in his mouth so that I was forced to call for another horse; in the meanwhile my lord Falkland (more gallantly than advisedly) spurred his horse through the gapp, where both he and his horse were immediately killed.'

Thus died that Philip Sidney of the Civil War, Lucius Cary, Viscount Falkland. He had billeted that night at an inn in Newbury, intent, it is believed, on dying in the field next day, distraught as he was with the miseries that his country was experiencing. An ostler saw him leap to his horse and, as he passed out through the narrow passage into the road, he saw him draw his sword. It was never sheathed again. . . .

The traditional spot where Falkland fell is known as Falkland Farm (or rather Garth, as it is now a private house). It is quite likely that his dead body was brought to this farm next day. But no great importance need be attached to this place-name; there were few houses about and it was almost inevitable that one of them should adopt the name; indeed, two have done so, the other being in a quite impossible place nearly a mile from the battlefield! Money, in his book, agrees that Falkland Farm is an improbable spot, but proceeds to place it in an even more improbable one, in the hedge above mentioned, where the infantry were sheltering, and which could not have been visible to the enemy. It is a pity that the hedges round the more probable spot have since been cut down.

As I have hinted above, the course of the battle was very confused and formless. The fortunes of the day swayed backwards and forwards, but the general trend seems to have been an attempt to turn the enemy's flank in each case, i.e. the southern flank upon the plateau. Fighting in the enclosed terrain in the meadows on the northern part reached a deadlock, and reinforcements were pushed by each side further south. The struggle thus centred about Round Hill and the edge of the plateau near Wash Farm. The tactical value of this edge for the Roundheads was considerable. Until they could obtain a firm foothold on the plateau their guns were practically useless. If they came into action at the foot of the plateau their view would be limited to the crest of the hill above them, whereas, once established on the top they could command a great deal of the plain to the north, and also the plateau itself. This illustrates and explains the intensity of the struggle for Round Hill and the Wash ridge (to the west of Wash Farm). At one period of the day the Royalist cavalry reached the gun position on the hill, but only managed to drag one gun away (probably a light 'Drake'). But for the most part the Royalists managed to retain the Wash Farm, and the Roundheads Round Hill.

Meanwhile the guns were hard at it, and it may be of significance that one place selected for the burial of the dead was in a direct line between the two batteries. (Both armies had a few guns down in the plain, but vision was so cramped there that they were comparatively useless.) Ultimately heavy guns (culverins) were in action on each side; this we know from the discovery of 15- and 20-lb. cannon-balls on the field.

Little more of value can be said about the fight. Some of the Royalist infantry lacked spirit, as we have seen; whereas the young troops of the London-trained bands performed splendidly, on the testimony of one of them that is generally accepted.

Darkness fell, and with it came the alarming news that the ammunition was running short in the Royalist army. Indeed, a Roundhead testifies of his opponents: 'Powder and shot was so far spent that they were not able to answer one shot for three.'

Fresh supplies of powder were expected from Oxford, but unfortunately they had not arrived. The King, who is variously reported as being (1) in the plain, (2) on the side of the hill, (3) leading a cavalry regiment forward, now decided that his army, lacking ammunition, would not be able to withstand a resumption of the attack next morning, and regretfully he gave the order to fall back on Oxford during the night. A man of sterner military calibre, such as Robert E. Lee, on the evening of Sharpsburg, might have decided to bluff it out next day, and had he done so it is by no means certain that Essex would have persevered with the fight. Certain it is that he completely lost touch with the royal army in the night, and next morning fired a single round into what he supposed were the hostile lines, oblivious of the fact that the King was by that time many miles to the north, crossing the battlefield of Ashdown—famous victory of his ancestor Alfred. But the silence on the part of the enemy soon disillusioned Essex and he resumed his march to London.

Losses on each side are problematical, but probably the Royalists lost the most; certainly their losses in the nobility were very high. But what was more significant was that the London-trained bands had proved that they could stand up to the Cavaliers on equal terms, and that Essex had attained his strategical aim. First Newbury was as much a victory for the Roundheads as Edgehill was for the Royalists.

SOME PROBLEMS OF THE BATTLEFIELD

I have already hinted that there are a good many disputable points about this battle. With all deference to Money's most useful book, I feel that it is largely responsible for this disputation. For one thing, he does not clearly define the boundaries of Enborne and Wash Commons, and as there are constant references to both of them it is difficult to trace out the operations with precision. (Perish the thought that he is not always quite clear on the subject himself!) In the second place, he locates Essex's headquarters at Biggs Hill, which is nearly three miles from Newbury to the south-west, in spite of the fact that Clarendon, who speaks of Biggs Hill, places it 'within less than a mile of the town'. The modern Biggs Hill is over a mile from Enborne, which was on the axis of the Roundhead advance, and the place where the artillery and baggage were parked. This Biggs Hill is, as shown on Money's map, on the extreme flank of the Roundhead position. The absurdity of such a position for a headquarters does not seem to have struck Mr. Money, the local historian. But I know of no battle in history where the commander of an army selected such a site for his headquarters. I am therefore forced to suppose either that Clarendon was misinformed or that there was another Biggs Hill near Enborne. There is a hill over 400 feet high one mile to the west of Enborne, quite a natural place for a headquarters, and one that might have been described as a 'big hill'—a term that might quite easily become transformed into Biggs Hill.[1] But whatever the explanation I simply cannot accept that Essex ever set foot on Biggs Hill that day. It follows that Skippon, his second-in-command, who also is mentioned in connection with Biggs Hill, was not posted outside the right flank of what I take to be the parliamentary position. If Skippon was on the right flank, how came it that he led an attack against the enemy on the river side (namely the opposite flank) in the course of the battle?

The result of Money's siting of the right flank on Biggs Hill is to land him in many difficulties in piecing the battle together; whereas, if we accept Enborne, on the axis of advance, as the Roundhead headquarters, events flow in a natural and easily understandable manner. As I have related, the two armies meet head-on, on the direct road between Kintbury and Newbury, and each extends bit by bit in the only feasible direction, namely to the south, and on to what is obviously the ground of supreme tactical importance for the battle, namely the plateau between Wash Farm and Round Hill, a hill that

[1] I am inclined to think that this is the solution: Clarendon was informed orally by a spectator, 'Essex had his headquarters on a big hill', and Clarendon thought he said 'on Biggs Hill'.

is rightly but quaintly described by one chronicler as 'the Hill of Greatest Concernment'.

My reasons for locating Round Hill where I do, I have already given; as also the spot where Falkland fell (but in this case with less assurance and precision; the absence of the old hedge lay-out makes the problem impossible of exact solution).

My explanation of how Round Hill came to be unoccupied, and how it was seized unobserved by the Roundheads is also conjecture, but I apply to it the acid test: is it a natural course of action? At first it appears inconceivable that Rupert's cavalry could have occupied Wash Farm and ridge while leaving Round Hill unoccupied. A simpler solution might be to accept the Royalist statement that the Wash position was not occupied by them till the morning. But this would conflict with their opponent's statement, and appears to be merely an excuse for a bad case of laxity. And yet it is in my view a natural laxity, when one pictures the conditions, as I have tried to envisage them. What appears to the student or historian, poring over his map, to be an impossible state of affairs is, alas, quite likely to happen in war. What the French call *friction de guerre*, plays a big part in military operations, and this incident of the Round Hill adds to the interest and instructiveness of the First Battle of Newbury.

THE BURIAL PITS

It is generally supposed that the dead were buried in three or more burial pits (marked as such on my map) in a field recently turned into a recreation ground. These 'pits' or mounds are almost certainly tumuli, in existence thousands of years before the battle. The evidence for them being burial places cited by Money, seems to be confined to the fact that in 1856 the levelling of these pits was taken in hand, but was stopped on the discovery of several bodies, together with battlefield relics. This proves that an unspecified number of the dead were buried in or beside one or more of the tumuli, but no more. There is evidence that dead were buried all over the place, in ditches, pits, and even a well. Probably the burial party, to save themselves trouble, scooped out recesses in the tumuli for the corpses lying around them. It is fantastic to suppose that they went to the enormous labour of heaping up these great mounds. There is scarcely a battle burial pit in the land that is raised perceptibly above ground level: and naturally so, for uncoffined corpses waste almost to nothing and the ground becomes level again. The most recent (nearly fifty years after Newbury) is at Sedgemoor, where the pits are now perfectly flat. Moreover, upwards of fifty cartloads of dead and wounded were taken into the town; others were taken to Oxford. Adding to all this the graves at Wash Farm and scattered over the battlefield it does not leave many for sepulture in the tumuli. The memorial stone on the easternmost tumulus is, however, as good a place as any to mark the battlefield and its victims.

CHAPTER XXXI

The Battle of Cheriton, 29 March 1644

THIS battle is unduly neglected and underrated. It was indeed the most considerable victory won by the Roundheads up till that date. Clarendon does not disguise the fact; he describes it as 'a very doleful entering into the beginning of the year 1644, and brake all the measures and altered the whole scheme of the king's counsels; for whereas he had before hoped to enter the field early and to have acted an offensive part, he now discerned he was to be wholly upon the defensive part, and that was like to be a very hard part too.'

At the opening of the year 1644 Royalist hopes ran high, and on 21 March Prince Rupert won a resounding victory at Newark. But the Roundheads were in high hopes too, and Sir William Waller with a well-found army of slightly over 8,000 all ranks, was entrusted with the mission of recovering the West Country. Simultaneously his old antagonist Sir Ralph (now Lord) Hopton, had the task of winning the counties of Surrey, Sussex, and Kent for the Royalist cause. By 20 March Hopton's army, also about 8,000 strong, was assembled at Winchester, while that of his opponent was approaching from the direction of Midhurst.

I have said that the latter army was well found. The same could not be said of the Royalist army, which was not only inadequately armed but consisted largely of recently raised levies from Hampshire: it no longer had the stiffening of the incomparable Cornish foot. It also contained some Irish regiments, and indeed some French troops. It was an ill-assorted combination and, to make matters worse, there was a question about the chief command. Lord Hopton was nominally in command, but the Earl of Forth, who might be described as Chief of Staff to the King, had recently joined the army as a 'volunteer' (bringing 2,000 'volunteers' with him), in order to give his old friend Hopton the benefit of his advice whenever he might require it. But it is an embarrassing thing to fight a battle with a superior general 'sitting in one's pocket' (as General Lanrezac found when Joffre 'sat in his pocket' during the Retreat from Mons in 1914).

Hopton courteously offered to give up the command to Forth, and the Earl with equal courtesy demurred. Eventually he consented to assume the responsibility, but as he was suffering from the gout and could not move far from his coach all the practical work continued to fall upon Hopton, without the actual responsibility being his. This was a vicious system, as we saw at Lansdown. An army should have a single commander and every man in that army should know who his commander is.

Sir William Waller, on the other hand, was in undisputed command of the Parliamentary army, and had been for a long time.[1] It was a well welded force, especially the cavalry, where the prestige of Sir Arthur Hazelrig's 'Lobsters' was still strong. Moreover, Waller was burning to avenge the mortifying defeat he had suffered in the previous summer, partly at the hands of Hopton's troops, at Roundway Down. Similarly Hopton was burning to wipe out the double setback he had recently sustained by a local defeat at Alton and the surrender of Arundel Castle to Waller. Both sides were thus confident and eager for battle. It is indeed asserted that Forth and Hopton issued a medieval challenge to their opponent to meet them in battle at a prescribed place and date. If so, Waller declined the challenge but was none the less resolved to fight whenever he could gain a favourable opportunity for it.

On 25 March the Parliamentary army was approaching East and West Meon from the east, whilst the Cavaliers were assembling at Winchester. From this city they suddenly advanced two days later and reached Alresford the same day. Here they were just in time to anticipate Sir William Balfour's body of horse which Waller had sent forward with the same objective. Balfour was forced to fall back to Hinton Ampner, 4 miles south of Alresford, where Waller's main body joined him.

There was bickering between the horse of both sides during the next twenty-four hours, while the two main bodies closed up to one another. By evening of the 28th the Cavaliers were drawn up along the ridge 2 miles to the south of Alresford, while the Roundheads were bivouacking in a large field at Hinton Ampner. Both armies made themselves ready for the arbitrament of battle on the morrow.

---

[1] Secretary Roe would seem to imply that Sir William Balfour, who had recently joined with a large contingent, shared the command, but that was not so.

THE TERRAIN

There is no dispute as to the site of this battle. Ample records and place-names and grave-pits pinpoint it.

Between Alresford and Hinton Ampner lies a horseshoe ridge; its 'toe' points eastward and its 'heels' westward, thus forming two ridges which join each other to the east. In the centre, representing the hollow sole of a horse's foot, is a vast but shallow amphitheatre or arena, nearly a mile wide. The northern ridge is rather higher than the southern one, rising 100 feet above the mean level of the 'arena' as we will call it. It was in this arena—fit site for a battle—that the fighting took place. This arena was for the most part open common land, whilst the slopes to north and south of it were thickly enclosed with fields and lanes, which may be compared to the tiers of seats surrounding an actual arena. The toe of the horseshoe was, and still is, covered by an extensive wood known as Cheriton Wood.

THE BATTLE

Although there are comparatively few controversial points and problems relating to this battle and although there is no question as to the exact site, it is not an easy battle to unravel and to describe. This is largely due, not to a paucity of sources, but to the very complexity and amount of detail that is comprised in a battle lasting practically the whole day, in which large forces of cavalry are continually on the move. It is difficult 'to see the wood for the trees'. The longest and most detailed history of the battle that has been written, that by the Rev. G. N. Godwin in *Hampshire in the Civil War*, suffers from this mass of detail. On the other hand Gardiner's account errs too much on the opposite side; I feel that he over-simplifies the course of events, and finds the clue to the whole battle in a certain tactical move on the part of Sir William Waller. I will try to steer between these two extremes.

When day broke on 29 March, 1644, both armies were equally resolved to fight it out. The Cavaliers had managed overnight to gain possession of the southern arm or ridge of the horseshoe, and an outpost line of horse under Sir George Lisle had been stationed there, while the remainder of the army took up position on the northern ridge. Here during the night Lisle was unmolested, for a Parliamentary council of war on the previous afternoon had resolved on retreat. But

with the dawn came a change of mind, though the exact reason for it
is in some doubt.

It was a misty morning and Waller opened operations by sending
a force from his London Brigade to seize Cheriton Wood. His reputed
'eye for country' here served him well, for this wood at the toe of
the horseshoe may be considered the key to the position. Whichever
side obtained control of it enjoyed the double advantage of being

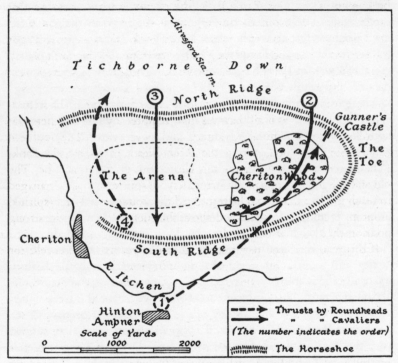

SKETCH-MAP 39.   CHERITON: THE BATTLE

able to gain the enemy's ridge by a covered line of approach and
without having to descend into the valley and attack uphill, and also
of being advantageously placed to threaten the flank of any hostile
force that attempted to advance straight across the arena.

The Roundheads were successful in obtaining a lodgement in the
wood, and this had the natural effect of inducing Lisle with his outposts
to fall back on to the main body, for fear of being outflanked and
cut off.

But Waller was not the only soldier on that field gifted with an 'eye for the country'. His old rival and friend Lord Hopton also possessed it, and as soon as he realized what Waller was aiming at he countered it with a still stronger force. Cheriton Wood was vital for both sides and a battle royal took place for it. Whereas Waller had sent only infantry to seize the wood, Hopton sent infantry and guns to recover it. The guns came into action on top of the ridge, above and only a short distance from the edge of the wood. (This spot came to be known as Gunners Castle.)[1] As the enemy emerged in somewhat ragged formation from the undergrowth the guns opened on them with deadly effect and they were driven back. Colonel Appleyard's foot crowned the good work begun by the guns and the Roundheads were completely ejected from the wood. The first round had been won by the King's army.

The Parliamentary army was visibly shaken by this early setback and it would seem as if all that was now required by the Cavaliers was to follow up their initial advantage and sweep down the southern ridge from the wood, taking the Roundheads in their right flank. (The sketch-map should make this clear.) But it was not to be. The old and cautious Forth had, unfortunately, in spite of his gout managed to reach the battlefield and he restrained the younger and high-spirited Hopton, preferring to stand and allow the enemy to attack the strong position that he now occupied.

If this plan had been persisted in all might yet have been well, for Waller, an easily discouraged man, might have reverted to the previous day's decision to retreat. But the course of battles is never foreseeable. When all the known and ascertainable factors have been duly weighed there still remain the unascertainable factors, what we may call the *imponderabilia* of the battlefield—the unpredictable interplay of human nature, which often makes or mars a well-laid plan. In this case it marred it. A youthful Royalist officer, Colonel Sir Henry Bard by name, contrary to all orders suddenly took it upon him to charge down into the arena at the head of his regiment, and up the other side against the enemy waiting in a prepared position. Gardiner in his account is kind to this undisciplined cavalryman, enlarging upon his patriotic zeal, 'burning to strike a gallant blow at the rebels he despised'. But this will not do. An army in which the officers are so regardless of their orders is like a cracked tool that may fall to pieces in your hand at any moment. Bard's cavalry regiment was isolated, and Sir Arthur Hazelrig, in a timely and brilliant manoeuvre, swung round their rear,

[1]Locally this spot seems to have been forgotten, but it is easy to identify it.

cutting off their retreat. Every man in the regiment was killed or captured.

Now this happened under the eyes of the rest of the army. It was hard to look on, leaving Bard's men tamely to their fate. Forth made his second change of plan, sending another regiment down to their succour. Much the same fate met this one. Regiment followed regiment down into the fatal arena in hasty ill-co-ordinated and spasmodic charges. A long, tangled, planless and formless struggle swirled round and round in the arena bottom. The advantage was all on the side of the defender, sitting securely behind his hedge or sallying out when an isolated troop of the enemy provided a suitable opportunity, the Parliamentary guns belching forth from the higher ground in rear.

Gradually the infantry were drawn in too, making the contest more involved and shapeless than ever. For several hours what can only be described as a gigantic 'dog-fight' went on in the arena. But of the many incidents recorded during this phase of the battle I will relate only one. This account, written by an eye-witness, is so graphic that it gives us a vivid picture of the conditions that prevailed. It was written by one Edward Walsingham, a gentleman in Sir John Smith's Regiment of Horse. Sir John was General of Horse in the Royalist army; he was that John Smith who had so enterprisingly recaptured the King's Standard at Edgehill, a feat for which he had been knighted. He was the hero of Edward, who calls him 'The Glory of our English Nation'. He relates how, when Sir John received Forth's order to commit the cavalry to action in the arena he was conscious that it would lead to disaster, and was much perturbed thereby; but, like a good soldier, proceeded to obey it. Indeed he in person led his own regiment into the attack.

Let the faithful Walsingham carry on the story.

'On therefore he goes, in heroick obedience, though expecting nothing else but what ensued. In distracted manner they are to charge a solid body of the Rebels' Horse, lying under the protection of both lanes and hedges lined with musketeers. Their cannons (where he is come almost within pistol shot with intention to charge in) flies off so freely that amazes his horse, the fire even flashing in his face causes him to rear and turns sidewise upon the enemy, who seeing his rider's power imployed to keep his saddle, and recover his horse let fly at him as thick as hail. And in this interim comes one amongst them clad in arms, like a lobster, who with his carbine gives him his third and mortal wound in his belly, on the left side beneath his armour. With this wound he falls, and with him the fortunes of the day. For no sooner was he down but, daunted with so disastrous an accident, they in a great disorder retreat, scarce any but his own Troop remaining on that wing, who resolving to die rather than lose so brave a leader, advanced to fetch him off, even to the enemies' nose, and despite of their gallantry brought off him, his horse and arms, whilst one of the Company in a brave revenge, riding up to the armed Monster [the 'Lobster'] and shoots him in the eye, sending him to answer for his detested feat in so base a manner wounding to death a Gentleman every way accomplished and worthy.' [1]

It must have been well on in the afternoon when the movement which decided the battle took place. It is related only by Colonel Slingby, in a short passage that has apparently escaped the notice of the various historians of the battle. In the course of the 'dog-fight' in the centre Royalist troops seem to have been gradually drawn away from their right wing. As it was on the open crest of the ridge every movement could be seen from the other ridge, and on the Parliamentary left wing a regimental commander took advantage of it. Swinging round his line to the right he outflanked the Royalist shortened right wing, and marching up the west end of the North Ridge forced a withdrawal. The Cavaliers fell back over Tichborne Down for one mile and took up a fresh position on the ground where they had bivouacked the previous night, on a slight ridge half a mile south of Alresford railway station. [2] The Roundheads dragged up some guns and after three discharges the Cavaliers again fell back.

But ere this happened the prescient Hopton had ordered the artillery to fall back, and all except two of his eleven guns got safely away. The Earl of Forth appears to have now given the order for a general retreat, and the whole Royalist army streamed to the rear through the streets of Alresford. Forth and Hopton and the bulk of the army took

[1] Walsingham's little book published in 1644 (and never reprinted) has the quaint title *Britannicae Virtutis Imago*. Walsingham described in touching terms the death of his hero a few hours later. 'He expressed in a mild manner that his death was now within a period, and conjured me by all the love and respect I owed him, to certify his dear Mother that he died with a quiet conscience, and a resigned mind, hoping likewise that she would not take his death with too much heaviness, but rather rejoice that she had a son to shed his blood for his Sovereign. A truly Christian and heroic speech which, though but short, comprised the very Elixir of true fortitude, loyalty and piety.'

[2] Secretary Roe claims for his master, Colonel Birch, the credit for initiating this move, and also one on the right wing, but his statement must be regarded as suspect.

the road to Basing House, which they reached that night; the remainder
made for Winchester.

Waller advanced next day to Winchester where the city, but not
the castle, surrendered to him. Soon all Hampshire was his, while
Forth fell back on Oxford. Clarendon's words were justified; the battle
of Cheriton 'altered the whole scheme of the King's counsels'.

COMMENTS

Gardiner is unaccountably kind to the Earl of Forth. On paper, at
least, it would seem that, with the capture of Cheriton Wood Hopton
had 'the ball at his feet', as he himself represented to Forth. But either
the nerve of the older man failed him or he played for safety, which
comes to much the same thing. 'Fortune is a woman', but unfortunately for the Royalist commander, Napoleon's well-known maxim
had not then been framed. Dame Fortune did not offer her favours
a second time.

It is curious that Waller was content to accept defeat in Cheriton
Wood and that he made no definite attempt to retake it.[1] For the
remainder of the day there seems to have been practically no fighting
in the wood. Not only must Waller be blamed for attempting nothing
in this vital sector, but Forth must also be blamed for not taking
advantage of it later in the day to intervene in the arena fight from
that direction. The fact probably is that his command post on the
centre of the northern ridge offered *too* good a view of the battle.
It was laid out beneath him; almost every movement could be seen,
and he would naturally become absorbed in what his own eye told
him to the exclusion of other interests and considerations. He became
too absorbed in the 'dog-fight', forgetful of everything else. Thus he
missed the opportunity to profit by the favourable position on his left,
and to rectify the unfavourable situation that supervened on his right
flank.

I cannot share the admiration of Gardiner for the action of Waller
in posting his cavalry at the foot of the slope on the edge of the arena.
Since only in the arena was there open ground favourable for cavalry
it was the obvious place in which to post them. He would have been
an imbecile to place them anywhere else (unless he placed them in
reserve); for everywhere the slopes were studded with small fields,
smaller apparently than they are to-day. (This surprising feature was

[1] Roe asserts that he did, but he is alone in this.

shared by First Newbury, where the terrain was more enclosed then than it is at the present day.)

In short I cannot detect any generalship of a particularly high order in either commander.[1] To what then must we attribute the victory, where place the credit? The immediate cause was, I believe, the happy manoeuvre of the Parliamentary left in their outflanking movement against the Royalist right; but more fundamentally I hold it due to the better quality, that is the higher standard of training and the greater coherence of the Parliamentary army. It was Waller's own army; he had trained the bulk of it and had led it himself; whereas the Royalist army was more heterogeneous, owning two masters, and consisting to a larger extent of fresh untrained troops. Discipline was better in Waller's army, and that old-fashioned military quality proved the decisive factor in the battle of Cheriton. There is a lot to be learnt from this battle.

Cheriton is the nearest battle to Camberley, and I commend it to the study of the Staff College.

[1] Secretary Roe seems, somewhat unexpectedly, to share my view—'It was indeed a victory, but the worst possible of any I ever saw.'

CHAPTER XXXII

The Battle of Marston Moor, July 2nd, 1644

NO two battles are alike. There may be some superficial resemblance between the three best known battles of the Civil War—Edgehill, Marston Moor and Naseby; for in all three, while the infantry fought it out in the centre the cavalry on the wings were having success on one flank simultaneously with disaster on the other, with the consequent result that the whole line of battle slewed round like a rugger scrum. But the similarity ends there. Of the three, that of Marston Moor had the most remarkable and the most unique features. A single quotation from a contemporary letter will show this: 'There were three Generals on each side. Within half an hour and less, all six took to their heels.'

At the first blush there would not appear to be so much to investigate in this as in the other big fights; the sources are numerous, and the exact site of the field of battle is quite clearly defined 'without a peradventure'. But when we examine it a little closer we find some nebulous features, and many obscurities, some of which have never been fully dealt with. So the examination of this battlefield should prove fruitful.

The strategy of the rival armies leading up to the battle shows the Cavaliers in a favourable light and the Roundheads at their worst. This is nothing to be surprised at when we are dealing with an allied force. The Scottish army under the old Earl of Leven was in alliance with the Parliamentary army, under Lord Fairfax and the Earl of Manchester. The Royalist commander, Prince Rupert, had just accomplished the virtual conquest of Lancashire, in a triumphant campaign of six weeks. Towns fell to him like so many houses of cards; and the fall of each town represented not only an accession to the prestige of the Royalist commander but a physical accession of strength as the wobblers flocked to the successful army. By the time he crossed over the backbone of England and entered Yorkshire on June 26th, 1644, his army was about 14,000 strong. He was on his way to the relief of York, where the Earl of Newcastle with 3,000 troops was being besieged by the allies, whose army totalled 27,000 men, half of them being Scots, and one-quarter belonging to Fairfax and Manchester respectively.

The news of the approach of 'Rupert of the Rhine' reached the besieging army on June 30th, and seems to have caused the allied commanders to lose their heads. Even though Rupert should succeed in joining up with Newcastle, the Royalists would still be outnumbered. But the Allies, who probably did not thoroughly trust one another, decided incontinently to abandon the siege and to concentrate their whole army against Prince Rupert, who was now reported at Knaresborough, ten miles west of York. July 1st therefore saw the allied army drawn up on Marston Moor, six miles west of the city, on the Knaresborough road. But only a small body of horse put in an appearance, 'amusing' them, and the next they heard was that Prince Rupert had slipped right past them and had relieved Newcastle in York.

It was probably Rupert's most brilliant manœuvre, and it put a fitting crown on his 1644 campaign. He had made a rapid encircling march, crossing the Ure at Boroughbridge and the Swale at Thornton Bridge, ultimately making use of a bridge of boats over the Ouse which had been constructed by the enemy three miles north-west of York, and which he captured by a quick dash. By nightfall on July 1st his army was in the northern outskirts of York, and Rupert and Newcastle were engaged in conference. The Allies had been outwitted and out-manœuvred.

The conference that ensued was a protracted one. The cautious Newcastle was opposed to a battle till some reinforcements had arrived. Rupert, fortified by a letter from the King, was clamant for a battle. Being the senior he had his way, and next morning, July 2nd, his army set forth to seek out the enemy on Marston Moor.

But the Allies had also been engaged in conference, and in their camp the voice of prudence prevailed. That is to say, fearing that the Royalists had offensive intentions against the eastern counties, they decided to fall back to the south-east ere they should be cut off from the Humber. It seems odd that the Scots should agree to leaving the enemy astride their line of retreat to Scotland. According to Fairfax they even proposed it. They were expecting reinforcements from Cheshire, which makes the direction of their march still more odd.

Tadcaster was the first town to be passed through, and the head of the army had almost reached that place when an urgent message was received by Leven from Fairfax, who was still with the rearguard covering the movement from Marston Moor, warning him that an attack appeared imminent. Leven, rather surprisingly, thereupon reversed his whole army and returned towards Marston Moor. This was a sudden reversal of policy. Fairfax had only seen hostile cavalry, and it was only to be expected that the enemy would throw out a cavalry screen, whatever their ultimate intentions were.

Unfortunately the accounts of this episode and of Leven's reasons for his action are scanty, but it looks as if the Allies had no clear-cut plan, and that Leven was over-borne by the vehemence of his younger colleagues. Yet he was a commander with a considerable reputation, probably the only really continental reputation of any British general at the time. He had been brought up under that great soldier Sir Horace Vere and had afterwards served under Gustavus Adolphus, and had encountered and worsted the great Wallenstein. Gustavus, indeed, made him a field-marshal. He was by this time 55 years of age.

However that may be, Fairfax had correctly sensed Rupert's intentions; possibly he received some information from spies that we know not of. Rupert also was having his troubles. Newcastle had somewhat reluctantly acquiesced in a battle, but did not rouse himself to get his men moving quickly, having wasted time looting the abandoned camp of the Allies,[1] and his contingent arrived very late on the field. It was not till after 4 p.m. that his whole force had reached the battlefield, where Rupert's troops had been drawn up for some hours.

THE BATTLEFIELD

As I have said, there is nothing doubtful about the position occupied by the two armies. It happened that both flanks rested upon villages which remain substantially as they were—Long Marston on the east, Tockwith on the west. To remove all possible doubt, the distance is given specifically as $1\frac{1}{2}$ miles, which it still is. Furthermore, a ditch bounding the moor is mentioned as dividing the two armies. The course of this ditch is well known, and in two places—where Atterwick Lane and Moor Lane cross it—it is still visible, and it is also marked by a hedge along most of its course.

[1] I prefer this explanation to the normal one—a dispute over pay for the troops.

On the Roundhead side the ground is very similar in appearance to what it was then: that is to say, a few large fields of arable, mostly under rye, sloping down gently for 1,200 yards to the ditch. This ditch bordered the moor, which was open and partly covered with gorse. It has since then been enclosed, but in summer the dividing line between the old arable and the old moor stands out strikingly owing to the yellow blaze of buttercups on the old moorland. This moorland, which was occupied by the Royalists is practically flat. Thus the Allies had the advantage of higher ground; but the Royalists had the advantage, such as it was, of occupying the actual ditch.

A word must now be said about this famous ditch. We are informed that it was 'wide and deep', but how wide or how deep I cannot discover. There was a hedge on the south side of the ditch, that is towards the enemy. This was unfortunate for the Cavaliers, for obviously they would like to line the hedge and have the ditch as an obstacle in their front. But now they had the option of putting the ditch behind them or having the hedge directly in its front, thus screening the approach of the enemy. No writer seems to have called attention to this awkward dilemma, either at the time or since; but I presume that one of two things must have happened. Either the occupiers, whilst waiting four hours for the battle to begin, levelled the bulk of the hedge, or else the ditch was only manned by outposts and the main line of resistance was at least 100 yards further back. For reasons that will appear presently I favour the latter alternative. But one thing can be said at this point. Though much has been written about the hedge at the beginning of the battle all records are silent about it once the fight has got well under way. In this it resembles the celebrated hedge at Poitiers which also disappears from the story once the two sides came into contact. Apart from the two spots mentioned above, all signs of the ditch have vanished, though I was informed on the spot that parts of it have only been filled in in recent times. An unspecified length on the western extremity of the ditch had however been filled in and the hedge levelled before the battle (whether a few hours before by the troops or some time before by the owners is not stated). In 1862 the ditch, where crossed by Moor Lane, is described in *Macmillan's Magazine* as 'a deep ditch'. It is still dimly visible at this point, but more clearly at the point where it is crossed by Atterwick Lane.

Here, then, we must picture the Royalist army drawn up, musketeers and a few light drakes lining the ditch, while the main line of resistance was about 100 yards behind, sufficiently close to bring the enemy under musket fire when they attempted to cross the ditch.

The Allies were drawn up in a parallel line some distance back from the ditch. Lord Leven, as commanding the largest contingent, was given the supreme command, and another experienced Scot, David Leslie, marshalled the line of battle. Though the road between the two villages is curiously absent from all the accounts, I feel certain that Leslie must have utilized it as a line of dressing for his front line. Thus they would be exactly a quarter of a mile from the ditch. This, though outside musket-shot, was well within cannon range, and it is not surprising to learn that there was a desultory cannonade by both sides in the course of the afternoon.

Leven's headquarters were by a clump of trees on the hill-top, now known as Cromwell's Plump. The original clump has since disappeared, the last tree being blown down in 1866.[1] We hear no mention of either side fortifying the houses in the two villages, but this is not to be wondered at, for such a procedure on the battlefield was quite out of fashion in the Civil War. It was the heyday of cavalry and battles were usually decided by that arm.

There is really nothing else that need be said about the battlefield at this point. It can best be surveyed from Cromwell's Plump on the hill-top, almost opposite Moor Lane and the memorial stone erected in 1939 by the Cromwell Association on the roadside.

ORDER OF BATTLE

Accounts on the side of the Allies are conflicting, but Professor Firth has, I consider, established the case for the order as given by Ashe, as opposed to that favoured by Gardner and earlier writers. According to these, Fairfax's foot were on the right and the Scots in the centre, but Firth places the Scots main body on the right, and this I accept. It is easy to see how confusion arose, for the Scots equalled, if they did not outnumber, the two English armies combined, and we are told that they were dispersed all along the line. On the right were Sir Thomas Fairfax's horse, and on the left Cromwell's horse. (Here it may be noted that I shall use the terms right and left as for the Allied army, and as the reader, with the north of the map on the top, would naturally see it.)

There is not the same doubt about the order of battle of the

[1] One account says 1839.

Royalists, for a plan of the line made by De Gomme is still in existence (in the British Museum). Of the infantry in the centre we need say nothing, except that Newcastle's Whitecoat regiments[1] formed the nucleus, and better infantry did not exist on either side. On the left Rupert placed his own horse, less a reserve in his own hands behind the centre. Lord Goring was in command of the horse on the other flank.

The guns on each side were placed for the most part in twos and threes in the intervals between the regiments, though as we have seen a few drakes were sited by Rupert along the ditch. He had 28 guns and his opponents had 25. The artillery on both sides played an insignificant part in the ensuing battle.

THE BATTLE

In most of the Civil War battles neither side evinced a desire to take the offensive. There were good reasons for this hesitation at Marston Moor. Newcastle, as already noted, was reluctant to fight at all, and Rupert no doubt was influenced by him to postpone the attack till the next day. Leven, on the other hand, holding the advantage of the higher ground was not anxious to forego it, especially as his opponents held the ditch, and that obstacle would be likely to impede and disarray his advance. Thus both sides sat narrowly eyeing one another till about 7 p.m. Prince Rupert then decided that the enemy had no immediate hostile intentions, so ordered up provisions from York for his troops and rode off to the rear to get some supper for himself, while Newcastle repaired to his coach to have a quiet smoke.

Suddenly, without any warning, the whole allied line advanced down the hill (they had previously pushed their line 200 yards forward so that only 250 yards separated the two lines). On the left there was a small preliminary action, which has occasioned much dispute. Some Parliamentary dragoons are said to have driven their opponents from 'Rye Hill', but the trouble is that there is nothing that could be described as a hill hereabouts. It has been conjectured to be just to the north of Tockwith village,[2] and in prolongation of the ditch, but this is mere conjecture, and local inhabitants do not seem to be aware of such a 'hill'. It may have been Rye *Hall*, not *Hill*. In any case,

[1] Frequently given in the singular, but there must have been several of them.
[2] Some modern maps of the battle show an imaginary hill here.

the affair is devoid of significance and we can pass it by. What is more to the point is that the dragoons cleared the opposing musketeers from the ditch on this flank (approaching it in a 'running march'), thus opening the way for the cavalry. Part of the ditch in this neighbourhood had been filled in, which made things still more easy for Cromwell's cavalry to charge.

Contrary to the usual practice I am going to describe events on the right flank first (though it should be borne in mind that the clash was practically simultaneous all along the line). As Fairfax's cavalry approached the ditch we may assume that the musketeers lining it fired one volley, and the drakes one salvo, and then fell back to their main line. Thus Fairfax got successfully across the ditch. But then his trouble began. The ground hereabouts was dotted with gorse bushes, which thus limited and split up his line, and made ordered progress difficult. Markham (on what authority I know not), states that all the ground between Atterwick and Moor Lanes was thus covered. There are also vague stories of ditches and hedges lined with musketeers. But there is also one very circumstantial story that is of an extraordinary nature, though it has been implicitly accepted by all writers without comment. It is in *A Full Relation*, attributed to a Captain Stewart. This account avers that 'there was no passage but a narrow lane where they could not march above three or four in front'. It had a hedge on one side and a ditch on the other, both being lined with enemy musketeers.[1] The account goes on: 'the enemy keeping themselves in a body, and receiving them by threes and fours as they marched out of the lane.' What are we to make of this? The picture conjured up is the absurd one of Fairfax's men marching up a narrow lane (Moor Lane) for 900 yards beyond the ditch, fired at at a range of a few feet the while *from both sides* and then being fired on again as they emerged. One would not suppose that many would be alive to emerge after this ordeal. Now Firth sees traces of a compilation, rather than a direct eye-witness story, in this *Full Relation*, and I can only suppose that the compiler has misunderstood some eye-witness or has exaggerated the story. For if Fairfax did emerge at the end of the Lane, which is generally believed to be at Four Lanes Meet (see Sketch-map 40) he would find himself some hundreds of yards behind Rupert's line of battle. It just does not make sense. I think we must ignore it, or rather water it down. What

[1] This hedge and ditch both exist still; the lane is known locally as Bloody Lane.

probably happened was that a few troopers who found themselves in the lane were peppered by the musketeers along the hedge, while the bulk of the cavalry were working their way through the gorse bushes on either side of the road, but chiefly on the right side.

Before they had gone far Fairfax's horse met the onrush of Goring's first line. Fairfax himself, at the head of 400 of his own men, charged them successfully and pursued his immediate opponents off the field.[1] Not so the remainder of his first line, many of whom were raw troops. Goring, ably seconded by Sir Charles Lucas, swept through them, putting them to headlong rout. Back over the ditch they hied and, not drawing rein, galloped over the hill in rear and right off the battle-field. Some of Goring's horse followed them for nearly two miles; others stopped on the hill-top to loot the baggage wagons, while the second line were kept in hand. But worse was to follow. In their mad rush to safety a portion of the defeated cavalry had galloped through and over the right of Leven's Scottish foot. Some of these were trodden to the ground, others joined in the panic flight. For panic it evidently was—all the chroniclers are emphatic on this point.

Panic spreads rapidly, unless taken firmly in hand immediately, and I suspect that there was some bad failure in leadership among the Scottish officers to account for this dire disaster. But the panic did not only spread from contagion; it was increased by Goring's second line which, wheeling to their right, now charged into the open flank of Lord Fairfax's foot, who had by this time advanced some hundreds of yards beyond the ditch. These followed the example of the Scots and fled too. Soon there were, on the admission of their own people, several thousand foot in mad flight from the field.

The scene must have almost beggared description—almost, but not quite. There happened to be a Cavalier taking a message to Prince Rupert from the South. He, as darkness was falling, found himself swept along in the wild stream, and he has left a vivid and unforgettable description. There is no space to give it here, but it may be read in *Original Papers*, by Carte, in a letter from a Mr. Trevor to Ormonde. Vicars, in *God's Ark*, puts it vividly in a few words, 'being amazed with panick feares', and Stockdale, whose account is in my opinion the most reliable of all, not excluding Chaplain Ashe's, admits that 'in all appearance the day was lost'.

---

[1] There is a tradition that, galloping through Huntergate, on the eastern edge of Wilstrop Wood, the fugitives rode over and killed a little girl.

Amid this fearful scene a remnant of the Scottish regiments stood firm; surrounded on three sides they kept their ranks, their pikemen forming a solid wall past which Goring's horsemen flung themselves in vain. But the pressure on them was prodigious and they were hard put to it to maintain themselves. Soon the breaking-point would come, unless speedy help were forthcoming.

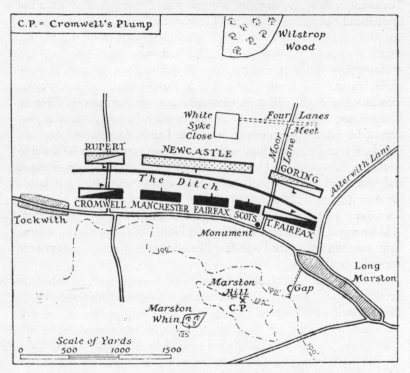

SKETCH-MAP 40. MARSTON MOOR: THE BATTLEFIELD

And now we take up the story on the left of the line, where we saw Cromwell's Ironsides about to charge over the ground opened up to him by the dragoons. Over the ditch they went, without losing their formation; on the flat moor beyond, here devoid of gorse, they encountered Rupert's first line of horse. The events of the next hour on this part of the field have been the occasion of fierce controversy from that day onwards. For something went wrong, and Scots blamed English and English blamed Scots, while each took the credit for the final upshot of the action. My reconstruction must therefore be taken with some reserve, though I feel happy as to its essential correctness.

In the first clash, then, Rupert's horse obtained the advantage; Cromwell's first line of Ironsides recoiled, he himself being wounded in the *back* of the neck, presumably in the act of recoiling. Temporarily shaken, he was led off the field into a house in the near end of Tockwith village, where his wound was dressed.[1] The situation immediately became serious, but Leslie, who commanded the second line of horse, charged Rupert's men in the flank and drove them back. Prince Rupert was not present in this first engagement, for he was at his supper, no doubt near his reserve regiment of horse in the centre of the line and well to the rear. Here he should no doubt have stayed, directing the battle. But Rupert was not of that nature. Seeing things going wrong among his darling cavalry, he took at least a portion of his reserve regiment with him and rushed to the rescue. *En route* he was met by some fugitive horse. In a towering rage he shouted at them: "Swounds! Do you run? Follow me?" A prolonged and bitter fight ensued, both sides now almost stationary. It lasted for almost an hour, Cromwell being off the field for most of the time. Lord Saye, a Roundhead, paid this generous tribute to his opponents: 'The enemy's horse stood very firm and long time, coming to a close fight with the sword, and standing like an iron wall, so that they were not easily broken.'

Eventually numbers told, Leslie's horse wrested the advantage from their opponents, and, slowly at first, then gathering momentum, they pushed their opponents off the battlefield.

While this strenuous contest was going on on the extreme left, Manchester's foot were at grips with Rupert's foot in the left centre. As the allied cavalry gradually made ground, Manchester's men were able to wheel slightly to the right and take the enemy in flank. At the end of an hour, say about 8.30 p.m., the sun being now set, the greater part of Manchester's line was facing to its right, and the cavalry were starting off in pursuit. At about this juncture, Cromwell, in the saddle once more, began to exert his influence and his restraining hand. Leaving Leslie's Scots to carry out the pursuit, he rallied his own horse and formed them up, facing to the right, and in prolongation of Manchester's foot. Thus the position was much as shown in Sketch-map 41. The whole line of battle had made a vast 'screw'

---

[1] The house is still pointed out, or rather the ruins of it; it was bombed by one of our planes during the World War.

as in a football scrum.　This was the situation described by Principal
Baillie and already given : 'all six generals took to their heels.'　Rupert
had had a narrow escape from capture ; Newcastle had not even time
to get back to his coach, which was taken with all his papers.　Goring,
however, at this moment was not in flight.　In the other camp, Leven
had got clear off the field, riding non-stop, according to some accounts,

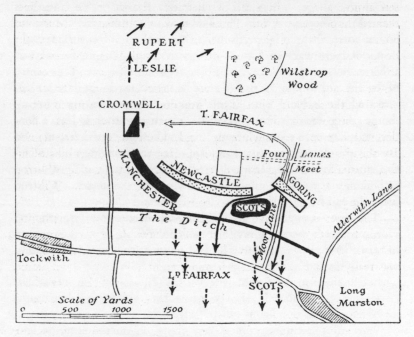

SKETCH–MAP 41.　MARSTON MOOR: THE CLIMAX OF THE BATTLE

as far as Leeds.　Manchester did not run far, and was soon back on
the field, bringing some fugitives with him, but Lord Fairfax is
reported to have fled to his own house at Cawood and to have gone
to bed.[1]　Has such an extraordinary situation ever been seen elsewhere in war ?　Probably the bulk of the Royalist horse and the bulk
of the allied foot were in flight simultaneously, and all the leading
generals on each side were wounded or in flight.　For besides Cromwell, Sir Thomas Fairfax too was wounded.　And this brings us back
to that doughty warrior and to the most dramatic moment in this or
any other battle of the Civil War.　It deserves a heading to itself.

[1] The story is denied by his biographer, but it is told circumstantially.

We left Fairfax somewhere behind the Royalist front line, with his 400 troopers pursuing a body of Royalist horse off the field. But his second line was in full flight; Fairfax, not attempting to rally his own party, returned to find out what had happened to the remainder of his command. But he was cut off by the triumphant cavalry of Lord Goring. Surrounded, wounded and unhorsed, he found himself almost alone amid a sea of enemies. Escape to his own lines seemed hopeless, and Sir Thomas took the desperate course of attempting a circuit right round the rear of the Cavalier army in the hopes of reaching Manchester's division. To do this it was essential to disguise himself. Now, in order to recognize friend from foe when the uniform of both sides was practically identical, the Allies wore white cap-bands (just as one side does in modern manœuvres). Fairfax therefore did what an umpire at manœuvres would have condemned; he removed his white cap-band and mingled with his enemies. By this simple ruse he passed unrecognized through the ranks of his foe, pursuing the course marked on Sketch-map 41, between Wilstrop Wood and White Syke Close. Somewhere on the modern Wilstrop Moor he joined up with Oliver Cromwell.

The latter was inactive at the moment, thereby drawing stinging words from Lawrence Crawford which have duly gone down to history. But though inactive he had got his Ironsides in hand, and was ready for any operation that might seem advisable. One would like a detailed picture of the young Fairfax, on foot, slightly breathless and with a gash across his face, greeting his comrade in arms, seated on his horse with a bandage round his neck. Life had been hazardous for both of them personally during the last hour, and their cause seemed hazardous now as Fairfax poured out his tale of woe. It was his first big battle and for Oliver it was only the second. But neither of these great men blenched. While there is life there is hope; while the Ironsides remain intact and unshaken no one may say the battle is over! Moreover Manchester's infantry, resolutely led by Lawrence Crawford, were also intact and victorious, unmoved apparently by the disaster on the rest of the field.[1]

The two generals put their heads together and a plan was evolved. Fairfax (lays no explicit claim to this plan, but at least it must have been made on the information supplied by him).

---

[1] But Manchester's reported absence from the field, even though temporary, makes one wonder if all the story has been told.

It was a simple plan, as such should always be; a complicated plan in the confusion of a battle has little chance, however good, of being carried out. The gist of the plan was that Cromwell with the horse should skirt round the rear, possibly guided by Fairfax on the route he had just followed. Arriving on the right wing, they would attack Goring and go to the help of the Scots who were still holding out. Meanwhile Manchester's foot on the other flank would attack the hostile infantry that were pressing upon the Scots. Professor Firth has argued as to whether these two operations were carried out simultaneously or not and has come to the conclusion that the cavalry attack upon Goring preceded the infantry attack. This is quite likely, if only because the horse, moving more rapidly and being more compact, would naturally get to grips sooner, unless a deliberate time-table (such as was unheard of in those times) were organized.

Cromwell therefore swept round the rear of the Royalist army (which was by now without a commander) and joined battle with Goring's horse. These were very scattered by this time, and no doubt in some disarray. Some of them were still attempting to penetrate the Scottish square as we may call it (for that is what it must have looked like by this time). Others were trickling back from the pursuit over the hill, rather exhausted and in no trim for another fight against a formed body of Ironsides. Cromwell promptly charged them and had not much difficulty in dispersing them. But note the extraordinary situation that had arisen. The two sides were exactly reversed: Cromwell was now charging from the very same spot and in the same direction as had his opponent Goring an hour before, while Goring's men were situated on the ground occupied by Fairfax at the opening of the battle. No wonder there was confusion in the ranks of both armies, bands of stragglers and fugitives from both armies using the same roads and tracks, dressed and armed alike, and inextricably mixed. To add to the confusion the sun had long set, though a harvest moon gave some help. Under such conditions he who takes the offensive in a resolute manner has a good chance of success. Cromwell was made for such a situation and he exploited it to perfection. What remained of Goring's gallant horse were swept away, and the pressure on the Scots' square was relieved. Not content with this, Cromwell now directed his attack against the hitherto intact Whitecoat regiments of Newcastle's army. Shortly afterwards Crawford, with some of Manchester's men, attacked the Whitecoats from the opposite flank. The double pressure was too much for these hard-tried men. They fell back slowly and steadily some few hundred yards till they entered the White Syke Close, a large field bordered with a ditch and hedge. The rest of the Royalist foot had by this time disintegrated. No doubt some of them had joined in the pursuit of the defeated Lord Fairfax, and had not been able to rejoin the field; but curiously little has come down to us about the action of these troops. Of the end of the Whitecoats, on the other hand, we have two graphic accounts. Nothing, on the testimony of their enemies, could exceed their valour: they did not testify to it themselves; they could not, for they did not live to do so. Scorning surrender, they died almost to a man. Out of a few thousand men, only a mere thirty or forty survived that fearful but glorious day.

The battle was over. In a few short minutes the situation had been transformed, and to two men above all is the credit due; to Sir Thomas Fairfax and to Oliver Cromwell. Marston Moor should be eternally connected with these two names.

★   ★   ★   ★   ★

Prince Rupert managed to collect the bulk of his cavalry in York next day and he marched out with them north-westwards back into Lancashire. But the infantry was completely destroyed and the Marquis of Newcastle, his spirit broken, took ship for Hamburg.

But it is significant of the degree of confusion and dismay in the allied camp that the victors sat down on the battlefield for nearly 48 hours and did not resume the siege of York till they had been joined by their Cheshire reinforcements.

COMMENTS

From almost every point of view the battle of Marston Moor was easily the most remarkable of the Civil War, if not of all the battles fought on English soil. It is hard to account for the excess of panic that swept through the ranks of the Allies. Whatever the various causes, we must allot the main share of the credit to Goring's magnificent troopers, and to his leadership of them. Unfortunately for his reputation Goring had few friends among the scribes. He was always painted as a debauchee; but a permanent drunkard could hardly have accomplished what he did, not only on this occasion. He cannot have been a physically soft man; he had no coach and six to convey him about at the minimum of exertion as had Newcastle. His deeds have remained largely unsung. But when we consider that his cavalry, practically unaided, had routed more than half the opposing army, that is to say a force more than three times as numerous as itself, and that he struck such a panic into his enemy that fugitives are reported as far from the field as Hull, Lincoln, Halifax and Wakefield, we get a fair measure of his achievement. Nor can we be surprised that in the darkness his scattered troopers were eventually driven off by the compact lines of Ironsides. We could well do with an account of Goring's personal motions during the battle; but a defeated army finds but few chroniclers: even Clarendon did not have the heart to compile an account of the battle. So we must abandon a profitless conjecture, only remembering that if Cromwell and Fairfax were the heroes of the victors, 'the drunkard Lord Goring' was the hero of the losers.

It is difficult to assess the work of Prince Rupert on this day. Once again the accounts are quite inadequate, and there is virtually nothing to add to what I have already related of his movements that throws any light on his conduct of the fight. It is to be feared that he merely let it take its course, being personally absorbed in the cavalry mêlée almost throughout the brief engagement. But his true spirit shone forth next morning. While Newcastle was making plans for his get-away, Rupert, finding his cavalry fairly intact, contemplated attacking his victorious enemies. When, on the previous day, someone expostulated at his wish to attack, he exclaimed: 'Nothing venture, nothing gain!' Nor do the eye-witnesses tell us anything material of Lord Leven, except his prolonged flight, and his natural remorse when hearing next day of the upshot of the fight. Indeed, the first news to reach London and Oxford was of a Royalist victory.

From quite another point of view the battle is unique. It was the only occasion during the Civil War in which English and Scots armies fought as allies on the same field (the Royalist army at Worcester was almost entirely composed of Scots). When two or more allies share in the same disaster one may be sure that there will afterwards be mutual recriminations. And even success leads to recrimination in alloting the credit. Such was the case after Marston Moor, and Cromwell was the centre of the controversy. There is no need to add here to what I have already said but it is worth while reflecting on this weakness which is inherent in such an army. Since, in the nature of things, the British Army fights its big battles with allies it is important to realize what hazards and pitfalls there are, and to take studious care to minimize them.

SOME FURTHER BATTLEFIELD PROBLEMS

Considering the comparatively large number of sources for this battle, and the very clearly defined line of battle, it might be supposed that the problems of the battle would be few and insignificant. But we must remember that exceptionally large numbers were present, more than in any other battle of the war and probably more than any other battle ever fought in England, with the single exception of Towton. Hence the number of witnesses is not large in proportion to the numbers engaged and the extent of the ground fought over. When we add to this the breakneck speed with which events succeeded one another, and the fact that the battle was fought in gathering darkness, it becomes easy to understand how scanty the material in reality is. For example, though the original line of battle is, as I have said, well defined and not susceptible to controversy, the scene of the decisive fighting is very conjectural. None of the sources help us here, though tradition mentions White Syke Close at the end. Thus we find Buchan placing the Scottish 'square' a few hundred yards south of the ditch, whereas I place it nearly 1,000 yards further north. I am influenced by the following considerations: (1) The Royalist foot gave ground at the beginning of the battle: that is, fell back from the ditch northwards. (2) Some of their guns were captured (which confirms point (1)) (3) If the Scots in their turn then fell back to the south of the ditch one might expect some reference to it, or to the ditch itself, but there is nothing. (4) Casualties must have been at least as heavy round the 'square' as anywhere on the field, yet there are no local traditions or signs of grave-pits to the south of the ditch. (Grave-pits are one of the best indications of the scene of the main fighting.) (5) If the main fighting took place to the south of the ditch the Whitecoats must have been there. In that case they had a retreat of over 1,000 yards to White Syke Close, fighting Crawford's foot all the way. Now Crawford started this attack from a spot well to the north of the ditch; if, then, the Whitecoats were to the south, his attack would have struck them in their right rear, tending to drive them further to the south, instead of to the north (to White Syke Close). (Sketch-map 41 will make this clear.) In short, it does not make sense. The only possible conclusion seems to be that the main engagement of Baillie's Scots was somewhere between White Syke Close and Moor Lane. All the known grave-pits point to the fighting taking place well to the north of the ditch. They are: Four Lanes Meet, White Syke Close, and the edge of Wilstrop Wood. Bullets have been found in the trees on the edge of the wood. This is only one of the problems that have to be solved, and I have entered into it in detail as an example of the obscurity that the original sources leave upon the battlefield, in spite of the apparent clarity of it when one reads a short account of the battle.

In relating the course of the battle I have not mentioned 'Cromwell's Gap'. This is pointed out about half-way up the hill from Marston village. But its significance is uncertain. One tradition is that Cromwell's men chased Goring's horse through this gap. R. N. Lawley, writing in 1862, says: 'Others say that it is where Cromwell's artillery was dragged'; adding inconsequently: 'but certain it is that to this day no thorn will grow there.' The connection of Cromwell's name with the spot is valueless; his name is almost invariably attached to any battlefield site that requires a name. It is of course not improbable that some Ironsides chased some of Goring's men back up the hill, but it throws no light on the course of the battle, hence I have ignored it.

CHAPTER XXXIII

The Second Battle of Newbury, October 28th, 1644

THE interest of this battle resides in its strategical rather than its tactical aspect. In this it is unique among all the battles of the great Civil War.

The situation leading up to the battle is somewhat involved and needs a map of Southern England by which to follow it. Stated in the broadest terms, the Royalist army, on its return from its victorious campaign in the west over the Earl of Essex, had by mid-October, 1644, reached Salisbury. The Roundheads at this moment had three separate armies in the field. The Earl of Manchester was at Reading, the Earl of Essex was reforming his defeated army at Portsmouth, and Sir William Waller was falling back before the King and was now at Andover. In addition the Roundheads had three sieges on their hands, Donnington Castle (a mile to the north of Newbury), Basing House (a mile east of Basingstoke), and Banbury. The approach of the Royal army seemed to threaten the first two. The very threat had this effect on the besiegers of Donnington Castle, who, faced by the resolute defence of Colonel Boys, abandoned the siege and fell back on Reading on October 18th. There remained Basing House. With the object of relieving it, the King resumed his advance on October 18th, driving Waller out of Andover the same day.

Meanwhile the three Parliamentary armies were steadily converging. On the 16th Manchester reached Basingstoke from Reading. On the next day Essex, advancing from Portsmouth, reached Alresford (12 miles south of Basingstoke), and on the 19th joined Manchester there. Meanwhile Waller was also drawing near from Andover, and on the 21st all three armies were united at Basingstoke. The total now concentrated came to 19,000 men, one of the largest armies on either side that had yet appeared in the field. But if formidable in numbers it was less so in its command. Instead of appointing one commander-in-chief for this army, the egregious Committee of Both Kingdoms placed it in commission under a council composed of Manchester, Essex, Waller and other officers, and even two complete civilians; (reminding one of the Dutch Deputies that accompanied Marlborough's army in the field).

Undeterred by this formidable concentration in front of him, the King pushed boldly forward and reached Kingsclere on October 21st. Here he was midway between the two threatened posts, Donnington Castle and Basing House. But he was too late to relieve Basing House, so he now turned north towards Donnington Castle, entering Newbury next day, the 22nd.

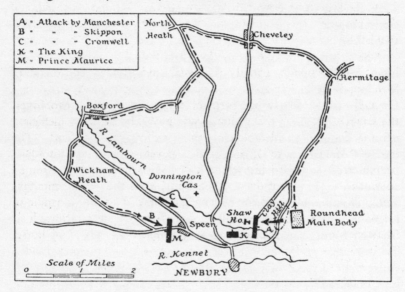

SKETCH–MAP 42.　NEWBURY II

From Newbury Charles sent a force of horse under the Earl of Northampton to the relief of Banbury, which was speedily effected by it. But this left him with only 9,000 men at Newbury. The Roundheads' Council of War decided to attack the Royalist army without further delay, and set out for the purpose on October 25th. Next day they were established on Clay Hill, one mile to the north-east of Newbury. (Sketch-map 42.)

Thus the situation on the evening of October 26th was that the Roundheads, 19,000 strong were confronting the Royalists, 10,000 strong, the two armies facing respectively west and east, immediately to the north of Newbury. It looked as if the King had been out-manœuvred; but there were certain points in his favour which appeared to justify his decision to stand his ground. The first was the natural strength of the position that he occupied. His right flank was protected by the river Kennet and the town of Newbury in which he kept a garrison; his left by a small tributary, the Lambourn, while still further to the left rear, stood the formidable Donnington Castle, under its heroic defender, Colonel Boys (whom the King knighted on the field for his spirited defence, shortly before the battle). So much for the flanks. The centre rested on a large house occupied by a Mr. Dolman and now called Shaw House. Round three sides of the garden, forming a sort of courtyard, were some ancient embankments.[1] The house formed a veritable fortress, like Hougoumont in a later and more famous battle. The Royalists had another but intangible advantage, namely the weak and divided command of their opponents. We have seen that the command was vested in a Council—a notoriously bad form of command in war. Moreover, the senior general on that Council was probably the most inefficient commander of a considerable army that ever fought in England. The Earl of Manchester, to do him justice, never set up to be a soldier; he preferred to regard himself as a civilian who had only assumed command at the call of duty. Apparently even the Parliamentarians were influenced by the desire to have a commander with 'a handle to his name'; whereas Cromwell, though fresh from his triumph at Marston Moor, was relegated to a subordinate command of horse. The Earl of Essex had gone sick and his army was itself given a divided command in the persons of Skippon and Balfour.

But this peculiar council now nerved itself to a remarkable decision —one that gives this battle its distinctive interest. Not liking the look of the Royalist position from the front, the council decided —on whose proposition does not appear—to attack it simultaneously from front and rear. To encompass this would entail a wide detour by the outflanking column owing to the position of Donnington Castle on the left rear—a site that might have been purposely selected to frustrate such a manœuvre. The route decided on was as follows: three miles north-east nearly to Hermitage—west, via Chieveley to North Heath—south to Winterbourne—west to Boxford—south to Wickham Heath—south-east to Speen. Total 13 miles. It was a bold decision to take, even though the Royalist army was in great inferiority; for the council could not have known the exact strength of their opponents, and the tendency is to overrate the size of the

[1] Incorrectly believed of old to have been thrown up for the battle.

opposing army. Including a period for rest and sleep the march would take the best part of 24 hours, and during that time the remainder of the army risked being attacked by the whole force of the Royalists. But this decision is a good example of the profound truth that in war risks *must* be taken. In actual fact there was never much prospect of the King attacking the main army during this period. By some means he managed to get wind of the flanking move, and in order to counter it he also divided his forces and detached Prince Maurice's detachment to occupy a position to the west of Speen, facing west.

The reserve, consisting of horse and the artillery train, was stationed in the open in a large field, which can still be identified, stretching from the northern outskirts of the town to the banks of the Lambourn river. Maurice took up his position on the rising ground just to the west of Speen village, and spent the morning of October 27th busily entrenching his position.

Meanwhile the outflanking force—Essex's army, under Skippon and Balfour, with Waller's and Cromwell's horse—was steadily plodding on its long, circuitous march. Skippon, Balfour and Waller appear to have shared the command—a strange arrangement! It had set out shortly after midnight and halted to bivouac at Heath End. This outflanking force constituted the greater part of the army—probably two-thirds of it, though exact figures are not given.

We must now for a moment consider the strategy of operations on 'exterior lines', such as this was: i.e. a concentric attack from two or more different directions. To make success probable, the army undertaking it should be in superior strength to its opponents, else there is the danger that the enemy, making use of his central position on 'interior lines', will attack and overwhelm each opponent in turn. To diminish the risk of this, and to add to the effectiveness of the blow, it is necessary that both forces should attack simultaneously. Therein lies the snag—or rather, there it used to lie before the days of improved communications, telegraphy and telephony, wireless, etc. For two widely separated forces, out of sight of each other, found it difficult, if not impossible, to co-ordinate their attacks. It is for this reason that the operation was so seldom attempted, and if attempted, so seldom was successful in olden days. Indeed, the second Battle of Newbury is the only clear-cut example of it in the course of the Civil War.

But in spite of the difficulties and hazards inherent in an operation on exterior lines in the seventeenth century, there remained one form of communication common to both ancient and modern times—sound. Manchester arranged very sensibly in my opinion, that Skippon should fire his cannon as a signal that he was in position and about to attack; on hearing that signal Manchester would also attack; thus co-ordination would be achieved in the simplest possible manner. It seemed almost foolproof—but nothing is foolproof in war.

THE BATTLE

Manchester attempted a feint attack in the early morning. The tendency of such attacks is either to be transparently feints, or to be pushed too far. The latter happened in this case and the attacking troops were only extricated with difficulty.

Skippon came into contact with Prince Maurice's detachment at about 3 p.m. The exact time is disputed; even to-day it is difficult to ascertain exact times of occurrences in the course of an encounter battle, and naturally it was much more difficult then. It is important to fix this moment though, in view of what transpired, and anyway it cannot have been far from 3 p.m. There remained two hours of daylight (it was November 9th New Style). If Manchester's attack was to prove effective against the strong Shaw House position there was no time to lose. But no sound came from that part of the field. Meanwhile the attack on Prince Maurice was being launched. In spite of their fatigue after their long march, the Roundheads attacked resolutely. The trenches to the west of Speen had not been completed, and the position was, after a sanguinary struggle, overrun, and the guns defending it, captured from Essex at Lostwithiel, were, by a curious coincidence, recaptured by Essex's own men. The Royalist foot was sent reeling down the road into and through the village of Speen, and even further. The situation for the Royalists looked critical. The King himself was with the Royal princes, standing at the head of his reserve in the open field, when some fleeing cavalry came charging past him. Charles did his best by his own personal efforts to rally them, but without marked success. At this critical moment a small reinforcement to either side would decide the issue, as so often happens in war. There was an obvious quarter from where it might be reasonably expected. Hitherto we have not spoken of the redoubtable Oliver Cromwell, whose cavalry had added such lustre to his name on the field of Marston Moor, only three months before.

He held the left, or northern flank of the line (Balfour held the southern) and hitherto had been but lightly engaged. Accounts as to his action on this day are conflicting. But though we cannot credit the assertion of Manchester that 'on that day there was no service at all performed by Cromwell' (for the two were at enmity), it does not seem that Cromwell exerted himself or intervened at this decisive moment. Excuses are made for him, the commonest being that his troopers were harried by the artillery fire from Donnington Castle. This will not do. Though we have no record of the number of guns in the castle it cannot have been very great; there was not room for a large number. Moreover, the fire of these guns was exceedingly slow, and even at the present day the cavalry would not constitute an easy target moving quickly across the front. The range was about 1,000 yards, and the most they can have effected was to be a 'nuisance value' to Cromwell's men. I conclude, therefore, that either Cromwell feared overmuch the potential danger residing in the armament of Donnington Castle, or else his heart, to put it bluntly, was not in the affair. He gives the impression of being slightly disgruntled on this occasion. Even the greatest of men suffer from human frailties.

Whatever the cause, Cromwell failed to effect a successful intervention; on the contrary it was a Royalist, Lord Cleveland, who seized this critical moment to charge with his brigade. The battle fluctuated uncertainly for some time, but it was decided in this sector by two further charges by Sir John Cansfield and the King's Life Guards. The Roundheads were hurled back to Speen, the King's personal safety was secured, and the battle on this portion of the front became stationary for the remaining few moments of daylight.

Meanwhile what was happening on the opposite side of the field? Again we are in the presence of controversy. The commonly accepted story is that Manchester refused, despite the reiterated appeals of those around him, to intervene, in spite of the engagement he had made to do so. But those who assert this do not explain how it then came about that Manchester *did* eventually intervene. Who, or what was it that caused him eventually to change his mind? Critics are silent on this point. In point of fact, his troops did attack, though as in the previous case it is impossible to ascertain precisely at what hour this happened. Partly these conflicting accounts are due to the fact that the precise moment of the commencement of such an attack is not clear-cut or clearly defined; there would be no established 'zero hour' with watches synchronized, and so on. One narrator might consider the beginning of the attack the moment at which the commander issued his orders for the attack; another might consider it the moment when they actually started to advance; a third, when they got to 'push of pike'. Moreover, the clash would come at slightly different moments in different parts of the front. What I suspect happened was that Manchester was so doubtful as to whether the attack would take place that day at all, that he did not issue any 'warning order' to his troops, preferring to wait until the moment actually arrived when he would issue the orders that seemed appropriate to the occasion. This would not be a prudent or far-seeing method of procedure (Manchester was a bad general), but that is very different from saying that the Earl of Manchester left his comrades in the lurch.

Assuming then that he set about launching an attack as soon as he heard the cannonade opening, it might easily take about one hour before the attackers actually came to blows with the enemy. His plan was not a particularly simple one; the attack was to be delivered by two columns, one to attack Shaw House from the north-east, and the other from the south-east. From the top of Clay Hill, where his troops were drawn up, to Shaw House is 2,000 yards. It would take the foot a good 30 minutes to cover this distance, without any delays, once they had been marshalled in order. An allowance of one hour is not in the least excessive to allow from the time when Manchester, having formed his plan, sent it out to the recipients, to the time when the first clash occurred. If Skippon's attack started at 3 p.m. that means that Manchester's, under these circumstances, would materialize at about 4 p.m. which is probably what actually occurred. The sun sets at 4.2 p.m. on that day, and the moon had not risen. The fight therefore took place in the gathering darkness, as is agreed on all hands. My contention receives support from Simeon Ashe, the Earl's chaplain. According to this worthy, Manchester was able to see from Clay Hill the attack on Speen (the contours show that this should be possible) and 'animated with this encouraging sight, the Earl prepared to descend to the more difficult work of forcing the strong position at Dolman's house'. Money states that Manchester, 'busy with his preparations for advancing in force, rode to and fro and spiritedly addressed his men'.

So the attack was launched, while still the action was in full swing on the opposite flank. Thus were the two essential conditions of an operation on exterior lines—superior numbers, and a simultaneous attack—observed. The enemy was thus not in a position to turn his

central position to account by concentrating against first one and
then the other of his opponents. I can find no evidence that Charles
even attempted this. His reserves in the field to the north of Newbury
nearly midway between Shaw House and Speen, were in a good
position to execute this if they got the chance, and were given enough
time; but the nearly simultaneous hostile attack rendered that impossible. What then saved the Royalists? Undoubtedly the night.
Manchester's attack, after a homeric contest in the garden of Shaw
House, was decisively repulsed, and some of his troops were chased
back as far as Clay Hill; but the far more serious attack on the west
would have completely borne down its vastly inferior opponents,
despite the intervention of the guns at Donnington Castle, had darkness not put an end to the battle. Thus was a risky and enterprising
plan justified by its success.

The King, who had decided that morning that if he were attacked
on both sides he would slip away to the north by night and try to regain
Oxford, carried out his plan to the letter. He left his guns in Donnington Castle, and while he himself with an escort rode to join Prince
Rupert at Bath, the army marched through the night, over King
Alfred's famous battlefield of Ashdown, to Wallingford, and reached
Oxford next day. Meanwhile the Roundheads were fast asleep, and
when morning dawned were still ignorant of the departure of the royal
army. The upshot of First Newbury had repeated itself.

PROBLEMS OF THE BATTLEFIELD

This battlefield, unlike that of First Newbury, presents few
problems. The three key points, Shaw House, Speen Village, and
Donnington Castle are all unambiguous. It is an extremely easy
battle to follow either on foot or in a car. All that is necessary is to
leave Newbury by the Hermitage road, and after crossing the Lambourn you come to Shaw House. Inside the house you may see the
bullet mark in a first-floor room which, tradition relates, nearly hit
the King. Round the garden the old embankment is still in existence.
Immediately beyond the garden to the east is a knoll surmounted by a
water-tower. From here Clay Hill, from which Manchester attacked,
is plainly visible, and the course of this attack can easily be followed.
A short walk through the village of Donnington then takes up up to
Donnington Castle. From the battlements of the Gatehouse, or even
from the ground at its foot, the Speen battle can be followed in detail.

It requires but little imagination to picture the excitement of the Royalist gunners as they spotted the approach of the Parliamentary army. It would be visible for over a mile along the ridge before it contacted Maurice's entrenchments. A few shots were fired at this point, the range being about 1,800 yards. Then when Cromwell's troopers appeared in the meadows almost at their feet the excitement must have been intensified, the range shortening to 800 yards. Sir John Boys, possibly accompanied for part of the time by the King himself, no doubt stood in the corner of the nearest (south-west) turret of the gatehouse, with his eye glued to his 'perspective glass'— if he possessed one. In short, the layout is so straightforward that no further space need be devoted to describing this battlefield.

CHAPTER XXXIV

The Battle of Naseby, June 14th, 1645

NO battlefield on English soil, apart from Hastings, is more famous than Naseby. It stands precisely in the centre of the country. Yet, how many people ever visit it? Until quite recently not a stone, not a mark, existed to indicate to the traveller that he was passing over a famous field (for the so-called Naseby Obelisk, erected in 1825, is situated a good mile from the site of the battle). The Cromwell Association have now erected a memorial to commemorate the charge of Oliver Cromwell that settled the issue, but this, useful though it be to attract the attention of the passer-by, is some 500 yards to the west of the correct site.

On the other hand, the battlefield is well documented on both sides—particularly the winning side, as may be expected; and there are few controversial points in connection with either the site or the course of the battle. Furthermore, thanks to the modern road from Sibbertoft to Naseby, it is easy to find the battlefield. This simplifies and shortens my task.

There is, however, one exceedingly knotty point that has never been fully cleared up (it has been slurred over by all historians except Gardiner) to which I shall devote a good deal of attention, for the episode is curious and almost unique. For the moment I will only indicate it. Two armies are approaching one another on the same road. They are only three miles apart, and a head-on collision on that road seems inevitable, unless one of them suddenly turns tail. Yet both armies, as if by mutual consent, side-slip nearly 1½ miles to the flank, and there form up and engage in battle. I know no exact counterpart of this; yet the question as to why they performed this curious evolution is still unresolved. I hope to throw some light on it in due course.

PRELIMINARY MOVES

We will take up the story at the moment when the New Model army of Parliament was abandoning the siege of Oxford, while King

Charles with his army was stationed irresolutely at Daventry, 35 miles to the north. The strategy of this brief campaign shows Charles, for the first time in the war, in a poorer light than his opponents. It was the old story of divided councils. Rupert was for going North to attack the Scots, while Digby favoured a concentration in the south in order to attack Fairfax's New Model army, and later to make an incursion into the eastern counties. As a result the King remained undecided at Daventry, while collecting further supplies for the succour of Oxford.

This was the situation when on June 5th, 1645, Fairfax broke up his camp before Oxford and advanced north-east to Newport Pagnell. From this moment the Roundheads out-manœuvred the Cavaliers. To what was this change due? To three events that followed in three successive days. On June 8th, Fairfax's council of war resolved to make the Royalist army their fixed objective. On the 9th, Parliament gave their general a completely free hand in conducting his operations (hitherto he had been subject to their directives); and, on the 10th, Oliver Cromwell was appointed to the New Model army as Fairfax's lieutenant-general, or second-in-command.

A new spirit of enterprise and clear-cut policy was thenceforth visible in the Parliamentary ranks.

The hesitation that had hitherto been so evident was in great measure due to the fact that the New Model was a brand-new army and an 'unknown quantity'. Many people, knowing what it afterwards achieved, assume that it was from the first a fine army, forgetting, or not being aware of the fact, that it was quite correctly described at the time by a Cavalier as consisting for the most part of 'raw, inexperienced, pressed soldiers'; for Parliament had to resort to compulsion in order to fill the ranks. But in two material points they were superior to their opponents—in leadership and in numbers. The combination of Fairfax and Cromwell was a formidable one, as Marston Moor had shown. The King had nothing to show against it, for Lord Astley, with his 66 years, was too old for the field, while Prince Rupert, if not too young at 25 years, was too independent. As for numbers, the Roundheads had a superiority of nearly two to one— 14,000 to 7,500, a scale of odds that the God of Battles usually favours. As for that third important factor, morale, it is, as always, difficult to be dogmatic. The King's recent capture of Leicester had certainly raised the morale of his army and its officers were openly contemptuous of their opponents, but the timely arrival of Cromwell had put fresh heart into the New Model, and both sides were equally confident of victory in the impending ordeal by battle.

To resume the narrative. On June 12th, Fairfax, pursuant to his new plan, advanced by the south of Northampton to Kislingbury, eight miles east of Daventry, driving in the royal picquets. The King was at that moment not prepared to fight in the open, and, breaking up his camp, he retreated hurriedly by night 18 miles north-east to Market Harborough, *en route* for Newark. Fairfax spotted the move betimes and set off in pursuit next day, the 13th. By nightfall he had reached Guilsborough, four miles south of Naseby, while his vanguard entered Naseby and captured some Cavalier patrols feasting at a long table in the inn.[1]

This startling news was brought to the King in the middle of the night. He rose and called a council. In the early hours of June 14th it met. At this council it was decided that the enemy was too close upon their heels to avoid a fight, so it was resolved to hold the high ground two miles to the south of the town as a defensive position. This position ran from East Farndon to Oxendon, extending for two miles and covering the road from Naseby it formed a very strong position, just made for the purpose. Here the Cavalier army was drawn up well before 8 a.m. From it the view to the south was not impeded by the tall hedges and numerous trees that now abound, and the ridge immediately to the north of Naseby was in full view. So also must have been a number of hostile horsemen on the ridge at about that time. But either because they were only a few in number or because the light was bad, Rupert sent his scoutmaster to report on the disposition of the enemy.[2] This feeble individual came back shortly afterwards declaring that he had been two or three miles forward and could see no enemy. Rupert flatly disbelieved this report, and did the obvious thing a young, energetic commander would do under such circumstances—he went forward himself, taking with him a body of horse of unspecified numbers.

The precise course of events during the next two hours forms the great controversial point of the battle—the 'side-slip' of both armies that I referred to in my opening paragraph. Here I will follow the example of Gardiner, who, in view of its importance and complication, in order not to destroy the smooth course of the narrative, relegates

[1] This table is now kept in the north aisle of the church.

[2] It cannot have been much later than 6 a.m., and there was probably a ground mist.

discussion of the point to an appendix. I therefore relegate it to the end of this chapter, here merely relating the course of events as I see them.

Fairfax broke up camp shortly after 3 a.m. and at the moment when the Royalists were ascending the East Farndon Ridge, he was ascending the Naseby ridge, four miles to the south. Each army discerned the motions of the other, though dimly.

It was now evident to Fairfax that the King, contrary to expectation, had arrested his retreat; but it was not yet clear whether he was merely awaiting attack on the East Farndon ridge, or whether he himself intended to attack. As a preliminary precaution Fairfax decided to occupy a position covering Naseby, and rode forward, accompanied by his lieutenant-general (Cromwell), to reconnoitre for such a position. Crossing the ridge-top he dropped down into the valley. The ground was boggy and a little stream crossed the road, about a mile south of Clipston (see Sketch-map 43). He was contemplating occupying this position, covered by the stream and the boggy ground, when Cromwell intervened. The enemy were strong in cavalry, but this was no cavalry ground, he observed, being an experienced horseman himself. Rupert, he sensed, would either turn the position or else remain on the defensive on the high ground to the north, declining action. This would not fit in with the Parliamentary plans. It would be better to occupy the ridge in rear, he urged; this would tempt Rupert across the valley and he would be obliged to charge uphill at them.

Fairfax saw the force of the contention, and agreed to it. At this moment his army was strung out on the line of march, the rear portion being still in column of route, gradually closing up on to the rendezvous near the village. Here the head of the army had halted, less the vanguard cavalry who had escorted the two generals forward on their reconnaissance.

Thus it came about that, at the moment when Rupert with his escort of horse was approaching Clipston, Fairfax with his escort was withdrawing up the hill to the Naseby ridge. Rupert, seeing this retrograde movement, imagined quite naturally that the enemy were going to occupy the ridge. He at the same time took note of the boggy ground beyond Clipston in front of the hostile position, and decided, as Cromwell had guessed, that it would not do to commit his cavalry to such ground. From the ridge to the north of Clipston, however, he could see what looked more promising terrain away to the right, by which his horse might ascend the Naseby ridge. It would be in the nature of a flanking movement, and would incidentally give him the advantage of the windward position, no mean advantage in the days of black powder. Sending back an urgent message to the army

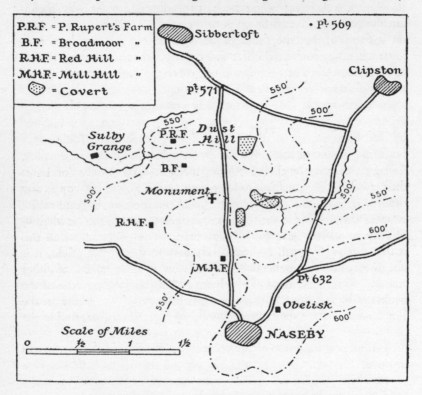

SKETCH-MAP 43.   NASEBY: THE BATTLEFIELD

to follow in his tracks, Prince Rupert therefore struck off to his right, and hit the Sibbertoft—Naseby road probably near point 571, one mile south of the village.[1]

Rupert's flanking move was spotted from the Naseby ridge and Fairfax divined his intention. In order to forestall him he decided to side-step to the same flank. The result of this decision was that both armies were by 9 o'clock moving westwards on almost parallel lines. This move involved a side-step of about one mile for the leading troops.

[1] One account says that Rupert was guided there, so it may be that a local inhabitant informed him of the possibilities of the Broadmoor position.

This brought them to an open valley between the two ridges, where the valley was at its shallowest and the slope at its most gentle. At this point, now called Broadmoor, there is no stream, for it is on the great 'divide' of England (though even less perceptible than the 'divide' at Hastings). Here both armies decided practically simultaneously to stand and take up position.

It forms a fine site for a battle, with two parallel ridges, now joined by the modern Sibbertoft—Naseby road along the invisible 'divide', the Avon having its sources just to the west of the road, and the Ise (flowing into the Wash) to the east.

THE BATTLEFIELD

The changes in the appearance of the ground since 1642 are as follows. Practically all the existing hedges except Sulby (or Lantford) Hedges (of which more later), are new. So are the copses and the few farmhouses. On the other hand the furze-bushes and rabbit warrens that abounded on the eastern edge of the field in the vicinity of Naseby Covert have long disappeared. The net result of all this is that though it is still comparatively easy to identify the field, it is not as easy to get a general bird's-eye view of the position of either side as it was at the time of the battle. This is especially true of the flanks: Sulby Hedges[1] on the west are on low ground, whilst on the east Naseby Covert tends to narrow the view. But the ground in the centre where the infantry fight took place is still comparatively open, and as it is nearly bisected by the modern Naseby—Sibbertoft road visitors travelling in either direction can easily get there, and recognize it when they have done so. But in order the better to identify the flanks, I produce a Sketch-map (44) showing the present fields and farms and copses. Reverting now to Sketch-map 43, on which are shown the important contours, 500, 550 and 600 feet, it will be seen that the road running north from Naseby passes through two slight dips before sinking into the valley of Broadmoor. The second of these dips is very slight and is described in one account as a 'ledge', an expressive term denoting a slight break in the general declivity.

It was just in front of this ledge that the Parliamentary army was at first arrayed by Skippon (as shown on Sketch-map 44). Fairfax, however, came up and decided to withdraw the line behind the

[1] The plural indicates a double hedge. It marked the parish and Sulby estate boundary.

ledge, whilst it was being marshalled, in order not to proclaim his dispositions to the prying eyes of the enemy. (Had Wellington this procedure in mind when at Waterloo he kept most of his infantry lying down just behind the crest?)

This incident is of significance as it shows (what some of the sources seem to deny) that the Roundheads started to take up their position

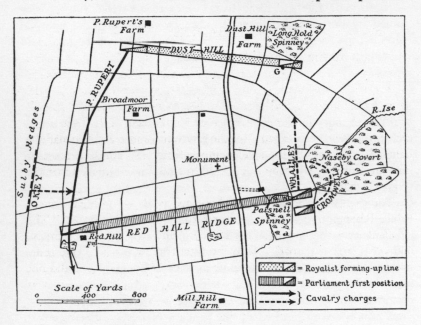

SKETCH-MAP 44.　NASEBY: THE BATTLE

before the Cavaliers. If it had been the other way, Fairfax's withdrawal behind the ledge would have been pointless, for it would have been too late.

This brings us to the Royalist army. We have seen how Rupert sent a messenger back from Clipston, calling the whole army forward. It followed pretty closely in his own footsteps, being seen at intervals as it crossed the crests. On reaching the Sibbertoft road, where Rupert had been waiting for it for an hour, it turned south and found itself on the Dust Hill ridge. From here the advanced troops of the hostile army could be seen straight across the valley. If Rupert had had hopes of turning the hostile flank and coming upon them from the west along the top of the ridge, he must have been disappointed, for he had been forestalled. A frontal attack, straight across Broad-moor Valley, was the only thing left to him. Still, this terrain was a great improvement on the Clipston position, the ground being firmer and the slope up which his horse would probably have to charge being much more gentle. In short, Prince Rupert was justified in being satisfied with the position.

THE BATTLE

As soon as the Royalist army reached Dust Hill, Lord Astley proceeded to deploy the foot in line, whilst Prince Rupert marshalled the horse. In this book we are not concerned with orders of battle, names and numbers, and it must suffice to say that Rupert himself took the right wing cavalry, Lord Astley commanded the infantry in the centre, while the cavalry on the left were under Sir Marmaduke Langdale. Owing to the sudden move from East Farndon most of the guns had been left behind; a few light pieces, however, did manage to join in the battle.

The extreme right flank was about 200 yards west of the present Prince Rupert's Farm, i.e. 1,000 yards to the right of the road. The left flank probably rested on the southern tip of Long Hold Spinney, 600 yards from the road. Thus the total front was nearly one mile. For an army of 7,500 this was quite as wide as desirable, and did not allow of a strong reserve. Such reserve as the King possessed was mainly of horse, and was about 800 strong. The King's own post would be near Dust Hill Farm, whence he could get a good general view of the field.

The Parliamentary army was drawn up in the same formation and on the same frontage, except for one detail on the western flank. The ground falls away rather sharply to the right, and is what the French call *accidenté*. Cromwell, who commanded the cavalry on this side, probably formed up his horse in consequence slightly behind the infantry line in order to keep to the higher ground. The infantry in the centre, under Major-General Skippon, were (when drawn back) just behind Red Hill ridge. The cavalry on the left were under Ireton, the Commissary-General. Their left rested just short of the Sulby hedges. Behind Sulby hedges Cromwell placed 1,000 dragoons under Colonel Okey. This was a striking disposition since they were in front of the general line of battle, and perpendicular to it. Their object was to enfilade Rupert's horse when they charged.

Very nice, but very risky; for if Rupert 'fetched a compass' the dragoons might find themselves enfiladed, or even taken in reverse. Not only were Okey's dragoons perpendicular to the line, and out on an exposed flank, but they were well in advance of the line. Map 44 shows that the southern end of the hedge bends away while it is still 300 yards in front of the general line. If the dragoons took up 800 yards of frontage this would bring their left flank level with the modern Broadmoor Farm. No historian of the battle appears to find such an advanced position in the least extraordinary, but I find it hard to credit. I think the solution must be that Okey's troops only lined the southern half of the hedge, and spilled over as it were, to the south of it, making use of some furze bushes in the vicinity for cover. I show them thus in my map. It is clear from Okey's own account that they were not fully deployed when the battle commenced, and in addition some troopers were left to protect the horses.

Fairfax had all his guns up, but, remembering the small effect they had at Marston Moor, he did not rely on them, and they played an insignificant part in the battle.

By 10 a.m. both armies were ranged in battle order, over half a mile apart, the Broadmoor Valley separating them. Which would make the first move? At Edgehill the Royalists had deliberately forsaken their commanding position and had attacked; at Marston Moor their opponents had done the same thing. Considering that the King's army was so weak in numbers it would have been natural for him to stand on the defensive, and probably Lord Astley desired this course. But the impulsive Rupert once again decided the issue. With or without the concurrence of Astley he prevailed upon the King to order a general attack. It is more difficult to determine what Fairfax's real intention was. He must have seen the hostile advance from its start, and might have stood his ground on the 'ledge'. But he did in fact advance his line down the hill below the ledge. Was this in order to meet the enemy on the move, or merely to reoccupy his original line just in front of the ledge? It is impossible to say, but the latter seems the more likely, for his cavalry on both flanks made no sign of attacking at first. We must conclude that the battle was in essence an attack by the Cavaliers on the Roundheads. The chronology of this, as of all battles, is vague, and most writers assume that the first episode was the charge of Rupert's horse. I think it more likely that Rupert on this occasion allowed the foot to come to 'push of pike' before launching his cavalry across the valley. Seated on his horse near the present Prince Rupert Farm, he could see perfectly the progress of the infantry across the valley and up the gentle slopes to the hedge where the new memorial now stands. A few seconds later he would see the Roundheads streaming over the crest beyond it, and then the two lines becoming merged into one. Till this moment his eyes and those of most of his horse would be glued on the progress of the infantry. The clash would be the signal for his own advance. Sinking the hill and trotting across the valley in two lines, his cavalry would be abreast of their infantry in a very few minutes.

Opposed to him were Ireton's horse. Rupert's charge went a bit wide of the infantry line, though keeping inside the Sulby hedges, from whence he received a ragged fire which did not impede or divert the charge. Sweeping up the gentle slope at an increased pace, his first line crashed into the left of Ireton's line about Redhill Farm. The Roundhead horse were either killed or took to flight, and Rupert surged victoriously on for another mile till, in a hollow to the west of Naseby village, he came across the enemy's baggage camp.

The camp guard, however, put up a sturdy resistance, and valuable time was lost by the Cavalier horsemen in attempting to capture it. Mindful of his experience at Edgehill under similar circumstances, Rupert drew rein and exerted himself to collect his troopers and lead them back to the battle. This, as always, was a difficult and lengthy task, and the best part of an hour elapsed before he reappeared on the field, at the head of his victorious horse.

In this short space of time two crises had been witnessed elsewhere. The first was in the centre. In spite of the fact that they had the slope of the hill against them, the Royalist foot managed to push their opponents back over the crest in a retreat which soon began to have the aspect of flight. Skippon himself was wounded and the position had suddenly become critical. Fairfax saw his left wing dispersed and now his centre was giving way. In such a critical situation in the heat of battle Fairfax was at his best. Flinging forwards his reserves, and entering the turmoil himself, the Roundhead commander managed to bring the Royalist onset to a halt.

But this was not all. We have seen how Rupert, riding wide, had struck the left portion of Ireton's horse. The right portion was not touched, and after Rupert's charge had passed on, Ireton became aware that Skippon's infantry on his right were also falling back,

With an exemplary display of presence of mind and initiative the young Ireton justified his new command,[1] wheeled the remnant of his cavalry to the right and struck the Royalist infantry in their right flank.

But these splendid regiments of the King's army did not flinch at this unexpected attack. Though the numbers in their direct front were every moment getting greater, as Fairfax threw in his reserves, they yet spared a portion of their now attenuated ranks to counter this new danger. And well they did it; the cavalry attack was brought to a stand, and Ireton himself was wounded and taken prisoner.

But this was not the end of their troubles. When Rupert's horsemen had swept past them Okey's Dragoons 'gave up ourselves for lost men', for an isolated body of Royalist horse was also attacking their rear.[2] However, Rupert had disappeared, and now Okey perceived the action of Ireton's horse[3] against the Royalist foot, and recovering his head and showing a like initiative, he mounted his dragoons and charged the enemy—an interesting example of the gradual merging of dragoons (mounted infantry) into cavalry.

Even now the cup of the Royalist infantry was not full. Cromwell, as we have seen, had drawn up his foot somewhere to the rear and well up the hill. From this vantage point he calmly watched Langdale's troopers threading their way through furze bushes and rabbit warrens at the bottom of the hill. As they began to breast the rather steep rise Cromwell gave the signal, at exactly the right moment, and Whalley's horse thundered down the hill in greatly superior numbers and in an irresistible charge. There is no need to attribute Langdale's defeat to the insubordinate spirit that was rife in his Northern horse. No mounted troops alive could withstand a mounted attack over such ground if it was pushed with resolution. Langdale's horse were swept off the field, with the leading three of Cromwell's regiments in hot pursuit. Now came the dramatic moment of the battle. We have seen twice in the case of Rupert's horse how they disappeared from the field despite what the Prince could do to stop them. But Cromwell did stop the bulk of his horse and retained them on the field. How are we to account for the

[1] He had only received it that morning.

[2] There is only a single reference to this attack, but corroboration of it is perhaps supplied by a grave-pit, which for long puzzled me, marked on the O.S. map some 400 yards to the *west* of Sulby hedges, i.e. right outside the battlefield.

[3] In his account he says Cromwell, but he must mean Ireton.

difference? The usual course is to dismiss the matter with the observation that Cromwell's men were better disciplined. It is difficult to assess discipline nicely and I suspect that most people assume from the result that their discipline must have exceeded that of the Cavaliers. Yet Rupert's men were at least as experienced as Cromwell's and *a priori* they were as well disciplined.

No, I think the difference can be accounted for in a simple manner. In the first place, though the details of the charge are, as always, obscure, it seems that whilst the left of the line under Whalley clashed with Langdale, the right of Cromwell's front line, outflanked the Royalists and wheeled to their left, thus striking them in their left flank. Langdale's men would retreat to their rear whilst a portion of Cromwell's (under Rossiter, to be explicit) were still facing at right angles to this line, and thus had in front of them the still intact hostile infantry. The sight of this new foe would naturally check their pace, and enable Rossiter to get them under control again, whilst Whalley's men continued their gallop straight to their front. Thus, no superhuman power of control on the part of Cromwell was either necessary or possible.

In the second place Cromwell's troopers outnumbered Langdale's by nearly two to one; Oliver could therefore afford to let the three leading regiments under Whalley disappear off the battlefield and yet retain ample forces in his second and third line for any further action.

I suspect he allowed a good distance to intervene between his first and second lines, and that he sat on his horse at the head of the second line and remained stationary until he saw the upshot of the charge of the first line. This would only be a matter of seconds and as the victorious horse galloped off the field in much the same manner as had Rupert's only a few moments previously on the opposite flank, Cromwell, seeing his opportunity, wheeled his second, followed by his third line to their left without appreciably advancing. This would bring their right shoulders on to the spot now marked by the northern edge of Paisnell Spinney, whence they would be in prolongation of the line of Royalist infantry. Thus an advance to their new front would take them into the Cavalier's exposed flank, albeit charging slightly uphill. During this operation Rossiter's men would, of course, be on their right flank.

It was at this point, I fancy, that Cromwell's personal part in the battle was played. He sent his second and third lines to the attack

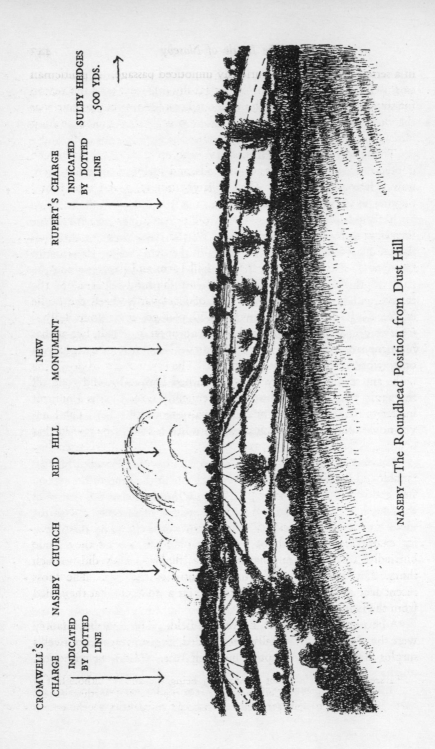

CROMWELL'S NASEBY CHURCH RED HILL NEW RUPERT'S CHARGE SULBY HEDGES
CHARGE   MONUMENT INDICATED 500 YDS.
INDICATED   BY DOTTED
BY DOTTED   LINE
LINE

NASEBY—The Roundhead Position from Dust Hill

in a series of waves. In a curiously unnoticed passage, 'A gentleman of Publike Employment' (probably Rushworth) explains the reason for this success. 'That which made our horses so terrible to them was the thickness of our reserves, and their orderly and timely coming on, and not one failing to come on in time'.[1]

The unfortunate Royalist infantry, who up to date had given such good account of themselves against odds, and against the ground, were now beset on three sides. They began to give way and soon found themselves back in the valley.

Only one thing could now save the devoted Royalist infantry—intervention by the King's reserve. Charles realized this himself and started to lead them forward towards the left flank. Picture this movement, starting from near Dust Hill Farm and passing along the front edge of Longhold Spinney. When the head had reached the eastern end of the spinney, the Earl of Carnwarth seized the bridle of the King's horse, exclaiming: 'Will you go upon your death?' Charles was quite ready, if need be, to go upon his death, but at that moment some unknown person shouted: 'March to the right' (in other words, in the reverse direction). The cry was passed down the ranks and the whole body of horse turned files about and rode off at a rapid pace. Now, as we have frequently noticed, it is a difficult matter to halt or control a body of cavalry from the rear. The King was now in the rear, and it speaks well for his control of the reserve that in a space of 400 yards he managed to pull them up. By this time they were back nearly where they had started from, and it was still perfectly feasible to return to the charge. But for some unrecorded reason Charles did not do so. The presumption is that his councillors overbore him; but it is useless to speculate. What, however, should be noted is the unfair way history has treated the Royal reserve. Gardiner, for example, asserts without a particle of evidence that they 'rode hurriedly' to the rear in what he calls a 'flight'. They did no such thing, they merely returned to the centre of the line. The most recent account (written in 1938) goes so far as to assert that they 'fled from the field'.

A curious pause now set in over the field. The Royalist infantry were by this time practically surrounded, for some of Cromwell's surplus horsemen had swept round their rear. The King witnessed,

[1] I see no reason to doubt Rushworth being the author, although it is curious that in his *Historical Collections* he uses Sprigge's account rather than his own. Both were present at the battle—no doubt with the baggage.

as a pathetic and powerless spectator, the tragedy that was now enacted in the valley some 600 yards in front of him. It was the end of his infantry—and for all practical purposes the end of his reign. Surrounded and left to their fate by their comrades of the other arms, the remnant of the regiments of foot one by one laid down their arms. Their ammunition had doubtless all been expended and their case was quite hopeless. All fought it out to the end, extracting the reluctant admiration of their opponents thereby.

It must have been during this sad episode that Rupert led back to the field the greater part of his cavalry. He would have liked to put all to the touch with one final desperate charge. Desperate it would have been, and the upshot not in doubt; for by now his horse were wearied and not in a condition to sustain a rapid gallop. Occasions when the same cavalry charge twice within a short period are few in number. Rupert's horse were not equal to this supreme test and the Prince was constrained, like his King, to gaze upon the tragedy, a hopeless eye-witness, powerless to intervene.

After the last regiment had laid down its arms, and Fairfax, having methodically marshalled his infantry, began to move forward once more, the King recognizing that the end was come, turned his horse and rode from the field.

Oliver Cromwell conducted a pursuit of 18 miles to the gates of Leicester.

Never had there been so complete a victory in a major battle in this land since the battle of Hastings.

PROBLEMS OF THE BATTLEFIELD

I.—THE FLANK MARCHES

And now we come to discuss in detail the chief problem presented by the battle of Naseby, namely, which side initiated that strange flank march before the battle, and why? Or did each, by some extraordinary coincidence execute it simultaneously, and irrespective of the other? The only historian who has discussed this problem is Gardiner. He devotes considerable space to it in the appendix to his *Great Civil War*, but does not appear to be very decided in his conclusions. He was aided by that thorough student of the Civil War, Colonel, W. G. Ross, whose conclusions are also recorded in Gardiner's appendix. I have found both of great help in my own examination of this problem. It has caused me more difficulty in coming to a conclusion than almost any other problem of our battlefields, but after much cogitation I have at length arrived at the conclusion given above in the narrative. For the evidence is nicely balanced on both sides, i.e. for Rupert initiating the movement or for Fairfax. Let us first give the evidence. It consists in the main of four passages, two in favour of each view—passages that appear at the first blush to be mutually and irreconcilably contradictory.

The two in favour of Fairfax are:

1. The Royalist Slingsby in his *Diary*, who asserts that Rupert 'sees their horse marching up on the side of the hill to that place where-after they embattled their whole army'. This clearly implies that Rupert saw the Roundheads making their flank march from the Clipston road to Red Hill.

2. One 'W. G.' in the *Thomason Tracts* (E 372 (22)) states on the evidence of his own eyes and ears that Cromwell 'did advise that the battalion (line of battle) might stand upon such a ground, though it was begun to be drawn upon another place, saying "Let us, I beseech you, draw back to yonder hill which will encourage the enemy to charge us, which they cannot do in *that* [other] place without absolute ruin".'

The precise meaning of this is obscure, depending on the location of Cromwell when he uttered the words. If Gardiner is correct in placing it on the forward edge of the Naseby plateau on the Clipston road (Point 632 on the O.S. map), 'yonder hill' would presumably be Red Hill. Both these passages therefore point to the same conclusion, namely that Fairfax moved from the Clipston road to Red Hill before and irrespective of Rupert's motions.

The passages in favour of Rupert being the initiator of the movement are:

1. Slingsby again. From Rupert's position near Clipston, 'Being hindered of any near approach, by reason of the place between us and them was full of burts (? burys) and water, we wheeled about, and by our guides were brought upon a fair piece of ground, partly corn and partly heath, under Naseby, about half a mile distant from the place'.[1]

This seems clear evidence that Rupert moved first, with the intention of crossing the valley at a more convenient place, *not* as a result of seeing his opponents making a trek in that direction.

[1] Distances in miles were apt to be underestimated in those days: Broadmoor is 1½ miles from Naseby.

2. Rev. J. Sprigge, Fairfax's chaplain, writing in *Anglia Rediviva*, states that while the army was being drawn up on the Clipston road position, 'the enemy's army, which before was the greatest part of it out of view, by reason of the hill which interposed, we saw plainly advancing in order towards us; and the wind blowing somewhat westwardly, by the enemy's advance so much on their right hand, it was evident that he designed to get the wind of us, which occasioned the general to draw into a large fallow field on the north-west side of Naseby'.

This is an equally clear indication that the initiative came from Rupert and that Fairfax merely conformed. What are we to make of such seemingly irreconcilable testimony?

The governing consideration seems to be that the side acting on the defensive is the least likely to have moved first. For consider the situation. The two armies were opposed to each other on the same road, Market Harborough—Naseby. Whichever army decided to stand on a defensive position would scarcely abandon this road and move to its flank unless its opponent had already started to do so. This, on the grounds of Inherent Military Probability (my 'IMP'), is to my mind conclusive of the matter.

Assuming, therefore, that Rupert took the initiative in the flank march, how are we to account for and reconcile the two statements to the contrary?

Take Slingsby first. Either Rupert mistook the withdrawal of the Roundhead advanced troops from the Clipston bottom for a flank march (which if his observation-post was slightly to the west of Clipston, say about Point 569, might easily happen), or Slingsby got a bit out in his chronology and forgot that it was *after* Rupert had started his own movement that he spotted the enemy's. Of the two, I prefer the first supposition. As for 'W. G.', if Fairfax and Cromwell were well forward at the foot of the hill at the time Cromwell made his suggestion, the ridge, on which is the obelisk, could correctly be described as 'yonder hill'. I have adopted this explanation in my narrative.

II.—A FURTHER NOTE ON THE TERRAIN

As I have already said, there is little that is controversial about the site of the battle, and I have indicated in the course of the narrative most of the points that arise. There remain but a few minor points.

One is the site of the grave-pit marked at G on my Sketch-map 44, taken from the O.S. map. It would seem to indicate that much of the slaughter took place some hundreds of yards further north than I locate the last stand of the Bluecoat Regiment (namely in the valley). The simplest explanation is that only a small number of the fallen are buried there and that the majority of the graves are in the valley. There are a number of depressions in the ground in the valley near Broadmoor Farm, a likely enough place. The outlying grave to the west of Sulby Hedges I have already accounted for. As for Prince Rupert's Farm, I like to think that it enshrouds a tradition, for it stands precisely where one would expect the Prince to have his headquarters immediately prior to the battle.

Local tradition is meagre and vague. I was pointed out an old oak a few hundred yards north-west of Prince Rupert's Farm, and my informant told me with neutral nonchalance that either Cromwell or Rupert hid up it.

Of battlefield memorials I have already mentioned the obelisk erected by John Fitzgerald in 1825, which can only be accounted for on the supposition that either it marks about the highest spot in the vicinity of the battlefield, or that the worthy John felt that the battle *ought* to have been fought there—with which sentiment I agree.

The modern monument to Cromwell, erected by the Cromwell Society, is 100 yards to the west of the Sibbertoft road and visible from it. I do not know the reasons for its location there. According to my reckoning Cromwell's charge was a good 500 yards further east, as already mentioned.

CHAPTER XXXV

The Battle of Langport, 10 July 1645

THE battle of Langport put the seal on the victory of Naseby, for that victory was incomplete in itself, although 4,000 of the small Royalist army of 7,500 had been captured; a still greater army might yet be put in the field if time were allowed to concentrate the forces scattered in the west, and in various garrisons.

But time was just what the victorious Sir Thomas Fairfax had no intention of allowing them. After pursuing the Royalist army to Leicester he laid siege to that town and captured it on 18 June. Meanwhile Lord Goring was besieging Taunton, where Robert Blake was putting up a valiant resistance. London clamoured for it to be relieved and Fairfax, who had now been given a free hand by Parliament, resolved to attempt its relief. He had already got as far south as Marlborough when this decision was made. The date was 28 June, and he had done the 113 miles from Leicester in a week, not bad going in the hot weather that prevailed. But still better was to come.

Fairfax could not be sure how long Taunton would hold out and he decided to take no risks, but to march to its relief with the maximum speed. This was all the more necessary inasmuch as the direct route was barred by several Royalist garrisons; Devizes, Bath, Bristol, Bridgwater. Fairfax therefore elected to approach it from the south, at the same time changing his base for supplies to the sea coast, at Lyme and Weymouth.

On Monday, 30 June, the forced march began. Twenty miles were covered the first day and the army billeted in Amesbury that night. Next day the army marched out to Stonehenge and then south-west to Bower Chalk. On Wednesday Blandford was reached. On Friday the army was at Beaminster (7 miles south of Crewkerne), having come via Dorchester. This represented a five days' march at 17 miles per day —in hot weather too. Here totally unexpected news reached it: Goring had suddenly abandoned the siege of Taunton and marched towards Yeovil.

It is now time to turn to the Royalist army. Unfortunately nearly all the eye-witnesses' accounts of this campaign come from the Parliamentary side, and the brilliant but unpredictable Goring has not left us his own account. We are thus reduced to guessing what was in his mind at any given moment, and his movements were on the surface so curious that we are left very much to conjecture and I.M.P. It is, however, fairly safe to presume that the reason for abandoning the siege was the news of the approach of Fairfax, for the Roundhead could muster 16,000 men, when General Massey's army in the west had joined it, whilst the Cavaliers were slightly less than half this number. But why, having abandoned the siege, did he march right across the front of the pursuing army and occupy a line that laid Bridgwater open to the enemy's attack? For the line he took up was that of the river Yeo from Langport to Yeovil, a wide front of 12 miles in a straight line, but much more measured along the windings of the river. True the river Yeo was only fordable in places and there were only three bridges in this sector, those of Load Bridge (opposite Long Sutton), Ilchester, and Yeovil. But a long river line is a treacherous thing to hold, as all military history shows, and the truth of this was soon to be witnessed.

Fairfax on 5 July concentrated his infantry at Crewkerne, opposite the centre of this line and distant 10 miles from it, while he sent his cavalry forward to gain touch with the enemy. Following them himself, and taking his cavalry commander Oliver Cromwell with him, the Roundhead leader made a personal reconnaissance of the hostile position along the river Yeo. He found all the bridges down, so decided that the line could not be rushed, and that a concerted plan must be made.

Next day, Sunday, the main army rested (Fairfax always rested on the Sabbath whenever possible). Meanwhile outlying contingents were continuing to come in. On Monday the 7th Sir Thomas made another reconnaissance, after which he assembled a council of war. It was the almost invariable custom on both sides in the Civil War to hold a council of war before deciding on battle. On this occasion it was decided to force the crossing of the river on the right, at Yeovil, with infantry while cavalry watched the remainder of the front. This was done, the weak detachment of cavaliers in Yeovil fell back without fighting and the river line was gained without firing a shot. Again we cannot say what was Goring's intention, and whether Yeovil was given up under his orders or not. Not only was Yeovil abandoned but Ilchester also, the Royalist army concentrating on Langport.

By Tuesday evening the Roundheads were across the river and in occupation of Ilchester. There a report reached Fairfax that Goring had left Langport with a large proportion of his cavalry and was marching in the direction of Taunton, presumably with the intention of attacking that town. This looks on the face of it an astonishing move, for what general in possession of his senses will divide his forces just when an immensely superior army is approaching, and go off with one portion to raid a town 12 miles away? The situation seemed to offer an opening to Fairfax. Either he could take advantage of the reduction in the opponent's army in his immediate front and spring on it before Goring

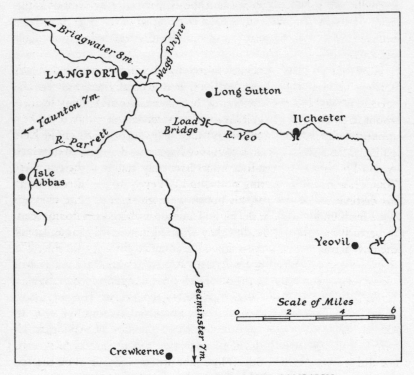

SKETCH-MAP 45.   LANGPORT: THE CAMPAIGN

could return to its aid, or he could pursue the detached force with the bulk of his own army and pulverize it between his field army and the garrison of Taunton.

But Fairfax did neither of these things. Instead he sent General Massey with his detachment of 3,600 men to pursue Goring's horse, while concentrating the remainder of his troops at Long Sutton, just north of the Yeo and 3 miles east of Langport. Massey departed apparently in the early morning of the 9th and silence descended upon his movements. As time wore on Fairfax began to get anxious and sent a further force of cavalry and dragoons to reinforce Massey, and when during the afternoon he heard distant sounds of firing, he sent a further reinforcement, thus making up Massey's force when concentrated to a total of 5,500.

Meanwhile Massey had engaged the Royalist detachment. His movements had been very slow, but in the afternoon he had bumped unexpectedly into the Cavaliers at Isle Abbotts, 7 miles south-west of Langport, and had surprised them. They galloped back into Langport, pursued most of the way by Massey's troopers, who took some prisoners.

Now this is a very curious episode, and will repay close investigation. The report that reached Fairfax is generally accepted by historians, from Gardiner downwards, but there are some baffling features about it. In the first place, if Goring had intended on 8 July to make a mounted dash upon Taunton and take it by surprise, he could have galloped the dozen miles in a couple of hours that day, instead of which we find his horse twenty-four hours later only half-way there, a mere hour's ride from his starting point, and not even on the direct road to his destination. Moreover, his horses were grazing, and the troopers were feeding, bathing, or sleeping. These astonishing facts do not seem to perturb most historians, but they worried me—until I came, late in the day, across the only eye-witness's account on the Royalist side, *The Memories and Reflections of Sir Richard Bulstrode*. Here quite a different picture is presented, and as Bulstrode has every appearance of being a truthful scribe, one is disposed to accept it—especially as it makes sense. From the account of this Cavalier writer, the close companion of Lord Goring, it is clear that there was never any intention of making an attempt on Taunton; nor did the commander accompany it in person, nor did it set out on the 8th. (No doubt orders were issued on the 8th and a spy probably got hold of them.)

What happened was that on the morning of the 9th a force of three cavalry brigades under the command of Lieut.-General Porter marched out of Langport in a south-westerly direction and halted at Isle Abbotts, 6 miles away. Bulstrode does not tell us the object of this operation, but, judging by after events it seems that it was a deliberate stratagem intended to puzzle and delude the enemy and to induce him to divide his forces. In this it succeeded, better even than Goring can have hoped, for it resulted in no less than 5,500 troops being detached from Fairfax's army. It is a fair presumption that Porter's orders were to await the approach of the enemy, and then to fall back into the town. But Porter carried out his orders badly, and suffered in consequence. As soon as Goring heard the firing he must have galloped out of the town, for he arrived on the scene in time to be met by streams of galloping horsemen, on the road back to Langport. Bulstrode's words are: 'The alarm being brought to General Goring, he immediately marched in person to his succour, rallied the horse that were flying, stopped the enemy's career who were eagerly pursuing, and made a handsome retreat, without which the best part of our army had been lost that day. And when our general met Lieut.-General Porter in the rear flying with the rest, His Excellency turned to me and said: "He deserves to be pistolled for his negligence or cowardice." ' But Porter was his brother-in-law, and he escaped being disgraced. Indeed, nowadays the odium for the affair is usually placed upon Lord Goring.

That night Goring, possibly upset by this disaster to some of his best troops, decided to fall back on Bridgwater. But it was to be done in an orderly manner and in his own time. The slowest moving units must start first; i.e. the baggage and the guns. He estimated that he could, if necessary, hold out in the strong position that he occupied on the eastern outskirts of the town during the daylight without the support of artillery, except for two small pieces that he ordered to stay behind. The artillery departed early in the morning of 10 July, and the remainder of the army took up position to defend themselves. This position must now be described.

THE TERRAIN

The little town of Langport lies on slightly rising ground on the north bank of the rivers Parrett and Yeo at their point of junction. One thousand yards east of the town is the church of Huish Episcopi with its beautiful lofty tower. From its summit a splendid view can be obtained of the battlefield. The Royalist position ran along the near side of a little brook sometimes called the Wagg Rhyne that runs through Pibsbury Bottom and crosses the Long Sutton road about 700 yards east of the church. The slope down to the brook is very gentle and is equally so up the far side. But further to the left, or north, it is steeper and the watercourse runs through a slight ravine, thus making it a fair obstacle for mounted troops. On the day of the battle a good deal of water was coming down, and the ford by which the road crossed the brook was 'up to the horses' girths.'[1]

[1] So it was reported, but probably with exaggeration.

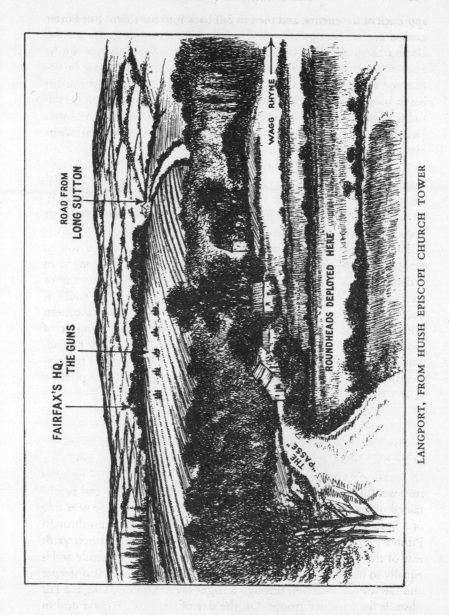

LANGPORT, FROM HUISH EPISCOPI CHURCH TOWER

The country beyond the brook was open, but on the near side was enclosed, and the road was lined with hedges. Musketeers lined these hedges and also hedges along the line of Pibsbury Bottom, while cavalry were posted on the slight ridge in rear, and the two guns were brought into action at the top of the slope covering the ford (or 'pass' as it was called in all accounts). The right flank was covered by the deep river Yeo. Thus the position was a reasonably strong one by nature. Lord Goring placed himself at the head of the Horse overlooking the 'pass', and awaited events with confidence.

In the other camp a council of war had been held in the early morning, the problem being how to bring the enemy to battle. Whilst the council was in session, however, news was brought that the enemy was evidently intending to hold his ground, so the problem was solved; the enemy invited an attack; an attack he should have.

THE BATTLE

The rival commanders agreed in one thing—the key to the position was the pass. We may wonder why this should be so, for the infantry at least could have crossed the Pibsbury Bottom anywhere, and there does not seem any reason why the whole position could not have been turned from the north. But when both commanders are agreed there must be some compelling reason, hidden from the modern historian, that ruled out these two expedients. Everything therefore centred on the pass. Goring's measures to defend it seemed adequate; Fairfax's measures to attack it were equally thorough. His first step was to silence the two cannons that commanded the pass. This was a comparatively easy matter; the Roundhead guns were deployed in a line along the ridge that runs parallel to the Wagg Rhyne and a few hundred yards from it. The position is quite obvious. From here the range to the two lone guns was about 700 yards. An overwhelming fire was concentrated upon these unfortunate pieces, 'the cannon playing their part as gallantly as ever I saw gunners in my life', declared the enthusiastic Colonel Lilburne, though it was a one-sided duel. By noon the Royalist artillery was silent and the next step was put in hand. This was an attack by musketeers on the hostile musketeers lining the hedges and the pass itself. A hot and stubborn contest developed, lasting a good hour before the Roundheads effected a crossing of the stream and a firm lodgement on the far side.

Now was the time for the decisive operation of the day, one which everything else had led up to. It was no less than a cavalry charge on a frontage of four yards, the width of the narrow lane leading to and from the pass. It was indeed a 'pass'; there was just room for four horses abreast, knee to knee, and no more—unless all the eye-witnesses have exaggerated. The horsemen were called 'the forlorn hope' and such they must have seemed. Fairfax gave the order direct to Cromwell, and the latter detailed the three troops of Major Bethell of his old regiment. Down the hill galloped the gallant band, Bethell at their head; through the ford they splashed, and up the gentle slope on the far side. They received a ragged fire from some musketeers in the hedges on the upper part of the slope but it did not check their progress. Without drawing rein, or even deploying (as far as one can tell) the leading troop crashed straight into the front ranks of the waiting cavaliers, and broke them. The second troop meanwhile managed to deploy out of the lane, and having done so charged in its turn, and overthrew the second line of Royalist horse. But Goring had more behind; the three Parliamentary troops were in fact in the heart of the enemy's position and once the momentum of the charge was spent there was no hope of further progress. Gradually by the force of numbers they were overborne, and began to fall back.

But not for long. Three more troops under Major Desborough were coming up the hill to their support. On reaching the top Desborough swung his squadron round to the north, and then wheeled to the left upon the open left flank of the Cavalier horse, who recoiled from the shock. But this was not the last shot in Fairfax's locker. His musketeers were also co-operating in a beautiful manner and added their fire and weight to the combined assault. It proved too much for the Cavaliers; after a fierce and fairly prolonged hand-to-hand contest they gave way, split up into small segments and dissolved in flight. The bulk of them retreated over the river-bridge and took the road to Bridgwater; Goring himself, accompanied by the faithful Bulstrode, made off to the north and reached Bridgwater late that night, 'overjoyed' to find that the greater part of his army had already arrived there.

But the defeat though not complete broke the morale of the Royalist army of the West, which was no longer capable of making a stand against the all-conquering Roundheads, and the First Civil War was virtually over.

COMMENTS

The leadership of the two commanders in this, the last pitched battle of the First Civil War, was in marked contrast. Sir Thomas Fairfax was a sound tactician; no general on either side had yet equalled him in the conduct of a battle; on every single occason of which we have detailed record he distinguished himself by coolness, courage, and good judgement. But as a strategist his record was not brilliant. Of Lord Goring it can be said that his handling of his troops in the battle was not brilliant but his strategy before the battle was masterly. I have taken some time in coming to this conclusion for there are many puzzling elements in his conduct of the campaign, but if the interpretation of them that I give above is correct, there can be no doubt that he out-manoeuvred his opponent. Consider the matter on the widest and simplest grounds. He found himself confronted by an army of 14,000 while he could only muster a little over 7,000. Yet when the final battle was fought he had nearly 7,000 to his opponent's 10,000. He had achieved this by his so-called dash for Taunton. The upshot of this was that he misled his opponent, threw him off his balance and induced him to divide his army, with three rivers—the Isle, the Parrett, and the Yeo —separating them at the critical moment of battle; for Massey had not rejoined and his troops had no influence on the decision. Nor does it appear that Fairfax gave him any specific orders to co-operate. This might have been done by approaching Langport from the west, and thus threatening the enemy's retreat. But in the event Massey's 5,500 troops were wasted. Although Goring had lost 500 men he had deprived his opponent of the use of 5,500, so the 'Taunton dash' had paid a good dividend. He was on interior lines, and he made good use of the fact.

Fairfax had taken the bait offered him. In fact he appears to have been a little bit 'rattled' by the surprise move of his opponent. A Roundhead eye-witness writes of Goring 'dancing from side to side of the river'. A good simile; Goring led his opponent 'a song and a dance'.

But tactically we can have nothing but admiration for Fairfax's handling of the battle. His action in launching a cavalry force four abreast through a defile commanded by the enemy's fire may appear almost foolhardy; but it succeeded, and that is the acid test. Fairfax had guessed correctly what was on 'the other side of the hill', and that after all is the supreme gift in a general. To put it in another way, he calculated correctly the relative forces and values of the two sides; his experience and judgement of war had served him in good stead, and he reaped his reward by a sterling victory. On paper it might look that the cavalry attack was bound to be defeated, but he calculated the incalculable; that is, he judged aright the effect of relative morale; and it was superior morale in the Parliamentary army that above all won the victory.

It is time that Goring received his due. Clarendon, who was no soldier, was strongly prejudiced against the 'debauchee', as he is always vaguely dubbed, and no one has taken up the cudgels on his behalf. Yet there is good contemporary testimony that Lord Goring was something more than a Royal favourite. Colonel Bulstrode, as we have seen, was in close contact with him in the Langport campaign, and he has something of interest to say of the man who so signally defeated Fairfax's wing at Marston Moor. On the subject of his 'debaucheries' he openly admits that Goring 'strangely loved the bottle'[1] (though there is no evidence that it in any way incapacitated him physically when operations in the field took place). Of his capacity as an officer Bulstrode has this to say: 'Goring was a person of extraordinary ability, as well as courage and was without dispute as good an officer as served the King, and the most dexterous in a sudden emergency that I have ever seen.' Bulstrode may have had in mind, when he wrote this, the disaster to General Porter's troops on 9 July. Goring no doubt allowed his troops to pillage; but as he had no money with which to pay them, it is likely that had he not allowed them to fend for themselves (i.e. to pillage) they would have dispersed and he would have been left without an army at all.

'THE PASS'

In 1895 Major G. F. Browne, in an excellent article on the campaign, suggested that the pass was not on the site of the modern road but further to the north. His grounds were that there is no hill up from the brook on the line of the modern road, but there is one a few hundred yards further north. I disagree; there is a perceptible slope; admittedly it is a very gentle one, but ancient chroniclers and writers were prone to exaggerate physical features, partly because they had only a limited vocabulary, and lacked the refinements of meaning that our more extensive vocabulary makes possible, and partly because features become enlarged in the memory in the course of time. The line of the modern road is the most natural line for a road linking Huish and Long Sutton; it existed at least as early as 1807, and it is only natural to suppose that there was always a road between Pibsbury and Huish. Such a

[1] This may be partly due to the fact, as pointed out by Peter Young, that he had a game leg, acquired at the Siege of Breda.

road would tend to follow the gentlest gradient instead of swerving to the north and crossing the brook in what might be called a ravine. The matter is of no great importance, but if we accept the modern road it makes it easier to picture the battle, and reconstruct every detail of it on the ground.

CHAPTER XXXVI

The Battle of Worcester, September 3rd, 1651

WORCESTER is unique among battles fought in England as being conditioned by a river crossing. The river Severn figures prominently in the battle; in fact it is its backbone, so to speak. The throwing of a bridge across it in the face of the enemy at the outset of the battle made possible a remarkable and successful manœuvre. But like most of our English battlefields it can boast of no visible memorial, unless the river Severn itself may so be deemed. Yet it was this battle that made possible the Protectorate. Cromwell spoke true when he wrote: 'It is, for aught I know, a crowning mercy.' It nearly placed the English crown upon his own brow. On the other hand but for the pillaging propensities of the Scottish troops on their march through England, which antagonized the country people, Charles II might have ascended the throne nine years earlier than he did.

To explain how a battle came to be fought outside the walls of Worcester we must hark back to August 6th, 1651, when King Charles (he had been crowned at Scone) crossed the border and marched on Carlisle, leaving Cromwell with his army in Scotland. The situation was a precarious one for Parliament. There was no army between Charles and London, merely scattered militia and a small force under Fleetwood at Banbury. The Council of State, however, acted resolutely and rapidly. They ordered a concentration of all available troops at Coventry. This town was a sound choice, for it was sufficiently far from the border to give time for the collection of a considerable force, yet was sufficiently far north to prevent the home counties from being overrun.

Meanwhile the Scottish army was pushing steadily south. Only a disappointing handful of English joined the King's colours, and most of this handful was dispersed in a short action at Wigan. Furthermore many Scots began to desert, till the strength of the army was under 16,000.

Lambert had hurried south from Scotland, his horse covering 200 miles in four days, and he reached Warrington first, while Cromwell with the main army followed through Yorkshire.

At Warrington Charles had an appreciable success, hurling Lambert back from the river bridge. The latter who had orders not to get unduly committed, 'went running' to Uttoxeter and thence to Coventry, leaving the road to London open to the invaders.

But Charles did not take advantage of this situation. He realized that his army could be outnumbered by at least two to one, and that it would be fruitless to attempt to penetrate as far south as London till he had recruited fresh forces. Wales and the West of England were traditionally royalist; the King therefore determined to halt at Worcester while recruits were being enlisted. In this he probably showed sound judgement. Unfortunately, the recruits were not forthcoming, and the longer he dallied at Worcester the greater the hostile strength that would be collected against him. It was a cruel dilemma—one for which there does not appear to be any obvious solution.

Advancing through Whitchurch, Newport, Wolverhampton and Kidderminster, the Royalist army entered Worcester on August 22nd. Here Charles set up his standard—nine years to the day since his father had set up his standard at Nottingham. And it was Nottingham that his opponent General Oliver Cromwell entered that very same day. A curious coincidence.

The Parliamentary armies now began to close in on the doomed Scots. On the 24th Cromwell was at Warwick, 25 miles to the east, and on the 27th he reached Evesham, 16 miles to the south-east, where Fleetwood joined him. Cromwell was now at the head of an army 30,000 strong, twice the strength of his opponent; and he was on the direct road leading from Worcester to the capital. Unless he made a big blunder 'the ball was at his feet'.

The Lord General realized the strength of his position. Time was now on his side, for outlying contingents were continually coming in and his army was swelling and would be likely to continue to swell. His aim was not merely to defeat and drive back his antagonists, but to annihilate them. It was the easier to plan this inasmuch as his antagonist was stationary, and looked like remaining stationary. Cromwell therefore proceeded deliberately and methodically to weave the web that should enmesh the enemy in its toils. The first step was to block the way of escape to the south and west into

Wales. On August 28th, therefore, Lambert was sent off with a small force to seize the bridge over the Severn at Upton, 11 miles to the west of Evesham and 11 miles south of Worcester. This bridge had been destroyed by the Royalists, but a single plank was left in position, and by a brilliant *coup de main* Lambert secured the bridge on the morning of August 29th. The Royalists retired hurriedly on Worcester, and took up a position on the northern bank of the river Teme.

THE TERRAIN

The river Severn runs north and south with Worcester on its eastern bank. Two miles south of the city it is joined from the west by the Teme, a swift-flowing river, about ten yards wide, with very steep banks about ten feet deep along most of its course. There were bridges at Powick and Bransford, and a ford somewhere between the two. The angle of the ground between the two rivers is flat meadow-land and was much intersected by hedges, as it still is. It is another peculiar coincidence that the first as well as the last shots of the two civil wars were fired on precisely the same ground, in these meadows. The situation was also not entirely dissimilar. On each occasion a Parliamentary army advanced on Worcester from Evesham, the city being held by the Royalists. On each occasion the battle that ensued took place in the meadows immediately north of Powick bridge. There the similarity ends. In 1642, Prince Rupert came dashing south to the help of the threatened garrison of Worcester, and unceremoniously and impetuously swept his opponents helter-skelter over the bridge or into the river. On the second occasion the bridge had been destroyed (as for its northern two arches). So also had Bransford bridge and Bewdley bridge over the Severn, 15 miles north of Worcester.

Half a mile south of Powick bridge there is a slight ridge on the brow of which Powick church is built. From its tower a fine view of the ground can be had, stretching right up to the walls of Worcester. Most prominent point in the landscape is the great tower of Worcester Cathedral, from where (incidentally) an even better view of the battlefield can be obtained. One mile to the east of the city is a long ridge, now almost completely built over. The northern end of this ridge is called Perry Wood, and the southern end Red Hill.

Turning now to the city itself: in those days it was a walled and gated city. The defences had been dismantled at the end of the First

Civil War, but Charles set to work feverishly to repair them. There is also a hillock just outside the east wall that the King fortified, naming it Fort Royal. A few guns were mounted on it.

THE RIVAL DISPOSITIONS

It is possible from a study of the King's disposition to gather his plan of action. Apart from the garrison of the city and of Fort Royal, which may be considered as part of the city, he kept no troops on the east side of the river. The sole bridge left intact was that which connected the town with the western bank and the suburb of St. John's. This, added to the fact that the bridges to north and south had been destroyed, as well as those over the Teme, makes it clear that the King's intentions were purely defensive. He was endeavouring to cover himself by the two rivers. Such a position must have appeared a strong one. Rivers always appear strong defensively, but military history teaches that there is no such thing as an impregnable river position; a mountain chain is generally much stronger. Be that as it may, the Royalists set to work to construct defences not only round the city but in the meadows between it and the Teme, facing south. The reserve foot was stationed in the western suburb of St. John's and Leslie's horse in rear of the city.

We turn now to the plans and dispositions of the Parliamentarians. It will be remembered that they outnumbered the Royalists by about two to one. Even so, it was a ticklish problem to approach and attack such a position from the east. It would involve a purely frontal attack on fortifications. This would not be promising, and might prove very expensive. If, on the other hand, that main attack was made from the south, on the far side of the river, the army would find itself divided in the presence of the enemy by an unfordable and unbridged river. The Severn hereabouts is a formidable obstacle, being about 40 yards wide, deep and swift, and with a high steep bank for the most part on the western side. From the top of the Cathedral tower which Charles might be assumed to make use of, this division of forces would be manifest, and if Charles possessed sufficient generalship, and his army sufficient manœuvrability, he would have it in his power by a swift transference of troops from one side of the river to the other, to concentrate superior force against one or other of the opposing wings.

Cromwell assembled a council of war on the 31st, at which no

TEME BRIDGE

SEVERN BRIDGE

WORCESTER—Juncture of Severn and Teme from the South, showing the position of the two bridges

doubt this knotty point was discussed and the solution decided upon. This was that the difficulty was to be overcome by constructing bridges over the rivers in the very face of the enemy—a novelty in English warfare. This might seem a desperate venture but there was no other obvious solution. 'Nothing venture, nothing have.' Careful plans were therefore made in order to minimize the risk. First a search had to be made for boats of a suitable size (for a pontoon bridge was the only type possible under the circumstances). Fortunately there does not seem to have been a shortage of such boats. In those days river navigation was fairly brisk, more so than at the present day. Twenty 'great boats' were collected in the lower reaches of the river and towed up to Upton. Here they were assembled during the next few days, together with the necessary planks and what Carlyle describes as 'aquatic and terrestrial artificers'. These boats were to be towed upstream to the junction of the Severn and Teme, where two bridges were to be constructed, one across either river, and quite close to the junction. (Sketch-map 46.)

These bridges should go far towards solving Cromwell's problem, for not only would the one allow Fleetwood (in command on the western bank) to cross the Teme, but the other would allow Cromwell to reinforce him at pleasure from the main army which would be on the eastern bank.

The whole plan depended for its success on the ability to throw these two bridges in the presence of the enemy. It seems to us a hazardous project, depending for its success on supine inactivity on the part of the Scottish troops in position in the meadows and in sight of the proposed crossing places. It was perhaps the most risky operation of war ever attempted by Cromwell, and one could wish that more details as to its execution were available.[1]

Cromwell allotted Fleetwood 11,000 men for his attack, and with the remainder he approached the eastern side of the city in slow cautious marches.

THE BATTLE

By the evening of September 2nd all was ready, and the next day, the 3rd, was selected for the attack. Whether this date was a coincidence or was designed, does not appear from the documents,

[1] I have searched the P.R.O. and the MSS. Room of the British Museum without being able to discover any relevant unprinted source.

but it was the first anniversary of the great victory over the Scots of Dunbar. No doubt this fact was present in the minds of the troops and that their morale was correspondingly raised, while that of the Scots was lowered.

Fleetwood's task was to advance from Upton to the Teme, towing

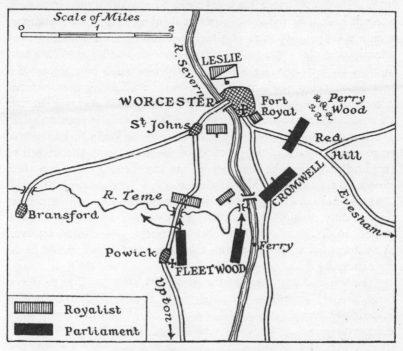

SKETCH–MAP 46. WORCESTER

the 20 great-boats as he went. This was presumably done with tow-ropes and man-power. The distance allowing for the bends is a good eight miles and the current is swift. The progress must have been very slow.[1] There were unspecified delays during the advance, but it is easy to imagine their nature. No doubt they were due to the tow-ropes breaking and suchlike mishaps on the water. The result was that although Fleetwood's column departed from Upton between 5 a.m. and 6 a.m., it was after 2 p.m. before they reached the river Teme.

Only a portion of Fleetwood's column was to cross by the pontoon

---

[1] On the last occasion that I visited the river junction I was lucky to witness some barges being towed upstream by a powerful tug. It gave one a good idea of the formidable nature of the task.

bridge; the remainder, and the bigger portion, were to try and force their way across the Powick bridge. How they expected to do this is not clear, for two arches of the bridge had, as already related, been destroyed. Probably a plank had been left across the broken arches as in the case of Upton bridge in order to allow of its passage by patrols and the rearguard. This rearguard had made a stand in the graveyard of Powick church. Here a brief engagement took place, and the 'bullet' marks on the base of the church tower are still visible—the only existing relic of the battle. These so-called bullet marks are too big for normal bullets, and I suspect they were made by cannon-balls fired from drakes, the smallest field piece. Whatever they be, the marksmanship must have been good, for they are 'grouped' in the exact centre of the base of the church tower. One is even tempted to think that the gunners may have been firing 'blind', taking the church tower for their target. Church towers have an irresistible attraction for gunners!

After taking Powick church, Fleetwood's men were naturally held up by the bridge. Ultimately they seem to have got across chiefly by the ford a mile higher upstream. Certainly all the horse must have crossed there. A fierce fight ensued in the very meadows where Rupert's cavalry had charged so spiritedly nine years before. Gradually, the Scots were driven back in this part of the field from hedge to hedge till they were almost back at St. John's.

Meanwhile, the boats had at last reached their rendezvous at the river junction. Here they were divided. Probably five boats were allotted to the Teme bridge and 15 to the Severn bridge. There is no sign of the bridge now, which is not surprising considering that they were pontoons, hurriedly assembled and probably only for foot and horse. There is no mention of guns crossing.[1]

A 'forlorn' was pushed across the river, presumably by small boats, as a preliminary, in order to throw back the hostile patrols from the river bank before bridging operations could commence. These patrols evidently gave the alarm, and reinforcements were sent up from the reserve at St. John's, but the bridges were constructed with most remarkable speed. According to Cary, they took only 30 minutes to construct. This must be an exaggeration.[2] On the other hand, if

[1] It is hard to credit the statement in Mr. J. W. W. Bund's *Civil War in Worcestershire* (1905) that 'the remains of Cromwell's bridge over the Teme were, within recent years pulled up and sold for firewood.

[2] Mr. Bund, on the other hand, writes of 'four day's hard work'. *op cit.*

they had taken much longer it is equally difficult to understand why the Scottish infantry in the meadows did not interfere with the work and drive back the 'forlorn' into the river and put to flight Carlyle's 'aquatic artificers'. The whole affair is astonishing, though it seems to have passed almost unremarked by the historians. This episode is alone sufficient to make the battle of Worcester memorable as a military feat.

According to one account the bigger bridge, that over the Severn, was finished first—another curious fact if true. Nor is it clear whether Cromwell originally intended that the main crossing should be made by his or by Fleetwood's troops. It is however asserted that he himself led his men over the bridge, into the meadows on the far side, where they were presently joined by Lambert's contingent of Fleetwood's column.[1]

It is now necessary to hark back and trace the movements of the King on this momentous day. An exasperating silence broods over most of the movements of Charles I in his battles; not so in the case of his son. We can follow him in some detail. Starting out very early that morning, evidently possessed by some vague foreboding, the King rode right round the position. He must have made a prolonged and minute inspection for he did not get back to his quarters till about noon. All was quiet, no sign of the enemy's approach had been reported. The King dismounted at his lodging, entered and partook of some luncheon. Less than an hour later he was roused by the sound of firing, presumably from the direction of Powick church. He then did the natural thing under the circumstances: he ascended the Cathedral tower to see for himself. From here he must have got a distant view of the skirmish at Powick church, and one report states that he also discerned the bridge-building operations. He therefore descended, mounted his horse and rode over to Powick bridge. Here he gave strict orders that the bridge must be held at all costs. He then rode over to the reserve of foot at St. Johns's, and addressed to them a few animated words. He then returned to the city.

On reaching the city Charles once more ascended the Cathedral, accompanied by his staff. From here he watched the unrolling and extension of the battle, and from here he could see his troops in the

[1] Ludlow in a rather obscure passage says that Lambert at first demurred at crossing the river.

valley almost at his feet being steadily pushed further and further back, till they were not far from the city walls.

All this time Cromwell's main body on the eastern side of the river had shown no activity beyond cannonading the Fort Royal from the slopes of Perry Wood. It must have appeared to Charles that Cromwell was staking all on the western attack, and dangerously denuding his right wing. A mediocre commander, seeing his centre being driven in at his very feet, as it would seem, would use his reserve to aid the threatened point and put in a counter-attack. But the King did no such thing. An opportunity seldom vouchsafed to a commander in battle was now open to him. His opponent's army was divided into two portions, divided by a river and a single bridge; the right wing was being continually weakened in order to reinforce the left. Here was the chance for a smashing counter-blow. By concentrating all available troops against the isolated right wing the Royalists might yet wrest victory from defeat. It was a brilliant conception, and Charles proceeded to carry it out brilliantly. Descending from the tower once more and collecting every man he could lay hands on (Leslie's cavalry would not take part), Charles placed himself at their head and sallied out through the Sidbury or eastern gate, and delivered a fierce attack on the surprised Parliament troops. These were mostly raw militia, and they recoiled from the blow. The Royalists advanced, carrying all before them and effected a lodgment on Red Hill.

It was a critical moment. It looked like a sudden debacle in this part of the field. But Oliver Cromwell rose to the height of his military stature here, just as he had done at the crisis of Marston Moor. Word was·brought him of the disaster that was overtaking his main body on the other side of the river. Instantly forming his resolution, he called off his troops engaged with the Scots, leaving Fleetwood to finish the work there, and himself galloped back across the bridge and joined his retreating militia. He arrived in the nick of time. The battle swayed in the balance for three hours more, though details are lacking. It was touch and go. Cromwell himself admitted that the battle was 'as stiff a contest for four or five hours as ever I have seen'. But numbers and good generalship told; the Scots were pushed back gradually down the hill, and through the Sidbury gate into the city. The King at one point lost his horse. An unpublished and anonymous account in the P.R.O. describes the scene so:[1] 'The King being

[1] *C.S.P.* (*Dom.*) d. 17/9/1651.

closely pursued, and our men stopping the passage, was forced to quit his horse and climb up our half-raised mount (Fort Royal?), and there so encouraged our foot that the enemy retired with loss.' He then fell back into the city, where 'taking a fresh horse, he rode to the cavalry with the intention of rallying them. . . . David Leslie rode up and down as one amazed, or seeking to fly, for they were so confused that neither threats nor entreaties could persuade them to charge with His Majesty. What became of His Majesty afterwards I know not, but God preserve him for certainly a more gallant prince was never born'.

It was a case of *sauve qui peut*. The Scottish cavalry had behaved badly and refused to counter-attack. As darkness fell they, leaving the infantry to their fate in the city, took to their heels. The infantry were all killed or captured to a man, while the fleeing horse secured a few more hours of freedom. To continue the anonymous account: 'We of the horse, trampling one upon another, much readier to cut each others throats than to defend ourselves against the enemy. . . . We had no guides so we often lost our way, but yet reached Newport 30 miles this side of Worcester, the next morning. . . . On Thursday night Lieut.-Gen. Middleton and Leslie left us, or willingly lost us.'[1]

COMMENTS

The conduct of King Charles during the battle, though not before, is to be admired. Of his physical bravery there is ample evidence, culminating in his leading the counter-attack in person. His great sin was that of allowing, or at least not preventing, widespread looting by his Scottish soldiery, south of the Mersey. This conduct alienated his potential adherents in England, without whom his cause was hopeless. Charles recognized this from the first. A letter in the Public Record Office states that the King 'says he was deceived by the English, for he would never have thought of entering England but he was led to expect a general rising'.[2] The same letter described how he felt himself 'let down' by the Scots. 'The King complains much of the Scotch. . . . He says, at the battle of Worcester, where he had

[1] Newport is a good 40 miles from Worcester, so it was an astonishing performance. This remarkable letter was written on Sept. 17th, the writer having been captured at Preston.

[2] *C.S.P.* (*Dom.*) *d.* Nov. 1st, 1652.

12,000 of them, only 5,000 fought as they should. He accuses David Leslie and Middleton of want of courage and conduct, if not of treachery. This was why he left them . . . the night of the battle, fearing they would betray and deliver him up, if attacked by any pursuing parties.' Possibly he was not unmindful of the treatment his father had received at their hands.

As for his conduct of the battle, I have already expressed my admiration. The Royalists were acting on interior lines, and the King took full advantage of this favourable position, and just at the right moment. He realized that it must be an 'all-out' blow, and quite properly he decided to lead it himself. The opposing commander, as we have seen, also decided to lead what was intended to be the decisive attack in person.

Considering that most of Leslie's horse had no stomach for the fight, it is, on the whole, surprising that the Royalist army maintained the fight for so long as five hours.

Oliver Cromwell also acquitted himself well, not only in the actual battle, but in the preliminary moves. His pursuit from Scotland was a good example of a prolonged forced march, his army being driven along by the influence of his own fierce resolution and animated by his own fiery spirit. The weather was stiflingly hot, so he marched his troops in 'shirt-sleeves order', impressing countrymen to carry the soldiers' coats. By such means he was enabled to march at a speed of upwards of 16 miles per day.

There was perhaps one weak point in his plan for the battle. While the main attack was proceeding he left the whole of his right wing idle. These were his worst-trained troops, consisting largely of militiamen, but if they were fit to take part in a battle they were at least fit to make a holding attack on the enemy in their front. This would have had the effect of using up some of the Royalist troops that were later employed in the counter-attack. But the Lord General was quick to rectify this mistake and his rapid and decided transference of a large force from the left to the right in the course of the battle was the most striking tactical manœuvre made by him in the course of his military career. The nearest approach to it in our history was perhaps Marlborough's transference of the bulk of his English contingent from right to left at the battle of Ramillies. The parallel is not exact, for in the latter case it was an offensive move, whereas Cromwell's was the result of an appeal for help. Nevertheless, it stamps him as a great tactician.

To sum up we may say that from the penultimate battle fought on English soil, both the King and the King-breaker emerged with credit.

PROBLEMS OF THE BATTLEFIELD

Contrary to the usual run of English battles, there are practically no problems here—that is, no soluble problems. Owing to the present built-up nature of the ground in the eastern suburbs of Worcester it would be fruitless to attempt to identify the exact localities where the evening struggle took place, beyond saying that it was on the slopes of Perry Wood and Red Hill. The location of the two bridges is precisely defined by Cromwell's statement that they were 'within pistol shot' of one another. Allowing for slight exaggeration, we should expect to find traces of them within 100 yards of the river junction. Being only of a temporary nature, and made of boats there could be no piles existing to mark the spot; but what one would expect to see are ramps cut into the banks on the west bank of the Severn and on both banks of the Teme, for there the banks are practically precipitous and about twelve feet high. If any vehicles or even horses were to get up the far bank, considerable ramps, of which there is not a sign, would be necessary. Both Cromwell and Downing state positively that horses did get across, so the complete disappearance of the ramps must remain a mystery. The fighting must, however, have been chiefly dismounted, working largely by 'push of pike' from hedge to hedge. All the accounts stress this hedgerow fighting.

Not only are the banks steep but the approach from the eastern side descends a steep cliff called Bund's Hill. There is, however, a ravine cutting into this cliff, about 200 yards above the river junction by which troops could approach, and another practicable slope just north of the existing ferry. The best way to approach the scene is now by the ferry, and then along the eastern bank. The old Powick bridge is still in existence (except the northern portion) but it is no longer used for the main road, which crosses the Teme 100 yards downstream. The main fighting in the meadows took place over featureless ground, and there is little to be gained from walking over it; moreover it is somewhat inaccessible. The dramatic point is undoubtedly the river junction. Mr. Bund, in his book, laments the fact that the battle has no tangible memorial. I would suggest that if such a memorial is ever erected it should be at this spot. It should be sited on the eastern bank of the Severn, precisely at the spot where the bridge was built. With its aid we could then conjure up a vision of the soldiers 'running down on to the bridge', led by a sombre figure with plumed hat and drawn sword—'old Noll'.

CHAPTER XXXVII

The Battle of Sedgemoor, July 6th, 1685

SEDGEMOOR is notable as being the last battle fought on English soil, and important inasmuch as if the King's forces had been defeated we might now have a different reigning House. It thus occupies a niche of its own. It is also notable as containing some features almost unique in English warfare.

A good deal has naturally been written about it, and its outlines are tolerably accurately established. But in spite of this, and of the fact that it is the most recent of our home battles, the actual battlefield has changed more than almost any other except Wakefield, and it is consequently very difficult to identify the exact localities referred to in the records. Two of these localities play a prominent part in the battle, yet they are either vaguely or incorrectly sited in all modern accounts and maps. I refer to the Langmoor Rhine and the Bussex Rhine. The explanation of this curious fact is that the whole area of the battlefield has been redrained since the battle, the old drains or rhines being replaced by modern drains. Alongside many of these drains, 'droves', or slightly raised cart-tracks, have been made. This matter will be dealt with in due course.

On June 11th, 1685, the Duke of Monmouth had landed at Lyme in Dorset. Hastily collecting a scratch army, he had advanced on Bristol. Frustrated there and at Bath, he had turned at bay a few miles south at Philips Norton, where he won the penultimate battle fought on English soil. But he had shot his bolt and fell back towards Bridge-water, followed by a superior Royalist army. This was the situation when on July 3rd he entered Bridgwater, depressed and despondent.

Though he had conducted the campaign heretofore with skill everything had gone against him. The gentry in the West had not risen in his favour; there had not been risings in other parts of England and a rising in Scotland by Argyle had just come to naught. His little army was disheartened, disillusioned and dwindling, its morale was at a low ebb, and its spirit was rapidly evaporating. Unpaid, badly shod, ill-armed and untrained, it had no expectation of success if pitted against the royal army in the field. Monmouth was at his wits end; only two courses seemed to remain—to make a dash to the north, in the hopes of joining up with friends in the Welsh Marches, or to fly the country. For two days he remained at Bridgwater, gloomily revolving the matter in his mind and debating it with his friends. We will leave him for the moment thus employed and turn to the other camp.

The King's army, following up the retreat of Monmouth in a leisurely manner, reached Somerton on July 4th, and hearing of the presence of the Rebels at Bridgwater, pushed on early next day to Weston Zoyland. Just north of this village a young officer discovered a good defensive position protected by the famous Bussex Rhine, a great drain about 20 feet in width, generally filled with water but at the moment dry, though boggy in most places.[1] Covered by this rhine the army pitched its tents and went into bivouac.

The commander of the royal army was a French Huguenot, Lord Feversham. He had had a fair grounding in soldiering on the Continent, but this was his first independent command. His second in command was John Churchill, afterwards Duke of Marlborough; he had commanded the advanced guard of the army in the opening stages of the campaign, and had acquitted himself well, though there had been no scope for brilliant manœuvring or battles during that period. In numbers the army was inferior to that of the Rebels, containing 1,800 against 2,900 foot, 700 against 800 horse and 17 against 4 guns. But it was the pick of the regular army: in fact it *was* the regular army. Every regiment, save the Scots Guards and the Buffs, that had been raised in 1661 by Charles II was present; consequently all the senior regiments of the army were now engaged for the first time. It will be convenient to tabulate them.

CAVALRY

1685 Title.	Subsequent Title.
The King's Horse Guards	The Life Guards
The King's Regiment of Horse	Royal Horse Guards
The Royal Dragoons	The same

[1] This identical position had been occupied in turn by Goring and Fairfax during the Civil War forty years previously.

INFANTRY

1685 *Title.*	*Subsequent Title.*
1st Regiment of Foot (2 battalions)	Grenadier Guards
2nd Regiment of Foot	Coldstream Guards
Dumbarton's Regiment	The Royal Scots
Trelawney's Regiment	The King's Own
Kirke's Regiment	The Queen's Royal Regiment

The heavy guns had been left at Devizes for want of horses to draw them. Nevertheless the lighter guns, as we see, greatly outnumbered the Rebel guns. They consisted of:

2 12-pdrs.
9 demi-culverin
4 6-pdrs.
2 minions

There were in addition 1,500 Wiltshire Militia, but Feversham left them three miles in rear, suspecting their loyalty.

The King's army, cheerful and loudly confident, pitched their tents whilst Feversham posted outposts as follows: at Burrow Bridge over the river Parret on his left rear; up the main road towards Bridg-water; in front 50 musketeers; and 150 horse under Sir Francis Compton in Chedzoy. These might be described as purely defensive outposts; in addition he sent out a special patrol of Life Guards under Colonel Ogelthorpe to Bawdrip, with orders to report any attempt by Monmouth to slip past up the Bristol road. Thus the position seemed adequately guarded, especially as the odds seemed in favour of Monmouth resuming his retreat to the West.

It was not deemed necessary to entrench the position, but the tents were aligned about 100 yards behind the Bussex Rhine, thus providing space to form up in a defensive line on the offchance of the enemy attacking during the night. Infantry patrols were also sent out a short distance in front of the Rhine, and an inlying picquet of 100 men guarded the camp. The horses not required for patrol work were stabled in the village, but Feversham ordered them to be kept ready saddled. Evidently he was not quite easy in his mind.

The guns were parked on the left of the infantry line, and about 400 yards from it, so placed that they could command the Bridgwater road if necessary. The artillery horses seem to have been stabled in the village.

The afternoon passed quietly and after dark, at 11 p.m., Lord Feversham rode forward to visit the outposts in order to see that they were properly placed and alert. He must have had some inkling that the Rebels might attempt a night attack, improbable though that seemed. He started on the left, and ended up in Chedzoy. Colonel Compton reported 'All quiet'. It was past midnight and pitch dark, with a thick mist rising off the moors all around the village. After chatting with the officers for some time, Feversham rode back to the camp. It was now about 1 o'clock in the morning of July 6th. Soon after arrival in camp a messenger reported from Ogelthorpe that he had moved up the hill from Bawdrip village, but that as he still could hear nothing he was moving forward down the road towards Bridgwater. Feversham approved of this action, and shortly before 2 a.m. he went to bed in a cottage in the village, first removing his cravat.[1] Where Lord Churchill slept history does not relate.

Leaving the slumbering camp of the royal army we must now return, in space and time, to Bridgwater in the early afternoon.

Unbeknown to the Royalists their motions at Weston Zoyland had been overlooked. A Chedzoy farmer named Sparks had climbed the church tower, 'perspective glass' in hand, and with it had watched Feversham's troops approaching Weston and later setting out their camp. Being friendly disposed to the rebels (though the parson dissuaded any open attachment), Sparks sent word of this momentous event to Monmouth by his servant, one Richard Godfrey.[2] When Godfrey arrived in Bridgwater the Duke was in the act of crossing the bridge, intending to lead his army back to Bristol. Godfrey delivered his message and Monmouth promptly climbed the church tower to see what he could see for himself.[3]

Godfrey assured the Duke that there was 'a way round', and offered to lead the army by it. Monmouth hesitated. He assembled a council

[1] Macaulay's reference to Feversham's actions is: 'Even at this momentous crisis he thought only of eating and sleeping.'

[2] Sometimes called Newton, after his mother. He was illegitimate.

[3] A local tradition which reaches me at fifth hand records that he spent some time walking round the embattled parapet before he managed to spot the camp. This seems to render improbable the well known story that he identified his old regiment from the church tower. I had always marvelled that he could recognize such details at a distance of nearly four miles.

of war. It also hesitated, and inquired whether the hostile camp was entrenched. Naturally Godfrey did not know, but the good-natured fellow undertook to find out. This he did, and returned to say that there was no sign of digging. If he said nothing about the Bussex Rhine (which is far from certain) he probably reasoned that as it was dry at that time of year, it would not be an appreciable obstacle for the infantry—*and he would be right.*

Thus reassured, Monmouth decided on the desperate venture of a night approach and night attack—one of the most difficult operations in war—taxing even the most highly-trained troops.[1] The most drastic, even draconian orders for maintaining silence were issued. Anyone making the least noise was immediately to be stabbed by his neighbour. These orders had their effect and the rebel army marched out in the darkness in complete silence.

The route followed is shown on Sketch-map 47. The army took the Bristol road, the foot leading, followed by the four guns, and in rear the horse. It was eleven o'clock when the army set forth. After 2½ miles they halted at the foot of Knowle Hill. Here the baggage wagons and one gun were detached up the Bristol road, ready for the march on Bristol as soon as the night's battle should be won. The army then turned to its right along what is still sometimes called War Lane, otherwise Marsh Lane. Thus the village of Chedzoy, occupied by Compton's men, was safely by-passed. Near Peasey Farm the ammunition wagons were parked. It was now about 12.30 a.m. and they were passing Bawdrip, half a mile on their left, where Ogelthorpe's troopers were sitting. Not surprisingly these neither saw nor heard anything; nor, as we have seen, did Feversham and the patrol in Chedzoy. Thus the Rebel army passed unknowingly between the two dangers on their right hand and on their left. The horse were now leading; indeed, it is not clear why they did not take the lead from the outset. Passing Peasey Farm the army emerged on to the moor. A cavalry patrol appeared near them. The column halted in trepidation, but the patrol passed on without spotting them. They were now approaching a big drain called the Langmoor Rhine. It lay ¾ mile south-east of Chedzoy; a ford by a line of stepping-stones,

---

[1] It is a curious fact that Lord Wolseley who had so successfully attempted this very operation at Tel-el-Kebir should write an account of Sedgemoor, in which he criticised Monmouth for attempting what he had himself succeeded in. Yet he rightly calls it 'the most deadly but the most difficult of military operations'.

and marked by a huge boulder called Langmoor Stone, afforded the only possible crossing for horsemen. Godfrey, of course, knew this ford, but in the darkness and fog he could not at first find it. The range of vision was only 50 yards. The column was obliged to halt for what must have seemed an infinity of time to the nerve-strung Monmouth. It was perhaps 1.45 a.m. and Feversham just getting into bed. But watches could not be consulted in the darkness, and it is useless to conjecture as to the exact time or duration of the delay.

At length Godfrey hit upon the ford, and the army started to cross. The cavalry did this successfully, and two out of the five foot regiments had followed suit when a pistol shot rang out. Discovered! What was to be done? A hasty consultation, and Monmouth sent Lord Grey forward with the cavalry, promising to follow with the foot as speedily as possible. The plan was for the horse to cross the Bussex Rhine by the upper of two 'plungeons', or crossings, that existed one on each flank of the hostile camp (see Sketch-map 47). They were then to attack the infantry camp from the flank while the foot attacked in front. It was estimated that meanwhile the troopers' horses would be stabled in the village some hundreds of yards away, so that no danger need be feared from that quarter. This flank was purposely selected for attack because it was known (probably the maligned Godfrey had spotted it) that the Royalist guns were all on the other flank, guarding the Bridgwater road.

In an emergency of this nature a quick, clear-cut and simple decision is essential, and it is difficult to see what other decision Monmouth could have come to, unless he were to abandon the whole enterprise. Once the hostile army had been alarmed immediate and speedy action was imperative. But had the enemy been alarmed? It is always assumed that they had. But this idea probably emanates from faulty location of the Langmoor Rhine. The matter is dealt with at the end of this chapter; here I will only observe that most modern maps show the Langmoor Rhine only a few hundred yards in front of the Bussex Rhine, and hence the sound of the pistol shot would be likely to arouse the camp. But in reality it is almost exactly one mile away, and a stray pistol shot would scarcely carry that distance. The same misconception as to the distance has led Mr. Maurice Page, who has written the most careful and detailed account of the battle, to criticize Monmouth for not immediately forming line instead of continuing his march in column. Under the circumstances I am

satisfied that Monmouth was right not to attempt to form line at that
juncture. The result of this attempt would probably have led to
confusion and disaster. Instead he hurried forward in what was a
diagonal approach to the camp, taking—whether by good luck or

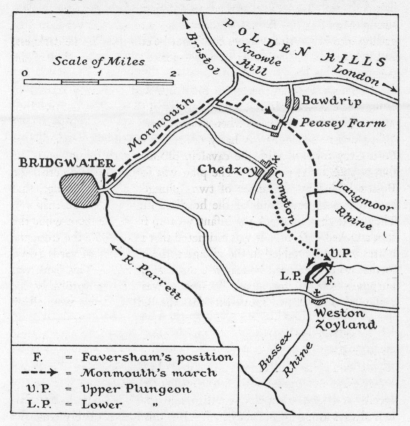

SKETCH-MAP 47. SEDGEMOOR: THE PRELIMINARY MOVES

good eye for ground—absolutely the right direction. It is indeed a
marvel how he accomplished it. It is a common complaint of visitors
to the ground that it is extremely difficult to locate any points or to
find one's way in that flat, featureless country. If this be so in daylight
and with the help of a good map, consider what a formidable problem
it must have been in the middle of a foggy night without a map or the
possibility of striking a match! Moreover, Monmouth no longer
had the services of a guide. Godfrey seems to have started off with the

cavalry; but as they trotted forward into the darkness the poor Godfrey was naturally left behind. He disappeared completely from the scene—and, after a few brief hours of fame, from history.

Grey had trotted forward with his cavalry, having only the haziest idea of the distance to the Bussex Rhine, though Godfrey presumably had indicated its general direction.

But, if the camp had not yet taken alarm the vedette on the Langmoor Rhine that had fired the pistol shot had. A trooper galloped to his headquarters in Chedzoy shouting: 'The rebels are close at hand, thousands of them, horse and foot.' Quickly Colonel Compton took action. First he despatched a trooper to warn the camp. This man galloped back and 'standing on the outside of the ditch called with all possible earnestness to the Scots Regiment to beat up their drums, and tell them the enemy was come; and having repeated it at least twenty times as loud as he could, rides back the way he came'. Oh, excellent trooper!

The second step Compton took was to collect as many of his 150 horsemen as he could and lead them out of the village by the south, in an endeavour to cut across the head of the rebel army, and get to the upper plungeon first. A glance at the map will show that the line of his march should take him across that of the Rebels. That is just what happened. In the dark he bumped into Grey's right flank, between the Langmoor and Bussex Rhines. There ensued some confused fighting and spirited night charges which quite defy accurate description. To describe the course of events in a cavalry action in daylight is difficult enough; in the night it is quite impossible. There seem, however, to have been at least two mounted contacts (they can hardly have been organized charges in the fog and darkness) between Compton and Grey. The net result was that though Compton was himself wounded and outnumbered he did manage to gain the upper plungeon before the enemy. Crossing it he formed up his men and awaited attack.

He did not have long to wait. Grey's troopers, who not only were themselves ill-trained but their horses also, had lost all semblance of order in the confusion and excitement of the night action. They somehow stumbled or blundered on till they were pulled up by the Rhine. Naturally they did not hit it off exactly opposite the plungeon. Some therefore turned to the left and some to the right. Grey, who was by now utterly powerless to control or guide his men, followed what seemed to him the larger portion, just as a huntsman in a wood who can hear but not see follows what sounds like the body of the pack when it divides.

About 300 horsemen had turned left, and thus encountered the plungeon, with Compton's Life Guards standing on the opposite side guarding it. A fairly prolonged struggle for the crossing ended, as might be supposed, in the defeat of the Rebels. Meanwhile the 'body of the pack' had turned to their right[1] and were riding along the side of the ditch looking for a way over. But before they could reach the lower plungeon they had to run the gauntlet of the whole Royalist camp, which was now thoroughly aroused.

Opposite the Guards they were challenged: 'Who are you for?' 'The KING!'

'Which King?'

'King Monmouth, God with him!'

'Then take that with you.' And a volley rang out.

The horses did what they will normally do under such conditions (only feebly dissuaded by their mounts): that is, they swerved away from the bullets, and broke into a gallop. This became unruly and uncontrollable as its speed increased and as the horses became more and more maddened with excitement. The hard-mouthed moorland horses bore the bewildered rebel rustics into the midst of their own foot, and confusion became worse confounded. Andrew Pascall's map tells the tale: about midway between the Langmoor and Bussex Rhines, it reads: 'Place where Grey's horse were fired on by their own people.' This fire had the natural effect of still further dispersing the rebel cavalry. They disappeared into the darkness and the hapless Grey was reduced to following, in the vain hopes of eventually collecting and bringing them back to the battlefield.

One cannot withhold sympathy for a brave soldier [2] in such a humiliating position, one that was not of his own making. Yet Lord Grey has been mercilessly criticized by numerous 'arm-chair critics' who have probably never had the experience of a night operation on horseback in the fog, especially with a completely raw body of troops.

Meanwhile the Royalist foot had sprung to arms, and formed up

[1] The mist was now not so thick and the lighted portfires of Dumbartons may have drawn them in that direction.

[2] A few days previously he had risked his own life in Wells Cathedral, protecting the altar from desecration. Lord Wolseley's charge of cowardice is unfounded.

in line just behind and parallel to the Rhine. Lord Feversham was also aroused after a mere half-hour in bed. If Lord Grey has been made the scapegoat for the Rebel defeat the Huguenot general has been made the scapegoat for the Royalist surprise. He is accused of dallying over his toilet, adjusting his cravat 'before a paltry cottage mirror'. I wonder who was the eye-witness of this action! But it is inherently probable. The commander had made judicious and adequate dispositions. Like Drake at Plymouth he might say: 'There is time to adjust my cravat and time to defeat the rebels too.' And there *was* time.

Before Feversham arrived on the scene, Churchill had altered the infantry dispositions slightly. Correctly sensing that the attack was coming from the right front and that the regiments on the left were likely to be wasted, he moved them across to the rear of the centre and right. This seems a common-sense manœuvre.

We left Monmouth hurrying his infantry (still in column) frantically forward at a sort of ambling double, and being charged through by some of Grey's wild horsemen. He was right to hustle, for if the attack by the two arms was to be co-ordinated there was no time to be lost. Here some critics have gone astray through supposing that he had only a short distance to traverse. He had, in fact, more than a mile, and hasten as he might he could not arrive opposite the ditch till the cavalry action was over. Still, he arrived earlier than he would have done had he attempted to advance that long distance in line. Such an attempt under the conditions that prevailed would have led to loss of direction, to clumping in some places, to dispersion in others, to confusion and probably even to some portions of the line firing on other portions.

The precise manœuvre by which he turned his column into line is not clear. His approach was a diagonal one, and it is on the whole most probable that when he got within 100 yards of the ditch he merely faced each regiment to its left. This would bring them into line, and a slight and probably instinctive wheel to the right would bring the line parallel to the ditch opposite the Royalist centre.[1]

In the course of this manœuvre two battalions, whether intentionally or not, formed in rear; thus leaving a frontage of three battalions. The alarm having been given it was no longer possible to rush the

---

[1] The best evidence on this interesting point (never discussed by historians) is Wade's *Confession* and Dummer's maps. Dummer was an officer in the King's Artillery.

camp, nor was Monmouth able to induce his men to advance any further once they had formed line. They merely stood and fired from a stationary position. According to Sir John Dalrymple they 'formed themselves into a solid body, laying their shoulders close to each other, and every man encouraging his neighbour, they advanced, fought, stopped and died together', like the Anglo-Saxon 'shield-wall' at Hastings, mining picks replacing battleaxes.

It was a fire-fight at a range of about 100 yards. But it must have been largely unaimed fire and a great waste of ammunition on the part of the raw and excited country lads. The natural result was that after an hour's firing ammunition began to run short, and the cry went up: 'Ammunition, ammunition! For the Lord's sake ammunition!' Messengers were sent hot-foot to bring up the ammunition wagons which had been halted near Peasey Farm (no doubt because of the noise they would have made if they had accompanied the column.) But the ammunition came not. A mob of Grey's disorderly horsemen had galloped through the baggage wagons and the panic spread to the drivers, who turned and drove away to the rear.

And what about the artillery? The story is soon told. The three rebel guns had followed as best they could, and a position was found for them between the second and third regiments by their Dutch commander at a distance of 116 paces from the ditch, opposite the Guards. The unusual precision of this siting is given by Capt. Dummer, who after the battle no doubt rode over to them, filled with professional curiosity, and paced the distance from the ditch. Firing from this position they were able to employ slightly oblique fire against the opposing foot, and the Guards suffered fairly heavy casualties.

Meanwhile the Royal artillery had not intervened in the action. As we have seen they were posted on the extreme left flank. When the two left regiments were moved to the right the guns were left several hundred yards from the scene of action. The discipline of the drivers (probably impressed civilians) was bad, and considerable delay was caused in trying to find and rout them out of their comfortable billets in the village. Their horses also were not forthcoming. But a *Deus ex machina* appeared in the person of the militant divine, Bishop Mews of Winchester, who, once a soldier himself, became one again as soon as he smelt powder. Bringing out his own coach-horses he personally supervised their hooking into the limbers and even took part in placing the guns in action in the required spot. No wonder he was afterwards described as 'fitter for a bombardier than a bishop'. The required spot was obviously somewhere whence they could engage and silence the impudent and annoying rebel cannon. Six guns were therefore brought up to the centre of the line and succeeded in accomplishing their task.

Lord Feversham, from the moment of his arrival on the scene, took charge and from then onwards controlled the fight with a firm hand. Every move he made was, as far as one can judge, a sound one. How far he consulted or was influenced by his second in command cannot be said. But the two were old friends and comrades both in the Royal Court and on the tennis court. Moreover they had both served under Turenne at the battle of Entzheim. There is no sign of any difference of opinion between them at any stage of the campaign, and it is only reasonable to surmise that the future victor of Blenheim exerted his influence to good purpose during the battle. Be that as it may, Feversham's first order was that the foot should not attempt to cross the ditch till daylight, an eminently sensible injunction. Further, realizing that musketry in the dark was a waste of valuable ammunition, he forbade any firing at first. (Later he modified the order.) Meanwhile the Rebels were firing rapidly and wildly; most of the bullets passed harmlessly overhead.

As soon as it began to get light enough to reconnoitre (i.e. about 4 a.m.) Feversham crossed the ditch by the lower plungeon, taking some cavalry with him. With these he felt and then pressed the Rebels' right flank. Whilst he was so employed Colonel Ogelthorpe rode up. He had ridden via Chedzoy to the gates of Bridgwater, and finding to his astonishment that the Rebel army had marched out, he hastened straight back to the camp with the news. Though Ogelthorpe has been condemned in unmeasured terms for failing to discover Monmouth's march, Feversham was evidently satisfied with his conduct. For he took the Colonel with him back across the ditch, handed over to him some cavalry and sent him across the upper plungeon to attack the enemy in their left flank, thus showing complete confidence in his military capacity. Ogelthorpe delivered a number of spirited charges, which eventually pushed in the rebel left and enabled him to capture the three guns.

By this time it was broad daylight and the Duke of Monmouth was able to survey the scene and appreciate the situation. The son of Charles II had, on the testimony of his opponents, conducted himself courageously and well. But he had now to make a painful

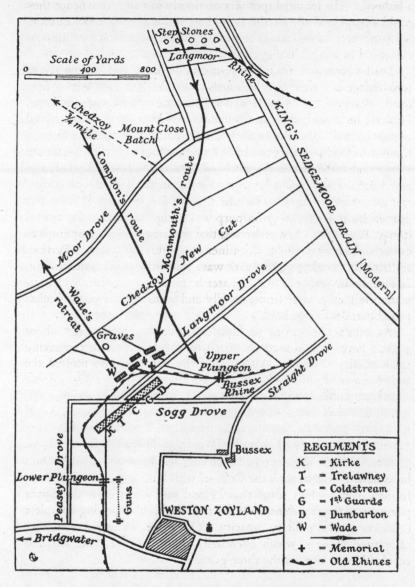

SKETCH-MAP 48. SEDGEMOOR: THE BATTLE

decision.[1] To his experienced eye it was clear that the situation was hopeless. His musketeers were now silent, having run out of ammunition after $1\frac{1}{2}$ hours' firing, and there was no sign of the ammunition wagons arriving. Both his flanks were being pushed in by the Royalist horse and musket and cannon fire from across the ditch was becoming heavier and more accurate as the light improved. Monmouth judged that there was no possible hope of victory, and he judged correctly. He was thus faced with two alternatives: to stand his ground till overrun, or to take flight. If he stood his ground he might meet a soldier's death, but on the other hand he might be only wounded, in which case he would be captured and probably beheaded. What good would that be? On the other hand, if he took to flight he might live to fight another day. To extract his whole army from the fight he judged to be impossible; they were so closely beset by the hostile cavalry that dismounted men had no hope of getting away, and their own cavalry had long since vanished. Thus he was driven to the unpalatable conclusion that the second course was the only possible one.

While the Duke was divesting himself of his armour, preparatory to flight, Lord Grey, with a small body of troopers reappeared on the field, after endeavouring to round up and bring back to the field his errant cavalry. A hasty consultation ensued and Grey agreed to accompany his master in flight. Together with a few companions they mounted and made off, striking for the Polden Hills. A local tradition relates that in the course of this flight the Duke leaped a ditch 17 feet wide. No doubt the distance has been exaggerated, but the tradition probably indicates that he had to cross some ditch on the moors, probably the Langmoor Rhine, in his gallop for the Polden Hills. Arrived there, he passes out of the story of the battle and so out of this chapter.

In the above account I have put down what probably passed through the mind of the unfortunate Duke, and have presented the best possible case for an act that, however, we look at it, is bound to stink.

The rest of the pathetic story can be told in a few words. Feversham, taking his time and no risks, was watching the enemy closely. Presently (in his own words) 'the pikes of one of their battalions began

[1] 'Drear and doom-like was the dawn to Monmouth' (Churchill's *Marlborough*).

to shake, and at last open'. The opportunity for which he had been waiting was at hand. He gave the equivalent of the order 'Up Guards and at 'em': in other words, he ordered the whole line of infantry to advance to the attack across the ditch. The order was promptly acted upon, whilst the cavalry renewed their assaults on the flanks.

But the long-suffering Rebels had reached the breaking point. They broke. Wade, who commanded the leading (right) regiment, fell back with what remained of his regiment, some 600 yards across the moor, over the drain—a continuation of the Langmoor Rhine —which divided (and still divides) it from the arable land to the north. Here, in a field of corn, he made a final stand. It did not last long; Wade was captured and his men killed or dispersed. The Wiltshire militia came rushing up to join in the congenial task of shooting up the stragglers.

The last battle fought on English soil had witnessed a very pretty example of the triumph of trained men and skilled leaders over stout-hearted amateurs.

COMMENTS

It will doubtless have been noticed that in the foregoing account I have not adopted the popular conception of the respective parts played by the guide and by the Bussex Rhine. The luckless Godfrey is generally represented as losing his head and his way, and also of failing to inform Monmouth of the existence of the Bussex Rhine. The only evidence in support of this belief is a statement made by James II, who was not present himself. There are sufficient indications that Monmouth *was* aware of the rhine, and took it into his calculations when elaborating his plan. Moreover, the credit should probably go to Godfrey for the correct report that the Royalist guns were isolated on the extreme left flank.

As for the importance of the Bussex Rhine, we have seen that it was dry, and that it was not impassable to the infantry. It was only horsemen who had to cross by the plungeons. It was not the existence of the rhine, nor a mistake on the part of Richard Godfrey that brought defeat and disaster to Monmouth's faithful followers, but good leadership and the cool discipline and literally that 'two o'clock in the morning courage' that is so typical of the Regular British Army

It is always easy to criticize unsuccessful generals. In this case it was found possible to criticize a successful one. Feversham became almost a figure of fun in London, and historians, following Macaulay, have done little to redeem his character and conduct. Yet if my facts are correct there seems little ground for fault-finding. His army no doubt was suffering from over-confidence, but he was scarcely to blame for that. Indeed, he did his best by cautious and methodical measures to offset it. No general can have much practical control over troops whilst engaged in night fighting, but once daylight had come I can feel nothing but admiration for his measures and actions which concluded with a nice piece of co-operation of all arms. Of his lieutenant-general, all that can be said is that everything that is known is to his credit. One would be glad of John Churchill's own account of this battle. Unfortunately he seems to have shared the repugnance of that other great Duke 'to fight his battles over again'.

Ogelthorpe is usually made the scapegoat, and Page treats him with a mixture of contempt and derision. I have expressed my doubts on this point in the narrative. Let me add something which shows this maligned soldier as remarkable in at least one respect. After fighting or marching practically all night and part of the next morning, and taking part in at least two charges, he was accorded the high honour of carrying Feversham's despatch on the battle to London. He set off the same day and arrived on the very next morning, early enough for someone in touch with the Court to write a letter containing accurate details of the battle, even including some facts that can only have been obtained from captured enemies. Thus this battle-worn man must have covered 150 miles in less than 24 hours. I do not grudge his knighthood to Sir Theophilus Ogelthorpe.

What are we to say of the defeated general? Here also it is easy to denigrate and deride. But if we view the whole campaign coolly and dispassionately, trying to forget its infamous ending, we must award praise rather than blame. It is noteworthy that James II, himself a good judge of a soldier, thought highly of his nephew's conduct of the campaign. Sir John Reresby in his *Memoirs*, writes: 'The Duke of Monmouth had from the very beginning of this desperate attempt behaved with the conduct of a great captain, and was allowed even by the King, who in my hearing said that he had not made one false step.' Lutterell testifies that 'Monmouth lighted off his horse and took a half-pike and charged at the head of the foot and briskly, several times'. This seems to dispose of reflections on his physical courage. Monmouth's plan, whereby his whole army should concentrate upon the hostile infantry before the horse and guns could come to their assistance, was a brilliant one. But it required a higher degree of training than his motley army possessed.

In resolving on a night attack it cannot be denied that Monmouth gambled. So did Napoleon on many occasions. And so do nearly all great generals at one time or another. It is for the weaker side to gamble. Monmouth was right to gamble, for Feversham was the stronger. Nor can we deny the Duke our meed of praise, for the degree of discipline and training that in a few brief weeks enabled his army to make a night approach of five miles in two hours, undetected, landing up at the desired point. Any other troops than the senior regiments of the English army might well have panicked in that early morning alarm. Instead, 'such was the extraordinary cheerfulness of our Army that they were almost as readily drawn up to receive them as a pre-informed expectation could have posted them, though upon so short and so dangerous a warning'.

But the last word must be one of pity and admiration for those poor deluded, misguided country rustics who believed that their Protestant religion was in danger and who were prepared to risk their limbs in its defence, even though armed with mining picks, forks and bludgeons. Thus Englishmen can look back upon this last battle fought on 'England's pastures green' with satisfaction and pride.

PROBLEMS OF THE BATTLEFIELD

No battlefield in England is more difficult to find than that of Sedgemoor—that is if one approaches it in the only way an historian should, namely in the steps of the Duke of Monmouth's devoted army. Thus only will you get that real thrill that every battlefield should impart to the intelligent visitor. The reason is obvious: Monmouth marched for 2½ miles across the moor without passing a single human habitation, and, following in his steps to Peasey Farm, the visitor will have the same experience. On top of this, the landmarks that might have guided him are gone, and the face of the countryside is changed. Finally, though a memorial-stone has been erected on the centre of the battlefield, it is in summertime screened from the road (or 'drove') by a thick hedge; nor is there any indication on the roadside to indicate its proximity. I, even when aware of its approximate situation, have walked past it unawares, and many visitors have departed in despair without locating it at all.

But there is worse to follow. Even if you are fortunate, or

keen-sighted enough, to spot the memorial, there is still nothing to indicate the course of the Bussex Rhine, without which it is impossible to site the Royalist line, or indeed to reconstruct the battle at all.[1]

I have therefore been at some pains to compile a map that should show both the ancient course of the drains, and also the modern lay-out of droves and fields and drains. Early in this pursuit I discovered that Page's map marks the Langmoor Rhine in the wrong place; it is out by nearly 1,000 yards, and unfortunately his map has been followed by subsequent writers, including Mr. Winston Churchill. This is a matter of some importance, because if we accept Page's map the cavalry encounters between Grey and Compton do not make sense. (Possibly that is why Mr. Churchill slurs over them in his account.)

Before his death Page did discover his mistake and in a note in *Somerset and Dorset Notes and Queries* for 1935, p. 241, gives the location as marked on my Sketch-map 48. I have visited the spot in the month of August and, when you know where to look, it is just visible. It is faintly visible from the air. Unfortunately the new map that has been prepared for Page's book still shows it in the old place. I fancy I have discovered the reason for the mistake: the six-inch ordnance map names the drain that runs 400 yards to the north of the Bussex Rhine 'Langmoor Rhine', and I was myself misled by this when I examined this map. But a lucky reference to the 25-inch map showed the name as 'Chedzoy New Cut'. I show it by this name in my sketch-map. I also show a line of stepping-stones to the north of Langmoor Rhine and parallel to it, as it is shown in the contemporary map of Rev. Andrew Paschall, the vicar of Ched-zoy at the time, who should know. All signs of the stones, as also of the Langmoor Stone, have vanished.

Coming now to the still more important question of the course of the Bussex Rhine, I have consulted all possible sources of information and, armed with them, I have gone over the ground, trying to trace its course. At first I was not hopeful of success. Asking a farmer near where I adjudged it should run, he replied vaguely: 'Somewhere yonder', with an equally vague wave of the hand. I subsequently discovered that the distance of the rhine from the spot where we were standing was under 50 yards!

[1] Page's little book does include a primitive diagram, showing the droves, but it is sadly inadequate, and omits the Bussex Rhine, whilst his general map is of too small a scale to assist in this respect.

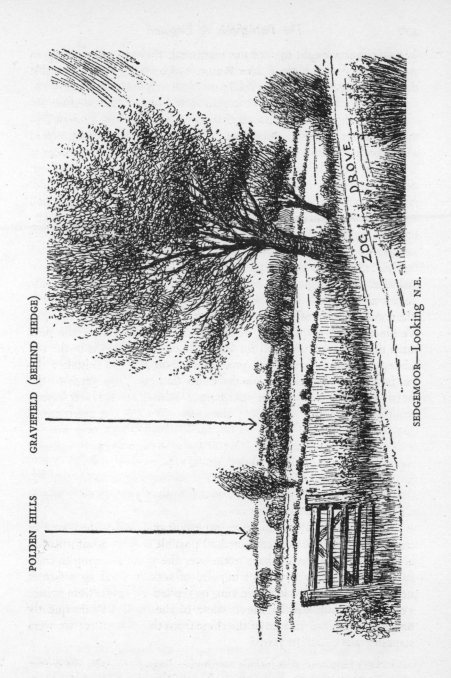

POLDEN HILLS   GRAVEFIELD (BEHIND HEDGE)

ZOG DROVE

SEDGEMOOR—Looking N.E.

I will not weary the reader by enumerating all the scraps of evidence that produced the course of the rhine as shown on my map, but must thank the Air Ministry for providing me with air photos of the ground, from which I have been able to corroborate most of my conclusions.

The memorial-stone was erected about 1930, made of Cornish granite, flanked by four smaller stones and two white poplars which are visible from the drove, even though the stone may not be.

The memorial does not mark the site of the chief grave-pit, as is sometimes supposed. I have it on the authority of the owner of the land, Mr. Oliver Reed (who helped to excavate the grave in the 'eighties), that it lies two-thirds of the way up the field from the drove. Incidentally, this field is quite modern; a photograph of the excavators shows a completely open moor. Assuming that the Royalist line of foot was parallel to the rhine, as shown in Paschall's and Dummer's maps, and about 100 yards from it, it must have run almost along the modern Langmoor Drove. If my reconstruction is correct it is easy to understand why the First Guards suffered more from artillery fire than Dumbarton's Regiment on their right; for the Rebel guns would find the Guards directly opposite them. As for the position of the Royalist guns, I have been somewhat perplexed. Paschall shows them almost alongside of the foot. But we are told that they were about 500 yards away, and that they covered the Bridgwater road. Now, no contemporary source shows this road, but I imagine that it ran as shown on the earliest map I have been able to consult, that of 1782. If so, it crossed the Bussex Rhine some hundreds of yards below the lower plungeon. This enables us to site the guns well away from the foot. This is partially corroborated by Dummer's map, and I have little doubt that they were approximately as shown on Sketch-map 48.

It still remains to explain how to get on to, and to follow, the course of Monmouth's night march. There is little to be gained by traversing the early portion through Peasey Farm.[1] Rather go through Chedzoy. Any bus from Bridgwater towards Bristol will put you down at the end of the Chedzoy lane. The church is worth a visit (but do not believe the story that the grooves on the church wall were made by Rebels sharpening their swords. The grooves were

---

[1] Page describes the early uneventful part of the march, and just when it begins to get interesting he blandly remarks: 'But probably the visitor will prefer to go straight to Weston Zoyland,' leaving his protegé stranded a Peasey Farm!

almost certainly made centuries earlier by the village archers.) The view from the church tower is disappointing owing to the number of trees, but Weston church tower can be picked up.

Leave the village by the cart-road going south-east. At 500 yards there is a fork; take the left-hand track. (It is marked on the one-inch map.) After half a mile it strikes a drove. Turn right, and 350 yards along this drove is a gate on the left. Another 40 yards is a small oak tree. Langmoor Rhine crosses the drove at this point; and it can be faintly descried to the left, crossing into the far corner of the field. (It is visible in the air photo.) Follow its course and in the field corner you find yourself to your surprise on the banks of a broad river. It is the King's Sedgemoor Drain, cut in 1795 to carry the upper waters of the river Cary into the Parrett three miles below Bridgwater. From here, if you are prudent, you will follow the drain for 1,000 yards, striking to the right after passing five fields, along Langmoor Drove. But you can try your luck across the moor if you feel like it.

APPENDIX

A NOTE ON ARMS AND ARMOUR

THOUGH the emphasis of this book is on fields of battle rather than on personal incidents of the fighting it may be as well to append a note on the armour and weapons in use at the various periods.

For the DARK AGES little can be stated positively except what archaeology has to tell. No doubt the army of Arthur retained some vestiges of Roman arms and armour. That is to say, the better-provided warriors would have some sort of helm and mail-shirt, the spear and double-edged sword being the chief weapons. Cavalry formed a prominent part of the army. The Saxon army, on the other hand, consisted entirely of infantry. Their weapons were the spear, sword or dagger, and light missile axes.

By the time of Alfred the Great, armour was beginning to appear in the Saxon ranks, but there was still an absence of cavalry, as also of bowmen. The Danes brought with them two features afterwards adopted by the English at HASTINGS, the double-handed axe, and the 'shield-wall', or line of footmen armed with kite-shaped shields, which took the place of the old round shield.[1] Mail armour down to the knee was worn by most of the Normans and by Harold's House carls. Spears or lances and swords still formed the main personal weapons, but cross-bowmen now appeared in the ranks of the invaders. There was in fact a great variety of missile weapons used on both sides.

The two centuries that elapsed between Hastings and Evesham produced no striking advance in weapons, unless we should mention the crossbow which played a fairly prominent part in the Barons' War. But in the field of personal armour great progress was made. The mail-shirt or hauberk became steadily longer till the knight was protected by mail-armour (vulgarly known as 'chain-mail,) to the feet. His helmet gradually covered his face till by the time of King John his head was completely encased in it. At the same time the surcoat, adorned with heraldic devices, made its appearance, thus

[1] The Shield-wall was also used by the Anglo-Saxons at Maldon, A.D. 991.

adding to the 'panoply of war'. As armour grew stronger the need for shields became less and they gradually diminished in size, becoming round again instead of kite-shaped.

This period witnessed the heyday of cavalry, whose mounted action usually decided the battle. But a new weapon had arrived by the time of Shrewsbury, which wrested the predominance from the cavalry—the longbow. A man could, by dint of much armour, protect himself from the arrow, but not so his charger. He was thus reduced to dismounting and fighting on foot. The appearance of the longbow had a further effect; it speeded up the improvement in personal armour, leading directly to the introduction of plate-armour, which was proof against its arrows.

Thus when we reach the battle of Shrewsbury we find plate replacing mail, and when we reach the WARS OF THE ROSES the metamorphosis is complete: the knight is as effectually encased in armour as a sardine in a tin.

But the days of the longbow were numbered. The introduction of artillery, after a long period of doubt, proved fatal to it. Guns were first used in the field at the battle of Crécy, but during the first half of the Hundred Years War, though useful against fortresses, they were little more than playthings in the field. Thanks, however, largely to the efforts of Jean Bureau, a French artilleryman of the fifteenth century, they were now beginning to prove effective in the field. They were used in small numbers in the chief battles of the Wars of the Roses, and though not very decisive they did succeed in killing an armoured man where the longbow was now generally powerless to do so.

Thus the process continued through the century till, by the time FLODDEN was fought, the artillery had quite usurped the part hitherto taken by the longbow. Apart from a small number of footmen armed with the very ineffective 'hand-gun', the infantry had thus returned to the weapons used at Hastings—lance and sword. Of these the lance or pike had acquired the pre-eminence in the ranks of the Scots, and on the English side its counterpart in the bill or halberd.

The century that elapsed between Flodden and the Great Civil War saw a steady continuance of the above tendencies. Artillery had, by this time, entirely ousted the bow, with the natural result that armour was rapidly disappearing. For the stoutest plate-armour could not keep out a cannon-ball. First leg protection went, then the breastplate, last of all the helmet. This last was worn fairly generally throughout the war, and corselets or breastplates by a variable portion of the troops and by practically all the senior officers of both sides at the start, though discarded later on in the war. Yet though artillery was now an integral part of all armies, it did not play a big part in any of the battles. The cavalry was now the queen of the battlefield—especially the Cavalier cavalry. Armed with sword and pistols, its officers mounted on thoroughbreds, Charles's horsemen in the opening stages of the war swept all before them; in the latter part of the war, Cromwell's Ironsides redressed the balance. Dragoons were employed on both sides, and played the part of mounted infantry. This brings us to the infantry arm, which was still the backbone of the army. Both sides were similarly armed, two in every three carrying the musket, and the third man the long pike. The heavy musket was fired from a portable rest at the beginning, but this was later abandoned and Firth supposes that with the disuse of the rest the musket was shortened and lightened.

Lastly we come to Sedgemoor. In the intervening period the bayonet had been introduced, and though it was temporarily withdrawn before the battle its influence remained: the *raison d'être* of the pike had vanished, for the musket could now do its work in addition to its own. Moreover, the substitution of flintlocks for matchlocks still further enhanced the supremacy of the musket. Thus, though the pike was still in use (Monmouth himself wielded a half-pike at the crisis of the battle) the army as a whole presented an appearance that had not materially altered till quite modern days, with the introduction of the rifle, machine-gun and mechanical transport.

SELECT BIBLIOGRAPHY TO
THE BATTLEFIELDS OF ENGLAND

THIS bibliography is divided into two parts. As explained in the Preface, no attempt is made at a comprehensive citation of all the many sources and commentaries which must be consulted if one is to arrive at the truth when treating of events in the distant past. Section 'A' is therefore intended merely to indicate the half-dozen or so sources that I personally have found most useful in writing each chapter; Section 'B' is confined, with rare exceptions, to recording those modern books, dealing with the battle in question which contain some contribution to the matter in hand, together with an attempt to indicate the degree of that contribution. For fuller information consult the bibliographies in the volumes of the *Cambridge Medieval History*.

ABBREVIATIONS

R.S.	—	Rolls Series
B.M.	—	British Museum
H.M.C.	—	Historical Manuscripts Commission
C.S.P.	—	Collected State Papers

CHAPTER II: BADON

A.

De excidio et conquestu Britanniae by Gildas (Ed. Plummer, 1896).
Historia Britannorum by Nennius (Ed. Plummer, 1894).
Historia Ecclesiastica by Bede.
Anglo-Saxon Chronicle (Ed. Earle and Plummer. R.S., 1892).
Historia Regum Britanniae by Geoffrey of Monmouth (Ed. Griscom, 1929).
De gestis regum Anglorum by William of Malmesbury (R.S., 1887).

B.

Perhaps it would be as well at the outset to warn the reader who is unacquainted with the subject of Arthur's battles that he will have to read snippets from a large number of books and articles if he wishes to form an independent opinion on this very debatable subject. For example, I have had to consult over 40 different books or articles before writing the above account. I will here cite what I consider the half-dozen most helpful books. To start with, for the historicity of Arthur, go to the three standard modern authorities: *Anglo-Saxon England* by F. M. Stenton (1945), *History of the Anglo-Saxons* by R. H. Hodgkin (1935), and *Roman Britain and the English Settlement* by Collingwood and Myres (1936). For the historical value of Geoffrey of Monmouth, consult the editorial notes in Geoffrey of Monmouth (supra).

For a general history of Arthur, *Arthur of Britain* by E. K. Chambers (1927), supplemented by *The Last Age of Roman Britain* by E. Foord (1925), though the latter rejects the Wiltshire site and prefers Badbury Ring.

For the identification of Badbury, see *The Battle for Britain in the Fifth Century* by T. D. Reed (1944). For local conditions, *Historical Geography of England before* 1800, edited by H. C. Darby, Chap. III, by S. W. Wooldridge (1936). For strategical considerations consult the *Ordnance Survey Map of Roman Britain*.

CHAPTER V: ASHDOWN

A.

De Rebus Gestis Aelfredi by Bishop Asser (Tr. C. Jane, 1926).
Anglo-Saxon Chronicle (*supra*).
Chronicle of Robert of Gloucester (R.S., 1886).
Chronica ex Chronicis by Florence of Worcester (Tr. Forrester, 1854).
De Gestis by William of Malmesbury (*supra*).

B.

One of the best and most easily available military commentaries is *Alfred the Great, the Truthteller* by B. A. Lees (1915). *Life and Times of Alfred the Great* by C. Plummer (1902) is a standard work, but disappointingly short for Ashdown. A good translation of Asser's *Life of Alfred* (from the Latin) is that edited by L. C. Jane (1908), with useful notes. *White Horse Hill* by L. V. Grinsell (1939) gives a succinct *résumé* of the controversy over the site, and a good bibliography. Oman's *England before the Norman Conquest* might also be studied. But the real sources of information and comment are articles in various technical journals, such as *Transactions of the Newbury Field Club*. The best military comment is that by W. H. Simcox in the *English Historical Review*, published as long ago as April, 1886.

CHAPTER XI: HASTINGS

A.

Gesta Guillelmi Ducis by William of Poitiers (Ed. Duchene, 1619).
De Bello Hastingensis Carmen by Guy of Amiens (Ed. Petrie).
Poem Descriptive of a Tapestry by Baudri, Bishop of Dol.
The Bayeux Tapestry (King Penguin, 1943. A life-size reproduction in the Victoria and Albert Museum).
Gesta Normanorum Ducum by William of Jumièges (Ed. Marx, 1914)

N.B.—The above are the five completely contemporary sources. There are at least thirteen other sources (including the rhymed romances of Wace), but over 90 per cent of the reliable facts are contained in the above.

B.

Anglo-Saxon England by F. M. Stenton (1945) gives the latest and probably the best account of the battle. Unfortunately it is short—the account in his *William the Conqueror* (1908) is longer. *Proxime accessit* Sir Charles Oman's *Art of War in the Middle Ages* (2nd Edition, 1924). Sir James Ramsay's *Foundations of England* (1898) is carefully compiled and documented, but he adopts a line of his own regarding the English position. Preferable is R. H. Hodgkin's *History of the Anglo-Saxons* (1935), but it lacks a map. Finally, H. B. George's *Battles of English History* (1895) is, like all his writings, well out of the ruck. General Fuller's chapter on the battle in his *Decisive Battles* (1940) has some valuable comments. The excellent account by General James in the *R.E. Journal* for January, 1907 cannot be classed as 'easily available.'

I have not cited Freeman's *magnum opus*, *The Norman Conquest* (1869), for it is both too lengthy for the average reader, and many of his conjectures no longer meet with favour.[1]

A German, W. Spatz, published *Schlacht von Hastings* in 1896.

[1] Professor Stenton acutely observes in his *Anglo-Saxon England*, p. 703 that there are 'many points in which his narrative forces discrepant pieces of information into an unreal synthesis'.

It had some influence on our historians as regards the numbers of troops engaged. It has no map and has never been translated. The best examination of the ground is contained in *Domesday Tables* by F. H. Baring (1909). Those who wish to read the original chroniclers in modern English will find them at the end of C. Dawson's *Hastings Castle* (1909), together with a useful, short bibliographical note. I have no space for the large number of articles (and in any case they are not readily available to the average reader).

CHAPTER XIV: EVESHAM

A.

Chronicle of Walter of Hemmingburgh (or *Hemingford*) (Eng. Hist. Soc., 1848).

Chronicle of Thomas Wykes (R.S., 1864).

Chronica et Annales by William of Rishanger (R.S., 1865).

Chronicon de duobus bellis by William of Rishanger (R.S., 1876).

Chronicle of Lanercost (Ed. Stevenson, 1839).

Chronicle of Robert of Gloucester (Ed. Wright R.S. 1887).

Chronicle of Melrose (Mailros) (Ed. Stevenson, 1835).

MS. Laud, Misc. 529 ff. 63 (Bodleian).

MS. 10 Bri. Royal Lib. B.M. (Tr. E. H. Review, 1896, p. 520).

Chronicle of John of Oxnead (Oxenede) (R.S. 1859).

Chronicle by a Monk of Lewes. MSS. Cott. Tib. A.X. B.M.

B.

Start with Sir James Ramsay's *Dawn of the Constitution* (1908). It has the best map and bibliography. That and Sir Charles Oman's *Art of War* (2nd Edition, 1924) cover the ground between them. For long the standard work was *The Barons' War* by W. H. Blaauw (1st Edition, 1848, 2nd Edition, with valuable appendix by C. H. Pearson, 1871). Unfortunately Blaauw is more interested in persons than military operations. The same applies to *Simon de Montfort* by Charles Bémont (translated into English, 1930). The author is the leading authority on de Montfort, but evinces little interest in military things, devoting only two pages to the battle. Finally, *Life of Simon de Montfort* by G. W. Prothero (1877), is a painstaking account, but his description of the battle is unconvincing.

Only a few of the original sources, of which there are a large number, have been translated into English.

CHAPTER XVII: SHREWSBURY

A.

Annales Ricardi et Henrici Quarti (Walsingham) (Ed. Riley R.S.).
Recueil des Croniques (Jean de Waurin) (Ed. Harvey R.S. 1864).
Origginale cronikul of Scotland (Andrew of Wyntoun) (Ed. Amours 1903).
Chronicle of John Hardyng (Ed. Ellis 1812).
Chronicon of Robert of Usk (Ed. Thompson 1904).
Chronicle of England (Capgrave) (Ed. Hingeston R.S.).
Chronicon Regum Angliae (Otterbourne) (Ed. Hearne 1732).

B.

Easily the best known and most accessible book is Sir James Ramsay's *York and Lancaster* (1892), and though I disagree with his conclusions profoundly, as explained above, the book is admirable for its careful collection of facts and for its references. Its real rival is J. H. Wylie's *Reign of Henry IV* (1884). But the most recent contributions to the subject are contained in the 1903 volume of *Transactions of the Shropshire Archaeological and Natural History Society* (1903), (available in the London Library), which gives Wylie's address and paper read on the battlefield at the Quincentenary celebrations. The great expert on the battlefield was the Rev. F. G. D. Fletcher, whose revised guide-book to the battlefield and church was also published in 1903. Earlier accounts appear in Owen and Blakeway's *History of Shrewsbury* (1825), *Visits to Fields of Battle in England* by Richard Brooke (1857), and *Battles and Battlefields of England* by C. R. B. Barrett (1896), which follows Ramsay closely. But the literature on this important battle is surprisingly sparse.

CHAPTER XVIII: FIRST ST. ALBANS

A.

Registrum Abbatiae. . . . (Whethamstede) (Ed. Riley R.S. 1872).
Paston Letters (Ed. Gairdner, 1904).
Parliamentary Rolls, v.
MS. of Sir William Stoner (Ed. J. Nayley, 1824).
An English Chronicle (Ed. Davies, 1856).

B.

Singularly little has been written about the battle of recent years. Sir Charles Oman scarcely mentions it in his *Art of War*, and only devotes a dozen lines to it in his *Political History of England*, but he remedies the omission in his *Warwick the Kingmaker* (1893) with a fairly full account. *Battles and Battlefields in England* by C. R. B. Barrett (1896) gives a good straightforward account of the fighting, but with no map. This is rectified by Ramsay in his *York and Lancaster* (1892) with a useful old map. The most detailed account is unfortunately not easily obtainable; written and published in St. Albans by C. H. Ashdown, it is entitled *Battles and Battlefields of St. Albans*. It can be studied in St. Albans Free Library.

CHAPTER XX: SECOND ST. ALBANS

A.

Annales Rerum Anglicarum (W. of Worcester) (Ed. Stevenson R.S. 1864).

Three 15th Century Chronicles (for Gregory's Chronicle) (Ed. Gairdner, 1880).

An English Chronicle (Ed. Davies, 1856).

Registrum Abbatiae . . . (Whethamstede) (*supra*).

Chronicle of the Abbey of Croyland (Ingulph).

Chronicle of Lancaster and York (E. Hall) (Ed. Ellis 1809).

B.

The authorities for this battle are much the same as for First St. Albans. Oman's account (q.v.) is rather short. Ramsay's is longer (*supra*) and again has a map. Barrett's (q.v.) account is somewhat perfunctory, and again we have to depend chiefly upon Ashdown (*supra*) The fact is, as readers will have realized, it is a most difficult battle to make anything of, and most historians slur over it. I cannot wholeheartedly recommend any account.

CHAPTER XXI: TOWTON

A.

Chronicle . . . (Hall) (*supra*).

Anglicae Historiae . . . (Polydore Vergil) (Ed. Ellis 1844).

Croyland Chronicle (Continuatio) (Tr. Riley 1864).

'Hearne's Fragment' in *Chronicle of the White Rose* (1845).

Gregory's Chronicle (*supra*).

Annales Rerum Anglicarum (Worcester) (*supra*).

Registrum Abbatiae . . . (Whethamstede) (*supra*).

Paston Letters (Ed. Gairdner, 1904).

B.

Modern, or comparatively modern, books on Towton are more numerous than in the case of most other medieval battles. I have found most generally useful *Battles Fought in Yorkshire* by A. D. H. Leadman (1891), though the disposition of troops shown in his map is rather fanciful. Closely following it I should place the article by C. Ransome in *English Historical Review* (1889). Our old friend Richard Brooke (1857) has still something useful, particularly regarding topographical details. There is a well-documented article by Sir Clement Markham in the *Yorkshire Archaeological Journal* (1889), though that unfortunately can hardly be classed as 'easily accessible'. The account in *Edward IV* by C. L. Schofield (1923) is adequate and is well documented. The accounts by Sir Charles Oman in his *Warwick the Kingmaker* and *Political History* are both rather short and lack maps. Sir James Ramsay has, as usual, an admirably clear map. Lastly, Hereford George is as sensible as ever in the few remarks he offers on the battle in his *Battles of English History*.

CHAPTER XXII: BARNET

A.

Historie of the Arrivall of Edward IV in England (Ed. Bruce 1838).
Chronicle of the First Thirteen Years of the Reign of Edward IV (Warkworth) (Ed. Halliwell 1829).
Chronicle . . . (Hall) (*supra*).
Anglicae Historiae (Polydore Vergil) (*supra*).
New Chronicle of England (Fabyan) (Ed. Ellis 1811).
Paston Letters (*supra*).

B.

Ramsay's *York and Lancaster* as usual contains the most detailed account, and as usual has the best map. Unfortunately, it is vitiated for the reason given above. There are few satisfactory accounts. The best are those of Oman in his *Warwick the Kingmaker* and, in a slightly shorter but more accessible form, in his *Art of War*, Vol. II. Almost equally good is *Edward IV* by L. Stratford. Some useful local tradition can be found in an article by F. C. Cass in the *Journal of the London and Middlesex Archaeological Society* (1882).

The account by H. B. George in his *Battles of English History* is short but, as usual with this author, to the point.

CHAPTER XXIII: TEWKESBURY

A.

The same as Barnet.

B.

It is uncommonly difficult to make any useful suggestions. Ramsay's account in his *Lancaster and York* I have dealt with. Easily the best account, that by Canon Bazeley, I have also referred to; but it is inaccessible to the average reader, being hidden away in the 1903 volume of the *Transactions of the Bristol and Gloucester Archaeological Society*. It is particularly valuable for the topographical information contained in it. Bazeley also is the only writer to note the existence of the 'hillock', though he does not, in my opinion, make clear its true significance. He does not appear to have studied *Hall's Chronicle* which, incidentally, Ramsay also ignores. Bazeley also follows the universal fashion of attacking Somerset's generalship. As so often happens in military history, the defeated general died on the field before he had a chance to explain his motives and actions, and posterity does not attempt to repair the omission. In my opinion Lord Wenlock, not the Earl of Somerset, was 'the villain of the piece'.

Visits to Fields of Battle in England by Richard Brooke (1857), though not founded on original sources, has some topographical details, such as the discovery of relics in Bloody Meadow, Lower Lode Ferry, and Gupshill. C. R. B. Barrett follows Ramsay. H. B. George is obviously influenced by Ramsay, but struggles to break away from him.

CHAPTER XXIV: BOSWORTH

A.

Chronicle . . . (Hall) (*supra*).
Croyland Chronicle (*Continuatio*) (*supra*).
Song of the Lady Bessie (In Harl. MSS. 542, f.34 B.M.).
Anglicae Historiae (Polydore Vergil) (*supra*).
Chronicle of John Stowe.
Ballad of Bosworth Field (Michael Drayton).

B.

The literature of the battle is more considerable than that of most battles in the Wars of the Roses. The account which I have found

most helpful is that by Professor Gairdner in *Archaeologia*, Vol. LV
(1896), which unfortunately comes outside the definition of 'easily
accessible modern books'. His *Richard III*, written 18 years earlier
(1878), is much inferior to it, and that of Sir Charles Oman in the
Political History of England (1906) must be given premier place, though
it contains no map. It is closely followed by Sir Clement Markham's
Richard III (1906).

All these books are much indebted (as I am) to the real historian
of the battle, W. Hutton, whose second edition (1813), edited by J.
Nichols, contains much valuable new material, including a transcript
of the curious and important *Richard the Third His Deathe*, by the Lord
Stanley, which is itself a transcription in the hand of Stowe of a copy
in the possession of one Henry Saville, who must be Sir Henry Saville,
the historian, contemporaneous with Stowe. I have only checked a
few passages in the B.M. Manuscript, but it seems to have been
accurately done by Nichols. Richard Brooke's *Visits to Battlefields*
(1857) is well annotated, and can sometimes be picked up in second-
hand bookshops. I have referred to poor Sir James Ramsay's account
in his *Lancaster and York* (1892). It is his last bow—and his last
imbecility—on the battlefields of England. C. R. B. Barrett, in
Battles and Battlefields in England (1896), follows, as usual, his mentor
Ramsay, but provides the only sketch of Richard's Well that I
know of. (It is for this reason that I include my own sketch of it in
the text.)

CHAPTER XXVI: FLODDEN

A.

Letters and Papers of Henry VIII (Ed. Brewer).
Letters and Papers Foreign and Domestic: Henry VIII.
Chronicle . . . (Hall) (*supra*).
La Rotta Scozzese (Italian poem), (Tr. Mackenzie in *The Secret of
Flodden*) (*see infra*).
Letter to Cardinal Bainbridge (In C.S.P. Venetian, ii).
Letter from Brian Tuke to R. Pace . . . (Roxburghe Club).
A Trewe Encountre . . . (Contemporary tract).
The Scottish Ffielde (Ballad) (Ed. Federer).
History of Scotland (J. Leslie).
Rerum Scotticorum (Geo. Buchanan).

B.

Two accounts, each superlative in its own way, are those by Sir Charles Oman and Dr. W. Mackay Mackenzie. The first occurs in *The Art of War in the Sixteenth Century* (1937); the latter is *The Secret of Flodden* (1931). I have been particularly indebted to the latter, and I consider that the author has made good his main contention that the defeat of the Scots was primarily due to faulty armament and formation; the Swiss pike proved their undoing. The book contains an invaluable list of original sources. For more recent contributions one must go to the *History of Northumberland* by K. H. Vickers (1922).

C. R. B. Barrett, in his *Battles and Battlefields* (1896), makes a valiant attempt to indicate the precise localities, a matter that is strangely slurred over by so many historians. *The Romance of Northumberland* (1906) by A. G. Bradley, contains a pleasantly written chapter on the battle, though he belongs to the Sandyford school. The same applies to *Highways and Byways* by P. A. Graham (1920), whose conception of the battle differs greatly from my own. Lastly we come to two books that I have referred to in the text, *The Battle of Flodden* (1931) by Lieut.-Colonel the Hon Fitzwilliam Elliot, and G. E. T. Leather's *New Light on Flodden* (1937). These two books seek to establish the fact that the Scottish army was in the act of retreating when surprised by the English.

CHAPTER XXVII: EDGEHILL

A.

Thomason Tracts, Nos. 21, 53, 124, 126, 128.
Memoirs of the Life of Edward Ludlow.
Memoirs of Prince Rupert (Warburton).
Bulstrode's Memoirs.
Original Papers (Carte).
The Verney Memoirs.
Memorials of John Hampden.
Memoirs of the Reign of Charles I (Sir C. Warwick).

B.

The battle of Edgehill is, as might be supposed, better furnished with accounts than most other battles; but, once again, as is usually the case, the best accounts are the least easily accessible. Quite the best is the comparatively brief account by Godfrey Davies in *English His-torical Review* (1921). That by Colonel W. G. Ross in the same periodical for 1887 was very good for its period, but fresh material has been since unearthed. For the topography of the battlefield the most informative source is an article in the now defunct *Illustrated Naval and Military Magazine of* 1890 by Rev. G. Miller; but as even the British Museum does not possess a copy the quest is rather hopeless. (There is a copy in the R.U.S.I.) The same author's *Rambles Round the Edgehills* (1900) contains much of the above material. *Shakespeare's Land* by Ribton-Turner contains the best map. The most detailed account is that in E. A. Walford's *Edgehill* (1923), published at Banbury.

Of the more popular accounts, that of Buchan in his *Cromwell* is good, being based on Godfrey Davies, though I do not agree with his siting of the field. Baldock's *Cromwell as a Soldier* has some good points, but Gardiner's *Great Civil War* is disappointing and not quite accurate. It is a pity that Firth did not write a full-length account of the battle.

CHAPTER XXX: FIRST NEWBURY

A.

Thomason Tracts, Nos. 69, 70.
Life of the Earl of Essex (R. Codrington, 1646).
The Great Rebellion (Clarendon).
Historical Collections (Rushworth).
Historical Discourses (Walker).

B.

I have already referred several times to Money's standard work, *The Battles of Newbury*. Though indispensable for a study of local detail and topography, it must be read with caution, and the hill features on its map ignored. As an account of the battle it is also difficult to follow, for it is discursive and repetitive. A better book in many ways is an older one, probably not easily procurable: *History and Antiquities of Newbury and its Environs*, published anonymously in 1838. From it I got the story of the cannon-ball that landed in Enborne. (All the damage it did was to remove a roasted pig from between two diners in the village!)

Gardiner's account in his *Great Civil War* is good as far as it goes, but is rather short. Unfortunately he was bear-led round the battle-field by Money, and converted to some of his questionable conclusions. Apart from recourse to original sources, probably not available in most public libraries, there is no other detailed account of the battle.

CHAPTER XXXII: MARSTON MOOR

A.

Thomason Tracts, Nos. 2, 3, 21, 54, 343.
A Short Memorial (Sir T. Fairfax).
Original Papers (Carte).
God's Ark (J. Vicars).
Memories (Denzil Holles).
D'Ewe's Diary.
Letters and Journals (Robert Baillie).

B.

To four modern writers we owe the research work on the battle. Other writers follow one or more of these four pretty obviously. The four are: (1) C. R. Markham, in his *The Great Lord Fairfax* (1870); (2) S. R. Gardiner, in his *Great Civil War* (1889); (3) Colonel W. G. Ross, in *English Historical Review* (1890), where he established the numbers and order of battle; (4) C. H. Firth, in *Transactions of the Royal Historical Society* (1898).

Of modern accounts *Cromwell as a Soldier* (1899) by Colonel T. S. Baldock contains some useful military comments. *Battles and Battle-fields in England* by C. R. B. Barrett (1896) is quite a good detailed and thoughtful account. Buchan's account in his *Cromwell* (1934) is brilliant as ever, and incorporates Firth's conclusions. The last account, *The Lord Fairfax* by M. A. Gibb (1938), gives full credit to Sir Thomas Fairfax (as such a book should) but it is rather short.

CHAPTER XXXIII: SECOND NEWBURY

A.

Thomason Tracts, No. 13, 18, 22, 23.
D'Ewe's Diary (Harl. MS. 166).
Diary of Capt. Symonds.
Historical Collections (Rushworth).
Historical Discourses (Sir E. Walker).

B.

The modern literature of this battle is singularly sparse and inadequate. Of Money's *Battles of Newbury* I have spoken under First Newbury. His florid style abounds in such passages as: 'Many a brave trooper fell, nevermore to draw sword again in the cause of parliament.' On the other hand his book is indispensable for local detail, tradition, relics, etc. Moreover, he gives useful and lengthy extracts from the primary authorities.

Gardiner's *Great Civil War* is of course reliable, but it is dreadfully short in its description of the battle. Other readable accounts are in *Cromwell as a Soldier* by Major T. S. Baldock, and *Battles and Battlefields in England* by C. R. B. Barrett. Hilaire Belloc makes some sound comments on the battle in his *Oliver Cromwell*.

CHAPTER XXXIV: NASEBY

A.

Thomason Tracts, Nos. 22, 25, 28, 38, 262, 288, 372.
Anglia Rediviva (Sprigge).
Diary (Sir H. Slingsby).
The Burning Bush (Vicars).
Historical Discourses (Sir G. Walker).
Great Rebellion (Clarendon).
Memoirs of Prince Rupert (Warburton).

B.

This is a simple matter. It is a case of 'Eclipse first; the rest nowhere'. S. R. Gardiner is first, with his *Great Civil War*, Vol. II, written in 1889. All subsequent accounts lean heavily on this classic work, sometimes omitting various details, but seldom adding anything new. Of the pre-Gardiner era easily the best work is Markham's *The Great Lord Fairfax* (1870), but copies are scarce. Of modern accounts, that of Buchan in his *Oliver Cromwell* (1934) is the most readable. Also worthy of notice is *The Lord General* by M. A. Gibb (1938).

Here again it is a pity that Firth (who seems to have been more interested in organization and training than in the actual battles of the war) did not give us a full account of this epoch-making battle.

CHAPTER XXXVI: WORCESTER

A.

Nicholas Leadman's Diary.
Thomason Tracts, Nos. 641, 1034.
C.S.P. Domestic, 4/9/51. 'Cmee. of State to General Monk.'
C.S.P. Domestic, 17/9/51. 'Relation of the Defeat of the King's army.'
A Perfect Diurnal (Cromwelliana).
Mercurius Politicus (Cromwelliana).
Memorials (Whitelock).

B.

Having regard to the importance of the battle it is surprising that it is not better documented, nor more fully dealt with by historians. It would seem that they have been mesmerized, as it were, by the drama of the King's personal adventures, and have concentrated on the events immediately following the battle, at the expense of the battle itself.

The most detailed modern account is contained in *The Civil War in Worcestershire* by J. W. W. Bund (1905). The best purely military account is that of Colonel T. S. Baldock, *Cromwell as a Soldier* (1899). Both Buchan and Barrett are too brief to be of much practical use.

The full story of Worcester has yet to be written.

CHAPTER XXXVII: SEDGEMOOR

A.

N.B.—As no book gives a satisfactory bibliography of this battle, and as references (particularly those in Macaulay's well-known account) are obscure, I will give more details than usual.

Feversham's Report (Anon) in H.M.C. Stopford-Sackville, i, 16.
James II's account in Misc. State Papers, ii, 305.
'*Mr. Wade's Confession*', in Harl. MSS. 6845 fol. 264 (B.M.).
'*Mr. Wade's Further Confession*', in Misc. State Papers, ii, 315.
Journal of Edward Dummer, ADD MSS. 31956 (B.M.).
Memoirs of Sir J. Dalrymple, i. (1790).

Reliquiae (Richard Baxter, 1696).

'*Lord Grey's Confession*', in Lansdown MS. 1152, fol. 310 (B.M.).

'*Examination of W. Williams*', in Lansdown MS. 1152, fol. 277 (B.M.).
(Further examinations on succeeding folios.)

'*Paschall's Letter*', in Ballard MS. 48, fol. 74 (Bodleian).

Letter from H. Seherer to Lord Dartmouth, H.M.C., 11th Report, Pt. 4,
App. V, 126.

Compleat History of England (White Kennet, iii, 42).

Hardwick State Papers, ii, 205.

James II (J. S. Clarke, 1816).

History of England (Oldmixon, 1730).

Memoirs (Sir J. Reresby, 1875).

Clarendon Correspondence (Ed. Singer, 1828).

Letter from Charles Bertie to Lady Rutland, ADD MS. 38012, fol. 27*b*,
(B.M.).

A Brief Historical Relation (N. Luttrell, 1857).

MSS. of Mrs. Stopford-Sackville, H.M.C., 9th Report, Pt. III, p. 4.

PLANS OF THE BATTLE:

1. Paschall's map, in Ballard MS. 48, fol. 74 (Bodleian). A copy
in Hoare's Bank.

2. Dummer's plan, in ADD MSS. 31956 (B.M.).

B.

This battle is, as may be supposed, quite well documented (though some of the sources are difficult to identify and unearth). But we are dealing with books, not documents. Here we meet with disappointment, for, as I have explained, the ground has changed so much that a plan of the modern field superimposed on the old map is essential to the visitor; and that none of the books provide. The most thorough modern investigator was the late Maurice Page, who claimed to have established the course of the Langmoor and Bussex Rhines; but he did not show the exact course of the latter in his book and the former he misplaced, and in this he has been copied by more recent writers. Nevertheless, his *The Battle of Sedgemoor* (1930) remains the best detailed account we possess. Unfortunately his military judgements are open to question. The other really detailed account is that of Lord Wolseley in his *John Churchill, Duke of Marlborough* (1894). He had not all the sources that are now available, which possible accounts for his severe criticism of Lord Grey.

Of shorter accounts, Mr. Churchill's *Marlborough*, permeated with his usual acumen and military insight, is *facile princeps*. A pity it is not longer.

King Monmouth by A. Fea (1902) is a sound, thorough piece of work, but contains no bibliography. (No book yet published contains that.) The only other modern book worth noticing is *James, Duke of Monmouth* by Elizabeth D'Oyley (1938) which gives an adequate summary of the battle. *Battles and Battlefields in England* by C. R. B. Barrett (1896) contains too many errors to warrant recommendation.

SELECT BIBLIOGRAPHY TO
MORE BATTLEFIELDS OF ENGLAND

THE following brief notes on the main sources for the battles included in this book are designed, not for the expert or for the historical student, who will require a much more exhaustive list, but for the general reader who may be curious as to where to look for the main outlines of the story. Any reputable library should be able to produce these sources at sight, except for a few that are specially listed and indicated.

CHAPTER I: CARADOC'S LAST FIGHT

The Greek historian Dion Cassius gives the general setting for the story of Caradoc's last battle, writing however 170 years after the event. The only contemporary source is that of Tacitus, in his *History of Agricola*, from which I have freely quoted. For the rest, we are confined to military geography and to the implications of Inherent Military Probability. The early Norman chroniclers are quite useless for the purpose.

CHAPTER III: DEORHAM

Our main, in fact our only real, source is the *Anglo-Saxon Chronicle*. *Ethelwerd's Chronicle* copies it almost word for word. Nennius is completely silent on the battle, and the early Norman chroniclers carry us no further. Were it not for the useful and identifiable place-names it would be quite impossible to make anything at all of the battle.

CHAPTER IV: WANSDYKE AND ELLANDUN

For Wansdyke there is no written evidence at all. Considering the importance of the battle of Ellandun it is surprising how little attention is paid to it by the early chroniclers. Florence of Worcester does not even mention it by name, and Henry of Huntingdon only gives one original fact about the battle. The *Anglo-Saxon Chronicle* is disappointingly meagre. In fact we have only one real source, that of the *Annlese de Wintonia*, or Winchester Annals edited by H. Luard in the Rolls Series (1865). Fortunately the place-names are sufficiently explicit to locate the approximate site of the battlefield. The rest is 'reasoned conjecture'.

CHAPTER VI: ETHANDUN

Another extremely important battle that has disappointingly meagre sources. Such as they are they have been mentioned in the text. The *Anglo-Saxon Chronicle* of course comes first. *Ethelwerd's Chronicle* has only a single sentence on the actual battle, and Asser is incomprehensibly reticent. The early Norman chroniclers are somewhat more expansive, but their accounts seem to be mere embellishments of the above-named sources. It is doubtful if they posses any independent sources.

CHAPTER VII: BRUNANBURH

As befits its importance the battle of Brunanburh provides almost an *embarras de richesses* after the barren waste surrounding the preceding battles. About a score of accounts and references can be found in the early chroniclers and charters, but the gist of the story is contained in the following half-dozen, the two first-named being much the most detailed. *Anglo-Saxon Chronicle*, *Egil's* (Norse) *Saga*; the *Annals of Ulster*, and the three early Norman chroniclers. Florence of Worcester, Simeon of Durham, and William of Malmesbury, who at last provide some really independent material. The main contributions of the above are indicated in the text.

CHAPTER VIII: MALDON

Here we are back again in the desert—or should be were it not for the Poem of Maldon, which alone gives us greater details of a battle than of any previously fought on this soil. There are a large number of editions of the Poem and translations of it, the latest edition being that of E. V. Gordon published in 1937 (2nd edition, 1949). Professor Gordon lists a baker's dozen of sources, but all except the Poem and the contemporary *Vita Oswaldi* deal with the setting rather than with the battle itself. There is in fact a singular silence on the battle in the chronicles. William of Malmesbury, for instance, does not even mention Britnoth by name. Danish sources are all silent about the battle. Finally, the *Anglo-Saxon Chronicle* confines itself to the single sentence: 'This year was Ipswich plundered and very shortly afterwards was Alderman Britnoth slain at Maldon.' The *Vita Oswaldi* describes the conduct in the battle of the 'glorious leader Britnoth'; but all other details of the battle are confined to the Poem.

CHAPTER IX: ASSINGDON

Here the sources are fairly plentiful, which is not surprising as we are getting near Norman times. Thus Florence of Worcester, William of Malmesbury, and Henry of Huntingdon all contribute something of interest. But the main sources are the *Anglo-Saxon Chronicle* and the *Encomium Emmae Reginae*. The latter was written for Emma, Queen of Ethelred the Unready and afterwards of Canute, by a Flemish priest who had once met Canute. It is a valuable and impartial account, possibly because the Queen might be said to 'have a foot in each camp'.

CHAPTER X: STAMFORD BRIDGE

The main sources are four in number, though most of the details of the actual fighting are usually taken from a single one, and that the least reliable. This is the *Saga of Harald Hardrada* contained in the *Heimskringla*. I have made but little use of it. The *Anglo-Saxon Chronicle* account is meagre, but is redeemed by the story, contained only in a late supplement to MS. D, of the episode on the bridge. Florence of Worcester repeats this story with additional detail which may be substantially true. The only other independent source seems to be Henry of Huntingdon, but he adds little. The fact is our sources are extremely scanty when compared with those for the battle of Hastings, which immediately followed it.

CHAPTER XII: NORTHALLERTON

The sources for this battle are numerous and diffuse, but disappointing. As mentioned in the text, the ecclesiastical aspect was what interested our ancestors, and as the chroniclers were for the most part monks, it is not surprising that they dwell on this aspect of the contest rather than on the military details of the battlefield. Most of the monastic chronicles can therefore be omitted from this brief list. We have now practically finished with the Norman chroniclers (only Henry of Huntingdon remains) and new names appear: Henry Knighton, Roger Hovedon, Thomas Wykes, Walter Hemingford (or Hemingburgh), Matthew Paris, and Roger of Wendover; but the main authorities are the monkish writers Aelred, abbot of Rievaulx, and Richard, prior of Hexham. Henry of Huntingdon comes third. See the Rolls Series for all these.

CHAPTER XIII: LEWES

The battle of Lewes is unusually well served with sources. About a dozen might be listed, but the greater part of the material is provided by the three Chronicles of Walter of Hemingburgh (or Hemingford), Thomas Wykes, and William of Rishnger, who also wrote an account of the battles of Lewes and Evesham under the title *De duobus bellis.* Unfortunately these chronicles have never been translated out of the original Latin, and I have relied mainly upon translations of important passages made for me by a friend. Other chronicles useful to a lesser degree are those of Melrose (or Mailros), of John of Oxnead (or Oxenede), and of a 'Monk of Lewes'. Again see the Rolls Series.

CHAPTER XV: NEVILLE'S CROSS

The best accounts of the battle are contained in two letters. That of the prior of Durham cathedral, Fossor, is addressed to Thomas, Bishop of Durham, a draft of which is printed in the Rolls Series under the heading *Papers and letters from the Northern Registers.* The other, as mentioned in the text, is from Thomas Samson, and is found in Bodleian MS. 302. The regular English chroniclers of the period all give very brief accounts, but the *Chronicle of Lanercost* has a good deal to say about the early stages of the campaign, as might be expected. The two standard Scottish sources are the poem of Andrew of Wyntoun and the *Scottish Chronicle* of John of Fordun, which is disappointingly brief.

CHAPTER XVI: OTTERBURN

When starting to study this battle I found the sources so puzzling that I decided to clarify them in the body of the text. Here therefore it only remains to tabulate them, adding another to make the half-dozen. They are: Froissart's *Chronicles,* John de Fordun's *Scottichronicon,* Walsingham's *History of the English,* John Hardyng's *Chronicle,* Andrew de Wyntoun's *Originale Cronikil;* Ranulph Higden's *Polichronica;* and Henry Knighton's *Chronicle.* The two ballads of Chevy Chase and Otterburn are contained in Percy's *Reliques of Poetry.*

CHAPTER XIX: BLORE HEATH

One could give an imposing list of authorities for this battle, if we include the Tudor historians of the next century, Grafton, Hall, Hollinshed, and Stow. But these writers copied from one another in a shameless manner, and for all practical purposes they can be reduced to one

—Edward Hall. The other main source for the battle is John de Waurin, the Burgundian. A few minor details can be obtained from a version of the Brut, known generally as *Davies' English Chronicle*, since it was brought to light by him in 1856, also in J. Whethamstede's *Register*, and in Fabyan's and Polidore Vergil's chronicles. But even in the aggregate they add but little to the two first-mentioned sources.

CHAPTER XXV: STOKE

As indicated in the text, much the most important source for this battle is the account by the Herald in the army of Henry VII. This is quoted by Leland in his *Collectanea* iv, 210, and is given in full in Appendix IV of *Visits to Fields of Battle in England*, by Richard Brooke (1857), and also quoted in part in *The Battle of Stoke Field*, by R. P. Shilton (1828). The original is given as 'a MS. in the Cottonian Library', and is headed 'A Shorte and a brief Memory by License and Correcion . . .' The other main source is Polydore Vergil. The Elizabethan historians quote from him almost exclusively, adding here and there a few touches of their own. Francis Bacon, deploring the scarcity of reliable authorities, was reduced to doing the same.

CHAPTER XXVIII & XXIX: LANSDOWN AND ROUNDWAY DOWN

The sources for these two battles are practically the same, as is not surprising, for they took place in the same area, between the same contestants and within a fortnight of one another. It will therefore be convenient to group them together.

There are a large number of reports of these two battles. They are largely contained in the *Thomason Tracts*, a contemporary collection of tracts, broadsheets, and newspaper cuttings made by Edward Thomason. They are kept in the North Library of the British Museum. They are all catalogued under the letter E; the most useful are: E 60 (8), (9), and (12), E 61 (6). *Bellum Civile* contains the accounts by Hopton and Slingsby. Atkyns's account is in *The Vindication of Richard Atkyns*. It includes a graphic and amusing relation of his pursuit and capture of Sir Arthur Hazelrig at Roundway Down. Waller's *Recollections* only contain a sentence or two, which is most unfortunate. Mercurius Aulicus is mentioned in the text, also Sir John Byron's account of Roundway Down. As this most valuable account is difficult to find in the British Museum catalogue I will give the press mark: it is 1103. d. 77 (5). Finally Clarendon's *The Great Rebellion* is indispensable.

CHAPTER XXXI: CHERITON

With the same two contestants, Hopton and Waller, we may expect the same or similar sources; and we get them: *Bellum Civile*, Clarendon and the *Thomason Tracts*: Nos. 27 (4) and 77 (14), are the chief ones. But we get in addition good accounts; from the Cavalier side Sir Edward Walsingham's book described in the text; from the Roundhead side, *Military Memoir of Colonel John Birch*, published anonymously, but written by his secretary Roe. The above, with a few details in Rushworth's *Collections*, provide a clear and full description of the battle.

CHAPTER XXXV: LANGPORT

Langport is particularly well documented. Of course there is Clarendon, and he is well backed up on the Cavalier side by Sir Richard Bulstrode's *Memories and Reflections*, referred to in the text. On the Roundhead side we have *Anglia Rediviva* by Joshua Sprigge, who was Fairfax's chaplain. A source commonly cited, *The Burning Bush consumed*, by J. Vicars, has no merit, being evidently complied from the numerous broad-sheets and letters contained in the *Thomason Tracts*. The chief of these are: 285 (10), 292 (18, 28, and 30), 293 (1, 2, 3, and 8). The net result of all these is a remarkably clear and vivid description of the battle.

INDEX